CRIMINAL JUSTICE IN CANADA

Third Edition

CRIMINAL JUSTICE IN CANADA

Third Edition

Colin Goff
University of Winnipeg

THOMSON

NELSON

Australia   Canada   Mexico   Singapore   Spain   United Kingdom   United States

THOMSON

NELSON

**Criminal Justice in Canada,
Third Edition**

Colin Goff

Editorial Director and Publisher:
Evelyn Veitch

Executive Editor:
Joanna Cotton

Marketing Manager:
Lenore Taylor

Senior Developmental Editor:
Edward Ikeda

Production Editor:
Natalia Denesiuk

Senior Production Coordinator:
Hedy Sellers

Copy Editor & Proofreader:
Karen Rolfe

Creative Director:
Angela Cluer

Cover and Interior Design:
Katherine Strain

Cover Image:
© RYUICHI SATO/Photonica

Compositor:
Andrew Adams

Printer:
Transcontinental

Statistics Canada information is used with the permission of the Minister of Industry, as Minister responsible for Statistics Canada. Information on the availability of the wide range of data from Statistics Canada can be obtained from Statistics Canada's Regional Offices, its World Wide Web site at http://www.statcan.ca and its toll-free access number 1-800-263-1136.

National Library of Canada Cataloguing in Publication Data

Goff, Colin H., 1949–
    Criminal justice in Canada / Colin Goff. — 3rd ed.

Includes bibliographical references and index.
ISBN 0-17-622504-8

1. Criminal justice, Administration of—Canada. I. Title.

HV9960.C2G63 2003
364.971   C2003-903068-7

To Sarah, Buddy, and Robley

CONTENTS

LIST OF EXHIBITS

LIST OF FIGURES

LIST OF TABLES

Public interest in the operation of the Canadian criminal justice system has grown dramatically during the past two decades. This continuing interest is not surprising, considering the attention given to issues such as how best to control crimes of violence, the role of the judiciary, whether our correctional system is doing an effective job, and whether our laws sufficiently deter crime and criminals. At the same time, there are demands for increased rights for victims, increases in the number of police officers, and harsher penalties for convicted offenders. Not surprisingly, students are demanding more postsecondary courses in criminal justice, with the result that colleges and universities today are graduating large numbers of students who will be employed in our criminal justice system.

This increasing interest led me to introduce more information about our criminal justice system in the criminology courses I was teaching. The popularity of this approach made it apparent that there was a great need for a comprehensive introductory course and accompanying text about criminal justice. *Criminal Justice in Canada* was written to fill that need and to provide an accurate account of the basic features of our criminal justice system.

This text describes the formal processes of our criminal justice system and shows how these reflect the basic structural and procedural components of our system. This approach involves a discussion of the major criminal justice agencies and the way those agencies operate to identify, apprehend, process, and control offenders. The book covers what most experts consider to be the central facets of our criminal justice system. It does not aim to describe every feature and nuance of each criminal justice agency, but rather to highlight those policies, legal cases, and decisions that shape the operation of the various agencies in fundamental ways. Criminological research studies are also included, as are federal and provincial government evaluations and policy efforts. In the third edition, some of the most recent developments and controversial aspects of our system are included: anti-terrorist legislation; attempts to control sexual offenders; recent Supreme Court of Canada decisions on, for example, the possession of child pornography and strip searches; and the operation of our court system.

NEW TO THE THIRD EDITION

The third edition of *Criminal Justice in Canada* features many changes since the text was first published. A significant new crime control philosophy, restorative justice, has appeared, as have new policing styles, sentences available to judges, and correctional policies. And while many of the traditional aspects of our system remain the same, new legal challenges and court decisions have necessitated this edition. The following is a chapter-by-chapter list of changes to the third edition.

- **Chapter 1** now includes a chart of the due process and crime control models as well as a discussion of antiterrorist legislation.
- **Chapter 2** contains new sections featuring discussions on the rule of law, the principles of fundamental justice, *mala en se* and *mala prohibita* offences, as well as an update on anti-gang legislation.
- **Chapter 3** continues to reflect the major philosophies that form the basis of the criminal justice system, with examples focusing upon how each approaches the issue of sexual offenders.
- **Chapter 4** contains updated trends and patterns of Canadian crime statistics as well as a new section on public perceptions of the criminal justice system.

- **Chapter 5** includes the following new topics: the history and development of policing in Canada, zero tolerance policing, and the police use of DNA.
- **Chapter 6** features new material on the debate surrounding racial profiling and more information about police accountability.
- **Chapter 7** contains new sections on investigative detention, strip searches, and police interrogations.
- **Chapter 8** has new sections on the functions of our courts and the prosecutorial screening process as well as the issue of race in the selection of jurors.
- **Chapter 9** features discussions on forms of punishment and the sentencing process as well as new data on sentencing patterns in Canada.
- **Chapters 10, 11, and 12** have been restructured to account for new alternative sentencing policies as well as developments in the area of corrections. Chapter 10 reflects the contemporary trend of Canadian federal authorities to use the community as a site for offenders to serve their sentences, such as conditional sentences. Chapter 11 features a discussion on new generation jails, as well as new sections on federal women's correctional facilities and the role of correctional institutions in our society. Additions to Chapter 12 include a discussion of the reintegration approach, which guides the federal correctional system, updated recidivism statistics, as well as use of the "faint hope" clause.
- **Chapter 13** includes information about the *Youth Criminal Justice Act*.
- **Chapter 14** explores various contemporary issues facing our criminal justice system, including hate crimes and courts that specialize in the sentencing and treatment of drug offenders.

ANCILLARY MATERIALS

Available to instructors is a robust support package consisting of the following items.

- An **Instructor's Manual** (0-17-641622-6) includes chapter summaries, teaching suggestions, learning objectives, key terms/key people, and InfoTrac exercises.
- New to this edition is a **Test Bank** (0-17-641621-8) that contains multiple-choice and true-false questions for each chapter. The Test Bank is also available in a Windows version of **MicroTest III** (0-17-641620-X). This easy-to-use assessment and tutorial software allows instructors to create, deliver, and customize tests in minutes.
- Also available to instructors is a new **video** (0-17-641619-6) that includes clips from CBC that illustrate the issues and concepts discussed in the text. Discussion topics for each video clip are included in the Instructor's Manual.
- **PowerPoint** presentation software (0-17-641623-4) is another feature that is new to this edition. The software is available to assist instructors in managing lectures. Instructors will have the ability to add, delete, or modify the slides according to their individual requirements.
- One last support item for both students and instructors is a **Web site** containing quiz questions, links to topics from each chapter, and other criminal justice resources. This Web site can be found at www.goffcrimjustice3e.nelson.com.

ACKNOWLEDGEMENTS

Writing a text on an area as diverse as the Canadian criminal justice system involves the efforts of a number of individuals. In particular, two individuals deserve recognition for their help in seeing this project through to publication. Robert Bangs of the RCMP gave up his personal time to offer his expertise, and it was much appreciated. In addition, the comments, insights, and meticulous work provided by Sarah Goff were invaluable, and her dedication, enthusiasm, and persistence contributed to the quality of the final manuscript.

Other thanks go to the librarians at the University of Winnipeg, especially those who work in Interlibrary Loans. I would also like to recognize Gil Geis and Frank Cullen, colleagues and teachers who have unfailingly supported my work.

Many individuals who work at Nelson deserve recognition. The enthusiasm, patience, tact, and positive support given by Edward Ikeda, Senior Developmental Editor, throughout the whole project made it enjoyable. The editorial skills, suggestions, and detailed work by Natalia Denesiuk, Production Editor, were always appreciated. Other individuals at Nelson who contributed include Evelyn Veitch and Joanna Cotton, as well as those regional sales representatives whose comments and feedback played such an important role.

Finally, the reviewers of this and past editions deserve special mention for their detailed comments. I appreciate their efforts, and many of their suggestions were incorporated into the final text. Reviewers included Susan Reid-MacNevin, St. Thomas University; Lynne Scott, Durham College; Anthony Micucci, Memorial University of Newfoundland; Anne-Marie Singh, University of Guelph; Kevin Haggerty, University of Alberta; Sandra Bell, Saint Mary's University; Marilyn Belle-McQuillan, University of Western Ontario; Gerald Flannigan, Fanshawe College; Ian Hepher, Lethbridge Community College; Reginald M. McLean, barrister and solicitor; Julian Roberts, University of Ottawa; Gordon Rose, Simon Fraser University; Vicki Ryckman, St. Lawrence College; Bob Tulloch, Sault College; Jim Anderson, John Abbott College; W.R. Anderson, Durham College; Gina Antonacci, Humber College; Rick Linden, University of Manitoba; David MacAlister, Kwantlen University College; Chris McCormick, St. Thomas University; Scott Nicholls, Humber College; T.A. Rudolph, Lethbridge Community College; K.R. Spencer, University of Alberta; and Brian Young, Camosun College.

ABOUT THE AUTHOR

Colin Goff received his MA in Sociology from the University of Calgary and PhD from the University of California (Irvine). Since graduating, he has taught at Simon Fraser University, the University of New Brunswick (Fredericton), and the University of Winnipeg. His areas of research include all aspects of the criminal justice system, corporate and white-collar crime, the history of criminology, and Aboriginal justice. In addition to *Criminal Justice in Canada*, he has published *Corporate Crime in Canada* (with C. Reasons) and *Corrections in Canada*. He has also published numerous articles on the work of Edwin H. Sutherland (many with Gil Geis), the development of criminology as a discipline in the early 20th century, and case studies involving corporate crime in Canada, particularly those occurring in the Atlantic provinces. He is currently studying the impact of the introduction of community policing, the development of Aboriginal police services, and the rise of sociological criminology in the United States during the late 1920s and early 1930s. He has also completed, with the assistance of Gil Geis, a manuscript on the early work of Edwin H. Sutherland in criminology.

CHAPTER 1

An Overview of the Criminal Justice System in Canada

CHAPTER OBJECTIVES

✓ Identify the major agencies of the criminal justice system and discuss the role of each in processing the accused through the criminal justice system.

✓ Outline the structure of the criminal justice system.

✓ Examine the operation of each criminal justice agency within the formal structure of the criminal justice system.

✓ Discuss the importance of the "informal" criminal justice system and the ways it affects the legal rights of defendants.

✓ Contrast the crime control and due process models.

The criminal justice system in Canada comprises three major agencies: the police, the courts, and the correctional system. Although many differences separate these agencies, they operate together in a formal manner and follow legal procedures developed to guide their actions. This formal system has an informal side as well; each agency operates in accordance with its goals and mandates, sometimes to the detriment of the other agencies as well as to the rights of those charged or convicted. This chapter begins by identifying the major components of the Canadian criminal justice system and the cost of operating them. It then outlines the formal and informal operations found within that system.

The *Latimer* Case

On 24 October 1993 the RCMP arrived at the farm of Robert Latimer, in Wilkie, Saskatchewan, in response to a call concerning the death of his 12-year-old daughter, Tracy. She was suffering from a severe form of cerebral palsy, which had left her physically and developmentally disabled and in extreme pain, a condition that could not be helped by medication. Robert Latimer's actions were the result of his decision to deliver her from the constant pain and suffering he felt she would experience throughout the remainder of her life. Eleven days later he confessed to the police that he had planned his daughter's death by poisoning her with carbon monoxide after placing her in the front seat of his pickup truck and feeding through the front window a hose connected from the exhaust pipe. From the outside of the pickup he watched her die. He informed the police that he had also timed her death as he watched. Latimer drew a diagram for the RCMP officers of the apparatus he used to pipe the exhaust fumes into the truck cab.

Based on the evidence supplied to the police by Mr. Latimer, he was charged with first-degree murder. During the trial, which was held in nearby North Battleford, Saskatchewan, Latimer's lawyer used the defence of necessity for his client (a legal defence usually reserved for cases involving imminent danger), arguing that his client was attempting to prevent a tragedy greater than the one of Tracy's death. In November 1994, the jury, having deliberated less than four hours, acquitted Latimer of the charge of first-degree murder but found him guilty of second-degree murder. He was sentenced to life in prison, with no chance of parole until he has served 10 years of his sentence. His lawyer filed an appeal, which was granted by the Saskatchewan Court of Appeal. In the meantime, Latimer remained free on bail.

Latimer's appeal was rejected by the Saskatchewan Court of Appeal on 18 July 1995. The majority, while stating that the defendant acted in order to relieve his daughter's suffering, ruled that he acted "as a self-appointed surrogate decision-maker [and] he was not entitled to take the criminal law into his own hands and terminate her life." However, the Appeal Court justices were not unanimous in their thinking about the appropriateness of the 10-year minimum wait before Latimer could apply for parole. The dissenting judge wrote that Latimer's sentence "exposes a stark inequality in the administration of justice in Canada in this sphere of wrongdoing."

Several issues arose regarding the case over the next few months. It came to the attention of Latimer's lawyer that the RCMP had tampered with the jury at the instruction of the Crown prosecutor trying the case. It was discovered that the prosecutor had requested the police to canvas some individuals whose names appeared on the jury list before the jury selection in order to determine what, if any, their views were on mercy killing. This decision by the prosecutor was a "incomprehensible error," as it led to questions about juror impartiality and fairness (Paciocco 1999: 56). On 26 June 1996 the Crown prosecutor was charged with attempting to obstruct justice (he was later acquitted). Once again there was an appeal, and this time the Supreme Court of Canada ruled, on 6 February 1997, that the jury's verdict of guilty must be set aside, and ordered a new trial due to the prosecutor's "flagrant abuse of process and interference with the administration of justice" (*R. v. Latimer* 1997: 240).

For Latimer's second trial, the Crown chose to proceed on the charge of second-degree murder. Since this was not a double-jeopardy situation, the Crown could have proceeded on a first-degree charge if it thought it could get a first-degree conviction with a new jury. The jury in the second trial convicted Latimer of second-degree murder. But during deliberations the jury asked the judge a question that would have a critical impact on this case: Could Latimer be given a sentence that was less than the mandatory minimum of 10 years before being eligible for parole? After all, Karla Homolka, who received a sentence of 12 years for her part in the heinous killings of young women in southern Ontario, could potentially be granted full parole after serving just one-third of her sentence.

Was this action of the jury appropriate? Although it convicted Latimer of second-degree murder, on 5 November 1997, the jury felt that a 10-year wait for eli-

gibility for parole would be too long in his case. Instead, jury members recommended that Latimer become eligible for parole after serving only one year of his sentence. In addition, Latimer's lawyer asked the judge to grant a constitutional exemption from the mandatory sentence, arguing that the length of the sentence for second-degree murder for what he called "a rare act of homicide that was committed for caring and altruistic reasons" constituted a breach of his client's constitutional right to be free from cruel and unusual punishment. The trial judge agreed with the logic of both the jury and defence lawyer, concluding that a life sentence and a 10-year waiting period before parole eligibility were unconstitutional under the circumstances. He granted Mr. Latimer a constitutional exemption from the mandatory minimum sentence and imposed a sentence of two years less a day, with one-half of the sentence to be served at Latimer's farm under house arrest. The judge based this sentence on a weighing of what he thought were the appropriate facts in this case—the personal characteristics of the defendant, the gravity of the offence, the circumstances surrounding it, and the potential impact a 10-year sentence would have on the defendant (Roberts and Cole 1999). Another factor in the judge's decision was the significant public support (over 2500 letters of support had been received) Mr. Latimer had received following his first conviction. The trial judge, who described Latimer's actions as "compassionate homicide," issued his decision on 1 December 1997.

Both Latimer and the Crown appealed the ruling. Latimer felt the sentence was too severe, and the Crown felt it was too lenient. The Saskatchewan Court of Appeal, on 23 November 1998, rejected the defence appeal by upholding the conviction. It also accepted the Crown's appeal by overturning the lower court sentence, reinstating the minimum 10-year sentence, and calling Latimer's actions "inexcusable." Latimer's lawyer sought leave to appeal both the conviction and the sentence to the Supreme Court of Canada. On 6 May 1999 the Supreme Court agreed to hear the appeal.

Three issues were addressed by the Supreme Court:

1. Did the trial judge mishandle the defence of necessity, resulting in an unfair trial?
2. Was the trial unfair because the trial judge misled the jury into believing it would have some input into the appropriate sentence?
3. Does the imposition of a mandatory minimum sentence for second-degree murder constitute "cruel and unusual punishment," and, as a result, should Mr. Latimer receive a constitutional exemption from the minimum sentence of 10 years?

On 18 January 2001, the Supreme Court gave its reply, and it adhered to the established principles of law by answering "no" to all three questions.

- For the first question, the justices wrote "the defense of necessity is narrow and of limited application in criminal law. In this case, there was no air of reality to that defense."
- For the second question, the Supreme Court decided "the trial judge did not prejudice the appellant's rights in replying to a question from the jury on whether it could offer input on sentencing."
- In its decision on the third question, the Supreme Court concluded "the mandatory minimum sentence for second-degree murder in this case does not amount to cruel and unusual punishment within the meaning of s. 12 of the *Canadian Charter of Rights and Freedoms*. The test for what amounts to 'cruel and unusual punishment' is a demanding one and the appellant has not succeeded in showing that the sentence in his case is 'grossly disproportionate' to the punishment required for the most serious crime known to law, murder."

The Supreme Court decision meant that Mr. Latimer had to serve the mandatory minimum sentence of 10 years before he could apply for parole. In its decision, the Supreme Court noted Mr. Latimer's attempt to conceal his activities from the authorities, his lack of remorse, his daughter's vulnerability and the "important role" a mandatory minimum sentence has in symbolically denouncing murder, particularly when there was significant planning and premeditation of the event (Thomas 2002). The Supreme Court also noted the considerable amount of public support for Mr. Latimer and took the unusual step of stating that Parliament could exercise its powers of granting a royal prerogative of mercy in this case by reviewing the circumstances surrounding the death of Tracy Latimer.

If the Supreme Court had decided in favour of Mr. Latimer, the impact of such a ruling on our criminal justice system would be immense. Trial judges could impose sentences less severe than the mandatory minimum if they believe the minimum sentence constitutes cruel and unusual punishment.

Following the decision by the Supreme Court of Canada, one poll reported that 73 percent of Canadians were in support of Latimer, believing that the mandatory sentence is too harsh. Forty-one percent of those polled stated that mercy killing should not be illegal (Sallot 2001). But people with disabilities and their advocates argue that Latimer is guilty of murder and that he should serve the mandatory minimum for his actions (Martin 1995; Roberts 1997). In addition, advo-

cates of people with disabilities argued this case should not be approached from the accused's point of view but rather from the perspective of the disabled victim in the interest of promoting the equality of persons with disabilities (Enns 1999; Peters 2000).

The *Latimer* case touches on a significant number of issues about crime and punishment, in particular the criminal process from prosecutorial discretion to sentencing (Roach 2000). These issues will be addressed in upcoming chapters. Chapter 4 includes an overview of public perceptions of our criminal justice system; Chapter 10 features a more detailed discussion of the public perception of sentencing. Section 12 of the *Charter of Rights and Freedoms* (cruel and unusual punishment) is reviewed in Chapter 2. Chapter 8 discusses the role and decision-making powers of juries. Home confinement is discussed in Chapter 10. Finally, a discussion of corrections, whether or not Latimer would benefit from treatment, and whether he would need to be reintegrated into society can be found in Chapter 12.

THE OPERATION AND ROLE OF THE CANADIAN CRIMINAL JUSTICE SYSTEM

Canada has developed a number of major agencies—the police, courts, and corrections—designed to protect the public from individuals who violate the law. These agencies comprise a vast network of organizations and facilities charged with the investigation, detection, prosecution, and punishment of offenders. They are linked together in what is commonly called the criminal justice system. Viewing the operation of criminal justice as a system allows us to comprehend the "interdependency of the parts of the entire process" since "many factors influence each decision and decision maker in the justice process" (Travis 1990: 34). Conventional wisdom holds that all the parts of the criminal justice system interact with one another in a coordinated fashion, although this image is not completely accurate. These agencies are related in the sense that they are involved in the apprehension and control of criminals, but "they have not yet become so well coordinated that they can be described as operating in unison" (Senna and Siegel 1995: 11).

Very few, if any, of the other agencies in our society provoke as much debate as our criminal justice system. Concerns about the operation and role of the major agencies of this system occur almost daily, since it is this system that determines the fate of the accused. These agencies and the people employed by them work

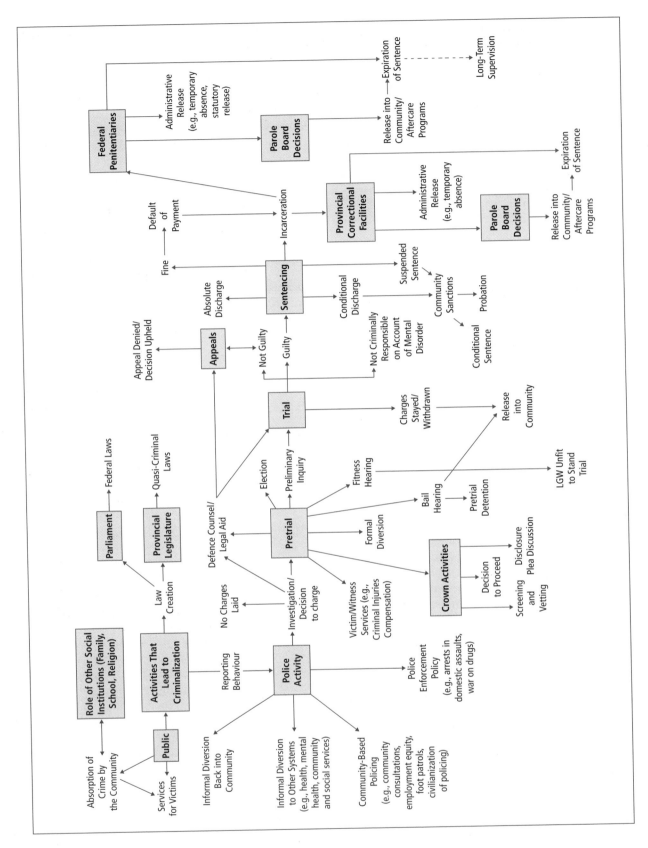

FIGURE 1.1

Overview of the Operation of the Canadian Criminal Justice System

Criminal Justice in Canada

toward detecting and apprehending those individuals who violate the law, determining whether or not they committed the crime(s) in question, and punishing those found guilty.

Our criminal justice system is, in reality, a vast organization of independent government agencies organized into three general categories—the police, the courts, and corrections. As Figure 1.1 shows, this system involves different types of police organizations, levels of courts, and correctional facilities, as well as a variety of federal statutes (such as the *Criminal Code* and the *Youth Criminal Justice Act*).

The Purpose of the Criminal Justice System

The purpose of the Canadian criminal justice system can be divided into three general areas of study: the control of crime, the prevention of crime, and the maintenance of justice. Controlling crime is possible in part by the arrest, prosecution, and punishment of those individuals who commit crimes. This system also anticipates that actions related to controlling crime will achieve the second goal, the prevention of crime. This is largely accomplished by punishing offenders in the hope they will refrain from committing crime in the future (i.e., specific deterrence) and by warning others that if they commit a criminal act, they too will be punished when caught (i.e., general deterrence). The third goal is achieving justice, a difficult task since justice is difficult to define in concrete terms and potentially involves conflicting views about what is "fair" and "just" in our society.

As we saw in the discussion about the *Latimer* case, different groups and individuals interpret justice in different ways. Achieving collective agreement about a definition of justice is an impossible task in our society. Although all members of our society share certain legal rights, these same rights may conflict with each other at certain times. Concerns about disorder in our society have led to questions about the appropriate response to homeless people in our society (see Chapter 2). Determining which rights should have precedence in any given situation can involve difficult conclusions. There is no doubt that our criminal justice system has given minimal importance to the rights of certain groups in our society over the decades, such as the rights of minority group members who are victims of hate crimes or the rights of women who are victims of violence.

In general terms, justice means that all citizens are equal before the law and that they are to be protected from arbitrary decisions made by those working within our criminal justice system (Rawls 1971). This view

holds that justice is connected to fairness since we want our laws to be written, administered, and enforced in a fair manner. Fairness within the criminal justice system refers to the balance between the state's interest in apprehending criminal suspects and the public's interest in avoiding unnecessary government inference in the lives and activities of individuals (Albanese 1999).

The three major agencies of the Canadian criminal justice system are supposed to achieve justice by making fair decisions. Sometimes their actions are interpreted by all parties as fair and just while, at other times, serious questions are raised about their actions. An overview of the formal operation of each of these agencies and how they are supposed to guarantee justice to citizens will be presented later in this chapter, but our attention now turns to exploring the notion of "criminal justice."

WHAT IS CRIMINAL JUSTICE?

We have just seen that the study of our criminal justice system involves the study of the police, courts, and corrections and that individuals are processed through these agencies. However, we also need to know what criminal justice is. In Canadian society today, when most people speak of justice they refer to the fairness about how our criminal law system operates, a view that is informed by three different assumptions.

The first assumption refers to the fact that guilt, innocence, and the sentence should be determined fairly, in accordance with the available evidence. Second, punishment should fit the offence as well as the offender. Finally, like cases should be treated alike and different cases treated differently (Law Reform Commission of Canada 1977). This view of criminal justice currently guides most Canadians' thinking regarding the most appropriate form for justice in our society. It is most closely related to what is called the justice model (see Chapter 3). Why should we be concerned about fairness and equality in our criminal justice system? We don't want unfairness and inequities since we don't want any biases against individuals or members of groups. When we talk about bias, two words are commonly used: "disparity" and "discrimination."

Disparity

Disparity refers to a difference, but one that doesn't necessarily include discrimination. Our concern with disparity in our criminal justice system occurs when inconsistencies appear due to illegitimate factors being used in the decisions made by the authorities. Legitimate factors include appropriate legal criteria such as the seriousness of the offence and the prior record of the offender. These are considered to be legitimate reasons for differences in our treatment of alleged offenders and those convicted of a crime within our criminal justice system since they are specifically concerned with the criminal behaviour of the offender. Illegitimate factors are extralegal factors, such as race, religion, and gender, which involve decisions about the group one belongs to and are unrelated to the criminal activity of any particular individual. For example, our criminal justice system is not supposed to operate or decide about a person's criminality on the basis of social class. If we did, it is entirely possible that middle- and upper-class individuals who commit crimes would be sentenced to serve their sentence within the community while members of the working class would receive a prison sentence.

Discrimination

Discrimination refers to the differential treatment of individuals based upon negative judgments about their perceived or real membership with a group. If discrimination occurs, something about an individual (e.g., his religion and/or race) overrides his other qualities (e.g., innocence, education, and abilities). Different types of discrimination each have the potential to influence fairness in a variety of different ways within our criminal justice system. Systemic discrimination refers to discrimination (e.g., race and/or gender) existing in all aspects of the operation of our criminal justice system. This means that discrimination can consistently be found in the rates of arrest, the type of charges laid, the decision to prosecute or stay charges, and in the conviction rates and types of sentences given to those convicted without any significant variation over a selected time period. Provincial inquiries of the treatment of racial minorities within the Canadian criminal justice system during the 1990s (e.g., the Manitoba Aboriginal Justice Inquiry) reported the existence of systemic discrimination.

Institutionalized discrimination is concerned with the issue of disparities appearing in the outcomes of decisions that are the result of established (i.e., institutionalized) policies existing within the criminal justice system. These policies do not directly involve consideration about the extralegal factors of individuals, such as their employment status, race, gender, or religion. The main issue here is very much one of system outcomes or results rather than any intent to discriminate against a specific individual or member of a group accused of a criminal offence. One example are those decisions made within the criminal justice system based upon the employment status of those accused of a crime and who are applying for bail. A policy granting bail made on the basis of the employment status of the accused can be legitimized on the basis of research showing that employed persons are better risks for showing up for their trial than those who are unemployed. But what if most men are employed and very few women are? Since women are disproportionately overrepresented among the unemployed, they are more likely to be denied bail. The result is referred to as a gender effect, which means that discrimination is the result of a policy that is not concerned with the gender of those who apply for bail. Discrimination in this case is the result of a policy; it does not exist because of individuals who are prejudiced.

Contextual discrimination refers to discrimination that occurs in certain contexts or situations. This refers to the organizational policies within criminal justice agencies such as the police and courts. One example of contextual discrimination occurs when a police service fails to enforce the criminal harassment (or anti-stalking) provisions of the *Criminal Code* simply because the police officers foresee the complainant dropping charges before the case enters the courts. Another example is when a judge sentences the members of one racial minority group more harshly when they victimize the members of another racial group but less severely when they victimize a member of their own racial group.

Individual discrimination occurs when an individual who is employed within the criminal justice system acts in such a way that discriminates against the members of certain groups. For example, police officers can discriminate against members of a certain social class and/or ethnic groups by arresting them in all circumstances while giving warnings to members of others social classes and/or ethnic groups.

Substantive and Procedural Justice

How does our criminal justice system operate to make sure that its decisions are fair and equal and do not discriminate? The answer is found in part by looking at what our society considers to be the most important components of justice. The first component is called substantive justice, specifically the accuracy or correctness of the outcome of a case. If the criminal suspect is in fact guilty, a verdict of "guilty" is a just decision. However, if the suspect is in fact innocent of the charge, then the verdict of "not guilty" is just. Substantive justice is primarily concerned with the truthfulness of the allegation, the accuracy of the verdict, and the appropriateness of the sentence. The high standards we demand of the agencies operating within our criminal justice system to make correct decisions are the result of our concern with substantive justice.

The second component is procedural justice or issues involving the fairness of the procedures used to arrive at the verdict of a case. If fair procedures aren't used, the trial is not just regardless of whether or not substantive justice was attained. For example, a person who is in fact guilty could have violated the law (substantive justice) but if unfair procedures were used somewhere during the investigation and/or trial, any conviction is unjust according to procedural justice. This situation is brought to our attention when a higher court, such as a Provincial Appeal Court or the Supreme Court of Canada, rules there was a problem with the procedural fairness with a case (e.g., whether or not the interrogation of the suspect by the police followed appropriate procedures). In Canada today, issues relating to procedural justice are more common than those involving substantive justice.

Although it is possible to analytically separate procedural from substantive justice, they are closely related. Our system of criminal justice attempts to ensure all individuals charged with and convicted of a criminal offence are treated fairly because we think of procedural justice as the best way to guarantee substantive justice. In fact, our criminal courts operate on the theory of the adversarial system, an approach that values procedural justice (e.g., a fair trial) as the best way to attain substantive justice in criminal trials.

The Adversarial System

An adversarial system of justice consists of three central characteristics. The first is that both parties involved, each in the hope that it will win the case, have the right to argue about what evidence is considered by the court.

A prosecutor (representing the state) is concerned initially that justice is done (for example, that charges are laid only where enough evidence exists to support them) and then with the successful prosecution of the case. The trial must be heard by an impartial fact-finder—the judge—who is trained in the law and who is not involved in the presentation of evidence or the questioning of witnesses. This latter characteristic is designed to guarantee that the defendant receives a fair trial. The judge ensures that the appropriate questions are asked and that the rules of a criminal court case are followed.

In theory, all levels of our court system operate on the basis of an adversarial system, in which the Crown prosecutor and defence lawyer oppose each other and debate the facts of the case. The goal of the adversarial system is to search for the truth, specifically the determination of the guilt or innocence of the accused. This system was designed to ensure that the accused's fundamental legal rights are protected, the trial is fair, and the final decision is impartial. Critics of this image (e.g., Ericson and Baranek 1982) argue that it operates only in theory and that the legal protections given to the accused are ignored or plea-bargained away by defence counsel and the prosecutor. As such, "legal justice" does not exist. Instead, most defendants receive what is referred to as a form of "bargain justice," where the accused is encouraged to plead guilty in return for a reduced sentence or the dropping of a number of charges. These critics believe the final result is a court system in which the vast majority of the accused plead guilty before any item is contested in the open court. Guilty pleas usually involve a reduction in the number of charges or a recommendation to the judge that the sentence be reduced. Significant issues have been raised about the benefits and limits of the adversarial system of justice, and these are outlined in Exhibit 1.1.

EXHIBIT 1.1 Benefits and Limitations of the Adversarial System

BENEFITS OF THE ADVERSARIAL SYSTEM

- A clear division exists among the various actors and agencies.
- As much evidence as possible is looked at in each case, particularly as it benefits each side, since each is committed to winning.
- The legitimacy of the criminal justice system is promoted through the appearance of fairness operating throughout the criminal justice system.

LIMITATIONS OF THE ADVERSARIAL SYSTEM

- The opposing sides often cooperate in order to reach a desired result, thereby undermining procedural justice in favour of efficiency.
- The length of a trial becomes a concern, since each side has to present as much information as possible in the hope that it will be able to win the case.
- Relevant evidence may be excluded if the judge considers that its use will violate the *Charter of Rights and Freedoms*.

THE STRUCTURE OF THE CRIMINAL JUSTICE SYSTEM

In order to understand the structure of the Canadian criminal justice system we need to look at its three major agencies. As indicated by Figure 1.1, this system is, in reality, a vast number of agencies organized into three major categories: the police, the courts, and corrections.

The Police

Policing is the responsibility of the federal, provincial, and municipal governments in Canada. Although police agencies have varying organizational structures and differing mandates, they usually cooperate with each other should the need arise. There are three main levels of police agencies in Canada: municipal, provincial, and federal. The most common type of police agency is found at the municipal level. These include police services whose sworn police personnel are hired by the municipal government as well as those municipalities that contract out their policing services to the Royal Canadian Mounted Police (RCMP) and provincial police forces (e.g., the Ontario Provincial Police). In 2001, almost 67 percent of all sworn police personnel working in Canada were employed by municipal police services (Filyer 2002). Municipal police services are located in almost every major Canadian city, including Vancouver, Calgary, Edmonton, Winnipeg, Toronto, Montreal, and Halifax. The 10 regional police services located in southern Ontario (e.g., the Halton Regional Police and the Peel Regional Police) are also classified as municipal police services. Those municipalities that contract out their policing services with the RCMP include larger cities, such as Burnaby and North Vancouver, B.C., but many of these municipalities included cities with a population of between 50 000 and 100 000 persons. All provinces have some municipal police services with the exception of Newfoundland and Labrador, Yukon, Northwest Territories, and Nunavut.

Each province is responsible for developing its own municipal and provincial policing services (Young 1994). This means a province may require any city within its jurisdiction that reaches a certain population size (e.g., any city over 10 000 people) to form and maintain its own municipal police service. Provincial police services involve the enforcement of all relevant laws within those areas in a province not under the control of a municipal police service. Besides the RCMP operating at the provincial level in most provinces, there are currently three police services that

A police officer carries marijuana plants seized from a private residence.

provide policing at the provincial level in Canada: the OPP, the Sûreté du Québec, and the Royal Newfoundland Constabulary.

The federal government, through the RCMP, is responsible for enforcing laws created by Parliament. The RCMP is organized under the authority of the *Royal Canadian Mounted Police Act* and is part of the portfolio held by the Solicitor General of Canada. The RCMP, while involved with municipal and provincial policing across Canada, is also charged with other duties such as enforcing federal statutes, carrying out executive orders of the federal government, and providing protective services for visiting dignitaries. In addition, the service also operates forensic facilities and an educational facility located in Ottawa (the Canadian Police College) as well as the Canadian Police Information Centre (CPIC), the automated national computer system used by all Canadian police services.

In 2001, there were 57 107 sworn police officers in Canada, an increase of 1153 from the previous year. In addition, there were 19 992 civilians employed by the various police organizations. Ontario had the largest number of sworn police officers (22 176), followed by Quebec (13 927) and British Columbia (6895). Most police officers work at the municipal level, including the RCMP and OPP (67 percent), followed by provincial policing (24 percent), federal policing services (8 percent), and RCMP contracts (1 percent) (Filyer 2002).

The Courts

The criminal courts across Canada process significant numbers of cases each year. During 2000–01, the adult criminal courts in eight provinces and the territories processed 375 466 cases (a 5 percent decrease compared to 1995–96) involving a total of 816 449 charges (Thomas 2002).

All provincial court systems in Canada, with the exception of Nunavut, have three levels, though their formal titles differ by province (Russell 1987; Mewett 1996). There are the lower courts, called the provincial courts in most jurisdictions, although in Ontario they are referred to as the Court of Justice and in Quebec as the Court of Quebec. At the next highest level are the Superior Courts, usually known as the Court of Queen's Bench or Supreme Courts (Trial Division). In Ontario these courts are called the Superior Court of Justice, and in Quebec they are known as the Superior Court. The highest level of criminal court in any province or territory is the Appeal Court. The Nunavut Court consists of a single-level trial court. Superior Court judges hear all criminal, family, and civil matters. This system was introduced in order to simplify the structure of the courts, improve accessibility to the court, and reduce the travel of judges. The court with the greatest authority in any criminal matter is the Supreme Court of Canada.

The provincial courts are the first courts most Canadians encounter when charged with a criminal offence. These courts are typically organized into specialized divisions that deal with different areas of the law. For example, a province may decide to divide its provincial court into a criminal court, family court, small-claims court, youth court, and family violence court. These courts deal with the majority of criminal cases, including violations of the *Youth Criminal Justice Act*, disorderly conduct, common assaults, property offences, traffic violations, municipal bylaws, and provincial offences.

Provincial criminal court dockets are crowded with cases. The courtrooms themselves have an air of "assembly-line justice," as defendants line up to enter the courtroom—only to have their cases summarily dispatched. Defendants in these courts rarely contest their cases in front of a judge. Researchers and observers report that most defendants who enter the provincial courts plead guilty to the charges during their initial appearance or find the charges either stayed (postponed indefinitely) or withdrawn by a prosecutor (Ericson and Baranek 1982; Wheeler 1987; Ursel 1994; Desroches 1995). Desroches (1995: 252) reported that 90 percent of the 70 robbers he interviewed pleaded guilty in provincial court, quickly averting any argument over the charges in an open courtroom. Most indicated they pleaded guilty simply because they wanted to "get the thing over with." Most criminal cases in Canada end up being heard in the provincial courts, which handle the routine criminal cases. This is the extent of most Canadians' involvement in our court system.

For the majority of indictable offences (i.e., offences that carry a maximum sentence of over six months) the accused has the right to be tried in either the provincial court or the Superior Court. The Superior Courts have to hear certain indictable offences such as first- and second-degree murder according to law (see Chapter 2). These courts also hear the appeals of cases decided at the provincial court level. A fundamental constitutional right in Canada guarantees those individuals charged with a criminal offence that during all stages of a trial their legal rights are protected. These rights include the right to representation by a lawyer, the right to a speedy court trial, the right to face and cross-examine the accuser in court, as well as the opportunity for the accused to testify on his own behalf (see Chapter 2).

The highest level of court in a province or territory—the Appeal Court—hears appeals from the Superior Courts and occasionally from provincial courts. These courts do not try criminal court cases; rather, they deal with issues concerning the possibility of procedural errors and sentence lengths. Defendants rarely appear in cases heard in Appeal Courts. Instead, lawyers representing the Crown and the defendant argue the case before a panel of Appeal Court judges.

Corrections

Once an accused is found guilty, she may be sentenced to a term in the federal or provincial/territorial correctional system. In Canada, the correctional system involves a vast array of facilities, agencies, and programs. The responsibility for adult corrections is divided between provincial/territorial governments and the federal government. Provincial and territorial governments are responsible for any individual serving a term of incarceration under two years and all noncustodial sentences (e.g., probation). The federal government, through Correctional Service of Canada, is responsible for any adult sentenced to a prison term of two years or more. If someone is sentenced to a term of two years or more but decides to appeal the conviction or sentence, she will first be incarcerated in a provincial facility. Those individuals who waive their right to an appeal are sent to a federal institution to start serving their sentence.

The total number of adult offenders incarcerated in a federal or provincial/territorial facility declined by 3.6 percent during 1999–2000. The average number of adults serving a custodial sentence in Canada on any given day during 1999–2000 totalled 31 624, a 2 percent decrease compared to the previous year. To house adult offenders, there are currently 212 correctional facilities located across Canada. Of these, 69 (17 of which are designated as community correctional centers (e.g., community residential centres) are operated by the federal authorities. The other 143 facilities operate within the jurisdiction of provincial/territorial governments, and they have a total capacity of 19 547, of which 80 percent are designated as secure institutions and the remaining 20 percent as open institutions (e.g., halfway houses) (Lonmo 2001).

Most of the individuals in the correctional population are serving all or part of their sentence under community supervision. Community supervision comprises various types of parole, probation, statutory release, and temporary absences. A total of 121 100 offenders were serving their sentence on some form of community supervision in 1999–2000. The majority of these offenders (102 100, or 82 percent) were sentenced to a term of probation, while the remaining 19 000 individuals were serving a conditional sentence or were participating on a conditional release program (e.g., parole, statutory release, or temporary absence). In 1999–2000, the total correctional population (including those incarcerated and/or serving their sentence on either probation, a conditional sentence, or conditional release program) was 152 800.

When we think of an individual serving a period of time in a Canadian correctional facility we usually think of an inmate (typically a male) serving a long period of incarceration. This image is only partly accurate. Most inmates are male; adult female offenders accounted for 9 percent of those individuals sentenced to a term of incarceration in a provincial/territorial facility and 5 percent in a federal facility in 1999–2000. However, most of those incarcerated serve relatively short sentences. In the provincial/territory jurisdictions, almost 75 percent received a sentence of incarceration of less than three months while at the federal level 67 percent of the 4221 admissions for the same year were for between two and four years.

The correctional system has been criticized by the public as well as by other criminal justice personnel for decisions that reflect an apparent disregard of public safety (Harris 2002). Critics point to what they consider to be high recidivism rates as an indication of the failure of institutions to rehabilitate offenders. The critics also claim that correctional officials are easily fooled by inmates, and as a result some who should remain incarcerated are released, resulting in higher crime rates. The correctional system, however, continues to play a number of important roles in the criminal justice

system. Some of these roles may seem contradictory—deterring crime, incapacitating those convicted of serious crimes, and rehabilitating offenders. Despite differing opinions about how to deal with offenders, the correctional system reinforces society's disapproval of their actions.

PROCESSING CASES THROUGH THE CANADIAN CRIMINAL JUSTICE SYSTEM

The Formal Organization of the Canadian Criminal Justice System

According to the Law Reform Commission of Canada (1988), a key function of our criminal justice system is to bring offenders to justice. At the same time, our legal system has created a number of legal rights and protections for those accused of crimes. Various fundamental principles exist to ensure that no arbitrary actions violate these principles. Our criminal justice system is based on the presumption of innocence of all defendants and is supposed to conduct itself in a manner that is fair, efficient, accountable, participatory, and protective of the legal rights of those arrested and charged with the commission of a criminal action.

An integral part of these guarantees is found in what is known as "criminal procedure." Criminal procedure is concerned with the way criminal justice agencies operate during the interrogation of suspects, the gathering of evidence, and the processing of the accused through the courts. Criminal procedure also ensures that the agents of the state act in an impartial and fair manner in their search for truth. Our system of criminal procedure is divided into two major parts: pretrial procedure and trial procedure.

Pretrial Criminal Procedure

Arrest, Appearance Notice, and Summons

The main purpose of arresting someone is to ensure the accused appears in a criminal court, where that person's guilt or innocence is determined. Another purpose of arrest is to prevent the commission of any further crime. With or without a warrant, police officers can arrest a suspect for violating the law.

A warrant is issued after a crime is committed when the police, during their subsequent investigation, collect enough evidence to give themselves reasonable and probable grounds to suspect that a certain person committed the offence. Once the evidence is collected, the police must go to a justice of the peace and lay an information against the suspect, indicating why they feel it is in the public interest to arrest the suspect. Once the arrest warrant is signed, the police execute the order by arresting the individual named on the warrant. Most warrants are issued only for the province in which the police investigated the crime. A Canada-wide warrant is issued only after an individual fails to appear in court after being charged with a violent or serious property offence. Even without a warrant, police can arrest an individual. This generally occurs when police officers have no chance to lay an information, such as when they discover a crime in progress (see Exhibit 1.2).

Whether the accused is granted bail or is held until the trial, almost all criminal prosecutions in Canada start with an information. As Mewett (1996) points out, an information serves two important purposes in the Canadian legal system. First, it compels the accused to appear at court on a specific date and at a designated time. Second, it forms the written basis for the charge that the accused faces in court.

Police officers need not arrest an individual when the offence in question is either a summary conviction offence or an indictable offence that does not allow the accused to choose a jury trial. Nor do police officers need to arrest a suspect

1. when they are certain the suspect will appear in court at the designated time and date;
2. when the prosecutor can proceed by way of a summary or indictable offence (that is, a hybrid offence);
3. when the offence involves a charge of keeping a gaming or betting house, placing bets, or keeping a common bawdyhouse.

Police may issue an appearance notice to a suspect or request a justice of the peace to issue a summons. A police officer at the scene of the crime will give the suspect an appearance notice. In these cases, the police officer hands the accused a form with information pertaining to the offence as well as the time and place the accused has to appear in court to answer the charge (or charges). The police officer must lay an information with a justice of the peace as soon as possible thereafter. Another alternative to an arrest is a summons. Here, the accused is ordered to appear in court by a justice of the peace. The summons must be handed to the accused by a police officer or person granted special powers by

---

EXHIBIT 1.2   Arrest Without a Warrant

Section 495(1) of the *Criminal Code* identifies five situations when a police officer can arrest without a warrant:

1. When an officer discovers an individual in the process of committing any criminal offence;
2. When an officer knows the individual has committed an indictable offence;
3. When an officer has reasonable and probable grounds that the accused has committed an indictable offence;
4. When an officer has reasonable grounds to believe an indictable offence is about to be committed; and
5. When an officer reasonably believes that there is an outstanding warrant for the arrest of an individual.

---

provincial authorities. It can also be left at the accused's last known address with an individual who appears to be at least 16 years of age. When this document is served, the accused is compelled to appear in court at a designated time and place (Barnhorst et al. 1992).

Detention

After an individual is arrested, the police have a number of decisions to make about the suspect. For one, they have to determine whether the person arrested should be held in custody before the trial. The law in Canada states the accused must be released unless there is good reason for keeping her in detention. The police cannot hold an individual for an undetermined reason; s. 9 of the *Charter of Rights and Freedoms* states "Everyone has the right not to be arbitrarily detained or imprisoned." In addition, s. 10(a) states "Everyone has the right on arrest or detention to be informed promptly of the reasons therefor." If the arresting officer decides that the accused is to be formally detained, the officer in charge at the police station to which the accused is taken has the discretion to release the suspect. The officer usually exercises that discretion unless the suspect is charged with a criminal offence punishable by imprisonment of five years or more, unless the suspect is felt to pose a threat to the public, or unless the suspect is believed unlikely to appear in court. If the officer decides that the accused is to remain in custody, the accused must be taken before a justice of the peace within 24 hours or, if this is not possible, at the earliest possible time. While the accused is in detention, the police may take fingerprints and photographs if the individual is charged with an indictable offence.

Bail or Custody

The purpose of bail is to ensure that the accused appears at her trial while permitting the accused to participate in the development of her defence. In Canada today, the *Criminal Code* requires all individuals arrested to be brought before a justice of the peace, who decides if the accused is to be released before her trial. This hearing, commonly referred to as the bail hearing, is formally known as the judicial interim release hearing. The justice of the peace is expected to release the accused unless the prosecutor supplies evidence to show either that the individual should not be released or that conditions should be attached to the release. Those charged with first- and second-degree murder can be released on bail only by a Superior Court judge.

Bail is considered such an important part of Canadian legal process that s. 11(e) of the *Charter of Rights and Freedoms* guarantees the right of the accused "not to be denied reasonable bail without just cause." According to s. 515(10) of the *Criminal Code*, bail may not be granted when it can be shown to be in the public interest or necessary for the protection or safety of the public, and where denial is necessary to ensure the appearance of the accused on the designated date of the trial. In certain circumstances, it is up to the accused to inform the judge why she should be released pending her trial.

Trial Procedure

The First Court Appearance

In most jurisdictions, the accused is arraigned—that is, hears the charges brought against her and enters a plea in response—not at the first appearance in court but at the preliminary hearing or at trial. Young offenders, however, are often arraigned at the first appearance. During the arraignment the accused is brought before a provincially appointed judge. At this time the court clerk reads all formal charges, and the accused (or her lawyer) makes her initial plea.

Sometimes defence counsel or the prosecutor indicates to the judge that she is not ready to proceed. This usually happens in cases that involve complex issues, where more time is needed to prepare the defence or prosecution. In such cases the presiding judge agrees to set aside the case until a later date. During such a postponement, the conditions that governed the accused individual before his initial appearance will apply. Because the *Charter of Rights and Freedoms* guarantees the right to a trial within a reasonable period of time, the accused may be asked to waive for the record this *Charter* right before the court proceeds further (see

Chapter 8). Only for that particular adjournment is the right waived; it can be raised again with respect to subsequent delays. If the accused won't waive the right, the case must be heard within the specified time period.

If a plea of "not guilty" is entered, a trial date is specified. However, if the accused decides to enter a plea of "guilty": the judge sets a sentencing date and decides whether the accused is to be held in custody until sentencing. If the accused pleads "not guilty," an information is drafted; but before the trial takes place, the accused may have the right to a preliminary inquiry. (An indictment is drafted only if the case goes to the Supreme Court.)

The Indictment and Preliminary Inquiry

In cases where the charge involves an election indictable offence—that is, when the accused has the right to choose between trial by judge alone and trial by judge and jury—an estimated 80 percent of the accused in Canada give up their right to a preliminary inquiry and go directly to trial. And approximately 80 percent of these cases end with the accused pleading "guilty" on first appearance in court. However, the accused has the right to a preliminary inquiry, which is held prior to the formal trial of a case in court. A provincial court judge hears preliminary inquiries. Summary conviction offences proceed differently in our court system, and they don't involve a preliminary inquiry.

The function of a preliminary inquiry is not to determine the guilt or innocence of the individual charged with a crime but rather to determine if there is enough evidence to send the accused to trial. During a preliminary inquiry, a prosecutor attempts to show the judge that enough evidence exists for a criminal trial. The prosecution has the power to call as few or as many witnesses as it feels necessary to prove to the judge that a case merits a trial. Once a witness testifies for the prosecution, defence counsel has the right of cross-examination.

The defence, too, has the right to call witnesses to support its claim of innocence. If the defence proves to the judge that the prosecution doesn't have a good case, there won't be a trial. Thus, a good defence during the preliminary inquiry can lead to the discharge of the accused. The defence also may call witnesses to get their testimony on record, especially if witnesses are sick or about to leave the country. The evidence provided by these witnesses during the preliminary inquiry may be used during the trial. Most preliminary inquiries last less than a day, and only rarely does a preliminary inquiry end in a judicial decision to discharge the accused or withdraw the charges. An inquiry is important to a defendant because it reveals much of the evidence that the prosecution will use against her during the trial. The defendant may then decide to plead guilty. In a study by the Law Reform Commission of Canada (1984), 71 percent of preliminary inquiries resulted in a plea of guilty once the case reached the court trial.

If the judge decides enough evidence exists to proceed to a trial, the offence for which the accused is to stand trial is then written in the form of an indictment. The indictment, a formally written allegation that states that the accused has committed a particular offence, replaces the information, and it forms the basis of the prosecution.

However, even if the judge decides to discharge the accused, the accused is not acquitted. A discharge simply means that insufficient evidence exists at this time to proceed to trial. As Mewett (1996: 82) points out, a discharge means "the accused cannot be tried on that information and that proceedings on that information are terminated." If, at a future date, new evidence is produced that strongly indicates the accused was involved in the crime, the prosecution usually proceeds by way of a direct indictment instead of requesting another preliminary inquiry. Whatever the avenue chosen, the Attorney General or a senior official in the provincial Justice department is required to give personal approval of the Crown's actions.

The Trial

For most indictable offences the accused can elect trial by judge alone or by judge and jury. Some exceptions apply, such as first- and second-degree murder charges, where the accused must be tried by judge and jury unless both the defendant and the Attorney General of the province agree to proceed by way of judge alone. Some indictable offences are considered so minor (for example, gaming offences) that in almost every circumstance they are heard by a judge alone.

In Canada, the accused has the right to change her mind about the type of trial she wants, although certain restrictions apply. In a reelection, as this process is called, an accused who initially selected trial by a provincial court judge has 14 days to change her mind and request a trial by a judge and jury. If she originally selected trial by judge and jury, the accused has 15 days after the completion of the preliminary inquiry to change her mind and select a trial heard by a provincial court judge alone.

Once the indictment is read to the accused in court, the accused has to plead to the charge(s) by entering a plea of either "guilty" or "not guilty." If the accused pleads "not guilty," the prosecution has to prove the defendant is guilty of the specified offence beyond a reasonable doubt. In this situation, no reasonable amount of doubt concerning the guilt or innocence of the accused can be left unresolved. If reasonable doubt exists, the accused is acquitted of all charges.

Sentencing

If the accused is found guilty, the judge has numerous sentencing options available. The sentences most commonly used in Canada include a discharge (either absolute or conditional), probation, incarceration, suspended sentence, and fines. A judge may decide to combine two of these sentences, such as a period of incarceration with a fine. The sentence depends in large part on the charges that the individual was found guilty of and the prior record of the offender. In a few instances a judge has no choice in setting the penalty. For example, if the judge finds an offender guilty of a charge of first- or second-degree murder, she must sentence the accused to life imprisonment.

In many instances, a judge also relies on a presentence report compiled by a probation officer to assist in the determination of the sentence. This report may evaluate such things as the employment record of the offender and any family support. A judge may use other sources of information such as a victim impact state-

Marie Deschamps is the latest appointment to the Supreme Court of Canada, replacing Madame Justice Claire L'Heureux-Dubé in August 2002.

CHAPTER 1 An Overview of the Criminal Justice System in Canada

Supreme Court justices pose for an official photograph at the Supreme Court in Ottawa Monday, Sept. 30, 2002. Front row (left to right): Justice John Major, Justice Charles Gonthier, Chief Justice Beverley McLachlin, Justice Frank Iacobucci, and Justice Michel Bastarache. Back row (left to right): Justice Louis LeBel, Justice William Binnie, Justice Louise Arbour, and Justice Marie Deschamps.

ment, information given about the accused at the sentence hearing by the Crown prosecutor or the defence lawyer, and any mitigating or aggravating circumstances surrounding the commission of the crime. These can be significant factors in determining the final sentence.

Incarceration

If the sentence involves a period of incarceration, the offender is sent either to a provincial jail or a federal institution. If she is sentenced to a federal institution, the offender can apply for day parole six months before she is eligible to make an application for full parole. Full parole is possible for most offenders after they complete one-third of the sentence or serve seven years, whichever period is shortest. Most offenders in Canada do not serve the full term of their sentence; if they don't receive full parole, most receive statutory release after serving two-thirds of their sentence. While they are incarcerated, offenders can receive some form of rehabilitation or treatment. Though the amount of treat-

ment given to offenders varies, programs are designed to help offenders reintegrate into society. After their release, offenders on parole must contact their parole officer on a regular basis. They may be required to spend some time in a halfway house or under some other form of community supervision.

THE INFORMAL OPERATION OF THE CRIMINAL JUSTICE SYSTEM

The Criminal Justice Funnel

Another approach to explaining the processing of cases through the criminal justice system is referred to as the "criminal justice funnel." When a crime is committed and the offender is charged by the police, the case enters the top of the funnel and then passes through ever-narrowing stages of the funnel until it exits. Sometimes this exiting occurs at the bottom of the funnel when the offender is sent to a correctional facility, but it could also happen higher on the funnel, such as when all charges are dropped because a witness refuses to testify or because the prosecutor feels the charges are insufficient. Between the top and bottom of this funnel, then, are key decision-making points, where a caseload potentially can be reduced.

Although the actors and agencies in our criminal justice system are controlled by the formal rules of law, there is considerable leeway in how they operate and how activities are allocated and carried out. According to those who study the informal criminal justice system, the criminal justice system is best thought of as a process. This view emphasizes the key decision points that cases pass. Each decision point is, in effect, a screening stage that involves a series of routinized operations and whose efficacy is gauged primarily by its ability to move the case to its next stage and a successful conclusion. The processing of individuals through our criminal justice system then becomes a system of human resource management. In this system the various actors go about their daily activities without stepping on toes and bending informal social and agency rules. Part of this system is dedicated to the search for simple solutions; simple routine justice treats similarly situated defendants in the same ways. The central element of this informal system corresponds more to the personal and political needs of justice personnel than to any abstract concept of justice or the rule of law.

All members of criminal justice agencies involved in the detection, prosecution, and sentencing of offenders may use their discretion in many professional matters (see Exhibit 1.3).

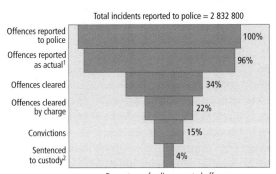

1. An offence is considered to be "actual" when, following an initial investigation, the police confirm that a criminal offence has occurred. An offence is "cleared" when the police are satisfied they have identified an offender. However, it may not be possible to lay a charge against the offender because he/she is dead, under age 12, has diplomatic immunity, is already in prison, etc. If, in the view of the police, it is possible to lay a charge against an offender, the offence is cleared by charge.
2. Includes secure custody only for young offenders and any custodial sentence for adults.

Source: Reproduced from Statistics Canada, *Juristat,* Catalogue 85-002, vol. 17, no. 13, November 1997, p. 1.

FIGURE 1.2
Caseload within the Canadian Criminal Justice System, 1996

Figure 1.2 illustrates the caseload of the criminal justice system at work in Canada during 1996. Of the total caseload for that year (there were 2 832 800 incidents reported to the police) only 22 percent of these offences were cleared by charge by the police (meaning that the police charged an accused). Of these cases, only two-thirds were convicted in court, and, of those, just over 25 percent of the offenders were sentenced to custody in either a provincial/territorial or federal correctional facility.

The Courtroom Workgroup

While the actors and agencies in our criminal justice system are theoretically controlled in their use of authority by the rule of law, there is considerable discretion used by the various actors. When the argument is made that the criminal justice system is operating on the basis of informal as opposed to formal rules, attention is focused upon what is called "the courtroom workgroup." One important feature of this group is that everyone involved cooperates with each other; that is, the members establish shared methods and values that assist the

---

EXHIBIT 1.3 Discretion within the Criminal Justice System

POLICE
Enforce the law
Investigate crimes
Search and seizure
Arrest suspects

PROSECUTORS
File charges on the basis of evidence brought to them by the police
Reduce charges
Drop cases
Plea-bargain

JUDGES
Decide to eliminate certain pieces of evidence

CORRECTIONAL OFFICIALS
Set a conditional release date (e.g., parole)

group to achieve their goals. Another important feature is that the needs of the members take precedence over concerns about the fairness and equity of how the system is operating. The relationships among the individuals composing this group have a significant impact on the day-to-day operations of the various criminal justice agencies as well as the outcomes of each individual case. The actors function on the basis of their own professional needs as well as the needs of their particular agency. The impact of this group has a significant impact upon the daily operation of our justice system as well as the type of justice administered to and experienced by both offenders and victims.

The police, for example, have the function of collecting sufficient evidence to lay charges, thereby allowing the case to pass into the hands of a Crown prosecutor. Of course, Crown prosecutors can't try a case if the police don't collect enough evidence to lay a charge. Similarly, at the parole stage, parole board members decide whether to release an inmate directly into society, to place her in a community facility, or to keep her institutionalized. Each decision is crucial. If an error is made, members of the public may be placed at risk or an innocent person may be incarcerated for a crime she didn't commit.

The criminal justice system does not inevitably secure a conviction in all cases of those who are charged with a crime and tried in court. At each stage in the system, the number of accused persons is reduced, sometimes because they plead guilty or because charges are dropped on account of insufficient evidence (see Figure 1.3).

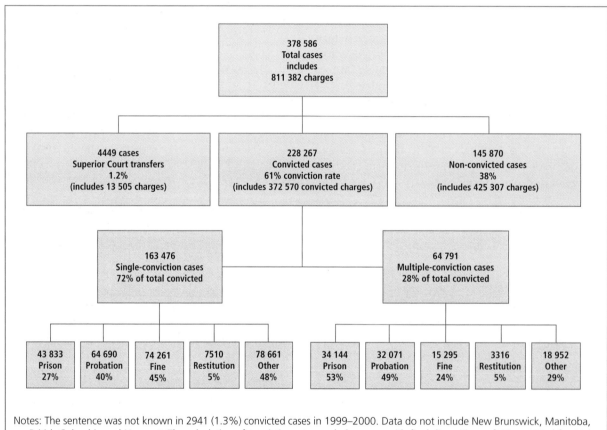

Notes: The sentence was not known in 2941 (1.3%) convicted cases in 1999–2000. Data do not include New Brunswick, Manitoba, British Columbia and Nunavut. The calculation of conviction rates excludes cases with final dispositions of "Committed for trial in Superior Court" and "Re-election to Provincial Court" (1.2% of disposed cases). Since Alberta and Yukon provide the survey with Superior Court data, transfers to Superior Court are not final dispositions for these two jurisdictions. Non-convicted equals Total minus Superior Court transfers minus Convicted. More than one sentence can be imposed in a charge or a case resulting in a conviction; therefore, the percentage total is greater than 100%.

Source: Statistics Canada, *Juristat*, Catalogue 85-002, vol. 22, no. 2, March 2002, p. 6.

FIGURE 1.3

Adult Criminal Court Processing of Federal Statute Cases with Type of Sentences Imposed, Nine Provinces and Territories in Canada, 1999–2000

Figure 1.3 illustrates how many cases and charges disappeared during the adult criminal court processing of federal statute cases for nine provinces and territories in Canada during 1999–2000. Thirty-eight percent of the cases for that year (involving just over 52 percent of all the charges) did not result in a conviction. Overall, a conviction was obtained in 61 percent of the 378 586 total cases heard in court. One-third of all these cases were stayed or withdrawn while only 2 percent concluded with the accused being acquitted.

Reporting the Crime

Some people who have been victimized in a crime may not realize they have been victimized; others who have been victimized realize what has happened but don't report the crime to the police. For example, victims may decide not to report a property crime because they feel it isn't worth the effort. Police forces themselves may refuse to investigate a property crime or fraud case because they feel it is too minor or because they stand only a slight chance of discovering the perpetrator. It may not be feasible for the police to investigate the theft of a bicycle, though it is worth a few hundred dollars, or a bad cheque under $100, because of the amount of time required to investigate the crime and the low probability of solving the case. But if the police accept the complaint, an occurrence report is recorded.

Recent victimization studies in Canada reveal that a substantial number of victims of violent crimes do not report these crimes to the police. In the Canadian Urban Victimization Survey (Statistics Canada 1985), the four most common reasons given to researchers by victims about their reasons for not reporting an incident to police were, in order of priority, "too minor," "the police couldn't do anything," "inconvenience," and "nothing taken." The survey discovered that victims didn't report 62 percent of the sexual assaults, 55 percent of the robberies, and 66 percent of the assaults committed against them. Questions about victimization included in the 1993 national General Social Survey found that 90 percent of sexual assaults, 68 percent of assaults, 54 percent of vandalism, 53 percent of robberies, 48 percent of motor vehicle thefts or attempted thefts, and 32 percent of all break and enters were not reported to the police. In total, only 42 percent of the above 10 types of criminal incidents were reported to the police (Gartner and Doob 1994).

In the most recent General Social Survey, Besserer and Trainor (2000) found victims continued to report only a minority of the offences committed against them to the police overall, with only 37 percent of the 10 criminal incidents included in the survey being reported to the police. The main reason these crimes were not reported was that the incident was not considered to be important enough (59 percent of the unreported responses) and because the victims felt the police couldn't do anything (50 percent) (see Chapter 4).

Recording of the Incident as a Crime by the Police

Even if the police are contacted about a possible criminal act, they may decide after an investigation that an official report and the laying of formal criminal charges is not required. Such cases are categorized as "unfounded," which means that, after a preliminary investigation into the incident, the police decide a crime was neither attempted nor actually committed.

There are many reasons an incident may be classified as "unfounded" by the police. Ericson (1982), in his study of policing in the Toronto region, discovered that patrol officers used many tactics to record an incident as "unfounded." Often they did not "officially record an incident because, in spite of their efforts, they are frustrated by the complexities and the lack of citizen assistance in sorting them out." In addition, Ericson found it rare for a minor complaint, such as a traffic accident involving damage under $200, to be recorded as a crime.

Patrol officers reacted quite differently when they were contacted by victim–complainants about one or more of four different types of complaints considered "major"—interpersonal incidents, property disputes, automobile disputes, and "other" disputes, according to Ericson. When one of these complaints was reported, the police officially recorded the event as a crime in 52 percent of their investigations. Official reports were more likely to be made in incidents where property damage or loss occurred. Incidents were also more likely to be recorded as crimes when no personal injury to the victim was involved. Interpersonal disputes, however, were often not officially recorded as crimes. The reason for this was that "a prior relationship between a victim and a suspect substantially decreases the probability that the suspect will be convicted if charged" and "there are usually greater problems in sustaining a charge for assault arising out of interpersonal conflicts" (Ericson 1982: 119). As a result, officers "routinely dealt with interpersonal troubles by informal means, while property-related troubles were more routinely processed as officially-determined crimes."

Laying a Charge

Once a suspect is identified and there is sufficient evidence to lay an information, the incident is considered to be "cleared by charge." Incidents may also be classified as "cleared otherwise" in cases where the complainant declines to proceed with the charges or when the suspect dies before a charge can be laid.

If a suspect is present at the scene when the police arrive, and the officer decides the complaint has merit, one would think that the individual would be arrested, taken to the police station, interrogated, and subsequently charged with a criminal offence.

According to Ericson (1982), however, patrol officers didn't always arrest an identifiable suspect even when they decided a crime had been committed. Of the 392 individuals formally classified as "criminal suspects," Ericson found that no further formal action or report was taken against 137 of them. Official reports were made on 40 other suspects, but again no further action was taken against them for a variety of reasons. Thus, almost half of the individuals classified as "criminal suspects" were not processed to the next stage of the criminal justice system. Only 107 (or 27 percent) of the criminal suspects were arrested and subsequently formally prosecuted.

More recently, Rigakos (1997) studied the responses by police officers in one police organization in the lower mainland area of British Columbia. These incidents required a mandatory arrest response according to both provincial and departmental policies. Yet, police officers said they rarely arrested offenders even when

1. The woman complainant presented them with a signed protection order;
2. The male in violation of the court order remained at the scene;
3. The complainant requested that the police officer arrest the offender, and
4. A zero tolerance domestic violence policy was in effect in their police service.

Overall, police officers arrested the suspect in only 35 percent of the cases involving criminal peace-bond breaches and 21 percent of the instances involving civil order violations.

Bail (Judicial Interim Hearing)

One of the most important components of the criminal justice system is whether or not the accused receives bail. Many concerns were raised during the 1960s about the relationship between the ability of an accused to pay bail and the judicial determination of his guilt or innocence. Studies conducted in the United States—which influenced Canadian policy on the granting of bail—pointed out the ramifications of such an approach: only 18 per-

cent of individuals jailed pending trial were acquitted, while 48 percent of those granted bail were acquitted (Vera Institute of Justice 1992). In response to these concerns about the relationship between bail and the outcome of a trial, Canada passed the *Bail Reform Act* (1972), which allowed an accused to be released on his own recognizance if he promised to appear in court on the date of his trial, if he was considered a good member of the community, and if he had not committed a serious or violent crime.

However, in a series of studies conducted within a decade of the enactment of the *Bail Reform Act*, Canadian researchers discovered many accused persons who were eligible for bail still didn't receive it and that their denial of bail significantly increased their chances of being convicted and receiving a longer sentence (Koza and Doob 1975). In addition, Hagan and Morden (1981), who studied individuals held in detention while awaiting a bail hearing, found that detention increased their chances of being found guilty and of subsequent incarceration.

Canadian law states that an accused person can be detained before trial only if the accused might not appear for his trial or if there is a risk that the accused will commit another offence while awaiting trial. However, Kellough (1996), in her study of bail hearings in Toronto during 1992, concluded that "the norm of conditional release operates differently in practice than in theory." Kellough notes that many applicants were denied bail not because of concern about their posing a possible threat to society or because they failed to appear at trial when scheduled. Rather, she points out, many are detained for "secondary grounds"—that is, for reasons other than community safety and appearance at a trial on the specified day.

Prosecution

Research has consistently revealed that the greatest amount of attrition of major or indictable cases within our criminal justice system occurs between the time the police lay a criminal charge and the time a prosecutor decides to accept the case and take it to court. The common assumption holds that prosecutors accept any case in which the police decide there are "reasonable and probable grounds" that a crime was committed and the individual charged did in fact commit it. But prosecutors review most, if not all, of the cases involving serious crimes handed to them in order to assess the quality of the evidence before they proceed to the courtroom. And concern about the quality of evidence collected by the police leads prosecutors to stay the charges or to drop them altogether (Petersilia et al. 1990).

Factors other than evidentiary issues may be involved in a decision to prosecute a case, however. For example, issues related to the role of witnesses and victims can have an impact on the prosecution of cases. In their interviews with Crown prosecutors in Manitoba, for example, Gunn and Minch (1988) discovered that approximately 10 percent of cases were not prosecuted because the victim of a sexual assault decided not to proceed to trial. The decision not to proceed, according to the prosecutors, came from the fear of testifying in court, the fear of revenge, pressure from family and friends, because of the prior relationship with the offender, or because of sympathy for the offender.

Even at the prosecution stage, cases usually remain in the hands of the police until they are scheduled to be heard in provincial court. What the police tell the prosecutor about a case can therefore have a significant impact on any decision made about proceeding with the case (Wheeler 1987).

The police have also been found to strike deals with offenders in order to gain information about other crimes and criminals. Here too the police can have considerable impact on the decision a Crown prosecutor makes about the charges or sentence in any particular case. Defence lawyers often negotiate with the police on their client's behalf, and after an agreement has been reached the police confirm the agreement by discussing it with the Crown prosecutor (Klein 1976; Ericson and Baranek 1982). As a result, criticism has been aimed at the control that police have over many minor court cases. This control means that prosecutions in such cases "are not as subject to checks and balances as formal legal procedures would have it. In only a tiny fraction of cases does the accused actually have a trial. In the vast majority, the 'trial' is the plea bargaining session and the accused is not allowed to attend" (Wheeler 1987).

Sentencing

As noted previously, most accused persons in Canada plead guilty on first appearance in provincial court, thus eliminating the opportunity to argue the facts of the case with the prosecution. In Desroches' (1995) study of robbers, the reasons given by accused persons for pleading guilty were numerous. Some people simply wanted to "get the thing over with," while others had already given the police a statement admitting their guilt. Other people believed that the police had enough evidence to convict them anyway or that a trial might actually lead to a longer sentence. Still others agreed to a guilty plea prior to the court case in the hope they would receive a lenient sentence. Whatever their hope, most considered their sentence too harsh. As one convicted robber said, "You can molest children or kill somebody in this country and get a slap on the wrist. But don't you dare steal our money or we'll put you in prison and throw away the key" (Desroches 1995: 253).

This inmate was referring to discrimination against some offenders in the matter of sentencing. Certainly it would seem logical to expect the perpetrators of the most serious crimes to receive the harshest sentences, but this is not always the case. Extralegal factors such as race, gender, age, and social class may become significant when sentencing decisions are made by the judge. Research results may differ in various parts of Canada, but studies have found that race is a significant factor in the type and length of sentencing of offenders. For example, Correctional Service of Canada statistics consistently reveal that an Aboriginal is more likely to be sent to federal prison than a white with a similar criminal record and prior record (Moyer et al. 1985). The Ontario Commission on Systemic Racism came to a similar conclusion in 1995 when it compared sentences among black offenders and offenders from other racial backgrounds in the Toronto criminal courts (Roberts and Doob 1997). Studies in Manitoba (Hamilton and Sinclair 1991) and Alberta (Alberta Task Force 1991) reported Aboriginal offenders were more commonly sentenced to a correctional facility when controlling for prior record and type of offence among all offenders. Other researchers have pointed out that the poor may not be able to afford quality legal representation and as a result receive harsher sentences (Winterdyck 2000).

VALUES AND THE CRIMINAL JUSTICE SYSTEM

If the informal processing of the accused through our criminal justice system disturbs you, you will no doubt question the values of the system. Social scientists agree that all individuals possess values, i.e., ideals or ultimate aims and standards about what is desirable; our criminal justice system also holds values. Packer (1968) developed two models of our criminal justice system, both of which represent very different value systems.

The Due Process and Crime Control Models of the Criminal Justice System

What do we want our criminal justice system to achieve? The answer to this question is not as straightforward as it might seem. Certainly most, if not all, individuals in our society want our system to be fair and just. Yet how will these ideals be attained? Herbert Packer, who was both legally and academically trained, attempted to answer this question by developing two ideal models of criminal justice. One showed how criminal justice should work and the other showed its appropriate goals. He called these two models the due process model and the crime control model. In Packer's view, the main concern of the due process model was prioritizing the rights of the suspect. Packer felt the mechanism to best accomplish this is an accurate, fair, and reliable system of laws and legal procedures. Of great importance to this approach is the fact that, at every step of the way within the justice system, the rights of the suspect or accused are not violated and that only the guilty are punished. In contrast, the crime control model emphasizes the control and suppression of criminal activity. This control is maintained by a criminal justice system that focuses on speed, efficiency, and incarceration for those found guilty. Because of its emphasis on the repression of criminal behaviour, the crime control model cannot be effective if delays occur as a case moves through the legal system and if negotiated outcomes, such as plea bargains, come into play. On rare occasions innocent persons are found guilty, but the model maintains that such incidents are more than countered by the deterrent impact of the justice system (see Exhibit 1.4).

The Crime Control Model

According to Sykes and Cullen (1992) the crime control model is best characterized by such statements as "get tough on crime" and "the criminal justice system is weak on criminals." It holds that the most important goal of the criminal justice system is to reduce crime by incarcerating criminals for lengthy periods of time. This reduces lawlessness and protects the rights of law-abiding citizens. To achieve this goal, the criminal justice system operates like an assembly line—it moves offenders as efficiently as possible to conviction and punishment so that effective crime control is attained. Certainty of punishment is reached through mandatory sentences, longer prison terms, and the elimination of parole.

The crime control model rests on the presumption of guilt; that is, most individuals who are arrested are in fact guilty. Thus the model puts great trust in the decisions made by criminal justice officials, who wish to protect society. The model assumes that these individuals make few, if any, errors, since most defendants are guilty. Each stage of the criminal justice system involves a series of uniform and routine decisions made by officials. Finality is important to officials, because it means

there are few problems with the system and, as a result, few challenges to the system. Support for the use of discretion throughout the system is a key feature of this model, since legal technicalities reduce the efficiency of punishing offenders. If the criminal justice system is allowed to run as efficiently as possible, a reduction in the crime rate results. Consequently, concerns for legal rights should not be allowed to erode the system's ability to reduce crime. Furthermore, when issues about the administration of justice come into conflict with the protection of society, the crime control model errs in favour of the protection of the rights of the law-abiding citizenry.

The Due Process Model

In contrast to the crime control model, the due process model emphasizes the protection of the legal rights of the accused. The most important goal of the model is not to reduce crime but to see that justice is done—specifically, by protecting the legal rights of the accused. This ensures that innocent people are not convicted. If they are, a serious wrong has occurred somewhere in the justice system, and it needs to be corrected immediately. The best way to protect the rights of the accused is to limit the powers of criminal justice officials in order to avoid potential wrongdoing. The operation of this criminal justice system is much different from the crime control model—it's like an obstacle course.

In a due process model, before people are arrested, prosecuted, and convicted, every attempt is made to ensure that accused persons are treated with fairness and that justice is served. All offenders are presumed innocent, regardless of their apparent guilt. Criminal justice officials are constantly monitored, since they are likely to abuse their power and to make errors in judgment when processing and convicting individuals. The high-profile cases of Donald Marshall and Guy Paul Morin both involved officials who convicted innocent people (Harris 1986; Makin 1993). As a result of these abuses, legal controls were introduced to make sure that officials don't abuse their power.

It is difficult, if not impossible, for the criminal justice system to reduce crime, say the supporters of this model, because the criminal sanction cannot prevent all criminal activity from occurring, so justice should not be sacrificed in the name of crime control that is largely beyond reach. Issues that bring the administration of justice into disrepute are of great concern to the due process model, and even if an accused is factually guilty, the fact that a member of a criminal justice agency violates the criminal procedures governing its operation means the offender is allowed to go free.

Due Process or Crime Control?

While these models are idealized and do not exist in reality as Packer presented them, they do help clarify the expectations individuals have of the criminal justice system (see Exhibit 1.4). For example, after the terrorist attacks in the United States on September 11, 2001, most Canadians wanted the federal government to introduce strong measures in order to counter the threat of terrorism in this country (see Exhibit 1.5). Public opinion polls found that 80 percent of Canadians wanted mandatory fingerprinting and identification cards for all Canadians, while a majority of citizens were supportive of giving the police extraordinary powers although this could mean that their home telephones could be tapped and their mail screened. They also informed the pollsters that they wanted an end to policies that favoured immigration. By January 2002, however, this support for the crime control model to deal with terrorism had decreased, with the public now informing the pollsters they favoured new immigration and that they were not as supportive of giving the police and security forces more legal powers to more effectively combat terrorism. In part because of the changing public perceptions of terrorism, by late May 2002 the federal government withdrew some of the most contro-versial proposals dealing with terrorist activities, such as giving the Cabinet powers allowing them to infringe on the civil rights of individuals living in Canada without any involvement of Parliament (Fife 2002b). Instead, they replaced the most onerous pieces of the proposed law with less harsh measures.

SUMMARY

The study of criminal justice has developed into a major field of study over the past 30 years. It combines different disciplines—criminology, law, psychology, political science, and social welfare—in an attempt to gain a better understanding of the crime problem, of how to improve the operation of the various criminal justice agencies, and of the most effective way in which to punish criminals. Much effort has gone into improving our knowledge of crime and determining how our agencies should fight crime, but the enterprise is extremely costly, and the costs rise each year.

Criminal justice can be viewed as a system as well as a "funnel." As a system it functions in a formal and highly visible manner, with all the major agencies working together as a coordinated unit. In its actual operation, the criminal justice system resembles a

---

EXHIBIT 1.4   A Comparison of the Due Process and Crime Control Models

Crime Control Model	Due Process Model
Goals	**Goals**
Deter crime Protect citizens and the community Punish offenders "Assembly-line" (efficient) justice	Protect individuals from the powers of the state Enhance legal rights of the accused Fairness, equality, and justice
Policies	**Policies**
Increases in the number of police officers Increases in the number of correctional facilities Increases in sentence length Guilty until proven innocent Give criminal justice agencies more legal powers	Limit and control the powers of the police Limit discretion and control the activities of Crown prosecutors and judges so that all accused are treated fairly Ensure the powers of all the agencies are controlled
Purpose	**Purpose**
Reduce the number of criminals on the street	Ensure that the rights of the defendant are protected
Case example	**Case example**
R. v. Hall (2002 SCC 64) The Supreme Court upheld the trial judge's decision to deny bail to Mr. Hall in order to maintain public confidence in the criminal justice system. Mr. Hall was charged with first-degree murder.	*R. v. Feeney* ([1997] 2 S.C.R. 117). In this case, a murder suspect was arrested without a warrant, an action the Supreme Court felt was not legitimate. As a result, the Court ruled against the police, restricting their powers of search.

EXHIBIT 1.5 The Anti-Terrorism Law: Crime Control or Due Process?

Laws usually evolve in a deliberate manner in our society. However, this approach changed immediately after 8:45 a.m. on the morning of September 11, 2001, when American Airlines Flight 11 was flown into the north tower of the World Trade Center in New York City by hijackers. Many Canadians began to ask whether or not we could have been better prepared for such actions. More specifically, could this action have somehow been prevented by laws in this country? And how should we react to these actions if they were to occur in this country? Even in this situation, when almost all Canadians demanded some form of legal response, creating new legal powers is not as straightforward as would seem at first glance.

THE GOVERNMENT'S RESPONSE

After September 11, the federal government introduced two pieces of legislation designed to deal with terrorism in this country. The first, introduced on 15 October 2001, was the Anti-Terrorism Act (known as Bill C-36), which created measures to (1) identify, prosecute, convict, and punish terrorists and terrorist organizations as well as (2) give new investigative powers to law enforcement and security agencies. Some of the measures directed toward terrorist organizations included

- defining and designating terrorist groups to make it easier to prosecute terrorists and their supporters;
- making it an offence to knowingly participate in, contribute to, or facilitate the activities of a terrorist group or to instruct anyone to carry out a terrorist activity or an activity on behalf of a terrorist group;
- creating tougher sentences and parole supervision for terrorist offenders; and
- cutting off financial support for terrorists by making it a crime to knowingly collect or give funds to them, either directly or indirectly.

Bill C-36 also proposed to give law enforcement and security agencies new extensive and powerful investigative powers to collect information about and prosecute terrorists and terrorists groups, including

- making it easier to use electronic surveillance against terrorist organizations;
- creating new offences targeting unlawful disclosure of certain information of national interest;
- amending the Canada Evidence Act to guard certain information of national interest from

disclosure during courtroom or other judicial proceedings;
- within certain defined limits, allowing the arrest, detention, and imposition of conditions of release on suspected terrorists for 72 hours without charge to prevent terrorist acts and save lives; and
- creating investigative hearings compelling individuals who have information about a terrorist organization to disclose that information to a judge even in the absence of a formal trial.

The second piece of legislation (Bill C-42) was introduced in November 2001, and proposed to give broad powers to the government in times of crisis. In particular, Bill C-42 proposed that special powers be granted to federal ministers in order that they could respond immediately to terrorist threats without waiting for authorization from the Cabinet (Fife 2002a). This meant that Cabinet ministers would now have the power to issue executive orders to deal with security threats but these would not be subject to the same parliamentary overview process needed for all other situations as currently provided by the Emergencies Act. In addition, the Minister of Defence was given the power to declare any area in Canada a "temporary military zone" for up to one year and allow the Canadian Forces to "forcibly remove" anyone from the area during that time.

Support for these stronger measures was not, however, held by all Canadians. Many observers voiced concerns over both pieces of proposed legislation, particularly that civil liberties would be a casualty of the "war against terrorism." Civil liberties can be defined as those rights guaranteed to Canadians by the Charter of Rights and Freedoms and they include, among others, freedom of religion, freedom of association, and freedom to expect a certain amount of privacy.

One concern was the racial profiling of suspects. Would specific groups be targeted more often than others, often with little or no evidence to back up suspicions (Choudhry 2001)? After September 11, it was obvious that some private citizens were racially profiling and then attacking those whom they considered responsible. Many of these attacks were directed at Muslims or South Asians who were mistaken for Muslims. Sixteen bomb threats were made against mosques, and two mosques and a Hindu temple were burnt. In Ottawa, an Arab-born teenager was brutally assaulted, while other Muslims across

Canada reported that they were the recipients of taunts and threats (Blackwell 2002).

Despite criticisms, perhaps the most important problem for the federal government came from the Supreme Court of Canada. Its decision in a case involving the issue of whether or not police could keep some of their investigations secret from the public, in particular by ordering a publication ban of their activities, dealt a blow to the proposed secrecy provisions of Bill C-36. The Supreme Court ruled that the use of publication bans to insulate police conduct from public scrutiny seriously "deprives the Canadian public of its ability to know of and be able to respond to police practices ..." (Chwialkowska 2001b). As a result, questions were raised about the potential that the deceptive police tactics contained in Bill C-36 would in many cases be illegal. But John Manley, then Minister of Foreign Affairs, stated that "either nothing changed on September 11 or everything changed." He went on to say that without the controversial powers of arrest given to the police, "it might be impossible to prevent a terrorist activity even if we had the information [that it was to occur]" (Chwialkowska 2001a).

The question then becomes, how, how much freedom are we willing to trade for security? In some areas, the proposed legislation received general support, such as increased security in airports and more thorough screening processes in many government agencies. But what about giving the police more powers and allowing the preventive detention of suspected terrorists? Within a few weeks of its introduction, opposition to Bill C-36 reached significant levels, ending the hope of the federal government to fast-track this legislation through Parliament. At the beginning of November 2001, many of these criticisms were voiced at the Security of Freedom conference held at the University of Toronto and later

in the publication of many of the speeches presented. At this conference, the criticisms of Bill C-36 included that it forwarded an overly broad definition of terrorist organizations, that it could lead to racial profiling, and was likely to undermine civil liberties and minority rights (Borovoy 2001; Daniels et al. 2001). Due to these concerns, Bill C-36 was revised and presented to Parliament on 20 November 2001. While the proposed legislation still contained several controversial components, such as broader police powers, significant changes were made in an attempt to reassure critics, "civil libertarians and ethnic groups who fear a trampling of individual rights" (Chwialkowska 2001c). In its revised form, Bill C-36 was able to deal with many of these criticisms and gain the support of most of its initial critics, and it received Royal Assent on 18 December 2001. However, it took 218 days from the passage of the act for the federal government to officially designate the first organizations as terrorist organizations. All seven of the groups were identified as Sunni Muslim organizations with connections to al-Qaeda, the group directly or indirectly linked to attacks on the United States (Curry 2002).

In April 2002, the federal government withdrew Bill C-42 to replace it in a few weeks with new "softer" legislation. The provision giving the defence minister the power to declare any area of Canada a temporary military zone was eliminated. In addition, that section of the proposed legislation granting Cabinet ministers the power to impose martial law without any checks or balances from Parliament was to be altered in the near future when a new bill would be presented to Parliament. However, the legislation was redrafted and sent back to Parliament the next week, with the provisions giving Cabinet ministers significant powers largely intact (*The Globe and Mail* 2002).

---

funnel, in the sense that many crimes are committed but relatively few individuals are convicted. The highest-profile cases are representative of the formal operation of the criminal justice system, with lawyers debating the facts and an impartial judge ensuring that the rules of legal procedure are followed. Most individuals don't enjoy the luxury of a formal trial, however. Their cases are resolved during their initial appearance in court or, if a trial is conducted, in a matter of hours or days. Thus, two opposing models of the criminal justice system emerge.

According to the crime control model, criminal law establishes an important difference between the

law-abiding and the law-breakers. Those who support the crime control model say the focus should be on the capture, processing, and control of individuals who break the law. In contrast, the due process model emphasizes the legal rights of individuals. This model's adherents believe that the legal system is in fact an obstacle course; they place emphasis on the rights of the accused. Even if the accused is factually guilty, the prosecution must prove the legal guilt before the accused can be convicted and punished. In the due process model, the operation of all agencies in the criminal justice system are open to investigation and questions about their actions.

Discussion Questions

1. Do you think the measures introduced by the federal government to combat terrorism will prevent such actions from occurring? What civil liberties are you willing to give up to ensure this?

2. Discuss the relative strengths and weaknesses of the crime control model.

3. Discuss the relative strengths and weaknesses of the due process model.

4. Discuss the effort made to reduce crime in our society. What stops us from attaining a crime-free society? Is a high crime rate the price that our society must pay to have legal rights?

5. What should be the predominant function of the police in contemporary society?

6. Should we try to control the discretion of our criminal justice agencies? If we do, and succeed, what would the impact be?

7. Why don't victims report their crimes to the police? Have you or members of your family ever witnessed or been a victim of a crime and not reported it? If so, why was the crime not reported?

Suggested Readings

Ericson, R.V., and P.M. Baranek. 1982. *The Ordering of Justice: A Study of Accused Persons as Dependants in the Criminal Justice Process.* Toronto: University of Toronto Press.

Harris, M. 2002. *Con Game: The Truth about Canada's Prisons.* Toronto: McClelland & Stewart.

Hartnagel, T.F., ed. 1998. *Canadian Crime Control Policy: Selected Readings.* Toronto: Harcourt Brace Canada.

Paciocco, D.M. 1999. *Getting Away with Murder: The Canadian Criminal Justice System.* Toronto: Irwin.

Roberts, J.V., ed. 2000. *Criminal Justice in Canada: A Reader.* Toronto: Harcourt Brace Canada.

Vallee, B. *Life with Billy.* 1986. Toronto: Seal Books.

References

Albanese, J. 1999. *Criminal Justice.* Boston, MA: Allyn & Bacon.

Alberta Task Force. 1991. *Justice on Trial: Report of the Task Force on the Criminal Justice System and Its Impact on the Indian and Metis People of Alberta.* Edmonton: Attorney General and Solicitor General of Alberta.

Barnhorst, R., S. Barnhorst, and K. L. Clarke. 1992. *Criminal Law and the Canadian Criminal Code,* 2nd ed. Toronto: McGraw-Hill Ryerson.

Besserer, S., and C. Trainor. 2000. *Criminal Victimization in Canada, 1999.* Ottawa: Statistics Canada.

Blackwell, T. 2002. "Racial Tension Peaked after Sept. 11 Attacks." *National Post,* 16 July, A7.

Blumberg, A. 1979. *Criminal Justice: Issues and Ironies,* 2nd ed. New York: New Viewpoints.

Borovoy, A. 2001. Does the Antiterror Bill Go Too Far?" *The Globe and Mail,* 20 November, A17.

Choudhry, S. 2001. "Protecting Equality in the Face of Terror: Ethnic and Racial Profiling and s. 15 of the *Charter.* In R.J. Daniels et al. (eds.) *The Security of Freedom: Essays on Canada's Anti-Terrorism Bill.* Toronto: University of Toronto Press, pp. 367–82.

Chwialkowska, L. 2001a. "Police Get Vast Power of Arrest." *National Post,* 15 October A1–A2.

———. 2001b. "Secret Police Tactics Public's Concern, Court." *National Post,* 16 November, A4.

———. 2001c. "Liberals Put Leash on Terror Law." *National Post,* 21 November, A1–A6.

Curry, B. 2002. "Al-Qaeda heads list of official terrorist groups." *National Post,* 24 July, A2.

Daniels, R.J., P. Macklem, and K. Roach (eds.) 2001. *The Security of Freedom: Essays on Canada's Anti-Terrorism Bill.* Toronto: University of Toronto Press.

Desroches, F.J. 1995. *Force and Fear: Robbery in Canada.* Scarborough, Ont.: Nelson Canada.

Enns, R. 1999. *A Voice Unheard: The* Latimer *Case and People with Disabilities.* Halifax: Garamond.

Ericson, R. 1982. *Reproducing Order: A Study of Police Patrol Work.* Toronto: University of Toronto Press.

———. 1981. *Making Crime: A Study of Detective Work.* Toronto: University of Toronto Press.

Ericson, R., and P.M. Baranek. 1982. *The Ordering of Justice: A Study of Accused Persons as Dependents in the Criminal Process.* Toronto: University of Toronto Press.

Fife, R. 2002a. Liberals Bow to Terror-Bill Critics." *National Post,* 25 April, A6.

———. 2002b. "Canadians Lose Fear of Terrorism." *National Post,* 6 July, A1–A6.

Filyer, R. 2002. *Police Resources in Canada, 2001.* Ottawa: Statistics Canada.

Gartner, R., and A.N. Doob. 1994. *Trends in Criminal Victimization, 1994.* Ottawa: Statistics Canada.

Gunn, R., and R. Linden. 1994. "The Processing of Child Sexual Assault Cases." In J.V. Roberts and R.M. Mohr, eds., *Confronting Sexual Assault: A Decade of Legal and Social Change*. Toronto: University of Toronto Press, pp. 84–112.

Gunn, R., and C. Minch. 1988. *Sexual Assault: The Dilemma of Disclosure and the Question of Conviction*. Winnipeg: University of Manitoba.

Hagan, J., and C. Morden. 1981. "The Police Decision to Detain: A Study of Legal Labelling and Police Deviance." In C.D. Shearing, ed., *Organizational Police Deviance: Its Structure and Control*. Toronto: Butterworths, pp. 9–28.

Hamilton, A.C., and C.M. Sinclair. 1991. *Report of the Aboriginal Justice Inquiry of Manitoba, Volume 1*. Winnipeg: Province of Manitoba.

Harris, M. 2002. *Con Game: The Truth About Canada's Prisons*. Toronto: McClelland and Stewart.

———. 1986. *Justice Denied: The Law versus Donald Marshall*. Toronto: Totem Books.

Kellough, G. 1996. "'Getting Bail': Ideology in Action." In T. O'Reilly-Fleming, ed., *Post Critical Criminology*. Scarborough, Ont.: Prentice-Hall, pp. 159–83.

Klein, J. 1976. *Let's Make a Deal: Negotiating Justice*. Toronto: D.C. Heath.

Koza, P., and A.N. Doob. 1975. "The Relationship of Pre-Trial Custody to the Outcome of a Trial." *Criminal Law Quarterly* 17: 391–400.

Landsman, S. 1983. *The Adversary System: A Description and Defense*. Washington, D.C.: American Enterprise Institute.

Law Reform Commission of Canada. 1988. *Compelling Appearance, Interim Release, and the Pre-Trial Detention*. Ottawa Law Reform Commission of Canada.

———. 1984. *Questioning Suspects—Working Paper 32*. Ottawa: Minister of Supply and Services.

———. 1977. *Our Criminal Law*. Ottawa: Minister of Supply and Services Canada.

Lonmo, C. 2001. *Adult Correctional Services in Canada, 1999*. Ottawa: Statistics Canada.

Makin, K. 1993. *Redrum the Innocent*. Toronto: Penguin, 1993.

Martin, D. 1995. "Tracy's Right to Life Was Taken from Her." *Winnipeg Free Press*, 3 August: A7.

Mewett, A.W. 1996. *An Introduction to the Criminal Process in Canada*, 3rd ed. Scarborough, Ont.: Carswell.

Paciocco, D.M. 1999. *Getting Away with Murder: The Canadian Criminal Justice System*. Toronto: Irwin Law.

Packer, H.L. 1968. *The Limits of the Criminal Sanction*. Stanford, Calif.: Stanford University.

Peters, Y. "Reflections on the Latimer Case: The Rationale for a Disability Rights Lens." *Saskatchewan Law Review* 64, no. 2: 631–43.

Petersilia, J., A. Abrahamse, and J.Q. Wilson. 1990. "The Relationship between Police Practice, Community Characteristics, and Case Attrition." *Police Studies* 1, no. 1: 23–38.

Rawls, J. 1971. *A Theory of Justice*. Cambridge, MA: Belknap Press of Harvard University Press.

Report of the Commission on Systemic Racism in the Ontario Criminal Justice System: A Community Summary. 1995. M. Gittens and D. Cole, co-chairs. Toronto: Queen's Printer for Ontario.

Rigakos, G. 1997. "Constructing the Symbolic Complainants: Police Subculture and the Nonenforcement of Protection Orders for Battered Women." *Violence and Victims* 10: 235–47.

Roach, K. 2000. "Crime and Punishment in the *Latimer* Case." *Saskatchewan Law Review* 64, no. 2: 469–90.

Roberts, D. 1997. "Latimer Sentence May Go to Top Court." *The Globe and Mail*, 1 December: A6.

Roberts, J.V. 2001. *Public Fear of Crime and Perceptions of the Criminal Justice System*. Ottawa: Solicitor General of Canada.

———. 1994. *Criminal Justice Processing of Sexual Assault Cases*. Ottawa: Juristat.

Roberts, J.V. and D.P. Cole, eds. 1999. *Making Sense of Sentencing*. Toronto: University of Toronto Press.

Roberts, J.V, and A.N. Doob. 1997. "Canada." In M. Tonry (ed.), *Ethnicity, Crime, and Immigration: Comparative and Cross-National Perspectives*. Chicago: University of Chicago Press, pp. 469–522.

Russell, P. 1987. *The Judiciary in Canada: The Third Branch of Government*. Toronto: McGraw-Hill Ryerson.

Sallot, J. 2001. "Latimer Sentence Too Harsh, Poll Told." *The Globe and Mail*, 11 January.

Senna, J.J., and L.J. Siegal. 1995. *Essentials of Criminal Justice*. Minneapolis–St. Paul, Minn.: West.

Statistics Canada. 1994. *Violence Against Women Survey*. Ottawa.

———. 1985. *Victims of Crime: Canadian Urban Victimization Survey*. Ottawa: Solicitor General of Canada.

Sykes, G.M., and F.T. Cullen. 1992. *Criminology*, 2nd ed. Fort Worth, Tex.: Harcourt Brace Jovanovich.

The Globe and Mail. 2002. "Where the Antiterrorism Bill Still Falls Down." 1 May, A14.

Thomas, N.E. 2002. "Sentencing Murder: Did Robert Latimer Deserve the Mandatory Minimum?" *Canadian Criminal Law Review* 7, no. 2, 93–118.

Travis, F. T. 1990. *Introduction to Criminal Justice*. Cincinnati: Anderson.

Ursel, J. 1994. *The Winnipeg Family Violence Court*. Ottawa: Statistics Canada.

Vera Institute of Justice. 1992. *Programs in Criminal Justice Reform*. New York: Vera Institute of Justice.

Wheeler, G. 1987. "The Police, the Crowns, and the Courts: Who's Running the Show?" *Canadian Lawyer*. February.

Young, G. 1994. "Trends in Justice Spending—1988/89 to 1992/93." Ottawa: Statistics Canada.

Court Cases

R. v. Latimer (1995), 99 C.C.C. (3d) 481 (Sask C.A.)

R. v. Latimer (1997), 112 C.C.C. (3d) 193 (S.C.C.)

R. v. Latimer (1997), 121 C.C.C. (3d) 326 (Sask Q.B.)

Criminal Law and Criminal Justice in Canada

CHAPTER OBJECTIVES

✓ Understand the ways criminal law can be established, including common law, case law, and statute law.

✓ Comprehend what offences are included in the three main categories of crime.

✓ Consider the difference between substantive and procedural laws.

✓ Recognize the basic principles used by legislatures and the courts in developing and interpreting substantive laws.

✓ Understand what protections are given to the accused by the *Charter of Rights and Freedoms.*

T o many people, the criminal justice system is a system exclusively concerned with the enforcement of the law, the processing of accused violators of the law, and the punishment of individuals convicted of violating the law. However, understanding how the criminal justice system works also involves studying, investigating, and questioning the role of law in our society. There are many aspects of the law that have an impact upon the processing of the accused, including

• the legal aspects of determining whether or not an individual has broken the law;
• the technical grounds for assessing such activities;
• how we make laws in Canada; and
• the legal protections given to the accused as he progresses through the criminal justice system.

To gain a complete picture of the operation of the Canadian criminal justice system, it is crucial to know something about the source, nature, purpose, and content of law in our society, as well as differences among types of laws.

There are two major terms used to study the role and practice of criminal law in our criminal justice system. The first is substantive criminal law, which refers to the body of legislative actions defining those actions that will be punished by the state if they are violated. In essence, substantive criminal law is the legal definition of crime in our society, that is, it involves the study of criminal statutes that define precisely what is illegal in our society. The main components of most criminal laws are *mens rea, actus reus,* and harm (all of which will be discussed later in this chapter). Although laws provide the framework for defining criminal acts, the various actors involved in the criminal justice system have to interpret these laws. Sometimes they interpret the laws in question with no controversy, but their decisions become major issues when someone appeals the outcome or public opinion decidedly opposes the formal decision.

The second type of criminal law is procedural criminal law, which is defined as the way in which the rights and duties of individuals may be enforced. It is concerned with the criminal process, that is, the legal steps through which an offender passes. Examples of procedural criminal law include the rules of evidence, the law of search and seizure, and the right to counsel. These are procedural safeguards designed to protect the accused. These safeguards can be found in the *Charter of Rights and Freedoms* (which will be discussed later in this chapter) as well as in the *Criminal Code* and the common law. Many people use the shorthand "due process" to refer to procedural criminal law. Whatever term is used, it is an important part of our criminal justice system because it signals "the primacy of demonstrating legal guilt rather than factual guilt and raises a number of obstacles to conviction in order to protect the rights of criminal suspects" (Hiebert 2002: 135).

Most procedural law is found in sections 8 through 14 of the *Charter of Rights and Freedoms*. In Canada, the drafters of the *Charter of Rights and Freedoms* preferred not to use the terms "due process" or "procedural criminal law." Instead, they preferred the most common reference in use today: "principles of fundamental justice." According to s. 7 of the *Charter* (see below) individuals cannot be deprived of life, liberty, and security of the person without the principles of fundamental justice being followed. As a result, the Supreme Court has been ruling on cases involving procedural issues that are not found in sections 8 through 14, but at the same time involve issues surrounding fundamental justice.

What are these principles and where are they found? The Supreme Court has stated that they are "to be found in the basic tenets of our legal system and that it is up to the courts to develop the limits of these tenets" (Barnhorst et al. 1992: 10). This means that the courts decide whether or not each case follows the principles of fundamental justice or if it involves a violation. Since the introduction of the *Charter*, the Supreme Court has decided on what is to be included as a principle of fundamental justice. Some of these areas are disclosure (see below), the right to silence, the right to a fair trial, and the right not to make self-incriminating statements.

The constitutionality of substantive criminal law and procedural criminal law has been ruled on in many criminal court cases since the introduction of the *Charter*. Following is a discussion of the development of Canada's sexual assault laws, where both of these types of criminal law have had to be examined and, in some cases, redrafted after rulings by the Supreme Court of Canada.

Prior to 1983 the offences of sexual aggression were dealt with in sections 139 to 154 of the *Criminal Code*. These offences were found in Part IV of the *Criminal Code*, which dealt with "Sexual Offences, Public Morals and Disorderly Conduct." Courts recognized four principal offences as offences related to rape. Rape itself was one of them. The key provision of the *Criminal Code* dealing with rape was found in s. 143. It stated that before a person could be found guilty of rape, the following general conditions would have to be established:

1. The complainant had to be female.
2. The accused had to be male.
3. The complainant and accused were not married to each other.
4. Sexual intercourse occurred.
5. The act of intercourse occurred without the consent of the woman.

The other three principal offences in Part IV were attempted rape (s. 145), indecent assault against a female (s. 149), and indecent assault against a male (s. 156). The penalties for these four offences were life, 10 years, 5 years, and 10 years, respectively.

Many criticisms were raised against these laws over the decades, including the argument that they reflected "the gender dichotomy and cultural perceptions of gender relations that were functional to the male status maintenance" (Los 1994). As a result, Canada enacted new legislation (referred to as Bill C-127) on 1 January 1983. Bill C-127 reflected a number of significant changes, including the reclassification of sexual assault and placement of it in Part VIII of the *Criminal Code* ("Offences against the Person and Reputation"), which emphasizes that "sexual assault involves physical violence against another person." Other significant changes included the recognition that victims may be either male or female and that spouses can be charged with sexual assault. The legislation also established protections for women against cross-examination in criminal court trials on their past sexual history.

The law covering sexual assault was written in order to represent different degrees or level of harm. Sexual assault is classified into three levels according to the seriousness of the incident. Level 1 sexual assault (s. 271) refers to incidents in which the victim suffers the least physical injury; it carries a maximum punishment of 10 years imprisonment. Level 1 is the most common charge for sexual assault. Ninety-seven percent of all sexual assault charges in 1998 were level 1 (Tremblay 1999).

Level 2 sexual assault (s. 272) involves the use of a weapon, threats to use a weapon, or bodily harm; it carries a maximum punishment of 14 years imprisonment.

Level 3 sexual assault (s. 273) involves wounding, maiming, disfiguring, or endangering the life of the victim. An offender convicted of this offence can receive a maximum term of life imprisonment. Level 1 sexual assault is a hybrid offence, so a Crown prosecutor has the power of discretion to proceed by way of indictment or summary conviction. That decision has a huge impact on the offender in terms of penalties; if the prosecutor proceeds by way of indictment, the maximum punishment is 10 years incarceration, but if the case proceeds by way of summary conviction, the maximum punishment is 18 months. Canada's sexual assault law has been the focus of much debate since its inception.

Probably the most controversial aspect of the new sexual assault law was in the provisions restricting the ability of the accused to introduce evidence concerning the victim's past sexual conduct. Evidence of the victim's sexual reputation became inadmissible (s. 277). The victim's sexual history with persons other than the accused also became inadmissible unless it was required to counter the prosecution's evidence concerning past sexual conduct, to prove the identity of the perpetrator, or to establish the sexual activity with others on the same occasion (s. 276). Pre–1983 legislation made it an ordeal for the victim of a sexual assault to testify in court because the reputation and prior sexual history of the victim could be held against her. As a result, many sexual assaults were not reported to the police since the trial itself "could be almost as agonizing to a victim of sexual assault as the offence itself" (Bowland 1994: 245).

Many legal changes and challenges to the sexual assault legislation have taken place over its brief history. In 1991, for example, the Supreme Court of Canada struck down s. 276 of the *Criminal Code*, ruling that it favoured the victim at the expense of the accused. In their decision involving the cases of *R. v. Seaboyer* and *R. v. Gayme*, two men who were accused of rape argued successfully that their right to a fair trial had been violated, since they were prevented from questioning the complainant about her prior sexual conduct. The following year amendments were passed by Parliament through the introduction of Bill C-49, which outlined "the legal parameters for determining the admissibility of a victim's past sexual history as evidence in sexual assault trials" (Mohr and Roberts 1994: 10). In addition, the issue of "implied consent" was eliminated as a defence, and actual consent is now required.

Three years later in 1994, the Supreme Court of Canada accepted the argument of "extreme drunkenness" as an appropriate defence to general-intent crimes including the crime of sexual assault. In this case, *R. c. Daviault*, the Supreme Court of Canada overturned a Quebec Court of Appeal decision denying this defence. The decision made by the Supreme Court was based largely on the assumption that the intoxication of the defendant was so extreme that the situation would rarely arise again. During the next few months, a number of men charged with sexual assault successfully defended themselves by using this defence. As a result, the federal government passed amendments in 1995 to the *Criminal Code* that eliminated this defence for offences requiring general intent, such as sexual assault and assault, but not specific intent, such as murder.

Later that same year, in a 5–4 decision, the Supreme Court ruled that a woman's counseling records had to be handed over to a judge if the defence persuades the judge that the records may contain information useful in the defence of the accused. This ruling occurred in *R. v. O'Connor* in the belief that eliminating such records (which would give the complainant her right to privacy) would violate the defendant's right to a fair trial. After this decision it became a common practice for judges to order full disclosure of records.

As a result of the *O'Connor* decision, the federal government passed new legislation (Bill C-46) in 1997 restricting the full disclosure of records. This bill created a two-stage process for judges to determine whether or not the victim's records would be disclosed to the defendant. In the first stage of review, the new law compels the accused to convince the trial judge that the documents are likely relevant to his defence. The judge also has to consider if it is "necessary in the interests of justice" to view them. In November 1999 the Supreme Court upheld Bill C-46 in *R. v. Mills*.

In that same year, the Supreme Court threw out a case involving sexual assault where the victim's counseling records had been destroyed. The decision in this case, *R. v. Carosella*, placed any third-party records on the same standard as police and Crown prosecutor documents. The federal government then passed amendments to Bill C-46 attempting to clarify when records concerning the victim should have restricted access by introducing a two-stage application process. In the first step, trial judges have to decide whether the sought-after record was likely to be of sufficient relevance to the defence. The second step involves balancing information contained in the document with the position forwarded by the defence on the basis of its importance to the defence with the threat that its exposure might pose to the complainant's right to privacy, dignity, and security of the person.

In the fall of 2000, the Supreme Court unanimously upheld the 1992 law (Bill C-46) restricting defence lawyers in their questioning of sexual assault victims about past sexual history. The Supreme Court ruled that forcing the victim to give evidence about her past sexual history "invades her right to privacy and would discourage the reporting of crimes of sexual violence" (Anderssen 2000: A7). In this case (*R. v. Darrach*) the defendant argued he had been denied a fair trial because he was unable to raise specific aspects of his prior sexual relationship with the complainant during the trial. Mr. Darrach argued that he had formed the "honest but mistaken belief" that the incident was consensual. His argument failed to influence the Supreme Court that the evidence was of significant probative value.

Critics of these rulings argued they resulted in unfair trials for men accused of sexual assault as they are "sometimes totally unable to raise relevant facts and arguments" (*National Post* 2000: A19). Supporters of the law countered that lawmakers had created "a fair way to keep prejudicial myths about women out of the courtroom while preserving the right of the accused to a fair trial" (Chwialkowska 2000: A4).

SOURCES OF CRIMINAL LAW IN CANADA

Canadian criminal law is derived from British common law. Thus, the structure of our criminal law is modelled closely on the British experience. Common law is an important source of our criminal law and is an important component of substantive law in Canada. Common

law originated during the reign of King Henry II (1154–89) as a result of his desire to establish a strong central government. Part of his vision was a court system that tries cases on the basis of laws passed by the government and that are applicable to all citizens. To this end, he appointed judges to a specific territory (or circuit) to hear cases in order to ensure that the "King's Law" was administered and enforced. Over time, judges exchanged information about their legal decisions, and this growing body of knowledge slowly began to replace laws based on local customs. In the traditional system, serious crimes such as murder, rape, and assault were viewed as wrongs between private citizens. Judges began to redefine these as wrongs against the state—that is, as criminal offences. A common law gradually developed, forming legal principles that were equally applicable to all citizens regardless of local customs or the geographic location of their residence.

Another significant change emerged about this same time, when a system gradually developed where judges decided cases on the basis of previous judgments in similar cases. Crimes had general meanings attached to them, and most people knew what was meant by "murder" and other criminal offences. This shared

---

EXHIBIT 2.1 Sexual Assault Legislation in Canada

Since the enactment of sexual assault legislation in 1983, numerous changes have occurred:

1991: The Supreme Court of Canada rules that the law favours the victim at the expense of the accused (*R. v. Seaboyer* (1991) and *R. v. Gayme* (1991)). The Supreme Court strikes down s. 276 of the *Criminal Code,* which limits the questioning of victims in sexual assault trials by the defence.

1992: Bill C-49 is passed, allowing sexual history to be introduced in a case but only when strict guidelines are used. It also provides a legal definition of consent specific to the offence of sexual assault.

1993: The Supreme Court accepts the extreme drunkenness defence in sexual assault cases (*R. c. Daviault*).

1995: The *Criminal Code* is amended (Bill C-72) to disallow the extreme-drunkenness defence for a number of violent offences, including sexual assault.

The Supreme Court rules that counseling records of the victim must be produced when requested by the court (*R. v. O'Connor*).

1996: An Alberta judge rules that the new law covering the disclosure of third-party

therapy or counseling records is unconstitutional, as it places too much of the burden of proof on the accused.

1997: The Supreme Court of Canada decides that when a sexual assault victim cannot produce her counseling records at the request of the court, the case must be thrown out of court (*R. v. Carosella*).

The *Criminal Code* is amended (Bill C-46) to introduce guidelines that instruct all parties on when the sexual assault victim's records are relevant during a trial.

1999: The Supreme Court of Canada upholds, in *R. v. Mills,* the constitutionality of the Bill C-46 provisions.

The Supreme Court of Canada, in *R. v. Ewanchuk,* rejects the defence of implied consent.

2000: The Supreme Court of Canada, in *R. v. Darrach,* upholds the provision of the sexual assault law restricting defence lawyers in their questioning of sexual assault victims about their past sexual history.

Sources: Bowland (1994); Los (1994); Majury (1994); Roberts and Mohr (1994); and Makin (1999).

---

knowledge resulted in a practice that continues today in our system of criminal law: deciding trials on the basis of precedent that would be followed, even if it were not necessarily binding, in future decisions. This practice evolved into a principle or rule, called *stare decisis* ("based upon situations of similar facts"), which requires the judiciary to follow previous decisions in similar cases. Today, judges in Canada still follow precedent. This generally means that the lower courts must follow the decisions of higher courts, and courts of equal rank should try to follow one another's decisions. Thus, by process of making decisions in case after case, and guided by the rule of precedent, these early English judges created a body of law that applied to all the people of England. This law was then common to all.

Today, the principle of *stare decisis* is still in use. If one criminal court has to make a decision, the judge will search out how other courts have reached their decision in similar cases and these will probably be used as a guide. This principle lends itself to stability in the legal system since it allows one to predict how a court will probably decide a case. However, this practice does not necessarily lead to a rigid system of criminal law because a judge can make a ruling that deviates from existing precedent. This can happen when, for example, conditions in a society have changed, allowing a judge to feel warranted in departing from existing precedents.

Written Sources of Criminal Law

Originally, common law was uncodified, which means that the law was not written down and preserved in a central location This meant that judges had to discuss the rulings among themselves, a situation that often led to long waiting periods before a final judgment was given. This system proved to be extremely cumbersome and led to the creation of written sources of the criminal law.

Contemporary Canadian criminal law has four main sources: the *Constitution,* statute law, case law, and administrative law. Because Canadian criminal law is modelled closely on the British experience, and makes use of British legal precedents and procedures, changes were gradually introduced when it became apparent that some legal issues facing Canadians were inapplicable to the British experience and British precedents and procedures. Clearly, some of the legal issues facing Canadians were called for made-in-Canada alternatives.

The *Constitution*

The fundamental principles that guide the enactment of laws and the application of those laws by the courts are found in the *Constitution Act.* Thus, only the federal government can enact criminal laws and procedure. However, a criminal law may be found to be unconstitutional "if it infringes upon a right or a freedom protected under the *Canadian Charter of Rights and Freedoms* and if it cannot be justified under s. 1 of the *Charter* as a reasonable and demonstrably justified limit on a right" (Roach 1996: 3).

Statute Law

Another source of criminal law is statutes. Statutes are laws that prohibit or mandate certain acts. These laws are systematically codified and placed in a single volume, such as our *Criminal Code.* Most offences are updated over time to include more detailed definitions of a criminal act. In order to change the existing law, governments have either to modify existing laws or introduce new ones by enacting statutes. Statute law is today considered to be the most important source of law in Canada, and it is through the use of statutes that criminal law is created, changed, or eliminated (see Exhibit 2.1).

The power to enact statute law in Canada is divided among the federal government (that is, Parliament), the provinces, and municipalities. However, only Parliament has the power to enact criminal law. Statute law always overrules case law, except in conflicts over the *Canadian Charter of Rights and Freedoms.* The *Charter* allows citizens the right to possess certain rights and freedoms "that cannot be infringed upon by the government" and so "limits the legislative authority of the government" (Barnhorst et al. 1992: 7–8). In Canada, all statutes are consolidated approximately every 10 years when Parliament replaces the existing statutes with revised versions.

Case Law

Case law involves the judicial application and interpretation of laws as they apply in any particular case. Every time a judge in Canada makes a decision in a court case, she has the discretion to interpret the relevant statutes. Statutes may need to be interpreted because they are stated only in general terms, and the court case may call for a specific meaning. For example, a judge may decide all previous decisions are problematic because they are outdated or vague, given the facts of a case at hand. As a result, the law may be redefined to make it reflect specifics. Once a judge makes a decision that changes the traditional legal definitions, an appeal is usually made to the Provincial Court of Appeal in that jurisdiction. The Appeal Court decision too will likely be appealed, to the Supreme Court of Canada, and if the Supreme Court refuses to hear the case, the ruling made by the Provincial Court of Appeal stands. However, if the Supreme Court decides to hear the case, that ultimate decision becomes law.

Administrative Law

Another source of criminal law is administrative regulations. These regulations are considered to have the power of criminal law, since they can include criminal penalties. These laws are written by regulatory agencies that have been given that power by governments to develop and enforce rules in specific areas, such as the environment, competition policy, and protection from hazardous products. Violations of administrative laws are sometimes referred to as regulatory offences. The federal government, provinces, and municipalities can enact them.

The Rule of Law

From the review of these differing written forms of criminal law, it is easy to see their applicability to our criminal justice system. Yet, questions abound about their use. For example, many people ask whether laws can be used by powerful groups to gain personal advantages through the criminal law. It is a clear possibility, but according to the rule of law, in our system of justice there is a "sense of orderliness, of subjection to known legal rules and of executive accountability to legal authority" (*Resolution to Amend the Constitution* (1981)). This means society must be governed by clear legal rules rather than by arbitrary personal wishes and desires. Central to this meaning is that no one individual or group have a privileged exemption from the law. Everyone is subject to the laws that have been introduced by the government. To protect our society from these individual or group self-interests, the rule of law ensures that laws are created, administered, and enforced on the basis of acceptable procedures promoting fairness and equality. The rule of law plays a central role in our society as it "forms part of the supreme law of our country, binding on all levels of government and enforceable by the courts" (Billingsley 2002: 29).

The basic elements of the rule of law include the following:

- *Scope of the Law.* This means that there should be no privileged exemptions to the law; all persons come under the rule of law. There are political and social aspects to this statement. Government under law is the political component (both the government and public officials are subject to the existing law). The social aspect is equality before the law.
- *Character of the Law.* This means that the law should be public, clear enough so that most people can

understand it, and relatively clear and determinate in its requirements.
- *Institution of the Law.* In our legal system, this means that there are certain rules that the institutions of the law must produce in order for the law to be fair and just. These include an independent judiciary, written laws, and the right to a fair hearing.

The *Canadian Charter of Rights and Freedoms*

One of the most important additions to our Canadian legal system was the *Canadian Charter of Rights and Freedoms,* enacted on 17 April 1982. The *Charter* differs from common law and statute law because it applies mostly to the protection of the legal rights of criminal suspects and convicted persons, the powers of the various criminal justice agencies, and criminal procedure during a trial. It is a complex piece of legislation, and only parts of it deal with issues relevant to the criminal justice system. However, the sections concerned with the operation of the justice system have had a tremendous impact on criminal procedural issues in Canada, especially as they apply to the rights of the accused and the powers of criminal justice agencies involved in the detection and prosecution of criminals (see Exhibit 2.2 on page 36).

Since its introduction, the *Charter* has played an important role in establishing and enforcing certain fundamental principles related to the operation of the criminal justice system, such as the protection of due process rights, a fair trial, and freedom from cruel and unusual punishment. The *Charter* divides these legal principles into a series of different sections. Section 7 is the most general; it guarantees no individual will be denied his basic rights in Canadian society "except in accordance with the principles of fundamental justice" as specified by s. 1 of the *Charter*.

Sections 8 to 10 of the *Charter* deal with the rights of individuals when they are detained and arrested by the police. Section 8 provides everyone with the right to be secure against unreasonable search or seizure. It involves the protection of citizens' property and privacy against unwarranted intrusions by state agents. This section of the *Charter* has led to a significant amount of case law since most criminal trial evidence is collected by the police, and the appropriateness of how they obtained the evidence is often raised in court. Although this section is concerned with an individual's right to privacy, this right has to be balanced with the interest of the police to conduct searches and seize evidence as a part of their law enforcement activities. Section 8 is therefore referred to as a "relative" right, since an individual is protected only against unreasonable searches and seizures.

The Supreme Court set out the basic framework for police searches and seizures in one of its earliest decisions after the introduction of the *Charter* (*Hunter v. Southam, Inc.* (1984)). In its decision, the Supreme Court agreed that individuals have a right to be secure from an unreasonable search and seizure and established that certain procedural elements had to exist in order for the police to operate. One of these elements is the need for prior authorization of a search. As a result, the police are now required to justify their need to search by producing sworn evidence that meets an objective standard. The Supreme Court also recognized there are exigent circumstances (such as a "hot pursuit") when the police need not have a warrant approved prior to their actions. Other limitations include the threat or danger that evidence connected to a crime will be destroyed or removed, if a person has contacted the police because of an emergency, or if the police are involved in a reasonable search.

Section 8 is designed to protect all reasonable expectations of privacy, which are not to be ignored even when an individual is caught committing a crime. In *R. v. Duarte* (1990), the police placed a body-pack recorder on an informer to record a conversation with a suspect. No warrant was obtained since the police assumed it was legal since one of the individuals involved had given his consent to be taped. The Court ruled that the other individual had the right to a reasonable expectation of privacy. Similar conclusions were reached in *R. v. Wong* (1990) and *R. v. Kokesch* (1990) where the police had acted prior to obtaining a warrant. In the former case, the police made a surreptitious video surveillance tape, while in the latter the police conducted a search around a person's house to see if the suspect was growing marijuana. It is important to note that s. 8 applies to personal information (where an individual has a right to be protected from intrusive activities by the authorities) as opposed to commercial records (which are not subject to this protection).

Section 9 guarantees that everyone has the right to be free from arbitrary detention or imprisonment. This means that the police do not have complete discretion to detain citizens, but rather they have to follow an objective standard determined by the federal government. One area that was brought to the attention of the Supreme Court involved the issue concerning the provincial power of the police to conduct random "spot checks" in order to look for impaired drivers. In *R. v. Hufsky* (1988), the Supreme Court ruled that randomly stopping a driver was in fact an arbitrary detention

under s. 9 of the *Charter* since it represented total discretion on the behalf of the police officer as to whom would be stopped. However, the Court then stated that randomly stopping a driver thought to be impaired could be justified under s. 1 of the *Charter* due to the importance of highway safety and the need to protect other citizens from potential harm. The Court ruled that the police should possess reasonable suspicion based on objective standards (*R. v. Duguay* (1989)).

In order to detain and arrest someone, the police must have reasonable grounds for their actions or they will judged as arbitrary and in violation of s. 9. The case of *R. v. Simpson* (1993) questioned the meaning of reasonable grounds for an arrest. In this case, a male was observed by a police officer leaving a house reputed to be inhabited by persons selling drugs. As he was driving away, the police officer pulled over the suspect and asked to see his driver's licence and registration. The man informed the officer he was driving without a valid driver's licence. He was arrested and subsequently charged with driving while under suspension. The officer then continued her search under the assumption he had bought drugs at the residence and discovered several grams of crack cocaine, leading to additional charges. When the case reached court, all charges were dropped because the police officer was ruled to have conducted an improper investigation violating the suspect's s. 9 *Charter* rights. Educated "guesses" do not form the basis of reasonable grounds to arrest someone.

Section 10 deals with certain specific rights given to individuals when they are detained by the police. These rights are found in the three subareas of this section. Section 10(a) stipulates that everyone has the right to be informed as soon as possible of the reasons for his arrest. Both the arrest and detention of an individual represents a significant intrusion into that person's life, and it is a basic right for him to know why he has been arrested and detained (*R. v. Borden* (1994)). Section 10(b) states "Everyone has the right on arrest or detention to retain and instruct counsel without delay and to be informed of that right," and this section has been one of the most controversial sections of the *Charter*. Its purpose is to control police conduct after initial charges have been laid against the suspect. In *R. v. Therens* (1985) the Supreme Court ruled that evidence obtained by the police without first informing the suspect of his right to a lawyer could not be used. This interpretation was expanded in *R. v. Manninen* (1987), when the right to legal counsel was extended to all persons detained by the police. Law enforcement officers were later instructed they had to inform anyone in their custody how she could exercise this right before being questioned. In *R. v. Brydges* (1990), the Supreme Court

LEGAL RIGHTS

1. The *Canadian Charter of Rights and Freedoms* guarantees the rights and freedoms set out in it subject only to such reasonable limits prescribed by law as can be demonstrably justified in a free and democratic society.

7. Everyone has the right to life, liberty and security of the person and the right not to be deprived thereof except in accordance with the principles of fundamental justice.

8. Everyone has the right to be secure against unreasonable search or seizure.

9. Everyone has the right not to be arbitrarily detained or imprisoned.

10. Everyone has the right on arrest or detention

    (a) to be informed promptly of the reasons therefor;

    (b) to retain and instruct counsel without delay and to be informed of that right; and

    (c) to have the validity of the detention determined by way of habeas corpus and to be released if the detention is not lawful.

11. Any person charged with an offence has the right

    (a) to be informed without unreasonable delay of the specific offence;

    (b) to be tried within a reasonable time;

    (c) not to be compelled to be a witness in proceedings against that person in respect of the offence;

    (d) to be presumed innocent until proven guilty according to law in a fair and public hearing by an independent and impartial tribunal;

    (e) not to be denied reasonable bail without just cause;

    (f) except in the case of an offence under military law tried before a military tribunal, to the benefit of trial by jury where the maximum punishment for the offence is imprisonment for five years or a more severe punishment;

    (g) not to be found guilty on account of any act or omission unless, at the time of the act or omission, it is constituted an offence under Canadian or international law or was criminal according to the general principles of law recognized by the community of nations;

    (h) if finally acquitted of the offence, not to be tried for it again and, if finally found guilty and punished for the offence, not to be tried or punished for it again; and

    (i) if found guilty of the offence and if the punishment for the offence has been varied between the time of the commission and the time of sentencing, to the benefit of the lesser punishment.

12. Everyone has the right not to be subjected to any cruel and unusual treatment or punishment.

13. A witness who testifies in any proceedings has the right not to have any incriminating evidence so given used to incriminate that witness in any other proceedings, except in a prosecution for perjury or for the giving of contradictory evidence.

14. A party or witness in any proceedings who does not understand or speak the language in which the proceedings are conducted or who is deaf has the right to the assistance of an interpreter.

EQUALITY RIGHTS

15. (1) Every individual is equal before and under the law and has the right to the equal protection and equal benefit of the law without discrimination and, in particular, without discrimination based on race, national or ethnic origin, colour, religion, sex, age or mental or physical disability.
(2) Subsection (1) does not preclude any law, program or activity that has as its object the amelioration of conditions of disadvantaged individuals or groups including those that are disadvantaged because of race, national or ethnic origin, colour, religion, sex, age or mental or physical disability.

ENFORCEMENT

24. (1) Anyone whose rights or freedoms, as guaranteed by this *Charter,* have been infringed or denied may apply to a court of competent jurisdiction to obtain such remedy as the court considers appropriate and just in the circumstances.
(2) Where, in proceedings under subsection (1), a court concludes that evidence was obtained in a manner that infringed or denied any rights or freedoms guaranteed by this *Charter,* the evidence shall be excluded if it is established that, having regard to all the circumstances, the admission of it in the proceedings would bring the administration of justice into disrepute.

extended the police duty to advise individuals of their right to legal counsel by giving the accused a reasonable length of time to retain and instruct counsel. The police now have to refrain from questioning any suspect until a reasonable opportunity exists for the accused to exercise his right.

However, certain limits have been placed on the rights of the accused to obtain legal counsel. In *R. v. Tremblay* (1987) and *R. v. Ross* (1989), the Supreme Court decided that the rights set out in this section of the *Charter* are not absolute, ruling that a suspect's right to retain and instruct counsel must be exercised diligently by the suspect. This means that a suspect cannot refuse the chance to contact legal counsel, be questioned by the police, and then complain about having said things he should not have because no lawyer was present. Furthermore, in *R. v. Thomsen* (1988), the Supreme Court decided that a motorist requested to provide a breath sample is not entitled to request and then wait for legal counsel to appear due to the necessity of protecting the public.

Section 10(c) is concerned with *habeas corpus,* a common law remedy against the unlawful detention of a suspect. This allows an individual who is detained to request an assessment to see if she is being unlawfully detained. The rights provided by this rule of common law are guaranteed by other *Charter* provisions, including the right to be secure from arbitrary arrest and detention and the right not to be denied reasonable bail.

The *Charter* also is concerned with the activities of the courts. Although s. 7 of the *Charter* provides the basic guarantee that everyone has the right to life, liberty, and security, s. 11 outlines the rights of individuals charged with a criminal offence as they proceed through the criminal courts. Since a court trial is a complex process, this section is divided into nine components and deals with issues concerned with the presumption of innocence, court delays, and the right not to be denied reasonable bail. Section 11(a) involves the police's informing the accused of the precise nature of the charges she faces without unreasonable delay. This is designed to assist the accused to challenge the proceedings if they are unlawful or to prepare a defence if the case is proceeding to court. This section also has the impact of defining and narrowing the proceedings, "thereby limiting the scope of the prosecution and the power of the police" (Sharpe and Swinton 1998: 167).

Section 11(b) includes the right of the defendant to be tried within a reasonable time limit (*R. v. Askov* (1990)). However, the Supreme Court has made a distinction about pre-charge and post-charge delay. For example, over the past few years a number of charges have been laid against individuals years after the alleged incident. The Supreme Court has ruled that a delay in charging an individual will rarely lead to a successful challenge about an unreasonable delay (*R. v. Mills* (1986)), although unexplained or unjustified delays may lead to a successful challenge (*R. v. Kalanj* (1989)).

Section 11(c) protects the accused from having to testify during his trial, while section 11(d) deals with the "presumption of innocence" in a fair and public hearing until proven guilty by an independent and impartial tribunal. Concerns about the presumption of innocence led the Supreme Court of Canada, in *R. v. Oakes* (1986), to strike down a section of the *Narcotic Control Act* that presumed the guilt of the accused, since it demanded that the accused prove to the court he did not possess a narcotic for the reason of trafficking. The other parts of s. 11 give the accused the right to reasonable bail (s. 11(e)), the right to a jury trial for any offence where the maximum punishment is for five years or more (s. 11(f)), that an individual's act or omission can be construed as an offence only if it was illegal at the time of the offence (s. 11(g)), give protection to individuals from double jeopardy (s. 11(h)) and to punish the accused on the basis of the penalties that were available only at the time of the offence (s. 11(i)).

Section 12 protects individuals from any form of cruel and unusual punishment. The criterion that has to be judged in this case is whether the punishment is excessive—that is, violates our standards of decency. In *R. v. Smith* (1987), the Supreme Court ruled laws mandating a minimum of seven years punishment for importing narcotics were in violation of this section of the *Charter*. The justices' reasoning was based on the fact that this section of the relevant act included too many activities in its prohibition as it did not distinguish between small amounts of drugs to be used for personal consumption and large amounts for trafficking. Although the Court did not provide a precise definition of "cruel and unusual punishment," it regarded the minimum sentence disproportionate in comparison to the seriousness of the offence.

Other minimum sentences have been upheld by the Court, such as the mandatory minimum punishment of seven days suspension for driving while under suspension (*R. v. Goltz* (1991)). Indefinite sentences for those classified legally as dangerous offenders have also been upheld by the Court (*R. v. Luxton* (1990)).

As a result of the cases in this section, guidelines have been established to keep punishments from becoming grossly disproportionate. These guidelines indicate whether a punishment is needed to achieve a valid penal purpose, whether a sentence is based on proper guidelines, and whether appropriate alternatives are available. An indeterminate sentence given to a person considered a dangerous offender is not a violation of this section and neither is a long period of incarceration before parole after the offender is convicted of murder, since incarceration does not violate our standard of what we consider to be decent.

Section 13 protects witnesses from self-incrimination and having charges laid against them as the result of their statements. The right given to the witness in this section is restricted to not having the evidence given in one trial used against them in a later trial in order to prove their guilt (*R. v. Mannion* (1986); Sharpe and Swinton 1998). However, in *R. v. Kuldip* (1990) the Supreme Court decided that evidence given at a previous trial could be used to later cross-examine a witness in order to assess his credibility as an accused. Section 14 guarantees the accused and any witnesses the right to an interpreter and that the interpreter translate the key testimony in full rather than simply summarizing the accused's statements (*R. v. Tran* (1994)).

Sections 15(1) and 15(2) are concerned with equality rights and specify the need for the equal protection of all persons within our system of justice as well as equality before and under the law. Section 28 guarantees that rights of equality extend to both women and men.

Section 24 deals with remedies in the criminal process in the event of any violation of the above rights. Section 24(1) allows for a stay of proceedings so a prosecutor cannot proceed with the case. This remedy is not common, as it is considered to be an extreme measure and the Supreme Court has stated that it can be applied only in "the clearest of cases ..." (*R. v. O'Connor* (1995)).

The most common remedy for a violation of a *Charter* right in the criminal process is found in s. 24(2). This section outlines a test to determine whether the rights of the accused have been infringed and the justice system brought into disrepute because of illegal evidence. The purpose of this section is not to control the conduct of the police but rather protect the integrity of the judicial system. This section protects the accused by excluding evidence illegally collected by the police and used during the trial. However, there is no one specific rule for the police to follow. The Canadian system stands markedly in contrast to the approach developed in the United States where a strict law known as the exclusionary rule makes it illegal to use evidence collected in an improper manner. The courts in Canada decide on a case-by-case basis whether or not it is possible to enter evidence into court. A number of questions must be asked prior to excluding or admitting any evidence. The first asks whether the evidence in question was obtained in a manner that infringed or denied any rights of freedoms guaranteed by the *Charter*. The

second asks whether or not the admission of the evidence "would bring the administration of justice into disrepute."

The closest the Supreme Court has come to establishing a test to determine the admissibility of evidence is found in *R. v. Collins* (1987). The Court adopted the "reasonable-person test," which asks the question, "Would the admission of the evidence bring the administration of justice into disrepute in the eyes of a reasonable man, dispassionate and fully apprised of the circumstances of the case?" (Stuart 1994: 82). The Supreme Court summarized the specifics of this test the following year in *R. v. Jacoy* (1988):

> First, the Court must consider whether the admission of evidence will affect the fairness of the trial. If this inquiry is answered affirmatively, "the admission of evidence would *tend* to bring the administration of justice into disrepute and, subject to a consideration of the other factors, the evidence generally should be excluded" ... One of the factors relevant to this determination is the nature of the evidence; if the evidence is real evidence that existed irrespective of the *Charter* violation, its admission will rarely render the trial unfair.

Section 7: The Principles of Fundamental Justice

In addition to the rights of guaranteed by the *Charter* reviewed above, the Supreme Court has used s. 7 of the *Charter* to introduce and subsequently require certain procedural rights that are not specifically guaranteed by sections 8 through 14 of the *Charter* after determining that the principles of fundamental justice are broader than the rights provided by the *Charter*. The rulings made in this context have had—and continue to have—a significant impact upon the processing of defendants through the criminal justice system. Four areas have been affected: the right to silence, disclosure, the right to make full answer and defence, and the detention of those persons found not guilty by reason of insanity.

The Right to Silence

In *R. v. Hebert* (1990) an undercover police officer posing as a fellow prisoner engaged the accused in a discussion about his activities. The officer was placed in the same cell in order to initiate conversations about the alleged offence and obtain incriminating evidence because the suspect had refused to make a statement to the police after receiving instructions from legal counsel. The Supreme Court ruled that in this case the *Charter* protections of s. 10(b) (the right to legal counsel) and s. 11(c) (the right against self-incrimination) didn't apply. The Court, however, continued, saying that the principles of fundamental justice implicitly included a broader right to silence and that the police cannot use their "superior powers" in an attempt to overstep the accused's decision to invoke his legal rights. The use of an undercover agent was ruled as "trickery," designed to deprive the accused of his choice to remain silent. The accused has a right not to be deprived of life, liberty, and security of the person except in accordance with the principles of fundamental justice, and in this case these rights were violated by the police. In a subsequent case, the police hired an inmate (who was then placed in the same cell) to talk to the alleged offender in order to elicit incriminating evidence (*R. v. Broyles* (1991)). The Supreme Court applied the same principle as in *Hebert*, ruling that this action violated the principle of fundamental justice.

The Right of Disclosure

Due to a number of cases where the Crown failed to give all the relevant evidence in its possession to the defence, leading to questions about the administration of justice, the Supreme Court, in *R. v. Stinchcombe* (1991), ruled that s. 7 imposed a duty on the prosecution to disclose all the evidence it will be using in the trial as well as any other evidence the defence may find useful. This ruling has had a tremendous impact upon the activities of both the prosecution and the police (see Exhibit 2.3 on p. 41 for a further discussion of disclosure).

The Right to Make Full Answer and Defence

One of the most significant common law rights provided to a defendant is the ability to question the complainant during a criminal trial. This became an issue in the sexual assault trials of *R. v. Seaboyer* (1991) and *R. v. Gayme* (1991) mentioned earlier in this chapter. The *Criminal Code* provision excluding the accused's right to question the victim about her prior sexual conduct during the trial was found to be in violation of the principles of fundamental justice. The Supreme Court determined that a complete ban was excessive as it could lead to a failure for the accused to provide a legitimate defence. And although the Supreme Court ruled that this *Criminal Code* provision violated the principles of fundamental justice, it ultimately accepted strict guidelines detailing the specific circumstances in which such questions would be allowed.

The Detention of Those Individuals Found Not Guilty by Reason of Insanity

The principles of fundamental justice apply at the post-trial as well as the pre-charge stages of the criminal justice system. The law governing the detention of those found not guilty by reason of insanity until recently stated that if an individual was found to be unfit to stand trial she would be confined without a hearing and held indefinitely at "the pleasure of the Lieutenant-Governor." This meant that the accused could be held without the benefit of a trial to determine whether or not she was actually guilty of the offence in question (McKay-Panos 1998/99). This confinement amounted in most cases to an indefinite period of detention as there was no provision for a hearing or for any procedural protections.

In *R. v. Swain* (1991) the Supreme Court ruled that this action violated s. 7 of the *Charter* and told the provinces to change their legislation to alleviate this situation. The following year, the federal government mandated the creation of provincial review boards to take over this decision-making authority. One activity of review boards is to hold hearings no later than every 12 months to review those individuals who are subject to their authority.

THE NATURE OF CRIME

Canada practises a federal system of criminal law, which means that all criminal law is passed by the federal government. Different approaches—general and legal—are used to explain what a crime is in our society.

According to the general level, a crime can be defined as any action

1. that is harmful;
2. that is prohibited by the criminal law;
3. that can be prosecuted by the state;
4. in a formal court environment;
5. for which a punishment can be imposed (Senna and Siegel 1995).

The legal definition of crime involves a mental and physical element as well as "attendant circumstances," or a causal link between the act and the harm that results. It also specifies that certain aspects of the criminal act in question must be proven in a court of law. Our criminal law is based on seven principles traditionally determined and followed by legislators and the courts, and these essential features must exist in every criminal act. These principles are summarized by the

Robert Sharpe leaves court after being found guilty of possessing pornographic photographs and innocent of two pornography charges related to his writings.

term *corpus delecti*, which means literally "the body of the crime." In order to convict someone, it is the duty of the state in most cases to prove each of the following seven elements:

1. legality;
2. *mens rea*;
3. *actus reus*;
4. concurrence of *mens rea* and *actus reus*;
5. harm;
6. causation; and
7. punishment.

As Jerome Hall (1947: 17), a famous American jurist, noted, "[the] harm forbidden in penal law must be imputed to any normal adult who voluntarily commits it with criminal intent, and such a person must be subjected to the legally prescribed punishment."

Legality

Legally, a crime is defined as "an intentional act or omission in violation of the criminal law, committed without defense or justification and sanctioned by the state …" (Tappan 1966: 10). This means that an act, to be considered criminal, must be "forbidden in a penal law" (Brannigan 1984: 25). The idea is that there can be no

crime unless a law forbids the act in question. This is embodied in the phrase *nullum crimen sine lege*, or "no crime without a law."

Mens Rea

The *Criminal Code* assumes that the act of becoming involved in a criminal act results from a guilty mind. This is referred to as *mens rea*, or the mental element of a crime. *Mens rea* is commonly defined as the "guilty mind," although it is often referred to as *intent*. It rests on the idea that a person has the capacity to control his behaviour and has the ability to choose among different courses of action. Many people may fantasize about committing "the perfect crime," but no crime is committed until some action is taken to realize this fantasy. In addition, a person is not culpable (that is, blameworthy) unless he intends to commit an act prohibited by law or to avoid doing something that the law requires him to do. Police officers and judges are often asked for forgiveness by an accused on the grounds that the accused, in committing a harmful act, "didn't mean to do it."

Intent is commonly confused with *motive*, although the two concepts are distinct. Intent refers to an individual's mental resolve to commit a criminal offence; motive refers to the reason for committing the actual illegal act. Although motive is distinct from *mens rea*, Barnhorst et al. (1992: 40–41) claim it is relevant to the criminal justice system in two ways. First, motive provides evidence of intent by establishing a reason why a person committed a crime (for example, out of greed or jealousy). Second, motive may assist a judge in sentencing the accused in the same way—by giving a reason why the person committed the crime. According to Barnhorst et al. (1992: 41), the accused may receive a lighter sentence if there was a good reason for committing the crime (for example, mercy killing, as opposed to killing someone out of greed for an inheritance).

The intent to commit a crime may take either of two forms, each of which requires a different amount of proof. Some offences require only *general intent*, which means that *mens rea* is inferred from the action or inaction of the accused. In these crimes (for example, homicide) there is no need for the prosecution to prove, through an independent investigation, the state of the defendant's mind at the time of the offence. It is necessary for the prosecution only "to prove that the accused committed the prohibited act intentionally and with the necessary knowledge of the material circumstances" (Verdun-Jones 1989: 120). For example, the intent to commit a homicide is inferred from the fact that the accused pointed a weapon at the victim and discharged

EXHIBIT 2.3   The *Charter* in Action: *R. v. Stinchcombe* (1991)

Disclosure is one of the most important features of our criminal justice system. According to the Law Reform Commission of Canada, disclosure of relevant information among all the parties involved in a court case is an important factor in the fairness and efficiency in the administration of the Canadian justice system. In the words of the Law Reform Commission of Canada (1974: 1),

> Fairness and efficiency in the administration of justice depend in large measure upon the quality of information available to litigating parties. In Canadian law pre-trial disclosure and discovery are commonplaces of civil procedure, designed to expedite the resolution of a dispute by refining the issues to be debated at trial and minimizing the risk of surprise. Our rules of criminal procedure, however, do not provide for such disclosure, although the preliminary inquiry is commonly used by defense counsel as an opportunity to discover the strength and the scope of the Crown's case.

However, clear-cut guidelines on exactly how disclosure should operate were never developed. The lack of any principles governing disclosure was one of the most important legal issues that emerged from the investigation into the wrongful conviction of Donald Marshall in Nova Scotia. Marshall was wrongfully convicted of murder and spent almost 12 years in prison, largely due to the fact that information given to the police was not passed onto the defence. One of the problems with the original court case was the lack of disclosure between all the parties involved during both the pretrial actions and subsequent trial (Brucker 1992). The investigation following Marshall's release found that the police and the prosecution had withheld information from the defence. That withholding, together with the failure of the defence counsel to seek disclosure from the Crown, was a major contributing factor in the wrongful conviction. According to the final report on Marshall's wrongful conviction, if "the police are not candid in their dealing with Crown prosecutors, the whole policy on disclosure may go for naught. It is trite to say that a dishonest cop who wishes to subvert the system may do so, and rules are not likely to completely contain such abuse" (House of Commons Debates 1986). As a result, recommendations were made by the Royal Commission of Inquiry into the Wrongful Conviction of Donald Marshall in the hope that guidelines on disclosure would emerge and that the authorities would comply with them in order to achieve the "sound administration of criminal justice ..." One of the problems with this case was the lack of clear directives concerning the role of disclosure during the prosecution.

The guidelines for disclosure emerged from the decision reached by the Supreme Court of Canada in the case of *R. v. Stinchcombe* (1991). This case involved an Alberta lawyer who was convicted in the Alberta Provincial Court of misappropriating funds from a client. Stinchcombe argued the client had actually made him a business partner and, as a result, he had done nothing wrong. Stinchcombe appealed his conviction to the Alberta Court of Appeal, but the appeal was dismissed. The Supreme Court of Canada decided to hear the case, however, perhaps because it saw the opportunity to create clear directives concerning disclosure in criminal trials.

The key issue concerned a taped statement given to the RCMP by Stinchcombe's secretary, which was given to the police after the preliminary inquiry but before the actual trial. The tape supported the claim that Stinchcombe was innocent. The Crown prosecutor informed the defence of this taped statement but declined to indicate the exact nature of its contents. In addition, the secretary refused all offers to be interviewed by the defence. During the trial, defence counsel discovered that the secretary wouldn't be called as a witness by the Crown. As a result, the defence requested that the judge make the Crown disclose the contents of the taped statement. The judge refused, since there was no obligation on the part of the Crown either to put the witness on the stand or to disclose her statements.

The Supreme Court of Canada overturned the decision made by the lower court. In a unanimous 7–0 vote favouring Stinchcombe, it ruled that Crown prosecutors must disclose to the defence any information in serious criminal matters that is capable of affecting the accused's ability to prepare a defence—and to do so early enough to allow the accused time to prepare that defence. However, this rule is not absolute and is subject to judicial interpretation. For example, the police are not required to give the names of any informant who supplies them with information relevant to a case. The Supreme Court decision is based on the fundamental right of the

Continued on next page

EXHIBIT 2.3 The *Charter* in Action: *R. v. Stinchcombe* (1991) ... *continued*

accused to give full answer and defence to the charges. However, the Supreme Court also ruled that "the defense has no obligation to assist the prosecution and is entitled to assume a purely adversarial role."

While *Stinchcombe* created guidelines about disclosure for both the police and prosecutor, what about guidelines for the defence counsel? This issue came before the courts recently in the trial of Ken Murray (*R. v. Murray* (2000)). Mr. Murray was the first lawyer hired to defend Paul Bernardo whose crimes (along with his wife, Karla Homolka) had made national headlines. Following a 71-day search of their residence by the police, Bernardo instructed Mr. Murray to find some videotapes he'd hidden in the house. About a month later, Mr. Murray viewed the six horrific tapes and, despite their damaging content, decided they could be used to direct some of the attention from the crimes away from his client (Ms Homolka had already struck a plea bargain with the Crown). For the next 17 months, Mr. Murray kept the videotapes in his possession, but did not inform the authorities about them or their contents. About a month before the trial, Bernardo suggested to his lawyer that the tapes shouldn't be used in his defence. Faced with an ethical dilemma, Mr. Murray withdrew from the

case, and the lawyer who took over handed them over—through an intermediary—to the police (Blatchford 2000).

Mr. Murray was charged under *Criminal Code* s. 139(2) for attempting to wilfully obstruct the course of justice since he failed to disclose the tapes to the police. Part of Mr. Murray's defence rested on the grounds that the Law Society of Upper Canada's Professional Conduct Handbook states only that a lawyer must not suppress "what ought to be disclosed." In June 2000, Mr. Murray was acquitted of the charges in the Ontario Superior Court as the trial judge ruled there was reasonable doubt concerning Mr. Murray's actions "after considering the accused's evidence in the context of the evidence as a whole" (Blatchford 2000: 33). As a result of this trial, the Law Society of Upper Canada created a panel to establish ethical guidelines for lawyers concerned about holding incriminating evidence (Abbate 2000). But some legal commentators felt that the practical lesson to be learned from this case "may simply be not to touch anything that smells of evidence" (Editorial 2000: 409).

Sources: Law Reform Commission of Canada (1974); Tochor and Kilbeck (1999); Abbate (2000); Blatchford (2000); Editorial (2000).

---

it. The offence of homicide is found in s. 222 of the *Criminal Code:*

> 222(1) A person commits homicide when, directly or indirectly, by any means, he causes the death of a human being.
>
> (5) A person commits culpable homicide when he causes the death of a human being
>
> (a) by means of an unlawful act ...

Therefore, the elements of culpable homicide are (1) the unlawful death (2) of a human being (3) by another human being.

Specific intent requires that the prosecution prove beyond a reasonable doubt the intent specified in the statute's definition of the elements of a crime. These offences are identified by phrases such as "with intent" or "for the purpose of ..." (Barnhorst et al. 1992). In these cases the prosecution must prove "not only an intention to commit an actus reus of the crime in question but also the 'intention' to produce some further consequence beyond the actus reus" (Verdun-Jones 1989: 121). For the offence of breaking and entering, the element of intent to commit an indictable offence typically must be established separately from the act of

breaking and entering. According to s. 348(1)(a) of the *Criminal Code*, the prosecution must prove that an individual not only intended to commit the offence of break and enter but did so "with the specific intent to commit an indictable offence such as theft," although "it is not necessary to show that the person actually committed an indictable offence" (Barnhorst et al. 1992: 39).

> 348(1) Every one who
>
> (a) breaks and enters a place with intent to commit an indictable offence therein,
> (b) breaks and enters a place and commits an indictable offence therein, ... is guilty of an indictable offence ...

In the case of breaking and entering, therefore, the elements of the crime are (1) the breaking (2) and entry (3) of a dwelling house (4) of another (5) with the intent to commit an indictable offence therein.

In addition to the concepts of general and specific intent, there are three distinct levels or degrees of *mens rea*, ranging from the most to the least culpable states of mind—*intent, knowledge,* and *recklessness*. The highest level of culpability is purposefully or intentionally causing harm, and such offences are identified with the word "intent." These offences are indicated in the *Criminal Code* by words such as "intentional" and "willful" and refer to those actions that purposefully or intentionally cause harm. For example, a person commits theft when he takes or converts (see definition below) anything with the intent of depriving the owner or person who has a special interest in it.

322(1) Every one commits theft who fraudulently ... converts to his use or to the use of another person, anything, whether animate or inanimate, with intent ...

Knowledge is used to indicate that the accused possessed an awareness of a particular circumstance. For example, if someone utters a threat to another individual, the question is whether the accused knowingly stated the threat. According to s. 264.1 of the *Criminal Code*

264.1(1) Every one commits an offence who, in any manner, knowingly utters, conveys or causes any person to receive a threat

(a) to cause death or bodily harm to any person;
(b) to burn, destroy or damage real or personal property; or
(c) to kill, poison or injure an animal or bird that is the property of any person

Recklessness refers to a situation in which an individual violates a law simply by lacking the appropriate care and attention about something he is doing. For example, if an individual decides to practise shooting a weapon in a crowded school yard during the lunch break and kills a child, he may argue that he did not have the intention to harm anyone. Yet he would probably be charged with the criminal offence of manslaughter because he was acting with reckless disregard for the safety of those around them. Recklessness is a requirement for the offence of criminal negligence.

219(1) Every one is criminally negligent who

(a) in doing anything, or
(b) in omitting to do anything that it is his duty to do, shows wanton or reckless disregard for the lives or safety of other persons.

Some defences in court can be made on the basis that the *mens rea* element does not apply. The issue here is the notion of criminal responsibility, and Canadian law allows certain persons to be unable to form the mental state necessary to commit a crime. This means that an individual might be excused for committing an action that would normally be classed as criminal. For example, children under 12 years of age cannot be charged with a criminal offence in Canada. *Mens rea* is also lacking when people commit a crime in self-defence or while under duress.

Actus Reus

Another criterion that has to be met before a criminal charge can be laid against a suspect is an action known as *actus reus*. This is the physical or action element of a crime, and it is generally referred to as the "guilty act" or "evil act." In the *Criminal Code*, *actus reus* usually refers to the physical act performed by the accused—a punch, shove, or similar type of action directed against another individual. The actor, and the actor alone, is responsible for his actions. In other words, a person cannot blame someone else for his criminal act. However, an attempt is being made to modify this idea, as some legislators and crime control officials argue that parents who are in control of their children should be subject to criminal prosecution for the illegal acts committed by the children over whom they have control.

While *actus reus* usually involves the commission of an illegal act, it refers also to the failure to do something—in other words, an omission of an act when the *Criminal Code* specifies there is a duty to act. Sections 219 and 220 of the *Criminal Code*, for example, refer to the offences of criminal negligence and criminal negligence causing death:

219(1) Every one is criminally negligent who

(a) in doing anything, or
(b) in omitting to anything that it is his duty to do, shows wanton or reckless disregard for the lives or safety of other persons.

(2) For the purposes of this section, "duty" means a duty imposed by law.

220. Every one who by criminal negligence causes death to another person is guilty of an indictable offence and liable ... to imprisonment for life.

For some criminal offences a person doesn't have to become physically involved in an action, as might be commonly thought. The *Criminal Code* specifies that in certain circumstances the mere act of talking (or speech) can be interpreted as a physical act. In fact, a crime can be committed by speech (as opposed to thought) in our legal system. Section 465 of the *Criminal Code* specifies it is illegal for two or more persons to agree to commit a crime. If both individuals are in agreement about the plan, the act of criminal conspiracy has transpired. In addition, s. 131 of the Criminal Code specifies an individual is guilty of a criminal offence when he commits perjury, and s. 222(5) states any individual who causes the death of another individual through threats, fear of violence, or deception is guilty of a crime.

Concurrence between *Mens Rea* and *Actus Reus*

While not an "official" element of a crime, concurrence requires that "intent both precede and be related to the specific prohibited action or inaction that was or was not taken" (Brown et al. 1991: 68). Concurrence is usually not considered a controversial issue, since in most instances the connection between act and intent is obvious.

Harm

Our legal system places importance on the belief that conduct is criminal only if it is harmful. This ideal is "reflected in the notion of due process, which holds that a criminal statute is unconstitutional if it bears no reasonable relationship to the matter of injury to the public" (Territo et al. 1995: 33–34). This means there has to be a victim for the action to be harmful. Others argue that if the offence is a "victimless" crime—for example, gambling, abortion, prostitution—it is "not the law's business" (Geis 1974). The basis for this view is that victimless crimes violate morality, not the law, and that making them illegal doesn't contribute to the good of society.

Although criminal harm may result in physical injury, it is by no means restricted to physical injury. Physical injury is not inflicted when perjury is committed, for example, though perjury is considered harmful. Criminal law must deal with intangibles, such as harm to public institutions and the harm that occurs as a result of feelings of concern about one's well-being. For example, Canada's anti-stalking law is concerned with protecting citizens from criminal harassment (see Chapter 3). Canada has also developed "hate laws." These are usually attached as a sentence enhancement to acts of violence or a crime against property committed because of the victim's race, gender, or sexual preference (see Chapter 14).

Causation

Causation refers to crimes that require that the conduct of the accused produce a specific result. In other words, as long as the act (or omission) of the accused started a series of events that led to harm, causation has occurred. Important concerns have been raised about causation when the *mens rea* and the *actus reus* are separated over a

lengthy period of time. In some cases it is easy to see the harm that results from an act, but it is not easy to establish the *mens rea* element. This is particularly true for actions generally referred to as corporate crime.

Take, for example, an employee who is told that because the spraying of a particular chemical mixture is "safe," she is not required to wear safety equipment. If the individual dies immediately after applying the chemical, concurrence could easily be determined. But what if the worker suffers no ill health for 15 years and then suddenly dies from a blood disease that is associated with exposure to the chemical? The lack of concurrence would make it difficult to prove that a crime was committed. This situation may be further complicated by the fact that many other workers applied the spray at the same time without contracting a terminal disease, or that some suffered from seemingly unrelated illnesses.

Punishment

The law must state the sanctions for every crime in order that everyone be aware of the possible consequences of certain actions. The *Criminal Code* therefore specifies the sanctions for every crime. In Canada there are sanctions for two types of offences: indictable and summary conviction offences.

THE CLASSIFICATION OF CRIMINAL OFFENCES

In Canada the federal government decides how to classify a crime and determines the penalties attached to each offence. Canada classifies crimes in two ways, both of which involve legal and general definitions. Legal classifications include indictable offences, summary conviction offences, and hybrid offences, while general classifications refer to offences used by police and other criminal justice agencies to classify criminal offences, such as violent crimes or property crimes.

Summary Conviction, Indictable, and Hybrid Offences

Summary conviction offences are generally punished by a period of incarceration not exceeding six months and a maximum fine of $2000, although for some offences (such as sexual assault level 1) the Supreme Court of Canada has increased the maximum punishment to 18 months. Summary conviction trials are always heard by a provincial court judge. In addition, charges for summary conviction offences must be laid within six months of the commission of the offence. If a period of imprisonment is part of the sentence, the offender serves the sentence in a provincial facility.

In contrast, there are three methods of trial for indictable offences. The less serious indictable offences (for example, most gaming and betting offences) are also known as absolute jurisdiction indictable offences. The accused has to be tried by a provincial court judge. The most serious crimes (for example, first- and second-degree murder) are referred to as Supreme Court exclusive indictable offences. They must be tried by a federally appointed judge and a jury in a provincial Superior Court. In some cases, the accused may request that the case be heard by judge alone, but this request has to be permitted by the provincial Attorney General or Minister of Justice. For all other indictable offences, the accused can choose to have the trial by a provincially appointed judge with or without a jury, or by a federally appointed judge with or without a jury. These offences, which make up the majority of indictable offences in Canada, are known as election indictable offences. If convicted of an indictable offence, the accused may receive a variety of sentences. Some offences (for example, homicide) bring life sentences, while for others (for example, sexual assault) punishments depend on the degree of harm inflicted on the victim. Few minimum punishments are stipulated by the *Criminal Code*, so it is up to the judge to select the appropriate sentence up to the severest allowable by law.

Hybrid offences (e.g., sexual assault level 1) give prosecutors the discretion to decide if they wish to proceed with a case as a summary conviction offence or an indictable offence. The prosecutor's decision is formally based on such factors as the previous record of the offender as well as any mitigating factors (for example, the social status of the offender) or aggravating factors (for example, crimes involving violence) associated with the crime. In reality, the prosecutor's decision can be influenced by police officers. In Ericson's study of Peel Regional detectives he found they were able to "fundamentally affect the outcome of a case both in terms of what the accused is convicted of and in terms of sentencing" (Ericson, in Wheeler 1987: 27). However the final decision is reached, it has a significant impact on most of the procedures that apply to the accused. For example, the decision determines

1. possible appeals;
2. the maximum length of the sentence;
3. whether a fine may be imposed in addition to imprisonment; and
4. whether an offender can serve her sentence in the community.

THE SERIOUSNESS OF CRIME

Legal Responses to Violent Crimes

Criminal statutes prescribe punishments that reflect the seriousness of the crime committed. Some offences in the *Criminal Code* recognize different levels of violence, together with differences in the maximum amount of punishment applicable to each. Examples of single offences with gradations of seriousness within are homicide and sexual assault.

The offence of sexual assault consists of three offences, the least serious of which is found in s. 271 of the *Criminal Code*. This is a hybrid offence, so if the Crown prosecutor elects to proceed by way of an indictable offence, the maximum length of punishment is 10 years. However, the Crown prosecutor has the discretion to proceed by way of summary conviction, and the accused, if convicted, faces a maximum punishment of 18 months. For a person convicted of sexual assault of the next-highest level of seriousness—s. 272 of the *Criminal Code*, which addresses sexual assault with a weapon, threatening bodily harm, or causing bodily harm—the maximum length of the prison term is 14 years. The most serious form of sexual assault, dealt with in s. 273 of the *Criminal Code*, involves the charge of aggravated sexual assault. An individual convicted of this offence can receive the maximum sentence of life imprisonment (Roberts and Mohr 1994).

In contrast to sexual assault, homicide is divided into four categories in the *Criminal Code*. A person who commits homicide, according to s. 222, "directly or indirectly, by any means … causes the death of a human being." This section specifies that only culpable homicide is punishable. Once the police have determined that a homicide is culpable, they can lay one of the following charges: first-degree murder, second-degree murder, manslaughter, and infanticide.

First-degree murder is planned and deliberate. However, an individual can be charged with first-degree murder even if the act wasn't planned and deliberate when the victim is a police officer, a prison guard, an individual working in a prison setting, or "is another similar person acting in the course of duty." In addition, a charge of first-degree murder can be laid if the act was planned or deliberate and if anyone dies during the commission of one of the following crimes: s. 76—hijacking an aircraft; s. 271—sexual assault; s. 272—sexual assault with a weapon; s. 273—aggravated sexual assault; s. 279—kidnapping and forcible confinement; and s. 279.1—hostage taking. All murder that is not

Maurice (Mom) Boucher, leader of the Hells Angels in Quebec, is shown being escorted by the police after his arrest in 1997. He was found guilty of two charges of first-degree murder and one charge of attempted murder in April 2002.

first-degree murder is second-degree murder (Silverman and Kennedy 1993).

The charge of manslaughter can be laid if the Crown prosecutor is unable to establish all the elements of murder. Usually a charge of manslaughter is laid when the death in question (an accidental death) is caused either by an unlawful act, such as assault, or by criminal negligence. Manslaughter is an indictable offence, and the maximum punishment is life imprisonment.

Infanticide is one of the rare sections of the *Criminal Code* that specifies the gender of the alleged perpetrator of the crime. This charge can be laid only against a "female person" when she "causes the death of her newly-born child." A newly born child, in the eyes of the law, is a person under one year of age. The maximum punishment for the offence of infanticide is five years in prison. This law is based on the reasoning that a woman may be "mentally disturbed of giving birth … and thus less responsible for her actions. In this situation, the law mitigates the severity of punishment for what would otherwise be murder or manslaughter."

The punishment for both first- and second-degree murder is life imprisonment. There is an important difference between the two, however, and that is the possibility of release on parole. At the sentencing of a person convicted of second-degree murder, the judge can state that the accused is eligible for parole after serving a designated amount of time of the sentence. A judge currently has the right to grant an offender eligibility for full parole after serving 10 years. An individual convicted of first-degree murder must serve life imprisonment. However, the law stipulates that individual must serve a minimum of 25 years of the sentence before applying for full parole.

In theory, any individual convicted of first- and second-degree murder spends the rest of his life in prison; that is, there is no guarantee of his ever leaving a federal correctional institution. However, since 1991, most persons convicted of first- and second-degree murder still serving their sentence after 15 years can apply for a judicial review of parole ineligibility under s. 745.6 of the Criminal Code for the purpose of receiving parole (also referred to as the faint-hope clause) (see Chapter 12). The jury decides whether to allow the application for reducing the number of years before the person receives parole. If it agrees to do so, the National Parole Board reviews the case and agrees or refuses to grant parole. By 2000 most individuals sentenced for the crimes of first- and second-degree murder who had applied for early release under this section of the Criminal Code received the right to apply for a reduction in their sentence length. Of the first 103 applicants under s. 745.6, 84 were successful in obtaining a parole board hearing, and 25 of the applicants were informed they could apply for parole immediately (Stein and Antonowicz 2001).

Mala en Se and Mala Prohibita Offences

Criminologists discuss the social functions of the law using two common terms: *mala en se* and *mala prohibita*. A criminal act is referred to as *mala en se* when an act is illegal because most law-makers and the public agree that the actions in question are wrong and that they should be criminalized. *Mala en se* offences are usually referred to as "natural crimes" because they offend the "natural" principles of what is good in a society. To some individuals (e.g., Brown et al. 2001), these offences "hardly need legal sanctions to forestall widespread violations." "If the threats of legal punishment were removed, moral feelings and the fear of public judgement would remain as powerful crime prevention forces, at least for a limited period" (Andenaes 1966: 957). These offences are thought to be universal, that is, the offences included in this area, such as murder, are outlawed in every society and culture. However, in our society there are exceptions. Our legal system, for example, excuses a homicide in certain extreme situations, such as in the case of self-defence or duress.

In contrast, *mala prohibita* refers to those actions that are wrong only because they have been made illegal through the creation of a statute—that is, they are "human-made laws." The actions in question are not considered to be an inherent wrong, but rather are made a wrong because they violate some moral principle.

What is a wrong in this area varies between societies and cultures. *Mala prohibita* offences are considered to be more responsive to threats of legal sanction, with conformity being fully reliant on those formal sanctions, since there are no informal sanctions (Brown et al. 2001). There are many debates in this area of our law as to what exactly should be sanctioned, and by how much. Our values and norms change over time, leading to debates over what is to be considered as a criminal act. The origins of Canada's narcotic and marijuana legislation and the present debate concerning whether or not simple possession of marijuana should be decriminalized is an example of how social values can change, with the resulting concerns over how best to control marijuana.

CRIMINAL LAW REFORM

During the past few decades the federal government has introduced and revised various substantive laws and ruled on countless procedural issues in an attempt to deal with contemporary issues. At the same time, new concerns have been raised that change the way we have traditionally granted legal rights in our society. The result is that a particular action that was legal 25 years ago is now a criminal offence. For example, can we create laws that can realistically control the organizational activities of gangs as well as determine the types of organizations they may join? Can activities such as panhandling in public areas be banned in order to reduce the perceived disorder on the streets? If the answer to these questions is "yes," can we then realistically develop meaningful punishments for individuals who become affiliated with gangs and/or involved with criminal gang activity as well as those persons who wish to panhandle on public streets?

Anti-Gang (Criminal Conspiracy) Legislation

In their attempt to resolve the gang dilemma and appease the public and law enforcement, the federal government of Canada developed anti-gang legislation (Bill C-95) in 1997. This law applies to "any or all of the members of a gang which engage in or have, within the preceding 5 years, engaged in the commission of a series of such offences." An accused found guilty of participating in a criminal organization can receive a maximum of 14 years in prison. The highlights of the new anti-gang measures include the expansion of the rights of police officers in order to combat this problem:

- *Participation in a criminal organization:* Anyone guilty of a criminal act performed for the benefit of or in association with a criminal organization is subject to tougher penalties that are referred to as "sentence enhancements." For example, a known gang member convicted of a violent crime will be subject to a much longer sentence than a person acting alone. A *criminal organization* was redefined as any group, association, or other body consisting of five or more persons who have as a primary activity the commission of any of a series of indictable offences punishable by a sentence of five years or more. This offence of belonging to a criminal organization is punishable by up to 14 years in prison.

- *Explosives offences:* An individual will be guilty of an offence if he possesses explosives for the benefit of, or at the direction of, a criminal organization. Anyone using explosives to commit murder will be guilty of first-degree murder. This offence is punishable by up to 14 years in prison (which is more than the maximum for possession of explosives). This sentence will be a consecutive sentence, added to any other offence.

- *Peace bonds:* A judge, on application of an Attorney General, can issue a restraining order that places strict conditions on a gang leader prohibiting his association with other known gang members or visiting known gang hangouts. If this order is breached, the gang leader could be sentenced to a jail term. The suspect does not have to commit an offence to be subject to the gang peace bond.

- *Electronic surveillance:* The police now have greater access to electronic means of surveillance in order to observe the movements and actions of gang members. Previously, the police had to convince a judge they needed electronic surveillance as a "last resort." The limits on wiretap authorizations can be extended from 60 days to one year.

- *Proceeds of crime:* This allows for the seizure and forfeiture of the proceeds from all criminal organization activities on conviction. Property such as weapons and vehicles used in the commission of a crime can also be seized, as well as property such as a gang clubhouse built or modified for the purpose of facilitating the commission of criminal organization activities. Police can also obtain a court order to access income tax information of those being investigated for participating in a criminal organization.

- *Bail:* Anyone charged with a criminal organization offence is subject to pretrial detention unless he can prove that it is not justified. Previously, the onus was on the Crown prosecutor to show why the person should be detained.

- *Sentencing:* Any evidence of an offence committed for the benefit of, at the direction of, or in association

CHAPTER 2 Criminal Law and Criminal Justice in Canada

with a criminal organization will be considered by a judge at sentencing as an "aggravating" factor that can lead to a longer sentence. Judges can also delay parole eligibility for anyone convicted of a criminal organization offence.

- *National and regional coordinating committees:* Six national coordinating committees on organized crime are in place across Canada (Newfoundland, the Maritimes, Quebec, Ontario, the Prairies, and British Columbia/Yukon) to share information and assist in the enforcement efforts against gangs.

The first application of Canada's anti-gang legislation occurred in Winnipeg, Manitoba, where 35 men, alleged members of the Manitoba Warriors street gang, were arrested after a year-long police operation involving up to 120 officers. Gang members were charged with drug and weapons charges, along with provisions found in the federal anti-gang legislation that target participating in a criminal organization. All of those charged were denied bail, with the exception of the last individual to have a trial (this person received bail after all of the others had pleaded guilty). Two of the accused had charges stayed against them in exchange for their testimony. Of the remaining 33 accused, the Crown secured 32 convictions on drug charges, and they received sentences ranging from time served to nine years in prison. Only two of the 33 individuals pleaded guilty to participating in a criminal organization, and both had extra time added to their sentences (McIntyre 2000). The cost of this trial was enormous—over $10 million from beginning to end.

Despite the fact that at least 14 individuals had been convicted under the anti-gang provisions, many individuals argued that the law needed to be amended to make it a much better legal tool to control criminal organizations. Critics objected to this law, arguing that the legislation was "bad law" and that it was unlikely to "solve the problem of biker or other gangs committed to rebelliousness and lawlessness (Stuart 1997: 216)." These critics believe that Canada already has strong laws, rendering the various provisions of the law unnecessary.

Most critics, however, argued that the anti-gang legislation was too difficult to apply and needed to be amended in order to make it more effective. Taking a strong crime control stance, these individuals made comments that the existing law was inadequate to effectively control such activities. For example, the president of the Canadian Police Association was quoted as saying "we're not winning the war. Things are going out of control and it's time to do something about it." Some parliamentarians felt the police are "handcuffed by ineffective laws and ineffective programs," while an organized crime specialist stated that Canada has become a centre of global crime activity "in part because of federal regulations and laws" (Humphreys 2001: A4).

In April 2001, new anti-gang legislation (Bill C-24) was tabled in the House of Commons. Some of the issues raised about the first law were addressed, and other new sections included sweeping new powers being given to law enforcement agencies and the courts. The most important changes include a new definition of "criminal organization," new criminal offences, and more powers to law enforcement officials.

- *Definition of a criminal organization:* Prosecutors faced a difficult task trying to convict someone based on the first definition. The proposed amendment defines a criminal organization more loosely, as a group of three of more people who have committed a crime for financial gain.
- *The criminalization of participation in a criminal organization:* This law expands the definition of participation in a criminal organization; it is no longer necessary for an individual to break the law. This change has the objective of making it easier for prosecutors to charge noncriminals such as accountants who knowingly work for criminal organizations. The maximum sentence for participation is five years.
- *The criminalization of benefiting from a criminal organization:* Anyone who is found guilty of committing a crime for the benefit of a criminal organization will face a maximum sentence of 14 years.
- *The criminalization of directing others to commit crimes.* Gang leaders will now face a maximum sentence of life imprisonment for directing others to commit crimes, whether or not their instructions are followed.

Other amendments included the proposals that the police be given new wiretapping powers and that undercover investigators possess immunity from all of their investigations. (Immunity would extend beyond the investigations associated with criminal gangs.) The police were also given the power to authorize their own activities (rather than receiving preauthorization from a judge) because their work now requires them to make split-second decisions. In addition, the police were given immunity from committing crimes in their pursuit of charges but they could not intentionally or recklessly cause death or bodily harm, obstruct justice, or commit sexual offences. Bill C-24 received royal assent in December 2001 and became law in 2002.

Officials working in crime control expressed their happiness with these amendments, stating that these provisions will make investigators more proactive and enable them to be more effective in preventing crimes committed by those who work in and for criminal organizations, They added that prosecutions will now be

Many groups are well organized and have come under increasing criminal justice scrutiny through new legislation passed to combat organized-crime groups.

easier and sentences will be much harsher. However, critics pointed out that this new law has created expansive powers for the agents of the state. According to Don Stuart, a law professor at Queen's University, one of the biggest problems with the law is the fact that the police can now break the law. "Police authorizing police to break the law is a perversion of the rule of law" (Chwialkowska 2001). Others critics point out that this legislation is similar to the anti-terrorist legislation (see Chapter 1) and would not be more effective in controlling gang-related activities but instead have the effect of eroding the civil rights of Canadians (Daniels et al. 2001).

The *Safe Streets Act*

Concern about the relationship between disorder and crime has become a major issue during the past 20 years, ever since the publication of the "broken window" thesis in 1982 (see Chapter 5). This has led cities to pass bylaws and the Province of Ontario to enact legislation prohibiting activities believed to contribute to disorder. Vancouver and Winnipeg passed bylaws (in 1998 and 1995, respectively) focusing on controlling "aggressive" panhandling in certain locations at certain times in an attempt to eliminate disorderly behaviour that some feel threatens the safety of citizens. Ontario passed the *Safe Streets Act* in 1999, which attempts to control similar behaviour as well as any type of solicitation from involving a "captive audience" in certain locations. All three of these pieces of legislation have created controversy and led to court challenges based on questions about their constitutionality.

The *Safe Streets Act* defined soliciting in an "aggressive manner" as a manner likely to cause a 'reasonable person' to be concerned about her personal

safety. It also identified numerous activities that are automatically considered to involve aggressive soliciting.

Some of these activities are

• threatening the person with physical harm;
• obstructing the path of the person who is being solicited;
• using abusive language during or after solicitation; and
• continuing to solicit a person in a persistent manner after the person has said that he doesn't want to give any money.

The act also identifies specific places and situations where an individual cannot solicit a "captive audience." Examples of these places and situations include

• using or waiting to use a pay telephone or a public washroom facility;
• using, waiting to use, or departing from an automated teller machine;
• in or on a public transit vehicle; and
• in a parking lot.

The punishments vary according to jurisdiction but all include a fine or a short period of confinement. In Vancouver, the maximum fine is not to exceed $2000, and in Ottawa the maximum fine is $5000. In Winnipeg, the fine is not to exceed $1000 or a jail term of up to six months. In Ontario, the *Safe Streets Act* specified that the first conviction is to be a fine not exceeding $500 while subsequent convictions involve fines of up to $1000 and a jail term of no more than six months.

This legislation has led to great debate and controversy. In British Columbia, the B.C. Public Interest Advocacy Centre is heading a constitutional challenge of the city bylaw. The Public Interest Law Centre in Winnipeg also challenged the city bylaw on similar constitutional grounds. Critics of these bylaws and the *Safe Streets Act* argue that these laws discriminate against the poor and are essentially a continuation of legislation that, over the centuries, has attempted to outlaw similar types of activities by using various terms such as "vagrancy," "tramps," "hoboes" and the "homeless." In addition, they argue that these laws are vague, since they do not define in any specific way exactly what types of activities are outlawed (Hermer and Mosher 2002). Others (e.g., Ruddick 2002) note this legislation, in particular the *Safe Streets Act*, has so many prohibitions that it has the effect of controlling the places that homeless people pursue their activities. Such laws, they point out, focus upon those least able to defend themselves or pay any fines (thereby raising the possibility of a jail sentence). These critics also approach the problems addressed from this legislation within a broader context, saying that the real problem that should be the focus of attention is the true extent of poverty, the elimination of welfare programs, and the lack of adequate housing.

Supporters of the *Safe Streets Act* argue that many citizens want these types of laws as they fear disorder and its effects. In addition, they believe street crime increases as the result of these activities, making city streets even more unsafe. To control activities in certain places and times, in their opinion, is not a blanket prohibition and the law controls only certain undesirable actions in very specific locations. Safer streets, they point out, emerge as a result of both more order and controlling activities that make people more fearful.

Eighteen months after the *Safe Streets Act* was introduced, over 100 individuals had been charged with an offence. In August 2001, 80 of the individuals charged decided to challenge the constitutionality of the act. The facts surrounding the activities of 13 of these individuals were agreed upon by defence counsel and the Crown (the other 67 individuals had their charges withdrawn). In this challenge (*R. v. Banks*), nine of the individuals were charged with "soliciting on the roadway," while three were charged under the provincial *Highway Traffic Act*, and one was charged for soliciting "in a persistent manner."

SUMMARY

Our criminal justice system is founded on the protection of law-abiding citizens through the operation of the law. In essence, the criminal justice system develops, administers, and enforces the criminal law. What constitutes a crime is defined by the federal government, but the actual administration of justice is in the hands of provincial governments; thus, one can find variations in the operation of our legal system across Canada. Crimes are categorized as indictable or summary conviction offences, depending on their seriousness.

Our understanding of criminal conduct changes over time. Today the *Criminal Code* is a complex document, because our knowledge of criminal behaviour has increased dramatically during the past decade. In recent years, for example, Canada has passed laws designed to combat organized groups such as gangs and panhandlers. These legal charges can be procedural or substantive in nature. (Changes in the rules of the processing of the accused through the criminal justice system reflect procedural concerns.)

In our system of law, all individuals are considered innocent until proven guilty. To determine guilt, the prosecution must prove beyond a reasonable doubt that the accused possessed *mens rea* and committed the act in question. No matter what standards our criminal justice system has to employ in the courtroom, the perception of our legal system held by the Canadian public differs from that of our legal professionals. In general, the public consider violent actions to be more serious offences than property crimes.

Discussion Questions

1. Explain precedent and the importance of the doctrine of *stare decisis*.

2. Identify the four sources of Canadian criminal law.

3. What is a crime? When are individuals criminally liable for their actions?

4. What are the elements required to establish a guilty mental state, or *mens rea*?

5. Discuss the kinds of crime classifications that we use in Canada. Should we use other classifications, such as an offence index or a white-collar-crime index?

6. Can you think of any laws that should be revised and made stronger? How would this help to control the behaviour you have in mind?

7. Do you think Crown prosecutors should have the power to determine if a hybrid offence should proceed as an indictable offence or a summary conviction offence?

8. Do you think simple possession of marijuana should be decriminalized?

9. Can you think of any examples of when an act has been made illegal (*mala prohibita*) but then made legal again?

10. Do you think the punishments for summary conviction offences should be made harsher?

Suggested Readings

Barnhorst, R., S. Barnhorst, and K.L. Clarke. 1992. *Criminal Law and the Canadian Criminal Code,* 2nd ed. Toronto: McGraw-Hill Ryerson.

Boyd, N. 1998. *Criminal Law: An Introduction,* 2nd ed. Toronto: Harcourt Brace Canada.

Hiebert, J. L. 2002. *Charter Conflicts: What Is Parliament's Role?* Montreal: McGill-Queen's University Press.

Mewett, A.W. 1996. *An Introduction to the Criminal Process in Canada,* 3rd ed. Scarborough, Ont.: Carswell.

Roach, K. 1996. *Essentials of Criminal Law.* Concord, Ont.: Irwin Law.

Roberts, J.V., and R.M. Mohr, eds. 1994. *Confronting Sexual Abuse: A Decade of Legal and Social Change.* Toronto: University of Toronto Press.

Verdun-Jones, S. 1999. *Canadian Criminal Cases: Selected Highlights.* Toronto: Harcourt, Brace Canada.

References

Abbate, G. 2000. "Lawyers to Get Code of Conduct on Evidence." *The Globe and Mail,* 30 November, A8.

Andenaes, J. 1966. "The General Preventive Effects of Punishment." *University of Pennsylvania Law Review* 114: 949–83.

Anderssen, E. 2000. "Supreme Court Upholds Rape-Shield Law." *The Globe and Mail,* 13 October, A7.

Barnhorst, R., S. Barnhorst, and K.L. Clarke. 1992. *Criminal Law and the Canadian Criminal Code,* 2nd ed. Toronto: McGraw-Hill Ryerson.

Billingsley, B. 2002. "The Rule of Law: What Is It? Why Should We Care?" *Law Now* 26, no. 5: 27–30.

Blatchford, C. 2000. "Ken Murray's Not-So-Excellent Adventure." *Canadian Lawyer* 24, no. 10: 28–33.

Bowland, A.L. 1994. "Sexual Assault Trials and Protection of 'Bad Girls:' The Battle between the Courts and Parliament." In J.V. Roberts and R.M. Mohr, eds., *Confronting Sexual Assault: A Decade of Legal and Social Change.* Toronto: University of Toronto Press, pp. 241–67.

Brannigan, A. 1984. *Crimes, Courts, and Corrections: An Introduction to Crime and Social Control in Canada.* Toronto: Holt, Rinehart, and Winston.

Brown, S.E., F.A. Esbensen, and G. Geis. 2001. *Criminology: Explaining Crime and Its Context.* Cincinnati: C.J. Anderson.

Brown, S., F. Esbensen, and G. Geis. 1991. *Criminology: Explaining Crime and Its Context.* Cincinnati: C.J. Anderson.

Brucker, T.M. 1992. "Disclosure and the Role of the Police in the Criminal Justice System." *Criminal Law Quarterly* 35: 57–76.

Chwialkowska, L. 2001. "Judge's OK Not Needed for Officers to Break Law." *National Post,* 22 December, B4.

———. 2000. "Rape-Shield Law Upheld by High Court." *National Post,* 13 October, A4.

Daniels, R.J., P. Macklem, and K. Roach, eds. 2001. *The Security of Freedom: Essays on Canada's Anti-Terrorism Bill.* Toronto: University of Toronto Press.

Desroches, F.J. 1995. *Force and Fear: Robbery in Canada.* Scarborough, Ont.: Nelson Canada.

Editorial. 2000. "Smoking Guns: Beyond the Murray Case." *The Criminal Law Quarterly* 43, no. 4: 409–10.

Geis, G. 1974. *Not the Law's Business.* New York: Schocken.

Hall, J. 1947. *Theft, Law and Society,* 2nd ed. Indianapolis: Bobbs-Merrill.

Hermer, J., and J. Mosher. 2002. *Disorderly People: Law and the Politics of Exclusion in Ontario.* Halifax: Fernwood.

Hiebert, J.L. 2002. *Charter Conflicts: What Is Parliament's Role?* Montreal: McGill-Queen's University Press.

Humphreys, A. 2001. "Anti-Gang Law to Get Tougher." *National Post,* 5 April, A4.

Johnson, H. 1996. *Dangerous Domains: Violence against Women in Canada.* Scarborough, Ont.: Nelson Canada.

R. v. Kuldip, [1990] 3 S.C.R. 618, 61 C.C.C. (3d) 385

R. v. Luxton, [1990] 2 S.C.R. 711, 58 C.C.C. (3d) 449

R. v. Manninen (1987), 34 C.C.C. (3d) 385 (S.C.C.)

R. v. Mannion, [1986] 2 S.C.R. 272, 28 C.C.C. (3d) 544

R. v. Mills, [1986] 1 S.C.R. 863, 29 D.L.R. (4th) 161

R. v. Mills, [1999] 3 S.C.R. 668

R. v. Murray (2000), 186 D.L.R. (4th) 125 (Ont. S.C.J.)

R. v. Oakes (1986), 24 C.C.C. (3d) 321 (S.C.C.)

R. v. O'Connor, [1995] 4 S.C.R. 411

R. v. Ross, [1989] 1 S.C.R. 3

R. v. Seaboyer, [1991] 2 S.C.R. 577, 7 C.R. (4th) 117, 66 C.C.C. (3d) 321

R. v. Simpson (1993), 79 C.C.C. (3d) 482 (Ont. C.A.)

R. v. Smith (1987), 34 C.C.C. (3d) 97 (S.C.C.)

R. v. Stinchcombe, [1991] 3 S.C.R. 326, 68 C.C.C. (3d) 1

R. v. Swain, [1991] 1 S.C.R. 933

R. v. Therens (1985), 18 C.C.C. (3d) 481 (S.C.C.)

R. v. Thomsen (1988), 40 C.C.C. (3d) 411 (S.C.C.)

R. v. Tran, [1994] 2 S.C.R. 951, 117 D.L.R. (4th) 7

R. v. Tremblay (1987), 37 C.C.C. (3d) 565 (S.C.C.)

R. v. Wong, [1990] 3 S.C.R. 36, 60 C.C.C. (3d) 460

Crime Control Philosophy and Criminal Justice Policy

CHAPTER OBJECTIVES

✓ Understand the differences and similarities among the six different punitive models of criminal justice in terms of the criminal sanction and operation of the major components of the criminal justice system.

✓ Understand the differences between the two different nonpunitive models in terms of the criminal sanction and operation of the major components of the criminal justice system.

✓ Identify the differences between the punitive and nonpunitive approaches to crime control in society.

✓ Recognize the basic elements of an Aboriginal justice system and how they differ from all other approaches.

✓ Recognize how each of these models approaches the general category of "sex offenders."

S ix distinct philosophies underlie our criminal justice system. Two of these—deterrence and rehabilitation—have traditionally guided criminal justice. Deterrence emerged in the 18th century, and rehabilitation gained prominence in our criminal justice system in the early 20th century. During the past 25 years these two philosophies were joined by two others: selective incapacitation and the justice model. Selective incapacitation focuses primarily on those individuals labelled as "dangerous," while the justice model is probably the dominant criminal justice policy today, as it forms the basis of the *Canadian Charter of Rights and Freedoms.* Recently, restorative justice and Aboriginal justice systems have been proposed as an alternatives to the traditional approaches used in Canadian society. Although restorative justice has been embraced by the federal and provincial governments, the possibility of separate Aboriginal justice systems has led to much controversy.

One of the major questions facing policy-makers is how best to control criminal behaviour. In an attempt to achieve this control, policy-makers face an array of choices; for example, they may want to examine the possibility of rehabilitating offenders. Or they may want to create and introduce prevention programs in an attempt to stop the criminal activity in question before it starts. In some cases, it could be better to sentence the offenders to very long periods of incarceration, which would protect society over the long term. Depending on the type of offence, it may be better to consider an alternative approach, such as restorative justice. No matter which approach is taken, the legal rights of the offenders in question have to be considered.

Today there are a number of alternatives available for controlling sex offenders. These include community notification laws and sex registries. Ontario was the first jurisdiction in Canada to introduce a registry (in April 2001) of those individuals convicted of sexual assault, child molestation, and other sex offences. Names are added to the registry when an offender is released. British Columbia followed the Ontario approach a few months later. These policies were due largely to public concern about the exploitation, assault, and murder of children by sex offenders. The Ontario registry requires all those convicted of a sex offence to register with their local police within 15 days of moving into a community, enabling the police to access the names and addresses of convicted pedophiles released into the community. Failure to do so will lead to fines of up to $25,000 and/or a jail term for a first offence (Mackie 1999).

In the first 12 months of its operation, the Ontario registry placed over 5000 names on its list. One shortcoming of this Ontario approach is that when an offender leaves Ontario, he is no longer required to register his address.

The federal government has introduced two pieces of legislation designed to assist the monitoring of convicted sex offenders released into the community. In 1994, the National Screening System was introduced, which allows volunteer and other community organizations access to criminal records of applicants for positions of trust with children and vulnerable adults. The second piece of legislation was Bill C-7, which created a special flagging system within the Canadian Police Information Centre for those offenders who have been pardoned of offences against children and vulnerable adults. Both of these pieces of legislation have been strongly criticized. According to an OPP spokesperson, both lack a search capability: "Without a name of the offender you can't do anything" (Elliott 2001). Another criticism was that the system does not force offenders to report their latest change of address. It wasn't until February 2002 that the Solicitor General of Canada announced, after two years of intense pressure from federal opposition parties, provincial governments, and public organizations that the federal government would introduce a national registry system, which it did in the fall of that year. It is proposed that this new national system will require all convicted sex offenders to register their new addresses, along with other information such as name changes, with local law enforcement officials when they move. This system will also allow police investigators to search by geographical area, such as postal code, so that when a sex crime is committed they will be able to quickly determine whether anyone who has been convicted of a similar offence lives in that area (Clark 2002).

Despite significant support for such laws, four criticisms have been raised. First, some argue these laws are based on "a false sense of precision" since the prediction of sexual reoffending is not very accurate at this time (Hefferman et al. 1995). Others believe notification may create "a false sense of security that may actually expose children to risk" (Steinbock 1995). Another criticism focuses on the disregard for sex-offenders' privacy rights for the purpose of protecting the public. Finally, some argue these laws ignore the fact that treatment programs for sex offenders in our federal correctional system are inadequate and need to be expanded, since many offenders are reconvicted of sexual crimes (Marshall 1993). However, experts in the field of child molestation argue that critics of these types of laws have a "terrible time accepting that this is a reality. They still can't believe it" (Rogers, in Mackie 1999, A1).

This chapter presents different ways of understanding the how each of the crime control philosophies potentially influences the criminal justice system. First, the four major contemporary criminal justice policies—the justice model, deterrence, selective incapacitation, and rehabilitation—are presented. This discussion precedes a review of the two most recent models to emerge—restorative justice and Aboriginal justice systems. Second, each of these crime control philosophies differs in its approach to a similar issue— the best way to deal with the crimes that are generally referred to as "sexual offences" and those individuals who commit them.

CRIME CONTROL IN CANADA

One of the most common complaints made against the criminal justice system is that it is too soft on criminals. Critics readily point to a series of shortcomings—criminals who are granted parole and then commit more crimes, plea-bargaining, lenient sentences imposed by judges, and police officers who warn offenders instead of arresting them. Left unchecked, critics argue, these factors contribute to rising crime rates. Others argue that parole boards make informed decisions concerning prisoners, that plea-bargaining is beneficial to the successful conclusion of criminal cases, and that judicial discretion in sentencing is an asset. These individuals feel that extraneous social issues that can't be controlled by the criminal justice system, such as family breakdown, contribute the most to the increasing crime rate.

These opinions spill over into significant publicpolicy debates. Should there be mandatory sentences for all convicted criminals? Should convicted violent offenders never be allowed out of prison? Should pleabargaining be banned? Should police budgets be increased dramatically to hire more police officers, who in turn investigate and apprehend more criminals? Finally, should judicial discretion be banned outright or at least closely controlled?

Many observers say it would be extremely difficult, because of the complexity of the criminal justice system today, to introduce clear policy directives that would influence that system's operation. The informal operation of the system, as well as self-interests of the various groups that work within it, would make improvement difficult. Despite these real-life questions, the major crime control models discussed below are conceptualized in an ideal manner.

CRIME CONTROL PHILOSOPHY AND CRIMINAL JUSTICE POLICY

Four major philosophies guide the operation of our criminal justice system: the justice model, deterrence, selective incapacitation, and rehabilitation. Because these philosophies are constantly being revised and updated, many people speak of "neo-deterrence" and "neo-rehabilitation" systems. Although legislators and other policy-makers use these models to guide their policies, none of the philosophies alone exclusively guides the operation of our criminal justice system. Usually two or more are combined. For example, when the *Young Offenders Act* came in force in 1984 it was grounded almost exclusively in the strategies of the deterrence and justice philosophies. Combining models leads to confusion about which strategy is most important approach in a given situation, raising questions about what leads to the success or failure of any particular crime control initiative.

These philosophies address different issues, although some share certain conceptual features. For example, only rehabilitation focuses on the criminal actor, so it emphasizes the individual treatment of most convicted criminals. The other three philosophies focus, albeit in different ways, on the criminal act. For example, the justice model focuses exclusively on the criminal act committed by the alleged perpetrators, and punishment is based on the seriousness of the offence. The deterrence and selective incapacitation philosophies, like the justice model, focus on the act, but with the purpose of preventing future crimes. In contrast to the justice model, however, the issue of the current criminal offence is of secondary importance.

Each of these four philosophies can be clearly described, and though some overlap exists among some of them, they are better known for their differences. Price and Stitt (1986) developed a framework to compare the philosophies and policies, showing how each strategy approaches crime control through criminal sanctions followed by their concomitant policy implications. The following description of the four philosophies follows the Price and Stitt outline.

THE JUSTICE MODEL

History

The justice model, though a recent creation, has had a significant impact on the operation of the criminal justice system. The first major document to offer support for the justice model appeared in *Struggle for Justice* (1971), written by the American Friends Service Committee. This committee, developed as a response to an analysis of a prison riot in the New York City area, recommended the criminal justice system be guided by the ideals of justice, fairness, and the need to protect human rights and dignity. It recommended the elimination of the discretionary powers held by prosecutors, the judiciary, and parole boards.

One of its most important recommendations was the need for the sentence to fit the offence, and not the offender. All individuals convicted of a certain offence must receive the same sentence, although the committee did recommend that repeat offenders be given longer sentences than first-time offenders for the same crime. This message was repeated by Marvin Frankel, a U.S. federal judge, whose book *Criminal Sentences: Law without Order* (1972) recommended that the principles of objectivity, fairness, and consistency be the basis of the operation of the justice system. He also argued that criminal offences be ranked according to their severity and that punishments reflect the severity of the crimes.

Perhaps the most influential argument for the creation of a justice model–based criminal justice system came from the Committee for the Study of Incarceration. Its book, titled *Doing Justice* (1975), proposed the creation of sentencing guidelines based on the seriousness of the crime and the prior record of the offender. In addition, it proposed shorter punishments for most crimes as well as the expansion of alternative sanctions.

The first criminal justice systems based on the justice model emerged in the United States during the 1970s and early 1980s. Maine enacted its new legislation in 1975, followed by California (1976), Minnesota (1981), Pennsylvania (1982), and Washington (1984). Although these states varied in the particular manner in which they developed their systems, they shared a number of features, namely the elimination or control of prosecutorial discretion, the abolition of individualized sentencing practices, limited treatment programs for prisoners, and the termination of early-release programs such as parole (Griset 1991). During the late 1980s in Canada, the Canadian Sentencing Commission (1987) proposed a similar approach but it was never introduced into public policy.

The Criminal Sanction

According to the justice model, the essential factor "is to punish offenders—fairly and with justice—through lengths of confinement proportionate to the gravity of their crimes" (Logan 1993). The punishment must be proportionate to the crime—specifically, the most serious crimes deserve the most severe punishments, in accordance with the doctrine of proportionality. In addition, the rights of the accused must be guaranteed by due process protections from arrest to incarceration (Hudson 1987).

The justice model assumes a direct relationship exists between the seriousness of the offence and the severity of the punishment. Ideally, any personal circumstances of those individuals involved in the crime are ignored. The only information the justice model needs to know about an offender is the accused's prior record. This "ensures the individual is not made to suffer disproportionately for the sake of social gain" and that "disproportionate leniency" as well as "disproportionate severity" are not allowed (von Hirsch 1976; Hudson 1987). An example of a violation of the principle of proportionality involves a mandatory five-year period of incarceration to punish parking violators as the punishment far outweighs the seriousness of the offence—that is, it is assumed that parking violators could be dissuaded by other, lighter sanctions, such as towing or fines.

In Canada, the federal government determines the proportionality of sentences that link a criminal offence to its punishment. Although it is easy to conclude a violent criminal should receive a more severe punishment than a parking violator, developing a comprehensive scale of proportional punishments is a difficult task, given the wide variety of crimes found in our *Criminal Code*. Should a person who sexually assaults a child receive a longer sentence than a person who robs a bank at gunpoint? Much discussion about which offences are the most harmful is required to create a workable system of punishment based on proportionality since the seriousness of crimes and the unpleasantness of crimes are not objective facts.

The justice model's major contribution to the area of punishment is its support of the creation and proliferation of alternative sanctions, such as when a convicted person is allowed to serve part or all of the punishment in the community. Alternative sanctions in the justice model are preferred for minor offences. Thus, any individual who is convicted of an offence in those categories designated as minor usually receives an alternative sentence allowing him to serve his sentence in the community. Community service orders and probation

orders are favoured for many first- and second-time property offenders. This means many offenders don't serve time in a prison facility, unless of course the number of their prior convictions grows to the point to where they will be incarcerated. Dangerous violent offenders, however, will always be incarcerated for the longest periods of time, even if they have no prior convictions.

One significant aspect about the justice model is that it guarantees due process rights for all persons accused of committing a crime. Both pretrial, trial, and post-trial procedural rights are guaranteed, so each suspect receives protections to ensure that criminal justice officials do not overextend their powers. In addition, anyone under investigation or charged with an offence is presumed to be factually innocent before proven legally guilty. Thus, although someone may admit to police investigators that she committed the crime (that is, factual guilt), that person's guilt nonetheless has to be established (that is, legal guilt) in a court of law. Due process ensures that only the facts of the case are at issue, evidence is collected according to the rules established by the courts, formal hearings with impartial arbitrators are held, and procedural regularity is maintained. Extralegal issues are considered to be inconsistent with the issue of fundamental justice.

The Operation of a Justice Model–Based Criminal Justice System

The main concern of the justice model is the elimination or control of discretion within the criminal justice system, particularly as exercised by prosecutors, the judiciary, and members of the parole board. Supporters of the justice model argue the major barrier to the attainment of justice is the discretion held by the major agencies within the criminal justice system. Concerns about discretion lead to concerns about the protection of rights for all the accused. Their solution is to operate the justice system in a fair and equitable manner. The main policy recommendations of justice model advocates are (1) to eliminate or control discretion and (2) to enhance due process protections for all who enter the criminal justice system.

The role of the police is pivotal, because their decisions affect all other groups involved in the later stages of the crime control process. In the justice model the police will allocate most of their resources to investigating crimes classified as the most serious. Justice model considerations also will direct the way the police react to a crime, with minor offenders being recommended for

EXHIBIT 3.1   Have Legal Rights of Sex Offenders Gone Too Far?

There will always be a debate between those who advocate the legal rights for the accused and those who argue that crime control should take precedence in judicial decisions. But can one side be taken too far? Many Canadians feel the courts have been excessive in their protection of the accused, to the detriment of protecting society. In particular, criticism has been directed at the Supreme Court of Canada and some of its recent decisions to expand the rights of the accused. This has led supporters of crime control to argue that Canada's top court is focusing too much on the principles of justice in their decisions while ignoring the reality of horrific crimes committed by sex offenders. Some of the most controversial decisions made by the Supreme Court in this area follow.

R. v. BORDEN (1994)

This case is known for its impact upon the legal system to create a law under which bodily substances can be legally taken by the police for DNA analysis (see chapters 5 and 7). Police in Nova Scotia were investigating two sexual assaults that occurred within a few months of each other. The police arrested a suspect for the second sexual assault and believed that the same individual had committed the first sexual assault, a case that involved a 69-year-old woman in Nova Scotia. Police requested a blood sample from the accused, but informed Borden, the suspect, that they wanted it only for the second sexual assault investigation. The police didn't inform him they wanted to use the DNA analysis in connection with the sexual assault on the senior citizen as well. DNA linked Borden to both sexual offences. He was convicted and sentenced to six years' imprisonment, based on the results of the DNA test. The Appeal Division of the Supreme Court of Nova Scotia overturned Borden's conviction on the grounds that his legal rights were violated under s. 8 of the *Charter of Rights and Freedoms,* which controls unlawful search and seizures. The Crown appealed this verdict, but the Supreme Court of Canada agreed in a 7–0 ruling that the DNA evidence could not be admitted as evidence because the police did not tell Borden that the blood sample and the subsequent DNA analysis could be used against him. Although the suspect had voluntarily signed a consent form for the police, the Supreme Court ruled that the proper test was not consent but rather whether or not the suspect had enough information to give up the right to be secure from unreasonable seizure. It was up to the police to inform the suspect that they were going to use his consent

for a DNA test for both offences, not just the second one.

R. v. SWIETLINSKI (1994)

A convicted murderer who applied for early parole eligibility (see Chapter 12) was found to have been denied a fair hearing because the Crown prosecutor was found to have consistently and improperly appealed to the jury's passions. Swietlinski was convicted of the first-degree murder of Mary Francis McKenna in 1976. He had stabbed her 132 times with five different knives. Although sentenced to a minimum of 25 years in a federal correctional facility, Swietlinski applied for early parole under s. 745 of the *Criminal Code,* which sets out a process for those convicted of first-degree murder to apply for parole eligibility after 15 years.

Swietlinski was granted the hearing, but during the proceedings the jurors were subject to "appeals" directed at their "passions" by the Crown prosecutor. The prosecutor told the jury, among other things, not to forget the victim in their decision, saying that "she doesn't have a chance to come before a group of people to ask for a second chance." Furthermore, the minimum-security prison where Swietlinski was incarcerated was described as "too comfortable," and "his residency there was reward enough for good conduct in jail." Surprisingly, the lawyer representing Swietlinski took no exception to these and other similar comments made by the prosecutor. Ultimately, the jury refused the accused's request for the possibility of early parole.

The Supreme Court, in a 5–4 ruling, agreed with Swietlinski that he was denied his right to a fair hearing and therefore deserved another jury review. The majority ruling was based on the opinion that the Crown prosecutor's role at a review hearing is much the same as it is at criminal trials—to assist the judge and jury in making decisions that lead to "the fullest possible justice" while avoiding "any appeal to passion." The minority ruling was based in large part on the silence of Swietlinski's lawyer, a silence that the jury interpreted as agreeing that the prosecutor's comments were not unfair.

R. v. SHARPE (2001)

In 1995, Sharpe was found possessing child pornography. In 1996 he was charged with violating Canada's child pornography laws after police seized books, manuscripts, a computer disc,

Continued on next page

CHAPTER 3 Crime Control Philosophy and Criminal Justice Policy and photographs (Persky and Dixon 2001). At his trial in November 1998, Sharpe argued that two sections of Canada's child pornography law violated the constitutional freedom of expression guarantees (s. 2 of the *Charter of Rights and Freedoms*). The B.C. Supreme Court judge, Mr. Justice Shaw, agreed with Sharpe's defence and ruled that the child pornography section of the *Criminal Code* (which makes simple possession of such items a crime) was illegal since it violated s. 2 of the *Charter*. The British Columbia government appealed the ruling, but on June 30, 1999, the B.C. Court of Appeal (by a 2–1 vote) ruled in favour of Mr. Sharpe, finding the section of the *Charter* in question too broad. The case was appealed to the Supreme Court of Canada, and,

in January 2001, the Court overturned the B.C. ruling and upheld (in an unanimous ruling) the child pornography law. However, the justices also specified that certain exceptions existed: works of artistic merit and works of the imagination by a private individual as well as photographic depictions of oneself. The case was returned to British Columbia to be retried and, on 16 March 2002, Sharpe was convicted of two charges of possession of child pornography but acquitted of the two charges of possessing written child pornography. On 2 May 2002, Sharpe was sentenced to four months home confinement.

Sources: Fine (1994a); (1994b); (1994c); (1997); Persky and Dixon (2001).

---

diversion or other similar types of alternative sanction programs. Arrest and prosecution is more likely if the individual commits a serious crime and has an extensive criminal record.

Prosecutors would then have to prosecute the accused on the basis of all charges laid. This means plea-bargaining would be eliminated or strictly controlled by guidelines enacted by the legislative authorities. In reality, however, plea-bargaining has proved to be difficult to ban. The state of Alaska banned all forms of plea-bargaining in 1975, but the policy lasted only a few years, because, among other problems, the ban had no influence on the disposition of cases involving serious crimes. In addition, other criminal justice agencies (notably the police) increased their discretion prior to laying any charges (Rubenstein et al. 1980). The most popular policy has been to permit some plea-bargaining but to control it by developing strict guidelines to govern its use as it allows prosecutors to bargain with the accused about their knowledge of other, more serious, crimes or to gain evidence about other criminals who would otherwise not be charged.

Supporters of the justice model argue that the problem with traditional sentencing approaches is the great amount of discretion held by judges. This discretion led to a concern about discrimination in sentencing, as some defendants received more severe punishments apparently on the basis of their group characteristics—such as race or gender—instead of their crimes. To eliminate this problem the justice model favours a determinate sentencing approach, in which all judges are required to follow sentencing guidelines. When deciding how much punishment a convicted offender receives, judges are to be influenced by the crime committed and the offender's

prior record. Once the seriousness of the crime and prior record are established, the judge will refer to the sentencing guidelines to determine the actual sentence. The research evaluating whether or not judges follow sentencing guidelines has found that they do so (Marvell and Moody 1996; Kramer and Ulmer 1996).

The seriousness of the crime and the blameworthiness of the offender are the most significant criteria in determining the type of correctional facility or diversion program to which an offender is sent. Canadian correctional facilities are classified by security risk—maximum, medium, and minimum—with the most serious of all offenders being sent to a Special Handling Unit located in Quebec (see Chapter 11). Because most sentences in Canada specify only the maximum amount of time an individual must serve before release, the decision about the exact length of an inmate's period of incarceration is actually made by the parole board rather than a judge. The discretionary powers held by parole boards are of concern to the justice model advocates too, since those boards can decide to release inmates prior to serving the full length of their sentence. The justice model's solution is either to eliminate the parole board altogether (by eliminating parole) or to remove it from the decision to release an inmate. In the latter case, the parole board is responsible only for parole supervision. It is conceivable, however, that the elimination of parole could lead to prison overcrowding, since no prisoners would be released early. To prevent overcrowding, convicted criminals would serve their entire sentences, but the length of the sentences would be shortened. When the justice model was instituted in Minnesota, almost all sentence lengths were reduced. The exception was first-degree murder, which remained punishable by a mandatory life sentence. The only exceptions to these policies would be the reduction of a sentence by 15 percent in exchange for an inmate's good behaviour during incarceration. Finally, while treatment programs are offered to inmates, such programs are limited in scope and voluntary in nature.

DETERRENCE

History

Deterrence is the oldest of the four major criminal justice philosophies. Its roots are in 18th-century Europe, where two reformers, one Italian (Cesare Beccaria) and the other English (Jeremy Bentham), proposed significant reforms to the criminal justice system. They argued that the goal of the criminal justice system was to prevent future crimes by individuals who were caught and punished for their crimes (that is, specific deterrence) and by members of the broader society who might contemplate committing a crime (that is, general deterrence).

Faced with a system that was biased and barbaric, Beccaria wrote *On Crimes and Punishment* (1764) in the hope of achieving reforms that were equitable and eliminated favouritism. It is important to note that Beccaria's recommendations became the source of modern criminal justice systems, including those in Canada and the United States. His book became the first widely read text that demanded due process rights be placed throughout the criminal justice system, that sentences reflect the harm done to the state and the victim, and that punishments be quick, certain, and contain a degree of deterrence. His major recommendations (Beirne and Messerschmidt 1991: 290) were as follows:

- The right of governments to punish offenders derives from a contractual obligation among its citizens not to pursue their self-interest at the expense of others.
- Punishment must be constituted by uniform and enlightened legislation.
- Imprisonment must replace torture and capital punishment as the standard form of punishment.
- The punishment must fit the crime. It must be prompt and certain, and its duration must reflect only the gravity of the offence and the social harm caused.

Bentham argued that legislators need to calculate the amount of punishment needed to prevent crimes and punish criminals. This system, which he referred to as a calculus, could include both positive sanctions (rewards) and negative sanctions (punishment). In addi-

tion, he argued the criminal justice system should operate in a manner that allows it to catch suspects with certainty, process criminal cases in a speedy yet efficient manner, and to punish those convicted of a crime with an appropriate (not excessive) amount of punishment.

An important basis of this approach was the reformers' strong belief that all people are rational, that is, they possessed free will. Criminals differ from law-abiding persons only because they choose to engage in criminal as opposed to noncriminal activities. Over time, however, legislators have recognized a number of limitations to those arguments. Today most Western legal codes recognize limits to criminal responsibility, including such factors as age, duress, and mental disorder.

Today, the deterrence model assumes that people participate in an action only after a careful consideration of its risk (or costs) and its benefits (or rewards). Punishment is supposed to induce compliance with the law, since people fear punishment and do not want to jeopardize their stake in conformity. In the deterrence model, then, the rationale for punishment is to affect future behaviour rather than to inflict pain.

In reality, however, not all criminal action has been found to be governed as the result of a careful consideration of the costs and benefits, as some of it is unplanned and habitual. Some individuals choose to avoid becoming involved in illegal behaviour because they lack the skills or opportunities to commit an act. At the same time, rational choice is involved in some criminal activity. Some offenders try to minimize the risks by planning their crimes, and they select their targets on the basis of what they are to gain. However, many of these individuals make poor selections as they lack good information or overestimate what they will gain. They may also underestimate the risk of punishment. In addition, many offenders have been found to act on impulse.

The Criminal Sanction

A criminal penalty might act as a negative inducement, discouraging people from engaging in behaviour that violates the law. According to Grasmick and Green (1980), deterrence is in reality the threat of legal punishment, or fear of physical and material deprivation from legally imposed sanctions. Deterrence is an objective phenomenon, as it implies a behavioural result of the fear a potential offender feels because that person thinks his illegal act may lead to capture and punishment. Supporters of the deterrence doctrine hope any individual contemplating a crime will be deterred because of the certainty, or risk, he will be caught and punished. Deterrence is also a perceptual phenomenon in the sense that potential criminals decide not to commit crimes on the basis of their perception that they may be caught and punished. According to Gibbs (1975: 2), a strong advocate of this model, deterrence is defined as "the omission of an act as a response to the perceived risk and fear of punishment for contrary behavior."

The deterrence approach assumes a direct relationship between the certainty of punishment and the severity and swiftness of punishment. The severity is achieved at a level that maximizes its deterrent effect—that is, "the pain of punishment would exceed the pleasure of the offense for a majority of potential offenders" (Price and Stitt 1986: 26). The deterrence philosophy places great emphasis on the efficient operation of the criminal justice system, namely the reduction of court delay as well as the time between arrest, preliminary inquiry, and court trial (Feeley and Simon 1992). Yet, researchers report they have found individuals have imperfect knowledge of the maximum sentences for various crimes. Behaviour choices are based on varying perceptions about the severity of sanctions, the certainty with which they believe the punishments will be used, and how swift the punishment will be (Sherman and Berk 1984; Decker et al. 1993).

According to Chambliss (1969), some crimes are more easily deterred than others. Instrumental or goal-oriented behaviour, such as robbing a bank, is more easily deterred than expressive behaviour that results from the inner needs of the offender, such as a violent outburst that leads to violence. This distinction between instrumental and expressive act is not easy to make: a person might commit a robbery to gain a sense of superiority over others (an expressive act) rather than to gain any material item (an instrumental act). Chambliss also stated that the success or failure of deterrence is linked to the offender's commitment to crime. Offenders who are highly committed to a criminal lifestyle are more difficult to deter than those offenders who do not see crime as a way of life.

The Operation of a Deterrence-Based Criminal Justice System

Any deterrence-based criminal justice system would introduce policies to attain the greatest certainty of capture, swiftness of prosecution, and, in cases of conviction for a crime, severity of punishment. The goal of this system is the prevention of future crime. More emphasis is given to the protection of society and the law-abiding public than to the protection of individual rights of defendants. To ensure that the justice system and its agencies work to their maximum efficiency, more money would have to be spent on all criminal justice agencies. More police officers, prosecutors, judges, and correctional personnel would be hired, and more facilities such as jails, courts, and prisons built. Further, the government would have to revise existing statute laws and pass new ones that would grant more powers to the police in the areas of investigation and apprehension, with the sole purpose of increasing the chance that suspected criminals are caught. Essentially, the criminal justice system would push offenders as efficiently as possible through conviction to punishment.

The number of police officers and resources involved in crime detection within a deterrence-based criminal justice system would increase, since police are the front-line agency in the "war on crime." Police patrol tactics would change to ensure that the maximum deterrent effect could be achieved by a highly visible patrol vehicles. Police officers would be better educated and better trained, and receive the latest technology in order to increase the certainty of capture of criminals. But not all the new resources given to the police would be involved in actual crime-fighting. Procedural laws that inhibit the police during their search for and arrest of criminals would be reduced. Emphasis would be placed on crime control and factual guilt. If, for example, a police officer accidentally violates the right of an alleged offender during an investigation, this violation would probably be overlooked, assuming the individual in question is guilty of the offence.

The deterrence doctrine also supports the prevention of crime. As a result, more money would be given to proactive policing activities, such as the Neighbourhood Watch, Operation Identification, and Crime Stoppers programs. These programs, because they involve members of the community in the fight against crime, enable police to spend more time in the pursuit of criminals, thereby increasing the probability of capture and subsequent punishment.

Deterrence advocates the control of all forms of plea-bargaining. Price and Stitt (1986: 27) point out controlling plea-bargaining "could be the greatest single step to increase both certainty and severity of punishment." In addition, suspects awaiting trial would find it more difficult to receive bail, since they are presumed guilty. This means that most of the individuals arrested are guilty, particularly as they move past arrest and into the court system (Packer 1968). As was the case in the justice model, prosecutors would pursue all charges laid against a defendant by the police.

EXHIBIT 3.2   Deterring Criminal Harassment (Stalking)

HARM AND CRIMINAL HARASSMENT

In the early 1990s a number of well-publicized incidents of men stalking and harassing women with whom they once had relationships led to tragic results. Terri-Lynn Babb, for example, was killed in broad daylight in Winnipeg by a man who was once a patient at the hospital where she was employed. Her death, and others like it, led to demands that the federal government create a new statute that would outlaw stalking, formally known as criminal harassment. Parliament passed this legislation in August 1993.

The federal Minister of Justice at the time, Pierre Blais, informed the House of Commons (House of Commons Debates 1993) it was now against the law to "repeatedly follow someone; spend extended periods of time watching someone's home or place of work; make repeated phone calls to someone or her friends, make contact with someone's neighbors or co-workers; and contact and possibly threaten someone's new companion, spouse or children." According to Hackett (2000), the intention of this law was to protect victims of stalking and to deter stalkers from threatening their victims. Johnson (1996: 199) points out that this law is not to punish criminal conduct that "hasn't yet occurred, but to punish harm that has already been perpetrated by virtue of the psychological harm of the threat of violence and injury, and fear of what the person might be capable of doing." Critics argued the new legislation presented a passive view of victims and that Justice Minister Blais had not consulted with interested parties prior to the drafting of the legislation (Cairns-Way 1994).

The law on criminal harassment, found in s. 264 of the *Criminal Code,* states

(1) No person shall, without lawful authority and knowing that another person is harassed or recklessly as to whether the other person is harassed, engage in conduct referred to in subsection (2) that causes that other person reasonably, in all the circumstances, to fear for their safety or the safety of anyone known to them.

(2) The conduct mentioned in subsection (1) consists of:

(a) repeatedly following from place to place the other person or anyone known to them;

(b) repeatedly communicating with, either directly or indirectly, the other person or anyone known to them;

(c) besetting or watching the dwelling-house, or place where the other person, or anyone known to them, resides, works, carries on business or happens to be; or

(d) engaging in threatening conduct directed at the other person or any member of their family.

In terms of punishment, criminal harassment was defined as a hybrid offence with a maximum penalty of five years imprisonment. The maximum period of imprisonment was increased to 10 years in June 2002.

Since the introduction of this legislation, a number of changes have been made to the existing *Criminal Code* provisions. In 1996, an amendment specified that any person charged with criminal harassment can be prohibited from possessing a firearm or ammunition. In 1997, other amendments were passed, including treating as an aggravating factor at sentencing the violation of a restraining order by a person convicted of stalking. In addition, murder committed during the commission of a stalking act could result in a first-degree murder conviction even if it was not possible to prove that the murder was planned. Nine homicides occurred from 1997 to 1999 that involved criminal harassment as the precipitating offence. In each of these homicides, the victim was a female who was being stalked by a recently separated spouse, ex-husband, or ex-lover. Despite these laws, the number of stalking incidents continues to increase across Canada. Between 1996 and 1999, the number of stalking incidents reported to 106 police forces increased from 4071 to 5382 incidents. In 2000, the number of such incidents continued to increase, reaching 6249 in 2000 (Hackett 2000; Logan 2000).

According to information collected by the police, in 1999 women were stalked most frequently by an ex-spouse (37 percent) followed by casual acquaintances (25 percent) and then by a current or ex-boyfriend (15 percent) and strangers (8 percent). For males, the greatest threat came from casual acquaintances (44 percent), followed by business acquaintances (13 percent), strangers (12 percent), and an ex-spouse (11 percent) (Hackett 2000).

Judicial discretion would be eliminated; governments would provide judges with a system of mandatory determinate sentences. This would lead not only to the uniformity of punishment but also to the certainty that an individual receives a designated punishment. However, in contrast to the justice model, most sentences under a deterrence approach would become longer, in order to impress on individuals contemplating a crime that, if caught and convicted, they would be punished severely.

Parole would be abolished. More prisons would be built to house those guilty of an offence and to discourage potential criminals from committing a criminal offence by making them fearful of being caught and incarcerated. Risk assessments of offenders would become normal practice. Offenders would be placed into groups based on their predicted future behaviour. In the deterrence model, all sanctions are viewed in terms of their effectiveness at reducing the risk of further offences. At one extreme is secure incarceration; at the other is probation, with levels of intermediate punishments between (Morris and Tonry 1990).

SELECTIVE INCAPACITATION

History

Selective incapacitation is a policy that attempts to separate high-risk offenders from low-risk ones, and incarcerate for a lengthy period of time those who are most likely to be dangerous once they are released. This philosophy is very recent in terms of its use in our criminal justice system, emerging as a major force in the 1970s. James Q. Wilson, a prominent criminologist, gave this model strong support in his book *Thinking about Crime* (1975). He wrote that serious crimes could be reduced by about one-third if each individual convicted of a violent crime received a sentence of three years and were not paroled. Then a study conducted by the Rand Corporation of San Francisco, titled *Selective Incapacitation,* appeared in 1982. During their investigation researchers devised a system they felt successfully separates those offenders who should be "incapacitated" because they pose a long-term threat to society from those who should serve shorter sentences because they could be successfully reintegrated back into society once released.

In this study, Peter Greenwood studied 2190 prison and jail inmates in California, Texas, and Michigan. He discovered that the offenders who had committed the most crimes had the following characteristics:

Selective incapacitation advocates support much longer prison terms for criminals who have committed serious crimes. The photo above was taken inside a Supermax correctional institution in the United States.

1. an earlier conviction for the same offence;
2. imprisonment for more than one-half of the two years prior to the current arrest;
3. a conviction before the age of 16;
4. previous commitment to a juvenile institution;
5. use of heroin or barbiturates during the previous two years;
6. use of heroin and barbituates as a juvenile; and
7. unemployment for half or more of the preceding two years.

Greenwood claimed that a sentencing approach based on this philosophy could reduce robbery by 15 percent and reduce prison populations by 5 percent. The imprisonment of an increased number of chronic offenders would be more than offset by the elimination of low-risk offenders from prison. This report received great attention, since it suggested that more effective crime control could be achieved at less cost. Another study, titled *Making Confinement Decisions,* was published by the United States Justice Department in 1987. This report concluded that, assuming the average chronic offender committed 187 crimes a year, a saving of $430 million could be made annually if these individuals were sentenced to lengthy periods of incarceration (Walker 1994).

Despite these claims, critics argued that many errors would be made since prediction is not an exact science. This means that there are some individuals who wouldn't commit another crime while some who were considered to be a good risk would, in fact, commit serious crimes soon after being returned to the community. For example, Zimring and Hawkins (1988) have argued that the reduction in crime promised by the supporters of selective incapacitation has not materialized. They claim these figures are based on estimates of the number of crimes a chronic offender remembered he committed each year. Many of the critics' harshest criticisms are based on their claim that attempts at reducing crime may be limited by a number of factors. These include problems in the identification of high-risk offenders and the possibility that one offender, if arrested, is simply replaced by another. If the offender who is incarcerated is a gang member, the gang may continue to commit the same amount of crime. While selective incapacitation would no doubt have some limited influence on the crime rate, its success would be dependent on the ability of the criminal justice system to identify chronic offenders in the early stages of their career (Visher 1995).

The Criminal Sanction

The selective incapacitation approach focuses on those few individuals who commit the greatest number of crimes, whether property crimes or violent crimes. Most attention to date has been placed on individuals classed as chronic, career, or repeat offenders.

According to the criminal sanction approach, the crime rate is a function of the total number of offenders minus those imprisoned (that is, incapacitated), multiplied by an average number of crimes per offender. Therefore, by incarcerating chronic criminals for long periods of time, the crime rate is lowered.

Research has shown that relatively few offenders are responsible for the vast majority of violent offences. An example of that research is a work by Wolfgang, Figlio, and Sellin, titled *Delinquency in a Birth Cohort* (1972), called "the single most important piece of criminal justice research in the last 25 years" (Walker 1993: 55). Focusing on 10 000 juvenile males born in

Philadelphia in 1945 and living in that city between the ages of 10 and 18, the researchers measured crime as the number of times the police took a juvenile into custody. They discovered that nearly 35 percent of all males had a record of an offence. At least 627 of these males had committed at least five offences. Even more important was the discovery that only 6 percent of the males in the study accounted for over half of all offences committed by the entire group and that the same 6 percent accounted for well over half of all violent crimes. Other studies (Hamparian et al. 1978; Shannon 1988; Tracy et al. 1990) turned up similar findings for both juveniles and adults. These studies identified small groups of high-rate offenders who were responsible for most criminal offences as well as most violent crimes.

The selective incapacitation philosophy does not apply to all offenders; it focuses only on those who are deemed the most dangerous to society. A key feature of this approach is that individuals are considered dangerous not only because of their deeds in the past but because of the crimes they are likely to commit in the future. Future crimes are determined either by the number of prior convictions or by the number of crimes that similar offenders committed once they were released from prison.

In 1990 the Solicitor General of Canada recommended the elimination of parole for those convicted of dealing drugs. This policy was to be instituted if members of the National Parole Board suspected convicted drug dealers "will commit further drug offences after release from prison." Such individuals were to be denied parole—were to be punished, in essence, for crimes they had not yet committed. An example of this type of philosophy is found in the state of Washington's "sexual predator" law, which allows the state to "indefinitely lock up anyone who has committed at least one violent sex crime—after he has served his time." Legislation has now been introduced in Canada to incarcerate and/or carefully control in the community those who are considered to be potential high-risk offenders (see Exhibit 3.3).

Although there is no doubt support for such policies, there are potential pitfalls in such legislation as well as problems associated with implementing them. The most serious criticism of the selective incapacitation of violent offenders is that the criminal justice system lacks the capacity to accurately predict future violent behaviour. This criticism directly challenges the legitimacy of selective incapacitation as a legal sanction. The legal maxim "It is better that 10 guilty persons escape than one innocent suffer" embodies the value that our society places on individual liberty. Judges would be given the

Canada has used various laws allowing the indeterminate confinement of those individuals considered as dangerous offenders over the past 50 years. In 1947, the term "habitual offender" was introduced in the *Criminal Code*. In 1977, this term was replaced by a section called "dangerous offenders" in an attempt to highlight the perceived "dangerousness" of the offender. Between 1977 and 1997 when an offender was declared a "dangerous offender," a judge could sentence that individual to either a determinate or indeterminate sentence. The law was once again changed, with determinate sentences being eliminated as a sentencing option. Today, a finding of "dangerous offender" automatically leads to an indeterminate sentence. The dangerous offender classification was upheld by the Supreme Court of Canada in *R. v. L. (T.P.)* (1987).

The current dangerous offender provisions in the *Criminal Code* allow court officials to evaluate patterns of offending over time. Although it is possible for an offender to become classified as a dangerous offender after committing one offence, most dangerous offenders have extensive criminal histories. There are three possible criteria for a finding of "dangerous offender" in s. 753 (1)(a) of the *Criminal Code:*

(1) (a) that the offence for which the offender has been convicted is a serious personal injury offence described in paragraph (a) of the definition of that expression in s. 752 and the offender constitutes a threat to the life, safety or physical or mental well-being of other persons on the basis of establishing

   (i) a pattern of repetitive behaviour by the offender, of which the offence for which he has been convicted forms a part, showing a failure to restrain his behaviour and a likelihood of his causing death or injury to other persons, or inflicting severe psychological damage on other persons, through failure in the future to restrain his behaviour,

   (ii) a pattern of persistent aggressive behaviour by the offender, of which the offence for which he has been convicted forms a part,

showing a substantial degree of indifference on the part of the offender respecting the reasonably foreseeable consequences to other persons of his behaviour, or,

  (iii) any behaviour by the offender, associated with the offence for which he has been convicted, that is of such a brutal nature as to compel the conclusion that his behaviour in the future is unlikely to be inhibited by normal standards of behavioural restraint; or

(b) that at the offence for which the offender is convicted is a serious personal injury offence described in paragraph (b) of the definition of that expression in s. 752 and the offender, by his conduct in any sexual matter including that involved in the commission of the offence for which he has been convicted, has shown a failure to control his sexual impulses and a likelihood of his causing injury, pain or other evil to other persons through failure in the future to control his sexual impulses.

As of the end of September 2000, there were 276 dangerous offenders—265 were serving indeterminate sentences. All of these offenders are male, and over 90 percent of them are sex offenders. The Solicitor General of Canada produced the following profile of sex offenders in this country. At the time of the offence that led to them being classified as a dangerous offender, the average educational attainment was 8.5 years; 48 percent were single, 95 percent were Caucasian, and 63 percent were unemployed. Ninety-two percent had been convicted of a sexual offence, and the victim for 86 percent of these individuals was a female. Fifty-nine percent of these offenders victimized an individual under the age of 16, and brutality was evident in 70 percent of the cases. On average, these men were first arrested at 16 years of age, 75 percent had a juvenile record, and 88 percent had previously served a term of incarceration. Seventy-three percent of them had previously failed on a conditional release program.

Source: Solicitor General of Canada (2001).

power "to prevent violent offenders … and drug offenders from obtaining parole until they have served half of their sentences." Those identified as dangerous are to be incarcerated longer than those who are not. For

Price and Stitt (1986: 28), this means that "two offenders could commit the same act but receive different sentences because one is thought to be more likely to commit that or a related act in the future."

The Operation of a Selective Incapacitation–Based Criminal Justice System

According to Price and Stitt (1986), a criminal justice system based on the selective incapacitation approach is based on the idea that the best predictor of future behaviour is previous behaviour. The criminal justice system would operate on the basis of the deterrence doctrine for the vast majority of offenders. However, once an individual enters the system and is considered to be dangerous, the system assigns special resources and individuals to process the case as quickly as possible. Therefore, only some of the resources of the criminal justice system are dedicated to the selective incapacitation approach.

Further, because it contains such a narrow interest, this approach is easily attached to any of the other three models. Such is the case with the state of Washington, which employs the justice model for the majority of its offenders but also exercises a sexual predator law to ensure that certain sex offenders are not released for a long time. In reality, then, this is the most specific of all the models in the sense that it looks only at a selective group of criminals.

The role of the police would be to arrest suspected offenders, conduct a careful background check, and then place offenders in a pretrial detention centre if they are considered to be chronic offenders. Plea-bargaining would be eliminated, enabling prosecutors to process all such cases as quickly as possible in order to ensure that offenders aren't released back into the general population. Judges would have little discretion in these cases. Once an offender is considered to be a chronic offender, he would be sentenced to a lengthy determinate prison term. Parole would be abolished, and the correctional system would become little more than a holding facility for such offenders. Policies such as "three strikes and you're out" are consistent with the selective incapacitation approach.

THE REHABILITATION APPROACH

History

Supporters of this model assume that the source of crime is determined by factors outside the control of the individual. They argue that since criminals don't freely choose their behaviour, punishment is the wrong policy. Instead, they recommend the individualized treatment of offenders in the hope that the causes of their criminal

behaviour are discovered and eliminated. As Allen (1981: 2) points out, a primary purpose of the rehabilitative approach is to influence "the characters, attitudes, and behavior of convicted offenders, so as to strengthen the social defense against unwanted behavior [as well as] to contribute to the welfare and satisfaction of the offenders."

The rehabilitation approach places more attention on the offender than on the criminal act itself. Criminal sanctions are to be tailored to treating the needs of the offender rather than "based on considerations of social harm and deterrence" (Cullen and Gilbert 1982: 34). To facilitate this approach, the indeterminate sentence becomes an essential policy, namely that offenders are to remain in prison for as long as it takes to find the appropriate "cure."

To facilitate an individual-based justice system, probation and parole were introduced along with indeterminate sentences during the late-19th and early-20th centuries. The idea guiding these policies was that the type of punishment (probation or incarceration) would be decided by an offender's need for treatment. If it was decided that the individual needed treatment, the duration of that person's punishment "would be determined by his or her behavior after sentencing as much as by the crime itself" (Clear 1995: 460). Inmates who showed improvement would be released earlier than those who resisted treatment or who failed to respond to the prescribed treatment. Treatment at the turn of the 20th century involved "programs of work, moral instruction, discipline, and order," all designed "to develop those personal habits that were prerequisites to a useful law-abiding life" (Carrigan 1991: 356).

Probably the test most often used to evaluate the success of rehabilitation programs is whether the offender recidivates—that is, is convicted of another offence after his sentence is completed. A Correctional Service of Canada (1999b) report indicated that, five years after they had successfully completed full parole (see Chapter 12), 27.6 percent of former inmates were returned to a federal institution for reoffending. In addition, 39.6 percent of those who served two-thirds of their sentences and were then released on statutory release were reconvicted of another offence. The debate about the worthiness and effectiveness of rehabilitation continues to this day between the advocates of rehabilitation and the other three models.

The Criminal Sanction

Supporters of the rehabilitation philosophy believe it is necessary to look at the criminal and discover the reasons he committed a crime. Once it is discovered what led to the criminal behaviour, an appropriate criminal sanction would be applied. Therefore, punishment would be flexible, based on the needs of the individual. This means that two individuals could commit the identical crime but end up with completely different punishments—perhaps because one individual needs a lengthy treatment program while the other needs another type of treatment. A rehabilitation system is best described as discretionary, with all court and correctional agencies having the power to determine the type and length of sentence to individualize the punishment.

It is important to note that after being subject to a lengthy period of criticism, rehabilitation appears to be gaining support. In a national survey in the United States, researchers discovered that prison wardens—though they felt the maintenance of custody and institutional order was their top priority—indicated that the rehabilitation of offenders was a more significant goal than punishment and retribution (Cullen et al. 1993).

The Operation of a Rehabilitation-Based Criminal Justice System

Whereas the other models considered discretion unnecessary and counterproductive, rehabilitation wishes to enhance the discretionary powers of the main agencies of the criminal justice system. Since the focus of this model is on the needs and welfare of the offender, each agency has to make decisions to enhance the chances of the individual's return to society as a better person.

As Price and Stitt (1986) point out, this aim to rehabilitate means the criminal justice system would have to focus on the criminal more than on the act committed. Agencies would intervene in the offender's life in order to change the offender, in the hope that the pressures that forced the individual to commit crime are reduced and finally eliminated. Much of the emphasis of the rehabilitation model of criminal justice is thus located at the sentencing and correctional stages of the criminal justice system.

The police role would not change dramatically. Police would continue to arrest criminals and lay charges. Prosecutors would be allowed to plea-bargain as much as they wish and would encounter few if any restrictions in this connection. A case would easily be terminated or the total number of charges reduced if the prosecutor felt it would be in the best interests of the offender. Prosecutors would rely on the presentence report and make recommendations on the type of treatment needed. Both the prosecutor and judge would

make use of this report during the sentencing of the offender.

Judicial discretion is essential to the rehabilitation approach. Prior to handing out a sentence, the judge would receive a presentence report from a probation officer. Any recommendations made in this report would be carefully considered by the judge in the sentencing decision, as would any statements made by the defence lawyer and the Crown prosecutor. The sentence would reflect the "best interests" of the offender and would involve an indeterminate sentence that best fits the needs of the offender. As such, offenders would have to serve only the minimum length of their sentence. Under a rehabilitation approach, the correctional system and its related services would probably become the most important agencies of the criminal justice system. Parole services would be expanded, since they would individualize the treatment program for each offender. This individualization would add discretion to the system, since offenders could be released at any time by the parole board after serving the minimum sentence.

Correctional services within the prison would become more treatment-oriented also. As Exhibit 3.4 reveals, the correctional system would focus on discovering the needs of offenders before it proceeded with a course of treatment. Since treatment is personalized, it could take a long time before that treatment is successful for any individual. Thus, not only might the type of treatment services vary for each offender but also the length of that treatment.

ABORIGINAL JUSTICE AND RESTORATIVE JUSTICE SYSTEMS: AN INTRODUCTION

Both Aboriginal and restorative justice systems represent a significant shift from the above-mentioned crime control philosophies. Central assumptions of both these models include the demand that government give up its monopoly over responses to crime to those who are directly affected—the victim and the offender. In addition, both models involve people in a circle to eliminate the type of hierarchial relationship that exits in our everyday legal system (Roach 1999). Another goal that both share is the rebuilding or restoration of the relationship between victims and offenders in a process that allows both parties to participate (Van Ness and Heetderks Strong 1997). Aboriginal justice differs in that it also includes the idea that crime devastates the quality of life in communities. As a result, Aboriginal

Debate has flourished during the past few decades regarding the best way to control criminals convicted of sexual offences in our society. Is it better to selectively incapacitate offenders or to rehabilitate them? In 1995 there were just under 4000 federal inmates who were classified as sex offenders. Incarcerating these individuals cost roughly $50 000 a year in 1995, and sex offenders at that time averaged about four years in custody. Other costs (such as court costs, legal costs, victim compensation, and hospitalization) add approximately $25 000 to the overall total. Of course, these costs do not consider the emotional trauma experienced by the victims. In contrast, the direct cost of providing sex offender treatment programs is approximately $7400 a year. As Williams (1995) points out, reducing recidivism by 40 sex offenders in a year would pay for future programs as well as preventing future victim suffering.

Only a few studies to date demonstrate that treatment can effectively reduce the recidivism rates of sex offenders (e.g., Marshall and Barbaree 1989). Some jurisdictions and groups cite this evidence to promote harsh punishments as the only alternative that "works" by keeping sex offenders from recidivating. However, this ignores the fact that almost all sex offenders will be released once they have completed their sentence and if they are not treated, many may likely recidivate. If successful sex offender treatment is discovered, the recidivism rates will be much lower.

The first significant comparison of the differences espoused by those who favour rehabilitation and selective incapacitation came from an analysis conducted by Greenwood et al. (1996). They estimated that the expected reduction in crime rates for both rehabilitation and selective incapacitation programs would be about 20 percent. However, they concluded that the cost savings of rehabilitation programs were substantial—selective incapacitation programs would cost about $5.5 billion per annum while rehabilitation programs would cost less than one-fifth that. Petersilia (1992) as well as Cullen and Applegate (1997) also pointed out that there are other significant differences between these two approaches. Rehabilitation programs, they argue, are more concerned with public safety because they lead to greater reductions in reoffending rates when offenders are released.

Other correctional experts now question the

Despite the creation of a national sex offender registry, longer sentences for sex offenders, and better rehabilitation programs, victims such as the one pictured here live in fear of their assailants attacking them once released.

success of deterrence-based punishment systems, arguing that they have only a marginal positive effect and do not save any money in either the short or long terms (for example, Clear 1994; Spelman 1994). Problems have been discovered in deterrence-based punishments, most notably the failure to properly implement programs. Many so-called get-tough programs fail to attain an appropriate level of certainty of punishment. Jones and Goldkamp (1993), for example, found in the U.S. jurisdictions they studied that many offenders who failed court-mandated drug tests were not punished, because of overcrowded courts and prisons. Because of the lack of certainty of punishment, high levels of deterrence were not found. Many observers argue that deterrence-based punishments fail to significantly reduce recidivism rates because they do not focus on any of the known predictors of recidivism,

Continued on next page

CHAPTER 3 Crime Control Philosophy and Criminal Justice Policy such as antisocial values and the influence of negative peer groups (Andrews and Bonta 1998). Others believe that "the deterrence approach ignores the criminological evidence showing that the roots of crime among serious offenders typically extend to childhood or early-adolescent activities, where youths develop propensities and associations that stabilize their involvement in crime" (Cullen and Applegate 1997: xxi).

Threats and long sentences may have minimal impact on these predictors because they focus on punishment and ignore behavioural aspects of offenders. This debate over the appropriate approach to reducing recidivism rates has been a central issue for over 25 years in the field of corrections, ever since the publication of Martinson's work, which questioned the success of rehabilitation programs (see Chapter 12).

Extensive empirical data now exist indicating that rehabilitation programs work—if they are well designed and effectively implemented. Paul Gendreau, a professor of psychology at the University of New Brunswick, has found that "appropriate" treatment programs can reduce recidivism rates by 53 percent after the offenders had been released for two years. Gendreau, along with Professor Don Andrews of Carleton University, discovered the most successful programs are those that employ behavioural modification techniques that reward prosocial behaviour and "target those anti-social attitudes and values that fuel criminal behaviour." Gendreau said these techniques vary. In some corrections settings, prisoners are given more privileges or money for prosocial behaviour. In many cases, he said, efforts are made to influence an offender's thinking by using role-playing to change his values (Freiberg 1990).

Gendreau and Goggin (1996) found that better results for rehabilitation-based programs result when programs operate with optimal theoretical integrity: programs that are properly

constructed, operated by qualified and well-trained staff members who provide intensive treatments, and evaluated by experts in the field of behavioural intervention. In their research analyses of rehabilitation-based programs, Gendreau and Goggin report that those programs with therapeutic integrity are much more successful than those programs that ignore or contain only partial amounts of program integrity. This difference leads to significant differences in recidivism rates; programs with proper therapeutic integrity reduce recidivism by 20 to 35 percent compared to between 5 and 15 percent for those without program integrity.

Developments in the area of sex offender treatment have meant lower recidivism rates for those individuals released into the community on a conditional release program. In a study of a treatment program for high-risk sex offenders (recidivist rapists and pedophiles serving a federal sentence) at the Correctional Service of Canada's maximum security Regional Psychiatric Centre (Prairies), the members of the treatment group were compared to another group of federal offenders released from federal correctional facilities for three years. The treatment group had a 59 percent lower rate of sexual recidivism than the comparison group, even though they were followed up for more than two years longer. At the same time, however, the research found no differences when the group were compared to a similar program that involved provincial sexual and nonsexual offenders. Other studies report little or no differences between treatment and comparison sex offender programs.

Sources: Martinson (1974; 1979); Marshall and Barbaree (1988); Freiberg (1990); Petersilia (1992); Jones and Goldkamp (1993); Clear (1994); Spelman (1994); Belanger and Earls (1995); Nicholaichuk (1995); Williams (1995); Gendreau and Goggin (1996); Greenwood et al. (1996); Cullen and Applegate (1997); Andrews and Bonta (1998).

justice redefines the formal role and operation of the various criminal justice agencies to an informal approach. Rather than focusing on the punishment of offenders, this approach supports a healing process between victims, offenders, and the community. It is a fundamental belief of Aboriginal justice systems that local communities should be able to direct what happens to offenders who commit crimes within their boundaries.

ABORIGINAL JUSTICE SYSTEMS

Many Aboriginal communities have traditionally emphasized restorative justice. The Supreme Court of Canada, in *R. v. Gladue* (1999) (see Chapter 9), commented that, in general terms, restorative justice may be described as an approach to remedy crime in which it is understood that all things are interrelated and that crime disrupts the harmony that existed prior to its occurrence, or at least that it is felt should exist. The appropriateness of a particular sanction is largely determined by the needs of the victims, and the community, as well as the offender. The focus is on the human beings closely affected by the crime.

In the past decade there was much discussion about the creation of formal Aboriginal justice systems throughout Canada. Such systems, specifically those administered by an Aboriginal court, have become a major area of interest, as they would honour traditional methods of resolving conflict. Many officials accept the notion of an Aboriginal justice system, but there has been much controversy over the form this justice system should take. In December 1991, for example, the Law Reform Commission of Canada published a report that supported the notion of an Aboriginal justice system, but it did not give any indication about the type of system it supported. The commission (1991: 5) did, however, discuss the reasons such a justice system was needed in Canada:

> From the Aboriginal perspective, the criminal justice system is an alien one, imposed by the dominant white society … not surprisingly, they regard the system as deeply insensitive to their traditions and values: many view it as unremittingly racist.

A few months after the Law Reform Commission released its report, federal Justice Minister Kim Campbell rejected the possibility of a separate system of Aboriginal justice in Canada, saying that such a system would be a "cop-out." She favoured a system that integrated aspects of the traditional Aboriginal value system into the broader Western legal system. In March 1996, the federal government decided to adopt Campbell's position. It continued to reject the idea of Aboriginals establishing their own justice system and creating their own criminal law by stating unequivocally that the *Charter of Rights and Freedoms* applies to Aboriginal peoples as much as to all other Canadians. It recommended that Aboriginals be given a greater role in sentencing Aboriginal offenders and in assisting in the development of alternatives to prison.

Some provincial governments have also rejected the idea of separate legal systems. To date, most Aboriginal systems in Canada have worked with the existing criminal justice system in order to accommodate their own approach to justice. In Manitoba, for example, the Aboriginal Justice Inquiry recommended sweeping changes in the criminal justice system but they failed to materialize. The provincial government turned down a proposal for an Aboriginal court in January 1993, proposing instead a three-year pilot project that would include "the first comprehensive approach to combine Aboriginal methods of conflict resolution with rules and procedures of the existing system." This would involve Aboriginal judges, magistrates, and paralegals "handling summary convictions—that is, crimes where the maximum penalty is six months in jail and a $2000 fine—accepting guilty pleas, imposing sentences and dealing with the *Young Offenders Act*." Although a new provincial government elected in 1999 announced it was realistically exploring this idea, it ultimately decided against a separate justice system, leading one of the original authors of the Aboriginal Justice Inquiry to speculate that such a system would never be introduced (Hamilton 2001).

In contrast, the Saskatchewan provincial government decided early on to accept a recommendation from its Indian Justice Review Committee that a separate system of justice for Aboriginal peoples be established. Among the first steps taken by the government was the creation of a justice-of-the-peace program on nine northern reserves. This move toward a parallel justice system was seen as a drive toward the development of an Aboriginal justice system.

Models of Aboriginal Justice Systems

How would an Aboriginal justice system operate? What shape would it take? There are numerous views on what constitutes the most effective system, but "fundamental is the belief that the system must be faithful to Aboriginal traditions and cultural values, while adapting them to modern society" (Law Reform Commission of Canada 1991: 7). Other essential components of an Aboriginal justice system include the interests of the collectivity, the reintegration of the offender into the community, mediation and conciliation within the community, and the importance of the role of community elders and leaders (Law Reform Commission of Canada 1991).

According to Meyer (1998: 44), each Aboriginal community may develop and practise justice systems that differ, but they all "focus on reparations and making the parties 'whole' after the injury." Another common aspect is the avoidance of blaming the offender for the harm she has caused. Instead, an attempt is made to repair the injury and make the community whole again. These approaches see the need to choose persuasion over coercion to restore the parties involved. They also recognize the necessity of having respected community members serve as decision-makers.

Manitoba's Aboriginal Justice Inquiry found that the meaning of justice in an Aboriginal society differs substantially from that of the broader society. Instead of an adversary system that attempts to "prevent or punish harmful or deviant behaviour," the Aboriginal system of justice attempts "to restore the peace and equilibrium within the community, and to reconcile the accused with his or her own conscience and with the individual or family who has been wronged." Thus, the underlying notion of Aboriginal justice systems when dealing with crime was "the resolution of disputes, the healing of wounds and the restoration of social harmony" (Hamilton and Sinclair 1991).

Other provinces too explored the possibility of a separate Aboriginal justice system. Alberta examined the issue through its Task Force on the Criminal Justice System and Its Impact on the Indian and Metis People of Alberta. The final Alberta report, titled *Justice on Trial* (the Cawsey Report), recognized important differences between the traditional Anglo and Aboriginal approaches to justice. It noted that the Aboriginal model incorporates different goals (Bryant 1999: 20–21):

1. to focus on problem solving and the restoration of harmony;
2. to use restitution and reconciliation as a means of restoration;
3. to use community acts as a facilitator in the restorative process;
4. to impress the offender with the impact of his action on the total;
5. to take into consideration the holistic context of an offence—its moral, social, economic, political, and religious and cosmic considerations;
6. to remove the stigma of offences through conformity;
7. to recognize remorse, repentance, and forgiveness as important factors; and
8. to have offenders take an active role in the restorative process.

Ross (1994: 262) has identified two essential features of Aboriginal justice systems:

1. a dispersal of decision-making among many people, as suggested by a regular emphasis on consensus decision-making, and a regular denunciation of such hierarchical decision-making structures as those created by the *Indian Act*; and
2. a belief that people can neither be understood nor assisted so long as they are seen as isolated individuals ... people must be seen as participants in a large web of relationships.

A number of central components of Aboriginal justice systems have been identified. One is healing, which allows the spiritual needs of the individual to be addressed. Another is "cultural imperatives." According to Clare Brant, a Mohawk psychiatrist, these consist of four major rules in conflict suppression that maintain harmony in the group. They form the very basis of Aboriginal life in communities. The four rules (Hamilton and Sinclair 1991) are

1. the ethic of noninterference, that is, the promotion of "positive interpersonal relationships by discouraging coercion of any kind, be it physical, verbal, or psychological";
2. the rule of noncompetitiveness, which acts to eliminate internal group conflict by "averting intragroup rivalry";
3. emotional restraint, which controls those emotional responses that may disrupt the group; and
4. sharing, which means that those who were rich gave away much of their wealth to ensure the survival of the group.

Beyond these general characteristics lies much diversity. Green (1998), who studied Aboriginal communities throughout Saskatchewan and Manitoba, found four approaches in use, all of which involved community participation. These included sentencing circles, an elders' or community sentencing panel, a sentence advisory committee, and a community mediation committee. Both the circle and mediation are important elements in these practices, as they represent a more egalitarian approach, reflecting the communal nature of the community. These groups hear a variety of offences; some heard cases for which the period of incarceration is less than two years, and other communities dealt with more serious offences, such as sexual assault. All of these different approaches incorporated certain features of Aboriginal practices, including spirituality, grassroots consultations, community consensus, and sharing (Green 1998: 134).

Ross (1994) found Aboriginal justice systems used different approaches for dealing with offenders. The Hollow Water First Nation community, located in eastern Manitoba, developed its justice system by requesting that some of the practices of the Western legal system be "modified to accommodate ... what they wanted to continue doing on their own" (Ross 1994: 248). By comparison, the approach taken at Sandy Bay and Attawapiskat (both in Manitoba) requested that they be "granted roles within the Western legal system" in order to cooperate with selected functionaries of the Western legal system.

Both the Sandy Bay and Attawapiskat justice systems focus on integrating traditional Aboriginal values into the Western legal system by placing Aboriginal peoples into selected advisory roles. At Sandy Bay, the emphasis was placed on Aboriginals becoming involved not in the trial process but rather at the time of sentencing. An elders' panel acts with a provincial court judge or justice of the peace to deliver the sentence. Recommended sentences usually involve some interaction with the community, such as restitution and community service work. If an offender does not fulfill his obligation, he is "banished" to the Western legal system, where he is subject to incarceration.

EXHIBIT 3.5   Hollow Water Community Holistic Circle Healing

The Hollow Water First Nation operates a program dealing with sexual abuse. Known as the Community Holistic Circle Healing Program (CHCH), it combines a healing approach with the Western legal system. It grew from the need to find a concrete solution to the community problem of sexual abuse. In the past, when sexual abuse was detected, the police were called in to arrest the individual and, if found guilty in a court located outside the community, the offender was incarcerated in the provincial or federal correctional system. However, when offenders completed their sentences, many returned to Hollow Water and surrounding communities and continued to engage in sexual abuse. As a result, a number of community members met during the mid-1980s to set up a program to heal sexual abusers by keeping the offenders and victims within the local communities.

According to the protocol of this justice system, disclosure about sexual abuse is first made to a community team rather than to the police. This community team consists of volunteers, mostly women, including a child protection worker, a community health representative, the nurse-in-charge, representatives from both the local school division and community churches, as well as the local detachment of the RCMP. Criminal charges are laid as quickly as possible after disclosure of the act. The alleged offender is then given a choice: he can decide to proceed through the outside criminal justice system or proceed with the healing support of the team. Either way, he is ultimately sentenced in a court of law. Sentencing is delayed, however, if the individual decides to take part in the healing process.

There are four components to the CHCH. First, the CHCH is a community; it involves a coming together of all resources in the community. CHCH is available to any community members who are prepared to take full responsibility for their actions in the sexual victimization of another person. All members of the community are included as participants in the healing process. Second, the CHCH is holistic. That is, it attempts to deal with all parties involved,

including the victim, the victimizer, the families, and the community as well as all aspects of the imbalance (physical, emotional, and spiritual). Third, the CHCH is a circle. This is the strength of tradition. In the circle everyone is equal, and all similarities and differences are accepted. Within the circle, the power of one becomes the power of all. Finally, the CHCH is spontaneity from within. This involves the members following their hearts. The CHCH uses principles that the elders say would have been used in the past to deal with such issues. The traditional way was for the community to bring the issue out into the open; to protect the victim, in such a way as to minimally disrupt the family and community functioning; to hold the abuser accountable for his behaviour; and to give the opportunity for balance to be restored to all parties (Community Holistic Circle Healing 1997).

To be accepted into the healing program, alleged abusers must accept full responsibility for their actions and enter a guilty plea as soon as possible. The abuser then enters a program that involves 13 different steps "from the initial disclosure to the creation of a healing contract," and if the individual passes them, he proceeds to the cleansing ceremony (Ross 1994: 244). This process entails a painful stripping away of all the defences of the abuser over a long period of time; then the rebuilding of the individual begins. Each case is considered different and is handled accordingly. Incarceration (as long as it includes input from the community) can be used as a part of this process but only in those cases where the prognosis for healing is not good.

When the accused appears in court for sentencing, the team presents a report to the judge about the abuser's sincerity of effort and how much work, if any, still needs to be done. Where the Western court would sentence the offender to a period of incarceration, the healing circle fiercely rejects any recommendation of incarceration. Between 1986 and 1995, only five offenders had selected to be tried by the Western courts while 48 others chose to enter the CHCH program (Moon 1995).

At Attawapiskat, Ross found the elders in a different role during the sentencing of an offender. They hear the majority of the cases by themselves within a community court, complete with its own summonses and subpoenas. Charges, however, are laid in provincial court but are stayed and can be reactivated at once within a year if the offender fails to follow the sentence of the elders' court. Indeed, the cases the elders' court tries would not normally involve a period of incarceration. As in Sandy Bay, most of the sentences involve some form of community work.

The first Aboriginal court system in Canada opened in October 2000, on the Tsuu T'ina Nation, located near Calgary. Referred to as "the first comprehensive justice system in Canada, it encompasses the desire of the Tsuu T'ina people to address the glaring problems affecting First Nations people within Canadian criminal justice" (Bryant 2002: 16). Known as the Peacemaker Court, it is located on Tsuu T'ina lands, and it comprises a First Nations judge, Peacemaker program, and control over the administration of the court. The court structure blends a combination of Tsuu T'ina cultural traditions along with various components found within the broader Canadian provincial court system (Mildon 2001).

The court itself works on a similar basis as the Alberta provincial court system. It has the jurisdiction to look after summary conviction offences as well as those hybrid offences elected to be tried as summary conviction offences. Prior to any trial, however, all sessions begin with a Peacemaker (who has reviewed each case and who has an equal but different role to the crown prosecutor) reviewing and then requesting that suitable cases be transferred to the Peacemaker program. If the Crown prosecutor feels that this case should be held in the regular court, the outcome is decided by the First Nations judge. The mandate of the Peacemaker program, which is modelled after the Navajo Peacemakers approach, is "to resolve problems, investigate and discover the root causes of the behaviour which has translated into criminal activity or disharmony in the community or among families" (Bryant 2002: 17). The Peacemaking process focuses upon community harmony and restorative justice, and if this approach is successful, the Crown prosecutor withdraws the charges laid against the accused.

RESTORATIVE JUSTICE

The introduction of restorative justice is a significant new development in the philosophy of crime control. This approach proposes that a convict's conscience (that is, internalized norms) and significant others (friends, family, etc.) can be incorporated into deterrence to function as potential sources of punishment. Supporters of this approach believe they can influence criminal behaviour by decreasing the expected utility of criminal activity. They argue that deterrence doesn't need to be restricted to legal sanctions but can also include refraining from acting on the basis of fear or of negative consequences such as shame (Grasmick and Bursik 1990).

History

In his theory of restorative justice, Braithwaite (1989) develops what he calls "reintegrative shaming," a system of justice that is based on the idea that it is better to try to shame some offenders than try to punish them within the formal criminal justice system, because reintegrative shaming controls crime. Using the criminal justice system leads to stigmatization, creating outcasts of offenders, severing their ties to society, and actually increasing criminal behaviour. Stigmatization involves the processes of humiliation, labelling the offender as evil, and allowing the label of "criminal" to become the master status trait. In contrast, shaming is "disapproval dispensed within an ongoing relationship with the offender based on respect" (Braithwaite 1993: 1). This process involves the offender being confronted by victims and significant others in an attempt to moralize the offender and explain the harm the behaviour in question has caused. Disapproval of the offender's actions is counteracted by the community effort to build a moral conscience and strengthen social bonds (Makkai and Braithwaite 1994).

The key to reintegrative shaming, then, is to change the perception of the offender: instead of seeing the offender as someone to be punished (for example, through incarceration), an attempt is made to reintegrate offenders by holding a "shaming" ceremony in which offenders realize the pain they have brought to the victim, the community, and society. Shaming is more likely to be reintegrative and successful when a high degree of interdependency exists between victim and offender, such as a family, group of relatives, or the community of which the offender is a member.

Restorative justice is a new approach to justice in North America: its history is found in other nations, particularly Japan. Since the early 1950s Western social scientists have been fascinated by the high level of social order—defined as the extent of citizens' compliance to important social norms—found in Japan. This compliance is translated into a higher degree of social order and lower crime rates. Some (for example, Smith 1983; Befu

1990) argue that the phenomenon is due to the religious ideals associated with Confucianism, an idea traditionally accepted by most Western social scientists. However, other Confucian nations have a high degree of social disorder. Why, then, is Japan different?

Braithwaite (1989) points out that when someone is shamed in Japan, the shame is shared by the collectivity (for example, the family, friends, school, and workplace) to which the individual belongs. In addition, the criminal justice authorities in Japan, notably the police, work with the offender and victim in order to develop alternatives to formal punishment. According to Braithwaite, one of the powerful aspects of shaming is that social control is diverted back to the family, the community, and the social environment of the offender.

Hechter and Kanazawa (1993) believe the answer lies in Japan's high rate of social conformity—higher than that of, for example, Canada and the United States. They explain this high rate of conformity on the basis of three principles of social control. The first principle is that of dependence, which is defined as the extent to which a group is the most important source of reward. Individuals conform to group norms the more they are dependent on the group. The second factor involves visibility—the idea that behaviour that is easily observed and monitored by the group is more likely to conform to group norms. The final factor involves how strongly norms are upheld by the group. According to Hechter and Kanazawa, the greater that strength, the greater the social order and the lower the crime rate.

Restorative Justice Sanctions

Restorative justice sanctions are developed to represent the interests of the victim, the public, and the community. These sanctions are essentially alternatives to incarceration and generally involve sanctions served in the community or those that convey to the community the decision of the court. The purpose of these sanctions is to make the offender aware of the moral wrong he has committed and to indicate that no more such actions are expected. According to Karp (1998), three types of

---

EXHIBIT 3.6 Restorative Justice and Family Violence

In order to combat family violence, the police have most recently used mandatory arrest. Every jurisdiction in Canada has legislation instructing police to follow a "zero tolerance" approach to family violence. These punitive-based programs were instituted during the 1980s and 1990s but critics now question this policy. One of the researchers, Lawrence Sherman, whose work was instrumental in the creation of these programs, now questions them. A review of studies in the 1980s and 1990s led him to conclude that "mandatory arrests in domestic violence cases may cause more violence against women in the long run." If this is true, what is the best policy to combat these crimes? Some advocate the police being given more discretionary powers, but others argue this proposal will lead to an increase in the number of cases that are not prosecuted, leaving those responsible for the crimes alone, and able to commit more of this acts.

Some researchers have explored the possibility of using restorative justice as a potential tool to reduce the incidence of family violence. Most restorative justice occurs in minor property crimes, not violent crime. However, it appears that restorative justice can be successfully used to reduce family violence. A recent study of a restorative justice approach to family violence in Newfoundland reported a significant reduction in child abuse and neglect as well as the abuse of mothers and wives. Researchers found a 50 percent reduction in all types of abuse and neglect for the 32 families involved in the study compared to the preceding year. They also reported an increase in family support and enhanced family unity. In addition, the incidents for families involved in a comparison group who didn't receive restorative justice programs increased markedly. The lowest success rates were found in those cases where young persons were abusing their mothers.

The researchers, in an earlier study, reported that victims of family violence who participated in a restorative justice–based program had high levels of satisfaction. Ninety-four percent of family members were satisfied with the techniques used in the program, 92 percent said they were "able to say what was important," and 92 percent said they agreed with the intervention plan that was offered to them. On the basis of all their studies, the researchers were able to conclude that the program did lead to a sense of shame throughout the extended families.

Sources: Sherman and Berk (1984); Pennell and Burford (1996); Burford and Pennell (1998).

---

shaming sanctions are currently practised in North America. The first type (and the most common) is referred to as "public exposure sanctions." The purpose of this sentence is to bring the attention of the community and other parties to the offence, the offender, and victim. The object is to criticize the crime and therefore shame the offender.

A second shaming sanction involves debasement penalties. These typically involve shaming through embarrassment or humiliation. Usually the offender agrees to accept a penalty that forces her to reflect on the feelings that a victim may have experienced as a result of the offence. The third type of reintegrative shaming sanction, apology penalties, typically has the offender writing an apology or making a public statement about the offence and how wrong it was for her to commit it.

The Operation of a Restorative Justice–Based Criminal Justice System

The primary focus of restorative justice is not to determine guilt and punishment but to address a harm. This approach provides an alternative to the traditional adversarial system; however, only certain criminal acts are to be considered for processing in a shaming context, most commonly nonserious property crimes and minor forms of violent crime. Certain criminal justice personnel, such as a police officer or a court worker, recommend that a conference take place and start the process of diverting the case to a trained facilitator. Facilitators then arrange a conference that involves the offender and the victim. A key component of the conference is the voluntary involvement of both the victim and offender.

In addition, the offender must have accepted responsibility for his actions. An important part of the shaming process involves the recognition of the community, so supporters of both the victim and the offender are invited to take part in the shaming process as well as serve as a social support mechanism. Professionals and law enforcement officials who have been involved or have assisted either party may be invited by the facilitator, victim, or offender. While 10 to 12 participants is the norm, it is possible that 40 individuals or more attend a conference. This group is expected to arrive at a consensus on the outcome of the case.

Goals of the conferences include accountability, prevention, and healing. The benefits of this approach include the recognition of a larger group of people as victims, the involvement of a wider group of participants than is normally the case, and the acknowledgment of

the importance of the family in the offender's life (Umbreit and Stacey 1996). At the end of the meeting a consensus is reached on the best way to deal with the harm, and all participants sign a resolution document.

SUMMARY

The different approaches and models ofwjustice discussed in this chapter are concerned with reducing crime in our society. Although one model may appear superior to the others in its ability to achieve that goal, one philosophy alone probably couldn't achieve the goal in contemporary society.

It is probably wiser to think of an integrated philosophical approach to attack the problem of crime. The treatment of offenders and the protection of the legal rights of alleged perpetrators are important, but so are the rights of victims and the desire of citizens to live in a crime-free society. How then are these issues to be reconciled? As well, it is important to remember that not all offenders—for example, some dangerous offenders—can be treated. So some offenders can and should be incapacitated for long terms of imprisonment, if not for life.

Overall, however, it appears that although most people want punishment for offenders, they also want justice done and want to see the protection of due process rights granted by the *Charter of Rights and Freedoms.* Thus, Canadians should expect to see combinations of the various crime control strategies described above, with the resulting tensions, conflicts, and problems that such approaches bring.

The purpose of our criminal justice system can be interpreted in different ways. The different models that form the basis of our criminal justice system can be categorized according to whether they focus on the act or the actor. Three of the philosophies emphasize the criminal act and include demands that discretion within the system be removed. These models argue that the discretion of both the prosecutor and the sentencing judge be controlled by guidelines and that any deviations from these standards must be written down and forwarded to a review agency that assesses their validity. In addition, because prosecutors and judges have the power to shorten sentence lengths, advocates of the justice model support the elimination of parole.

The justice model, which forms much of the basis of our criminal justice system today, believes that the accused should be punished only after being found guilty in a court of law, regardless of the factual guilt of the accused. The philosophy's advocates also believe in the control of discretion and the elimination of parole, and so

TABLE 3.1 Differences in Justice Paradigm	
ABORIGINAL JUSTICE APPROACH	**AMERICAN JUSTICE PARADIGM**
Communication is fluid. Native language is used. Oral customary law learned as a way of life, by example.	The paradigm is vertical. Communication is rehearsed. English or French language is used.
Law and justice are part of the whole.	Written statutory law is derived from rules and procedure.
The spiritual realm is invoked in ceremonies and prayer. Trusting relationships are built to promote resolution and healing. Talk and discussion is necessary.	The paradigm features separation of power. The process is adversarial, conflict-oriented, argumentative. Isolated behaviour is considered—freeze-frame acts.
Problems are reviewed in their entirety; contributing factors are examined.	A fragmented approach is taken to process and solutions.
Comprehensive problem-solving is undertaken. No time limits are put on the process; it includes all individuals affected.	The process is time-oriented. Limits are imposed on the number of participants in the process and solutions.
All extended-family members are represented. The focus is on victim and communal rights. The process is corrective; offenders are accountable and responsible for change. Customary sanctions are used to restore the victim–offender relationship.	Representation is by strangers. The focus is on individual rights. The paradigm is punitive and removes the offender. Penalties are prescribed by and for the state.
Offender is given reparative obligations to victims and community.	Rights of the accused are defended, especially against self-incrimination. Society is vindicated.

Source: Melton (1998).

differ from advocates of the deterrence and selective incapacitation models, who believe that most prison terms should be short in length. In addition, advocates of the justice position believe in alternatives to imprisonment, especially for first-time offenders. The deterrence philosophy too supports the limitation of discretion throughout the criminal justice process, but it favours much longer periods of incarceration. Violent offenders are the focus of the selective incapacitation approach, which argues that the incarceration of these offenders reduces the rate of violent crime.

The only philosophy of punishment to focus on the actor is the rehabilitation model. Since offenders differ from one another, this approach favours discretion within the criminal justice system so that the "punishment fits the criminal." The goal of this model is the reintegration of offenders back into society, so a wide variety of programs is available for offenders both inside and outside correctional facilities.

The philosophy of restorative justice differs from the other mechanisms of social control, largely due to its emphasis on the involvement of both the victim and the community. Aboriginal justice systems, which are predicated largely on the principles of restorative justice, now operate in various locations across Canada. The communities using these Aboriginal tenets of justice are working to integrate their concerns with those of the Western legal system in order to assist in the social control of as many Aboriginal offenders as possible. These systems comprise a large number of groups and individuals, including elders, community members, the offender, the victim, and police officers.

Discussion Questions

1. Which philosophy of criminal justice do you think is most effective in controlling crime in our society?

2. What improvements would you make to our criminal justice system to reduce crime?

3. Why do you think that the majority of the models of criminal justice want to control or eliminate the discretionary powers of criminal justice agents? How would such control reduce the crime rate?

4. Do you think that increasing the number of police on the street, as advocated by the deterrence model, would effectively control crime?

5. Do you think Aboriginal communities should operate their own justice systems?

6. What, if any, Aboriginal principles of justice do you think are superior to those held by Western legal systems?

7. Why do you think Aboriginal justice systems are so successful, compared to the Western legal system, in processing and treating Aboriginal offenders?

8. Do you think restorative justice programs should deal with violent offenders on a regular basis?

Suggested Readings

"Aboriginal Justice." 1992. In *Canadian Journal of Criminology* 34, nos. 3–4.

Cullen, F.T., and K. Gilbert. 1982. *Reaffirming Rehabilitation*. Cincinnati: C.J. Anderson.

Duff, A., and D. Garland. 1994. *A Reader on Punishment*. New York: Oxford University Press.

Green, R. 1998. *Justice in Aboriginal Communities: Sentencing Alternatives*. Saskatoon: Purich.

Hart, M.A. 2002. *Seeking Mino-Pimatisiwin: An Aboriginal Approach to Healing*. Halifax: Fernwood.

Hudson, B. 1987. *Justice through Punishment: A Critique of the "Justice" Model of Corrections*. London: Macmillan.

Ross, R. 1996. *Returning to the Teachings: Exploring Aboriginal Justice*. Toronto: Penguin Books.

References

Allen, F. 1981. *The Decline of the Rehabilitative Ideal: Penal Purpose and Social Purpose*. New Haven, Conn.: Yale University Press.

Andrews, D., and J. Bonta. 1998. *The Psychology of Criminal Conduct,* 2nd ed. Cincinnati: Anderson.

Apospori, E., and G. Allpert. 1993. "Research Note: The Role of Differential Experience with the Criminal Justice System in Changes in Perceptions of Severity of Sanctions over Time." *Crime and Delinquency* 39: 184–94.

Beccaria, C. 1978. *On Crimes and Punishment.* Indianapolis: Bobbs-Merrill.

Befu, H. 1990. "Four Models of Japanese Society and Their Relevance to Conflict." In S.N. Eisenstadt and E. Ben-Ari, eds., *Japanese Models of Conflict Resolution.* London: Kegan Paul.

Beirne, P., and J. Messerschmidt. 1991. *Criminology.* San Diego, Calif.: Harcourt Brace Jovanovich.

Belanger, N., and C. Earls. 1995. "Sex Offender Recidivism Prediction." *Forum on Corrections Research* 8: 22–24.

Boerner, D. 1992. "Confronting Violence: In the Act and in the Word." *University of Puget Sound Law Review* 15: 525–577.

Braithwaite, J. 1993. "Shame and Modernity." *British Journal of Criminology* 33: 1–18.

———. 1989. *Crime, Shame, and Reintegration.* New York: Cambridge University Press.

Bryant, M.E. 2002. "Tsuu T'ina First Nations Peacemaker Justice System." *Law Now* 26, no. 4: 16–17.

———. 1999. "Sentencing Aboriginal Offenders." *Law Now* 24: 20–22.

Burford, G., and J. Pennell. 1998. *Family Group Decision Making Project: Outcome Report,* Volume 1. St. John's: Memorial University.

Cairns-Way, R. 1992. "The Charter, the Supreme Court and the Invisible Politics of Fault." *McGill Law Journal* 39: 379–400.

Canadian Sentencing Commission. 1987. *Sentencing Reform: A Canadian Approach.* Ottawa: Ministry of Supply and Services Canada.

Carrigan, D.O. 1991. *Crime and Punishment in Canada: A History.* Toronto: McClelland and Stewart.

Chambliss, W.J. (Ed.) 1969. *Crime and the Legal Process.* New York: McGraw-Hill.

Clark, C. 2002. "Ottawa to Create National Sex-Offender Registry." *The Globe and Mail,* 14 February, A1–A8.

Clear, T. 1995. "Correction beyond Prison Walls." In J.F. Sheley, ed., *Criminology,* 2nd ed. Belmont, Calif.: Wadsworth, 453–75.

———. 1994. *Harm in American Penology: Offenders, Victims, and Their Communities.* Albany, N.Y.: SUNY.

Committee for the Study of Incarceration. 1975. *Doing Justice.* New York: Hill and Wang.

Community Holistic Circle Healing. 1997. *History.* Wampigoux, Manitoba.

Correctional Service of Canada. 1999. "A Profile of Federal Community Corrections." *Forum on Corrections Research* 2, no. 2: 8–13.

———. 1999. *Basic Facts About Federal Corrections.* Ottawa: Public Works and Government Service Canada.

Cullen, F.T., and B.K. Applegate. 1997. *Offender Rehabilitation.* Aldershot: Ashgate.

Cullen, F.T., and K. Gilbert. 1982. *Reaffirming Rehabilitation.* Cincinnati: Anderson.

Cullen, F.T., E.J. Latessa, V.S. Burton, and L.X. Lombardo. 1993. "The Correctional Orientation of Prison Wardens: Is the Rehabilitative Ideal Supported?" *Criminology* 31, no. 1: 69–92.

Decker, S.H., R. Wright, and R. Logie. 1993. "Perceptual Deterrence Among Active Residential Burglars: A Research Note." *Criminology* 31, no. 1: 135–47.

Elliott, L. 2001. "Ontario Willing to Foot Bill for National Offender Registry." *Winnipeg Free Press*, 7 September, B4.

Feeley, M., and J. Simon. 1992. "The New Penology: Notes on the Emerging Strategy of Corrections and Its Implications." *Criminology* 30: 449–75.

Fine, S. 1997. "Top Court Extends Rights of the Accused." *The Globe and Mail*, 9 August, A1, A6.

———. 1994a. "Has the High Court Lost Touch with Reality?" *The Globe and Mail*, 8 October, D2.

———. 1994b. "Murderer Denied Fair Hearing, Court Says." *The Globe and Mail*, 1 October, A4.

———. 1994c. "Failure to Inform Suspect Invalidates DNA Evidence, Top Court Rules." *The Globe and Mail*, 1 October, A8.

———. 1994d. "Right to Seek Counsel Beefed Up." *The Globe and Mail*, 30 September, A1.

Frankel, M.F. 1972. *Criminal Sentences: Law without Order.* New York: Hill and Wang.

Freiberg, P. 1990. "Rehabilitation Is Effective if Done Well, Studies Say." *American Psychological Association Monitor* (September).

Gendreau, P., and C. Goggin. 1996. "Principles of Effective Correctional Programming." *Forum on Corrections Research* 8: 38–41.

Gibbs, J. 1975. *Crime, Punishment, and Deterrence.* New York: Elsevier.

Grasmick, H., and R. Bursik. 1990. "Conscience, Significant Others, and Rational Choice: Extending the Reference Model." *Law and Society Review* 24: 837–61.

Grasmick, H., and D.E. Green. 1980. "Legal Punishment, Social Disapproval and Internalization as Inhibitors of Illegal Behavior." *Journal of Criminal Law and Criminology* 71: 325–35.

Green, R.G. 1998. *Justice in Aboriginal Communities: Sentencing Alternatives.* Saskatoon: Purich.

Greenwood, P., T. Model, C. Rydell, and J. Chilsea. 1996. *Diverting Children from a Life of Crime.* Santa Monica, Calif.: Rand Corp.

Griset, P.L. 1991. *Determinate Sentencing: The Promise and the Reality of Retributive Justice.* Albany, N.Y.: State University of New York Press.

Hackett, K. 2000. *Criminal Harassment.* Ottawa: Canadian Centre for Justice Statistics.

Hamilton, A.C. 2001. *A Feather Not a Gavel: Working towards Aboriginal Justice.* Winnipeg: Great Plains Publishing.

Hamilton, A.C., and C.M. Sinclair. 1991. *The Justice System and Aboriginal People: Report of the Aboriginal Justice Inquiry,* Volume 1. Winnipeg: Queen's Printer.

Hamparian, D.M., R.S. Schuster, S. Dinitz, and J.P. Conrad. 1978. *The Violent Few: A Study of Dangerous Juvenile Offenders.* Lexington, Mass.: Lexington Books.

Hechter, M., and S. Kanazawa. 1993. "Group Politics and Social Order in Japan." *Journal of Theoretical Politics* 5: 455–493.

Hefferman, W.C., J. Klenig, and T. Stevens. 1995. "Megan's Law: Community Notification of the Release of Sex Offenders." *Criminal Justice Ethics* 14: 3–4.

House of Commons Debates. 6 May 1993. *Hansard* 132 (247): 19015–19024.

————. 26 May 1986. *Hansard* VI: 62.

Hudson, B. 1987. *Justice through Punishment: A Critique of the "Justice" Model of Corrections.* London: Macmillan.

Jerusalem, M.P. 1995. "A Framework for Post-Sentence Sex Offender Legislation." *Vanderbilt Law Review* 48: 219–55.

Johnson, H. 1996. *Dangerous Domains: Violence against Women in Canada.* Scarborough, Ont.: Nelson Canada.

Jones, P., and J. Goldkamp. 1993. "Implementing Pre-Trial Drug Testing at Two Experimental Sites." *Prison Journal* 73: 199–219.

Karp, D.R. 1998. "The Judicial and Judicious Use of Shame Penalties." *Crime and Delinquency* 37: 449–64.

Kramer, J.H., and J.T. Ulmer. 1996. "Sentencing Disparity and Departures from Guidelines." *Justice Quarterly* 13: 81–106.

Law Reform Commission of Canada. 1991. *Aboriginal Peoples and Criminal Justice.* Ottawa: Law Reform Commission of Canada.

Logan, C. 1993. *Criminal Justice Performance Measures for Prison.* Washington, D.C.: Bureau for Justice Statistics.

Logan, R. 2001. *Crime Statistics in Canada, 2000.* Ottawa: Canadian Centre for Justice Statistics.

McMahon, M. 1988. "Police Accountability: The Situation of Complaints in Toronto." *Contemporary Crisis* 12: 301–27.

Mackie, R. 1999. "Ontario Plans Registry of Rapists and Pedophiles." *The Globe and Mail,* 17 April, A5.

Majury, D. 1994. "*Seaboyer* and *Gayme*: A Study InEquality." In J.V. Roberts and R.M. Mohr, eds., *Confronting Sexual Assault: A Decade of Legal and Social Change.* Toronto: University of Toronto Press, pp. 268–92.

Makkai, T., and J. Braithwaite. 1994. "Reintegrative Shaming and Compliance with Regulatory Standards." *Criminology* 20: 361–413.

Marshall, W.L. 1993. "The Treatment of Sex Offenders." *Journal of Interpersonal Violence* 8: 524–30.

Marshall, W.L., and H.E. Barbaree. 1989. "The Long-Term Evaluation of a Behavioural Treatment Project for Child Molesters." *Behaviour Research and Theory* 26: 499–511.

Martinson, R. 1979. "Symposium on Sentencing: Part II." *Hofstra Law Review* 7: 243–58.

———. 1974. "What Works? Questions and Answers about Prison Reform." *Public Interest* 35: 22–54.

Marvell, T.B. and C.E. Moody. 1996. "Determinate Sentencing and Abolishing Parole: The Long-Term Impacts on Prisons and Crime." *Criminology* 34: 107–28.

Melton, A.P. 1998. *Indigenous Justice Systems and Tribal Society.* Washington, D.C.: National Institute of Justice.

Meyer, J.A.F. 1998. "History Repeats Itself: Restorative Justice in Native American Communities." *Journal of Contemporary Criminal Justice* 14: 42–57.

Mildon, M. 2001. "First Native Court Set Up in Alberta." *Law Now* 25, no. 5: 6.

Moon, P. 1995. "Natives Find Renewal in Manitoba Prison." *The Globe and Mail,* 20 July, A1–A4.

Morris, N., and M. Tonry. 1990. *Between Prison and Probation: Intermediate Punishments in a Rational Sentencing System.* New York: Oxford University Press.

Nicholaichuk, T.P. 1995. "Sex Offender Treatment Priority: An Illustration of the Risk/Need Principle." *Forum on Corrections Research* 8: 30–32.

Packer, H.L. 1968. *The Limits of the Criminal Sanction.* Stanford: Stanford University.

Pennell, J., and G. Buford. 1995. *Family Group Decision Making: New Roles for "Old" Partners in Resolving Family Violence.* St. John's: Memorial University, School of Social Work.

Persky, S., and J. Dixon. 2001. *On Kiddie Porn: Sexual Representation, Free Speech, and the Robin Sharpe Case.* Vancouver: New Star Books.

Petersilia, J. 1992. "California's Prison Policy: Causes, Costs, and Consequences." *The Prison Journal* 72: 8–36.

Price, A.C., and B.G. Stitt. 1986. "Consistent Crime Control Philosophy and Policy: A Theoretical Analysis." *Criminal Justice Review* 11, no. 2: 23–30.

Rand Research Corp. 1994. *California's New Three-Strikes Law: Benefits, Costs, and Alternatives.* Research brief. Santa Monica, Calif.: Rand Research Corp.

Richards, B. 1992. "Burden of Proof." *Wall Street Journal* 18 December, A1, A8.

Roach, K. 1999. "Four Models of the Criminal Process." *Journal of Criminal Law and Criminology* 89, no. 2: 671–716.

Ross, R. 1994. "Duelling Paradigms? Western Criminal Justice versus Aboriginal Community Healing." In R. Gosse, Y. Youngblood Henderson, and R. Carter, eds., *Continuing Poundmaker and Riel's Request*. Saskatoon: Purich, pp. 241–68.

Rubenstein, M.L., S.H. Clarke, and T.J. White. 1980. *Alaska Bans Plea Bargaining*. Washington, D.C.: Government Printing Office.

Shannon, L. 1988. *Criminal Career Continuity: Its Social Context*. New York: Human Sciences Press.

Sherman, L.W. and R. Berk. 1984. "The Specific Deterrent Effects of Arrest for Domestic Assault." *American Sociological Review* 49: 261–72.

Smith, R.J. 1983. *Japanese Society: Individual, Self and the Social Order*. Cambridge: Cambridge University.

Solicitor General of Canada. 2001. *High Risk Offenders: A Handbook for Criminal Justice Professionals*. Ottawa: Solicitor General of Canada.

Spelman, W. 1994. *Criminal Incapacitation*. New York: Plenum.

Steinbock, B. 1995. "A Police Perspective." *Criminal Justice Ethics*, 14: 4–9.

Tracy, P., M.E. Wolfgang, and R.M. Figlio. 1990. *Delinquency in Two Birth Cohorts*. New York: Plenum.

Tso, T. 1992. "Moral Principles, Traditions, and Fairness in the Navajo Nation Code of Judicial Conduct." *Judicature* 76: 1.

Umbreit, M., and S. Stacey. 1996. "Family Group Conferencing Comes to the U.S." *Juvenile and Family Court Journal* 47: 29–38.

Van Ness, D., and K. Heetderks Strong. 1997. *Restoring Justice*. Cincinnati: CJ Anderson.

Visher, C. 1995. "Career Offenders and Crime Control." In J.F. Sheley, ed., *Criminology*, 2nd ed. Belmont, Calif.: Wadsworth, pp. 515–33.

von Hirsch, A. 1976. *Doing Justice*. New York: Hill and Wang.

Walker, S. 1994. *Sense and Nonsense about Crime*, 3rd ed. Belmont, Calif.: Wadsworth.

———. 1993. *Taming the System*. New York: Oxford University Press.

Williams, S.E. 1995. "A National Strategy for Managing Sex Offenders." *Forum on Corrections Research* 8: 33–35.

Wilson, J.Q. 1975. *Thinking about Crime*. New York: Basic Books.

Wolfgang, M.E., R.M. Figlio, and T. Sellin. 1972. *Delinquency in a Birth Cohort*. Chicago: University of Chicago Press.

Zimring, F.E., and G. Hawkins. 1988. "The New Mathematics of Imprisonment." *Crime and Delinquency* 34: 425–36.

Court Cases

R. v. Borden, [1994] 3 S.C.R. 145

R. v. Gladue, [1999] 1 S.C.R. 688

R. v. L. (T.P.), [1987] 2 S.C.R. 309

R. v. Sharpe, [2001] 1 S.C.R. 45

R. v. Swietlinski (1994), 92 C.C.C. (3d) 449 (S.C.C.)

Trends, Patterns, and Perceptions of Crime in Canada

CHAPTER OBJECTIVES

✓ Understand the Uniform Crime Reporting system in Canada.

✓ Understand how violent and property crimes are differentiated.

✓ Follow the general trends of criminal victimization in Canada.

✓ Know the shortcomings of using crime statistics collected by official agencies.

✓ Understand the importance of public perceptions toward crime and the criminal justice system.

I f the criminal justice system is to effectively control and reduce crime, we need current and accurate information on the nature and extent of crimes in particular locations as well as across Canada. To understand the dimensions of any type of crime, we must measure crime in an accurate fashion. A number of different measures have been developed to assist officials and policy-makers to collect and interpret crime statistics. The police or other justice officials collect official crime statistics from crimes reported to them or by interviewing individual citizens about instances in which they were victimized. And while many individuals look at crime or victimization rates for a single year, others are concerned with trends—whether the numbers of crimes are increasing or decreasing over a period of years. As a result, many analysts study crime trends and how particular types of crime change over time.

The type of crimes studied and included in official government reports can change over time, such as the areas of criminal harassment (stalking) and home invasions. Gang-related homicides (defined as those homicides classified by the police as occurring due to gang activities and/or gang membership (e.g., motorcycle gangs, street gangs, youth gangs, or organized families/groups) are a recent area of interest. An investigation found an average of 22 gang-related homicides each year between 1991 and 1997. Between 1998 and 2001, however, the number of such homicides almost tripled, to an average of 58 victims each year. And it was found that although gang-related homicides decreased from 72 in 2000 to 62 in 2001, they still accounted for just over 10 percent of all homicides during each of those years. In 2001, the police estimated that two-thirds of these homicides involved drug trafficking or the settling of various issues, such as "turf wars." Firearms were involved in 74 percent of all the killings (Dauvergne 2002).

Each year in Canada, crime statistics about a variety of crimes are published. Perhaps the most anticipated crime statistics are the national crime statistics, which are usually released to the public during the early summer. Criminologists are interested in how much crime occurs, whether the overall crime rates increase or decrease, the rate of violent crime, which crimes are the most frequently committed, how many crimes are solved (or cleared) by the police, and which city can lay claim to the title of "murder capital of Canada." But what do these national crime statistics mean? What are the problems and limitations associated with these figures? Can the figures be manipulated? This chapter discusses the official crime reporting system in Canada. Official crime measures include police-generated crime data and data collected from victimization surveys. In addition, the chapter discusses unofficial methods of collecting crime data.

TRENDS IN CRIME RATES

One of the simplest questions asked about crime in Canada—but one of the hardest to answer—is whether the crime rate is decreasing or increasing. The question is difficult to answer because it depends on the type of crime data we are using. If they come from the police, they represent only those crimes reported to the police or those crimes the police discover themselves. If we use an alternative source of data, such as self-reports or victimization reports, are we any closer to the actual number of criminal incidents? While none of these three sources of crime data is accurate, attempts have been made over the years to study them to see how well they capture the true extent of criminal incidents.

WHAT THE POLICE SAY: THE UNIFORM CRIME REPORTING SYSTEM

The Uniform Crime Reporting (UCR) system started in Canada in 1961 and continues, with some modifications, to this day. The UCR is designed to generate reliable crime statistics for use in all aspects of law enforcement, and, in order to ensure reliability in the reporting of crime data, standard definitions are used for all offences. This approach eliminates variations in the definitions of offences between different parts of the country; all police agencies must submit their crime statistics in accordance with the UCR definitions. Since some offences are "hybrid" offences (see Chapter 2), the UCR does not make a distinction between indictable and summary conviction offences. The overall police-reported crime rate declined between 1991 and 1999, and then increased by 1 percent for the years 2000 and 2001. The increase in the police-reported crime rate was largely the result of a 4 percent rise in the number of offences reported in the category of "Other" *Criminal Code* offences (Savoie 2002).

In order to classify crimes, the police use a guidebook, *The Uniform Crime Reporting Manual*, which contains definitions of crime as determined both by the Canadian Association of Chiefs of Police and by Statistics Canada (Silverman, Teevan, and Sacco 1991). Between 1961 and 1988, all police departments in Canada summarized their crime data on standardized forms on a monthly basis and forwarded the forms to Statistics Canada. Since 1982 an affiliated agency, the Canadian Centre for Justice Statistics, has the responsibility of collecting and reporting these data. This organization produces the annual crime statistics as well as a bulletin known as *Juristat*. This publication is published periodically throughout the year, and features reports that provide insight into specialized areas of Canadian crime statistics as well as the operation of various aspects of the criminal justice system, such as corrections.

For the first 27 years of UCR operation, crime was reported on the basis of aggregated statistics. This survey, known as the Aggregate UCR Survey, is still used today alongside the revised system. It records the number of incidents reported to the police and includes the number of reported offences, the number of actual offences (excluding those that are unfounded), the number of offences cleared by charge, the number of adults charged, the number of youths charged, and the gender of those individuals charged. It doesn't include victim characteristics. This approach to collecting statistics has been criticized because it is "less useful for analytic purposes than information based on characteristics of individual crimes" (Silverman et al. 1991: 62).

A new system of collecting and reporting crime statistics was introduced in 1988, but it wasn't fully operational until 1992. The new system—referred to as the Incident-based UCR Survey, or UCR2—incorporated a key change, as it collected incident-based data rather than summary data and thus allowed for better analyses of crime trends. The Incident-based UCR system also added the following features:

1. information on victims: age, sex, victim–accused relationship, level of injury, type of weapon causing injury, drug and/or alcohol use;
2. information on the accused: age, sex, type of charges laid or recommended, drug and/or alcohol use; and
3. information on the circumstances of the incident: type of violation (or crime), target of violation, types of property stolen, dollar value of property affected, dollar value of drugs confiscated, type of weapon present, date, time, and type of location of the incident (Silverman et al. 1991: 62–63).

Another difference between the aggregate and revised Incident-based UCR systems lies in the number of police departments included in the study. The Aggregate UCR Survey includes every police force, while the Incident-based UCR Survey consisted of a sample of 154 police departments in nine provinces in 2001. The police departments included in the Incident-based UCR Survey are nonrepresentative, since 40 percent are located in Ontario and 31 percent in Quebec. And other than the police forces selected from Ontario and Quebec, the data used in the Incident-based UCR are collected from urban police services.

A crime typically becomes known to the police when a victim or sometimes a witness reports the criminal incident. At best, the police discover only a minimal number of all crimes by themselves, since many victims do not report the crimes committed against them. And when the police do receive a report of a criminal incident, they have to decide whether or not to record it as such. Sometimes they may not believe the report, or, even if they do believe it, may not feel that the incident in question really involved any criminal activity. Even if the police do believe that a crime occurred, they may be too busy to investigate it thoroughly or to complete all the necessary paperwork, especially if the incident in question is not that serious. If the police do not record it as a crime, it is not included on the official UCR system. One study found that about 6 percent of all information informally processed by the Edmonton police was lost between the call from the complainant and the records section; the corresponding figure for the Calgary police was closer to 20 percent. Differences in the crime rates between cities can be attributed to the structure, organization, and operation of the information systems operating within each police service.

Even if the police do record the crime, a case successfully solved by a charge is the exception rather than the rule. Unless the victim or witness can positively identify a suspect, or if the police are able to catch the alleged offender shortly after the offence was committed, it is unlikely they will catch the offender. Police don't have the time to investigate each criminal incident thoroughly and interview many witnesses or suspects, unless the crime is a serious one. Generally, the proportion of the total number of crimes solved is small. In 1996, for example, Canadian police services were able to solve 66.2 percent of all violent crimes compared to 17.7 percent of all property crimes and 71 percent of "Other" *Criminal Code* violations.

Another concern involves the accuracy of the UCR. How well does the UCR measure the crime rate in Canada? For the UCR to be accurate, citizens must report criminal activity to the police, and then the police must pass this information on to Ottawa. Criminologists have long been aware that this is a highly discretionary area. Citizens may not report a crime threat, for example, due to fear, and the police may also not report every crime that comes to their attention due to their discretionary powers. As a result of these concerns, numerous criticisms have been made against police-generated crime statistics. The most common of these criticisms are as follows:

1. There is an unknown (and no doubt large) amount of crime that is not reported to the police and, as a result, is not recorded in the UCR. This problem can be alleviated by the use of victimization surveys.

2. In a single series of criminal actions reported to the police, only the most serious crime in it is included in the UCR. The most serious offence is usually the one that carries the longest maximum sentence under the *Criminal Code*. If, for example, a male breaks and enters a house, sexually assaults a woman level 1, and then kills her (homicide), only the murder is recorded. Although break and enter and homicide both have a maximum penalty of life imprisonment, violent offences take precedence in the record over nonviolent offences. One exception to this approach is criminal harassment (stalking); all instances of this offence are recorded, not just those that are the most serious violation of a series (Hendrick 1995).

3. The overall crime totals misrepresent the crime rate in any given year. When we talk of an increase or a decrease in any given year, we are comparing the totals of all crimes included in the crime statistics to those totals of the previous years. But what if an increase in break and entering corresponds with a decrease in sexual assault level 1? Since one offence is classified as a violent crime and the other a property crime, critics argue that these two offences shouldn't have the same weight.

4. There are problems with the way the UCR records criminal incidents for some crimes. For nonviolent crimes, one incident is counted for every distinct or separate incident. But the UCR records violent incidents differently; for violent crime, a separate incident is recorded for each victim, so if one person attacks and assaults five individuals, five incidents are recorded. But if five people attack and assault one person, only one incident is recorded. Robbery is an exception: one robbery equals one incident, regardless of the number of victims. This is because a single robbery can involve many victims, so to record the robbery by the number of persons it victimizes would overstate the occurrence of robbery (Martin and Ogrodnik 1996).

Crime rates are a more reliable way to measure crime than total numbers of crimes because rates are not influenced by changes in the population, which can have a significant impact on the degree of risk faced by an individual. If, for example, you live in a town of 1000 residents where there were 200 break and enters, your chances of being a victim are one in five. But if you live in a community of 10 000 with 200 break and enters, your risk is reduced to one in 50, even though the number of break and enters is the same. Since the term "crime rate" is used so often, it is important to know exactly what it means. Crime rates are usually based on 100 000 population. This allows researchers to standardize and compare crime rates across Canada in any given year as well as across a number of years. For example, in 2001, when there were 554 homicides in Canada, the homicide rate dropped to a 32-year low of 1.78 per 100 000 population—a 41 percent reduction over 1975, when the rate was 3.03 per 100 000 population.

WHAT VICTIMS SAY: VICTIMIZATION DATA

One of the problems of using the UCR as the only basis for crime statistics in Canada is the fact that not all victims report crimes to the police. For example, in 1999, there were 2 357 771 crimes recorded by the police in Canada; in comparison, there were 8.3 million criminal victimization incidents involving only eight criminal offences (Tremblay 1999; Besserer and Trainor 2000). The exact number of unreported crimes is an unknown, but the number and type of these unreported crimes probably fluctuates from year to year. For example, the number of crimes that went unreported to the police in 1999 was estimated to be 78 percent for all types of sexual assaults and 67 percent for all household thefts (Besserer and Trainor 2000). The official crime rate generated by the UCR is only as accurate as the contributions made by the public—as well as the data the police decide to process. Asking members of the public about the crimes they do not report to the police contributes significantly to our understanding of the amount of crime. The benefits of victimization surveys therefore include

1. the potential to provide estimates of unrecorded crime;
2. the potential to identify the reasons victims do not report crimes to the police;
3. information about the impact of crime on victims; and
4. the identification of the population at risk (Hood and Sparks 1970: 5).

Victimization surveys were first used in Canada during the late 1970s and early 1980s in an attempt to gain more information about the volume, types, and rates of crime. The first national study was the Canadian Urban Victimization Survey (CUVS) conducted by the

federal government in the late 1970s in various urban centres across Canada. The survey revealed that huge numbers of Canadians living in these areas did not report crimes—including large numbers of violent crimes—to the police. For example, the survey found that victims did not report 11 000 sexual assaults, 27 000 robberies, and 185 000 assaults to the police. Since 1988, a national survey of personal risk related to criminal victimization was included as part of the General Social Survey program.

The General Social Survey (GSS) is based on a representative sample of about 10 000 Canadians aged 15 years or older, from the noninstitutionalized population in the 10 provinces. Selected by computer-assisted telephones using random dialing techniques, interviewers ask respondents about their experience with crime and the criminal justice system during the previous 12 months. There are a number of differences in how the UCR and the GSS collect data about crimes (see Table 4.1). One such difference is the ability of the GSS (as compared to the UCR) to discover information about crimes not reported by victims to the police. In 1993 and again in 1999, the GSS collected data on personal and household risk and examined the prevalence and social and demographic distribution of eight types of criminal victimization: sexual assault, robbery, assault, and theft of personal property (all of which are categorized as "personal crimes") break and enter and attempted break and enter, theft of household property, vandalism, and motor vehicle theft and attempted motor vehicle theft. The survey collected information in other areas of criminal victimization as well—including fear and perceptions of crime, police reporting, and perceptions of the criminal justice system.

The GSS surveys were not intended to substitute for the UCR but to complement it. Comparisons between the UCR and the GSS are of dubious value, because the ideas behind each system are different. While crime rates in the UCR came from reports of incidents of crime by the public to the police, those in the GSS come from reports of victimizations to survey interviewers. Therefore, GSS data originate from individuals who are actually victimized, and UCR data are based on criminal acts reported to the police. Because their sources of data differ, the GSS and UCR give us different information about crime in Canada.

Another use of victimization surveys is their ability to focus upon specific types of crimes. In 1993, for example, the federal government conducted a national victimization survey, the Violence Against Women Survey (VAWS), which focused upon the amount of violence committed against women in Canada.

TABLE 4.1 Comparison of the GSS and UCR Surveys

Survey Characteristics	General Social Survey (GSS) on Victimization	Uniform Crime Reporting (UCR) Survey
Survey type and coverage	Sample (in 1999) of about 26 000 persons aged 15+ in the 10 provinces	Census of all incidents reported by all police services in Canada
Historical data	1988, 1993 and 1999	Available continuously since 1962
Source of information	Personal account of criminal victimization incidents, whether reported to police or not	Criminal incidents reported to and recorded by police
Comparability of offence categories	Sexual assault	Comparable to total sexual assault in UCR
	Robbery	Not comparable. UCR includes robberies of business and financial institutions.
	Assault	Comparable to total assault in UCR
	Break and enter	Comparable to break and enter of a residence in UCR
	Theft of personal property Theft of household property	Not comparable. UCR does not distinguish between theft of personal and household property.
	Motor vehicle/ parts theft	Comparable to the UCR when theft of motor vehicle parts is removed from GSS
	Vandalism	Not comparable. UCR has a "mischief" category that includes a broader range of infractions.
Sources of error	Sampling errors (i.e., differences between estimated values for the sample and actual values for the population)	Public reporting rates to police
	Non sampling errors (e.g., inability of respondents to remember/report events accurately, refusal by respondents to report, errors in the coding and processing of data)	Police discretionary power, changes in policies and practice in relation to capturing all reported incidents

Source: Statistics Canada, *Juristat*, Catalogue 85-002, vol. 20, no. 10, November 2000, p. 4.

CRIMINAL VICTIMIZATION IN CANADA, 1988–99

General Trends and Patterns

According to Besserer and Trainor (2000), 25 percent of Canadians in 1999 were victimized by at least one crime during the previous 12 months, a percentage that was slightly more than that reported by respondents in 1993. Besserer and Trainor stated that the chance of victimization for Canadians 15 years and over in 1999 for the crimes of sexual assault, theft of personal property, household property theft, and motor vehicle/parts theft all increased, while the rates of robbery, assault, and break and enter all decreased (see Figures 4.1 and 4.2). This means that any individual's chance of becoming a victim of any of these violent crimes in 1999 was 5 percent. The possibility of becoming a victim of a property crime was much higher, at 30 percent. While these percentages may seem low, they hide more startling facts. First, the rate of victimization for some groups of people, such as those who live in

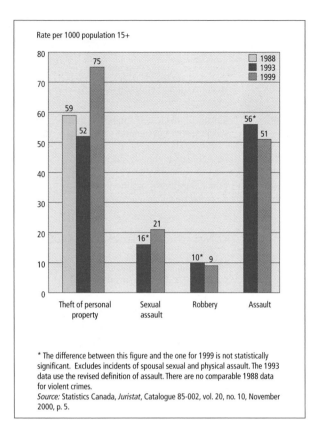

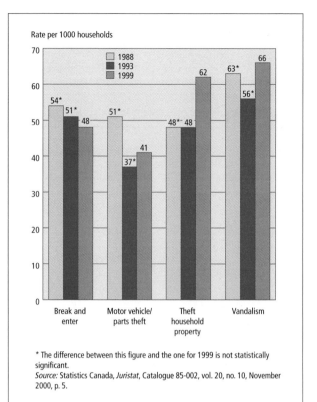

FIGURE 4.1

Rate of All Personal Victimization by Type of Incident, Age 15+, Canada, 1988, 1993, and 1999

FIGURE 4.2

Rate of All Household Victimization by Type of Incident, 1000 Households, Canada, 1988, 1993, and 1999

British Columbia, is much higher compared to other provinces. In 1999, for example, the rate of personal and household victimization in British Columbia was 33 and 23 percent higher respectively than the next highest provincial rates of victimization. Second, the risk of any one person being victimized during his lifetime is quite high; it is estimated that there is a 20 percent chance a person will have a motor vehicle stolen or vandalized during her life, and a 25 to 30 percent chance that someone will be a robbery victim (Besserer and Trainor 2000).

The rate of those offences categorized as personal victimizations in 1999 was 157 incidents per 1000 Canadians 15 years or older (see Figure 4.1). In this category, the rate of theft of personal property was the highest (75 per 1000 population), followed by assaults, sexual assaults, and robbery. In comparison, the overall rate of household victimization was higher than personal victimization: 218 incidents per 1000 households. Vandalism had the highest rate (66 per 1000 households), followed by theft of household property, break and enter, and motor vehicle/parts theft (see Figure 4.2).

Personal and Household Victimization

The following list provides certain principal findings of the 1999 GSS (Besserer and Trainor 2000):

Risk of personal victimization

- Women and men have similar overall risks.
- Personal victimization rates are highest for young persons (ages 15 to 24).
- Risks are highest for single and separated/divorced persons.
- Students have higher rates of personal victimization.
- Participation in more evening activities increases the risk level.
- Urban rates of personal victimization are higher than rural rates.

Risk of household victimization

- Homes in urban areas have a higher risk of victimization than homes in rural areas.
- Higher household income is associated with higher rates of household victimization.

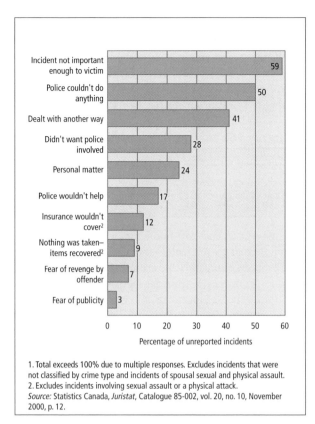

1. Total exceeds 100% due to multiple responses. Excludes incidents that were not classified by crime type and incidents of spousal sexual and physical assault.
2. Excludes incidents involving sexual assault or a physical attack.
Source: Statistics Canada, *Juristat*, Catalogue 85-002, vol. 20, no. 10, November 2000, p. 12.

FIGURE 4.3

Victimizations Not Reported to the Police, by Reason of Not Reporting

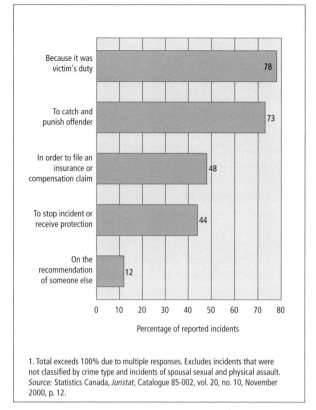

1. Total exceeds 100% due to multiple responses. Excludes incidents that were not classified by crime type and incidents of spousal sexual and physical assault.
Source: Statistics Canada, *Juristat*, Catalogue 85-002, vol. 20, no. 10, November 2000, p. 12.

FIGURE 4.4

Victims Report Incident Because "It Is My Duty"

- Rates are higher in those households with more people living in them.
- Semi-detached, row, and duplex homes have the highest risk of victimization.
- Tenants have higher risks than home owners.

The GSS also provides a profile of violent victim incidents for three offences—sexual assault, robbery, and assault—by providing information about the presence of a weapon and injury to the victim. Some of the findings made in this area and reported by the 1999 GSS include

- No weapons were present during the majority (68 percent) of violent crime incidents. Weapons were most commonly (40 percent of the time) used during robberies; the most common weapon used was a knife.
- Nearly one in five violent crime victims suffered a physical injury. In 1999, victims suffered an injury in 18 percent of violent crimes.
- Drug/alcohol abuse was a factor in 50 percent of violent crime incidents. Victims stated that the incident was most commonly related to drug and/or alcohol use by the accused alone (43 percent) or by the accused and victim (7 percent).

- Violence can be very disruptive to the victim's main activity. Forty-one percent of victims said the crime interrupted their main activity for one day, 40 percent said it affected them for two to seven days, and 8 percent for eight to 14 days.

Victimizations Not Reported to the Police

Of great interest to many who study crime are the reasons victims do not report crimes to the police. Figure 4.3 indicates that, in most cases, victims did not report crimes for reasons related to the perceived usefulness of reporting. Most victims who didn't report the incident to the police viewed the incident as not important enough to them to report it. The next two most common reasons were the belief that "the police couldn't do anything about it" and that it would be better to deal with offender "in another way" than involving the police. Besserer and Trainor (2000) found that most victims who informed the police about criminal offences did so because they viewed it as "their duty" followed by informing the police in order to "catch and punish the offender" (see Figure 4.4).

Victimization studies have a number of limitations, including the following:

1. *Underreporting to interviewers*. While victimization surveys always reveal more crime than the UCR does, they also underreport the crime rate. This is because many crimes are forgotten by victims or seem so insignificant to them that they do not report them (Sparks 1981).

2. *Response bias*. Critics of victimization surveys argue that the rate of underreporting is distributed unevenly in society. On the basis of race, whites are more likely than blacks to report having been victimized. In terms of education, college graduates are more likely to report their victimization than those with less education (Beirne and Messerschmidt 1991).

SELF-REPORT SURVEYS

Self-report surveys are a third source of data used by criminologists to study crimes not necessarily reported to the police. They are based on similar principles as victimization surveys, since people are asked directly about any criminal activities they may have been involved with during a certain time period, usually the previous year. Self-reports also include questions about subjects' attitudes, values, personal characteristics, and behaviours. The information obtained from them is used for various purposes such as measuring attitudes toward criminal offences and looking at the relationship between crime and certain social variables, such as family relations, income, and educational achievement.

One of the uses of this approach is to demonstrate the prevalence of offending by individuals who indicate they have committed a criminal offence in the time period under study. The subjects most commonly focused upon in self-report surveys are youths and drug offenders. Youths are usually questioned about issues besides their offending, such as how their friends, schools, and families potentially influence their law-breaking and/or law-abiding behaviours. Drug offenders are surveyed because many of them have committed numerous crimes in order to pay for the drugs they use.

Self-report surveys are also beneficial in that some researchers use them to focus on specific criminological subjects. Some researchers have used these surveys to study the age (referred to as "age of onset") at which youths first start offending. Frechette and LeBlanc (1987) studied male youths in Montreal and discovered that the annual rate of self-reported offending was approximately twice as high for those who started their involvement with youth crime earlier compared to those who started a few years later. Hagan and McCarthy (1992) studied the criminal activities of 309 homeless youths in Toronto during the late 1980s through self-reports, and reported that youths who had been homeless for one year or more were more likely to be involved in criminal activities.

CRIMES AGAINST THE PERSON

The violent crimes of homicide, attempted murder, assault, sexual assault, other sexual offences, abduction, and robbery make up the crime category of "violent crimes" or "crimes against the person." Although they made up only 13 percent of all crimes reported to the police in 2001, they constitute the offences that lead to the greatest physical harm and are typically the ones feared most by the public. In 2001 the overall violent crime increased by 1 percent over the previous year. Just over 309 000 violent crime incidents were reported to the police, an increase from the 302 000 reported in the previous year. The rate for all major categories of violent crime increased in 2001 with the exception of the category of attempted murders, which declined by almost 7 percent. The largest increases in violent crimes were experienced in the categories of assaults and sexual assaults (which increased by 1.3 percent and 0.7 percent).

According to police officials, Robert Picton is the focus of the largest serial killer investigation in Canadian history. By the end of October 2002, he had been charged with the deaths of 15 women.

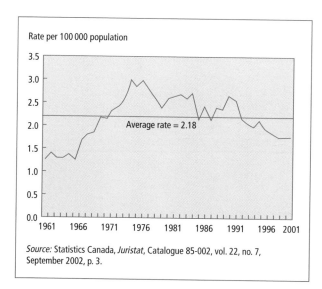

Rate per 100 000 population

Average rate = 2.18

Source: Statistics Canada, *Juristat,* Catalogue 85-002, vol. 22, no. 7, September 2002, p. 3.

FIGURE 4.5
Homicide Rate, 1961–2001

Murder

According to the Uniform Crime Reports, a murder occurs when an individual either causes the death of another human being or means to cause bodily harm the person knows is likely to cause death. There are four different types of murder in Canada: first-degree murder, second-degree murder, manslaughter, and infanticide. The incidence of murder has decreased gradually since 1975. Between 1975 and 2001, despite yearly fluctuations, the homicide rate in Canada gradually declined, reaching a rate of 1.78 in 2001, a decrease of 40 percent over the 26-year period (Dauvergne 2002). Therefore, an individual's risk of being a victim of homicide is less today than it was nearly 25 years ago (see Figure 4.5).

In 2001, knives and firearms were used in 33 percent of all homicides. The most common firearm used was a handgun. According to Dauvergne (2002), 87 percent of all solved homicides were committed by an acquaintance and family member, while the remaining 13 percent were committed by a stranger. Eighty-six persons in a family homicide were killed by a spouse. In addition, 39 children (under the age of 12) were murdered in 2001. Thirty children were killed by a parent, six were killed by another family member, and three were killed by a stranger. Twelve of these children were under the age of one year—infants under the age of one year continue to have the highest risk of being a victim of a murder compared to any other single age in Canada. (Infanticide occurs when a female causes the death of her newborn child, and her state of mind is disordered as a result of her having given birth.)

Sexual Assault

Sexual assault occurs when an individual is sexually assaulted or molested or when an attempt is made to sexually assault or molest an individual. A total of 24 419 sexual assault incidents were recorded by the police in 2001, accounting for less than 10 percent of all violent crimes. Between 1991 and 2001, the rate of reported sexual assaults declined from 109 to 78.6 per 100 000 population, a decrease of 27 percent. Females were assaulted most often by a casual acquaintance (33 percent), a stranger (26 percent), or a family member (25 percent). Male victims of sexual assaults tended to be much younger than females (the median age for males was 11 years compared to the median age of 17 for females) and they were most frequently victimized by a casual acquaintance (40 percent), a family member (30 percent), or a stranger (14 percent).

Assault

The category of assault is the most frequently occurring crime in the violent crime category. During the five-year period 1997 to 2001, the total number of violent crimes averaged 299 000 offences per year. During this same period, assault offences averaged 228 000 incidents per year, or about 76 percent of all violent offences. Of all assaults reported to the police between 1997 and 2001, the most common was common assault—assault level 1—which accounted for 82 percent of all assault offences. The next most frequent category was assault causing bodily harm, or assault level 2, which accounted for 17 percent of all assault offences, followed by aggravated assault, or assault level 3 (1 percent of all assault offences).

Data from the UCRs reveal that males and females are just as likely to be the victim of an assault. Females were most likely to be the victim of assault level 1 (52 percent), while males constituted 67 percent of the victims in both level 2 and level 3. Women were more likely to be assaulted by a spouse or ex-spouse (42 percent), a casual acquaintance (18 percent), or a close friend (12 percent). The assailants of men were most commonly strangers (37 percent) and casual acquaintances (33 percent).

Robbery

In 2001, robbery accounted for 9 percent of all violent crimes reported in the UCR statistics. Robbery is classified as a violent crime because it involves either real violence or the threat of violence. However, in about 75 percent of robberies, victims receive no physical injury, which implies they were threatened. Of the remaining victims, 22 percent receive minor physical injuries, and 4

CHAPTER 4 Trends, Patterns, and Perceptions of Crime in Canada percent suffer major physical injuries (i.e., an injury that required professional medical attention either at the scene or at a medical facility).

Criminal Harassment (Stalking)

On 1 August 1993 amendments to the *Criminal Code*—s. 264(1)—were introduced to protect persons from harassment. "Criminal harassment" occurs when an individual repeatedly follows or communicates with another person, repeatedly watches someone's house or workplace, or directly threatens another person or any member of that person's family, causing the person to fear for her safety or the safety of someone known to that person (see Chapter 2). The serious impact of stalking is illustrated by the fact that between 1997 and 1999, nine women were killed by a male when the precipating crime was criminal harassment (Hackett 2000).

In 1994, 3200 incidents of criminal harassment were reported to the police in Canada. In 1999, the number of criminal harassment incidents reported on the UCR2 increased to 5382. Seventy-seven percent of stalking victims were women, while most of the accused were men. For female victims, those arrested for criminal harassment in 1999 were, in relation to the victim, most commonly ex-husbands (36 percent) and casual acquaintances (25 percent). Male victims were harassed by a different profile of offenders: 44 percent of the accused were casual acquaintances, while 12 percent were either strangers and business acquaintances (Hackett 2000).

CRIMES AGAINST PROPERTY

Property crimes account for the majority of all serious crimes. Property incidents involve unlawful actions with the intent to gain property, but they do not

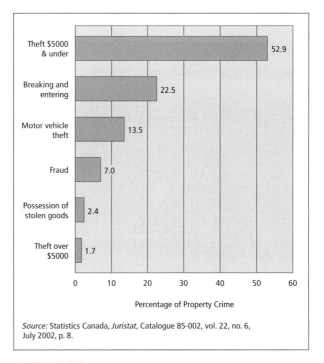

Source: Statistics Canada, *Juristat*, Catalogue 85-002, vol. 22, no. 6, July 2002, p. 8.

FIGURE 4.6
Property Crime, by Category, Canada, 2001

involve the use or threat of violence. Six crimes comprise the category of property crime: theft $5000 or under, theft over $5000, possession of stolen goods, fraud, breaking and entering, motor vehicle theft, and possession of stolen goods. Theft under $5000 is the most common property crime (see Figure 4.6). In 2001, 1.27 million property crime incidents were reported to the police. These accounted for 52 percent of all *Criminal Code* incidents, reflecting a general decline in property crimes since 1984. Rates for all types of property crime decreased in 2001 with the exception of fraud, motor vehicle theft, and the possession of stolen goods.

EXHIBIT 4.1 Home Invasions

In recent years, Canada has experienced a new criminal phenomenon of home invasions. While no official definition of this crime exists, it is normally characterized by the forced entry into a private residence while the occupants are home and involves violence against the occupants. Broadly defined, home invasion encompasses both robberies that occur at a place of residence and residential break and enters involving any other type of violent offence. Compared to the total number of robberies and break and enters reported to the police, however, those that are characterized as home invasions are rare.

Regardless, this type of crime is particularly frightening to the victim, as it involves an attack within the sanctity of one's home. A sample of police forces reporting to the Revised UCR reported 2470 of these incidents in 1996. Almost half of these involved robbery of the occupants. Police data suggest that the number of home invasions rose slightly from 1993 to 1994 (an increase of 1 percent) but decreased 10 percent in 1995 and 8 percent in 1996.

Source: Statistics Canada, *Juristat*, Catalogue 85-002, vol. 18, no. 5, 1998, p. 6.

Breaking and Entering

Breaking and entering occurs when a person enters a dwelling or other premise illegally to commit an indictable offence. Break and enter is considered to be the most serious of all property crimes. This is reflected in the severity of the sentencing provisions in the *Criminal Code*. The maximum penalty for an offender convicted of breaking and entering into a dwelling is life imprisonment. In comparison, the maximum punishment for breaking and entering into a business or any other premise is 14 years. In the UCR, breaking and entering is divided into three classifications: business, residential, and all other types (e.g., a barn). A recent concern has been the incidence of home invasions, which involve criminals breaking in when the residents are at home and physically attacking them (see Exhibit 4.1). In June 2002, in an attempt to combat this crime, the federal government passed legislation making home invasion an aggravating circumstance to be considered by judges at the time of sentencing.

Theft

Theft comprises two separate offences—"theft over" and "theft under" a certain dollar amount. In 1995 the cutoff point between the two offences was raised to $5000. Incidents of "theft under $5000" accounted for 53 percent of all property crimes in 2001. This percentage has been stable since 1998. Any change in reported incidents of theft under $5000 strongly influences the property crime rate and the overall crime rate, so high is the number of "thefts under" (Tremblay 1999).

Motor Vehicle Theft

Motor vehicle theft involves the stealing of a motor vehicle or the taking of it without permission. Theft from a motor vehicle is the theft of automobile accessories as well as personal property found within the vehicle. There were about 170 000 incidents of motor vehicle theft in 2001, a 5 percent increase from the previous year. Motor vehicle theft is an expensive crime; the 1993 General Social Survey reported that the total value of all vehicles stolen and the theft of motor vehicles was almost $600 million, compared to $73 million in losses from credit card fraud during the 1993–94 fiscal year (Morrison and Kong 1996).

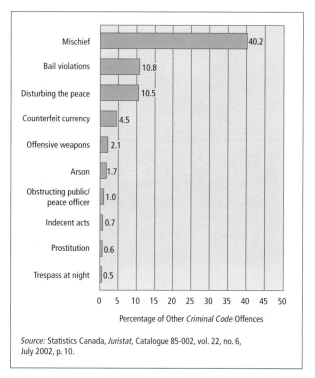

Source: Statistics Canada, *Juristat*, Catalogue 85-002, vol. 22, no. 6, July 2002, p. 10.

FIGURE 4.7

Selected Other *Criminal Code* Offences, by Category, Canada, 2001

OTHER *CRIMINAL CODE* INCIDENTS

Offences classified as other *Criminal Code* offences include arson, bail violations, disturbing the peace, mischief, offensive weapons, and prostitution. Almost 34 percent of all *Criminal Code* incidents recorded in 2001 included one of these offences. Offences in this category increased by 4.3 percent in 2001, due to large increases in both bail violations (an increase of 15.7 percent), offensive weapons charges (an increase of almost 13 percent) and disturbing the peace (an increase of 10 percent). There was also an increase of 3 percent in mischief, the most common offence in this category, as it accounted for 40 percent of all offences in this category during 2001 (see Figure 4.7).

OTHER TYPES OF CRIME

So far we have looked at only those crimes considered to be the most serious violent and property crimes. For obvious reasons, these receive the greatest amount of attention from the public, police, and politicians. Nevertheless, other types of crimes are emerging that

David Myers, former controller of WorldCom, is taken into custody by FBI agents. He was charged with fraud and conspiracy in the US$3.85 billion accounting controversy that hastened the company's collapse.

pose significant threats. They can be categorized as white-collar (or economic) crime, computer crime, organized crime, and hate crime.

White-Collar (or Economic) Crime

White-collar crime is a generic term that encompasses a variety of activities. Generally speaking, the term is used within the criminal justice system to describe crimes of fraud that are carried out during the course of a (seemingly) legitimate occupation. Most noteworthy is the fact that the criminals operating in this area carry out their activities in a deceitful form (as opposed to using force) in an effort to trick unsuspecting victims. Examples of white-collar crime receiving significant amounts of attention today are telemarketing fraud, consumer and business fraud, theft of telecommunication services, and counterfeit currency and payment cards (see Exhibit 4.2).

White-collar crime is costly, and the federal government estimates that in 1998 economic crime such as securities and telemarketing fraud cost Canadians $5 billion per year. Credit card fraud increased over 40 percent between 1996 and 1997—from $88 million to $127 million (LeMay 1998). And the illegal smuggling of tobacco, alcohol, and jewellery results in a loss of about $1.5 billion in government tax revenues per year.

Computer Crime

Since almost every business has at least one computer, computers have become a central component in the daily activities of most Canadians. Some individuals have discovered ways to use the computer as an instrument of theft or extortion. Others have used computers as an object, that is, to cause damage to hardware and software or to alter data in an unauthorized manner (see the discussion on cyber crime and using the Internet in Chapter 14).

EXHIBIT 4.2 Computer-Related Crime

From a criminal justice point of view, computers and the world of information technology offer numerous practical and legal challenges. They have created new crimes, offered offenders novel ways to achieve old objectives, and provided investigators with a new tool (whether the crime is computer-related or not). Computer-related crimes range from the theft of components to the actual use of various telecommunications tools, Internet access, and "hacking" techniques. The theft of computer components may be related to fraudulent practices; however, not all computer crimes are frauds.

There is a common misconception that the Internet has created a new type of crime. In fact, the Internet has provided a new arena in which traditional crimes such as hate propaganda, theft, and fraud can flourish. Furthermore, criminal organizations can use the Internet to access information, communicate, and facilitate criminal activities. The use of encryptions are often used to mask and hide illegal information.

Telecommunications fraud is a relatively recent development that enables organizations to access telecommunication services by some deceitful act. This is accomplished by technological manipulation (hacking, for example) or through the theft of activated cellular phones. Cellular telephones too can be put to fraudulent use, as when their computer components are modified to enable the user to duck the billing system.

Too often, victims of computer and telecommunication fraud are unable to provide meaningful assistance to police investigators. Many complex issues have rendered computer-related and cyber-related offences undetectable.

Source: Statistics Canada, *Juristat*, Catalogue 85-002, vol. 18, no. 4, February 1998, p. 9.

Senior Constable Don De Gray of Cornwall, Ontario, and a boater recover cigarettes dumped into the St. Lawrence River by thwarted smugglers.

Organized Crime

Organized crime involves a number of different criminal activities, all of which revolve around the provision of illegal goods or services as well as the infiltration of legitimate businesses. Most organized crime has emerged from the demand of illicit services and goods by the public. The crime of conspiracy (the planning of a criminal activity) characterizes nearly all organized criminal activity.

In Canada the government has introduced laws to govern such activities—for example, the *Proceeds of Crime (Money Laundering) and Terrorist Financing Act*—while in the United States law enforcement agencies have more sweeping laws (such as the Racketeer Influenced and Corrupt Organization (or RICO) provisions of the *Organized Crime Control Act of 1970*), which make it illegal for people to engage in an enterprise through racketeering activities. These laws are meant to make it difficult for people to organize to violate the law.

In 1998 the Department of Justice reported that, according to reliable sources, the illicit drug market is estimated to be between $7 billion and $10 billion per year. And each year between $5 billion and $7 billion is laundered (that is, the proceeds are disguised so as to make them appear to have originated from legitimate sources).

Hate Crimes

Hate crimes are those in which victims are threatened or assaulted purely on the basis of their race, ethnicity, religion, or sexual orientation. Hate crime legislation first appeared in the United States during the 1980s, when the number of hate crimes increased from 50 to 250.

This led to the creation of the *Hate Crime Statistics Act* (1990) by the U.S. government. The act requires that data about all hate crimes be collected. Previously, hate crimes were categorized by the most serious type of offence that occurred with them, such as murder or aggravated assault. Canada has also introduced hate crime legislation (see Chapter 14).

PUBLIC PERCEPTIONS OF CRIME AND THE CRIMINAL JUSTICE SYSTEM

As we have seen in this chapter, Canada has developed an elaborate system in the hope of ensuring a safe and just society. On any given day in 1999–2000, an average of 152 800 adults were under the supervision of correctional officials. Another 31 600 individuals, or roughly 20 percent of all those under correctional supervision, were in custody in either a provincial/territorial or federal correctional facility. And more than 7500 Canadians contacted the police on any given day to report a crime.

Because of the high visibility of the decisions made by the various agencies of our justice system, most Canadians have opinions about its effectiveness and/or failures. As a group, they pay, through their taxes, for most of the operation of this system. As consumers, they expect quick and just responses to their needs; as victims, they may suffer from the inadequacies of the system. They question whether or not current practices and policies are reaching their expectations. While the true impact of the public may be questionable, policy-makers are increasingly influenced by perceptions of public sentiment and the need to maintain public confidence in the criminal justice system.

But when we focus on the actual operation of the major agencies comprising the criminal justice system, what are Canadians' perceptions? Researchers have consistently reported that the public usually perceives the police in the most positive light when all the major agencies are compared. The 1999 GSS examined public attitudes toward the police, the courts, the prison and the parole system, and reported findings consistent with the previous surveys. In 1999, most Canadians (66 percent) felt the police were doing a good job, making sure citizens were safe (62 percent), enforcing the laws (60 percent), and providing information about how to reduce crime (54 percent). Forty-nine percent of the respondents considered the police to be doing a good job at responding to calls for service (Tufts 2000).

Overall, the level of satisfaction with the police was similar to previous findings in the 1988 and 1993 GSS.

When asked how they felt about the courts, more people perceived this agency to be doing a poorer job than the police. Only 41 percent of Canadians considered the courts to be making sure the accused was receiving a fair trial. Less than 25 percent of the public questioned felt that the courts were doing a good job of determining whether or not the accused is guilty (21 percent), assisting victims (15 percent), and providing justice quickly (13 percent) (Tufts 2000).

Overall, Canadians rated the prison system about the same as the courts. In 1999, 26 percent of the population rated the prison system as doing a good job at supervising and controlling inmates while 20 percent said the system was doing poorly in this area. Fourteen percent considered the prison system to be doing a good job in helping inmates become law-abiding citizens. In contrast, 28 percent considered the prison system to be doing a poor job of assisting inmates in this same area (Tufts 2000).

In the 1999 GSS, Canadians rated the parole system lowest of all the major criminal justice agencies in terms of doing a good job. Approximately 30 percent of the population felt the parole system was doing a poor job. Fifteen percent of those asked said they felt the parole system was doing a good job at releasing inmates who are not likely to reoffend, while 13 percent considered it was doing a good job supervising inmates on a conditional release program such as parole (Tufts 2000). However, many individuals overestimate the percentage of inmates successful in their attempts to receive parole as well as the number of offenders who, after being released on parole, commit another offence, typically a violent crime. These perceptions did not reflect the reality of the situation, since, for example, the failure rate for a conditional release program such as parole is much lower than the public thinks it is. And in most years, less than 20 percent of those individuals on parole commit a violent offence. Despite these negative perceptions about parole, the majority of the public informed the researchers that the parole system should be retained.

Canadians differ in their perceptions about whether or not any particular criminal justice agency is doing a good job. Tufts (2000) reported that women, rural residents, persons who have less than a high school education, those over the age of 65, people who are not recent victims of a crime, and those who are satisfied with their overall personal safety are more likely to have positive assessments of the police. In contrast, those most likely to rate the courts, the prisons, and the parole system in a positive way were male, younger (aged 15 to 24), possessed less than a high school education, and those who were most satisfied with their overall safety. However, it was found that those persons coming into contact with the police or the criminal courts (either as a victim or as perpetrator) had less positive attitudes toward them. Wortley (1994), in his study of black, Chinese, and white residents of Toronto, reported that police contact led to increasing perceptions of discrimination within the criminal justice system by blacks but not by members of the other two groups. And while he discovered that contact with the courts results in increases in the perceptions of discrimination for members of all groups, the biggest effect was felt by members of the black community.

Despite their concerns about the operation of our criminal justice system, most Canadians don't perceive crime and the issues that emerge from the criminal justice system to be of major importance when it comes to other social issues. This is illustrated by the number of surveys asking Canadians to identify the importance of a number of issues. A consistent finding of these surveys is that crime and criminal justice issues are not a major concern for most Canadians. For example, between 1990 and 2001, an average of 5 percent of Canadians identified crime and justice as the issue Canada's leaders should be most concerned about compared to 24 percent who rated the economy and 27 percent who identified unemployment as the most important national concern. In 2000, only 2 percent of the public identified crime as the top priority for the government, after health care (33 percent), education and the economy (both at 9 percent), unemployment (8 percent), and taxes (7 percent). Other studies have reported similar results. It is estimated that less than one-third of Canadians are "very concerned" about crime, compared to those who were "very concerned" about the health care system (68 percent) and child poverty (58 percent). This finding was reported by Environics Canada (1998), which found that during the previous 15 years the percentage of Canadians identifying crime as the most important problem was never higher than 5 percent. A revealing aspect of the lack of overall concern about crime and criminal justice is that in the summer of 2002 this issue was left off a survey developed by the Liberal Party's own polling firm studying Canadians' level of confidence in the government's handling of key social issues.

At certain times, however, Canadians reveal they are very concerned about crime and criminal justice issues. Just days after the September 11, 2001, attacks in the United States, 80 percent of Canadians were concerned about how our criminal justice system could deal with acts of terrorism and wanted the Canadian government to introduce substantial new laws to deal with this threat. This survey (Fife 2002) reported that the priorities of Canadians eight months after the attacks had changed to health care, high taxes, and government spending. In fact, some of the changes in the proposed antiterrorism law were done because public sentiment has shifted and the federal government decided the law would be too intrusive.

SUMMARY

Since the 1960s the traditional mechanism for collecting information about crime in Canada has been the Uniform Crime Reports. This information is based on crimes reported to police forces across Canada that are tabulated and summarized by the federal government. During the late 1980s this reporting system was revised to include incident-based data, such as information on the victims, the accused, and the circumstances of the incident.

Critics have pointed out a number of limitations in the Uniform Crime Reports. Among them are the facts that many victims don't report crimes to the police and that the police include only the most serious offence in a criminal incident involving numerous criminal actions. Questions have also been raised about the accuracy of police recording practices and how police "clear," or solve, many crimes. As a result of these criticisms, the federal government started to collect crime data from victims. During the past 15 years, the federal government has discovered that many violent crimes are not reported to the police by the victims. Despite these findings, the police are more likely to solve violent crimes than they are to solve property crimes.

In addition, the public perception of crimes has become an increasingly important component of understanding our response to crime. The 1999 GSS reports that while most Canadians felt that the police were doing a good job in combating crime, they did not have the same feelings toward both the courts and corrections. However, most Canadians do not consider crime to be a pressing issue, and so it is left off many public opinion polls.

Discussion Questions

1. Why did government officials revise the Uniform Crime Reports?

2. What are the three categories into which all crimes in Canada are placed? Do you think the government should develop new categories, such as a sexual offence category or a white-collar crime category? Why or why not?

3. Why is the clearance rate for aggravated assault lower than the clearance rate for first-degree murder?

4. Why do you think reports of sexual assault declined between 1991 and 2001?

5. What are the four categories of murder?

6. Why would a police force try to manipulate the number of crimes reported to the various categories?

7. Discuss the differences between the Uniform Crime Reports and victimization surveys.

8. What are the traditional criticisms of the Uniform Crime Reports system?

9. Why is it important to study the fear of crime? Should statistics on the fear of crime be incorporated into official year-end measures of crime as are statistics in the Uniform Crime Reports?

10. What is the importance of understanding how the public perceives the operation of the Canadian criminal justice system?

11. Why don't Canadians consider crime to be a major social issue?

Suggested Readings

Beare, M. 1996. *Criminal Conspiracies: Organized Crime in Canada*. Scarborough, Ont.: Nelson Canada.

Gartner R., and A.N. Doob. 1994. *Trends in Criminal Victimization: 1988–1993*. Ottawa: Canadian Centre for Justice Statistics.

Sacco, V.F. 1995. *Fear and Personal Safety*. Ottawa: Canadian Centre for Justice Statistics.

Silverman, R.A., J.J. Teevan, and V.F. Sacco, eds. 2000. *Crime in Canadian Society*, 6th ed. Toronto: Harcourt Brace.

Snider, L. 1993. *Bad Business: Corporate Crime in Canada*. Scarborough, Ont.: Nelson Canada.

Tremblay, S. 1999. *Crime Statistics in Canada, 1998*. Ottawa: Canadian Centre for Justice Statistics.

References

Beirne, P., and J. Messerschmidt. 1991. *Criminology*. San Diego, Calif.: Harcourt Brace Jovanovich.

Besserer, S., and C. Trainor. 2000. *Criminal Victimization in Canada, 1999.* Ottawa: Canadian Centre for Justice Statistics.

Dauvergne, M. 2002. *Homicide in Canada, 2001.* Ottawa: Canadian Centre for Justice Statistics.

Environics Research Group. 1998. *Environics: Focus Canada Report 1998-1.* Toronto: Environics.

Fedorowycz, O. 1999. *Homicide in Canada—1998.* Ottawa: Juristat.

———. 1995. *Homicide in Canada—1994.* Ottawa: Juristat.

Fife, Robert. 2002. "Canadians Lose Fear of Terrorism." *National Post,* 6 July, A1–A6.

Frechette, S., and M. Le Blanc. 1987. *Delinquances et Delinquants.* Chicoutimi: Gaetan Morin.

Gartner, R., and A.N. Doob. 1994. *Trends in Criminal Victimization: 1988–1993.* Ottawa: Canadian Centre for Justice Statistics.

Hackett, K. 2000. *Criminal Harrassment.* Ottawa: Canadian Centre for Justice Statistics.

Hagan, J., and B. McCarthy. 1992. "Streetlife and Delinquency." *British Journal of Sociology* 43, no. 4: 533–61.

Hendrick, D. 1995. *Canadian Crime Statistics, 1994.* Ottawa: Canadian Centre for Justice Statistics.

Hood, R., and R. Sparks. 1970. *Key Issues in Criminology.* London: Weidenfeld and Nicholson.

Janhevich, D. 1998. *The Changing Nature of Fraud in Canada.* Ottawa: Canadian Centre for Justice Statistics.

Johnson, H. 1995. *Children and Youths as Victims of Violent Crimes.* Ottawa: Canadian Centre for Justice Statistics.

Kong, R. 1998. *Breaking and Entering in Canada, 1996.* Ottawa: Canadian Centre for Justice Statistics.

———. 1994. *Urban/Rural Criminal Victimization in Canada.* Ottawa: Canadian Centre for Justice Statistics.

LeMay, T. 1998. "Credit-Card Fraud Epidemic Worsens." *National Post,* 18 December, D1, D4.

Martin, M., and L. Ogrodnik. 1996. "Canadian Crime Trends." In L.W. Kennedy and V.F. Sacco, eds., *Crime Counts: A Criminal Event Analysis.* Scarborough, Ont.: Nelson Canada, pp. 43–58.

Morrison, P., and R. Kong. 1996. *Motor Vehicle Crimes.* Ottawa: Canadian Centre for Justice Statistics.

Savoie, J. 2002. *Crime Statistics in Canada, 2001.* Ottawa: Canadian Centre for Justice Statistics.

Silverman, R., and L.W. Kennedy. 1993. *Deadly Deeds: Murder in Canada.* Scarborough, Ont.: Nelson Canada.

Silverman, R., J.J. Teevan, and V.F. Sacco, eds. 1991. *Crime in Canadian Society*, 4th ed. Toronto: Butterworths.

Skogan, W. 1981. *Issues in the Measurement of Victimization*. Washington, D.C.: Government Printing Office.

Sparks, R. 1981. "Surveys of Victimization—An Optimistic Assessment." In M. Tonry, ed., *Crime and Justice—An Annual Review of Research*. Chicago: University of Chicago Press, pp. 1–60.

Tremblay, S. 1999. *Crime Statistics in Canada, 1998*. Ottawa: Canadian Centre for Justice Statistics.

Tufts, J. 2000. *Public Attitudes toward the Criminal Justice System*. Ottawa: Canadian Centre for Justice Statistics.

Wolff, L. 1992. *Arson in Canada*. Ottawa: Canadian Centre for Justice Statistics.

Wortley, S. 1994. *Perceptions of Bias and Racism within the Ontario Criminal Justice System: Results from a Public Opinion Survey*. Toronto: Commission on Systemic Racism in the Ontario Criminal Justice System.

Wright, C. 1995. *Risk of Personal and Household Victimization*. Ottawa: Canadian Centre for Justice Statistics.

CHAPTER 5

Police Operations

CHAPTER OBJECTIVES

✓ Describe the three types of police agencies.
✓ Understand the two measures used to estimate the appropriate size of police forces.
✓ Understand the traditional organizational structure of the police force.
✓ Describe the preventive model of police patrol and new types of police patrols.
✓ Compare and contrast problem-oriented policing, community policing, and zero tolerance policing.
✓ Understand DNA legislation and its due process limitations.

The police are an important component of the criminal justice system, since anyone who is processed through the courts and ultimately convicted must first be arrested. The policing is role is crucial, as was noted by the Royal Commission on the Donald Marshall, Jr., Prosecution: "The police are, in effect, the first and main keepers of the integrity and fairness of the criminal justice system" (Hickman et al. 1989: 249).

This chapter begins with a history of the police followed by a description of the types of police agencies in Canada and an overview of the professional model of policing, the dominant model of policing from the 1930s to the 1970s. The central types of police operations—patrols and criminal investigation—are then reviewed. Later in this chapter emerging trends in policing—problem-oriented policing, community policing, zero tolerance policing, and Aboriginal police forces—are discussed. One of the most significant developments in policing during the past two decades has been problem-oriented policing (see below). This approach promotes the idea that the police should search for the root causes of crime in a community rather than simply respond to criminal incidents over and over again. It also stresses that some crimes may not be isolated incidents but rather reflect a pattern of similar activities within a neighbourhood or community. This means the police have to take a proactive stance by looking for the conditions that lead to crime.

One type of problem-oriented policing occurred in Toronto during the summer of 1999, when the police conducted the Community Action Policing Project. This program involved a selective deployment of police officers and resources to specific "trouble spots." Part of the project included targeting "suspicious-looking" persons. Some 950 of these "suspicious" individuals were arrested, with 4000 provincial tickets for mostly traffic infractions issued. The police also collected what they called "contact cards," which provided information about any individual stopped, whether that person was acting suspiciously or not. These cards were filled out on a voluntary basis, but if a person agreed to answer, she provided her name, address, and whether she had seen anything suspicious in the area recently. The information on these cards was entered into a database to be retrieved for current or future investigations.

Although the police and many citizens lauded this program, others criticized it. Some raised the issue of abuse of authority, while others suggested the police were mostly targeting the members of certain racial minority groups or other groups of people, such as the homeless, panhandlers, and squeegee kids (Appleby 1999). But how did this type of policing emerge? How proactive can the police be? And does this type of policing infringe on people's rights? Many questions surround the role of police in our society, including the amount of authority they should be given and how they try to counter criminal activity. Do they enforce the law in an equal or just manner, or do their activities infringe upon the rights of citizens and offenders?

THE HISTORY OF THE POLICE

The origin of Canadian police agencies, like our criminal law, can be found in early English society. Prior to the Norman conquest of England in the 11th century, there was no regular police force. The closest thing to a police agency was the pledge system, in which every person was responsible for assisting neighbours and protecting the village from thieves and other criminals. Groups of 10 families (known as "tithings") were set up in villages in order to police their own minor problems. Ten tithings were then grouped to a form a "hundred," whose affairs were looked after by a constable appointed by local nobles. The constable, considered by many to be the first "real" police officer, dealt with the most serious law violations. The hundreds were then amalgamated into shires (the equivalent of modern-day counties), and the top law enforcement official became known as shire-reeves, a position that (as the phonetics suggest) developed into the position of sheriff. The Crown or local landowner appointed this individual to supervise a specific area to maintain law and order and apprehend law violators.

In the 13th century, the watch system was created in order to protect the property of people in larger English towns and cities. Watchmen patrolled at night to protect citizens from robbers, ensure that citizens were safe, and detect fires. Watchmen reported to the area constable, who ultimately became the primary law enforcement officer. In the largest English cities, watchmen were organized within church parishes and were usually residents of the parishes they were hired to protect.

In 1326, shire-reeves were replaced by the justice of the peace, a position created to control an entire county. Over time, justices of the peace took on judicial functions. Later the position of parish constable emerged, and these individuals were expected to oversee criminal justice for parishioners. Parish constables were agents of the justice of the peace, and they supervised night watchmen, investigated offences, served summonses, executed warrants, and ensured the security of those charged with crimes before their trial. This system has been credited with starting the separation of the police from the judiciary, a system that has continued in our legal system for almost 700 years.

The Development of Modern Policing

By the mid-1700s, the city of London, England, did not have an organized law enforcement system. Crime was commonplace, and when crime became so common that it became unbearable, the only recourse open to city officials was to call in the military. Such actions were unpopular with the local populace, however, as the soldiers used their powers in most cases to maintain a system of harsh control over citizens living in the crime-prone areas, and they occasionally used firepower to gain control of disorderly situations. The military also came under the direct control of city officials, who abused the power of the military to gain their own ends. As a result, many citizens in London were suspicious of any formal attempt to control their activities.

Henry Fielding, Chief Magistrate of Bow Street in the mid-1700s, introduced an alternative to calling in the military. Fielding decided to form the Bow Street Runners (also referred to as "Thief Takers") in 1753, which consisted of volunteers who mainly retrieved stolen property. The Runners soon became so successful that they were hired out to control crime in various other locations across England.

This success, in conjunction with large numbers of migrants moving to London from the countryside, resulted in the British Parliament's debating the best way to handle criminal activity. But it wasn't until Sir Robert Peel was appointed to the position of Home Secretary that a formal plan was approved. In 1829, Parliament passed the *Metropolitan Police Act*, which continues to have an impact on policing. Many of its goals are still espoused by police agencies in Great Britain, Australia, New Zealand, and North America. As a result of this legislation, the London Metropolitan Police was created. The number of police officers was initially 1000, and members were easily recognized by their uniforms (which included blue coats and top hats). Peel's legislation included four operational philosophies for the police (who were called "bobbies" after their creator) (Guth 1994):

- to reduce tension and conflict between law enforcement officers and the public;

- to use nonviolent means in keeping the peace, with violence to be used only as a last resort;
- to relieve the military from certain duties, such as controlling crime; and
- to be judged on the absence of crime rather than by high-visibility police actions (Manning 1977).

The bobbies were so successful in controlling crime and disorder that they were soon copied throughout England, and ultimately in Canada and the United States.

The Early Canadian Police Experience

In colonial Canada during the 1700s and early 1800s, various law enforcement agencies were established. Prior to Canada becoming a member of the British Empire, settlers in Quebec created a system of policing that replicated the system in France. The first individuals involved in policing appeared in Quebec City in 1651. Twenty years later, Quebec City developed police regulations (Kelly and Kelly 1976). The first permanent constables under the control of their respective city councils appeared in both Quebec City and Montreal during 1833.

Settlers in Ontario municipalities followed the law enforcement system being practised in England. In 1835, the City of Toronto hired six men to be the first constables to police the municipality at night. Other Canadian cities gradually formed their own municipal-based police forces, including Halifax (1841), Hamilton (1847), St. John (1849), Victoria (1862), Winnipeg (1874), Calgary (1885), and Vancouver (1886).

The areas west and north of Ontario municipalities didn't undertake any organized form of policing. Most of these communities created policing systems based largely on what the populace had experienced in their homelands. The Hudson's Bay Company also formed its own type of policing system, approved by the federal government, in the areas surrounding its trading posts. In order to gain control over western lands, the North-West Mounted Police (NWMP) was established in 1873. It differed in its organization from the new municipal police forces, as its creators followed a structure based on the military model of the Royal Irish Constabulary, a system that was gradually adopted by all municipal police forces across Canada (Guth 1994). The purpose of the NWMP (renamed the RCMP in 1920) was to police and control the western areas purchased from the Hudson's Bay Company by the federal government in 1869 (Kelly and Kelly 1976; Browne and Browne 1973).

The Rise of Municipal Policing

The early municipal police departments had three major functions:

- maintain public order;
- control and prevent crime; and
- provide services to the community (Marquis 1994).

Perhaps the most significant development in this type of policing over the decades was in the area of communications. In their initial stages of development, municipal police officers had to personally meet or write notes delivered by police runners to communicate with each other. But the introduction of call boxes in the 1870s revolutionized policing. At first, patrol officers could simply signal their location to police headquarters. Later, call boxes were equipped with a bell system, allowing patrol officers to send different signals to headquarters, such as calling for backup or an ambulance. Finally, in the 1880s, telephones were placed in call boxes, providing a direct link between officers on the street and those at headquarters. Over the ensuing decades the police introduced more technology as it became available. Patrol vehicles, two-way communication systems, fingerprinting, a criminal record system, and the use of toxicology were all introduced during and after the 1920s. One of the biggest changes, however, was the separation of police officers from the community, a situation that was to last until the introduction of community policing in the late 1980s.

THE DISTRIBUTION OF THE POLICE IN CANADA

A total of 77 099 individuals were employed by police forces across Canada in 2001. Of this total, 57 107 were sworn police personnel and 19 992 were civilian employees. The number of police officers increased by just over 2 percent from the previous year. Between 1998 and 2001, the number of civilian employees increased by 3 percent.

There are three different jurisdictional levels of policing in Canada—municipal, provincial, and federal. In 2001, 38 009 (66.6 percent) of all police officers in Canada were involved with municipal police agencies. This total includes over 350 "independent" municipal police forces, employing 33 973 police officers, or 89 percent of all municipal police officers in Canada. There were also just over 200 RCMP municipal contract forces employing 4036 officers.

Provincial police agencies employed 13 573 police officers, or 23.7 percent of all police personnel in Canada. Provincial police forces enforce the Criminal Code and provincial statutes within areas of a province not serviced by a municipal police force. The three provincial police forces are located in Ontario (the Ontario Provincial Police), Quebec (the Sûreté du Québec), and Newfoundland (where the Royal Newfoundland Constabulary provides policing services to the three largest municipalities). For the other seven provinces and three territories, provincial policing is provided by the RCMP under contract.

The RCMP has complete responsibility in all provinces and territories for enforcing federal statutes, executive orders, security for dignitaries, and airport security. In 2001, 4069 RCMP officers (7.1 percent of all police officers in Canada) were involved in federal policing. Other responsibilities of the RCMP include forensic laboratory services, the operation of CPIC (an automated national computer system available to all police forces), and telecommunications services for data and radio transmissions to ensure all detachments receive current information. There were 1456 RCMP officers stationed at RCMP Headquarters and at the training facility as well as in departmental and divisional administration in 2001, accounting for 2.6 percent of all police officers (Filyer 2002).

The largest police agency is the Toronto Police Service, with 8579 police officers, or 15 percent of all police officers in Canada. Montreal is the next largest police service, with 5940 (10.4 percent of the total number of police officers). The only other police services comprising over 1000 police personnel in 2001 were Vancouver (2821 officers), Edmonton (1407), Calgary (1338), Hamilton (1203), Winnipeg (1201), and Ottawa (1107).

There is no single model for determining the appropriate size of a police force or its workload. One problem is determining the size of the appropriate population base; census figures are commonly used, but every large city in Canada experiences a substantial influx of persons on most days as people who live outside the city limits drive in for work or pleasure. The size of police agencies varies significantly across Canada, both in terms of personnel numbers and in the number of officers per person served. For example, in 2001, Thunder Bay had the highest number of police officers (247) for every 100 000 population, while Sherbrooke and Chicoutimi-Jonquière had the lowest numbers of police officers for every 100 000 population, at 111 and 119, respectively.

An aerial view of a farm in Coquitlam, B.C., belonging to suspected serial murderer Robert Picton. One hundred and thirty police investigators are involved in the search for evidence, a group so large that they are considered an RCMP detachment.

Two measures are generally used to establish the appropriate size of a police force by analyzing and identifying trends in the population. The most common measure used is the population-to-police-officer ratio, which compares the changes in the number of police officers to the changes in the Canadian population. By province/territory, the lowest number of police officers per 100 000 population in 2001 was found in Newfoundland and Labrador, with 144 police officers to 100 000 population. The highest rate among the provinces was Yukon (405 police officers for every 100 000 population), followed by the Northwest Territories and Nunavut (with 372 and 323 officers, respectively, for every 100 000 population).

The second technique used to evaluate the appropriateness of police force size is to compare the number of *Criminal Code* incidents (excluding traffic incidents) reported to the police with the number of police officers in the police force that handles those incidents. This ratio is used as an indicator of police workload (Young 1995). The number of *Criminal Code* incidents per police officer increased from 20 in 1962 to 51.1 in 1991. It has since declined, to 48.2 in 1995 and then to 41.2 in 2001.

THE ORGANIZATION OF THE POLICE

Police forces are bureaucracies, so in order to provide policing services as efficiently as possible, a model known as the professional model of policing emerged in the 1930s and remained dominant for the next four decades. This model was characterized by four organizational characteristics:

- a hierarchical differentiation of the rank structure, with the police chief holding the highest rank and probationary constables the lowest;
- functional differentiation, where job specializations, such as patrol, homicide investigation, traffic, and robbery, were developed to better deal with the crime problem;
- the routinization of procedures and practices, which were formalized and included in policy manuals that dealt with all aspects of the organization; and
- the centralization of command, in which "ultimate authority rests at the top of the police hierarchy, and decision making within the hierarchy is accountable up the chain of command, while being protected from outside influences" (Reiss 1992: 68–72).

These four characteristics remain in place today, although most police forces have attempted to shift their focus to a community policing perspective, an approach that, in theory, attempts to limit the top-down approach by eliminating many middle managers and giving patrol officers more discretion. However, since police forces operate on a paramilitary basis, it is difficult to eliminate the top-down approach.

Of particular importance to the professional model are specialist job roles. These roles allow the police to operate in a more efficient and effective manner. Large police departments are divided into various operational areas, including field operations, administration, and crime and support services. Each of these components is in turn divided into different specialties. For example, crime and support services can be broken into dozens of different units, including homicide, robbery, crime prevention, gang, and stolen-vehicles units. This type of job specialization continues in the first decade of the 21st century, with many large police forces creating specialized operations such as gang units and hate crime units.

In recent years, however, criticism arose regarding this type of organization, specifically that it fails to suit the social needs of contemporary society. For example, the number and complexity of police divisions and the lack of a clear relationship among them can lead to internal problems. For example, one division may inadvertently implement a program that overlaps with the activities of another. This overlap illustrates the problem with a traditional top-down approach to organizational structure, in which administrators tell supervisors what to do, then supervisors tell divisional commanders what to do, and they in turn tell subordinate police officers what to do, and then these officers talk to citizens. The problem with this approach for the organization is that there isn't enough information flowing from the bottom to the top, especially regarding the sentiments of the public. Other problems include the failure to promote personal ingenuity as well as the reduction of contact among the members of the police organization (Kelling and Moore 1988).

POLICE EFFICIENCY

Efficiency is typically measured by organizations by using statistical measures, and the police are no different than other organizations in this regard. For police organizations, the traditional measures of statistical efficiency are (a) response time and (b) arrest rates. Response time is defined as the time elapsed between a citizen's call to police and when the police arrive at the scene of the incident. The speed with which the police respond to calls for service is a traditional statistical measure of efficiency because it is seen as an effective response to crime control and prevention. If the police can respond quickly, the belief is that they will catch perpetrators at the scene of the offence.

The problem with using this as a measure of police efficiency is that citizens often wait several minutes before calling the police for assistance. And so by the time the police arrive the perpetrator has already fled the scene of the crime. Citizens have been found to take between five and 10 minutes to call the police from the moment the crime is committed. As a result, rapid response doesn't have the anticipated effect on either crime rates or police efficiency.

Management of Demand (Differential Response)

When police agencies realized that response time for nonemergency calls was not as important as the response time for emergency calls requiring immediate assistance, they began to develop systems that could distinguish between these emergency and nonemergency calls. These systems utilize what is referred to as management of demand or differential response. Management of demand for services requires the police to categorize citizen demands for services and then match these with differential police responses. This means that the police, after receiving a call for service involving an emergency, respond to it faster than a nonemergency call. There are a variety of differential responses developed by the police. For nonemergency calls, for example, they may take the report over the telephone, request that the citizen go and file a report at a community police office, or request the citizen to make an appointment when the level of calls for service is usually lower. This means the police are able to adjust workloads, enabling them to make better use of their resources.

Management of demand/differential response programs are now standard policy across Canada. For example, the Edmonton Police Service analyzed its calls for service and discovered "consistently, month after month … only about five percent of all incoming phone calls are high priority in nature" (Braiden 1993: 219). A similar study of the Halifax Police Service found that only 17 percent of incoming calls required an immediate police response, and many of these were false alarms (Clairmont 1990). If the police could identify the most serious criminal incidents, a rapid response might be the most efficient approach to apprehending the offender. In addition, by analyzing calls for service, police administrators are able to restructure their patrol activities without diminishing public satisfaction with the police, improving police efficiency since this change in operations didn't adversely affect the crime rate. This approach has also gained support because it allows some patrol officers to become active in other areas of police operations, such as criminal investigation and crime prevention, when demand for immediate response is low.

Arrest Rates and Efficiency

The second traditional type of measure of police efficiency is the arrest rate. Following the logic of the deterrence approach discussed in Chapter 3, it is assumed that arresting most offenders will prevent crime, and the crime rate will go down. This approach, which was accepted for decades by police administrators, is flawed because (as discussed in Chapter 4) self-report and victim surveys reveal that a significant amount of crime is not brought to the attention of the police. Another problem with using arrest rates as a measure of efficiency is the fact that many people are arrested but not all are prosecuted.

Some police administrators favour the clearance rate of crime as a better indicator of police performance. The clearance rate, or the percentage of crimes solved over a specific time period, allows the police to separate and analyze various categories of crime, such as violent and property crimes, from each other. The clearance rate for violent crimes is usually the highest, since many of

these offences are committed by persons whom the victim knows. In comparison, property crimes are often committed by strangers. For example, the clearance rate for homicides in 1999 was 77 percent, while the clearance rate for break and enters in the same year was only 16 percent. High clearance rates illustrate that the police response to that crime is good, while low clearance rates typically indicate that more resources could be applied to this area.

Table 5.1 presents the list of clearance rates for selected violent, property, and other *Criminal Code* offences from 1996. These figures show that just over 21 percent of all crimes known to the police were cleared by an arrest or "otherwise." That the figure is so low is due largely to the low proportion of property offences cleared. This means that only about one in five criminal offences led to an arrest.

Yet another performance indicator of police performance is the number of arrests made by the police that lead to prosecutions. A crime cleared by the police but not processed may be the result of decisions made by Crown prosecutors and have nothing to do with the police. Certain events are beyond the control of the police, such as witnesses and/or victims who are reluctant to testify, resulting in prosecutors deciding to stay the charges. But the fact that almost 67 percent of arrests lead to conviction overshadows some of the limitations found in other indicators used to evaluate police performance.

A more recent measure used to evaluate the performance of the police is that of fear reduction, which is considered by advocates of community policing the most important indicator of all. Reducing fear of crime in the community is viewed as a way to increase police–community interaction and allow the police to gain the trust of residents. In turn, this trust gives the police much-needed community support when it comes to reducing criminal activity or behaviours that can lead to criminal incidents.

Some successful techniques of fear reduction used by the police include

1. a community-organizing response team designed to build a community organization where none had existed before;
2. a program allowing victims of crime to be contacted by the police to inform them of the progress of the case and to offer them advice about victim services;
3. a police community service centre staffed by police officers and local community volunteers; and
4. the creation of neighbourhood activity programs for youths and young adults sponsored and operated by police officers and volunteers.

TABLE 5.1 Criminal Incidents by Clearance Status, 1996

| | Total Incidents | Cleared by Charge | Cleared Otherwise | | | | | Not Cleared[3] |
| | | | Complainant declines laying charges | Accused involved in other crimes | Departmental discretion | Other[2] | Total | |
		percent	percent	percent	percent	percent	percent	percent
Homicide[1]	292	59.2				5.1	5.1	35.6
Criminal negligence/other violations causing death	31	77.4				12.9	12.9	9.7
Attempt/conspire murder	495	67.5	0.6		0.8	1.4	2.8	29.7
Sexual assault—Total	8 867	41.2	8.2	0.1	5.5	4.3	18.1	40.7
Aggravated sexual assault	136	52.2	6.6		0.7	6.6	14.0	33.8
Sexual assault with weapon	280	47.9	2.5		0.4	1.1	3.9	48.2
Sexual assault	8 451	40.8	8.4	0.1	5.8	4.4	18.7	40.5
Nonsexual assault—Total	81 845	57.0	10.9		5.5	3.1	19.5	23.5
Aggravated assault	1 387	66.4	3.5		1.1	2.2	6.8	26.7
Assault with weapon/CBH[4]	16 556	62.9	6.0		2.5	2.0	10.6	26.5
Assault	59 858	53.3	13.0		6.6	3.4	23.1	23.7
Discharge firearm with intent	100	47.0	1.0		4.0	2.0	7.0	46.0
Assault peace officer	2 739	91.3	0.5		2.1	2.3	4.9	3.8
Other assaults	1 205	74.0	4.2		2.6	5.3	12.1	13.9
Assault—Total	90 712	55.5	10.6		5.5	3.2	19.3	25.2
Other sexual offences	1 174	42.4	7.3	0.3	5.5	11.0	24.1	33.5
Kidnapping/hostage taking	1 329	63.7	2.9		1.0	1.1	5.0	31.3
Abduction	243	28.4	4.5		10.7	5.3	20.6	51.0
Robbery	21 795	25.4	1.1	1.0	1.4	0.4	3.9	70.6
Extortion	614	48.2	8.1		4.4	2.3	14.8	37.0
Criminal harassment	4 256	46.3	16.2	0.2	5.1	3.9	25.5	28.1
Other	350	30.9	13.7	0.6	10.6	2.6	27.4	41.7
TOTAL VIOLATIONS AGAINST THE PERSON	121 291	49.6	8.9	0.2	4.7	2.8	16.6	33.8
Arson	6 078	8.0	0.6	0.1	3.7	3.3	7.7	84.3
Break and enter	207 536	8.6	0.5	2.0	1.3	0.5	4.2	87.2
Motor vehicle theft	98 673	6.9	0.6	0.7	1.0	0.3	2.6	90.6
Theft over $5000	15 854	8.1	0.8	1.0	1.4	0.5	3.7	88.2
Theft $5000 and under	418 522	12.6	1.3	0.4	2.7	1.0	5.4	82.0
Have stolen goods	13 353	87.7	0.7	0.6	3.0	2.3	6.6	5.7
Fraud	43 591	43.4	4.5	0.9	4.2	3.5	13.1	43.5
Mischief	147 074	7.2	1.5	0.1	1.8	1.0	4.4	88.3
TOTAL VIOLATIONS AGAINST PROPERTY	950 681	12.7	1.2	0.8	2.1	1.0	5.0	82.3
Prostitution	4 250	94.1	—	—	4.1	0.3	4.5	1.4
Disturb the peace	2 033	63.1	3.2	—	13.2	2.5	18.9	18.0
Public morals	3 137	28.8	3.1	0.3	5.4	1.9	10.6	60.7
Firearms, offensive weapons	4 327	68.4	1.2	—	8.9	3.2	13.4	18.2
Threatening/harassing phone calls	14 029	6.6	13.6	0.2	7.8	1.5	23.1	70.2
Offences against the administration of law	60 707	86.0	0.5	1.2	1.5	4.2	7.4	6.6
Other	38 122	28.5	10.6	0.2	5.9	2.8	19.5	52.0
OTHER CRIMINAL CODE VIOLATIONS—TOTAL	126 605	57.8	5.1	0.7	4.2	3.2	13.1	29.1
TOTAL CRIMINAL CODE (excluding traffic)	1 198 577	21.2	2.4	0.7	2.6	1.4	7.1	71.7

Source: Statistics Canada, *Canadian Crime Statistics* 1996, Catalogue 85-205, vol. 20, no. 10, December 1997, p. 71.

1. Homicide characteristics reported to UCR may not match those on the homicide data base. For detailed analysis on homicides in Canada, refer to the Homicide Survey.
2. Other types of "cleared otherwise" include suicide and death on the accused/complainant, reasons beyond the control of the department (e.g., policy), accused is less than 12 years of age, committal of accused to a mental facility, accused is in a foreign country, diplomatic immunity, or the accused has already been sentenced.
3. Not cleared is coded when an accused has not been identified in connection with the incident.
4. CBH is an abbreviation for causing bodily harm.

THE POLICE STYLE

The police role is changing in our society, from one involved predominately with investigating criminal incidents to one involving noncrime activities. The police are becoming more actively involved with crime prevention activities and addressing social problems. Police work can take many different forms, including peacekeeping, law enforcement, emergency medical treatment, etc. Police work is so involved that it cannot be limited to any one form but must encompass all types as parts of the policing process. Part of the socialization of police officers involves the development of a working attitude, or style, through which any individual officer approaches his job. Probably the most successful classification of these styles was created by Wilson (1968). He described four: the social agent, the watchman, the law enforcer, and the crime fighter.

- *The Social Agent:* This style sees the need for police officers to be involved in a range of activities that are not necessarily attached to law enforcement. Instead, officers see themselves as problem-solvers who work with community members. Generally, police officers working in this style are expected by residents to provide protection from outsiders and to respond to their concerns, whether they involve criminal violations or not. Police forces are also expected to direct their law enforcement actions toward strangers while giving local residents great latitude.
- *The Watchman:* The watchman style of policing is best characterized by its emphasis on the maintenance of public order. This style is tolerant of private matters between citizens as well as minor criminal offences. Much is left up to the citizens. If the police respond for a second time to an altercation at an address, they may separate the parties involved but are unlikely to make an arrest unless a major incident occurs. This style of policing involves the restoration of "disruptive situations to normalcy without arresting the citizens involved" and "the management of situational tensions." In these cases the police "move along" drunks to hostels instead of arresting them and escort mentally ill patients to their facilities if they wander away.
- *The Law Enforcer:* enforces all laws to the limit of her authority. All crime-related incidents and suspects are treated in accordance with the formal dictates of the law. This means that all suspects are arrested and charged if enough evidence is found, all traffic violators are issued tickets, and discretion is minimal. This approach involves investigating all criminal incidents; apprehending, interrogating, and charging suspects;

and protecting the constitutional rights of suspects as well, because the law states that this is what police officers are supposed to do.
- *The Crime Fighter:* The most important part of policing for those in this role is the detection and apprehension of criminals. They focus entirely on serious criminals, and they believe that without the "thin blue line" society would fall into chaos. They are opposed to any sort of social service function for the police as this diminishes their effectiveness.

THE PATROL FUNCTION

Police patrol is considered to be the backbone of policing, since all new police personnel are expected to spend the first years of their careers on patrol. Sir Robert Peel introduced police patrols in London, England, in 1829. Peel believed the presence of the police would prevent crime, and this idea became a basic assumption concerning the role and function of patrol officers. The basic purposes of police patrol have hardly changed since 1829, when Sir Robert Peel created the first formal police organization. These purposes include

- the deterrence of crime by maintaining a visible presence;
- the maintenance of public order and a sense of security in the community; and
- the 24-hour provision of services that are not crime-related (Walker 1992).

The first two of these purposes—deterrence and maintaining public order—are almost universally agreed upon as legitimate purposes for the police. The third purpose has been much more controversial, especially when community policing was introduced (see below).

The importance of police patrol cannot be underestimated. It continues to be the essential component of police agencies, since patrol officers are the officers who are visible to the public. The police patrol is designed to achieve a number of purposes, notably the maintenance of a police presence in the community, a quick response to emergencies, and the detection of crime (Langworthy and Travis 1994). Patrol officers fill an important public role because they are so visible in the community. Because they are mobile and located throughout a community, they are usually able to respond quickly to emergencies. Finally, officers on patrol are expected to observe what is going on in the community and prevent potential crime.

The main activities of patrol officers today are many and varied:

1. Deter crime by maintaining a visible police presence.
2. Maintain public order within the patrol area.
3. Enable the police department to respond quickly to law violations or other emergencies.
4. Identify and apprehend law violators.
5. Aid individuals and care for those who cannot help themselves.
6. Facilitate the movement of traffic and people.
7. Create a feeling of security in the community.
8. Obtain statements from crime victims and witnesses.
9. Arrest suspects and transport them to a police facility for investigation (American Bar Association, 1974; Cordner and Hale 1992).

Patrol officers are the most visible component of the police and perhaps of the whole criminal justice system. When a criminal incident occurs, patrol officers are usually the first to arrive and deal with the incident. They are typically seen in marked patrol vehicles but may also patrol on foot, bicycles, or horses. They perform their duties within a designated area, or beat, and rarely leave unless in pursuit of a suspect or to back up other patrol officers. Police beats are patrolled 24 hours a day by different shifts of officers. The activities of patrol officers are hard to enumerate, because their role is, in many ways, generalist—that is, a patrol officer performs a multitude of roles on the job.

Sometimes patrol officers receive a detailed assignment, such as traffic patrol or security checks at business establishments. Their typical role, however, is that of routine observation, in which officers drive around a particular beat and respond to citizens' calls for service. Most of the activities of patrol officers are unrelated to crime. Some observers have estimated that at least 80 percent of all calls for police assistance involve noncrime incidents. This means that officers on patrol commonly deal with issues such as neighbourhood disputes, animal control, noise complaints, and locating lost children.

Toronto police officer Nicole Campbell surveys the city from her "eye in the sky" position aboard one of the force's new helicopters on Sunday, 13 August 2000.

Incident-Driven Patrol

Two developments revolutionized police departments in the 1930s: the police patrol vehicle and two-way communications. New communications technology enabled police patrols to be in constant contact with headquarters, and the motor vehicle allowed them to respond to criminal incidents almost immediately. This led to a type of policing known as incident-driven policing, where the primary role of the police is to respond to citizens' calls for help. Since incident-driven policing was viewed as the most efficient way to organize patrols, police administrators moved all patrol officers into motor vehicles. In addition, it was assumed that the greatest deterrent effects in police operations were random patrols in a patrol beat along with rapid response to criminal incidents.

Incident-driven policing is also known as reactive policing; when the police receive an emergency call a patrol officer is immediately dispatched to the scene of the crime. Patrol officers are also involved with proactive policing by initiating their own crime control activities. Requesting information from citizens or stopping and questioning a citizen who looks like a suspect are examples of this approach to policing. When police departments decide to crack down on the street drug trade or street prostitution, or to set up fencing operations, they are engaged in proactive policing.

Proactive and reactive policing styles are thought to be separate functions of the police, but they may be used in conjunction with each other. For example, in a city experiencing an increasing number of break and enters, when a citizen calls the police after realizing that his residence has been broken into, the police respond by investigating the incident. At the same time, the police could respond proactively by analyzing all such recent incidents in the hope that a pattern emerges. If a pattern is detected, the police may be able to identify potential burglary sites and stake them out.

Deterrence through Patrol Officer Arrests

One of the most significant tests of the deterrent effect of the police has been the study of whether the arrest of an alleged offender reduces crime. Some critics have argued that any formal action by the police can have only a limited deterrent effect on criminal activity (Ross 1982; Walker 1985; Sherman 1990). However, some researchers believed that arrests made by police officers may in fact deter future criminal activity. Shapiro and Votey (1984), for example, discovered that an arrest for drunk driving increases the belief by the offender that he

will be rearrested if he drinks and drives again. Other researchers have not found support for the deterrent effect of arrest (Chamlin 1988).

Jaffe et al. (1991) reported that London, Ontario, police officers responded favourably to a change in arrest policy for domestic violence incidents. They found that in the year prior to the introduction of the mandatory arrest policy, charges were laid in only 2.7 percent of the occurrences involving wife assault. During the first year of the new policy (1981) this figure increased to 67.3 percent, and by 1990 it reached 89 percent. In addition, over the course of the study police officers were found to be less inclined to wait for the victims to file charges, deciding to take the initiative themselves. Choi (1994) discovered that Toronto police officers, as well as members of the Ontario Provincial Police, were more likely to arrest the domestic violence suspect when (1) the victim accuses the suspect of an assault; (2) the victim requests charges to be laid; (3) the suspect used a weapon during the assault; and (4) the suspect is hostile to the officers who attend. His study indicates that if police arrests are to have a deterrent effect on domestic violence, it is essential for victims to start the legal process by laying a formal complaint.

Methods of Police Patrol

As we have seen, while police officers are on patrol they can engage in numerous activities, such as traffic control, investigating complaints, and making arrests. Although these activities have been done for decades, the organization of patrol has recently taken a variety of approaches.

Directed Patrol

Directed patrol is the type of patrol in which officers spend some of their time in certain locations and watch for specific crimes. This type of patrol is usually a result of crime analysis information. Results of directed patrols indicate that the police can reduce the target crime, although it is not known if directed patrols actually reduce crime or force it into other areas.

One form of directed patrol is referred to as "hot spots" patrol. This requires an analysis of all incoming calls based on their geographical origin. The Neighbourhood Foot Patrol Program (NFPP) in Edmonton in 1987 was largely based on an analysis of calls for service. Through an analysis of 153 000 calls for service in 1986, the 21 "hottest" areas of the city were located. Over 80 percent of the calls in these areas came from repeat addresses. Twenty-one foot patrol officers were then permanently assigned to a beat that encompassed a hot spot. The presence of foot patrol officers was supplemented by 80 motor vehicle patrol officers. One year after the creation of the NFPP, the number of calls coming from those addresses that accounted for at least two calls the year before was examined. A slight reduction in the number of calls to repeat addresses (from 4014 to 3918) was noted, as well as a reduction in the total number of calls (from 21 001 to 19 612) (Koller 1990; Hornick et al. 1993).

Foot Patrol

Once the mainstay of police forces in the late-19th and early-20th centuries, foot patrol all but disappeared with the introduction of motor vehicle patrol in the 1930s. However, foot patrols began to reappear in the late 1970s in response to citizens' complaints about the lack of contact with patrol officers in motor vehicles. A common feature of foot patrols today is their emphasis on greater interaction with the community and the solving of underlying community problems that may lead to crime and disorder. Most municipal police forces in Canada today have foot patrols, although many forces maintain such patrols only in the downtown core or other densely populated areas.

An experiment involving foot patrol officers in Flint, Michigan, became the source of renewed interest across North America (Trojanowicz et al. 2001). An evaluation of the Flint Neighborhood Foot Patrol Program revealed that although foot patrol may reduce crime only slightly, it lead to a significant reduction in citizens' fear of crime and a positive change in police–citizen relationships. For example, it was discovered foot patrol lowered crime rates by about 9 percent in all categories of crimes except burglary and robbery, both of which increased by about 10 percent. Calls for service decreased by more than 40 percent and public support for the police increased. After four years, 64 percent of the citizens surveyed indicated they were satisfied with the police, and 68 percent felt safer in their neighbourhood.

Police forces in Canada have implemented a variety of foot patrols. In Toronto, Division 31 police commanders instituted foot patrols in the Jane–Finch area in 1977 to "defuse escalating tensions between the police and, in particular, members of the ethnic community" (Asbury 1989: 165). This area was selected for its long history of tension between police and community, its high population density, and its high rate of serious crime. Foot patrol officers designed and became involved in various "community-building" activities in an attempt to help residents increase community cohesion and gain control of their community. Some residents reported "a 1000 percent" (Asbury 1989: 165) improvement in the community after the introduction of foot patrols and felt much safer.

Another major foot patrol initiative came from the Edmonton Police Force and its Neighbourhood Foot Patrol Program (NFPP). Twenty-one foot patrol areas were selected on the basis of calls for service (see Directed Patrol, above). The results of this program have been mostly positive, but an evaluation of the program discovered that it worked best in stable middle-class neighbourhoods and not as well in the inner city (Bayley 1993). A survey of users of police services in these 21 beats revealed that foot patrol was favoured over motor vehicle patrol. In addition, foot patrol officers held a higher degree of satisfaction with their job than did motor vehicle patrol officers.

The evidence to date indicates that if foot patrol is to be successful, it must operate in locations with large numbers of community members, such as in shopping centres, high-density neighbourhoods, and the downtown core. The size of the foot patrol beat should be small, in some instances covering no more than a few blocks, thereby enabling the police to walk their beat area at least once a day (Trojanowicz et al. 2001).

Does Preventive Patrol Deter Crime?

One of the main purposes of police patrol is to prevent crime. That is, the presence of officers on general patrol in marked vehicles was assumed to prevent criminal activity, thereby reducing the crime rate. This assumption was one of the main principles of the professional model of policing, and as a result police organizations used marked patrol vehicles as their main operational activity to deter crime. During the late 1960s and early 1970s critics of the presumed effects of preventive policing argued that this mainstay of policing operations did not reduce the crime rate as espoused by its supporters. This assumption had never been empirically evaluated until 1972 and 1973, when the Kansas City Police Department conducted perhaps the most famous of all police patrol studies, the Kansas City Preventive Patrol Experiment (Kelling et al. 1974). The results of this study forever changed how patrol officers in marked vehicles were used in both Canada and the United States.

During the one-year evaluation, the police studied the effects of preventive patrols by applying different patrol strategies in different areas. Three types of patrol were instituted: reactive, proactive, and control (that is, preventive patrol). The reactive beats involved no preventive patrol activity whatsoever. Patrol officers who worked reactive patrol beats entered their beat only to respond to calls for assistance. When not responding to calls, the patrol officers patrolled neighbouring proactive police beats. Proactive beats were assigned two to three times the number of police patrol units through the addition of patrol vehicles from the reactive beats. Proactive patrols were highly visible, and the officers patrolled in an aggressive style, meaning they stopped vehicles and citizens if they felt there was reason to do so. The control beats maintained the normal level of patrols that were operational at that time—one car per beat.

Before this study started, most observers felt proactive patrols would be the most successful in reducing crime and improving citizens' feelings of safety, because of the greater number of patrol vehicles and the more aggressive patrol approach. But the results, after one year, did not support this idea. In fact, the results revealed that the different types of patrol did not affect (1) crime rates (as measured by the number of burglaries, motor vehicle thefts, thefts including motor vehicle accessories, robberies, and vandalism, all considered to be highly deterrable crimes), (2) citizens' attitudes toward police services, (3) citizens' fear of crime, or (4) rates of reported crimes. These findings were both revealing and controversial.

They were revealing because police departments had always considered routine preventive patrol to be the most effective approach to patrolling. Yet the results of this study concluded that preventive patrol was no more effective than reactive patrol, and adding more patrol units (as in the case of proactive units) does not automatically lead to a reduction of crime rates or citizens' fear of crime. As Klockars and Mastrofski (1991: 131) state, this experiment led to the conclusion that it "makes about as much sense to have police patrol routinely in cars to fight crime as it does to have firemen patrol routinely in fire trucks to fight fire." The results were controversial because they questioned traditional assumptions about preventive patrol. Although it is necessary to have police patrols, the presence of more patrol officers didn't lower the crime rates. This finding led to the "mayonnaise theory" of police patrol, which states that the quantity of police patrols is similar to the amount of mayonnaise required to make a sandwich (meaning having some mayonnaise is just enough). If an area has no patrol, starting one there will reduce the crime rate, but adding more patrols to an area that already has some appears to have little, if any, impact on crime. This study gave police managers a reason to maintain a constant level of vehicles on patrol, but at the same time it allowed administrators to experiment with alternative tactics and strategies.

According to Walker (1994), there are several reasons why increasing police patrols has so limited an impact on crime. First, patrol officers are spread so thinly across a beat that a patrol vehicle may be seen only on chance encounters rather than as a daily occurrence. Second, many crimes are not deterrable by police patrols. Crimes that occur in residences, such as murders, sexual assaults, and child abuse, won't stop because more police are patrolling the streets. Finally, some people are not deterred by increasing numbers of police. Robbers, for example, will change their approach to committing an offence rather than stop their criminal behaviour altogether (Desroches 1995).

CRIMINAL INVESTIGATIONS

Criminal investigation is the second main function of the police. After a crime is committed and the offender has left the scene, patrol officers conduct a preliminary investigation and then detectives take over in an attempt to find the offender. In most mid- to large-size police services today, detectives comprise approximately 15 to 20 percent of all personnel. Detectives have not been the focus of as much study as patrol officers, since the bulk of their work is law enforcement, and very little of their time goes into service and order maintenance activities. Detectives are usually organized in a different division of a police agency than patrol officers. Usually detectives are assigned to sections specializing in a particular type of criminal activity, such as vice operations (gambling, homicide, robbery, and prostitution) or support services, such as a polygraph operator. While most detective work is reactive, detectives are involved in proactive activities too, such as vice squads and sting squads. A vice squad may pose a police officer as a prostitute in order to arrest customers, or, in a sting operation, detectives may set up an operation that buys stolen goods and videotape everyone who brings in stolen goods.

One of the most important aspects of detective work has been technological advancement in such areas as DNA identification methods. These improvements in technology have allowed detectives to maintain their high clearance rate in certain criminal activities such as murders. Over 80 percent of all murders in Canada are solved by police in the year they were committed. In contrast, in the United States this figure dropped from a clearance rate of 86 percent in 1968 to 64 percent in 1998. The reason for the lower clearance rate in the United States is thought to derive from the fact that strangers are responsible for more murders than they were three decades ago and their identity is harder to detect (Parker and Fields 2000).

The Detective Function

The "ideal" criminal case is one where the offender is arrested at the scene by a patrol officer, there are numerous witnesses, and the suspect quickly confesses to her actions. Such cases are, of course, rare, and so detectives are typically investigate by collecting evidence through personal interviews of the victim and witnesses, doing background checks on potential suspects, and by waiting for an analysis of any forensic evidence available at the crime scene. According to Eck (1983), detectives categorize cases into three types:

- *Unsolvable cases:* these cases are considered to be "weak" in the sense that they cannot be solved regardless of the amount of effort put into investigation.
- *Solvable cases:* these cases can be solved with a moderate to considerable amount of investigation effort.
- *Already solved cases:* these cases have strong evidence and so can be solved with a minimum of investigation effort.

Studies have discovered that cases with moderate levels of evidence can be successfully solved. For example, Brandl and Frank (1994) examined a number of robbery and burglary cases and found that detectives were able to successfully solve most of the cases that had a moderate level of evidence.

If patrol officers are unable to solve a serious crime at the scene, detectives assume control over the case. The first step in the detection process is the preliminary investigation. If the case was committed some time previously, detectives will receive a file from the patrol division. But if the crime just occurred, detectives will arrive to secure the crime scene (i.e., the physical area that may contain potential evidence, such as weapons and any physical evidence such as fingerprints, bloodstains, clothing fibres, and hair samples that can be sent to forensics for analysis) (see Exhibit 5.1). Statements are also taken from any witnesses and photographs are taken of any relevant information. Any evidence collected is placed into evidence bags. In addition, investigators will commonly walk through the crime scene, trying to recreate the crime as it might have happened. This enables them to determine the location of the victim as well as the offender at the time of the incident, the place of entry and exit, whether there are signs of forced entry, etc. All relevant information must be documented by taking written notes.

If a suspect is arrested at the scene, detectives interrogate the suspect to provide prosecutors with enough information and evidence to prosecute. If the case remains unsolved, detectives and their superiors have to determine if they will pursue the investigation any further. This decision is based on what is referred to as "solvability factors," such as any witnesses or the available forensic evidence.

Aggressive Detective Investigation Tactics

Detectives solve a case through various means. In contrast to the mostly reactive actions of patrol officers, these actions are proactive in nature. If the case involves a significant piece of property, such as jewellery or an expensive motor vehicle, detectives may choose to set up a "sting" operation, so that the offender thinks the undercover officers (called "fences") are purchasing stolen property. The "buy" will be videotaped in order to make a strong case for prosecutors and also establish they conducted themselves within the parameters of the law.

Police may also decide to "go undercover" in order to obtain information concerning the crime. This is standard fare for certain types of crimes today, such as narcotic operations or criminal organizations. Or police may try to either get an individual to become an informant in an attempt to get the suspect to confess or get a member of the suspected group or criminal organization to become an informant. In recent years, the police have been able convince members of organized criminal groups to give them evidence about their activities, leading to arrests of significant individuals in the top echelons of these groups. Without this information, it would be almost impossible for the police to infiltrate these organizations, and, if they did, many more years before they could be a witness to any criminal activity. However, the use of informants has been carefully scrutinized in recent years by the Supreme Court of Canada since the police have used various "dirty tricks" to obtain confessions or other evidence.

POLICING MODERN SOCIETY

Due to concerns about the proper role of the police in contemporary society, police administrators and analysts began to study what was wrong with traditional styles of policing and to develop and experiment with new ones. By the mid-1980s, two decades of research had revealed the limits of traditional styles of policing: police patrols didn't reduce the crime rate, detectives didn't solve a lot of crimes, and arrests didn't necessarily deter would-be criminals. The majority of police work remained reactive, but that didn't seem to work well. Surveys discovered citizens didn't report crimes to the police and that victims had lost faith in the police to respond quickly

EXHIBIT 5.1   DNA and Criminal Justice

As pointed out earlier in this chapter, the role of forensics (i.e., the application of science to criminal investigations) plays a key role in the detection of criminals by the police. In fact, it has become a standard part of many police investigations, with many different techniques available to investigators. These include lighting a crime scene with ultraviolet light to detect hidden fingerprints, footprints, and blood stains. DNA has also been used to reopen cases where individuals have already been convicted of a crime and are serving their sentences. DNA analysis has assisted in the acquittal of persons already serving a sentence for the crime, including Guy Paul Morin, David Milgaard, and Thomas Sophonow. In the United States, by 2000 there were at least 74 cases in which DNA had established that an innocent person had been wrongfully convicted (Scheck et al. 2000).

DNA is deoxyribonucleic acid, the genetic material that carries the code for all living cells. DNA is useful to criminal investigators since the DNA of one individual is different from the DNA of all other individuals (except identical twins). DNA is therefore often called the "genetic blueprint" or "genetic code." Through DNA profiling, forensic scientists test DNA samples in order to test whether they match with the DNA profile of a known offender.

The first use of DNA to secure a criminal conviction occurred in England in 1986 in the case of Colin Pitchfork, who was convicted on the basis of DNA evidence for the murder of two schoolgirls. Two years later, the FBI in the United States successfully used it to establish guilt. In Canada, DNA was first used in 1989 by the RCMP in an investigation when the suspect denied any involvement in a sexual assault, although the victim identified him as the attacker. After learning of the results of the DNA test, the suspect pleaded guilty. The first Canadian case in which the DNA results were openly debated in court didn't occur until a few years later, when Alan Legere was convicted of four murders on the basis of DNA profiling (*R. v. Legere* (1994)).

Today in Canada, law enforcement agencies are allowed to collect DNA samples from offenders who have been convicted of specific crimes in order that they can be stored in a national database. Two pieces of legislation relevant to DNA have been passed by Parliament. The first piece of legislation (passed in 1995) established a statutory basis for securing DNA evidence, and the second created the national data bank, which was proclaimed in 2000. This latter piece of legislation also allowed law enforcement

officials to set up two databases, thereby allowing for the cross-referencing of information. The first database (the Crime Scene Index) contains DNA profiles from the bodily substances found at a crime scene, and the second database (the Convicted Offender Index) collects DNA profiles of individuals who have been convicted of specific crimes, such as murder, sexual assault, and break and enter. The legislation also allows for DNA samples to be taken from individuals who have already been convicted but are considered to be dangerous offenders or who have been convicted of more than one sexual offence or murder (Hiebert 2002). By the end of 2001, the DNA data bank contained approximately 8000 DNA samples, along with about 2000 samples from crime scenes. During this same time period, the information entered in the DNA database identified seven different crimes as having been committed by the same person and made 18 matches of convicted offenders to crime scenes.

DNA has transformed (some say revolutionized) many aspects of policing. One commentator stated that it is "a scientific miracle for human justice" that "shines the light of irrefutable truth into our courtrooms and juries" (Wickham 2000: 15A). The main issue raised concerned whether or not individuals who were arrested for committing crimes would be required to give a DNA sample prior to being convicted. In 1990 Ontario government officials suggested taking DNA samples from all those charged with a crime. They based their proposal on the fact that accused persons are denied liberty in other areas involving preconviction, such as the police taking fingerprints. The officials also wanted to have DNA samples taken from every person already incarcerated. However, federal legislation specifies that only those individuals convicted of specific crimes would have to give a DNA sample.

Other critics argued that DNA sampling would infringe upon the legal rights of offenders. Concerns focused on how the police would obtain consent from the suspect or whether they perhaps use an illegal seizure to obtain it. In *R. v. Borden* (1994), the Supreme Court of Canada ruled that the police had not given the suspect sufficient information about the charges before obtaining a DNA sample. To rectify this situation, Parliament introduced legislation (Bill C-104) authorizing the police to obtain a warrant to collect DNA evidence.

Sources: Blackwell (2000); Scheck et al. (2000); Wickham (2000); Royal Canadian Mounted Police (2001); Hiebert (2002).

and effectively. If the police did respond, many citizens remained uninformed about the case until they were notified to appear at a preliminary hearing or court trial. Further, officers became removed from the concerns of the neighbourhood, and as a result seemed unreliable, with the result that citizens didn't call the police to report crimes and lived with significant fear of crime (Sherman 1986).

At the same time, some communities took to hiring private security companies to protect them from criminals because of their lack of faith in the ability of the police to do so (Shearing 1992). As a result, some police administrators felt there was a need for fundamental change. What emerged is community policing, which attempts to close the gap between the police and the community.

There are many types of community policing, and almost all police forces in Canada practice at least some aspect of it. In fact, community policing is seen by many as the future style of policing. How did this new type of policing develop in such a short time?

The Broken Windows Model

The start of the community policing era can be traced to an article written by two police scholars (Kelling and Wilson 1982) in a popular American magazine. The article, titled "Broken Windows: The Police and Neighborhood Safety," appeared in a 1982 issue of *The Atlantic Monthly*. This article argued that the police cannot combat crime successfully themselves. Instead, community assistance and support is necessary—and, most importantly, the basic police role must change to allow for community involvement in policing. The

A police officer in Vancouver

article introduced the concept of disorder to policing, making the point that disorder, if left unchallenged, signals that no one cares. Disorder then increases and, as a result, crime (including violent crime) increases also. The police had traditionally ignored this element of community life, since it was not part of the professional model of policing.

The broken windows model argues that social incivilities (for example, loitering, public drinking) and physical incivilities (for example, vacant lots, abandoned buildings) cause residents and workers in a neighbourhood to be fearful of crime. This fear causes some residents to move out and others to live in fear and isolate themselves. The model has three components:

1. *Neighbourhood disorder creates fear.* Those areas in a city that are filled with criminals such as drug dealers are the areas that are most likely to have a high crime rate.
2. *Neighbourhoods give out crime-promoting signals.* This means that the appearance of a community can attract criminals. Deteriorated housing, disorderly behaviour, and unrepaired broken windows send the message that no one in the area cares about the quality of life. That message attracts criminals, who feel they can go about their business without interference from the local residents.
3. *Police need citizens' cooperation.* If the police are to reduce fear of crime and the crime rate, their policies must include the involvement and cooperation of local citizens.

This approach proposed that there is a significant correlation between disorder and perceived crime problems in a neighbourhood. This type of reasoning is found at the basis of Ontario's *Safe Streets Act* (see Chapter 2), which targets panhandlers, the homeless, and squeegee kids as significant sources of disorder. Proponents of these types of laws point to the research from community policing projects that have reported that both serious crimes and fear of crime can be alleviated by reducing disorder (Skogan 1990; Pate et al. 1986). The broken windows model recommends police administrators change some of their policies to include local residents in decisions about policing priorities in their neighbourhoods. This model also indicated that other areas of policing that had been largely ignored during the previous four decades would have to be reviewed to reduce the level of fear of crime, increase the levels of safety, and develop order maintenance policies. These should become the main focus of the police—patrol officers in particular.

Problem-Oriented Policing

In 1979 Herman Goldstein published an article in which he laid out a new style of policing that he called problem-oriented policing. This style of policing, according to Goldstein, represented a fundamental change in the way the police operate. Rather than spend most of their time responding to citizens' calls about criminal incidents, the police would direct their energy to the causes of crimes and complaints in an attempt to modify these sources. This involved a fundamental shift in the way the police operated. They began to study the underlying causes of crime, for unless those causes are modified or eliminated the problem will persist, leading to more criminal incidents and citizens' greater fear of crime.

What is a problem? Although it is easy to point to criminal acts as problems, the essence of problem-oriented policing are those situations that are perceived as leading to criminal activity. Five principles of problem-oriented policing have been identified, all of which take the police away from an incident-based focus to one that emphasizes the potential sources of criminal activity.

- A problem is something that concerns the community and its citizens, not just police officers.
- A problem is a group or pattern of incidents and therefore demands a different set of responses than does a single incident.
- A problem must be understood in terms of the competing interests at stake.
- Responding to a problem involves more than a "quick fix," such as an arrest. Problem-solving is a long-term strategy.
- Problem-solving requires a heightened level of creativity and initiative on the part of the patrol officer (Bureau of Justice Assistance 1993).

As problem-oriented policing came into practice, four stages in the problem-solving process were developed. The first is referred to as scanning, where a police officer identifies an issue and then assesses whether it really is a problem. In the second stage, analysis, the officer collects as much information as possible about the problem. In the next stage, response, all relevant information is collected by an officer to initiate the development and implementation of solutions. In the final stage, assessment, police officers collect information about the effectiveness of their approach, changing tactics if doing so is considered necessary, or even developing an entirely new approach.

Community Policing

One flaw of the problem-oriented approach is that the police didn't always include the community when studying a crime problem. As Moore and Trojanowicz (1988: 5) point out, community policing involves community groups, such as business people, residents, and school teachers, as "key partners … in the creation of safe, secure communities. The success of the police depends not only on the development of their own skills and capabilities, but also on the creation of competent communities."

The goal of this style of policing was not to fight crime but to encourage public safety and confidence, reduce citizens' fear of crime, and encourage citizen involvement. The development of community support would be facilitated by decentralized, neighbourhood-based policing operating out of mini-stations or storefronts.

An important goal of community policing is to reduce the fear of crime in the community. Fear of crime has been divided into three types. First is the intense fear suffered by the victims of crime as well as their family, friends, and neighbours. This fear comes from physical injury, property loss, economic costs (such as medical bills and loss of wages at work), and psychological trauma such as depression and anxiety. Some victims also suffer from what has been called "double victimization"—that is, when they report the crime they are treated as second-class citizens by agencies in the criminal justice system.

The second type of fear is known as the concrete fear of crime, which refers to fear of specific crimes, especially violent crimes. Studies have identified high-risk groups—people who live in large urban areas, the young, women, and racial minorities—who are most susceptible to concrete fear. They fear being sexually assaulted, physically assaulted, robbed, and murdered. The third type of fear—formless fear—is the feeling that one is unsafe. Research has found groups displaying the highest levels of formless fear include the elderly, the marginally employed, and those with low incomes. Studies focusing on the fear of crime note that while people are afraid of serious crime, they are just as concerned, if not more concerned, about petty crimes and social disorder. In the past, the police failed to understand that when people say they are afraid of crime, they are talking about all types of crime and disorder, not just serious, violent crimes (Trojanowicz et al. 2001).

To community police officers, the reduction in the fear of crime is an essential component of their job. It's also a way to increase citizen–police cooperation. A variety of techniques can be employed to reduce the fear of crime in a community, including a police–community newsletter, a police–community contact centre staffed by patrol officers and civilians, and a variety of programs in which police officers contact victims of crime to inform them of police action on the case. Whatever programs are developed, the most successful allow officers the time to identify key issues with local residents and to use both personal initiative and community input to solve problems. Although not all programs are successful, evidence shows that foot patrol officers are actually able to reduce the level of fear in the community.

Criticisms of Community Policing

Many evaluations have been made of community policing over its several-decades existence. Most observers recognize the benefits of community-based policing far outweigh its shortcomings, but a number of criticisms arise. These criticisms state that community policing is not necessarily the crime control panacea its advocates say it is, and problems remain. The first criticism is that community policing seems to include almost any type of proactive activity by the police since it lacks a comprehensive definition. The fact that it is a philosophy rather than a concise set of operational procedures is damaging to its overall integrity, since this has led to a dilution of this approach by police services introducing endless programs under this rubric.

A second criticism focuses on the amount of community policing that becomes part of the everyday operations of the police. Community policing has become a "buzzword," but critics point out that it may be more rhetoric than an approach that has taken over the operational philosophy of the police. They point to the fact that the two most common programs implemented by the police identified as community policing are the Drug Abuse Resistance Education (DARE) program and foot patrols, both of which existed long before community policing emerged.

Another criticism is that studies of community policing reveal that police officers spent more time on paperwork and other administrative duties than talking to members of the community or developing programs specific to the needs of the community (Parks et al. 1999). Others point out that community policing will never be accepted because it advocates a change in the command structure, thereby reducing the number of higher-level positions (Lewis et al. 1999). There are also problems associated with the police being able to define exactly what a community really is and that the roles of community police officers remain poorly integrated into the rest of the police organization (Halsted et al. 2000).

Zero Tolerance: Aggressive Policing

In recent years, policing has seen another emerging type of policing—zero tolerance policing. Zero tolerance policing is actually a variant of problem-oriented policing, but instead of combating a problem by analyzing various features about it within the community, the police decide to eliminate most of the analysis stage and apply traditional law enforcement methods to solve the problem. The central concern with this style of policing is order maintenance, and it narrows police attention to suppressing those individuals who are perceived as the main sources of disorder.

To eliminate disorder, the police decide to pursue an aggressive policy throughout certain designated neighbourhoods with disorder problems. This means a confrontive style of policing, as the police target those individuals they feel are responsible for disorder and incivility within the community.

Zero tolerance policing gained attention of police services across Canada and the United States after the results of this program were published by the New York City Police Department. This style of policing started shortly after Mayor Rudolph Guiliani took office in 1993, as he had promised the citizens of New York City that it would become a safe place to inhabit. He then hired a new police commissioner, William Bratton, who had previously been the police chief in Boston. Bratton radically altered the way the New York Police Department (NYPD) approached crime. He created the CompStat program, which placed crime data into the hands of precinct commanders. These individuals were held accountable if crime rates did not decline within a certain period of time, and they were replaced if their actions were not deemed adequate. Bratton also increased the powers of police officers to stop, search, and question individuals who had violated the law, even if their infraction was minor. He believed that by stopping and questioning suspects, the police might discover a weapon or information that could assist in solving a crime or prevent a crime from occurring. To accomplish these goals, a large number of police officers were hired, with the NYPD increasing its size by 39.5 percent.

The results of this approach to controlling crime and disorder gained international headlines just a few years later. Official police statistics indicated that there had been a dramatic reduction of 37.4 percent in the crime rate between 1990 and in 1995. Large reductions were recorded in homicides, robberies, and burglaries.

However, there was a price to be paid by introducing zero tolerance policing. Minority neighbourhoods were most often the target of this style of policing, and the number of civil rights complaints against the NYPD increased by 75 percent by the end of 1997. In the same time period, citizen complaints filed with New York's Civilian Complaint Review Board rose by 60 percent. Complaints against the police in cases where no arrests were made doubled by the end of the first year of the program. Amnesty International claimed that this new policing approach had increased police brutality and the use of unjustifiable force.

Despite these accusations, there was considerable interest in the NYPD's tactics because of the decease in the crime rate. Other cities rushed to introduce zero tolerance programs themselves. But although the zero tolerance approach reduced crime in New York (but led to an increase in the number of complaints) it was noted that remarkable reductions in the crime rate were also being recorded in other cities that had not introduced zero tolerance policing. Critics of the NYPD approach pointed to the program practised by the San Diego, California, Police Department (SDPD). It followed a more community-oriented approach to policing crime and disorder by trying to work closely with the community and develop a solution acceptable to both groups. The results of the SDPD program are interesting compared to those in New York City—between 1990 and 1995, both the number of complaints filed by citizens in San Diego and the crime rate dropped 36.8 percent—and the size of the SDPD increased by only 6.8 percent. One of the major determinants of success in San Diego was the effort of the police to rely on the community to participate in planning and crime prevention efforts. The approach taken by New York City, in contrast, alienated the residents of many communities (Greene 1999).

For a comparison of policing types, see Figure 5.1.

ABORIGINAL (FIRST NATIONS) POLICE FORCES

History

One of the earliest undertakings of Aboriginal police services took place in Quebec in 1978, when 25 Aboriginal reserves were policed by a semiautonomous police force known as the Amerindian Police. These forces were created to solve the Aboriginal communities' dependency on outside police forces, a dependency that "increases the likelihood of police interventions and 'criminalizes' behaviors that would not necessarily be considered criminal if other agencies were involved" (Hyde 1992: 370). Aboriginal police forces were founded to give a greater understanding of, and sensi-

tivity to, the issues that confront the peoples living in Aboriginal communities.

Amerindian Police force members were most commonly requested to perform a service function within the community. Approximately 6000 of the total 17 000 requests for police assistance recorded between 1978 and 1983 were for noncriminal incidents. Most were requests for services, with almost 45 percent of these calls resulting in police making referrals to other agencies, such as social and health services, probation officers, and psychiatric specialists. Hyde (1992: 370) believes that "peace keeping, crime prevention, and crisis-intervention functions of the police are, in part, the raison d'être for the establishment of the force."

The crimes committed usually involved the least serious *Criminal Code* and provincial offences. These include public order offences, interpersonal disputes, liquor and drug offences, and break and enters. The most typical police response to an incident is "no charge," meaning the police take no action, while the next most common response is "suspect detained," meaning an individual is detained by the police overnight (Depew 1992). As a result, the Amerindian Police played an important role in the area of crisis intervention as well as in the provision of social services. LaPrairie and Diamond (1992) found many criminal cases were dealt with by going beyond the measures available through the formal criminal justice system. They discovered that only about 33 percent of reported criminal or potential criminal offences were officially recorded, and only 12 percent of those officially recorded made it to court.

During the late 1980s and the early to mid-1990s numerous provincial and federal government inquiries, commissions, and reports focused in whole or in part on the issue of First Nations policing. All were unanimous in their evaluations of policing on First Nations communities—there were inadequate services and major problems regarding the lack of cultural sensitivity of the existing policing arrangements, discriminatory criminal justice techniques being used against First Nations peoples, and little if any crime prevention techniques being introduced into the communities. These reports were divided in their opinion about the best way to correct this situation. Some (e.g., Head 1989) felt that the best solution was to make changes to the existing system while others (e.g., Hamilton and Sinclair 1991) recommended a separate and First Nations–controlled policing service.

Recognizing the importance of Aboriginal police officers on reserves, the federal government created the First Nations Policing Policy in June 1991 to allow

Social Interaction or Structural Dimension	Traditional Policing	Community Policing	Problem-oriented Policing	Zero Tolerance Policing
Focus of Policing	Law enforcement	Community-building through crime prevention	Law, order, and fear problems	Order problems
Forms of Intervention	Reactive, based on criminal law	Proactive, on criminal, civil, and administrative law	Mixed, on criminal, civil, and administrative law	Proactive, uses criminal, civil, and administrative law
Range of Police Activity	Narrow, crime focused	Broad crime, order, fear, and quality-of-life focused	Narrow to broad—problem focused	Narrow, location and behaviour focused
Level of Discretion at Line Level	High and unaccountable	High and accountable to the community and local commanders	High and primarily accountable to the police administration	Low, but primarily accountable to the police administration
Focus of Police Culture	Inward, rejecting community	Outward, building partnerships	Mixed, depending on problem, but analysis focused	Inward, focused on attacking the target problem
Locus of Decision-making	Police directed; minimizes the involvement of others	Community–police coproduction; joint responsibility and assessment	Varied, police identify problems but with community involvement/action	Police directed, some linkage to other agencies where necessary
Communication Flow	Downward from police to community	Horizontal between police and community	Horizontal between police and community	Downward from police to community
Range of Community Involvement	Low and passive	High and active	Mixed, depending on problem set	Low and passive
Linkage with Other Agencies	Poor and intermittent	Participative and integrative in the overarching process	Participative and integrative depending on the problem set	Moderate and intermittent
Type of Organization and Command Focus	Centralized command and control	Decentralized with community linkage	Decentralized with local command accountability to central admission	Centralized or decentralized but internal focus
Implications for Organizational Change/ Development	Few; static organization fending off the environment	Many; dynamic organization focused on the environment and environmental interactions	Varied; focused on problem resolution but with import for organization, intelligence and structure	Few; limited interventions focused on target problems, using many traditional methods
Measurement of Success	Arrest and crime rates, particularly serious Part 1 crimes	Varied; crime calls for service, fear reduction, use of public places, community linkages and contacts, safer neighbourhoods	Varied; problems solved, minimized, displaced	Arrests, field stops, activity, location-specific reductions in targeted activity

FIGURE 5.1

Comparisons of Social Interactions and Structural Components of Various Forms of Policing

Source: Greene (2000), p. 311.

Aboriginal communities more control over the operations and management of policing on reserves (see Exhibit 5.2). The purpose of the First Nations Policing Policy is to improve the administration of justice and the maintenance of social order, public security, and personal safety in Aboriginal communities on reserves. The purpose and objectives of the policy are

1. to contribute to the improvement of social order, public security, and personal safety in First Nations communities, including that of women, children, and other vulnerable groups;

2. to provide a practical way to improve the administration of justice for First Nations through the establishment of First Nations police services that are professional, effective, and responsive to the particular needs of the community;

3. to ensure that First Nations peoples enjoy their right to personal security and public safety. Their safety and security will be achieved through access to policing services that are responsive to their needs and that meet acceptable standards with respect to the quality and level of service;

4. to support First Nations in acquiring the tools to become self-sufficient and self-governing through the establishment of structures for the management, administration, and accountability of First Nations police services; and

5. to implement and administer the First Nations Policy in a manner that promotes partnerships with First Nations based on trust, mutual respect, and participation in decision-making (Solicitor General of Canada 1999).

By 1995, 41 agreements had been signed with 180 First Nations communities. Three years later, 61 percent of the total First Nations population living on reserves—311 bands with a population of 219 000—were under the jurisdiction of the FNPP (Linden et al. 2001). Two options are available to First Nations communities under the First Nations Policing Policy. The first is called a "self-administered police service" (also referred to as a "stand-alone police service"), which allows a community or number of communities to have their own separate police force that is not affiliated with any other police force, whether federal, provincial, or municipal. The second option is to sign an agreement with an existing federal, provincial, or municipal police force.

Of the total number of First Nations communities who had signed an agreement by 1998, 194 (69 percent) were using a self-administered approach to policing (Linden et al. 2001). This approach involves fully trained officers of Aboriginal ancestry providing policing services to a community or communities. Agreements under the FNPP provide for appropriate mechanisms to balance the demands of protecting independent policing services from inappropriate political or partisan influences and allowing for appropriate police accountability. This has led to the creation of First Nations Police Boards and Commissions that administer services in accordance with established policing standards.

Depew (1992) and Metha (1993) point out the relevance of a community-policing approach to Aboriginal communities. This involves a commitment to community planning that takes into consideration "community-level political and economic development to ensure stability and coherence in local social organization and an appropriate legislative framework to sustain intergovernmental cooperation, coordination, and support for new native policing arrangements." However, they point out that the task may be difficult, given the erosion of the community and potentially limited community resources. A major issue is the extent to which a different style of policing—one informed by Aboriginal cultural traditions and "communitarianism" (LaPrairie 1992)—can be developed and autonomously practised in Aboriginal communities.

First Nations communities with high crime rates want their Aboriginal police officers not only to practise community policing but also to be skilled and effective at solving major crimes in their communities. Aboriginal law enforcement officers as well saw the need to have conventional policing skills to perform their jobs. A survey of Aboriginal police officers conducted by Murphy and Clairmont (1996) rated conventional police skills as very important, and indicated they had a need for greater skill training in both general and specialized law enforcement techniques. Some researchers (Hyde 1992; Landau 1996) have questioned the extensive funding that has gone into Aboriginal policing services, a policy they say leads to overpolicing. They believe some of these funds might be better spent on other social policies within the communities.

SUMMARY

Police forces have traditionally been organized in a militaristic way. Many questions arise about the effectiveness of policing, especially patrol work. Police officials have spent the past two decades experimenting with different patrol styles, some of which appear to be effective in catching criminals and deterring further criminal actions.

In order to improve their effectiveness, many police forces introduced community-based policing.

EXHIBIT 5.2   Principles of the First Nations Policing Policy

QUALITY AND LEVEL OF SERVICE

First Nations communities should have access to policing services that are responsive to their particular policing needs and equal in quality and level of service to policing services found in communities with similar conditions in the region. First Nations should have input in determining the level and quality of the police services they are provided.

RESPONSIBILITIES AND AUTHORITIES

Police officers serving First Nations communities should have the same responsibilities and authorities as other police force members in Canada. This means they should have the authority to enforce applicable provincial and federal laws (including the *Criminal Code*), as well as Band by-laws.

RESPONSIVENESS TO FIRST NATIONS CULTURES AND NEEDS

First Nations communities should be policed by such numbers of persons of a similar cultural and linguistic background as are necessary to ensure that police services will be effective and responsive to First Nations cultures and particular policing needs.

POLICE SERVICE OPTIONS

First Nations communities should have access to at least the same police service models that are available to communities with similar conditions in the region. They should also have input in determining the model appropriate to their community.

SELECTION OF POLICE SERVICE MODEL

The selection of a particular model of police service should balance the need for cost-effectiveness and the particular policing needs of First Nations communities.

IMPLEMENTATION OF NEW ARRANGEMENTS

New First Nations administered police services should be phased in over a number of years to facilitate a successful transition.

POLICE ACCOUNTABILITY AND INDEPENDENCE

First Nations communities should have an effective and appropriate role in directing their police service. Therefore, First Nations policing services should include police boards, commissions, and advisory bodies that are representative of the communities they serve. In addition to police management and accountability, these bodies should ensure police independence from partisan and inappropriate political influences.

POLICE OVERSIGHT

Policing mechanisms for First Nations communities should include: mechanisms for impartial and independent review of allegations of improper exercises of police powers and violations of codes of conduct; and mechanisms for grievance and redress on matters related to discipline and dismissal.

LEGISLATIVE FRAMEWORK

First Nations police services should be founded on a legislative framework that enables First Nations to establish, administer, and regulate their police service and to appoint police officers consistent with provincial norms and practices. The federal government will work with the provinces/territories and First Nations to promote legislation in support of First Nations policing where appropriate.

COST-SHARED ARRANGEMENTS

The federal and provincial governments, because they share jurisdiction, should share the cost of First Nations policing services. Within the funds available, the federal government should provide such funding support as is necessary to promote national standards and to support the aforementioned principles on the basis of consistent and equitable funding arrangements.

POLICE OVERSIGHT

Policing mechanisms for First Nations communities should include: mechanisms for impartial and independent review of allegations of improper exercises of police powers and violations of codes of conduct; and mechanisms for grievance and redress on matters related to discipline and dismissal.

LEGISLATIVE FRAMEWORK

First Nations police services should be founded on a legislative framework that enables First Nations to establish, administer, and regulate their police service and to appoint police officers consistent with provincial norms and practices. The federal government will work with the provinces/territories and First Nations to promote legislation in support of First Nations policing where appropriate.

COST-SHARED ARRANGEMENTS

The federal and provincial governments, because they share jurisdiction, should share the cost of First Nations policing services. Within the funds available, the federal government should provide such funding support as is necessary to promote national standards and to support the aforementioned principles on the basis of consistent and equitable funding arrangements.

Source: Solicitor General of Canada (1999).

Although the nature of this type of policing varies, most services include the elements of community involvement and problem-solving. These new approaches have led many police forces into a new era of policing in which they use their resources differently in an attempt to achieve better results. Although these new models have established themselves as the future of policing in our society, many issues have yet to be resolved. Police forces are reluctant to change their organizational structure, particularly in any way that would decentralize their decision-making authority and share that authority with the community.

In recent decades Aboriginal police forces have emerged in an attempt to deal more effectively with the issues facing individuals who live in Aboriginal communities. In many ways, the members of those forces are peacekeepers, because they combine the role of police officer, social worker, and community activist. The origins of Aboriginal policing are found in the community policing model.

Discussion Questions

1. What should be the primary function of the police in our society?

2. Should the police become more proactive? If so, how could this be accomplished, and what would the impact be?

3. What are the problems and benefits associated with a highly structured model of police organization?

4. Would there be benefits to a decentralized model of police organization? Why do you think many officers resist attempts to move police departments toward a community policing model?

5. Can the efficiency of detectives be increased? How?

6. Discuss the positive aspects of community policing for the police and the public. Can the police and community ever form a unified front to fight crime?

7. Discuss how problem-oriented policing led some police forces to practise zero tolerance policing.

8. Discuss the impact of Aboriginal police forces. What are the benefits of Aboriginal police forces? Should each province have a unified Aboriginal police force for all Aboriginal communities?

Suggested Readings

Chacko, J., and S.E. Nancoo, eds. 1993. *Community Policing in Canada.* Toronto: Criminal Justice Press.

Forcese, P. 1992. *Policing Canadian Society.* Scarborough, Ont.: Prentice-Hall.

Martin, M.A. 1995. *Urban Policing in Canada: Anatomy of an Aging Craft.* Montreal: McGill–Queen's University Press.

Metha, V. 1993. *Policing Services for Aboriginal Peoples.* Ottawa: Ministry of the Solicitor General.

Stansfield, R.T. 1996. *Issues in Policing: A Canadian Perspective.* Toronto: Thompson Educational Publishing.

Trojanowicz, R.C., V. Kappeler, and L. Gaines. 2001. *Community Policing: A Contemporary Perspective,* 3rd ed. Cincinnati: Anderson.

References

American Bar Association. 1974. *Standards Relating to Urban Police Function.* New York: Institute of Judicial Administration.

Appleby, T. 1999. "Target Policing Hits Uncertain Mark." *The Globe and Mail,* 18 October, A6.

Asbury, K.E. 1989. "Innovative Policing: Foot Patrol in 31 Division, Metropolitan Toronto." *Canadian Police College Journal* 13: 165–81.

Bayley, D.H. 1993. "Strategy." In J. Chacko and S.E. Nancoo, eds., *Community Policing in Canada.* Toronto: Canadian Scholars' Press, pp. 39–46.

Blackwell, T. 2000. "Collect DNA from All Charged with a Crime, Ontario Urges." *National Post,* 9 September, A4.

Braiden, C. 1993. "Community-Based Policing: A Process for Change." In J. Chacko and S.E. Nancoo, eds., *Community Policing in Canada.* Toronto: Canadian Scholars' Press, pp. 211–32.

Brandl, S., and J. Frank. 1994. "The Relationship between Evidence, Detective Work, and the Dispositions of Burglary and Robbery Investigations." *American Journal of Police* 13, no. 3: 149–68.

Brannigan, A. 1984. *Crime, Courts, and Corrections: An Introduction to Crime and Social Control in Canada.* Toronto: Holt, Rinehart and Winston.

Browne, L., and C. Browne. 1973. *An Unauthorized History of the RCMP.* Toronto: James Lewis and Samuel.

Bureau of Justice Assistance. 1993. *Problem-Oriented Drug Enforcement: A Community-Based Approach for Effective Policing.* Washington, D.C.: Office of Justice Programs.

Chamlin, M. 1988. "Crime and Arrests: An Autoregressive Integrated Moving Average (CARIMA) Approach." *Journal of Quantitative Criminology* 4: 245–55.

Choi, A. 1994. *An Examination of Police Intervention in Domestic Disturbances in a Canadian Context.* Lampeter, Wales: Edwin Mellen Press.

Clairmont, D. 1990. *To the Forefront: Community-Based Zone Policing in Halifax.* Ottawa: Canadian Police College.

Cordner, G.W., and D.C. Hale. 1992. *What Works in Policing? Operations and Administration Examined.* Cincinnati: Anderson.

Depew, R. 1992. "Policing Native Communities: Some Principles and Issues in Organizational Theory." *Canadian Journal of Criminology* 34, nos. 3–4: 461–78.

Desroches, F.J. 1995. *Force and Fear: Robbery in Canada.* Scarborough, Ont.: Nelson Canada.

Eck, J.E. 1992. "Criminal Investigation." In G.W. Cordner and D.C. Hale, eds., *What Works in Policing? Operations and Administration Examined.* Cincinnati: Anderson, pp. 26–33.

———. 1983. *Solving Crimes: The Investigation of Burglary and Robbery.* Washington, D.C.: Police Executive Research Forum.

Eck, J.E., and W. Spelman. 1987. "Problem-Solving: Problem-Oriented Policing in Newport News." *Research in Brief.* Washington, D.C.: National Institute of Justice.

Ericson, R. 1982. *Reproducing Order: A Study of Police Patrol Work.* Toronto: University of Toronto Press.

———. 1981. *Making Crime: A Study of Detective Work.* Toronto: University of Toronto Press.

Filyer, R.E. 2002. *Police Resources in Canada, 2001.* Ottawa: Canadian Centre for Justice Statistics.

Goldstein, H. 1979. "Improving Policing: A Problem-Oriented Approach." *Crime and Delinquency* 25: 236–58.

Greene, J. 2000. "Community Policing in America: Changing the Nature, Structure, and Function of the Police." In *Criminal Justice 2000*, vol. 3. Washington, D.C.: National Institute of Justice, pp. 299–370.

———. 1999. "Zero Tolerance: A Case Study of Police Policies and Practices in New York City." *Crime and Delinquency* 45: 171–88.

Guth, D.J. 1994. "The Traditional Common-Law Constable 1235–1829: From Bracton to the Fieldings of Canada." In R.C. Macleod and D. Schneiderman, eds., *Police Powers in Canada: The Evolution and Practice of Authority*. Toronto: University of Toronto Press.

Halsted, A., M. Bromley, and J. Cochran. 2000. "The Effects of Work Orientations and Job Satisfaction among Sheriffs' Deputies." *Policing* 23: 82–104.

Hamilton, A.C., and C.M. Sinclair. 1991. *The Justice System and Aboriginal People: Report of the Aboriginal Justice Inquiry of Manitoba, Volume 1*. Winnipeg: Queen's Printer.

Head, R. 1989. *Policy for Aboriginal Canadians: The RCMP Role*. Ottawa: Royal Canadian Mounted Police.

Hickman, Chief Justice T.A., Associate Chief Justice L.A. Poitras, and the Honourable G.T. Evans, Q.C. 1989. *Royal Commission on the Donald Marshall, Jr., Prosecution*, vol. 1. Ottawa: Ministry of Supply and Services.

Hiebert, J.L. 2002. *Charter Conflicts: What Is Parliament's Role?* Montreal: McGill-Queen's University Press.

Hornick, J.P., B.A. Burrows, D.M. Phillips, and B. Leighton. 1993. "An Impact Evaluation of the Edmonton Neighbourhood Foot-Patrol Program." In J. Chacko and S.E. Nancoo, eds., *Community Policing in Canada*. Toronto: Canadian Scholars' Press, pp. 311–32.

Hyde, M. 1992. "Servicing Indian Reserves: The Amerindian Police." *Canadian Journal of Criminology* 34, nos. 3–4: 369–86.

Jaffe, P., D. Reitzel, E. Hastings, and G. Austin. 1991. *Wife Assault as a Crime: The Perspectives of Victims and Police Officers on a Changing Policy in London, Ontario from 1989–1990*. London, Ont.: London Family Court.

Kelling, G.L., and M.H. Moore. 1988. *Perspectives on Policing*. Washington, D.C.: National Institute of Justice.

Kelling, G.L., T. Pate, D. Dieckman, and C. Brown. 1974. *The Kansas City Preventive Patrol Experiment: A Summary Report*. Washington, D.C.: Police Foundation Report.

Kelling, G.L., and J.Q. Wilson. 1982. "Broken Windows: The Police and Neighborhood Safety." *Atlantic Monthly*, 249.

Kelly, W., and N. Kelly. 1976. *Policing in Canada*. Toronto: Macmillan.

Koller, K. 1990. *Working the Beat: The Edmonton Neighbourhood Foot Patrol*. Edmonton: Edmonton Police Service.

Landau, T. 1996. "Policing and Security in Four Remote Aboriginal Communities: A Challenge to Coercive Models of Police Work." *Canadian Journal of Criminology* 38: 1–36.

Langworthy, R.H., and L.F. Travis. 1994. *Policing in America: A Balance of Forces.* Don Mills, Ont.: Macmillan.

LaPrairie, C. 1992. *Justice for the Cree: Communities, Crime and Order.* Nemaska, Que.: Cree Regional Authority.

LaPrairie, C., and E. Diamond. 1992. "Who Owns the Problem? Crime and Disorder in James Bay Cree Communities." *Canadian Journal of Criminology* 34, nos. 3–4: 417–34.

Lewis, S., H. Rosenberg, and R. Sigler. 1999. "Acceptance of Community Policing among Patrol Officers and Police Administrators." *Policing* 22: 567–88.

Linden, R., D. Clairmont, and C. Murphy. 2001. *Aboriginal Policing in Manitoba: A Report to the Aboriginal Justice Implementation Commission.* Winnipeg: Government of Manitoba.

Manning, P. 1977. *Police Work.* Cambridge, MA: MIT Press.

Marquis, G. 1994. "Power from the Street: The Canadian Municipal Police." In R.C. Macleod and D. Sneiderman, eds., *Police Powers in Canada: The Evolution and Practice of Authority.* Toronto: University of Toronto Press.

McIntyre, M. 1998. "Foot Patrols Cut Emergency Calls." *Winnipeg Free Press,* 15 February, A7.

Metha, V. 1993. *Policing Services for Aboriginal Peoples.* Ottawa: Ministry of the Solicitor General Research Division.

Moore, M., and R.C. Trojanowicz. 1988. *Corporate Strategies for Policing.* Washington, D.C.: National Institute of Justice.

Murphy, C., and D. Clairmont. 1996. *First Nations Police Officers Survey.* Ottawa: Solicitor General of Canada.

Parker, L., and G. Fields. 2000. "Unsolved Killings on the Rise." *USA Today,* 23 February, 1A.

Parks, R., S. Mastrofski, C. DeJong, and M.K. Gray. 1999. "How Officers Spend Their Time with the Community." *Justice Quarterly* 16: 483–519.

Pate, A., M.A. Wycoff, W.G. Skogan, and L. Sherman. 1986. *Reducing Fear of Crime in Houston and Newark.* Washington, D.C.: Police Foundation.

Reiss, A. 1992. "Police Organization in the Twentieth Century." In M. Tonry and N. Morris, eds., *Crime and Justice: A Review of Research,* vol. 15. Chicago: University of Chicago Press, pp. 51–98.

———. 1967. *The Police and the Public.* New Haven, Conn.: Yale University Press.

Ross, H. Laurence. 1982. *Deterring the Drinking Driver: Legal Policy and Social Control.* Lexington, Mass.: D.C. Heath.

Royal Canadian Mounted Police. 2001. *The National DNA Bank of Canada: Annual Report 2000/2001.* Ottawa: Royal Canadian Mounted Police.

Scheck, B., P. Neufeld, and J. Dwyer. 2000. *Actual Innocence: Five Days to Executing and Other Dispatches from the Wrongfully Convicted.* New York: Doubleday.

Shapiro, P., and H. Votey. 1984. "Deterrence and Subjective Probabilities of Arrest: Modelling Individual Decisions to Drink and Drive in Sweden." *Law and Society Review* 18: 111–49.

Shearing, C.D. 1992. "The Relation between Public and Private Policing." In M. Tonry and N. Morris, eds., *Crime and Justice: A Review of Research,* vol. 15. Chicago: University of Chicago Press, pp. 399–434.

Sherman, L.J. 1990. "Police Crackdowns: Initial and Residual Deterrence." In M. Tonry and N. Morris, eds., *Crime and Justice,* vol. 12. Chicago: University of Chicago Press, pp. 1–48.

———. 1986. "Policing Communities: What Works?" In A.J. Reiss and M. Tonry, eds., *Crime and Justice: A Review of Research,* vol. 8, pp. 343–86.

Sherman, L.J., J. Schmidt, D. Rogan, P. Gartin, E. Cohen, D. Collins, and A. Bacich. 1991. "From Initial Deterrence to Long-term Escalation: Short Custody Arrest for Poverty Ghetto Domestic Violence." *Criminology* 29: 821–50.

Skogan, W. 1990. *Disorder and Decline: Crime and the Spiral Decay in America's Neighborhoods.* New York: Free Press.

Solicitor General of Canada. 1999. *The First Nations Policing Policy.* Ottawa: Solicitor General of Canada.

Statistics Canada. 1997. *1996 Census Dictionary.* Ottawa: Industry Canada.

Trojanowicz, R., V.E. Kappeler, and L.K. Gaines. 2001. *Community Policing: A Contemporary Perspective,* 3rd ed. Cincinnati: C.J. Anderson.

Walker, S. 1994. *Sense and Nonsense about Crime,* 3rd ed. Belmont, Calif.: Wadsworth.

———. 1992. *The Police in America: An Introduction,* 2nd ed. New York: McGraw-Hill.

———. 1985. "Setting the Standards: The Efforts and Impact of Blue-Ribbon Commissions on the Police." In W.A. Geller, ed., *Police Leadership in America: Crisis and Opportunity.* New York: Praeger.

Wickham, W. 2000. "Don't Use DNA Test to Excuse Bad Idea." *USA Today,* 2 January, 15A.

Wilson, J.Q. 1968. *Varieties of Criminal Behavior.* Cambridge, MA: Harvard University Press.

Young, G. 1995. *Police Personnel and Expenditures in Canada—1993.* Ottawa: Juristat.

Court Cases

R. v. Borden, [1994] 3 S.C.R. 145

R. v. Legere (1994), 95 C.C.C. (3d) 139 (N.B. C.A.)

CHAPTER 6

Issues in Canadian Policing

CHAPTER OBJECTIVES

✓ Discuss the practice of police discretion.

✓ Examine the changing social composition of the police.

✓ Discuss the use of deadly force by and against police officers in Canada.

✓ Examine the amount and types of police misconduct and attempts to control these actions by outside agencies.

This chapter focuses on a number of different topics related to contemporary policing: first is a discussion of police activities that concern due process advocates, in particular those activities where the police may discriminate against certain groups of people, such as discretion, the use of force (including deadly force), and police misconduct. Through a review of the "police subculture," the reasons due process violations occur is also discussed. Second, the chapter addresses issues surrounding social composition of police agencies, such as who should be recruited as police officers. Are women and minority-group members treated fairly by the police agencies they work for? What types of experiences have they encountered as police officers? What is the relevance of a college or university education for police officers? And what about the treatment of racial minorities by the police?

In the fall of 2002, numerous black community groups and individuals accused the Toronto Police Service of "racially profiling" the members of their community.

Racial profiling occurs when a police action is initiated by a statistical profile of the race, ethnicity, or national origin of a suspect, rather than by any evidence or information that the suspect had broken the law. According to Callahan and Anderson (2001), racial profiling involves the police moving from the standard practice of "case probability" to "class probability." Case probability is defined as those situations where some factors relevant to a particular event are comprehended, and class probability describes those situations where enough is known about a class of events to describe it using statistics, but nothing about a particular event is known other than the fact that it belongs to the class in question. That is, before the police have evidence of a crime, they start to "investigate a high proportion of people of some particular race, ethnic group, age group and so on. Their only justification is that by doing so, they increase their chances of discovering some crime" (Callahan and Anderson 2001: 40). Class probability is also known as racial profiling, and once that occurs, "there is a strong claim that certain groups of people are being denied equal protection under the law" (Callahan and Anderson 2001: 39).

It is well known that racial profiling has been used in the United States for a number of years, and divisive points of view about whether or not it is targeting minority-group members have been raised. Supporters of racial profiling favour the crime control model discussed in Chapter 1 and defend its practice by saying it is an efficient approach to catching criminals since the police use the laws of probability to make the best use of their resources. Others say that its use is only one of many investigative tools the police use to estimate who is criminal. This line of thinking is referred to as "rational discrimination," as it relies on statistics that indicate a correlation between crime and race. Critics of racial profiling follow the logic of the due process model and argue that racial profiling involves discriminatory police actions against minority-group members. This is revealed, they argue, by empirical research investigating the race of those individuals charged with drug offences that reveals that Caucasians are more likely to be charged with possession of drugs than are African Americans or Hispanics. Skolnick (1994) points out that law enforcement involves stereotyping, a practice he feels is integral to the world of policing.

Introduction of Canada's new Anti-Terrorism Bill in late 2001 raised concerns about racial profiling in Canada (Choudhrey 2001). And in one Canadian court case, the issue of racial profiling was raised by the defence. This case involved an African American member of the Toronto Raptors basketball team, who was stopped for going slightly over the speed limit on a Toronto expressway. He was subsequently charged with and convicted of impaired driving. At his trial, his lawyer argued that Mr. Brown was the victim of racial stereotyping and had been stopped arbitrarily by the police because "black men in big cars must be criminals" (Mitchell 2002: 8). The judge dismissed the idea of racial profiling, calling such allegations "distasteful" and "really quite nasty, malicious accusations based on, it seems to me, nothing" (Mitchell 2002: 8). The trial judge convicted Mr. Brown, and the case was appealed to the Ontario Superior Court. There it was determined that in the lower court trial, race was a factor in the actions of the police officers. The Superior Court judge also noted that "Racism is a part of our culture and justice system."

POLICE DISCRETION

Discretion involves police officers using their judgment when deciding in which situations to intervene and which to ignore. The discretionary powers of the police have been the subject of appeals in court cases since the *Charter of Rights and Freedoms* was proclaimed in 1982. In fact, some lower court cases involving questions about police discretion have been appealed to and heard by the Supreme Court of Canada. The most significant case involving this issue to date involved a decision by the Saskatchewan Court of Appeal, which ruled that the police held too much discretionary power in their activities. Although the court agreed that the power for this discretion is found granted in the *Criminal Code*, it ruled that the police were using too much discretionary power in their operations. This was particularly the case when the police thought there were reasonable and probable grounds for believing the accused had committed an indictable offence (*R. v. Beare* (1988)).

On appeal, the Supreme Court of Canada disagreed with the Saskatchewan decision. It decided that "discretion is an essential part of the criminal justice system … [t]he Criminal Code provides no guidelines for the exercise of discretion in any of these areas. The day-to-day operation of law enforcement and the criminal justice system nonetheless depends upon the exercise of that discretion." This means that police officers are in a unique position to use discretion in their decisions about enforcing the law.

The Supreme Court also said discretion can be contested in court by an individual who feels the police used their discretionary powers in a wrongful manner. Section 24 of the *Charter* is a remedy for cases involving the use of discretion in an "improper or arbitrary" manner. And although it wasn't developed to deal specifically with police discretion, s. 15(1) of the *Charter* stipulates that numerous "extra-legal" factors are not to be considered within the law or the application of the law. Legal questions surrounding the discretionary powers of a police officer can be stayed on the basis of an abuse of process or as an infringement of equality as specified by equality provision (s. 15(1)) of the *Charter*:

> Every individual is equal before and under the law and has the right to the equal protection and equal benefit of the law without discrimination and, in particular, without discrimination based on race, national or ethnic origin, colour, religion, sex, age or mental or physical disability.

It is not common for a police officer's discretion to be brought into question during a case because the Supreme Court requires that a judicial stay be allowed only in cases where "compelling an accused to stand trial would violate those fundamental principles of justice which underlie the community's sense of fair play and decency" (*R. v. Mack* (1988)). If an appeal is made under s. 15(1), there has to be clear evidence of discrimination (*Andrews v. Law Society (British Columbia)* (1989); *R. v. Turpin* (1989)).

Studies of Police Discretion

The discretionary powers held by the police has been one of the most visible issues in policing for over 40 years. Researchers have studied the issue of police discretion and its relationship to the unequal enforcement of the law, specifically as it relates to possible discrimination of certain groups in our society. If discretion is used, it can create unfairness within the criminal justice system, violating the various due process protections designed to protect all citizens outlined in Chapter 2.

When deciding to invoke their powers (which may include discretion), the police typically consider three factors. The most important is the type of crime committed: the more serous a crime, the more likely the officer will use her legal powers to enforce the law. The second factor is the attitude of the citizen involved in the offence. If a suspect's manner is demeaning to the officer, chances are the officer will detain the individual and lay a charge against him. Finally, departmental policies can limit the amount of discretion a police officer will use in a given situation (see Exhibit 6.1 on page 137). During the past two decades, for example, zero tolerance policies have attempted to limit the amount of discretion used by officers when they respond to a domestic violence complaint (see Chapter 5). However, police officers do use considerable amounts of discretion, even when organizational policies say otherwise (see Chapter 1). As McKenna (2002: 120) points out, discretion "may be put forward as a general principle that it is virtually impossible to provide rules and regulations for police officer activity in the field.

Goldstein (1960), in one of the first analyses of police discretion, noted that a decision by a police officer to arrest a suspect "largely determines the outer limits of police enforcement." This statement reveals the power inherent within police discretion and illustrates that the police do not have to arrest everyone they find breaking the law. Discretion is the choice or decision—the judgment call—made by a police officer to make an arrest or not. In reality it is difficult for the police to arrest and charge everyone they catch breaking the law because they lack the resources to do so. As a result, a police officer may decide to give a warning or reprimand instead. Many citizens fully expect to be "let off" with a warning.

Police discretion becomes a factor when officers could use their powers of arrest or investigate an alleged criminal offence when available evidence indicates they should not. According to Roberg and Kuykendall (1993), police discretion involves three elements:

- deciding whether to get involved in an incident in the first place, although no choice may be available if the officer is responding to a citizen complaint;
- determining how to behave in any particular incident, or how to interact with the victim, witnesses, or the public; and
- selecting one of many alternatives in dealing with the problem.

In any given situation, a police officer may decide to do nothing, even though he observes the commission of a criminal offence or lets one person off with a warning while arresting another for the same offence.

Goldstein (1960) created two categories of police discretion based on the type of approach used to enforce the criminal law: (1) invocation discretion and (2) noninvocation discretion. Invocation discretion refers to situations in which a police officer decides to arrest an individual. Noninvocation discretion refers to situations in which a police officer can arrest someone but chooses not to. Goldstein was most concerned about noninvocation discretion, because such decisions have "low visibility" and are not reviewed by superiors. The low visibility of police discretion means that the police can, unlike other criminal justice agencies, "hide" or "obscure" their discretionary decisions. Thus, discretion "may sometimes deteriorate into discrimination, violence, and other abusive practices" (Senna and Siegel 1995: 233).

Factors Affecting Police Officers' Decision to Arrest

Most studies on police use of discretion focus on the specific factors that led to an officer's decision to make an arrest. According to Stansfield (1996: 142), the focus should not be on whether or not the police decide to use discretion but "which criteria police use when enforcing the law." The most common factors found to influence a police officers' discretion are situational variables, as well as a suspect's social class, age, sex, and race; the relationship between victim and complainant; the amount of respect or deference given to the police officer; the nature of the offence or problem; and the amount and quality of the evidence.

Situational Variables

The dynamics differ in any two situations, so police officers differ in the way they respond to incidents. The dynamic derives in part from the location of the incident. Police more often arrest suspects in public settings than in private ones. Still, a number of different agents can influence police use of discretion in these situations, such as the need to be in control of the situation, especially if members of the public are watching. The presence of other police officers is another influence on police discretion—if a police officer thinks other officers expect him to respond in a punitive manner, he will probably do so. Indeed, police officers working alone behave much differently than if they are working with a partner—they usually make more arrests, since they are concerned with gaining control of a situation as quickly as possible.

Community Variables

An important factor in police decision-making is the racial and social class composition of a community. Research conducted in Canada and the United States has found police officers make more arrests in minority and working-class communities. The police view these communities as locations where violent crimes are more likely to occur and where residents are more likely to challenge police authority. Police, as a result, are more suspicious and concerned for their safety when in these areas. These feelings revolve around the idea of a symbolic assailant—an individual who, the police believe, tends to be potentially dangerous or troublesome (Skolnick 1966; McGahan 1984).

Some communities have higher rates of reported crime, which can influence an officer's perception of danger. The greater the danger a police officer perceives, the more likely he will respond with an arrest. But, at the same time, police officers tend to ignore certain types of criminal activity in these areas, perhaps because of the greater amount of police work entailed or because they are more tolerant of minor violations. In addition, the attitudes of citizens in a particular community can influence police behaviour, since most police–citizen encounters result from a citizen's call to police. McGahan (1984) found that police form a "model" of troubled areas, which they use to predict the type of calls and the most appropriate response, allowing them to deal with threatening and problem aspects of the environment.

Extralegal Factors

Perhaps the most controversial issue connected to police use of discretion is whether the police take into account the race, class, and gender of the suspect when deciding to make an arrest—that is, whether police discretion favours the members of a certain social class or racial group.

The issue of race and police discretion in Canada has interested researchers for over 30 years. In one of the earliest studies conducted in this country, Bienvenue and Latif (1974) studied 1969 arrest data for the city of Winnipeg in order to determine if differences existed in the arrest and charge rates between Aboriginals and non-Aboriginals. They found Aboriginal women and men were overrepresented for all offences except drug and traffic violations. However, when the distribution of offences within each group was compared, Aboriginals were found to be arrested more often for minor offences and whites arrested more often for the most serious, indictable offences. Although these arrest patterns may reflect variations in socioeconomic status, Bienvenue and Latif suggest they are the result of police discretion.

This was evident when they looked at police decisions to charge, as Aboriginals were overrepresented for every type of charge at the time of sentencing. Numerous studies (e.g., Havemann et al. 1985; Hamilton and Sinclair 1991; Ontario Commission on Systemic Racism 1995; Mosher 1998; Forcese 1999) published since the work of Bienvenue and Latif have found race to be a determining factor in the police use of discretion.

Police discretion has also been found when extralegal variables other than race are studied. For example, Gunn and Minch (1988) found extensive use of police discretion in sexual assault cases in Winnipeg. Of the 211 charges laid against offenders, 122 (or 58 percent) were terminated, either because the police officer decided no sexual assault had occurred or because she foresaw difficulties for the complainant. Because police were using discretionary power to choose not to arrest or charge alleged offenders, mandatory arrest and charge policies in sexual assault cases is now policy in all Canadian police forces. In 1992 the Metropolitan Toronto Police Force required all its officers to lay charges when the evidence supported such an action; if officers did not lay a charge, they had to file a report indicating the reason for inaction.

Fleming (1981) discovered evidence of police discretion in his study of police decisions concerning whether or not they should proceed with an investigation after the victim of a violent crime was determined to be gay. Abell and Sheehy (1993: 225) note that when police investigate these crimes the "violence and homophobia and lesbophobia underlying it are often downplayed or excused." Assailants receive more lenient treatment simply because "their crimes are crimes against gay men or lesbians."

Other studies have found that the race and social class of the victim rather than the criminal is the basis for the police decision to use discretion. For example, Ericson (1982) discovered that when a crime involved property damage or theft, the police proceeded by way of arrest when suspects were poor and members of minority groups.

These studies have led some observers and researchers of police discretion to say that police discretion works against males, the poor, and members of minority groups while protecting women and those who are members of the privileged groups in our society. Others point to studies (e.g., De Lisi and Regoli 1999) that conclude that the police do not discriminate when they use their discretionary powers to arrest and charge members of certain groups. Instead, they say, legal variables (such as the seriousness of the crime and the prior record of the suspect) determine whether or not the police will arrest and charge a suspect.

EXHIBIT 6.1 Police Discretion and High-Speed Pursuits

The police have traditionally possessed considerable discretion in their decision to start a high-speed pursuit. However, this discretion has come under scrutiny in recent years because of the numerous serious accidents resulting from such pursuits. From the years 1991–95 in Canada, 19 deaths were attributed to 4200 pursuits. One-third of these chases resulted in collisions and 14 percent resulted in injuries (Bell 1999). Between 1991 and 1997, 33 persons (26 were suspects, one was a police officer, and the other six were bystanders) died in police chases in Ontario. In British Columbia, the RCMP and 12 municipal police forces were involved in 4468 high-speed pursuits between 1990 and 1997, and 21 people were killed and 748 injured as a result (Appleby et al.1999). In 1999, eight people died during police chases (Alberts 2000). And in the United States, the National Highway Safety Administration estimates that over 250 people are killed each year (about one-third of whom are bystanders) and over 20 000 injured as a result of high-speed pursuits by police officers (Mitchell 1990).

Most police departments in Canada and the United States now have written policies that govern high-speed pursuits. In Canada, these policies vary among jurisdictions, but they are similar in such key areas as public safety and the discharging of weapons. The safety of the public is supposed to be the most important consideration in any police decision to begin, continue, or end a pursuit. According to the Ontario Provincial Police policy, a police chase "shall be the choice of last resort and will be considered only when other alternatives are unavailable or unsatisfactory." The policy of the Royal Canadian Mounted Police (RCMP) on pursuits informs its officers to consider the seriousness of the offence before starting a pursuit, but "it is silent on what constitutes a serious offence" (Bell 1999). In addition, most jurisdictions prohibit police officers from discharging their weapons at or from a moving vehicle in an attempt to stop the fleeing vehicle.

Canadian police forces require their officers to believe that a criminal offence has been, or is about to be, committed before starting a chase and that the immediate apprehension of the vehicle and its driver outweighs the danger created by the chase. When a noncriminal offence is involved most police forces allow an officer to chase the vehicle but for only for the purpose of identifying the vehicle; once this is accomplished, the officer must stop the pursuit. The RCMP has

different policies, relying instead on the different types of pursuits. A "hazardous" pursuit begins when a motorist refuses to stop for a police officer. A "routine" pursuit occurs when the police speed, without using their sirens or lights, in order to gauge the speed or to intercept a fast-moving vehicle.

Many jurisdictions don't allow more than two police vehicles to engage in a pursuit at any given time. Restrictions also govern the instances in which a police officer can ram his patrol car into the fleeing vehicle (only in an extreme emergency or when a major crime is committed). Other jurisdictions require their police officers to have both their lights and sirens on during a chase. In British Columbia, if lights and sirens aren't on, officers must stop at all red lights and stop signs and observe the speed limit in school zones (Appleby et al. 1999).

Various alternatives have been tried to reduce the number of high-speed pursuits—some jurisdictions have increased the number of hours of training that police officers receive—but these initiatives have been criticized because they do not reflect real-life situations, in which officers must decide quickly whether to continue or end the pursuit. Other alternatives have been proposed for heavily populated areas. In Calgary, for example, the purchase of a helicopter by the Calgary Police Service in 1995 has assisted in pursuits. Since then, every pursuit involving the helicopter has ended in an arrest, and no accidents have occurred. Legal issues too are important in the determination of pursuit policies.

In an attempt to deter high-speed pursuits, Ontario and the federal government have introduced new offences in an attempt to stop motorists from fleeing police officers. Ontario, the first jurisdiction to introduce such legislation, in 1999, allows judges to suspend drivers' licences from 10 years to life in those cases where fleeing motorists cause death or injury. The federal government added a new offence to the *Criminal Code* in 2000 that provides for specific penalties against motorists who refuse to stop after being requested to do so by the police. This offence gives judges the power to impose penalties to a maximum of life imprisonment for motorists whose flight from police results in death. An incident causing injury has a maximum sentence of 14 years, and conviction for evasions could lead to a maximum sentence of five years (Alberts 2000; Laghi 2000).

Continued on next page

EXHIBIT 6.1   Police Discretion ... *Continued*

A number of studies have explored police officers' attitudes toward pursuits. Falcone (1994) reported that the police officers he studied in Illinois indicate that the seriousness of the offence was strongly associated with their decision to engage in a high-speed pursuit. Most officers answered that the most important reasons for stopping a pursuit were (in descending order) traffic conditions, certain speed zones, seriousness of the offence, and weather conditions. Alpert and Madden (1994) studied police supervisors in Florida, South Carolina, Nebraska, and Arizona, and found that they regarded the need to apprehend a suspect immediately as more important than the risks posed to either police officers or the public. Finally, Britz and Payne (1994: 130–31) found supervisors and patrol officers differed significantly in their "perceptions of policy, supervisory support, the adequacy of training, liability issues and discretionary issues regarding police pursuit." They also found that 38 percent of the police officers reported that the pursuit policy was difficult to understand and implement, 80 percent of the supervisors stated they had given no pursuit training whatsoever to their officers, and 35 percent of the officers who had been in pursuits had not reported them.

These conflicting positions may be the result of the varying techniques used by researchers to study this issue. An analysis of many studies led to the following conclusions as to why discretion is found in some situations and not others:

1. Most of these studies examine only a few factors that may influence police decision-making and do not attempt to explain it comprehensively.
2. Most do not cover a wide enough range of offences to account adequately for discretion in serious and nonserious cases.
3. Studies reporting on factors influencing police decisions in one city may not hold true for police decisions in other cities.
4. Many studies rely on responses to hypothetical scenarios rather than actual observations of police work.
5. Even factors that are found to be important in police discretion cannot be used to make accurate predictions more than 25 percent of the time (Albanese 1999: 187).

THE POLICE SUBCULTURE

All professions possess unique characteristics that distinguish them from other occupations and professions. Policing is no different. Police veterans and policing experts have long talked about certain factors, such as the nature of the job itself, that make police officers form a tight bond with one another. This leads to the so-called "blue curtain" (also known as the "blue wall of silence"), a term used to refer to the value placed on secrecy and the general mistrust of the outside world shared by many police officers. The blue curtain separates the police from the very citizens they are supposed to protect.

The police subculture is thought to consist of six basic values:

1. Police are the only real crime fighters. The public wants the police officer to fight crime; other agencies, both public and private, only play at crime fighting.
2. No one else understands the real nature of police work. Lawyers, academics, politicians, and the public in general have little concept of what it means to be a police officer.
3. Loyalty to colleagues counts above everything else. Police officers have to stick together because everyone is out to get the police and make the job more difficult.
4. It is impossible to win the war against crime without bending the rules. Courts have awarded criminal defendants too many civil rights.
5. Members of the public are basically unsupportive and unreasonably demanding. People are quick to criticize the police unless they themselves need police help.
6. Patrol work is the pits. Detective work is glamorous and exciting (Sparrow et al. 1990: 51).

These six values make it difficult for police officers to accept new ideas and innovative concepts, such as community policing. The police culture exists because of the dangerousness of the police profession and the need for the complete support and loyalty of other police officers.

Many feel police officers have formed a unique set of personality traits to help them in their work. They have often been criticized for these traits—cynicism, hostility, dogmatism, and conservatism—which are almost universally viewed as negative. These attitudes are thought to be influential in police decisions to arrest, and ultimately contribute to poor relationships with the community they serve as well as lead to police deviance and the greater use of deadly force. In particular, police cynicism is characterized by a rejection of the ideals of justice and truth, the very values that a police officer is sworn to uphold and protect. When an officer becomes cynical, he loses respect for the law and replaces it with other rules formed in and promoted by the police subculture. These values become more acceptable to some police officers because they think they give a better representation of the reality found in society today. Police cynicism exists at every level of policing, including police chiefs, and throughout all stages of a police career (Regoli et al. 1990). Where police cynicism becomes entrenched, the result can be increased police misconduct, corruption, and brutality (Regoli et al. 1979).

The existence of the police subculture has led researchers to ask how it starts in the first place, which led to a study of what is referred to as the "police personality." In turn, this led to questions such as whether or not police officers have different attitudes compared to the general public. How did they obtain these attitudes? Do the personality characteristics of police officers influence their discretion and performance on the job? Or do they learn them from other officers while on the job? These questions have led to numerous studies focusing on the police personality.

The term "police personality" refers to a value orientation that is unique to police officers or at least to some police officers. Some believe that the police are cynical—that is, motivated entirely by self-interest and pessimistic outlooks on human behaviour. But how do police officers become cynical? Is it because they hold different attitudes when they become members of a police force, or do they become that way once they have held the job and are exposed to negative public feelings and the police subculture?

The earliest studies explored the possibility that police officers are exposed to negative social events and public responses and, as a result, learn from other police officers how to best deal with them, notably by becoming part of the police subculture. Niederhoffer (1967) conducted the first major study of police cynicism when working as a police officer for the New York Police Department. He believed there were two types of police cynicism: (1) general cynicism, or cynicism directed against people in general, and (2) system cynicism, or cynicism aimed at the police organization itself. According to Niederhoffer, police officers embark on a policing career with a professional and committed attitude but experience frustrations on the job. This leads to disenchantment, which leads most officers to develop a cynical attitude. For a minority, however, it leads to a renewed commitment to the high standards they started with. The degree of cynicism of an officer, in

Niederhoffer's view, is determined by her age and experience.

He concluded that police officers become highly cynical after 7 to 10 years on the job. He also found that new officers were less cynical compared to those officers who had only a bit more experience. He found that almost 80 percent of new recruits questioned on their first day on the job responded that the police department was "an efficient, smoothly running organization," but less than two months later fewer than one-third held this view. In addition, he reported that college-educated patrol officers were more cynical than the other patrol officers, that cynicism decreased the closer police officers were to retirement, and that police administrators had the lowest levels of cynicism. Other researchers (e.g., Regoli et al. 1979; Langworthy 1987) have tried to test Niederhoffer's ideas on other police departments but have discovered it is difficult to measure cynicism accurately.

The development of police cynicism may have a damaging impact upon the job performance of a police officer. Feelings of cynicism appear to intensify the need to maintain respect and exert authority over others (Regoli and Poole 1979). And as this cynicism escalates, there can be a corresponding increase in citizens' distrust and fear of the police. This can ultimately result in the feeling that every contact with the public involves potential danger, a state of mind termed "police paranoia." All of these factors contribute to make the police conservative and resistant to change (Regoli and Poole 1979).

THE WORKING PERSONALITY OF THE POLICE OFFICER

Probably the most important result of Niederhoffer's study is that it led some researchers to investigate whether those who choose to become police officers possess personality characteristics that make them susceptible to cynicism. Skolnick (1966) conducted the classic work on the police personality. Like Niederhoffer, Skolnick believed that the police personality emerges from certain aspects of police work, such as danger and isolation, rather than from preexisting personality traits. Skolnick felt the constant danger of the job led police officers to be extremely suspicious of people, which has the effect of isolating them from the public. The fact that citizens constantly challenge their authority further isolates them. This has the effect of police officers' reacting to "vague indications of danger suggested by appearance," a feeling that is constantly reinforced by the police subculture. Police officers also feel strongly that the public don't support them; this leads to feelings of isolation, which in turn make police officers turn to one another for support (Skolnick 1994).

The work of Niederhoffer and Skolnick supports the view that the police personality emerges as a product of the strains and pressures found in their work. This view has become known as the socialization model. An alternative approach, referred to as the predispositional model, argues that the police personality is the product of the preexisting personality traits of police officers.

Bennett and Greenstein (1975) conducted one of the first tests of this latter model. They asked three groups of students at a university located in the United States—police officers (working toward their Bachelor of Arts degree), police science majors, and nonpolice science majors—to assign priorities to the values that serve as guiding principles in their lives. These values included equality, happiness, freedom, a sense of accomplishment, a comfortable life, etc. The researchers hypothesized that the police officers and police science majors would possess like value orientations. However, the opposite was true, which led to a rejection of this model. The researchers found that the police science majors were most like the nonpolice science majors and that the values of both of these groups were "markedly divergent from the value systems of experienced police officers." Other studies (for example, Cochrane and Butler 1980) yielded similar results.

Significantly, these studies show that any attempt to reduce value differences between the police and the community should be in the context of new training procedures rather than recruitment on the basis of personality characteristics alone. Further, the training of new recruits should emphasize the social and legal aspects of policing (such as awareness of different cultures as well as the use of discretion) rather than focus on changing personal values alone. Despite the evidence that shows police attitudes are learned on the job, most police forces today continue to rely on personality screening tests and similar interview questions in an attempt to screen potential candidates for police academies (Ash et al. 1990; Sanders et al. 1995).

HIGHER EDUCATION AND POLICING

With the demise of the predispositional model, researchers turned their attention to the effect of higher education on police officers. Police forces today often use higher education to reduce undesirable attitudes among individuals who want to become police officers (Rodriquez 1995). This strategy has led to research on the impact of higher education on police attitudes.

One of the earliest studies took the form of a questionnaire mailed to 100 members of the RCMP (Smith et al. 1969). These officers were divided into four comparable groups on the basis of age, education, and experience. Each of the officers was tested using two scales measuring attitudes (an authoritarianism scale and a liberal–conservative scale) and a personality test, to assess the degree of rigidity and flexibility of the officers. The results indicated that significant differences existed among officers on the basis of the level of education they had received. Senior officers who had not graduated from a university or college possessed authoritarian, conservative, and rigid attitudes, while those who had attained a degree did not share these attitudes. Other studies have yielded similar results. Roberg (1978), Murrell (1982), Meagher (1983) and Carter et al. (1988) reported that there are benefits of higher education for law enforcement officers, which include a more professional demeanour and performance as well as the ability to cope better with stress. Police administrators point out police officers with higher education

TABLE 6.1 Highest Level of Education for Police Officers, Canada, 1996

	Male (%)	Female (%)	Total (%)
Less than high-school diploma	6	4	5
High-school diploma	14	8	13
Trade and nonuniversity	13	8	12
Trade and nonuniversity with certificate/diploma	35	33	35
Some university	19	22	19
University with bachelor's degree or higher	13	25	14
Total	100	100	100

Source: Statistics Canada, *Juristat*, Catalogue 85-002, vol. 18, no. 13, November 1998, p. 8.

take greater initiatives in performing their tasks, receive fewer public complaints, and act more professionally when conducting their duties (Krimmel 1996). Table 6.1 illustrates the highest level of education for police officers in Canada in 1996.

POLICE USE OF DEADLY FORCE

If the police subculture is largely determined by the occupational hazards of policing, then its behavioural side can be expressed through the police use of authority. The use of this authority sometimes leads to misuse, which can lead to the use of deadly force.

Deadly force is defined as force that is used with the intent to cause bodily injury or death. Police use of deadly force refers to those situations in which the police use firearms in encounters with citizens. Nevertheless, citizens may be injured or killed as the result of other types of force used by the police. For example, choke holds, which can cause death, should be included in any definition of deadly force (Fyfe 1988). High-speed chases ending in death can also be seen as a type of deadly force; however, such cases are not included here because the deaths that occur are unintentional and often accidental.

Until 1995, the *Criminal Code* permitted the shooting of a "fleeing felon" without any concern if the suspect presented a danger to a police officer or other citizens (Roach 1999). This was challenged in a Toronto trial of a police officer who shot and wounded a black male suspected for purse snatching. In this case (*R. v. Lines* (1993)), the prosecutor successfully argued that the shooting was inconsistent with the victim's rights to life and security as specified by the *Charter of Rights and Freedoms*, specifically that it deprived both victims and potential victims of police shootings of life and security of the person since the *Criminal Code* "authorized lethal force regardless of the seriousness of the offence or the threat posed by presented by the suspect" (Roach 1999: 232).

As a result of the ruling in the Toronto case, Parliament introduced a new defence (found in s. 25(4) of the *Criminal Code*) authorizing police officers to use deadly force in order to prevent a suspect from fleeing if the officer "believes on reasonable grounds that the force is necessary for the purpose of protecting the police officer ... or any other person from imminent or future death or grievous bodily harm."

Section 25 of the *Criminal Code* authorizes Canadian police to use force, including lethal force, to deal with various situations that they come into contact with during their activities.

25. (1) Every one who is required or authorized by law to do anything in the administration or enforcement of the law

(a) as a private person,
(b) as a peace officer or public officer,
(c) in aid of a peace officer or public officer, or
(d) by virtue of his office, is, if he acts on reasonable grounds, justified in doing what he is required or authorized to do and in using as much force as is necessary for that purpose ...

(3) Subject to subsections (4) and (5), a person is not justified for the purposes of subsection (1) in using force that is intended or is likely to cause death or grievous bodily harm unless the person believes on reasonable grounds that it is necessary for the self-preservation of the person or the preservation of any one under that person's protection from death or grievous bodily harm.

(4) A peace officer, and every person lawfully assisting the peace officer, is justified in using force that is intended or is likely to cause death or grievous bodily harm to a person to be arrested, if

(a) the peace officer is proceeding lawfully to arrest, with or without warrant, the person to be arrested;
(b) the offence for which the person is to be arrested is one for which that person may be arrested without warrant;
(c) the person to be arrested takes flight to avoid arrest;
(d) the peace officer or other person using the force believes on reasonable grounds that the force is necessary for the purpose of protecting the peace officer, the person lawfully assisting the peace officer or any other person from imminent or future death or grievous bodily harm; and
(e) the flight cannot be prevented by reasonable means in a less violent manner.

Subsection (1) of s. 25 of the *Criminal Code* states that any individual, including a peace (police) officer, can use "as much force as is necessary" in the "administration ... of the law" if he "acts on reasonable grounds." Furthermore, if a police officer is to be justified in using deadly force, he must believe on "reasonable grounds" that it is necessary to use force in order to protect himself or an individual in his care from "death or grievous bodily harm."

Stansfield (1996; 2000) points out that this approach to deadly force raises a number of problems. First, the phrase "as much force as necessary" makes it appear that police can use as much force as they feel is necessary to resolve any particular incident. Second, it does not state exactly how much force should be used. In the first case where a police officer was convicted of manslaughter under this section of the *Criminal Code*, the police officer received a conditional sentence (see Chapter 10) and 180 hours of community service. This sentence was reached on the basis of the convicted defendant's previous record as a police officer and because he was given false information that the Aboriginal protestors at Ipperwash, Ontario, were in possession of weapons (*R. v. Deane* (1997)).

A number of mechanisms have been implemented to control the use of deadly force by police. Although the *Criminal Code* clearly states that a police officer does not have to be physically attacked before using potential deadly force, it does say that police officers have to follow a reasonableness standard for the use of force, namely that force is considered excessive when, after the officer has evaluated all the circumstances at the time of the incident, the force is determined to be unreasonable. However, even if police investigators and Crown prosecutors determine excessive force was used, it is still difficult to gain a conviction. Police officers who are witnesses to potential criminal offences committed by their colleagues have traditionally been reluctant to assist Crown prosecutors. As a result of this problem, the Ontario *Police Act* was repealed in 1990 and replaced with the *Police Services Act*, which stipulates that officers must now cooperate with any investigation. Three categories must be examined if the full extent of the issue is to be assessed:

1. *Death:* police use a deadly weapon, and as a result the individual dies.
2. *Injury:* the police use a deadly weapon, and the individual is wounded but does not die.
3. *Noninjury:* the police use a deadly weapon, and the individual against whom it is directed is not injured.

Roberg and Kuykendall (1993) feel that a fourth category should be added—the total number of times a police officer fires his weapon. An individual who is shot at and killed or wounded may be shot at many times, not just once, and so each shot must be counted. Geller and Scott (1991) found police officers miss their target 60 to 85 percent of the time. An officer who shoots six bullets at a suspect might miss the suspect altogether, or hit him once, injuring or killing him.

Data on the first category of deadly force is hard to find in Canada, since such records are not kept for public review. Unfortunately, case studies from newspapers cannot be analyzed with the purpose of studying anything beyond the dynamics of the situation, such as police regulations and the final results of any investigation (Forcese 1992). In contrast, figures can be obtained in the United States as a "cause of homicide" category has been published annually by the National Center for Health Statistics since 1949 in the subcategory of "police or legal" intervention. Between 1949 and 1990, police in the United States killed approximately 13 000 people. However, Sherman et al. (1979) point out that these statistics underestimate such incidents by 25 to 50 percent and that the real number is closer to 30 000 or 40 000.

Variations among Provinces and Cities

The frequency with which police use category 1 deadly force differs between provinces or territories. Between 1970 and 1981, the use of deadly force by police resulted in 119 deaths. Quebec experienced the greatest number of deadly force incidents during this period (37 percent), followed by Ontario (27.7 percent), and British Columbia (11.8 percent). However, when the number of deaths caused by police use of deadly force is measured by 100 000 population, the Northwest Territories had the highest rate (2.43 per 100 000 population), followed by Manitoba (1.18), and Quebec (0.70 per 100 000 population).

The size of a police force is thought to influence the police use of deadly force, which is thought to increase as the size of the police force increases. This idea is based on the argument that larger centres have more criminals, more crime, and more weapons, and that the police are more likely to intervene in those situations in which they think deadly force is the appropriate response. As Chappell and Graham (1985) found, between 1970 and 1981 there was no discernible evidence that such a relationship existed in Canada. Although they did not analyze their data in this matter, American researchers (Kania and Mackey 1977; Sherman et al. 1979) found a relationship between lack of social cohesion in a community (for example, high poverty and divorce rates) and police involvement in potentially dangerous situations.

Another important factor is the police organization itself—the organizational values, policies, and practices of police administrators. For example, the imposition of restrictive shooting policies will no doubt lead to a significant decrease in the use of deadly force.

Also, police training and police response to dangerous incidents may have an impact on the use of deadly force. For example, some police departments may tell their officers how to deal with certain incidents, such as whether to wait for backup support or to act in an aggressive manner (Fyfe 1988). Police forces do not always follow government recommendations to change their practices. In Ontario, the Task Force on Race Relations and Policing (Lewis 1989) recommended alternative types of interventions involving such procedures as better community relations, employment equity, and culturally sensitive training.

Research on Police Use of Deadly Force

The following discussion of police use of deadly force in Canada is limited to those few studies that have empirically analyzed this issue. Abraham et al. (1981) focused on the Metropolitan Toronto Police Force, Chappell and Graham (1985) looked at both national and British Columbia data, Stansfield (1996) looked at the Metro Toronto Police Force, while Parent and Verdun-Jones (1998) studied police shootings in British Columbia.

Abraham et al. (1981) studied the use of deadly force by Metropolitan Toronto police officers and described seven incidents as "confrontation situations." All victims were armed at the time of the shootings: one had a shotgun, another an inoperative shotgun; there were also two toy weapons, two kitchen knives, a gardening tool, and a police officer's nightstick. The key problem in all seven incidents was that the police involved themselves in a way that led to a confrontation, reflecting "fundamental training defects in the Metro police" (Abraham et al. 1981: 234).

In their study of police use of deadly force in British Columbia between 1970 and 1982, Chappell and Graham (1985: 110–11) reported all 13 victims were males aged 17 to 52. One victim was black, another was of Asian descent, and all others were white. Seven of the victims were armed at the time of the shooting, and two victims were not in possession of a weapon when confronted by the police (though they were in possession of a weapon at the time of their offence). Three individuals were not armed, while in the remaining case no weapon was discovered on the victim's body in the field, though an unloaded weapon was discovered tucked into his belt at the autopsy.

As Stansfield (2000) points out, these two studies found that many of the incidents mentioned above involved the use of deadly force by the police in fleeing-felon situations. Chappell and Graham (1985) reported that almost 40 percent of the fatal shootings they ana-

lyzed involved situations where the victims were fleeing the police. Stansfield (1996) found that in eight of the 14 shootings that occurred in Toronto between 1988 and 1991, the victims were shot while fleeing the police.

In contrast, Abraham et al. (1981) reported that all of the victims in their study were shot and killed while they were confronting the police. Parent and Verdun-Jones (1998) found that of the victims of police shootings in British Columbia between 1980 to 1994, almost half of the 58 deaths they analyzed were the result of the victim's unintentionally or intentionally provoking an officer to use deadly force. In "the majority of these cases, the individual's statements and actions clearly reflect their intention to commit suicide" (Parent and Verdun-Jones 1998: 438).

The issue of the race of the victims in police shootings has been raised numerous times. For example, the Ontario Commission on Systemic Racism (1995: 377) stated that "the number and circumstances of police shootings in Ontario have convinced many residents that they are disproportionately vulnerable to police violence." Between 1978 and 1995, 16 black males were shot by the police in Ontario, with 10 of them being shot fatally. Nine of these shootings led to criminal prosecutions; all ended with the officers charged being acquitted (Ontario Commission on Systemic Racism 1995: 377). Some cases involving the police use of deadly force and members of racial minority groups receiving national attention are the J.J. Harper case in Winnipeg (Hamilton and Sinclair 1991) and Richard Barnabe in Montreal (see Exhibit 6.2 on pages 147–48).

Deadly Force against Police Officers

Police officers can of course be the recipients of deadly force. The danger of their daily work was underscored in the summer of 1995 when a police chief in Quebec was shot and killed while responding to a domestic violence incident. The death of a police officer on duty is a rare event in Canada; on average, two or three officers are killed each year. In comparison, approximately 70 police officers a year are shot and killed each year in the United States.

Between 1879 and 2000, 363 police officers (a figure that also includes some penitentiary guards) died in the line of duty in Canada. The decade in which the highest number of police officers were killed was the 1980s: between 1980 and 1989, 63 officers were killed. Fifty-seven police officers died between 1960 and 1969 and 61 between 1970 and 1979 (Picard 1995). The Canadian Centre for Justice Statistics (1982) investigated the deaths of Canadian police officers over the years 1960 to 1979. During this period, 118 Canadian police officers were murdered. Most of these homicides were committed by firearms—handguns, rifles, shotguns, and sawed-off rifles. Between 1960 and 1991, 11 percent of all police officers killed were shot with their own, or a fellow officer's, firearm (Stansfield 2000).

POLICE MISCONDUCT

Police misconduct, or police deviance, is a term used in its broadest sense throughout the criminal justice literature (Martin 1993). It can be defined as "a generic description of police officer activities which are inconsistent with the officer's legal authority, organizational authority, and standards of ethical conduct" (Barker and Carter 1986: 1–7). Police misconduct can be subdivided into two categories: occupational deviancy and abuse of authority. Occupational deviancy is defined as "criminal and noncriminal [behaviour] committed during the course of normal work activities or committed under the guise of the police officer's authority" (Barker and Carter 1986: 4). Examples of police occupational deviancy include misconduct such as sleeping on duty, insubordination, and misuse of firearms.

Social scientists and social historians have investigated and reported police misconduct. Examples of police misconduct in recent years are not difficult to uncover. For example, in Quebec, charges in a drug case were thrown out after the judge discovered that the documents linking the shipment to the accused had been planted by Sûreté du Québec. Another incident involved a jury finding two Sûreté du Québec officers guilty of falsifying evidence in an attempt to prevent the daughter of one of them from being charged with drunk driving causing bodily harm (Tranh Ha 1999).

Police abuse of authority (often referred to as the use of excessive force) involves the use of various types of coercion when the police are interacting with citizens. According to Roberg and Kuykendall (1993: 200), four types of coercion are used by the police:

1. *verbal coercion:* the use of deceit, promises, threats, and derogatory language;
2. *physical coercion:* the use of the officer's physical strength and body;
3. *nonlethal coercion:* the use of a weapon instead of or in addition to the officer's body; and
4. *lethal coercion:* the use of a deadly weapon in such a manner that a person is likely to be seriously injured or killed

How common is the police use of excessive force? Claims have been made throughout the 20th century that Canadian police forces have used excessive force. Jamieson (1973) and Brown and Brown (1978) found that various police forces across Canada have harassed and intimidated striking workers. More recently, some Regina police force officers patrolled with unleashed police dogs during 1981–82; 52 Aboriginals and 33 non-Aboriginals were bitten (Forcese 1992).

Incidents of police use of excessive force are reported almost weekly by the media across Canada. But what form does this force take? Reiss (1974), in an American study, used college students to observe police–citizen interactions in high-crime areas in Washington, D.C., Chicago, and Boston. The students reported verbal abuse was common but that the excessive use of force was relatively rare, occurring in 44 cases out of the 5360 observations. There was little difference between the way police treated blacks and whites, and when force was used it was typically used selectively—against those who were disrespectful of the police or who disregarded police authority after they were arrested. Sherman and Cohen (1986) reported that police use of any form of violence was rare, and Bayley and Garofalo (1989) found that when police officers use force, it usually involved grabbing and restraining and rarely if ever involved the use of weapons.

Despite these research findings, widely publicized incidents of the police use of excessive force have continued to haunt police departments in Canada (Forcese 1992: 172–76). The police are frequently accused of relying on excessive physical force to obtain confessions from suspects (Hagan 1977) and that they "push the law to its limits, slip through the loopholes and employ technicalities" and cannot be trusted "to obey the rules society imposes on the way they question suspects" (Woods, in Martin 1993: 161). This situation has led Brannigan (1984: 57) to conclude that "the police appear to routinely trample over the rights of accused people." In 1976, as a result of allegations of excessive police force in the Metropolitan Toronto Police Force, a Royal Commission was created to investigate the charges. The commission chairman, Mr. Justice Donald Morand, concluded that six of the 17 incidents he studied involved the use of excessive force. And the Quebec Court of Appeal posthumously overturned the manslaughter conviction of Michel Jaffe, who spent five years in prison for the killing of a suspected drug-trafficker. The court overturned Mr. Jaffe's conviction when it heard his confession followed four hours of beatings (with telephone books) by Sûreté du Québec officers (Tranh Ha 1999).

A third type of police misconduct can be added to the two types already discussed. This involves the selective enforcement of laws amoug certain populations in Canada. These "routine incidents of misconduct reflect and reinforce race, class and gender bias in a myriad of ways" (Martin 1993: 149). The selective enforcement of the law as it applies to marginalized women, such as prostitutes, has recently surfaced in Vancouver with the disappearance of over 50 women and the charge that the police were indifferent to their disappearances.

"Problem" Police Officers

Some people believe that all police officers are involved with the illegitimate use of force while others argue that it is only a small proportion of officers who engage in such actions. Research by Lersch and Mieczkowski (1996) found that 7 percent of all police officers in the American police force they were studying were "chronic" offenders who received the majority (33 percent) of public complaints. The officers who received the majority of complaints were younger, less experienced, and were accused of using force after a proactive encounter they had personally initiated. Lersch and Mieczkowski also found these officers were actually praised by police administrators as more productive officers who were performing their duties to the best of their abilities—that is, citizen complaints were often interpreted as measures of productivity rather than a problem (Lersch and Mieczkowski 2000).

Police Accountability

Although a police department may have excellent training, practise culturally sensitive policing, and establish an excellent rapport with local residents, problems such as police misconduct and the use of excessive force will no doubt surface. In this case, the question then becomes, who shall police the police?

In some cases, a Royal Commission or an Inquiry will be struck to investigate a specific incident, although the actual occurrences of such government responses are rare. For example, a Royal Commission (the Royal Commission on the Donald Marshall, Jr. Prosecution) was appointed to investigate the wrongful conviction of Donald Marshall, Jr., a Mi'kmaq man who served almost 12 years of a sentence for a murder he did not commit. The Aboriginal Justice Inquiry in Manitoba focused upon the deaths of two Aboriginals in that province, Helen Betty Osborne and J.J. Harper. Although these reports were critical of some of the practices (or lack thereof) used by the police, investigations typically occur only after a lengthy period.

The most common ways to assure that the police are accountable for their actions are internal investigations, citizen oversight, and civil liability. Internal investigations involve the police themselves investigating the

potential wrongdoing by police officers. Many observers criticize this approach, arguing that it is inherently biased in favour of the police and that if an officer is found guilty of wrongdoing, the sentences are too lenient. A. Alan Borovoy, general counsel of the Canadian Civil Liberties Union, argues this approach is flawed since it "will scare off many potential complainants" and that "investigating officers will have a conflict of interest" (Borovoy 2000: A3). To illustrate his concerns, he points to the evidence collected by the Royal Commission on the Wrongful Prosecution of Donald Marshall, Jr. in which a RCMP officer appointed to evaluate the prosecution of Marshall soon after Marshall started to serve his sentence found no wrongdoing by the Sydney, Nova Scotia, investigators. When this issue was raised in the hearings conducted on this case years later, another member of the RCMP stated that "Police officers are like a fraternity. You feel a certain loyalty to one another." Similar scenarios have been found across Canada. In Winnipeg, the conclusions reached by an internal police review board established to look into the wrongful death of an Aboriginal man, J.J. Harper, by a Winnipeg police officer were criticized by an external inquiry. They found that the police attached "much more attention to protecting the officer than ... to uncovering the facts." And in Toronto, a police officer whose testimony helped incarcerate another police officer who had assaulted a prisoner was reportedly ostracized by other police officers, with the result that the officer left the force.

A second approach—and the most popular method used today—to controlling police misconduct is the creation of a separate civilian commission or review agency to investigate allegations of such behaviour. The goal of establishing an external citizen review board (sometimes referred to as civilian oversight) is to make the police accountable to the public. The first such organization was introduced as a preliminary act in 1981 in Toronto to allow the public the opportunity to make complaints directly to a nonpolice organization. This organization was created as a result of an investigation into the Metropolitan Toronto Police Force (as it was then known) by Judge D.R. Morand of the Ontario Supreme Court. He discovered evidence of false arrests, cover-ups, false charges, and conspiracy among police officers to protect one another from legal action. In 1984 this initial system was replaced by the *Metropolitan Toronto Police Force Complaints Act*. Its purpose is to investigate allegations of police brutality of Metropolitan Toronto police officers, and it attempted to strike a balance between the police in terms of investigating their own complaints and the need to independently investigate citizens' complaints against the police. In 1990, Ontario introduced a new *Police Services*

Act, creating the Special Investigations Unit (SIU), a group of individuals comprising civilians. The jurisdiction of the SIU was expanded to cover the entire province in 1992 (Wells 2000). The duties of the office were to

- review and, if necessary, reinvestigate complaints made by persons dissatisfied with decisions made by the police;
- monitor initial police complaints investigations and decisions made by police chiefs, the Ontario police commissioner, and decisions reached in internal disciplinary hearings;
- receive and record complaints from the public;
- refer cases to a civilian board of inquiry, if necessary, after reviews;
- conduct initial investigations into "two-force" complaints—allegations against officers from more than one force; and
- make recommendations to the police to improve police practices in order to avoid reoccurrence of certain types of complaints.

In order to carry out an investigation, the Public Complaints Commissioner was granted considerable powers of search and seizure as well as powers to subpoena witnesses and order hearings before a board of inquiry that held direct disciplinary powers. One-third of the board of inquiry were to be lawyers, one-third individuals jointly recommended by the Board of Police Commissioners and the Metropolitan Toronto Police Association, and one-third appointed by the Toronto City Council (McMahon 1988). Although these hearings were not criminal in nature, misconduct needed to be established beyond a reasonable doubt, a standard usually applied to criminal matters. Between 1988 and 1990, almost 98 percent of the cases in which civilians filed a complaint against police stemmed from an incident in which those civilians themselves were charged (Ellis and DeKeseredy 1996).

The annual reports of the Public Complaints Commissioner for the period 1988 to 1991 are summarized by Ellis and DeKeseredy (1996). Nonphysical and physical assaults by police accounted for about half of all complaints, with the most common complaint (43 percent) being the "failure to act according to police procedure," such as neglect of duty. Landau's (1994) study of the nature of allegations revealed that "improper police behavior" accounted for 49 percent of complaints, followed by physical abuse (34 percent), verbal abuse (32 percent), unprofessional conduct (29 percent), and neglect of duty (25 percent). The largest percentage of decisions by both the police chief and the Public Complaints commissioner for a 15-month period in 1992 and early 1993 resulted in "no action taken" because of insufficient

evidence, which accounted for 52 percent of all "resolved" complaints. Two other categories, "no further action—evidence supports officer" and "no further action—complainant lodged in bad faith," accounted for 16 and 23 percent of all complaints, respectively. Thus, no further action was taken in 70 (91 percent) of 77 decisions.

Of the 1915 incidents investigated, Ellis and DeKeseredy found most complaints to result from police–citizen contact on the street (48 percent). The next-largest categories were "residence," "police building," and "public place," which accounted for another 46 percent of the remaining incident locations. Landau obtained similar results, with just over 78 percent of all complaints coming from incidents "on the street or in public" (54 percent) and the complainant's residence (24 percent). Thirty percent of the complainants were black, 8 percent were Asian, and 4 percent were Hispanic, and the remainder were white. These rates are considered to be an "unreliable indicator of the current state of relations between police and visible minority, particularly black members of the community" (Landau 1994). Ellis and DeKeseredy (1996: 119) point out these rates "greatly underestimate the actual number of occasions in which blacks and other visible minority community members experienced racially or ethnically biased police conduct."

The third mechanism to controlling police misconduct is through civil liability. In this approach, individual police officers can be held liable for their misconduct and sentenced to a period of incarceration (although this rarely occurs), or the police service itself can be sued. In 1998, for example, a rape victim successfully sued the Toronto Police Service for failing to warn her that a serial rapist was attacking women in her neighbourhood. An Ontario court awarded her $220 000 (Gatehouse and Eby 2000). In another case, a British Columbia woman attempted to sue the RCMP for allegedly failing to protect her from a "shooting rampage" by her former husband that left her best friend dead and her daughter wounded. Even though an internal RCMP investigation found the officer in question did not conduct a thorough investigation, the B.C. Supreme Court dismissed her case (Sokoloff 2001: A9).

THE CHANGING COMPOSITION OF THE POLICE

During the past 25 years Canadian police forces have started to hire more women, visible-minority, and Aboriginal police officers in order to better serve their

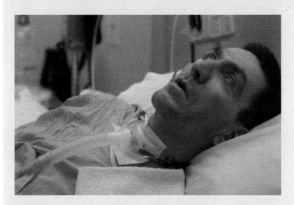

Richard Barnabe died in May 1996 after 29 months in a coma following a beating while in police custody.

In the early morning hours of 14 December 1993, Montreal taxi driver Richard Barnabe, depressed over the fact that he was not granted visiting rights to his son over Christmas, went to his church to talk to a priest. While banging on the building to awaken the priest, he accidentally broke a church window. When the police arrived after receiving a call from a citizen, Mr. Barnabe fled the scene and led police on a 10 kilometre pursuit through city streets at speeds exceeding 100 kilometres per hour. When Barnabe finally stopped his cab in front of his brother's house, he was arrested, taken to the local police station, and strip-searched with six police officers present.

When they began their strip search at 4:21 a.m., Mr. Barnabe was conscious and coherent enough to refuse medical assistance, but when the handcuffs were placed back on his hands 29 minutes later, he was bloodied and bruised and in full cardiac arrest. At hospital, he was diagnosed as having three broken ribs (that had been snapped from his spine), a skull fracture, bruises, a broken nose, a ripped sinus cavity, a tooth lodged in his throat, and suffering from irreversible brain damage, ultimately lapsing into a coma (Moore: 2000; Peritz 2000).

All the police officers involved in this case were suspended without pay, but received the equivalent of their take-home pay from their union, the Montreal Police Brotherhood. After a police investigation into the incident, the six officers were charged with assault causing bodily harm, a charge that carries a maximum 10-year sentence. A jury found four of the officers guilty as charged. Three were sentenced to jail terms of between 60 and 90 days. These sentences were intermittent, that is, they were to be served on weekends, allowing the officers to maintain their police jobs. The fourth officer convicted was ordered to perform 10 hours of community work in a palliative care hospital and given two years' probation. His sentence was lighter than the others because he arrived after the strip search had started and was implicated only in tying Mr. Barnabe's legs together. The fifth officer was acquitted, and the trial judge imposed a publication ban on the remaining officer's testimony and forbade any mention of his name or role in the events.

According to the Quebec Superior Court judge who heard the case, the sentences had "to reflect society's revulsion and the suffering of the officers from public scorn." Despite Mr. Barnabe's injuries, the judge ruled that "no gratuitous blows were delivered" and the actions of the police were "neither premeditated nor malevolent." In addition, he cited their lack of prior criminal records, the likelihood they would be fired from their jobs, and the poor training given to the officers. The judge also considered the fact that the officers were "not criminals in the normal sense of the word," posed no danger to society, and had already been punished and stigmatized by the media. However, the judge did add that the jail sentences were necessary to reflect "public revulsion" and that the "role of the court is not to please public opinion, but to dispense justice."

Although the lawyers for the four officers sentenced to jail terms felt the punishments were "reasonable and fair," they immediately filed appeals. Mr. Barnabe's sister considered the sentences to be "candy-coated" and demanded the officers be fired. Just one week before, her family received about $215 000 from the Montreal Urban Community Police Force in a civil lawsuit (Picard 1995: A1, A2).

Mr. Barnabe never regained consciousness and died in May 1996, 29 months after the beating. In 1997, Quebec's Police Ethics Committee effectively fired two of the officers while handing out maximum suspensions to two of the other officers. But on 6 March 2000, a Quebec Court Judge ruled that the two officers who were "fired" should instead be suspended for 240 and 300 days respectively. The judge "reproached the ethics committee for disregarding the fact that lawyers for both sides had recommended that disciplinary actions be limited to suspensions" (Peritz 2000: A3).

Continued on next page

Public reaction to the ruling was extremely critical. In addition, the Quebec Provincial Security Minister commented that he wanted the law changed so that officers convicted of criminal offences are automatically fired. A retired police chief commented that the two officers cannot return to duty and uphold the "credibility and duties " of police officers (Peritz 2000: A3). Mr. Barnabe's brother stated that this latest development led him to say that there is "a justice for the police, a justice for the rich, and a justice for the poor. My brother got the justice for the poor" (Peritz 2000: A3).

communities. For many people a police force that represents the sexual, ethnic, and racial composition of their community is "an essential feature in effective policing" and "provides a psychologically positive attitude on the part of visible minorities who have felt left out and alienated from the mainstream of society" (Jayewardene and Talbot 1990; Normandeau 1990). A police force that reflects the demographics of its community can be essential "in gaining the public's confidence by helping to dispel the view that police departments are generally bigoted or biased organizations" (Senna and Siegel 1995: 239).

In Canada, pressure to increase the numbers of women and visible minorities in police forces did not emerge until the 1970s, over 10 years after similar issues were raised in the United States. According to Forcese (1992), this change was the result of increasing numbers of visible-minority immigrants to Canada.

Christine Silverberg served five years as the chief of police of Calgary. She was the first woman to head a major-city police force in Canada.

Questions about the appropriate composition of the police were raised, among them whether the police are isolated from the community, how important it is to have visible-minority and female representation in police departments, and what type of individuals should be recruited as police officers. Although the responses to these questions differed, some police officials actively began to increase the number of visible minorities and women in their departments. In addition, the Royal Commission on the Status of Women made recommendations in 1971 that all police forces train and hire women. Their recommendations became the basis of the RCMP decision to train and hire their first female members in 1974. However, the integration of women and other minorities into policing has been a slow process.

Women and Policing

The number of women police officers in Canada has always been small until recently. Throughout the 1960s the percentage of female police officers remained below 1 percent, rising to 2 percent only in 1980. This figure increased to 3.6 percent in 1985, 6.4 percent in 1990, 10.9 percent in 1994, and 13 percent in 1996. While the number of sworn police officers has stayed about the same during the past few years (see Chapter 5), the number of women police officers has increased by several thousand. In 1997, women totaled 7495 sworn police officers.

Women police officers are gradually entering the upper echelons of police administration. In 1996, for example, 1.7 percent of all senior officers in Canada were women; by 2001, this figure had reached 3.5 percent. Women in noncommissioned ranks had increased their presence from 3.0 percent in 1996 to 6.3 percent in 2001. And in 1996, women comprised 13.5 percent of all constables; in 2001 that percent increased to 17.8 percent (Filyer 2002). The first woman chief of police was appointed in Guelph, Ontario, in 1994. In 1995 Calgary became the first Canadian city with a population over 100 000 to appoint a woman police officer to run its police force, Since that time women have been appointed commissioner of the Ontario Provincial Police and chief constable of British Columbia. In the RCMP, the first female detachment commander was appointed in 1990, the first commissioned officer in 1992, and the first commanding officer of a division in 1998.

Unequal Treatment

Before the increase in the number of women police officers in Canada during the mid-1980s, the role of women in policing was generally restricted to assignments involving social service issues, most commonly in the areas of juvenile and family violence. Women officers were seen as adding to specialized police activities and units as opposed to contributing to overall law enforcement duties. It was commonly believed at the time that men were more effective administrators and "were less likely to become irritable and over-critical under emotional stress" (Wilson and McLaren 1977).

Although these stereotypes of women and men in police work would ultimately be challenged, the initial breakthrough for equal treatment of women was the elimination of exclusionary physical requirements. For example, until 1979 the Ontario Provincial Police and the Ottawa Police Force turned down women applicants unless they were 5'11" tall and at least 160 pounds. Complaints to the Ontario government resulted in changes to these standards to accommodate the recruitment of more women (Forcese 1992). Police agencies started to advertise for more women interested in policing as a career. In 1987 the Metropolitan Toronto Police Force, which employed more than 5000 officers, had only 226 female sworn officers, approximately 4 percent of the total. The percentage of women in the RCMP, which didn't hire its first women officers until 1974, was 7 percent in 1988. Fourteen percent (or 2045) of all RCMP officers in 1999 were women.

Probably the most significant breakthrough for women police officers was the policy of employment equity. According to the federal government of Canada, employment equity is the purposeful identification of any significant differences between the participation levels and the population figures of four targeted minority groups—visible minorities, women, people with disabilities, and Aboriginals. Employment equity also aims to identify any employment policies and/or practices that disadvantage these groups. The legal foundation of employment equity is the *Canadian Human Rights Act* (1977). Section 15(1) of this act states that it is not discriminatory to start a program designed to prevent, eliminate, or reduce disadvantages experienced by individuals because of their race, national or ethnic origin, religion, age, sex, family status, marital status, or disability.

Some observers have noted that the major problem facing police departments is not recruiting women but rather keeping them. This is because "many police departments are locked in a 'timewarp' that perpetuates the myth that only men can do patrol" (Hale and Wyland 1993: 4). The presence of women in a traditionally male domain is threatening to many male officers, regardless of rank, and women are treated as outsiders, effectively preventing them from learning tasks that would help them to be promoted later (Padavic and Reskin 1990; Hunt 1990). Crawford and

Stark-Adamec (1994) studied why both women and men police officers left four major Canadian police forces. The reasons women gave for leaving their job as a police officer was to raise a family (56 percent), to move to another city (17 percent), to join a different police force (11 percent), or because of burnout/negative views on life (6 percent), feelings of inadequacy as a police officer (6 percent), and dissatisfaction with shift work (6 percent). Male officers, in contrast, left primarily due to a change in occupation (41 percent), disillusionment with policing or the criminal justice system (32 percent), burnout/negative views on life (23 percent), dissatisfaction with shift work (18 percent), family-related issues (9 percent), and danger inherent in the job (5 percent).

The Performance of Women Police Officers

When questioned about their experience on the job, the majority of women police officers feel they have to work harder than men to receive credit for their work. Most say that their competence is repeatedly questioned, they are judged by different standards, and any mistakes they make are attributed to their gender. This type of experience is found in many developed countries, not just Canada. Brown (1994) reports that this is the case in the United States, as do Holdaway and Parker (1998) in England and Winnifree and Newbold (1999) in New Zealand.

Some believe women police officers differ from their male counterparts in that they are more compassionate, less aggressive, and less competitive. They see their job from a different perspective and therefore develop different policing styles than do men. Citizens appear to prefer having a female officer respond to their complaints, especially those that involve domestic issues. In addition, women officers are more likely to possess the skills to reduce potentially violent circumstances. And, in the United States, financial payouts in civil lawsuits for cases involving police brutality and misconduct involving male officers exceed those involving women officers by a ratio of 43 to 1 (Spillar 2000).

Women Police Officers: Gender Conflicts at Work

Despite evidence (Balkin 1988) that shows female and male police officers perform equally, policewomen have sometimes experienced difficulty being fully accepted by their male colleagues. According to Balkin (1988: 33), male officers perceive policewomen to lack both the physical and emotional strength to perform well in violent confrontations. Overall, male police officers hold "almost uniformly negative … attitudes toward police-women." Petersen (1982) and Martin (1991) have pointed out that since male police officers associate masculinity with the use of physical force, and view the use of physical force as the defining feature of police work, they are concerned and threatened by women's successful integration into police work. However, Hunt (1990) reports that male and female police officers develop similar attitudes toward their occupational duties and job satisfaction.

This is not to say women officers no longer continue to experience gender conflicts at work. In her national assessment of women police officers in the United States in the 1980s, Martin (1991) found that a high percentage of female officers experienced some form of bias and that 75 percent of both new and experienced female police officers reported being victims of sexual harassment. In fact, a higher proportion (35 percent) of rookie women officers than rookie men officers (8 percent) reported their primary problem as new patrol officers was harassment by other police officers. This harassment included displays of pornography, jokes or comments based on sexual stereotypes of women, and remarks on women's sexuality. Crawford and Stark-Adamec (1994) made a similar conclusion in their study of 50 female and 68 male police officers and ex–police officers in four major Canadian police departments. Eighteen percent of the women in this study referred to sexually related problems on the job, including sexual harassment and sexual discrimination. The perception of the performance of women police officers is often based on gender stereotypes and, as a result, they are caught in conflicting situations, specifically the perception that they are physically weak and a risk in physical confrontations; if they are strong and aggressive, they are seen as an affront to the maleness of the policeman (Charles 1982).

Aboriginal and Other Visible-Minority Police Officers

Visible minorities "are those persons (other than Aboriginal persons) who are non-Caucasian in race or non-white in colour …" (Statistics Canada 1997: 5). Aboriginal persons refers to those "who reported identifying with at least one Aboriginal group, i.e., North American Indian, Métis or Inuit (Eskimo) and/or those who reported being a Treaty Indian or a Registered Indian as defined by the *Indian Act* of Canada and/or who were members of an Indian Band or First Nation" (Statistics Canada 1997: 5). Little has been written about visible-minority and Aboriginal police officers in Canada, in part because few have become police officers.

For example, in 1986, a total of 645 (1.1 percent) sworn police officers in Canada were members of visible-minority or Aboriginal groups. At the time, the largest group of visible minorities was located in Ontario, where 395 officers—1.9 percent of all sworn police officers in the province—were members of visible minorities; there were no visible-minority police officers in either Newfoundland or Prince Edward Island. By 1996 the percentage of visible-minority police officers had increased to 1725 officers (3 percent of the total number of police officers in Canada). Of this total, 1430 were males and 295 were females. At the same time, there were 1785 Aboriginal police officers (3 percent of the total number of sworn officers), of which 1430 were males and 355 were females. In 1989 the police force with the largest number of visible minorities was the Metropolitan Toronto Police Force, where 242 (or 4.2 percent) of all police officers were members of visible-minority groups. At that time the population of the jurisdiction policed by the Metropolitan Toronto Police Force was in excess of one million people. The largest number of visible-minority officers were constables (195, or 4.7 percent of all constables), followed by sergeants (18, or 2.0 percent), staff sergeants (8, or 2.7 percent), inspectors (2, or 4.4 percent), and staff inspectors (1, or 3.0 percent) (Suriya 1993). In 1988, the Sûreté du Québec had no officers who represented "minority communities." During 1997, in the Montreal Community Police Department, 2 percent of the police officers were members of visible minority groups (other than Aboriginals), 7.4 percent were members of ethnocultural groups, and 0.2 percent were Aboriginal (Jaccoud and Felice 1999).

The small number of visible minorities in Canadian police forces is a result of their limited access to the law enforcement profession. To date, studies have found that unrelated job requirements have deterred large numbers of visible minorities from applying to police forces across Canada (Jayewardene and Talbot 1990). For example, the debate over the wearing of turbans, as part of their uniform, by Sikh RCMP officers focused on the issue of RCMP tradition rather than the legal issue of whether the wearing of turbans interferes with the performance of duty. Hiring policies that create such obstacles for police officers have been termed a form of systemic discrimination, since these policies place an arbitrary barrier between an individual's ability and his employment opportunities in his chosen area of work (Abella 1984).

According to the *Employment Equity Act*, the goal of selecting the appropriate individual "has to be so structured as to increase the reliability of its objectivity" (Suriya 1993: 47). In his investigation of the recruitment process by Canadian police forces, Jain (1994) recommends the need for proactive recruitment methods, such as community outreach programs. These programs involve strategies such as providing visible-minority role models, trained recruiters, giving high-school presentations with visible-minority role models, and requesting high-school teachers and others to identify potential visible-minority candidates. Related issues include the reassessment of mental ability tasks, which may be biased against those not raised in Canada (or North America) and not male. Interviews may be a questionable component of the hiring process, since they have relatively low reliability (different interviewers reach different conclusions) as well as low validity (interview ratings and job performance scores are not closely related), and as a result involve subjective assessments and are "susceptible to the covert prejudices of individual interviewers" (Jain 1994: 105). Interviews have also been criticized because they are "not conducive to objective results" (Jayewardene and Talbot 1990: 6).

In addition, the Advisory Committee on Multicultural Police Recruitment and Selection of the Ottawa Police Force found that psychological tests, unless carefully reviewed, can readily lead to "many areas where sexual, religious, and cultural assumptions could lead to misinterpretations of the responses." Furthermore, they stress the importance of including an individual "with multicultural experience or training at the final interview as well as throughout the entire selection process." Wood (1989) reported that Ontario Task Force on Race Relations and Policing found that members of visible minorities consider policing a dead-end job with few promotional opportunities. The task force found that the "effective ceiling" for visible-minority promotions is the rank of staff sergeant. The task force also concluded that many visible-minority police officers have served for many years to obtain promotions "which have not been forthcoming."

Only limited analyses have explored racial minority communities across Canada to evaluate what residents expect from the police in terms of the racial composition of the police officers who patrol their neighbourhoods. One such study was Manitoba's Aboriginal Justice Inquiry, where the authors of the report wrote that Aboriginals "consider the police to be a foreign presence and do not feel understood by it. They certainly do not feel that the police operate on their behalf, or that the police are in any significant manner subject to a corre-

sponding Aboriginal influence in their communities" (Hamilton and Sinclair 1991: 597). Due to these concerns, the authors of the report recommended that police services in Aboriginal communities be delivered by professional regional Aboriginal police services that report to and service Aboriginal communities.

There are many benefits for increasing the number of Aboriginal and other visible-minority officers in police services in Canada. These include benefits for the police organization itself, such as improving the effectiveness of the police, preventing crime, and changing the image of the police for community members, especially youths (Jaccoud and Felices 1999).

SUMMARY

Police forces and their officers today face many critical issues as they develop policies, enforce the law, and interact with the public. One central issue is to effectively measure the overall effectiveness of the police. Some people assert that the police should arrest an individual whenever there is enough evidence, regardless of the infraction. This move toward a policy of "zero tolerance" has led to debate about the practice of police discretion. Studies of the arrest practices of the police in Canada indicate that the police do not "over-arrest" members of any particular group, but that situational and community factors play a crucial role in the decisions made by the police. Social issues too affect police operations.

Women and minority group members are entering police ranks in increasing numbers, and research indicates that their performance is equal to that of male police officers. However, the percentages of women and minority-group members on police forces still falls short of their percentages of the population. Still, as their numbers increase, an important issue becomes the number of women and minorities in the higher echelons of police departments.

Other critical issues are police use of deadly force and police deviance. Although the studies of deadly force are few, it is uncommon in Canada for the police to kill a citizen. More information is available on police deviance; recent initiatives by the province of Ontario reveal that many citizens have concerns about the police overextending their powers in their contact with citizens.

Discussion Questions

1. What are some possible negative and positive consequences of the police use of discretion?

2. Why is it difficult to formulate a clear policy to guide decision-making by police officers?

3. Why were women and minority-group members prevented from joining police forces throughout most of the 20th century in Canada? Compare the Canadian experience to that of the U.S. Are there any differences?

4. How do police officers' attitudes affect their performance?

5. Are women as effective as men in all types of police work? Why or why not?

6. Discuss why the police in Canada use deadly force less often than their counterparts in the United States.

7. Do you think police deviance is a serious problem? If yes, what is the best way to control it?

8. Do you think the police practise racial profiling? As a group? As individuals?

Suggested Readings

Forcese, Dennis P. 1992. *Policing Canadian Society.* Scarborough: Prentice-Hall.

Landau, Tammy. 1994. *Public Complaints against the Police: A View from Complainants.* Toronto: Centre of Criminology, University of Toronto.

Macleod, R.C., and D. Schneiderman, eds. 1994. *Police Powers in Canada: The Evolution and Practice of Authority.* Toronto: University of Toronto Press.

Marquis, G. *Policing Canada's First Century: A History of the Canadian Association of Chiefs of Police.* Toronto: Osgoode Society, 1993.

Northup, D.A. 1996. *Public Perceptions of Police Treatment of Minority Groups and the Disadvantaged in Metropolitan Toronto.* North York, Ont.: Institute for Social Research, York University.

References

Abell, J., and E. Sheehy, eds. 1993. *Criminal Law and Procedure: Cases, Context, Critique.* North York, Ont.: Captus Press.

Abella, R.S. 1984. *Report of the Commission on Equality in Employment.* Ottawa: Supply and Services Canada.

Abraham, J.D., J.C. Feld, R.W. Harding, and S. Skura. 1981. "Police Use of Lethal Force: A Toronto Perspective." *Osgoode Hall Law Journal* 19: 199–236.

Albanese, J. 1999. *Criminal Justice.* Boston: Allyn and Bacon.

Alberts, S. 2000. "Motorists Face Stiff Penalties for Fleeing Police." *National Post,* 8 February, A6.

Alpert, G.P. and T. Madden. 1994. "Police Pursuit Driving: An Empirical Analysis of Critical Decisions." *American Journal of Police* 13: 23–45.

Andrews, A.G. 1992. *Review of Race Relations Practices of the Metropolitan Toronto Police Force.* Toronto: Metropolitan Police Services.

Appleby, T. 1999. "Target Policing Has Uncertain Mark." *The Globe and Mail,* 18 October, A6.

Appleby, T., T.T. Ha, and R. Thomas. 1999. "Police-Chase Deaths Prompt Calls for Action." *The Globe and Mail,* 24 March, A3.

Ash, P., K.P. Slora, and C.F. Britton. 1990. "Police Agency Selection Practices." *Journal of Police Science and Administration* 17: 258–69.

Balkin, J. 1988. "Why Policemen Don't Like Policewomen." *Journal of Police Science and Administration* 16: 29–38.

Barker, T., and D.L. Carter. 1986. *Police Deviance.* Cincinnati: Anderson.

Bayley, D.H., and J. Garofalo. 1989. "The Management of Violence by Police Patrol Officers." *Criminology* 27: 1–21.

Bell, S. 1999. "RCMP Watchdog Wants Police Chases Only in Serious Cases." *National Post,* 14 December, A4.

Bennett, R.S., and T. Greenstein. 1975. "The Police Personality: A Test of the Predispositional Model." *Journal of Police Science and Administration* 3: 439–45.

Bienvenue, R., and A.H. Latif. 1974. "Arrests, Dispositions, and Recidivism: A Comparison of Indians and Whites." *Canadian Journal of Criminology and Corrections* 16: 105–16.

Borovoy, A. Alan. 2000. "Who Will Police the Police?" *National Post,* 6 June, A9.

Brannigan, A. 1984. *Crimes, Courts, and Corrections: An Introduction to Crime and Social Control in Canada.* Toronto: Holt, Rinehart and Winston.

Britz, M., and D. Payne. 1994. "Policy Implications for Law Enforcement Pursuit Driving." *American Journal of Police* 13: 13–42.

Brown, L., and C. Brown. 1978. *An Unauthorized History of the RCMP,* 2nd ed. Toronto: Lewis and Samuel.

Brown, M. 1994. "The Plight of Female Police: A Survey of NW Patrolmen." *Police Chief* 61: 50–53.

Callahan, C., and W. Anderson. 2001. "The Roots of Racial Profiling." *Reason* 33, no. 4: 36–43.

Canadian Centre for Justice Statistics. 1982. *Homicides of Police Officers in Canada.* Ottawa: Statistics Canada.

Carter, D.L., A.D. Sapp, and D.W. Stephens, 1988. "Higher Education as a Bona Fide Occupational Qualification (BFOQ) for Police: A Blueprint." *Policing: An International Journal of Police Strategies and Management* 7, no. 2: 1–27.

Chappell, D., and L. Graham. 1985. *Police Use of Deadly Force: Canadian Perspectives.* Toronto: Centre of Criminology.

Charles, M. 1982. "Women in Policing: The Physical Aspects." *Journal of Police Science and Administration* 10: 194–205.

Choudhrey, S. 2001. "Protecting Equality in the Face of Terror: Ethnic and Racial Profiling and s. 15 of the *Charter*." In R.J. Daniels, P. Macklem, and K. Roach, eds., *The Security of Freedom: Essays in Canada's Anti-Terrorism Bill.* Toronto: University of Toronto Press, pp. 367–82.

Cochrane, R., and A.J.P. Butler. 1980. "The Values of Police Officers, Recruits, and Civilians in England." *Journal of Police Science and Administration* 8: 205–11.

Crawford, B., and C. Stark-Adamec. 1994. "Women in Canadian Urban Policing: Why Are They Leaving?" In N. Larsen, ed., *The Canadian Criminal Justice System: An Issues Approach to the Administration of Justice.* Toronto: Canadian Scholars' Press.

De Lisi, M., and B. Regoli. 1999. "Race, Conventional Crime and Criminal Justice: The Declining Importance of Skin Color." *Journal of Criminal Justice* 27: 549–57.

Ellis, D., and W. DeKeseredy. 1996. *The Wrong Stuff: An Introduction to the Sociological Study of Deviance,* 2nd ed. Scarborough, Ont.: Allyn and Bacon.

Ericson, R.V. 1982. *Reproducing Order: A Study of Police Patrol Work.* Toronto: University of Toronto Press.

Falcone, D. 1994. "Police Officers and Officer Attitudes: Myths and Realities." *American Journal of Police* 13: 143–55.

Filyer, R.E. 2002. *Police Resources in Canada, 2001.* Ottawa: Canadian Centre for Justice Statistics.

Finckenhauer, J.O. 1975. "Higher Education and Police Discretion." *Journal of Police Science and Administration* 3: 450–57.

Fleming, T. 1981. "The Bawdy House 'Boys': Some Notes on Media, Sporadic Moral Crusades, and Selective Law Enforcement." *Canadian Criminology Forum:* 101–15.

Forcese, D. 1999. *Policing Canadian Society,* 2nd ed. Scarborough: Prentice-Hall Allyn & Bacon Canada.

———. 1992. *Policing Canadian Society.* Scarborough, Ont.: Prentice-Hall.

Fyfe, J.J. 1988. "Police Use of Deadly Force: Research and Reform." *Justice Quarterly* 5, no. 2: 165–205.

Gatehouse, J., and C. Eby. 2000. "Rape Victim and Family Sue Toronto Police Force for $4.5 Million." *National Post,* 12 October, A9.

Geller, W.A., and M.S. Scott. 1991. "Deadly Force: What We Know." In C.B. Klockars and S.D. Mastrofski eds., *Thinking About Police.* New York: McGraw-Hill, pp. 446–76.

Goldstein, J. 1960. "Police Discretion Not to Invoke the Criminal Justice Process: Low Visibility Decisions in the Administration of Justice." *Yale Law Journal* 69: 543–94.

Gunn, R., and C. Minch. 1988. *Sexual Assault: The Dilemma of Disclosure and the Question of Conviction.* Winnipeg: University of Manitoba.

Hale, D.C., and S.M. Wyland. 1993. "Dragons and Dinosaurs: The Plight of Patrol Women." *Police Forum* 3: 1–6.

Hamilton, A.C., and C.M. Sinclair. 1991. *The Justice System and Aboriginal People: Report of the Aboriginal Justice Inquiry of Manitoba, Volume 1.* Winnipeg: Queen's Printer.

Havemann, P., K. Couse, L. Foster, and R. Mantonovitch. 1985. *Law and Order for Canada's Indigeneous People.* Regina: Prairie Justice Research, University of Regina, School of Human Justice.

Holdoway, S., and S.K. Parker. 1998. "Policing Women Police: Uniform Patrol, Promotion and Representation in the CID." *British Journal of Criminology* 38: 40–48.

Hunt, J.C. 1990. "The Logic of Sexism among the Police." *Woman and Criminal Justice* 1: 3–30.

Jaccoud, M., and M. Felices. 1999. "Ethnicization of the Police in Canada." *Canadian Journal of Law and Society* 14, no. 1 (Spring): 83–100.

Jain, H.C. 1994. "An Assessment of Strategies of Recruiting Visible-Minority Police Officers in Canada: 1985–1990." In R.C. Macleod and D. Schneiderman, eds., *Police Powers in Canada: The Evolution and Practice of Authority.* Toronto: University of Toronto Press, pp. 138–64.

Jamieson, S. 1973. *Industrial Relations in Canada,* 2nd ed. Toronto: Macmillan.

Jayewardene, C.H.S., and C.K. Talbot. 1990. *Police Recruitment of Ethnic Minorities.* Canadian Police College.

Kania, R.R.E., and W.C. Mackey. 1977. "Police Violence as a Function of Community Characteristics." *Criminology* 15: 27–48.

Krimmel, J. 1996. "The Performance of College-Educated Police: A Study of Self-Rated Police Performance Measures." *American Journal of Police* 15: 85–95.

Laghi, B. 2000. "Bill Gets Tough with Those Who Flee Police." *The Globe and Mail,* 8 February, A9.

Landau, T. 1994. *Public Complaints against the Police: A View from Complainants.* Toronto: Centre of Criminology, University of Toronto.

Langworthy, R.H. 1987. "Police Cynicism: What We Know from the Niederhoffer Scale." *Journal of Police Science and Administration* 11: 457–62.

Lersch, K.M., and T. Mieczkowski. 2000. "An Examination of the Convergence and Divergence of Internal and External Allegations of Misconduct Filed against Police Officers." *Policing: An International Journal of Police Strategies and Management* 23, no. 1: 54–68.

Lersch, K.M., and T. Mieczkowski. 1996. "Who Are the Problem-Prone Officers? An Analysis of Citizen Complaints." *American Journal of Police* 15, no. 3: 23–44.

Lewis, C. (chair). 1989. *The Report of the Race Relations and Policing Task Force.* Toronto: Solicitor General.

McGahan, P. 1984. *Police Images of a City.* New York: Peter Lang.

McKenna, P.F. 2002. *Police Powers I.* Toronto: Pearson Education Canada.

McMahon, M. 1988. "Police Accountability: The Situation of Complaints in Toronto." *Contemporary Crises* 12: 301–27.

Martin, D. 1993. "Organizing for Change: A Community Law Response to Police Misconduct." *Hastings Women's Law Journal* 4: 131–74.

Martin, S.E. 1991. "The Effectiveness of Affirmative Action: The Case of Women in Policing." *Justice Quarterly* 8: 489–504.

Meagher, M.S. 1983. *Perception of the Police Patrol Function: Does Officer Education Make a Difference?* Paper presented at the annual meeting of the Academy of Criminal Justice Sciences, San Antonio, Tex.

Mitchell, L.P. 1990. "High Speed Pursuits." *Criminal Justice: The Americas,* vol. 2 (January).

Mitchell, T. 2002. "One Judge: Two Cases about Bias." *LawNow* 26, no. 5: 8.

Moore, L. 2000. "Police Who Beat Man into Coma Should Keep Jobs, Judge Says." *National Post*, 8 March, A5.

Mosher, C. 1998. *Discrimination and Denial: Systematic Racism in Ontario's Legal and Criminal Justice System, 1891–1961.* Toronto: University of Toronto Press.

Niederhoffer, A. 1967. *Behind the Shield: The Police in Urban Society.* Garden City, N.Y.: Anchor Books.

Normandeau, A. 1990. "The Police and Ethnic Minorities." *Canadian Police College Journal* 14: 215–29.

Ontario Commission on Systemic Racism in the Ontario Criminal Justice System. 1995. *Report of the Commission on Systemic Racism in the Ontario Criminal Justice System.* Toronto: Queen's Printer for Ontario.

Padavic, I., and B.F. Reskin. 1990. "Men's Behaviour and Women's Interest in Blue-Collar Jobs." *Social Problems* 37: 613–27.

Parent, R.B., and S. Verdun-Jones. 1998. "Victim-Precipitated Homicide: Police Use of Deadly Force in British Columbia." *Policing: An International Journal of Police Strategies & Management* 21: 432–48.

Peritz, I. 2000. "Montrealers Aghast at Barnabe Ruling." *The Globe and Mail*, 9 March, A3.

Petersen, C. 1982. "Doing Time with the Boys: An Analysis of Women Correctional Officers in All-Male Facilities." In B.R. Price and N.J. Sokoloff, eds., *The Criminal Justice System and Women.* New York: Clark Boardman.

Picard, A. 1995. "Police Get Weekend Jail Terms in Beating." *The Globe and Mail*, 14 July, A1, A2.

Regoli, R.M. 1977. *Police in America.* Washington, D.C.: R.F. Publishing.

Regoli, R.M., R. Culbetson, J. Crank, and J. Powell. 1990. "Career Stage and Cynicism among Police Chiefs." *Justice Quarterly* 7: 592–614.

Regoli, R.M., and E.D. Poole. 1979. "Measurement of Police Cynicism: A Factor Scaling Approach." *Journal of Criminal Justice* 7: 37–52.

Regoli, R.M., E.D. Poole, and J.D. Hewitt. 1979. "Refining Police Cynicism Theory: An Empirical Assessment, Evaluation, and Implications." In D.M.

Peterson, ed., *Police Work: Strategies and Outcomes in Law Enforcement.* Beverly Hills, Calif.: Sage, pp. 59–68.

Roach, K. 1999. *Due Process and Victims' Rights: The New Law and Politics of Criminal Justice.* Toronto: University of Toronto Press.

Roberg, R.R. 1978. "An Analysis of the Relationship among Higher Education, Belief Systems, and Job Performance of Police Officers." *Journal of Police Science and Administration* 6: 336–44.

Roberg, R.R., and J. Kuykendall. 1993. *Police and Society.* Belmont, Calif.: Wadsworth.

Rodriquez, M.L. 1995. "Increasing Importance of Higher Education in Police Human Resource Development Programs." *Criminal Justice: The Americas*, vol. 8 (April–May): 1–9.

Sanders, B., T. Hughes, and R.H. Langworthy. 1995. "Police Officer Recruitment and Selection: A Survey of Major Police Departments in the U.S." *Police Forum* 5: 1–4.

Senna, J.J., and L.J. Siegel. 1995. *Essentials of Criminal Justice.* Minneapolis/St. Paul: West.

Sherman, L.W., E.G. Cohen, and R.H. Langworthy. 1979. "Measuring Homicide by Police Officers." *Journal of Criminal Law and Criminology* 70: 546–60.

Skolnick, J. 1994. *Justice without Trial,* 3rd ed. New York: Macmillan.

———. 1966. *Justice without Trial.* New York: Wiley.

Smith, A.B., B. Locke, and A. Fenster. 1969. "Authoritarianism in Police College Students and Non-Police." *Journal of Criminal Law, Criminology, and Police Science* 58: 440–43.

Sokoloff, H. 2001. "Domestic Violence Victim Loses Suit against the RCMP." *National Post*, 6 June, A9.

Sparrow, M., M. Moore, and D. Kennedy. 1990. *Beyond 911: A New Era for Policing.* New York: Basic Books.

Spillar, K. 2000. *Gender Differences and the Cost of Police Brutality and Misconduct.* Los Angeles: National Center for Women & Policing.

Stansfield, R.T. 2000. "Use of Force by and against Canadian Police." In J.V. Roberts, ed., *Criminal Justice in Canada: A Reader.* Toronto: Harcourt Brace & Company Canada Ltd., pp. 70–76.

———. 1996. *Issues in Policing: A Canadian Perspective.* Toronto: Thompson Educational Publishing.

Statistics Canada. 1997. *1996 Census Dictionary.* Ottawa: Industry Canada.

Suriya, S.K. 1993. "The Representation of Visible Minorities in Canadian Police: Employment Equity beyond Rhetoric." *Police Studies* 16: 44–62.

Swol, K. 1998. *Private Security and Public Policing in Canada.* Ottawa: Canadian Centre for Justice Statistics.

Tranh Ha, T. 1999. "Quebec Police Officers Guilty of Falsifying Evidence." *The Globe and Mail*, 23 December, A3.

Wells, J. 2000. "The Watchdogs." *Toronto Life* 34, no. 16: 114–22.

Wilson, O.W., and R.C. McLaren. 1977. *Police Administration.* New York: McGraw-Hill.

Wilt, G.M., and J.D. Bannon. 1976. "Cynicism or Realism: A Critique of Niederhoffer's Research into Police Attitudes." *Journal of Police Science and Administration* 4: 40.

Winnifree, L.T., and G. Newbold. 1999. "Community Policing and the New Zealand Police." *Policing* 22: 589–618.

Wood, C. 1989. "Police: A Call for Racial Balance." *Toronto Star,* 12 April, A22.

Court Cases

Andrews v. Law Society (British Columbia) (1989), 56 D.L.R. (4th) 1 (S.C.C.)

R. v. Beare, [1988] 2 S.C.R. 387, 66 C.R. (3d) 97

R. v. Deane, [1997] O.J. No. 3578 (Ont. Prov. Ct.)

R. v. Lines, [1993] O.J. No. 3248 (Ont. Gen. Div.)

R. v. Mack (1988), 44 C.C.C. (3d) 513 (S.C.C.)

R. v. Turpin (1989), 48 C.C.C. (3d) 8 (S.C.C.)

Pretrial Criminal Procedures

CHAPTER OBJECTIVES

✓ Explain the key components of pretrial procedures.
✓ Consider the importance of the defendant's right to legal counsel.
✓ Discuss the rules governing search and seizure in Canada.
✓ Discuss the limitations and expectations placed on the police use of warrants.
✓ Understand the laws governing police use of electronic surveillance.
✓ Examine the laws controlling the police interrogation while the suspect is in custody.

Between an arrest and a trial lies a series of events that are essential in the processing of suspects within our criminal justice system. Pretrial criminal procedures are important because most criminal cases are never formally heard in the courts, but resolved informally. Although most Canadians have seen television courtroom dramas with juries, defence lawyers, and prosecutors arguing over details in front of a judge in a court room filled with spectators, these are infrequent events. As a result, it is important to study pretrial procedures in order to understand the events most individuals experience when they enter the criminal justice system.

This chapter focuses upon pretrial criminal procedures that involve the actions of the police from detaining a suspect until the case enters a criminal courtroom for trial. As you will see, a large number of procedures are necessary during this time, and many of these issues have ultimately been heard by the Supreme Court of Canada. One of the most important concerns at this stage of our criminal justice system is privacy; that is, what rights can individuals reasonably expect in our society without the police intruding into their lives? This question has led to a number of significant trials in recent years, and the Supreme Court has agreed to hear cases in this area in order to resolve important issues for both suspects and the police. Part of this controversy results from the fact that "privacy" is not mentioned in the *Charter of Rights and Freedoms*, and as a result the courts have had to interpret—and balance—this area of law between the rights of society to have effective police protection and the rights of suspects to their privacy. The issue of privacy was a central concern in *R. v. Feeney* (1997), and the ruling by the Supreme Court became one of its most controversial in recent years. In fact, a legal observer commented that the Supreme Court's action in this case was an unprecedented judicial action (Coughlan 1998).

In this case, a murder suspect was arrested without a warrant, and the decision of the Supreme Court (which was in favour of the defendant) led to a restriction of police search powers, which resulted in Parliament's having to pass new legislation concerning warrants. In fact, the decision in this case reversed a rule previously established by the Supreme Court—that police could enter a residence to make an arrest without a warrant.

At 8:20 a.m. on 8 June 1991, 86-year-old Frank Boyle was found murdered in his mobile home in the interior of British Columbia. The police officer who arrived at the scene concluded that, by the amount of blood, the murder had been extremely violent. A neighbour informed the investigating police officer that she had observed a man, Michael Feeney (who lived nearby), walking away from Boyle's truck after it had been driven into a ditch earlier that morning. Another neighbour told the officer he had seen Feeney enter a storage trailer at about 7 a.m. The officer knocked on the door of the storage trailer and yelled out "Police!" The officer heard nothing in response, entered without a warrant, and awakened the sleeping Feeney by touching him on the leg. Feeney's shirt and shoes were covered with blood, and money stolen from the deceased was located under the suspect's mattress. Feeney was later charged and convicted of second-degree murder.

However, on 22 May 1997 the Supreme Court of Canada, in a 5–4 ruling, decided the search was unlawful and ordered a new trial. The majority, following the due process model, felt the police officer acted on a hunch, since he admitted that he did not have reasonable grounds for arresting Feeney and should have obtained a search warrant while waiting outside the storage facility. The justices' ruling was based on the arresting officer's statement that at the time of his entering into the suspect's trailer, he had reason to believe that the suspect was involved in the murder, but he did not have sufficient reason to make an arrest (until he saw the bloodied clothing) (Hiebert 2002). The majority ruled that although the officer was correct in his "hunch" about the accused, it still did not legitimize his actions. Supreme Court Justice Sopinka wrote in his decision that "in general, the privacy interest outweighs the interest of the police and warrantless arrests in dwelling houses are prohibited" (*R. v. Feeney* (1997), para. 159). Another issue that concerned the majority of Supreme Court justices was the delay in the reading of Feeney's rights. They ruled it took too long for the officer to read Feeney his rights, as they felt as soon as the officer touched Feeney's leg to awaken him, Feeney was "detained," and the law requires that the rights of a detained person be read immediately.

The minority, supporting the crime control model, interpreted the actions of the officer quite differently, while placing it in the context of a concern for the victim. In their opinion, the police officer acted properly by ensuring that a murder suspect was not at large in the community. Madame Justice L'Heureux-Dubé stated that the majority had seen the action of police officers "as lawless vigilantes, flagrantly and deliberately violating the *Charter* at every turn" (*R. v. Feeney* (1997), para. 114). Her concern went beyond the police to the "helpless victim," who she considered had suffered from a "random" and "savage beating" (*R. v. Feeney* (1997), para. 117).

The Supreme Court ordered a new trial but ruled the bloody shirt and shoes and the money were considered to be inadmissable as evidence, because their con-

tinued use by the prosecution would bring the criminal justice system into disrepute. The ruling of the majority of Supreme Court justices was based on the fact that, up until this case, the common law permitted a police officer, under certain conditions, to enter a private dwelling to arrest a suspect without a warrant. But now the majority of justices ruled that the arresting officer was incorrect to believe there was reasonable grounds for an arrest and that he possessed reasonable and probable grounds to arrest the suspect. While the police officer was within the law of detaining as well as arresting a suspect as it existed up until this case, the majority of the Supreme Court justices now considered the existing rules to be insufficient.

The potential impact of this decision on police forces was so great that the Supreme Court allowed the previous rules governing warrants to continue for six months. Parliament responded to this by passing Bill C-16, which allows a police officer to enter a residence or other dwelling to make an arrest without a warrant if exigent circumstances exist, such as the need to prevent the loss or destruction of evidence, if she believes her warnings will lead to personal harm when she enters a dwelling and if there is an urgent call for assistance, particularly in the context of domestic violence.

This latter exception was affirmed in *R. v. Godoy* (1997), a case in which the police entered an apartment without a warrant after receiving a 911 call. A "nervous-looking man answered the door and suggested nothing was going on interest to them," but "the police pushed past him" (Makin 1998). They discovered the woman who had made the call. She was sobbing and had a badly bruised eye. She told the police the man who had tried to stop them at the door was responsible for her injury. The accused was acquitted at the lower court but on appeal was convicted by the appeal court. The accused argued that when the police entered his apartment they were infringing his constitutional right to be free of unreasonable search and seizure. The Supreme Court disagreed with the accused, throwing out his appeal.

Another exception to the decision made in *R. v. Feeney* involves the actions of police officers searching a motor vehicle without a warrant in certain circumstances. A warrantless search could in many situations mean that evidence would be ruled inadmissible. One such case occurred during October 1997 when a RCMP police officer on patrol arrested a man after he stepped out of a field of tall grass just outside Gimli, Manitoba. When questioned about his activities, the individual informed the police officer that he had gone into the field to relieve himself. After a quick search of the area, the officer discovered a bag that contained four kilograms of marijuana and arrested the man for marijuana trafficking. The officer then took the suspect to the police lockup in Gimli. The vehicle of the arrested individual was towed to an impound lot, where, six hours after the arrest, the RCMP discovered cocaine and a large amount of cash during a routine inventory check of the arrested individual's vehicle. The RCMP seized the cocaine and money. Defence counsel later argued that since the RCMP did not have a search warrant, the cocaine and money should be returned.

Was the RCMP search of the suspect's vehicle lawful? Should the cocaine and money found in the vehicle be returned? Or could it be used as evidence for another criminal charge? Once again, these questions involve the conflict between an individual's right to privacy and the need for the police to have some leeway in the gathering of evidence. In this case, the Supreme Court of Canada (*R. v. Caslake* (1998)) ruled the seizure of the cocaine and money was unjust because the search was not connected to the arrest itself. However, the court also ruled that the evidence should not be excluded. Not only did the police act in good faith, but the evidence caused no harm to the administration of justice. The court felt that "excluding the evidence would have a more serious impact on the repute of the administration of justice than admitting it … [for] the prosecution had no case without the evidence."

INVESTIGATIVE DETENTION

While many people consider an arrest to be the first step in criminal pretrial procedure, this is often not the case. This is because the courts in Canada have recognized the police's right to detain, interrogate, and search an individual even "where there is less than reasonable grounds to believe than an offence has been committed" (Bilodeau 2001/2002: 42). Today in Canada, the police can hold a person for questioning even if they do not have grounds for an arrest. However, the legality of detaining a person in this way depends upon the importance of the issue being investigated and the amount of intrusion that is necessary.

An investigative detention is currently defined as "a reactive power dependent upon a reasonable belief that the detained person is implicated in a prior criminal act" (*Brown v. Durham Regional Police Force* (1998)). The *Charter* is concerned about police officers misusing their powers, so s. 9 states that "Everyone has the right not to be arbitrarily detained or imprisoned." According to Bilodeau (2001/2002: 42–43), the police are allowed to detain an individual due to safety concerns. If, for example, a suspect runs from the police after leaving a crack house and being told to stop, the police are allowed to protect themselves by conducting a nonintrusive search for weapons. And if during this search illegal

drugs are discovered, the police officer can legally arrest the person without fear of having the case dismissed on a *Charter* challenge to have the evidence thrown out. A police officer risks having the evidence thrown out when he decides he is at risk when he actually isn't (e.g., when the individual in question doesn't run from the police after being requested to stop). Another limit on police powers in this area is when the police decide to conduct an intrusive search, such as a strip search (see below), which is more difficult to justify to the court. One example of an illegal police investigative detention occurs when a police officer observes an individual running away from the scene of a break and enter with a sack over her shoulder. The police stop her, take the sack from her, and discover expensive machinery parts. Soon they learn that the parts have been stolen, and they subsequently arrest the individual. Assuming that no threats to the police were made (i.e., their safety was not at issue), the search for the stolen property is illegal. While an officer is allowed to detain an individual to determine if she had been involved in a crime, this does give the police the right to make an intrusive search if it does not involve issues of safety.

So, why do the police conduct investigative detentions? As Nicol (2002: 234) points out, "the opportunity to stop and confront suspects is an invaluable tool." There are possible benefits to the police, such as allowing officers the time and opportunity to use other search powers they are allowed to use if the circumstances permit. If during their search of the individual they legally obtain evidence about a crime, police officers may then use a number of legal warrantless search and seizure powers they possess, such as the plain view doctrine (see below), in certain exigent circumstances. And, if the police, during an investigative detention, find enough evidence to formally arrest an individual, s. 495 of the *Criminal Code* permits them to conduct a search incident to an arrest (Nicol 2002). However, other *Charter* rights may come into existence for suspects or arrestees, such as those found in ss. 10(a) and 10(b) (the right to be informed promptly of the reasons therefor, and to retain and instruct counsel without delay, and to be informed of that right, respectively).

ARREST

An arrest involves the police power to restrain an individual—in effect, to deprive an individual of liberty. During the course of their duties, police officers may stop and question a large number of people for a variety of reasons. They may want to obtain information about a crime or question someone about what he is doing in a particular location.

To legally arrest someone, the police officer has to verbally inform the suspect that he is under arrest. An arrest also involves the taking of physical control or custody of an individual with the intent to detain that individual. This action will require the use of force if the individual being arrested resists being taken into custody. If a person being arrested willingly accompanies the police officer, the officer will have no need to make physical contact, but at the same time the arrested person must acknowledge that he is in custody. If there is no contact, a police officer has to make physical contact with the suspect. Section 10(a) of the *Charter of Rights and Freedoms* stipulates that "Everyone has the right on arrest or detention to be informed promptly of the reasons therefor."

A police officer must inform an individual of his rights the moment that individual becomes a suspect in the crime under investigation. If the suspect is not informed, any evidence obtained from the suspect is not admissible, will not stand the test of the *Charter*, and will put the administration of justice into disrepute. On detaining or arresting a suspect the police must read the following:

1. Notice on arrest: I am arresting you for … [briefly describe reasons for arrest].
2. Right to counsel: It is my duty to inform you that you have the right to retain and instruct counsel without delay. Do you understand?
3. Caution to charged person: You [are charged, will be charged] with … Do you wish to say anything in answer to the charge? You are not obligated to say anything unless you wish to do so, but whatever you say may be given in evidence.
4. Secondary caution to charged person: If you have spoken to any police officer or anyone with authority, or if any such person has spoken to you in connection with this case, I want it clearly understood that I do not want it to influence you in making any statement.

Arrest without a Warrant

According to s. 495(1) of the *Criminal Code* it is possible for a police officer to arrest someone without a warrant. A person may be arrested in this way who:

- is found committing any criminal offence (indictable, summary conviction, and federal statute);
- is about to commit an indictable offence, on the basis of reasonable and probable grounds;
- the police officer, on reasonable and probable grounds, believes has an outstanding warrant within the territorial jurisdiction in which the person is located; or
- the police officer knows has committed an indictable offence.

A police officer's power to arrest without a warrant is restricted by s. 495(2) of the *Criminal Code*, which states that no arrest shall occur where the public interest is satisfied and no reasonable grounds exist to believe the accused will fail to appear in court. This means that a police officer shall not arrest an individual without a warrant

1. for a summary conviction offence,
2. an indictable offence within the absolute jurisdiction of a provincial court judge, as listed in s. 553 of the *Criminal Code* (see Chapter 8), or
3. if the offence is defined as a hybrid offence.

Section 495(2) states:

495 (2) A peace officer shall not arrest a person without warrant for

(a) an indictable offence mentioned in section 553,
(b) an offence for which the person may be prosecuted by indictment or for which he is punishable on summary conviction, or
(c) an offence punishable on summary conviction, in any case where
(d) he believes on reasonable grounds that the public interest, having regard to all the circumstances including the need to

(i) establish the identity of the person,
(ii) secure or preserve evidence of or relating to the offence, or
(iii) prevent the continuation or repetition of the offence or the commission of another offence,

may be satisfied without so arresting the person, and

(e) he has no reasonable grounds to believe that, if he does not so arrest the person, the person will fail to attend court in order to be dealt with according to law.

Police officers then proceed to use one of three alternatives available to them. First, they have the option of issuing the suspect with an appearance notice or, second, they have the power to release the suspect with the intention of applying for a summons from a justice of the peace. Their final option is the possibility of releasing the suspect unconditionally. This means that the police officer, after determining the identity of the suspect, releases the suspect and, at a later date, either issues an appearance notice or is able to have a justice of the peace issue a summons.

Arrest with a Warrant

If the police intend to arrest someone with a warrant, they must suspect on the basis of reasonable grounds that the individual in question committed a crime and that the suspect's appearance cannot be compelled by a summons (see Chapter 1). To obtain a warrant, the police must ordinarily go before a justice of the peace and lay an information alleging that a criminal offence has been committed. Once the police are successful in obtaining an arrest warrant, an officer who executes the warrant should have it in his possession in case the suspect requests that he show it. In some situations, the police may be granted an arrest warrant that authorizes them to enter a private residence to arrest an individual if certain conditions are met (s. 529.1 of the *Criminal Code*). Police officers are also able to enter a private residence without a search warrant in certain circumstances, such as if they are in "hot pursuit" of a suspect (s. 529.3 of the *Criminal Code*). Obviously, an arrest can be made without a warrant if the police observe a crime being committed. But if the police decide they are going to detain the individual for a period of time, the suspect must be brought before a justice of the peace as soon as possible.

Section 503(1) of the *Criminal Code* states that when a justice of the peace is available within 24 hours of an arrest, the accused must be taken before him within this period of time—or, if a justice is not available, within a reasonable period. If the accused does not appear before a justice within a certain amount of time, the case may be terminated on the grounds of "unreasonable delay." The Supreme Court of Canada dealt with the meaning of "unreasonable delay" in *R. v. Storrey* (1990), where it was ruled that the police could delay this process for 18 hours so that a lineup could be put together. However, when an accused was detained for 36 hours (*R. v. Charles* (1987)) the Saskatchewan Court of Appeal ruled that it was a violation of s. 9 of the *Charter*.

CUSTODIAL INTERROGATION

The police can place an accused into custody at the time of his arrest, whether the arrest is on the street, in a house, in a police station, or in a police vehicle. It is recommended procedure to inform the suspect of his right to silence and counsel before the police start questioning. According to s. 7 of the *Charter*, everyone has the right to life, liberty, and security of the person, and the right not to be deprived thereof except in accordance with the principles of fundamental justice. Once arrested, many suspects choose to remain silent, and since both oral and written statements are admissible in court, police officers sometimes stop their questioning until defence counsel are present. However, the police can still ask certain questions, such as location of residences, place of work, etc. If the accused decides to answer the questions, she may decide to stop at any time and refuse to answer more questions until a lawyer arrives. Suspects may waive this right only if they are aware of what they are doing and are able to contact a lawyer at any time if they so wish.

Traditionally, Canadian courts have held that an out-of-court statement by an accused person constitutes appropriate evidence as long as the statement was given voluntarily. In *R. v. Pickett* (1975) it was determined that when an issue arises over the voluntariness of a statement, it must be proved beyond a reasonable doubt that the statement was voluntary. In essence, s. 7 of the *Charter* seeks to impose limits on the powers the state and its agents (such as the police) have over the detained individual. This protects the accused against the superior resources of the police; however, the police have the power to deprive an individual of her life, liberty, or security as long as they respect the fundamental principles of justice.

What concerns civil libertarians, defendants, and defence lawyers about police interrogations are the techniques used by police investigators to obtain information from a suspect and/or accused. If the police inform the person they are to question about her right to contact a lawyer (see below) and the offer is refused, the investigators may use a variety of strategies to get the suspect to provide the relevant information.

The police use a number of strategies to obtain information during custodial interrogations. These strategies have been devised by the police to convince suspects to voluntarily give information that could implicate themselves as the offender (Leo 1996). The first is referred to as the "conditioning strategy," whereby the officers provide an environment in which the suspect is encouraged to think positively of the interrogator(s) and subsequently cooperates with the authorities. By providing coffee and cigarettes, the suspect's anxiety level is lowered and a sense of trust is reached. The second technique is known as the "de-emphasizing" strategy, in which interrogators inform the suspect that rights are unimportant and the most important issue is to empathize with the victim(s) and his family(ies). One outcome of this technique is that the suspect rarely if ever thinks of stopping the interrogation in order to contact a lawyer for advice. The "persuasion strategy" refers to investigators informing the suspect that if he doesn't tell his side of the story at that time, only the victim's will be used during the trial.

EXHIBIT 7.1   Police Interrogations

For three hours RCMP Corporal Greg Bishop interviewed Shane Ertmoed, suspected in the killing of Heather Thomas, 10.

On October 1, 2000, a young girl vanished while visiting her father's townhouse complex in Surrey, British Columbia. Three weeks later, her body was discovered in a nearby provincial park. Twelve days later, on 3 November, the RCMP arrested a male suspect who lived in the same townhouse complex. The next day, a police officer started his interrogation (which was videotaped), ending later that day with the suspect confessing to the officer that he had killed the girl. The following exchange is taken from the transcript of the interrogation of the suspect. Before he started the interrogation, the police officer prepared a strategy with two psychologists. The police officer also used a nine-step style of interrogation that includes "behaviour observation questions" and "elimination questions" designed to evaluate a suspect's reaction. Notice how the investigator moves from strategy to strategy in an effort to make the suspect admit to the murder.

Police Officer: When you watch American TV, and you see the cops, they tend to be acting in a pretty brutal fashion at times, kinda threatening and menacing and all that stuff.

Suspect: Right.

Police Officer: We don't operate like that here.

[What follows is a discussion of the suspect's childhood in the interior of B.C., the suspect's job, sports, family members, and cars, all in an attempt to develop the conditioning strategy.

This continues for so long that the suspect asks the officer why he is asking these personal questions. Eventually, the police officer starts to discuss why the suspect was arrested. Questions then focus on the accused's alibi and then to the issue of guilt.]

Police Officer: We know that you did it. We will prove that you did it. We will prove it 10 times over [that] you left a trail of evidence that is unbelievable, OK? ... What would [your grandfather] want you to do here right now? He would want you to take some responsibility for your actions ...

Police Officer: Did you want her to die ... Is that the intent you had ahead of time? Were you trying to snuff her life out? Did you wanna see this kid suffer and die? [The suspect starts to cry.]

Police Officer: No ... I'm glad, buddy. My God, it's OK. And that's the best thing I have heard today ... was it intentional?

Suspect: Ah, no.

Police Officer: No? Did you wanna be close with her or did you wanna snuff her out?

Suspect: I didn't wanna hurt her at all.

[The police officer then questions the accused about whether or not he planned the murder in advance or if it just happened.]

Suspect: Just happened.

Police Officer: It just happened ... Did you feel bad after?

Suspect: Yeah. Suicidal.

Police Officer: You felt suicidal. Well you know what? You're gonna feel better now that you've let this out ...

[Later on, the suspect admits he killed the girl.]

Suspect: Before I knew it, she was dead. I didn't mean to hurt her at all.

During the trial, this line of questioning became a major issue. The accused's lawyer argued that his client gave a false confession as the result of improper police techniques. And when the accused took the stand, he stated to the court that the "intense interrogation ... made him feel that he had no options."

Source: Armstrong (2002), p. A5. Reprinted with permission from *The Globe and Mail.*

Exhibit 7.1 reveals, through the use of a transcript from an actual interrogation in British Columbia, a police officer trying to get obtain information from the suspect implicating him in the abduction and death of a young girl. During his trial, the accused told the court he felt "hopeless" after the police officer said "he had no doubt he was responsible for the death" of the young girl (Armstrong 2002: A5). According to Bailey (2002: A3), "within minutes" the interrogator had "what he wants," that is, the accused made a confession that he murdered the victim.

According to Williams (2000), while the *Charter* has significantly increased the rights of the accused within our criminal justice system, this has not led to significant changes during police interrogations. This is largely due to the fact that suspects do not appreciate "the nature and significance of their rights given problems with the clarity and adequacy of their communication" (Williams 2000: 224). Also, interrogations fall within the workings of the informal criminal justice system, and the police use a number of techniques that, while legal, are innovative in the sense that they are designed to get the suspect to confess to the crime. While these techniques are sometimes successful, they are not always so, as occurred in the case of Guy Paul Morin, who was charged and convicted (wrongfully) of the murder of a young girl at the end of an interrogation (Makin 1993: 184–208).

RIGHT TO COUNSEL

According to s. 9 of the *Charter of Rights and Freedoms*, everyone has the right not to be arbitrarily detained or imprisoned. But even if detention is justified, the right to legal counsel found in s. 10 of the *Charter* "emerges in the face of any detention" (Abell and Sheehy 1993: 269):

10. Everyone has the right on arrest or detention

   (a) to be informed promptly of the reasons therefor;
   (b) to retain and instruct counsel without delay and to be informed of that right; and
   (c) to have the validity of that detention determined by way of *habeas corpus* and to be released if the detention is not lawful

Section 10(b) of the *Charter* gives an arrested individual the right to contact a lawyer without delay. This means that when an accused requests counsel, that request must be allowed. A number of issues have arisen over this issue, including what the right to counsel encompasses, when and how the police must inform the accused of the right to counsel, what the accused must do to assert the right to counsel, and when it is reasonable to limit the right to counsel under s. 1 of the *Charter* (Abell and Sheehy 1993: 269).

The accused must be given a reasonable opportunity to consult a lawyer. The accused must also have the right to talk to legal counsel privately. However, the accused cannot delay the investigation by deciding to contact counsel after several hours. The burden is on the accused to prove that it was impossible to contact a lawyer when the police offer him the opportunity to do so (*R. v. Smith* (1989)).

The right to counsel in Canada is not absolute. It is available only to someone under arrest or being detained. In *R. v. Bazinet* (1986) the suspect voluntarily agreed to accompany the police to the police station. While answering questions about a murder, the suspect confessed to committing the crime. At this point, the police informed him of his right to counsel. On appeal, the court ruled that the police followed proper procedure, since there was no evidence to indicate that the accused felt he was deprived of his liberty and had to accompany the police.

But what happens once a suspect requests to see a lawyer? Can the police continue to interrogate him while he is waiting for the lawyer to appear? The answer depends on the type of question the police are asking. If the questions are "innocuous" (for example, requests for the accused's name and address), they are allowed. However, questions about the facts of the case are not allowed until legal counsel has talked with his client.

In *R. v. Manninen* (1983), the accused had requested to see his lawyer. However, a police officer continued to question him, asking the accused for the location of a knife that was allegedly used to rob a store. The accused then told the officers that he had only a gun while committing the robbery. The Ontario Court of Appeal ruled that this question was in violation of Manninen's rights, because it was "based on a presumption of guilt and the answer was devastating to the defence" and because it was asked "as if the appellant had expressed no desire to remain silent." As a result, the accused's admission of guilt was excluded.

In *R. v. Black* (1989), the accused was originally charged with the attempted murder of another woman. She contacted her lawyer by telephone, and a few hours later the victim died. Then the police advised her that she was being charged with first-degree murder. The accused requested to speak to her lawyer again, but the lawyer could not be reached. The officers then suggested she speak to another lawyer, a suggestion she refused. Shortly after, the police questioned the accused again, and she confessed to the crime. The Supreme Court ruled that since the accused had not waived her right to a lawyer, the police had violated her right to legal counsel, and consequently her statement was excluded from the evidence.

An individual may elect to give up the right to counsel but must appreciate the consequences of doing so. If he is not so instructed by the police, anything he tells the police will be excluded. In *R. v. Clarkson* (1986), a woman confessed to the police that she murdered her husband, even though her aunt, who was present during the questioning, told her to contact a lawyer. The accused was intoxicated at the time of the questioning. The Supreme Court later ruled the confession to be inadmissible, saying the police should have waited till she was sober to question her, since everyone must be fully aware of the consequences of waiving the right to counsel.

How long does an accused have to make a call? It depends on the seriousness of the charge. In *R. v. Smith* (1989), the accused was arrested for robbery and requested to contact a lawyer after 9 p.m. Finding only a business telephone number, the accused decided to try again in the morning, despite police recommendations that he call that evening. The accused refused. When the police questioned him later, he made a statement "off the record" that was later used as evidence to convict him. On appeal, the Supreme Court of Canada ruled the statement to be admissible, because the crime was not considered a serious offence. If it had been a serious offence, he should have been granted an additional opportunity to contact legal counsel.

COMPELLING APPEARANCE, INTERIM RELEASE, AND PRETRIAL DETENTION

After an individual is arrested, he may be taken to the police station where the police record the criminal charges and obtain other information relevant to the case. This process is commonly referred to as "lodging a complaint," and it usually includes a description of the suspect and, if necessary, circumstances relating to the offence. If the suspect was caught in the act of committing a crime (as opposed to being arrested by a warrant or summons), the arresting officer swears an information and presents it to a justice of the peace as soon as possible.

What happens to the accused depends on the charge. If the charge is a summary conviction offence, in all likelihood the accused is released immediately on his own recognizance and after a promise to appear in court on the trial date. This is standard operating procedure in Canada, and it expedites the processing of such cases and saves the police from searching for the accused to serve him with an arrest warrant or summons.

When an indictable or hybrid offence is involved, the police need reasonable and probable grounds for believing that a crime was committed. In all provinces except New Brunswick, Quebec, and British Columbia, Crown prosecutors do not review any charges before they are laid. This means that anyone (usually a police officer) who has reasonable and probable grounds for believing that an individual has committed an indictable offence can swear an information before a justice of the peace (s. 504 of the *Criminal Code*). The justice of the peace must accept the information and decide whether to proceed by way of a summons or arrest warrant (s. 507 of the *Criminal Code*).

The procedure of initiating charges has been criticized by the Law Reform Commission of Canada (1990: 70) as "a mere formality." As a result, the protections offered individuals through the *Charter* "are largely lost," and "the resources of the court can be wasted by the initiation of prosecutions that have little chance of success." However, the theory behind this process is to require the justice of the peace to evaluate the worthiness of the charge(s).

Unlike individuals charged with summary conviction offences, those charged with indictable offences are usually processed at a police station. The processing can involve fingerprinting and photographing the accused. Afterward, depending on the charge, the accused may be released on his own recognizance; however, if police believe that the individual may not appear at the court trial, they may keep the individual locked up in a jail cell or send him to a remand centre to await a hearing on the charges and bail. If the accused enters a guilty plea when the charges are read into court, he is admitting to all the elements of the crime, and the court will usually schedule a sentencing date. A plea of not guilty sets the stage for a trial, and such a case may ultimately involve a plea bargain.

If the accused is charged with what is referred to as a s. 469 crime—murder, for example—a Superior Court justice decides whether or not to order the accused into a detention facility (see Chapter 8). In these cases, a reverse onus applies—that is, it is up to the accused to show why he should be released. Among the reasons for detention are these:

1. The accused is charged with an indictable offence while already on judicial interim release or is in the process of appealing another indictable offence.
2. The accused commits an indictable offence but is not a resident of Canada.
3. The accused allegedly has broken a previous interim release order.
4. The accused has committed or conspired to commit an offence under ss. 5 and 6 of the *Controlled Drugs and Substances Act* (that is, trafficking, exporting, or importing).

In almost every case, the prosecutor has to show cause—to demonstrate that detaining the accused is justified (s. 515 of the *Criminal Code*). Our criminal justice system presumes that the accused should be released, and released without conditions, unless the Crown feels otherwise. In most cases that presumption means that the accused is released. The judge cannot impose any more control over the accused unless the prosecutor shows that it is necessary. Certain conditions—for example, an obligation to report to a police officer—may be imposed when the accused is released. The prosecutor may want the accused to enter into some form of recognizance. If the accused is released, the accused may be requested to deposit an amount of money with the court. A cash deposit is not preferred, since the accused may disappear after paying.

Our criminal justice system prefers that a surety (an individual who chooses to monitor the accused until the trial) agrees to be indebted to the court for a specified amount of money if the accused does not appear on the appointed date. The surety may have to provide a cash deposit if the accused fails to appear.

Alternatively, the accused may be requested to deposit an amount of money with the court. Both a surety and a cash deposit may be required if the accused is not a resident of the province or lives more than 200 kilometres from where he is being held. Of course, the accused may be detained if the justice of the peace feels it is necessary, but the reasons must be recorded.

The continued detention of the accused in custody can be justified only on one or more of the following conditions found in s. 515(10) of the *Criminal Code:*

(a) where the detention is necessary to ensure his or her attendance in court in order to be dealt with according to law;

(b) where the detention is necessary for the protection or safety of the public, including any victim of or witness to the offence, having regard to all the circumstances including any substantial likelihood that the accused will, if released from custody, commit a criminal offence or interfere with the administration of justice; and

(c) on any other just cause being shown and without limiting the generality of the foregoing, where the detention is necessary in order to maintain confidence in the administration of justice, having regard to all the circumstances, including the apparent strength of the prosecution's case, the gravity of the nature of the offence, the circumstances surrounding its commission, and the potential for a lengthy term of imprisonment.

In many cases, the suspect will be released but only after she agrees to certain conditions set by the court—for example, to reside at a particular residence or not to have communication with certain witnesses (s. 515(2) of the *Criminal Code*) (see Exhibit 7.2 on page 169).

BAIL REFORM

The *Bail Reform Act* (1972) created the system of judicial interim release described above. Amended four years later, the act is the basis for bail in Canada today. Its cre-

ation was largely the result of the Ouimet Committee, which recommended that suspects should not be placed in detention unless detention was the only means to ensure that the accused would appear in court. This recommendation was based on a Canadian study on pretrial detention and a U.S. study on how bail discriminates against the poor. In the Canadian study, Milton Friedland (1965) concluded that "the overwhelming majority of persons in Toronto charged with offences against the *Criminal Code* were arrested rather than summoned." In the 6000 cases he studied, Friedland found that the accused was arrested in 92 percent of the cases and that 84 percent of those arrested remained in custody until their first court appearance.

The U.S. study, referred to as the Manhattan Bail Project, took place in New York City in the early 1960s. The Vera Institute, a private, nonprofit research organization dedicated to improving the criminal justice system, designed an experimental pretrial program that investigated arrested individuals who could not afford bail in order to see how many would appear in court for trial after having been released back into the community following their initial court appearance. The researchers found that the appearance rate of those released on their own recognizance was consistently the same as or better than the rate of those released on monetary bail. As a result, release-on-recognizance programs were influential in changing the nature of the bail process across North America.

The Manhattan Bail Project also led to the introduction of different types of pretrial release. One such innovation became known as station house release, a process in which a suspect is issued a citation to appear in court at a later date, thereby bypassing the costly exercise of pretrial detention. This experiment showed that most suspects released back into the community appeared in court on the duly appointed date. As a result of these studies, "the prevailing view became that release should be available, regardless of financial circumstances, unless overwhelming factors preclude it" (Anderson and Newman 1993: 216).

The *Bail Reform Act* prefers most offenders be released into the community pending their trial. The new legislation instructed police officers to issue an appearance notice to the accused rather than arrest him unless officers felt the public was in jeopardy or the accused had committed a serious indictable offence. In addition, the officer in charge of the lockup must, for most offences, release the person charged and compel that person to appear in court by a summons, promise to appear, or on his own recognizance.

In addition, the legislation provides that a magistrate has to release the accused unless the prosecutor shows cause why the release should not occur. A process

There have been a number of criticisms made about the bail process in Canada. Hamilton and Sinclair (1991) reported that Aboriginals accused of a crime in Manitoba were more likely to be denied bail than non-Aboriginals and that they also spent a longer period of time in pretrial detention than non-Aboriginals. The Ontario Commission on Systemic Racism in the Ontario Criminal Justice System found that black accused were more likely to be remanded to custody than nonblacks. Kellough and Wortley's (2002) study of bail hearings in Toronto discovered that those who received negative personality assessments from the police were more likely to have their application for bail denied. And these police decisions helped explain racial differences in the area of pretrial detention.

SEARCH AND SEIZURE

Two sections of the *Charter of Rights and Freedoms* relate specifically to search and seizure. Section 8 states that "Everyone has the right to be secure against unreasonable search or seizure," while s. 24(2) points out that if evidence "was obtained in a manner that infringed or denied any rights or freedoms guaranteed by this Charter, the evidence shall be excluded if it is established that … the admission of it in the proceedings would bring the administration of justice into disrepute."

One of the most fundamental rights of Canadian citizens is the protection against unreasonable search and seizure. This right gives a citizen the right to be left alone by the government or its agents unless there are grounds that allow them to intrude. A *search* is the intrusion of a government representative into an individual's privacy, of which every citizen has reasonable and justifiable expectation. A *seizure* is the exercise of control by a government representative over an individual and/or item. Generally, a search warrant is required before a search of an individual or a place may be legally conducted. Three different legal areas govern searches and seizures in Canada: common law, the *Criminal Code*, and the *Charter of Rights and Freedoms*.

The common law is concerned with the search of persons as well as places. In most cases, the police must have a search warrant granted by the judiciary in order to search an individual. However, the common law gives police the right to conduct general body searches and searches of the immediate surrounding area (see the Doctrine of Plain View on page 175) when arresting a suspect. A body search includes combing out hair samples for forensic evidence but does not include the taking of blood samples, which is considered to be an

Every day, police vans enter the gated entrance to Toronto's Old City Hall, taking accused persons to their bail hearings.

known as the "ladder effect" determines if the accused should be released. This means that a prosecutor must, for most offences, convince the magistrate that a less severe release mechanism is not appropriate in any given case. The ladder is found in s. 515(2) of the *Criminal Code*, which establishes that almost every individual can be released on recognizance if he promises to appear for trial on a designated date. Unsecured bail does not require the defendant to pay money to the court, but he remains liable for the full amount if he fails to appear at the trial. Fully secured bail requires the defendant to post the full amount of bail with the court. However, the amount of bail cannot be fixed so high that it becomes, in effect, a detention order.

EXHIBIT 7.2 Pretrial Release in Domestic Abuse Cases

Our legal system sometimes makes special provisions in connection with judicial interim release. One such instance involves cases of spousal or domestic abuse. Because of zero tolerance laws on these types of abuse, the police cannot simply release the accused on an appearance notice. Usually they require a recognizance with certain conditions, such as:

- The accused must have no contact or communication with the complainant.
- The accused must not attend at the residence of the complainant.
- The accused must satisfy the court that he has another address at which to live.
- The accused may not possess firearms, ammunition, or explosives (and sometimes weapons such as knives).
- The accused must surrender any firearms acquisition certificate.

These restrictions are not always a deterrent to continued threats, fear of retaliation, and more violence, however. In a study of women in shelters across Canada in April 1998, less than one-third of all women had contacted the police or sought a restraining order. In an attempt to ensure that the recognizance conditions are followed, the complainant can request that a peace bond (formally known as a Judicial Recognizance Order) be ordered under s. 810 of the *Criminal Code*. If a defendant is found in violation of the peace bond, he may be found guilty of a summary conviction offence, with a maximum penalty of 12 months in jail and a $2000 fine.

According to the peace bond provision of the *Criminal Code*:

810(1) An information may be laid before a justice by or on behalf of any person who fears on reasonable grounds that another person will cause personal injury to him or her or to his or her spouse or common-law partner or child or will damage his or her property....

(3) The justice or the summary conviction court ... may, if satisfied by the evidence adduced that the person on whose behalf the information was laid has reasonable grounds for his or her fears,

   (a) order that the defendant enter into a recognizance, with or without sureties, to keep the peace and to be

of good behavior for any period that does not exceed twelve months, and comply with other such reasonable conditions prescribed in the recognizance ... the court considers desirable for securing the good conduct of the defendant; or

   (b) commit the defendant to prison for a term not exceeding twelve months if he or she fails or refuses to enter into the recognizance.

Another option is available to any woman who is legally married to the accused. The complainant can apply for a civil restraining order found in provincial statutes (usually within the jurisdiction of the Family Court) if the threats and violence continue or if she is in fear of the accused. The efficacy of this approach has been questioned in British Columbia (Rigakos 1997), the United States (Sherman 1992), and Australia (Stubbs and Powell 1989). Some provinces (for example, Alberta, Saskatchewan, and P.E.I.) have strengthened their legislation. However, criticism of restraining orders continues because not all of those restrained follow the orders. The report of the Joint Committee on Domestic Violence (1999) in Ontario detailed the problems surrounding civil protection orders. Among its recommendations on improving this system were the following:

- A breach of a restraining order must be prosecuted in the criminal court to reinforce to the public the necessity of complying with these orders. Criminal charges are rarely laid when an order is violated, and only a few cases ever reach criminal court.
- The language used in an order should be as specific as possible and include definitions of inappropriate behaviour.
- Police officers currently do not know when a restraining order has been served. It is recommended that all such orders be sent to Ottawa to be placed in the Canadian Police Information Centre (CPIC) computer. While orders are supposed to be sent to CPIC, this is not a consistent practice.
- Improve enforcement of a restraining order when shared or joint custody is ordered. Sometimes contradictory or conflicting orders are issued by a criminal court and a family court (for example, the former may impose noncommunication conditions while the latter permits access to children).

Continued on next page

EXHIBIT 7.2   Pretrial Release in Domestic
Abuse Cases ... *Continued*

One major concern of the judiciary is that preventive detention is based on the prediction that the accused will do something wrong in the future. In this sense, concern about detention is much like the concern raised about selective incapacitation (see Chapter 3). Such factors as previous criminal record and the seriousness of the current offence may lead a Crown prosecutor to request preventive detention. This is at best a difficult process since prosecutors may look past the current domestic abuse incident and predict on the basis of a perpetrator's prior record that he will obey a bail order with a condition to stay away from his wife and her residence. Such was the case in Ontario in 2000, when an estranged husband killed his wife while on bail. A coroner's jury reviewing this case recommended a number of changes to protect women from their abusive partners beyond bail and preventive detention orders, including an increase in the provincial housing allowance for women and their children escaping an abusive home, so that the family can live without fear of violence (Abbate 2002: A9).

invasive search. For an invasive search, special statutory authorization is required, and this is usually found in the *Criminal Code*.

Most of what the police do in this area of law is regulated by s. 487 of the *Criminal Code*. All police officers must obtain a search warrant by swearing an information under oath in front of a justice of the peace. Before issuing a warrant, the justice of the peace must decide whether there are reasonable grounds for believing that the objects in question will be found at the location in question and that these objects will prove to have been involved in the commission of an offence. The search warrant provides police officers with the power to search places but not individuals (which is covered by common law). Currently, a warrant can be obtained for:

(a) any items on or in respect of which an offence under any federal act has been committed;

(b) anything that will provide evidence of any evidence under federal legislation; and

(c) anything intended to be used to commit an offence against the person for which an arrest without a warrant may be made.

The police officer must specify the offence, describe the items as well as the place (or places) that will be searched, and explain how the search will turn up the items mentioned in the warrant application (Form 1 of the *Criminal Code*). The information provided to the justice of the peace by the police may be based on hearsay evidence and it may come from an unnamed source as long as there is evidence to support the reliability of the individual's evidence. Not all evidence is physical in the way that a weapon or stolen property is physical. For example, s. 487.05 of the *Criminal Code* authorizes a warrant that allows the police to obtain DNA samples from a suspect.

Do the police have the right to collect DNA samples anytime they please? (See Exhibit 7.3.) Can they conduct frisk searches whenever they want once an individual has been lawfully arrested? Should the police be able to use physical force or psychological intimidation beyond what is "reasonable" in order to accomplish the search? The answers to these questions are found in the laws governing search and seizure in Canada. Because the issue of search and seizure encompasses a variety of situations throughout the criminal justice process, notably the right to privacy by private citizens, debate exists over appropriate behaviour by the police or other government agents. As a result, the laws governing this area are constantly challenged in court.

Police officers have the legal right to seize items not mentioned in the warrant if the officers have reasonable grounds for believing those items were obtained by or used in the commission of an offence. Despite these legal restrictions, the Law Reform Commission of Canada (1991) maintains that the *Criminal Code* contains only minimal regulations covering search and seizure and therefore that a lack of certainty exists within the law itself.

REQUIREMENTS FOR SEARCH WARRANTS

The "Reasonableness" Test

This test, as it applies to searches and seizures, generally refers to the question of whether a police officer has overstepped his authority. Most searches are judged to be unreasonable if an officer lacks sufficient information to justify the search. The appropriate standard of proof is one of "reasonable and probable grounds" rather than proof beyond a reasonable doubt; in other words, a search warrant can be granted only if the request for it is accompanied by facts that indicate to the court that a crime has been committed or is being committed.

EXHIBIT 7.3 The Seizing of DNA Samples: *R. v. Stillman* (1997)

Early decisions by the courts across Canada took conflicting positions on the taking of DNA samples by the police. In Ontario, the Court of Appeal ruled in *R. v. Alderton* (1985) that the police could take hair samples for DNA testing as part of their powers of search incident to an arrest. In comparison, the New Brunswick Court of Appeal, in the case of *R. v. Legere*, a serial killer, held that the police violated s. 8 of the *Charter of Rights and Freedoms* when they took hair and bodily samples without a warrant or the consent of the accused. However, they admitted the evidence into court under s. 24(2) of the *Charter*. And in *R. v. Borden* (1994) the Supreme Court of Canada excluded DNA evidence that had led to the conviction of the accused of sexual assault (the samples in question did not involve semen). However, the police did not inform the accused that the samples would be used in their investigation and possibly be used as evidence. The Supreme Court decided that the accused had not waived his rights or consented to the taking of the samples by the police.

Following this case, legislation authorizing the seizure of bodily samples for DNA testing was quickly approved by Parliament. Authorization involves a judge's hearing an application for and granting a warrant if probable cause is present. But how far can the police go in terms of seizing a person's bodily samples? Can the police "conscript" an individual into providing them with self-incriminating evidence?

The Supreme Court then heard an appeal involving DNA used to secure a conviction of murder (*R. v. Stillman* (1997)). In this case, a 17-year-old New Brunswick youth had been convicted of the murder of a young woman. The victim had disappeared after a party she had left in the company of Stillman. Six days later her body was recovered. She had been raped and bitten on her abdomen and had died from blows to the head. Arrested just hours after the discovery of the body, Stillman met his lawyers at the police station. They instructed that Stillman not cooperate with the authorities in any request for bodily samples or in any interrogation. After the lawyers left, the police proceeded to violate this directive. They took the bodily samples they wanted from the accused and then interrogated him for an hour. When the police took a break in

their questioning they agreed to contact Stillman's lawyers and request their presence at the interrogation. In the meantime, the accused went to the washroom, blew his nose, and threw the used tissue into the wastebasket. The police seized the tissue for DNA testing.

When the police took their evidence to a Crown prosecutor to receive approval for a charge, the prosecutor refused, saying the evidence was still insufficient. Stillman was released, only to be rearrested a few months later. This time, the police obtained teeth impressions and an oral swab, a process that took about two hours to complete. This time the evidence was considered sufficient, and Stillman was subsequently found guilty of murder and sentenced in adult court to life imprisonment. As a 17-year-old, however, he could apply for parole after eight years. His conviction was upheld by the New Brunswick Court of Appeal.

On appeal to the Supreme Court, the defence argued that the teeth impressions and oral swabs were obtained improperly by the police. The Supreme Court ruled that the police had reasonable and probable grounds to suspect Stillman of the crime. However, the justices also ruled that the seizures could not be justified by the police as necessary because they could be thrown away or hidden. The majority of the justices considered the taking of the teeth impressions to be particularly offensive, although they were taken by a dentist. In the court's final decision, the hair and dental seizures were deemed the result of "the abusive exercise of raw physical authority by the police." The court also wrote that "If there is not respect for the dignity of the individual and the integrity of the body then it is but a very short step to justifying the exercise of any physical force of the police if it is undertaken with the aim of solving crimes." In addition, the court felt the seizure of the discarded tissue violated Stillman's right not to be subject to unreasonable search and seizure but should be admitted as evidence. Parliament responded to this decision by allowing for warrants to obtain bodily impressions if there are reasonable grounds for believing an offence had been committed and that it is in the best interests of the administration of justice to use them (see s. 487.091 of the *Criminal Code*).

Particularity

Particularity refers to the search warrant itself. A search warrant must specify the place to be searched and the reasons for searching it. When the police request a search warrant, the warrant must identify the premises and the personal property to be seized, and it must be signed by a police officer. The facts and information justifying the need for a search warrant are set out in an affidavit requesting the warrant.

Searches Needing a Warrant

The power to issue a search warrant is located in s. 487 of the *Criminal Code*. Before issuing a warrant, a justice must decide whether there are reasonable grounds for believing that the objects in question will be found at the location specified and that the objects will prove to have been used during the commission of an offence.

The issue of whether the police are required to obtain a warrant as a prerequisite to a search or seizure has been a key component of the Supreme Court of Canada's interpretation of s. 8 of the *Charter*. During the early years of the *Charter*, the courts took two different positions on the necessity of warrants. First, some judges and justices of the peace focused on the issue of the reasonableness of police conduct, meaning that a critical evaluation of the "reasonableness" of the search can, if the issue arises, be determined after the search or seizure takes place. The presence or absence of a warrant, or the information found in the warrant, is not always considered the most important criterion in determining whether the search or seizure was reasonable. The Law Reform Commission (1983: 83), in its study of search warrants in seven Canadian cities, concluded that "there is a clear gap between legal rules for issuing and obtaining search warrants and the daily realities of practice." In some locations, police gave only minimal information to support their request for a warrant and, as a result, provided the "adjudication no objective basis for making a judicial determination as to whether or not to issue a warrant." This does not mean that the police are involved in illegal searches but, rather, that proper procedures have not been followed, thereby raising concerns about the reasonableness of a search. The Law Reform Commission (1983: 86) concluded, after an analysis of all the documents, that

> no decisive relationship [exists] between the legality of the search and the eventual seizure of the specified item. This argues against the possibility that the widespread illegality of warrants is attributable to police decisions to search in inappropriate cases. Rather the indication is that the problem resides with adherence to procedures. In other words, the necessary factual basis for a search may well exist, but the warrant is nonetheless being issued improperly.

Other judges and justices of the peace interpreted s. 8 of the *Charter* differently. They emphasized that failure to obtain a warrant without all pertinent information is unreasonable except in the most extraordinary situations. In other words, the *Charter* exists to prevent unreasonable searches and seizures from taking place at all, not to determine if they were reasonable or unreasonable after the fact.

Invoking strict standards for warrants involving searches and seizures promotes adherence to the law in three ways. First, it requires police officers to make an objective assessment of the "reasonableness" of their evidence before they act. Second, it provides judges with the exact information a police officer has obtained to date, giving judges the basis to make a more informed decision on the legality of the warrant. Third, it provides a neutral and objective assessment of the evidence by a disinterested individual rather than the possibly more subjective view of a police officer "in the heat of the chase." According to advocates of the third position, a proper system for issuing search warrants can be accomplished only in a system of prior authorization, not one that uses subsequent validation.

This issue has not yet been resolved in Canada. In its decision in *Hunter v. Southam Inc.* (1984), the Supreme Court of Canada took the position that "for any type of search of premises, the person or a vehicle, the question is whether a warrant is feasible." Therefore, according to the Supreme Court, there may be exceptions to the requirement of a warrant in every case, since it may not be "feasible" to obtain one. In essence, the test is whether a warrant is feasible for any type of search of a place, person, or motor vehicle. This ruling protects citizens from unreasonable searches and seizures through a minimum-standards approach.

Warrantless Searches in Exigent Circumstances

A case involving a warrantless search is liable to be deemed illegal and therefore thrown out of court. However, in Canada, a warrantless search can be considered reasonable under some exigent (that is, immediate) circumstances. But when are such circumstances considered acceptable in Canada? When can a police officer conduct a search without a warrant? After all, the Canadian courts have ruled that the police cannot go on "fishing expeditions" for evidence. The circumstances of the case and how the police conduct their activities are critical.

After the *Feeney* decision (see above), the federal government introduced Bill C-16 to address that ruling. This legislation established two more exceptions to the legal requirement that a police officer obtain a search warrant before entering a dwelling (an existing exception allowed the police to enter a dwelling while they are in "hot pursuit" of a suspect). The two new exemptions are where a police officer

1. has reasonable grounds to suspect that entry into the dwelling house is necessary to prevent bodily harm or death to any person; or

2. has reasonable grounds to believe that entry is necessary to prevent the imminent loss or destruction of evidence.

In addition, illegal searches are not always ruled to be unreasonable. In *R. v. Heisler* (1984), for example, the Alberta Court of Appeal ruled that searching an individual's purse when the individual entered a rock concert was not illegal even though there had been no prior reasonable grounds. And in *R. v. Harris* (1987), Mr. Justice Martin of the Ontario Court of Appeal stated that minor or technical defects in a warrant would not automatically make unconstitutional a search or seizure under s. 8 of the *Charter*.

Drug convictions are sometimes appealed on the issue of warrantless searches. In such cases, police officers observe possession of the drug but don't have time to obtain a search warrant prior to the use or selling of it. In *R. v. Collins* (1987), police officers in British Columbia conducting a heroin investigation observed two suspects in a village pub. When one individual left to go to his car, the police approached him, searched the car, and found a quantity of heroin. Back in the pub, an officer approached the other suspect and proceeded to grab her by the throat to prevent her from swallowing any evidence. The suspect dropped a balloon containing heroin. The trial judge ruled the search unreasonable because the police had used unnecessary force. The Supreme Court of Canada, however, overturned this decision, stating there was nothing to suggest the collection of evidence in this manner made the trial unfair.

In determining the reasonableness of a search, the courts examine the following issues:

1. whether the information predicting the commission of a criminal offence was compelling;
2. whether the information was based on an informant's tip, and whether the source was credible; and
3. whether the information was corroborated by a police investigation before the decision to conduct the search was made

The police are to take into account the accused's past record and reputation, provided that such information is relevant to the circumstances of the search.

Searches Incident to an Arrest

Another exception to the search warrant requirement is searches incident to an arrest. This power is granted to the police by the common law and allows the police to search the suspect for weapons and evidence of a crime without first obtaining a search warrant. In order that a search incident to arrest be lawful, it is necessary that the arrest itself be lawful. This means that there must be reasonable grounds for believing that a suspect committed an indictable offence, meaning that the police cannot make an arrest purely on the basis of assisting their investigation.

The courts have allowed a search incident to arrest on a number of grounds, including

1. the need to protect the arresting officers;
2. the need to prevent the arrestee from destroying evidence in his possession;
3. the intrusiveness of the lawful arrest being so great that the incidental search is of minor consequence; and
4. the fact that the individual could in any event be subjected to an inventory search at the police station.

The Supreme Court of Canada unanimously agreed in *Cloutier v. Langlois* (1990) that most searches are to be based on reasonable and probable grounds but that searches incidental to arrest are not. In this case, the police stopped a motorist for making an illegal right-hand turn. The officers found that the motorist had several unpaid traffic fines. The driver became agitated and abusive toward the police, who then had him spread his legs by the car and frisked him. The motorist later sued the police officers for assaulting him. The Supreme Court ruled that reasonable grounds are not necessary for a frisk search incident to an arrest, and that such searches are necessary for "the effective and safe enforcement of the law ... [and] ensuring the freedom and dignity of individuals." In this case, the police were justified in believing that the search was necessary for their safety. In most cases, frisk searches at the time of arrest will probably be considered constitutional. In addition, searches of the immediate vicinity of a crime scene will generally be accepted if the search can be justified on the basis of "prompt and effective discovery and preservation of evidence" (*R. v. Lim* (1990)).

However, the courts have also stated that before conducting a frisk search the police must inform the suspect of his right to counsel. But the police do not have to wait until the suspect contacts a lawyer before a search is made.

The Supreme Court has established the following limits on the common law and the right to search an individual incident to arrest:

1. The police have discretion over whether a search is necessary for the effective and safe application of the law.
2. The search must be for a valid criminal objective (for example, to check for weapons or to prevent an escape).

3. The search cannot be used to intimidate, ridicule, or pressure the accused to gain admissions.
4. The search must not be conducted in an abusive way (see Exhibit 7.4).

There are exceptions to these rights. In *R. v. Tomaso* (1989), the accused appealed his conviction of dangerous driving, arguing that the police collected blood from his bleeding ear while he was unconscious in hospital. The blood sample revealed the accused was impaired at the time of the accident. However, the Ontario Court of Appeal determined the seizure was unreasonable—but only because the accused was not charged until two weeks later.

Warrantless Searches in Motor Vehicles

The Supreme Court of Canada has established that a warrantless search of a vehicle may be reasonable if grounds exist for believing that the vehicle contains drugs or other contraband. However, the power to search a vehicle without a warrant must be found in statute or at common law (for example, a search incident to a valid arrest).

The legality of searching motor vehicles has proved to be a difficult issue for the police. Can a police officer search the interior of a vehicle? Or a locked suitcase or

---

EXHIBIT 7.4   Strip Searches by the Police: *R. v. Golden*

In *R. v. Golden* (2001), the Supreme Court of Canada ruled for the first time on the lawfulness of a strip search. As Dickson (2002) points out, this case was significant because although the courts have ruled on the police searching private residences, the rules governing physical searches are less developed. In fact, the *Criminal Code* does not mention body searches. In its ruling the justices of the Supreme Court attempted to balance the reasonable expectations for privacy held by someone who has been arrested with those of the police. The issue in this case revolved around s. 8 of the *Charter*, which states that "Everyone has the right to be secure against unreasonable search or seizure."

In this particular case, police officers entered a Toronto café to arrest Mr. Golden, whom they believed was trafficking cocaine. After arresting him, the police patted down Mr. Golden but did not find any weapons or drugs in his possession. The police then decided to visually inspect (i.e., conduct a strip search) of Mr. Golden's underwear for drugs in the café. Mr. Golden was forced to bend over a table, and then the police made him lower his pants and underwear so that his buttocks and genitalia were exposed. The police were able to seize a bag of crack cocaine weighing 10 grams. Mr. Golden was arrested for possession of a narcotic for the purpose of trafficking (the police had observed Mr. Golden selling a substance similar to crack cocaine in their surveillance of the café).

At his trial, Mr. Golden argued that the case should be thrown out of court because, in his opinion, the police had conducted an illegal search on the basis of s. 8 of the *Charter*. The trial judge refused to accept this defence, found Mr. Golden guilty, and sentenced him to serve 14 months in a provincial correctional facility. Mr. Golden appealed his conviction to the Ontario Court of Appeal, which dismissed his appeal. However, the Supreme Court of Canada, in a 5 to 4 vote, overturned the conviction and acquitted Mr. Golden.

The Supreme Court, in its decision, noted that "a strip search will always be unreasonable if it is carried out abusively or for the purpose of humiliating or punishing the arrestee" (Dickson 2002: 36). The Supreme Court also decided that if the police were to conduct a routine strip search in good faith and with no violence involved, it will also violate s. 8 of the *Charter* in those cases "where there is no compelling purpose for conducting a strip search during an arrest" (Dickson 2002: 36).

However, the Court pointed out that the common law of search incident to arrest, which permits strip searches, does not violate s. 8 of the *Charter*. The common law ensures that such searches are carried out only where the police establish reasonable and probable grounds for a strip search for the purpose of discovering weapons and seizing evidence related to the offence for which the person was arrested. In addition, strip searches are to be done in a manner that preserves the dignity and privacy of the person arrested. While in this case the arrest was lawful and the strip search was related to the purpose of the arrest, the Supreme Court decided that the strip search was not carried out in a reasonable manner.

---

closed briefcase? In *R. v. Mellinthin* (1992), the Supreme Court of Canada ruled the accused's rights were violated when, at a police check stop, the accused was questioned about the contents of a bag. The suspect handed over the bag, which was found to contain narcotics. However, the officer had no suspicion that the accused was in possession of illegal drugs when he asked to search the bag. According to the Supreme Court, the purpose of a police check stop is to detect impaired drivers or dangerous vehicles, not to conduct unreasonable searches. In this case, there was no informed consent.

Other Types of Warrantless Searches

The Doctrine of Plain View

The police can search for and seize evidence without a warrant if the illegal object is in plain view. For example, if a police officer arrives at a home in response to an incident of domestic violence and notices marijuana on the coffee table, the officer could seize the evidence and arrest the suspect. However, if the officer suspects that more drugs are in the house, the officer would have to apply for and receive an authorized search warrant before investigating further. However, if an officer arrests a suspect in a kitchen, the kitchen cupboards can be looked into, but only with justification that the search was more than just a "fishing expedition." Justification clearly exists when there is a report of a weapon but no weapon is visible. A police officer who suspects the weapon was placed in a cupboard just before she arrived may decide to check all the cupboards.

Reasonable Grounds

If a police officer stops a motor vehicle because of a defective taillight and the driver leans over, the officer may become suspicious that an illegal item is being hidden. Nothing in the act of leaning over can, by itself, make a police officer suspicious, but when the officer talks to the motorist and the motorist appears nervous and says nothing, an experienced officer can come to the reasonable conclusion that the motorist is hiding something. This might give the officer reasonable cause to search the vehicle (Salhany 1986).

The rationale for "reasonable grounds" is found in s. 101(1) of the *Criminal Code*. It allows a police officer to search without a warrant when the officer believes he has reasonable grounds for believing that an offence is being committed or has been committed. The section also deals with prohibited weapons, restricted weapons, firearms or ammunition, and evidence that an offence is likely to be found on a person, in a vehicle, or in any place or premises other than a dwelling place. In *R. v. Singh* (1983), the accused fit the description of a suspect wanted for interrogation about a multiple shooting. The incident had occurred just a few minutes before, when the suspect was seen in the same vicinity. When stopped by police, the suspect had a noticeable bulge in his pocket and refused to make eye contact with the police. The police then searched the suspect and found the weapon used in the crime. In this case, the Ontario Court of Appeal ruled there was no unreasonable search and seizure as specified by s. 8 of the *Charter of Rights and Freedoms*.

Similarly, in *R. v. Ducharme* (1990), police officers noticed a man running into a lane with a full garbage bag at 3 a.m. When they stopped the individual, they noticed the man's hands were cut and bleeding. An officer searched the bag, without consent, and found 32 cartons of cigarettes. It was later reported that the glass door of a store had been broken and cigarettes stolen from inside. The accused was convicted, but the defence lawyer appealed the case, arguing that the officer had performed an improper search. However, the British Columbia Court of Appeal ruled that since the search occurred peacefully in a public place, no invasion of the body occurred; under incriminating conditions it was "reasonable" for the officer to search the garbage bag. It was not necessary to arrest the accused before looking into the bag. In this case and in *R. v. Ducharme*, the courts ruled police officers can search if they have reasonable grounds for suspicion.

Section 489 of the *Criminal Code* also permits police officers to seize items not mentioned on a warrant. The key issue here is that the officer has to believe on reasonable grounds that the item in question has been obtained by, or has been used in, the commission of an offence.

Consent Searches

Police officers may also make a warrantless search when an individual voluntarily consents to the search. Those individuals who choose to consent to a search are waiving their constitutional rights. Thus, the police may have to prove in court that the consent was voluntarily given to them.

The major legal issue in most consent searches is whether the police can prove that consent was given to them voluntarily. In *R. v. Wills* (1992), the Ontario Court of Appeal provided guidelines for judging whether voluntary consent was given:

1. The giver of the consent had the authority to give the consent in question.
2. The consent was voluntary in the sense it was free from coercion and not the result of police

oppression, coercion, or other external conduct that negated the freedom to choose whether or not the police should continue.

3. The giver of the consent was aware of his right to refuse to give consent to the police to engage in the conduct requested.
4. The giver of the consent was aware of the potential consequences of giving the consent.

ELECTRONIC SURVEILLANCE

The use of wiretaps to listen to conversations between individuals has had a significant impact on police work. These electronic devices allow people to listen to and record private discussions between people over telephones as well as through the walls and windows of houses. Using a variety of techniques, police are able to listen to private discussions and obtain information on criminal activity.

The earliest and most commonly used type of electronic surveillance is wiretapping. With an approved search warrant from the courts, police officers can listen to and record conversations over telephone lines. This evidence is considered admissible and has often led to convictions of the accused.

The Law of Electronic Surveillance

In Canada, the judiciary can authorize the interception of private communications and admit the information obtained as evidence. It appears that most applications for authorizations for electronic eavesdropping are accepted. Between 1985 and 1989, only three applications of a total of 2222 were rejected. According to the Solicitor General of Canada (1991), this low rejection rate reflects the facts that (1) strict procedures are being followed and (2) judges return an unknown number of applications to the police to provide more information about the case before any authorization is granted. The Solicitor General points out that almost every one of the 408 authorizations granted in 1989 involved conspiracies to commit serious drug offences. Electronic surveillance would appear to be a necessary feature in the fight against organized drug rings.

Charter defences have been used by drug offenders to argue the police use of electronic surveillance brings the administration of justice into disrepute. However, the Supreme Court has ruled that if the police act in good faith—that is, act in accordance with what they understand the law to be—the evidence should be admitted. In *R. v. Duarte* (1990), the Supreme Court of

Canada ruled on the issue of the police acting in good faith. In this case, members of the Ontario Provincial Police and the Toronto police force were involved in a joint investigation involving large quantities of cocaine. The investigation also involved a police informant and an undercover police officer. Both consented to having electronic surveillance equipment placed in the walls of the apartment occupied by the informant and paid for by the police. In this situation, a court authorization was not required by law, since both the informant and the undercover operator agreed to the use of such equipment. The lower court judge agreed with the defendant that the practice of conducting electronic surveillance by the police without judicial authorization, even when one of the individuals (as opposed to all of the participants) consents to the surveillance, violates s. 8 of the *Charter*.

Two other cases, both heard in 1990 by the Supreme Court of Canada, had a significant impact on the laws governing electronic surveillance. In the first one (*R. v. Wong* (1990)), the court determined that video surveillance of a location in which there is a reasonable expectation of privacy without prior judicial authorization is contrary to s. 8 of the *Charter*. And in *R. v. Garofoli* (1990), the court ruled that s. 7 of the *Charter* entitled the accused access to materials used to obtain an authorization of electronic surveillance, subject to editing.

STAY OF PROCEEDINGS

What happens when an individual commits a crime a number of years before the laying of charges? Judges in Canada have the discretion to stay the proceedings when they believe such a situation abuses the rights of the accused. A delay in the charging and prosecution of an accused for sexual offences cannot justify a staying of proceedings, however. Sometimes the information concerning a sexual offence will come to the attention of the police years after the reported incident occurred. Or the police may take months or years to decide that they have the reasonable and probable grounds to lay charges.

In *R. v. L. (W.K.)* (1991), the accused was charged in 1987 with 17 counts of sexual assault, gross indecency, and assault involving his two daughters and stepdaughter. The victims complained to the police in 1986, although the first incident had reportedly occurred in 1957 and the last in 1985. The trial judge stayed the proceedings, since to do otherwise would violate the right of the accused to fundamental justice. Both the British Columbia Court of Appeal and the Supreme Court of Canada ruled that the trial should not have been stayed. The Supreme Court ruled that the fairness of a trial is not automatically jeopardized by a lengthy precharge delay. In fact such a delay may favour the accused, since the police may find it more difficult to find witnesses and corroborating evidence, if needed.

In some cases the complainant may make charges of illegal sexual activity on the part of the accused but not wish the case to proceed to court and give evidence. This is what happened in *R. v. D.(E.)* (1990) and the police decided not to proceed with the charges on the condition the accused agree to have no more contact with the family. Four years later, the victims decided to press charges against the accused, and the police laid charges. The accused argued his rights had been violated, and the judge agreed that this case would constitute an abuse of process and ordered a stay of proceedings. The Crown appealed and won. The Court of Appeal rested its decision on the fact that the accused gave no formal statement to the police in 1984, talking to them on a "non-caution, no-charge basis." The Appeal Court stated that an abuse of process would have occurred only if the prosecution had unfairly reneged on the expectations it gave to the accused.

LEGAL AID

Section 10(b) of the *Charter of Rights and Freedoms* states that all Canadians have the "right to retain and instruct counsel without delay" for criminal cases. This right may involve the use of legal-aid lawyers for those who cannot afford to retain private counsel and who earn under a certain amount of money. In the earliest days of our criminal justice system, defence lawyers played an important role in the protection of the accused by providing free legal aid as an expression of social responsibility. In recent decades, however, formal legal-aid programs were developed, with the result that the legal-aid systems across Canada are "viewed both as an aspect of social welfare and an important component of an effective justice system" (Johnstone and Thomas 1998: 2).

Since the introduction of the *Charter of Rights and Freedoms*, the role of legal aid has changed. Today, s. 10(b) has been judicially interpreted to mean that any person arrested must be informed by the police of the existence and availability of duty counsel and legal aid in the jurisdiction (*R. v. Brydges* (1990)). This right was expanded in 1994 (*R. v. Pozniak*), when the Supreme Court of Canada ruled that when a toll-free number had been established by local or provincial authorities the police had to inform the detained individual that he could contact duty counsel or a legal-aid lawyer.

In recent years, *Charter* decisions have extended the use of legal aid in our criminal justice system. In addition to rights granted to the accused during her ini-

tial appearances in the Canadian criminal justice system, the rights of the defendant are recognized as well, including the entitlement to a legal-aid lawyer in certain conditions, as when an appeal of her case is heard or during parole revocation hearings. The right to legal aid continues to be expanded. In September 1999 the Supreme Court of Canada ruled that prisoners who face solitary confinement have a right to legal aid (Makin 1999).

Prior to a system of legal aid being introduced into our criminal justice system just a few decades ago, those defendants who could not afford their own lawyers were susceptible to local provisions concerning free legal representation. Such a system was clearly problematic, and many critics argued that this system discriminated against people on the basis of wealth and income. An important legal decision in the United States illustrated the problem of not having access to free legal counsel and led to the development of formal legal-aid systems in Canada. The case in question is *Gideon v. Wainright* (1963), which led to a U.S. Supreme Court decision considered to have had a greater impact on the criminal court process than any other Supreme Court case. Gideon was charged in a Florida state court with breaking and entering a poolroom. When he gave his plea, Gideon requested the court to appoint a lawyer to represent him. The court refused, since free legal representation was available only to persons charged with an offence punishable by death. Gideon argued that it was his constitutional right to be represented by a lawyer, citing the Sixth Amendment to the U.S. Constitution, which states, in part, that "in all criminal prosecutions, the accused shall enjoy the right … to have the Assistance of Counsel for his defense."

The state court judge refused Gideon's request, with the result that Gideon conducted his own defence. Defending himself as best he could with his limited legal knowledge, Gideon made an opening statement to the jury, cross-examined the prosecution's witnesses, called his own witnesses, and gave a concluding statement in which he argued that he was innocent of the charge. The jury found him guilty, and the judge sentenced him to five years in prison. Gideon appealed his case to the Florida Supreme Court, arguing that the state's refusal to appoint him legal counsel denied him his constitutional rights. The Florida Supreme Court upheld the conviction. Gideon then wrote a letter to the U.S. Supreme Court, which agreed to hear his case. They appointed him free legal counsel and ultimately agreed with his argument.

In Canada, the first province to provide a legal-aid system was Ontario, in 1967. The last was Yukon, in 1979. In 1973, the federal government started to provide funds to provincial legal-aid programs; to receive funding, a program had to offer criminal-law services when an accused was charged with an indictable offence or when the accused faced the loss of liberty or livelihood in a summary conviction offence. Governments are the major source of revenue for legal-aid plans. The cost of providing legal-aid services has increased dramatically in the past decade; in 1987–88 the total cost of legal-aid programs in Canada was approximately $260 million, increasing to $412 million in 1990–91 and over $600 million in 1992–93 before dropping to $536 million in 1996–97 and $512 million in 2000–01. The federal government has reduced its contribution significantly during the past few years, making provincial governments pay more of the costs. As a result, some provinces have stopped funding legal-aid programs, forcing provincial bar associations to pay for continued existence of the program. During 2002, defence lawyers in several Ontario cities proposed to stay away from court for one day to protest the fact that legal-aid fees paid to them have been frozen in that province for 15 years. And later that same year, the premier of British Columbia created a controversy when he announced that legal aid in that province would be reduced by 40 percent (Tibbetts 2002b).

According to a federal government evaluation of legal aid, the financial cutbacks to legal aid that occurred during the mid- and late-1990s have had a significant negative impact. Legal aid is now a "directionless program that is hampered by federal funding cuts, patchwork of services from province to province and no national standards to ensure poor people have access to justice." In addition, the report stated that legal aid "is only given to Canada's poorest of the poor—and only when they face jail terms if convicted" (Tibbetts 2002a: A5). Yet, legal aid is considered such an important component of ensuring access to justice for the poor that a legal-aid expert at the Canadian Bar Association commented that the federal government should establish minimum legal-aid standards. And Chief Justice McLachlin of the Supreme Court of Canada stated in 2002 that governments should treat legal aid as an essential service. These statements reflect the belief that all Canadians have the right to a fair trial, and "even in times of government restraint, certain basic duties are unavoidable" (Davison 2000: 16).

Some consider legal aid such an important part of our criminal justice system they feel it should become a *Charter* right to have mandatory legal aid since the *Charter* does not currently entrench the right to a publicly funded lawyer. The closest that the courts have ruled that there should be legal-aid assistance for an individual was in a 1999 Supreme Court decision that gave a mother the right to public funding in order to defend herself against provincial authorities from taking her children (*New Brunswick (Minister of Health & Community Services) v. G.(J.)* (1999)). Others argue that this right is extended in certain criminal cases, where judges are able to order legal aid for an accused who will serve time in a federal or provincial correctional facility if convicted.

Three models for providing legal aid for those who qualify are used in Canada. These are the judicare model, the staff system (also referred to as the public defender model), and a combination of these two approaches, called the mixed or combined approach. The judicare model operates in New Brunswick, Ontario, and Alberta. In this program, qualified legal-aid recipients receive a certificate and are allowed to select their own lawyer. The major benefits of this system are lower costs, the availability of services, and the efficiency inherent in having one lawyer handle the case from beginning to end. Usually lawyers are paid a set fee for their services, but this amount is typically too low to cover their costs. Rural areas are better served by this system, since the population base is too small to justify the maintenance of a permanent legal-aid office funded by the government. It is far less costly to allow clients to select legal counsel from those already in the area. Other benefits of this system are:

1. legal-aid recipients are able to select their own lawyer;
2. normal lawyer–client relationships can be maintained for poor defendants; and
3. clients can select lawyers they feel will best serve their interests (Burns and Reid 1981).

The staff system operates in Saskatchewan, Newfoundland, Nova Scotia, and Prince Edward Island. In this system, lawyers are in effect employees of the provincial government. One benefit of this system is that the lawyers involved are salaried—thereby assuring that the client receives competent legal counsel—and take no money for their services from their clients or their clients' families. Another advantage is that the public defenders representing a legal-aid case are able to contact other public defenders, allowing them to benefit from group resources and expertise. Private-practice lawyers can also be used in this model, especially when a conflict of interest arises or if a staff lawyer is unavailable for the case.

According to Burns and Reid (1981: 414–16), the benefits of this approach include

- better representation, because lawyers are specialists, with some becoming spokespersons for the poor;
- lower costs;
- greater efficiency, because it is centralized; and

- better service of the interests of clients, because lawyers are salaried and therefore do not need to use legal tactics that benefit them

The mixed system is practised in British Columbia, Manitoba, Quebec, the Northwest Territories, Nunavut, and Yukon. In these jurisdictions, the legal-aid recipient is given the right to choose legal counsel, either staff or private, from a panel of lawyers providing legal-aid services (Johnstone and Thomas 1998).

Does a person receiving legal aid have a greater chance of being convicted? In a study in which she compared judicare legal counsel and public defenders in British Columbia, Brantingham (1985) found no difference in terms of conviction rates (guilty outcome rates) and sentence severity (the amount and length of jail terms). However, she did discover that these two types of legal aid varied substantially on sentencing outcome. Specifically, judicare clients received more jail sentences or absolute discharges, while the clients of public defenders were given more sentences involving probation orders, restitution, community work orders, and fines. Brantingham (1985: 77) attributed these differences to the fact that clients of public defenders were sentenced after guilty pleas, "particularly guilty pleas following discussions between the public defenders and the Crown counsel."

Morse and Lock (1988: 36), interviewing Aboriginal offenders on their perceptions of the criminal justice system, heard considerable criticism of legal-aid lawyers. They pointed to the fact that legal aid "is overworked so lawyers tell 75 percent–90 percent of accused to plead guilty," and that there "is no real choice in who gets to act as your lawyer." Aboriginal offenders also complained that legal-aid lawyers do not invest much time in them and their cases and "often don't see them in custody until five minutes before appearing in court." Only 41 percent of the offenders indicated they were satisfied with their legal representation, while 48 percent said they were dissatisfied.

SUMMARY

Police officers have the power to use many different techniques to investigate and apprehend suspects. These include searches, electronic surveillance, interrogation, the use of informants, and the use of DNA evidence. Since the introduction of the *Charter of Rights and Freedoms*, the Supreme Court of Canada has placed many constitutional limits on the police. For example, the police are required to obtain properly authorized warrants to conduct searches except in clearly defined contexts. The police must follow these legal procedures exactly or risk the chance of losing the case for technical reasons.

The interrogation procedures of the police are carefully controlled. However, a number of issues continue to affect police conduct during interrogations, such as what type of procedures are used to obtain statements from suspects during this stage of the collection of evidence.

A significant issue for the accused is whether he receives interim release or is detained for part or all of the time preceding the trial. During the past 25 years, bail provisions have been loosened, allowing most individuals charged with a crime to be free while awaiting trial. However, recent crimes involving individuals released on bail have led to a reappraisal of the rules regarding bail, with the result that offenders charged with certain types of crimes are now refused any type of pretrial release.

Discussion Questions

1. Should guilty individuals go free because the police did not follow established legal procedures when they arrested the suspects?

2. Should evidence that is obtained illegally always be excluded from trial? Explain.

3. Do you think the police should be able to collect DNA evidence without any legal restrictions?

4. Should suspects have fewer constitutional rights? If so, what rights should be curtailed? Should the courts be more concerned with the rights of victims?

5. When can the police legally search a dwelling or person without a search warrant?

6. What would happen if police officers were required without exception to obtain a search warrant before they search any person or dwelling except in cases of hot pursuit?

7. Should legal aid be available to all individuals accused of a crime? Give reasons for your answer.

8. When should an individual be denied interim release?

9. What type of inequities, if any, exist in the bail system in Canada? In the legal-aid system?

Suggested Readings

Atreis, J., P.T. Burns, and J. Taylor, eds. 1991. *Criminal Procedure: Canadian Law and Practice.* Vancouver: Butterworths.

Cameron, J. 1996. *The* Charter's *Impact on Criminal Justice.* Toronto: Carswell.

Doob, A.N., P.M. Baranek, and S.M. Addario. 1991. *Understanding Justices: A Study of Canadian Justices of the Peace.* Toronto: Centre of Criminology, University of Toronto.

Pink, J.E., and D. Perrier. 1988. *From Crime to Punishment: An Introduction to the Criminal Law System.* Toronto: Carswell.

Stuart, D. 1996. Charter *Justice in Canadian Criminal Law.* Toronto: Carswell.

Velverde, M., L. MacLeod, and K. Johnson, eds. 1995. *Wife Assault and the Canadian Criminal Justice System.* Toronto: Centre for Criminology.

References

Abbate, G. 2002. "Jury Calls for Changes to Protect Women." *The Globe and Mail,* 9 February, A9.

Abell, J., and E. Sheehy, eds. 1993. *Criminal Law and Procedure: Cases, Context, Critique.* North York, Ont.: Captus Press.

Alberta. 1991. *Justice on Trial*. Edmonton: Task Force on the Criminal Justice System and Its Impact on the Indian and Métis People of Alberta.

Anderson, P.R., and D.J. Newman. 1993. *Introduction to Criminal Justice*, 5th ed. Toronto: McGraw-Hill Ryerson.

Armstrong, J. 2002. "Police Wrung out Confession, Accused in Murder Case Says." *The Globe and Mail*, 20 August, A5.

Bailey, I. 1992. "Do You Want Her To Die, Shane?" *National Post*, 22 July, A9.

Bilodeau, S. 2001/2002. "Investigative Detention." *LawNow* 26, no. 3: 42–43.

Birkenmayer, A.C., and S. Jolly. 1981. *The Native Inmate in Ontario*. Toronto: Ontario Native Council on Justice.

Brantingham, P. 1985. "Judicare Counsel and Public Defenders: Case Outcome Differences." *Canadian Journal of Criminology* 27: 67–81.

Burns, P., and R.S. Reid. 1981. "Delivery of Criminal Legal Aid Services in Canada: An Overview of the Continuing 'Judicature versus Public Defender' Debate." *UBC Law Review* 15: 403–29.

Canadian Centre for Justice Statistics. 1992. *Legal Aid in Canada: 1990–91*. Ottawa: Statistics Canada.

Coughlan, S.G. 1998. "Developments in Criminal Procedure: The 1996–97 Term." *Supreme Court Law Review* (2d)a: 285.

Davison, C. 2000. "A Right to Fairness: Legal Aid." *LawNow* 24, no. 4: 14–16.

Department of Justice. 2000. *The New Brunswick Aboriginal Duty Counsel Project*. Ottawa: Department of Justice.

Dickson, G. 2002. "Strip Searches." *LawNow* 26, no. 6: 36.

Ericson, R., and P.M. Baranek. 1982. *The Ordering of Justice: A Study of Accused Persons as Dependents in the Criminal Process*. Toronto: University of Toronto Press.

Fagan, J., E. Freidman, S. Wexler, and V. Lewis. 1982. *The National Family Violence Evaluation: Final Report*. Washington, D.C.: U.S. Department of Justice.

Fine, S. 1994. "Lawyers Object to Changes in Legal Aid." *The Globe and Mail*, 24 September, A1, A5.

Freidland, M.L. 1965. *Detention before Trial*. Toronto: University of Toronto Press.

Hamilton, A.C., and C.M. Sinclair. 1991. *Report of the Aboriginal Justice Inquiry of Manitoba*, vol. 1. Winnipeg: Queen's Printer of Manitoba.

Hiebert, J.L. 2002. *Charter Rights: What Is Parliament's Role?* Montreal & Kingston: McGill-Queen's Press.

Johnstone, R., and J. Thomas. 1998. *Legal Aid in Canada: 1996–97*. Ottawa: Juristat.

Joint Committee on Domestic Violence. 1999. Report. Toronto: Ministry of the Attorney General.

Kellough, G., and S. Wortley. 2002. "Remand for Plea: Bail Decisions and Plea Bargaining as Commensurate Decisions." *British Journal of Criminology* 42: 186–210.

Law Reform Commission of Canada. 1991. *Police Powers*. Report 33. Ottawa: Law Reform Commission of Canada.

———. 1990. *Controlling Criminal Prosecutions: The Attorney General and the Crown Prosecutor.* Ottawa: Law Reform Commission of Canada.

———. 1983. *Police Powers: Search and Seizure in Criminal Law Enforcement: Working Paper 30.* Ottawa: Law Reform Commission of Canada.

Leo, R.A. 1996. "The Impact of Miranda Revisited." *Journal of Criminal Law and Criminology* 86, Spring: 621–92.

Makin, K. 1999. "Punished Prisoners Win Access to Legal Aid." *The Globe and Mail,* 16 September, A3.

———. 1998. "Police Allowed to Enter if 911 Called, Top Court Says." *The Globe and Mail*, 4 December, A6.

———. 1993. *Redrum the Innocent.* Toronto: Penguin.

Mewett, A.W. 1992. *An Introduction to the Criminal Process in Canada,* 3rd ed. Scarborough, Ont.: Carswell.

Morse, B., and L. Lock. 1998. *Native Offenders' Perceptions of the Criminal Justice System.* Ottawa: Minister of Supply and Services.

Nicol, J.A. 2002. " 'Stop in the Name of the Law': Investigative Detention." *Canadian Criminal Law Review* 7, no. 2: 223–52.

Rigakos, G. 1997. "Constructing the Symbolic Complainants: Police Subculture and the Nonenforcement of Protection Orders for Battered Women." *Violence and Victims* 10: 235–47.

Salhany, R.E. 1986. *Arrest, Seizure, and Interrogation,* 3rd ed. Toronto: Carswell.

Sherman, L.W. 1992. *Policing Domestic Violence: Experiments and Dilemmas.* Toronto: The Free Press.

Solicitor General of Canada. 1991. *Annual Report on Electronic Surveillance as Required under Subsection 195(1) of the* Criminal Code *1989.* Ottawa: Minister of Supply and Services Canada.

Stubbs, J., and D. Powell. 1989. *Domestic Violence: Impact of Legal Reform in NSW.* Sydney, Australia: Bureau of Crime Statistics and Research.

Tibbets, J. 2002b. "Lawyers Hope to Make Legal Aid a *Charter* Right." *National Post,* 7 March, A9.

———. 2002a. "Legal Aid System Falling Apart, Justice Department Report Says." *National Post,* 19 February, A5.

Williams, J.W. 2000. "Interrogating Justice: A Critical Analysis of the Police Interrogation and Its Role in the Criminal Justice Process." *Canadian Journal of Criminology* 42: 209–40.

Young, G. 1994. *Trends in Justice Spending, 1988/89 to 1992/93.* Ottawa: Juristat.

Court Cases

Brown v. Durham Regional Police Force (1998), 131 C.C.C. (3d) 1, 21 C.R. (5th) 1 (Ont. C.A.); leave to appeal allowed (1999), 252 N.R. 198 (note) (S.C.C.)

Cloutier v. Langlois (1990), 53 C.C.C. (3d) 257 (S.C.C.)

Gideon v. Wainright, 372 U.S. 335 (1963)

New Brunswick (Minister of Health & Community Services of New Brunswick) v. G.(J.), [1999] 3 S.C.R. 46

Hunter v. Southam Inc. (1984), 14 C.C.C. (3d) 97 (S.C.C.)

R. v. Alderton (1985), 17 C.C.C. (3d) 204 (Ont. C.A.)

R. v. Bazinet (1986), 25 C.C.C. (3d) 273 (Ont. C.A.)

R. v. Black (1989), 50 C.C.C. (3d) 1 (S.C.C.)

R. v. Borden (1994), 92 C.C.C. (3d) 404 (S.C.C.)

R. v. Brydges, [1990] 1 S.C.R. 190, 53 C.C.C. (3d) 330

R. v. Caslake, [1998] 1 S.C.R. 51

R. v. Charles (1987), 36 C.C.C. (3d) 286 (Sask. C.A.)

R. v. Clarkson (1986), 25 C.C.C. (3d) 207 (S.C.C.)

R. v. Collins, [1987] 1 S.C.R. 265

R. v. D.(E.) (1990), 57 C.C.C. (3d) 151 (Ont. C.A.)

R. v. Duarte, [1990] 1 S.C.R. 30

R. v. Ducharme (June 13, 1990), Doc. CA010644 (B.C. C.A.)

R. v. Feeney, [1997] 2 S.C.R. 13

R. v. Garofoli, [1990] 2 S.C.R. 1421

R. v. Godoy (1998), [1999] 1 S.C.R. 311

R. v. Golden, [2001] 3 S.C.R. 679

R. v. Harris (1987), 57 C.R. (3d) 356 (Ont. C.A.)

R. v. Heisler (1984), 11 C.C.C. (3d) 475 (Alta. C.A.)

R. v. L.(W.K.) (1991), 64 C.C.C. (3d) 321 (S.C.C.)

R. v. Legere (1994), 95 C.C.C. (3d) 139 (N.B. C.A.)

R. v. Lim (1990), 1 C.R.R. (2d) 136 (Ont. H.C.)

R. v. Manninen (1983), 8 C.C.C. (3d) 193 (Ont. C.A.); affirmed (1987), 34 C.C.C. (3d) 385 (S.C.C.)

R. v. Mellenthin, [1992] 3 S.C.R. 615

R. v. Pickett (1975), 28 C.C.C. (2d) 297 (Ont. C.A.)

R. v. Pozniak (1994), 92 C.C.C. (3d) 472 (S.C.C.)

R. v. Singh (1983), 8 C.C.C. (3d) 38 (Ont. C.A.)

R. v. Smith (1989), 50 C.C.C. (3d) 308 (S.C.C.)

R. v. Stillman (1997), 113 C.C.C. (3d) 321; reversing (1995), 97 C.C.C. (3d) 164 (N.B. C.A.)

R. v. Storrey (1990), 53 C.C.C. (3d) 316 (S.C.C.)

R. v. Tomaso (1989), 70 C.R. (3d) 152 (Ont. C.A.)

R. v. Willis (1987), 37 C.C.C. (3d) 184 (B.C. Co. Ct.)

R. v. Wills (1992), 70 C.C.C. (3d) 529 (Ont. C.A.)

R. v. Wong (1990), 60 C.C.C. (3d) 460 (S.C.C.)

The Courts and Criminal Trial Procedure

CHAPTER OBJECTIVES

✓ Understand the organization of our court system.

✓ Understand the roles of the defence lawyer, Crown prosecutor, and judge.

✓ Understand that the court is designed to provide an impartial forum for the facts of the case.

✓ Discuss the role of plea-bargaining in the Canadian criminal justice system.

✓ Understand the fundamental rights of the accused.

✓ Discuss the way trials can vary and the implications of such differences for the accused as well as the legal system.

The courts play an important role in our criminal justice system. As discussed in Chapter 1, the definition of "criminal justice" favoured in Canada means that we expect the courts to identify the guilty and free the innocent, provide a deterrent to illegal activities, safeguard civil liberties of citizens, punish the guilty in relation to the seriousness of their crime(s), and rehabilitate criminals—all at the same time. And while, in this chapter, we will describe the major components of our court system, it is important to remember that very few individuals charged with an offence actually have trials like those we see on television dramas. During 1999–2000, for example, trial cases made up just 9 percent of all cases, compared to cases where the accused was convicted with a guilty plea (53 percent) and those otherwise terminated by the court without a trial (Pereira and Grimes 2002).

One major issue facing our legal system is increasing caseloads in our courts. In the past, this problem has usually been resolved by plea-bargaining, but this means that prosecutors, police, criminal defence lawyers, and judges still become involved. Alternatives that involve hearing cases outside the courts are now being created. This issue also led to the Supreme Court ruling in *R. v. Askov* (1990) that a delay of almost two years between the preliminary inquiry and the trial was unconstitutional. In the estimation of the Supreme Court, the "normal" delay should have been between six and eight months. As a result of the ruling, the Ontario legal system permanently stayed more than 100 000 charges.

Though the *Askov* ruling was made over a decade ago, the issue of court delay remains a critical issue in our legal system. For example, in January 1996 a B.C. man accused of sexually assaulting his adopted daughter for more than seven years had his charges dismissed because the case took too long to come to trial—33 months had elapsed from the time he was charged until his case was dismissed. In fact, the case ended only when Mr. Justice S.W. Hood of the British Columbia Supreme Court dismissed the charges, since the long delays violated the constitutional rights of the accused. The case was expected to take less than a day in court; only two witnesses—the father and the daughter—were scheduled to appear. Mr. Justice Hood indicated that guidelines provided by the Supreme Court of Canada indicate cases should take less than 10 months to move through the provincial court system and no more than another eight months to reach trial in a provincial Supreme Court. But in Campbell

River, B.C., where the trial was to be heard, the backlog of cases had increased to such a point that by late-1998 delays in setting hearings had stretched to seven months, from an average of two months in 1992. In this particular case, delays stretched to two years in the provincial court and more than eight months in the B.C. Supreme Court. Mr. Justice Hood commented that both the Crown prosecutor and defence counsel had tried to move the case forward and that the problem was not simply the backlog in the system. He pointed out that this case should have taken only two months to reach the provincial courts (Willcocks 1999).

The dismissal of this case due to delays is not an isolated incident. Case backlogs had grown to such proportions that other B.C. courts were routinely dismissing charges, including those involving violent crimes. A report in 1998 informed the Attorney General of British Columbia that more than 50 percent of the criminal cases in the province were more than six months old. The Attorney General of British Columbia at the time of Mr. Justice Hood's ruling, Ujjal Dosanjh, commented that the provincial government had recently reduced the delays in the system by hiring five new provincial court judges. He said that delays by defence lawyers contributed significantly to the problem.

The problem of delay in getting a case to be heard in court is a national problem. Despite attempts to speed cases along in the courts, between 1995–1996 and 1999–2000 there was a 9 percent increase in the overall median elapsed time from first to last appearance in court, growing from 77 to 84 days (Pereira and Grimes 2002). The efforts to ensure a speedy trial for the accused have led some to argue that justice is being sacrificed for efficiency. A number of efforts have been introduced to alleviate this situation. One such program involves the use of mediation services that settle disputes outside the courts by using a neutral third party. Other efforts include the introduction of "specialty courts" such as domestic violent and drug courts (see Chapter 14). Some critics also believe plea-bargaining has increased in recent years as one way to alleviate court congestion, although this has not been verified. Whatever the potential solutions, it is important to remember that advocates of the crime control model argue that speed and efficiency in the courts are benefits rather than shortcomings.

THE FUNCTIONS OF THE COURTS

In Chapter 1, the underlying values of our criminal justice system were seen to vary according to the crime control and due process models. These two models are also applicable to our court system. A third model (see below) has been developed in an attempt to provide an alternative perspective to our court system, and this approach is based on the values found in the informal nature of our criminal justice system.

The Due Process Model

The primary focus of our court system is to protect individual citizens from the unfair advantages held by the agents of the state. Rights guaranteed to individuals by the *Charter of Rights and Freedoms*, such as the right to a jury trial, the right to defence counsel, and the right to face the accuser in the courtroom, are viewed as "equalizers" so that the various parties in a court trial have as equal a footing as possible. This model also emphasizes the adversarial nature of our court system (see Chapter 1), in particular

1. a neutral and impartial decision-maker (a judge) making the decisions;
2. equal chances to the presented relevant evidence by both the prosecution and defence; and
3. a highly structured set of procedures (e.g., constitutional safeguards) that must be followed in a trial. It is through this system, due process advocates argue, that truth is discovered and upheld by the courts.

The Crime Control Model

This approach stands in contrast to the due process model by arguing that while safeguarding individual liberties is important, it is secondary to protecting society (and law-abiding citizens) from criminals. The police are not allowed to engage in abusive behaviour, but they are allowed by the courts to utilize devious techniques to outwit offenders. For the courts, a punishment role is emphasized, and it is the courts' responsibility to ensure offenders are punished for their actions and harms they have inflicted. The main goal of the courts is not to ensure the accused is given a "fair" chance, but to achieve justice through deterrence and lengthy punishments. Constitutional rights are used to protect the law-abiding citizen, rather than the accused.

THE BUREAUCRATIC FUNCTION

In this model, there is more of a focus on the day-to-day operation of the courts. This means that while punishing criminals and protecting their constitutional rights is still an area of concern, the main focus is upon the day-to-day activities of the court. Like other bureaucracies, issues such as speed and efficiency become paramount. As we saw at the beginning of this chapter, the length of court trials and their closure is of concern to the authorities. Because the backlog of cases is important (since a number of individuals each year are sentenced to serve their punishment in a correctional facility, but then released because they have already served a considerable—if not all— amount of time waiting for the trial to start), the real measure of success for a judge and the court system becomes their ability to move cases along rather than questioning whether or not justice has been served. For some observers, the real adversarial nature of our courts is not between the accused and the accuser, but between the ideal of justice and the reality of bureaucratic limitations (Feeley 1981).

THE ORGANIZATION OF CANADIAN CRIMINAL COURTS

The Canadian criminal justice system involves a variety of provincial and federal courts. In fact, there are 14 different systems at work in Canada—13 provincial/territorial courts and the federal government. Each of these court systems may differ from the others in certain ways (such as the case of Nunavut, discussed in Chapter 1) (see Figure 8.1).

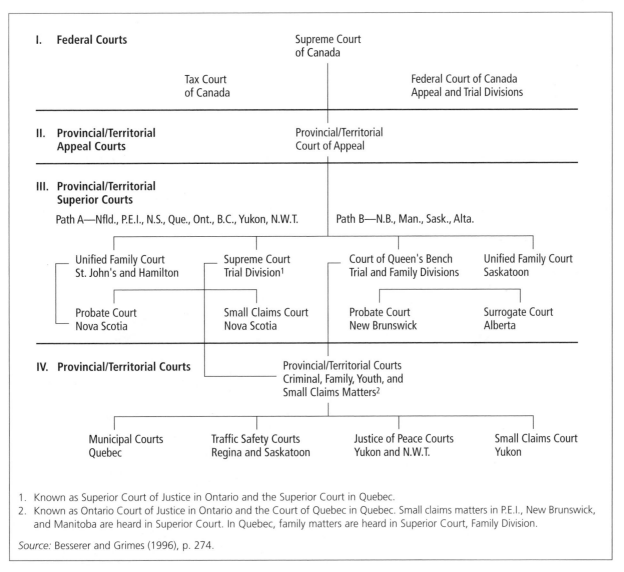

1. Known as Superior Court of Justice in Ontario and the Superior Court in Quebec.
2. Known as Ontario Court of Justice in Ontario and the Court of Quebec in Quebec. Small claims matters in P.E.I., New Brunswick, and Manitoba are heard in Superior Court. In Quebec, family matters are heard in Superior Court, Family Division.

Source: Besserer and Grimes (1996), p. 274.

FIGURE 8.1
Organization of the Canadian Courts

A brief overview of the basic principles of our court systems is necessary to understand how the courts in Canada are organized. Each court has a geographical jurisdiction; provincial and territorial courts are responsible to deal with those cases occurring within their boundaries, and the Supreme Court of Canada has jurisdiction over the entire country. Provinces and territories vary in their provision of court services, larger cities and towns have a permanent court (provincial/territorial courts and provincial/territorial Superior Courts), and, in rural areas, if there is no permanent court, services are offered by a circuit court.

Provincial courts are divided into courts of limited jurisdiction and courts of general jurisdiction. Courts of limited jurisdiction means that local courts are divided into a variety of areas that "specialize" in certain areas, such as motor vehicle violations. A judge sitting alone presides over and decides the proceedings. The majority of minor criminal cases are decided in these courts. Justices of the peace (or magistrates, as they are known in some provinces) are included in this level of courts. In most jurisdictions, these individuals are responsible for allowing law enforcement agents to swear an information in front of them as well as pro-

viding law enforcement agents with search and seizure warrants, summonses, subpoenas, and remand warrants (bail hearings).

Courts of general jurisdiction deal with the most serious criminal offences, and, depending on the type of offence, the case may be decided by a judge and jury or a judge sitting alone. In order to alleviate caseload pressures in these courts, some provinces have started to introduce what is referred to as special subject-matter courts. For example, a number of provinces now have courts that specialize in family violence while projects in Toronto and Vancouver are using courts specializing in drug offences (see Chapter 14). There are also Courts of Appeal in each province/territory; that is, courts that act as reviewing courts where a number of judges listen to and decide on cases where the convicted individual or the crown prosecutor is appealing a decision made by the lower courts.

The Supreme Court of Canada is essentially an Appeal Court, in the sense that it has authority over all provincial/territorial Appeal Courts as well as those cases that come from the federal court system. The Supreme Court has final authority over all public and private law in Canada. This includes all federal, provin-

The Supreme Court of Canada building, located in Ottawa

cial, and municipal law, as well as all common law, legislation, and constitutional interpretation (Bowal 2002). It hears about 105 to 140 cases a year, and over one-half of these cases are "hand-picked by subcommittees of three Supreme Court judges because they involve legal issues of general importance" (Greene et al. 1998: 100). The remaining cases comprise serious criminal cases that either the accused or the Crown has a right to have heard by the Supreme Court; these are known "as-of-right" appeals. These involve cases where there was a dissent over the case in a provincial/territorial Appeal Court concerning a question of law, or a provincial/territorial Appeal Court overturned a trial court acquittal.

The Supreme Court "creates" criminal justice policy in two different ways. The first is known as judicial review, which refers to the power of the Supreme Court to decide whether a law or policy created by a provincial/territory is constitutional. This is also referred to as the "lawmaker" role. For example, the Ontario *Safe Streets Act* (discussed in Chapter 2) is being appealed to the Supreme Court, where, if it is heard, a judgment will be made (i.e., a judicial review) of Ontario's legality to create this law. The second area is the Supreme Court's authority to interpret the law, (also referred to as the "law interpreter" role). In this role, the Supreme Court decides on the meaning of statutory laws when applied to specific situations. Many of the cases discussed or mentioned in the chapters of this text involve the Supreme Court's interpreting a specific piece of legislation or laws enforcement activity, such as search warrants (e.g., the *Feeney* decision on search warrants). Seven Supreme Court justices were recently asked about whether they saw one of the two areas as more important than the other, and all of the judges indicated that both were important (Greene et al. 1998).

It is common practice to refer to the "lower" and "higher" courts in Canada. The former refers to provincial courts, which try all provincial and summary conviction offences; Superior, or higher, courts hear only indictable offences. The higher courts also encompass the provincial Appeal Courts, such as the Ontario Court of Appeal. Appeal Courts are also known as the courts of last resort, meaning that they are the final authority in cases under their jurisdiction. Nonetheless, all individuals have the right to apply for leave to appeal to the Supreme Court of Canada, even if the provincial Appeal Court denies their application for an appeal.

THE COURT SYSTEM

The word "court" refers to a complex part of the criminal justice system. Prior to entering the courts, the only

elements of a case that exist are suspected criminal offences, allegations of wrongdoing, police investigations, charges, and issues concerning bail. The only proof required prior to a criminal trial is probable cause; in order to convict a defendant in a criminal case, a higher standard of proof—beyond a reasonable doubt—must be achieved. This higher standard is meant to ensure that only those individuals who are in found guilty (also referred to as legal guilt) are punished, not those who are thought to be guilty (also known as factual guilt). Higher standards of proof also contribute to high levels of public confidence in both the fairness and accuracy of the criminal justice system.

Once individuals who have been arrested enter their plea, they face a number of decisions that have a significant impact on the determination of guilt and innocence as well as any punishment in the event they are found guilty. While any defendant must make numerous decisions as he proceeds thorough the court system, four other categories of central participants emerge during the court proceedings: Crown prosecutors, defence counsel, judges and juries, and victims and witnesses. Only a court or a court-appointed official can decide to detain an accused prior to trial, and only the courts can decide on his guilt or innocence. In addition, the court must decide on the appropriate type and length of sanction. Note that the word "court" is used to refer to a number of different places or individuals. It can refer to a room where a case is being heard, to a group of judges (for example, the Supreme Court of Canada), or to a single judge.

A judge is an officer of the government who is in charge of a court of law. The duties of a judge include deciding which evidence can be admitted in trial, the appropriate questions to be asked, and any procedural issues that arise. In a jury trial, the judge has to charge (that is, instruct) the members of the jury about the evidence and charges prior to their adjourning to the jury room to decide on the guilt or innocence of the accused. If the trial is to be decided by judge alone, she determines the guilt or innocence of the accused.

THE COURT SYSTEM IN CANADA

Court procedures are controlled by law, tradition, and judicial authority. These procedures govern, among other things, who may speak, when they may speak, and in what order they may speak. In addition, what can and cannot be said in court is dictated by the rules of evidence, and the judge settles any question about the admissibility of the evidence.

The Daily Business of the Courts

Studies of the provincial courts across Canada have consistently shown that in the majority of cases the accused pleads guilty, during his first appearance in court, to the charge as laid (Hann 1973; Griffiths et al., 1980; Wheeler 1987). For example, Ericson and Baranek (1982) found 91 of 131 accused (70 percent) individuals pleaded guilty to at least one charge when they appeared in court. Only 21 individuals pleaded not guilty, with 15 found guilty on at least one criminal charge, while six were acquitted. Seventeen had their charges withdrawn or dismissed. In the remaining two cases, the accused persons did not appear in court to face the charges laid against them.

At the lower court level, the police have an important role in prosecutorial discretion. Crown prosecutors often have little time to prepare for a case, and for the sake of expediency they must rely on information provided by the police. In some instances, prosecutors follow the suggestions of the police officer involved in the investigation (Ericson 1981). Desroches (1995: 244) reports that the police work closely with Crown prosecutors "to avoid lengthy trials that tie up courts, judges, police officers, prosecuting attorney, and witnesses." If the police are successful in obtaining a statement of guilt from the accused, they can bargain with the defence counsel from a position of strength. In the majority of these cases (about 60 percent), offenders were given no concession for their guilty pleas. And those who were able to reduce the number of charges against them in return for a guilty plea were given no guarantee of a shorter sentence.

Prosecutors can of course decide to use their own discretion to stay proceedings, withdraw charges, or dismiss the charges altogether. They may decide, given the circumstances of a case, to use their discretion to expedite matters for the victims. Prosecutors have been found to use their discretion to settle cases before the trial in order to speed up the decision-making in the criminal justice system and to protect child victims from the trauma of appearing and testifying in court (Campbell Research Associates 1992). Other reasons for prosecutors' deciding not to prosecute a case include insufficient evidence, witness problems, due process problems, a plea on another charge, and referral to another jurisdiction for prosecution. For example, Vinglis et al. (1990) found that Crown prosecutors in Ontario withdrew charges in drinking–driving cases because witnesses were not available, errors were found in the technical requirements of the *Criminal Code*, the police failed to collect available evidence, the evidence did not substantiate the charge, or the information was improperly worded. Cases were also dismissed because the accused was charged in a number of different cases, the prosecutor decided to dismiss charges in exchange for a guilty plea, the accused agreed to attend a diversion program, or the accused was wanted for a more serious crime in another jurisdiction.

The Defence Lawyer

Defence counsel represents the legal rights of the accused in criminal proceedings. Though some people believe that the aim of the defence lawyer is to work out the best deal for his client with the prosecutor, it is in fact to ensure that the legal rights of his client are protected. To achieve this goal, defence lawyers typically examine all the evidence collected by the police in order to establish probable cause—the evidence that will be used by the prosecutor in the case as per the Stinchcombe rule (see Chapter 2)—so as to assess the strength of the Crown's case in the proving of the defendant guilty beyond a reasonable doubt. This examination can, of course, lead a defence lawyer into conflict with the police, prosecutors, witnesses, and victims, who may feel that they are being attacked. But the role of the defence lawyer is not to criticize anyone as an individual but to assess the validity and reliability of the evidence and testimony being used by the prosecutor.

The defence lawyer is also responsible for the preparation of the case and selecting a strategy with which to attack and question the prosecutor's case. Since most defendants are not trained in the operation of the law, they are unsure of how to proceed. A defence lawyer ideally helps his client to understand what is happening in court and the consequences of the charges if the client is found guilty. In some cases, the defence lawyer may hire individuals to investigate certain aspects of the case or contact other experts in the field to get a second opinion.

Some of the most significant work of the defence lawyer is his discussion of the case with both the police and the prosecutor. The defence has probably worked with the investigating officers and the prosecutors on previous occasions. Usually, they discuss the strength of their client's case and assess the chance of gaining a satisfactory plea bargain.

The defence lawyer represents the accused at all stages of the criminal justice process, including bail hearings, plea negotiations, and preliminary inquiries. If the trial will be decided by a jury, defence lawyers question prospective jurors. If their client is convicted, they argue for their client's receiving the lightest possible sentence. If they lose the case and are dissatisfied with the sentence or with a legal issue, they may file an appeal in the hope that a court of appeal agrees with their argument and either reverses the lower court's decision or reduces the sentence.

Throughout the trial process, the formal function of the defence lawyer is to "exercise his professional skill and judgment in the conduct of the case … [and] fearlessly uphold the interest of his client without regard to any unpleasant consequence to himself or any other person" (Martin 1970: 376). If the accused admits to the defence lawyer that she committed the crime in question, the lawyer, if convinced that the admission is true, can contest the case by objecting to such legal issues as the form of the indictment and the admissibility or sufficiency of the evidence. However, he cannot suggest that another individual committed the crime, nor can he introduce any evidence he believes is false or that has the purpose of establishing an alibi for the accused.

Criminal defence lawyers are commonly asked how they can defend someone they know is guilty. According to the Canadian Bar Association's (1987) Code of Professional Conduct, defence lawyers are required, even in those cases where they know their client is guilty as charged, to protect their client as much as possible. Our legal system insists that accused persons have the legal right to use every legitimate resource to defend themselves. This means that defence lawyers have to question the evidence given by witnesses called by the prosecution and attempt to point out that the evidence taken as a whole "is insufficient to amount to proof that the accused is guilty of the offence charged"—but "the lawyer should go no further than that" (Martin 1970: 376). Some view the role of defence lawyers as necessary to protect the integrity of our legal system; if they refuse to protect the guilty, "the right of a defendant to be represented by counsel is eliminated and with it the entire traditional trial" (Swartz 1973: 62).

The Crown Prosecutor

Crown prosecutors play a pivotal role in the courts, as they are responsible for presenting the state's case against the defendant. According to the Canadian Bar Association's (1987) Code of Professional Conduct, the prime duty of Crown prosecutors is not to gain a conviction but to enforce the law and maintain justice by presenting all the evidence relevant to the crime being tried in criminal court. For example, the prosecutor must disclose "to the accused or defence counsel … all relevant facts and known witnesses" that could influence "the guilt or innocence, or that would affect the punishment of the accused."

However, many prosecutors face the dilemma of maintaining an impartial role in the court and attempting to find the defendant guilty as charged. Grosman (1969: 63) says there is pressure on prosecutors to gain as many convictions as possible. This pressure to succeed at trial stems from two considerations. The first is that in order to "maintain his administrative credibility and to encourage guilty pleas the prosecutor must demonstrate that he is able … to … succeed consistently at trial." If he fails to demonstrate this ability, more cases would be taken to court, because the defence would feel that it had a good chance to gain a favourable result for its client. The second consideration is that "confidence in present administrative practices is maintained only if the acquittal rate is not substantial." Therefore, to maintain their credibility, prosecutors attempt to gain as many guilty verdicts as possible. As a result, caseload pressure forces prosecutors to decide on the outcome of a case more on the basis of expediency than of justice. This leads to criticism of the justice system as little more than an assembly line (see Chapter 1).

Some argue that this role makes prosecutors more powerful simply because it enables them to virtually define the parameters of a court case. For example, the prosecutor presents the Crown's side of the case in an opening address to the judge before the jury has heard anything else. While the opening address may be criticized in court, it makes a significant first impression. Karp and Rosner (1991: 74) argue that in the David Milgaard case the Crown prosecutor gave a "damning and convincing argument" to the jury, taking "full advantage" of the tradition that allows the Crown to speak first, and providing "a lengthy exposition of what he expected the forty-two witnesses to say when called to the stand."

Crown prosecutors can be viewed as the chief law enforcement officers within the provincial and federal court systems. They represent provincial or federal Attorneys General and Ministers of Justice in all phases of their work, from discussing a case with the police to making sentencing recommendations to the judge and sometimes filing appeals. The most obvious responsibility of Crown prosecutors is to try indictable and summary conviction offences in a court of law. They have a large number of responsibilities associated with the trying of cases, such as examining court documents sent by a variety of individuals, including coroners and the police, in order to determine if further evidence is required.

In addition, Crown prosecutors interview victims and subpoena witnesses to give testimony during the court trial. They also decide when not to try a case, even after the police have laid charges, by requesting an adjournment of the case until a future date, withdrawing the charges, or deciding to offer no evidence so that the court will dismiss the charges and the case (Osborne 1983; Law Reform Commission 1990).

Crown prosecutors are responsible for trying a wide spectrum of cases involving a variety of charges, including child sexual assault, domestic violence, and white-collar and property crimes. Because a Crown prosecutor may be assigned to one particular courtroom, as opposed to a specific case, a number of Crown prosecutors may work on a single case as it progresses through the court system. In recent years, however, a trend toward specialization has become evident, in which special prosecution units try only cases involving specific charges, such as financial or economic crimes and domestic violence.

For a variety of reasons, a prosecutor may decide not to proceed with a case despite the police believing charges should be laid against the suspect or have been laid already. In three provinces (British Columbia, Quebec, and New Brunswick), the police are required to allow prosecutors to review and approve evidence before charges are laid. In all other jurisdictions in Canada, charges can be laid without prosecutorial approval, although prosecutors may decide not to pursue the case at a later date For indictable offences, defence counsel may decide to contest the evidence at a preliminary inquiry in order to determine whether sufficient evidence exists to proceed to criminal trial. In such cases, the prosecutor attempts to show a judge that sufficient evidence does exist by reviewing the physical evidence and questioning and cross-examining witnesses.

The scope of prosecutorial work is extensive, as prosecutors' duties include the entire criminal justice system from investigation and arrest through bail and trial sentencing to appeals. One possible result of this involvement is overload. Gomme and Hall (1995) studied Crown prosecutors in one Canadian province between 1990 and 1992 to find out if prosecutors are subject to work-related strain. They found prosecutors routinely prosecuted six to 10 trials each day in provincial court five days each week. The number of trials increased to between 12 and 14 during peak periods. The impact of this workload "severely constrains the time available to undertake the careful preparation required to ensure that the quality of legal work meets prosecutors' personal and professional standards" (Gomme and Hall 1995: 193). They found prosecutors were susceptible to work overload and excessive strain, leading to questions about their professional effectiveness and whether justice is compromised.

Administering justice is a very human process, Mr. Justice Frank Iacobucci insists. "To say you can decide these questions without having any after-effect or sense of concern is just not accurate."

Judges

Judges uphold the rights of the accused and arbitrate any disagreements between a prosecutor and defence lawyer in a trial. In addition, judges may also act as triers of fact in cases and decide if the defendant is guilty or innocent; in such cases they also determine the type and length of sentence. Judges must be viewed as objective participants so that their decisions on rules of law and procedure are viewed as acceptable by all parties involved in the case.

Canada's constitution allows the federal Cabinet the power to appoint provincial Superior Trial Court judges, provincial and territorial Court of Appeal judges, federal court judges, tax court judges, and the judges of the Supreme Court of Canada. Provincial cabinets have the power to appoint judges in the provincial court system beneath the level of the Superior Court. The appointment of provincial court judges is determined by three different nonpartisan appointment procedures. In Ontario and Quebec, judicial nominating committees search out the best candidates and recommend them to the Attorney General for review and appointment; in Alberta and British

Columbia, provincial judicial councils screen applicants and then make their recommendations to the Attorney General; and in Saskatchewan and Newfoundland judicial councils make comments on the qualifications of candidates proposed by the Attorney General (Greene 1995). In the remaining provinces patronage continues to be evident in judicial appointments; in 1985 the Canadian Bar Association reported that patronage remained an important criterion in provincial court appointments (McCormick and Greene 1990). Russell (1987) points out that though many good lawyers were appointed judgeships in return for their favours, some inappropriate appointments were made also.

CRIMINAL TRIAL PROCEDURE

The criminal trial is the start of the adjudication stage of the criminal justice system, and it is the centrepiece of our court system (see Exhibit 8.1). If the accused pleads guilty, a date is set for the sentencing (see Chapter 9). However, if the accused elects to be tried in court, he has various alternatives, depending on the charge. One such possibility is trial by judge and jury. Jury trials are relatively rare in Canada, as only about 5 percent of all cases are heard at the Superior Court level. Since these are usually high-profile cases, they usually attract much media attention, which leads many members of the public to believe they are typical of what happens in the Canadian justice system.

EXHIBIT 8.1 Case Processing

There are many paths that a criminal trial can take as it makes its way through adult criminal court in Canada. These variations in case processing depend on several factors including the seriousness of the offences being heard, and the elections made by the Crown and the accused. For most cases, the trial process in adult provincial/territorial criminal courts will include some or all of the elements listed below.

First Appearance: The first appearance in court is usually a bail hearing in a provincial court, where the court must determine if the accused should be released pending trial. Most offences require the Crown to show that the accused is either a danger to the community or a risk to flee prosecution before a remand order is given. However, several offences are classified as reverse onus offences, where the accused must show cause why his detention is not justified—*Criminal Code* s. 515(6).

Crown Elections: The Crown is eligible to elect the type of proceeding for hybrid offences, which are also known as "dual procedure" offences. The defining *Criminal Code* sections for hybrid offences specify that the Crown may try the case in one of two ways; (1) as a summary conviction offence—the least serious offence type, which also carries a lower maximum penalty, or (2) as the more serious indictable offence. If the Crown elects to try the case as an indictable offence the accused faces the possibility of a prison sentence that, depending on the offence, ranges between no minimum sentence to life in prison.

Defence Elections: Where permitted under the *Criminal Code*, the accused may elect to be tried in adult provincial/territorial criminal

court or in Superior Court—with or without a jury. If the accused elects to be tried in Superior Court, a preliminary inquiry may be held. (See preliminary hearings below.) The defence is not eligible to elect the mode of trial for summary conviction offences, or offences identified under *Criminal Code* s. 469 or 553. These *Criminal Code* sections identify offences that are the absolute jurisdiction of a single court level, Superior Court and provincial/territorial court respectively.

Preliminary Hearings: The purpose of the preliminary inquiry process is to determine if there is sufficient evidence in the case to proceed to trial in a higher court level, Superior Court. The provincial court judge will commit the case for trial in Superior Court if the evidence is compelling and there is a reasonable expectation of a judgment against the accused. However, if the evidence is not convincing, the judge must stop the proceedings against the accused—and the court finding will be recorded as "discharged at preliminary." The preliminary inquiry process is a way for the accused to review all of the Crown's evidence before proceeding to the higher court. The defence is permitted to question all of the Crown witnesses and to review any prosecution exhibits related to the charges, which helps the accused's council prepare for trial.

Fitness Hearings: When the accused's mental health is brought into question, the court will order a psychiatric examination. In the fitness hearing that results, the accused will be found fit for trial or remanded in custody until the Lieutenant Governor of the province permits release.

Continued on next page

EXHIBIT 8.1 Case Processing ... *Continued*

Trial: The trial begins with the accused entering a plea of guilty, guilty of a lesser charge, not guilty, or special plea (i.e., previous conviction, previous acquittal, or pardon—*Criminal Code* s. 607). In some cases, the accused may refuse to enter a plea, and the court will enter a plea of not guilty on behalf of the accused. A guilty plea will usually result in an immediate conviction, but the court may also refuse to accept a guilty plea if that plea is given with conditions, or if the court feels that the accused does not understand that the plea is an admission of guilt. A plea of not guilty will result in a trial, where the evidence against the accused is heard and the court will make a judgment on that evidence. The final disposition, or decision, of the court will be either (1) guilty of the offence charged, (2) guilty of an included offence, (3) not guilty of the charged offence, or (4) not guilty on account of insanity. The court may sentence the accused immediately following a finding of guilt; however, the court may also delay the sentencing to a later date so that all relevant factors can be considered prior to imposing a sentence on the accused.

Source: Statistics Canada, *Juristat*, Catalogue 85-002, vol. 20, no. 1, March 2000, p. 6.

The Plea

In most cases an accused who appears in criminal court for an indictable offence enters what is known as a general plea—that is, a plea of guilty or not guilty (see Exhibit 8.2). Three other pleas (referred to as special pleas) are available to the accused: autrefois acquit, autrefois convict, and pardon. An estimated 90 percent of accused plead guilty prior to trial or when they appear in a lower court for the first time. If the accused pleads not guilty to an indictable offence (a common plea in the more serious and complex cases), a trial date is set that is acceptable to both the prosecution and the defence. In most cases, the accused is released under the same terms and conditions he was previously given.

What occurs next is determined by the type of charge—indictable, hybrid, or summary conviction. If the accused is charged with a summary conviction offence, the trial is held in a summary conviction court. The information is read to the accused, who is then asked if he pleads guilty or not guilty. If the accused pleads not guilty, a date will likely be set for a trial before a provincial court judge, since it is typical in larger communities that the court docket will be full that particular day. If the accused pleads guilty he will be sentenced immediately or remanded until the judge has the opportunity to hear submissions concerning the sentence. The *Criminal Code* allows for remands of up to eight days, unless the accused consents to a longer adjournment. (Accused in custody generally enforce their eight-day rights.) Even if the charge is for an indictable offence (for example, a gaming offence) because it is under the absolute jurisdiction of a provincially appointed judge (a s. 553 offence), the trial may proceed immediately (Mewett 1992).

Preliminary Hearing

Whenever the accused is charged with an offence that must be tried by a judge and jury, or when the accused elects to be tried by a judge and jury or by a judge alone, the next step is a preliminary inquiry or preliminary hearing. In reality, the accused waives the preliminary inquiry with the consent of the prosecutor, especially if the accused and her lawyer know what evidence the prosecutor will be using at trial. In Canada, the accused in most cases has the right to waive the preliminary inquiry. A defendant is most likely to waive a preliminary inquiry for one of three reasons:

1. The accused has decided to enter a plea of guilty.
2. The accused wants to accelerate the criminal justice process and have a trial date set as early as possible.
3. The accused hopes to avoid the negative publicity that might result from the inquiry.

The purpose of a preliminary inquiry is twofold:

1. to see if there is enough evidence collected by the Crown prosecutor (and by the defence, if it wishes to make the same determination) to proceed to a criminal trial; and
2. to protect the accused from being placed on trial unnecessarily.

During the preliminary inquiry, a provincial court judge or justice of the peace examines the evidence and hears witnesses in order to determine whether a reasonable jury (or a judge when there is no jury) would find the accused guilty. The intention of the preliminary inquiry is *not* to determine guilt. Therefore, the Crown prosecutor does not have to convict the accused but only

If the accused is charged with a Superior Court exclusive offence (a s. 469 offence), the presiding provincial court judge has no jurisdiction to try the case and so sets a date for a trial to be heard by a Superior Court judge. These cases must be heard by a Superior Court judge and jury unless, under special circumstances, the Attorney General of the province allows the case to be heard by judge alone. In all other criminal cases involving indictable offences the accused has the right to select trial by Superior Court judge alone or by provincial court judge alone.

In Canada it is possible to have a trial even if the accused pleads guilty. The Crown prosecutor usually makes a brief statement of the facts of the case to the trial judge court and provides other information he considers to be relevant to the case. At this time, the accused may disagree with certain or all aspects of the prosecutor's statement. The judge then enquires as to the nature of the disagreement. If the judge decides there is substance to the disagreement the judge advises the accused to withdraw his plea of guilty and instead enter a plea of not guilty. If the accused decides to plead guilty to a lesser offence, the judge may decide to proceed with the more serious charge if it arose from the same factual circumstances.

In these situations, the Crown prosecutor may decide to accept the guilty plea and not proceed on the original (and more serious) charge. The presiding judge doesn't have to accept this guilty plea, and if he doesn't, the trial continues with the original charge. Mewett (1992: 109) points out that the basis of a Crown prosecutor's decision to accept a plea of guilty to a lesser charge depends on a number of factors, including "the seriousness of the charge, avoiding the necessity for witnesses to testify, the public interest, the likelihood of securing a conviction on the more serious charge, and so on." Thus, a plea bargain made between the defence and prosecution may not be accepted by the trial court judge.

An individual's plea of guilty must be a free and voluntary act. The accused gives up her constitutional rights, including the right to cross-examine witnesses and to have a trial by jury (if applicable). However, a judge may decide to review the evidence, and if it appears that the accused wishes to change her plea, the judge has the discretion to allow the change. As a result, a judge must believe that the facts of the case warrant a plea of guilty and that the plea is made voluntarily by the accused. The accused, if not represented by defence counsel, must be informed of the right to make a plea voluntarily, and the judge may insist on the presence of a defence lawyer before the plea is accepted by the court. In addition, the judge has the right to allow the accused to withdraw a plea of guilty if she was "in a disturbed state of mind at the time" of the guilty plea (*R. v. Hansen* (1977)).

SECTION 469 OFFENCES

The offences listed below are the exclusive jurisdiction of Superior criminal courts:

- treason;
- alarming Her Majesty;
- intimidating Parliament or Legislature;
- inciting mutiny;
- seditious offences;
- piracy;
- piratical acts;
- murder;
- attempting to commit any of the above offences;
- conspiring to commit the above offences;
- being an accessory after the fact to high treason, treason, or murder;
- bribery by the holder of a judicial office; and
- crimes against humanity.

SECTION 553 OFFENCES

- theft, other than theft of cattle;
- obtaining money or property on false pretences;
- possession of property obtained, directly or indirectly, from the commission of an indictable offence;
- defrauding the public, or any person, of any item;
- mischief under subsection 430(4) of the *Criminal Code*;
- keeping a game or betting house;
- betting, pool selling, bookmaking, etc.;
- placing bets;
- offences involving lotteries and games of chance;
- cheating at play;
- keeping a common bawdy-house;
- fraud in relation to fares; and
- counselling, attempts to commit, or being an accessory to any of the offences listed above.

Source: Besserer and Grimes (1996), p. 277.

introduce sufficient evidence to make the guilt of the accused a reasonable conclusion.

The preliminary inquiry is conducted in much the same way as a regular trial. In most cases it is open to the public. The accused can request a prohibition of the publication of the proceedings either until charges are discharged or, if a trial is held, until the trial is over. The publication ban order is mandatory when requested by the accused at the opening of the inquiry, but discretionary when the prosecutor applies for it.

The prosecution presents its evidence and presents any witnesses. The accused has the right to cross-examine any or all witnesses and to challenge the prosecutor's evidence. It is not necessary for the prosecution to present all the evidence it has as long as it gives *sufficient* evidence to the judge that a reasonable case can be made against the accused. After the prosecutor presents his evidence, the judge must inform the accused that he has heard the evidence against him and ask whether he wishes to make a statement in response to the charge. Rarely does a defendant decide to discuss the evidence, but, if he does, whatever he says is written down and might be used against him during the actual trial. The next step allows the accused to call any witnesses he feels merit attention.

After all the evidence is presented to the court, the judge decides whether the prosecution has presented sufficient evidence to prosecute the accused. If the judge believes the evidence is sufficient, he schedules a trial; but if the evidence is insufficient, the charges are dropped and the defendant is freed. The judge weighs the evidence on the same basis he would use to assess the evidence at a criminal trial. Note that if the presiding judge decides there is insufficient evidence to proceed, he will discharge the accused. This discharge does not mean the accused is acquitted; rather, it means the accused cannot be tried on that information and the proceedings on that information are ended. If fresh evidence is brought to light about the case, the prosecution usually proceeds by way of a direct indictment, which allows the Crown prosecutor, after receiving the permission of the Attorney General or a Deputy Attorney General, to bypass the preliminary inquiry, allowing the accused to be indicted directly.

The Prosecutor Screening Process

Once the police arrest and lay charges against a suspect, it is not automatic that the prosecutor tries the case. For various reasons, many defendants are never brought to trial. Crown prosecutors "have virtually unfettered discretion as to when to charge, what to charge, when the charge should be reduced or dropped" (Stuart and Delisle 1994: 525). Therefore, the prosecutor has the power to decide whether a case is tried in court on the charges laid by the police, or whether to plea-bargain, stay proceedings, or dismiss the charges outright. In addition, the prosecutor has the discretion to proceed by way of indictment or summary conviction in hybrid offences. The prosecutor's discretionary powers exist at all levels of criminal trials. The courts have been reluctant to limit prosecutorial discretion—the Supreme Court of Canada held in *R. v. Beare* (1988) that prosecutorial discretion does not violate the principles of fundamental justice, stating that it is an essential component of our criminal justice system.

The prosecutor's decision to proceed with a case or not is a major source of case attrition (see Chapter 1). To decide what to do with cases as they come into the prosecutor's office, a screening process is used. Several factors may be involved during case screening:

- The most important factor in making a decision about whether to prosecute or not is not the prosecutor's belief in the guilt of the accused, but whether there is sufficient evidence for a conviction. If prosecutors decide there is strong evidence in the case (e.g., overwhelming physical evidence, a confession and a number of reliable and credible witnesses), the decision to prosecute is easier (Boland et al. 1992).
- Prosecutors have case priorities, that is, with all cases being hypothetically equal, the prosecutor will take a violent criminal to court before someone charged with vandalism. The record of the accused is also a significant factor. If the accused has a lengthy number of prior offences, the prosecutor will usually decide to prosecute him before a first-time offender. Sometimes prosecutors will decide to pursue all cases of a specific type, such as domestic violence, gang-related activity, or drinking drivers.
- A major consideration is the type of witnesses, that is, witnesses classified as uncooperative. For example, cases involving domestic violence may be dropped because the witnesses will not cooperate with the prosecutor. The likelihood of a violent crime being pursued in court is more likely when the crimes involve strangers rather than family members.
- The credibility of victims (or witnesses) can also influence the decision to proceed with a case. If the victim or witness is a prostitute or drug addict, and the defendant an upstanding citizen, prosecutors may be reluctant to have a trial, particularly a jury trial where 12 citizens decide on who is more trustworthy.
- A prosecutor may decide to drop a case against the accused if she will testify against someone else in another trial. For example, if the accused is a small-time drug dealer, the prosecutor may drop all charges for information leading to the arrest and conviction of a major drug supplier.

These case-processing decisions become integrated into a strategy for the prosecutor's office. A number of models have been developed to guide prosecutors when to proceed with the case to court and when to drop or stay charges (Jacoby 1979). These include:

- The transfer model, in which very little screening occurs, and prosecutors charge most of the accused after they receive the case from the police. The key factor here is the amount of resources available to a prosecutor's office: if they have ample resources, more cases will be heard in court.
- The unit model, in which individual prosecutors are given significant amounts of discretion to do as they like with each case. There is not much organizational guidance or specific policy given to prosecutors.
- The legal sufficiency model, in which cases are screened according to the legal elements of the case. If there are sufficient legal grounds, the case will probably be prosecuted.
- The system efficiency model, in which cases are disposed of in the quickest possible way. In this model, only those cases where there is a high probability of success will be prosecuted, and those that are not as clear-cut will be rejected as too time-consuming (even if they may end with a conviction) because there are not enough resources.
- The trial sufficiency model, where a case proceeds to court only if a conviction is likely. Resources are secondary, given the prosecutor's belief that the case will end in a conviction.
- The defendant rehabilitation model, in which the prosecutor's decision relies upon her assessment of the possibility that the defendant can be rehabilitated. In these cases, alternatives (e.g., treatment programs) are sought out before the case goes to court as long as the accused agrees to participate.

Plea-Bargaining

Plea-bargaining has been defined as the exchange of prosecutorial and judicial concessions for pleas of guilty (Alschuler 1968). In most cases it occurs prior to the start of the trial, but it can also happen during a trial when the defendant and defence counsel may think that they may get a better sentence than if the trial continues. Plea-bargaining agreements take several forms.

Charge-bargaining involves the following activities:

- the reduction of the charge to a lesser or included offence;
- the withdrawal or stay of other charges or the promise not to proceed on other possible charges; and
- the promise not to charge friends or family of the defendant.

A plea bargain for dropped charges is the dropping of extraneous illegal actions that are contained in the complaint. For example, the prosecutor may agree to drop an auto theft charge accompanying a drug offence.

Sentence-bargaining is another common form of plea-bargaining. Prosecutors and defence lawyers recommend to the presiding judge an appropriate sentence for the accused. Judges do not have to accept this recommendation, but they usually do. Sentence-bargaining usually includes the following:

- a promise to proceed summarily rather than by way of indictment;
- a promise from the Crown to make a particular recommendation in relation to sentence;
- a promise not to oppose defence counsel's sentence recommendation;
- a promise not to appeal against sentence imposed at trial;
- a promise not to apply for a more severe penalty;
- a promise not to apply for a period of preventive detention;
- a promise to make a representation as to the place of imprisonment, type of treatment, etc.; and
- a promise to arrange sentencing before a particular judge.

In sentence-bargaining, the prosecutor agrees to recommend a shorter sentence to the judge or to proceed in the court trial by way of summary conviction in a hybrid offence. For example, a Crown prosecutor may agree to proceed against an individual charged with sexual assault (level 1) on the basis of a summary conviction charge rather than an indictable offence.

In the case of fact-bargaining, the prosecutor and defence lawyer agree not to submit certain facts about the case or the background of the offender into court. In so agreeing, they hope that the accused receives a lighter sentence. Such a practice usually involves

- a promise not to volunteer certain information about the accused (e.g., information on the defendant's previous convictions); and
- a promise not to mention a circumstance of the offence that may be interpreted by the judge as an aggravating factor (and therefore making the accused deserving of a more severe sentence).

Label-bargaining is the attempt by defence counsel to prevent her client's being charged with an offence that carries a negative label (for example, child molestation) in exchange for a less socially objectionable one (for example, assault) by offering a plea of guilty.

Section 10(b) of the *Charter of Rights and Freedoms* states that an essential aspect of prosecutorial discretion lies in negotiating a bargain with defendants and their lawyers in a criminal case. In plea-bargaining, the defendant agrees to plead guilty to a criminal charge and receives some benefit in return (Law Reform Commission of Canada 1989: 2–3). Though an agreement may be reached by all the key actors involved in a trial, the judge is not legally bound to approve it. Plea-bargaining exists because it serves a variety of purposes (Wheatley 1974):

1. It improves the administrative efficiency of the courts.
2. It lowers the cost of prosecution.
3. It permits the prosecution to devote more time to more important cases.

Since prosecutors prefer to devote their time to serious crimes or to cases in which they have a good chance of securing a conviction, they may agree in other cases to accept a guilty plea to a lesser charge because it saves the court's time and money, and it reduces the risk of the prosecution's losing the case should it proceed to trial. In addition, the prosecutor may gain information about other criminals that will help solve other crimes.

The practice of plea-bargaining has been criticized and defended by a wide variety of individuals and professional bodies that work in the criminal justice system. The Law Reform Commission (1975: 14) referred to plea-bargaining as "something for which a decent criminal justice system has no place." Nine years later, however, it changed its view, calling plea-bargaining a normal practice in the criminal justice system, and in 1989 it commented that plea bargaining is not a "shameful practice" (Law Reform Commission 1989: 8).

The Right to a Jury Trial

Before a case is heard in court, the accused may have the right to decide if she wants to be tried by judge and jury or judge alone. In Canada, the right to a jury trial is found in s. 11(f) of the *Charter of Rights and Freedoms*, which states that any person charged with an offence has the right to trial by jury where the maximum punishment for the offence is imprisonment for five years or more. In *R. v. D. (S.)* (1992) this five-year rule was challenged by the accused, who was charged with an offence that carried a maximum punishment of less than five years. The court held that no principle of fundamental justice was violated, as no right exists that entitles the accused to a jury trial in every criminal case. Note too that the majority of indictable offences are electable, and many accused persons decide not to be tried by judge and jury.

Once an accused is convicted and further proceedings take place on the basis of the conviction, there can be no additional jury trial. For example, when convicted murderer Paul Bernardo was declared a dangerous offender, his defence lawyer made no attempt to have the case heard by both a judge and jury, since Bernardo had already been found guilty and, as such, was not an individual "charged with an offence" as specified in s. 11(f) of the *Charter*. This ruling was based on a previous case heard by the Supreme Court of Canada, which ruled that it is wrong to allow an individual already convicted to have the right later on to request a jury trial *R. v. L. (T.P.)* (1987).

Jury Selection

If the accused decides to be tried by a judge and jury, jury selection follows. Jury selection is a four-step procedure. Three of these occur outside the court and are a provincial responsibility; the fourth takes place in the court and is governed by federal legislation (the *Criminal Code*). The three out-of-court stages are:

1. the assembly of a source list of persons who may be qualified, under provincial law, to serve as jurors (most, but not all, provincial jury acts specify some or all of the sources to be consulted to prepare the list);
2. a determination of the identity of those on the source list who are qualified to serve, according to the relevant provincial jury act, and the disqualification or exemption from service of those on the list who, for various reasons, are usually also specified in the appropriate jury act; and
3. the selection from the names remaining on the source list of a jury panel, whose members are, as appropriate, summoned to appear in court in accordance with the procedures set out in each provincial jury act.

A list of initial candidates is compiled in ways that differ from province to province. This initial list, referred to as a jury array, provides the government with the names of citizens who are potential jurors. Each province has a jury act that specifies who may be selected for the jury array. Section 626 of the *Criminal Code* allows each province to determine the qualification for potential selection, but it precludes discrimination on the basis of sex.

A number of individuals from the juror list appear in court (the number varies widely from jurisdiction to jurisdiction), where there is an in-court selection process. The framework for this in-court procedure is found in s. 631 of the *Criminal Code*. The purpose of this process is to determine which of the prospective jurors are impartial. In contrast to the system in the United States, the trial judge in Canada does not have the authority to determine impartiality among prospective jurors. The judge can ask the assembled panel of prospective jurors whether, if selected, they might be unable to serve on the jury (because of a health problem, for example). The judge may excuse those who indicate they have concerns.

In Canada the decision to select a jury is held by two layperson triers. To select the first juror, two individuals are randomly chosen and sworn to serve as triers. The triers listen to prospective jurors as they respond in turn to questions approved by the court. The triers must decide, after each response, whether the candidate is impartial. Once the candidate is deemed to be impartial, he replaces one of the original triers, another prospective juror is then called forward, and the process continues until another impartial juror is found. However, even if the triers decide that a juror is impartial, either the Crown prosecutor or the defendant may exercise a peremptory challenge (see below), making the triers call another prospective juror. Once the twelfth juror is called, the jury is sworn.

There are two types of challenges in Canada: the challenge for cause (where a reason must be given for, and a determination made about, the validity of the challenge) and the peremptory challenge (where no questioning of prospective jurors takes place and where no cause need be stated as to why a potential juror is being eliminated). The purpose of both challenges is to eliminate jurors considered by either side to be unqualified or not impartial. In this process, potential jurors may be challenged by the prosecution and defence lawyer in order to assess their appropriateness to sit on the jury. Potential jurors may be questioned under oath about such things as their personal background, occupation, residence, interest in the case, and attitudes about certain relevant issues, though typically the court allows only one or two specific questions—approved by the trial judge—to be put. Any citizen who is thought to have a bias for or against the accused—for example, a person who is a friend of the accused or has already formed an opinion—will be eliminated.

If there is a challenge for cause, a reason must be provided and the judge must determine if the reason has merit. The usual approach is for either side to challenge for cause first, as the number of peremptory challenges is limited. A potential juror may be challenged if, for example, she was convicted of an offence and incarcerated for over 12 months, or is physically unable to serve on the jury, or cannot speak either official language of Canada, or is a non-Canadian or a landed immigrant. If a potential juror is challenged peremptorily, no reason need be given.

Challenges for cause are not common in Canada (Vidmar 1999). Most challenges are peremptory, but the number of such challenges is limited. Section 634(1) of the *Criminal Code* was changed in 1992 to allow both the prosecutor and defence to exercise 20 peremptory challenges when the accused is charged with high treason or first-degree murder, 12 challenges when the accused is charged with all other offences punishable by imprisonment of five years or more, or four peremptory challenges for all other offences. Different numbers of challenges are available to the Crown in cases where there are accused being jointly tried.

Historically, questions involving the potential racial bias of jurors have not been allowed in Canada. In 1993, the Ontario Court of Appeal was the first court to acknowledge the possibility of juror racial prejudice. In this case, a black male was accused of murdering a white male during a cocaine transaction in Toronto. In this case, (*R. v. Parks* (1989)), the Court of Appeal held that "it was essential for the accused to be able to ask potential jurors about their racial bias." The Court of Appeal hoped that "allowing one question would legitimate the trial process as fair and nondiscriminatory" (Roach 1999: 228). Many judges, however, interpreted this ruling as being applicable to only the Toronto area, but the Court of Appeal pointed out later that one question could be asked throughout the province. The Court of Appeal also clarified what type of question could be asked: general questions related to the offence in question could not be asked. This question cannot be used for trials involving defendants who were gay or Vietnamese due "to the lack of evidence of systemic discrimination against these groups."

This issue soon resurfaced; in *R. v. Williams* (1996), a trial judge in British Columbia refused to let an Aboriginal male ask potential jurors about their potential biases. This ruling was appealed to the British Columbia Court of Appeal, but it upheld the decision of the trial judge. This case was then appealed to the Supreme Court, which ruled in favour of the accused. And in *R. v. Mankwe* (2001), the Supreme Court held that potential jurors may be questioned about their views on blacks by the defence. This case involved a black male who was convicted by a jury of sexually assaulting a woman working for an escort agency in his apartment. The Supreme Court ordered a new trial, and his lawyer could ask potential jurors whether or not they believe that blacks

- commit more crimes in Canada than other Canadians;
- have a greater propensity to commit crimes of violence;
- are more likely to commit crimes of a sexual nature than other races; and
- have a greater tendency to lie than persons of other races do.

Only the trial judge has the right to "stand aside" a prospective juror, and then only in limited circumstances. A juror may ask to be stood aside by a judge for reasons of personal hardship or any other reasonable cause (s. 633 of the *Criminal Code*). Exempting a prospective juror allows the judge, in those situations in which a full jury has not yet been sworn, to call back jurors in the hope that both sides agree on their role as a juror. In these cases, however, the recalled jurors are subject to the same challenges as the other jurors (s. 641 of the *Criminal Code*).

In Canada, all juries consist of 12 individuals. Until 1992, Yukon and the Northwest Territories were allowed to select only six individuals. However, the Court of Appeal of the Northwest Territories held that such a jury was in violation of s. 15 of the *Charter*. The *Latimer* case discussed at the beginning of this book was tried by a jury of 11 since a judge has the power to discharge a juror because of illness or any other reasonable cause. A trial may continue as long as 10 jurors remain, but if the number falls below ten, the jury must be discharged and the process started over, as specified by s. 644 of the *Criminal Code*.

LEGAL RIGHTS AND CRIMINAL TRIALS

The purpose of a criminal trial "is for the prosecution to prove, according to law, the guilt of the accused" (Mewett 1992: 125). This means that the prosecutor must prove that the defendant committed the act in question and had the appropriate mental element when he committed the criminal offence. Every trial involves certain legal principles concerning the rights of the accused; these are specified in the *Charter of Rights and Freedoms* and in rules of evidence. These rights ensure the accused is given a fair trial. What follows is a discussion of the most fundamental rights accused persons possess in the Canadian legal system.

The Presumption of Innocence

According to s. 11(d) of the *Charter*, everyone has the right "to be presumed innocent until proven guilty according to law in a fair and public hearing." The burden of proving guilt in a court of law lies on the state (i.e., the prosecutor). Even if the accused is factually guilty, the prosecutor has to convince a judge or jury that the defendant is legally guilty.

The Right of the Accused to Confront the Accuser

The right of the accused to confront the accuser is essential to a fair trial, since it controls the type of evidence used in court. Hearsay evidence—that is, second-hand information—is accepted as evidence only in rare circumstances, such as for example, when it is information divulged by a dying person. This is what happened in a famous U.S. criminal case involving the Ford Motor Company and one of its vehicles, the Ford Pinto (Cullen, Maakestad, and Cavender 1987). In this case a deathbed statement made to a nurse by a victim of a traffic accident involving a Pinto led to that statement's being entered into the court record, despite that it could not be corroborated. As a result, crucial evidence was entered into the case, and it proved a major factor in the outcome of the case.

Furthermore, the accused (usually through his lawyer) has the right to cross-examine all witnesses and victims who testify against him. Cross-examination allows the defence to challenge any statement or testimony given by a prosecution witness or a victim, in the hope of discrediting such information.

Child sexual assault legislation allows a child to testify outside the courtroom when the accused is charged with certain sexual offences. Judges may allow a child to testify from behind a screen or via closed-circuit television from another room in the courthouse. However, the provisions found in this legislation protecting children from seeing the alleged abuser have not always been accepted outright by members of the judiciary. In *R. v. Ross* (1989), the Nova Scotia Court of Appeal upheld the constitutionality of the provision, ruling that "The right to face one's accusers is not in this day and age to be taken in a literal sense … it is simply the right of the accused person to be present in court…"

The use of videotape as the sole evidence of the victim's testimony, however, has proved to be more problematic. In *R. v. Meddoui* (1990), heard in the Court of Queen's Bench of Alberta, the trial judge accepted the videotape of the victim as evidence. However, in another case that same year (*R. v. Thompson* (1990)), the use of videotape was ruled as violating sections 7 and 11(d) of the *Charter*. In future, therefore, the use of videotape as *prima facie* evidence will likely be rare in Canadian courts.

The Right to a Speedy Trial

One of the most serious problems facing the courts today is delay in hearing a criminal case. Delay may result from a variety of legal options—plea-bargaining, procedural and evidentiary issues, and court cancellations. These delays may, however, contravene s. 11(b) of the *Charter*, which guarantees that any person charged with an offence has the right "to be tried within a reasonable time."

The right to a speedy trial is also considered to be a part of fundamental justice protected by s. 7 of the *Charter*. This right was clarified in *R. v. Askov* (1990) (see Exhibit 8.3). In this case, three men charged with weapons offences were denied bail in November 1983. The men were released on bail in May 1984, but their court trial was put over until September 1985, due to a backlog of cases. The lawyers for the accused argued

that their clients' right to a fair trial was unfairly violated by courtroom delays. The presiding judge agreed, but the Ontario Court of Appeal overturned that decision. However, the Supreme Court of Canada agreed with the trial judge. In addition, when the Supreme Court made its decision, it identified four factors for a judge to rule on when unreasonable delay had occurred:

1. *The length of the delay.* While no absolute time limit was identified by the Supreme Court of Canada, it ruled that "it is clear that the longer the delay, the more difficult it should be for a court to excuse it." This factor is to be balanced

---

EXHIBIT 8.3 The Right to a Speedy Trial (*R. v. Askov* (1990))

The case of *R. v. Askov* (1990) illustrates how the Supreme Court of Canada interpreted the right to speedy justice for the accused. This decision relates to s. 11(b) of the *Charter of Rights and Freedoms*, which states that any person charged with an offence has the right "to be tried within a reasonable time."

FACTS OF THE CASE

In November 1983 Askov (along with a few associates) was charged with the possession of a prohibited weapon, possession of a weapon for a purpose dangerous to the public, pointing a firearm, and assault with a weapon. He was denied bail in November 1983 but was released on bail in May 1984 on a recognizance of $50 000. A preliminary inquiry started in July 1984 lasted until September 1984. There was enough evidence to proceed to trial, but the trial wasn't slated to start for another year, due to scheduling problems. By then almost two years had passed since the charges were laid. The case was once again rescheduled to be heard in September 1986.

When at last the trial started, defence counsel argued it should be stayed because of the length of time the case had taken to come to trial (by then almost three years). The trial judge denied the request, stating that "insufficient institutional resources" were the source of the delay. This ruling was confirmed by the Ontario Court of Appeal.

DECISION

Askov appealed this decision to the Supreme Court, which heard the case in October 1990. The court ruled in favour of Askov, setting out a number of factors to be used by the courts when determining whether the delay for a case to

come to trial is excessive. These factors included the length of the delay, the explanation for the delay, the accused's waiver of rights, and prejudice to the accused. In addition, the court stated that a waiting period of five to eight months for a case to come to trial was acceptable.

SIGNIFICANCE OF THE CASE

The impact of the *Askov* case was described by a judge on the Ontario Court of Appeal as "staggering." In the six months following the court's decision, over 34 000 charges were stayed, dismissed, or withdrawn. This included 8600 impaired driving charges, 6000 cases involving theft under $1000, a substantial number of charges involving assaults and frauds, 500 sexual assaults, over 1000 drug offences, and thousands of violations of provincial statutes.

UPDATE

Seventeen months later, the Supreme Court of Canada, in *R. v. Morin* (1992), changed the acceptable waiting period to eight to ten months. It also introduced a number of other tests, making it no longer necessary for the prosecutor to prove that the delay was caused by the accused, that institutional delay was justified, or that the accused had waived his rights under s. 11(b) of the *Charter*. The median elapsed time for cases involving serious charges is longer. The longest median elapsed times for violent crimes are for cases involving, for example, sexual abuse (210 days), sexual assault (209 days), and homicide and related (178 days). Crimes against the Person offences, with an overall median of 126 days of elapsed time, take 50 percent more time to complete than Crimes against Property offences, which have an elapsed time of 84 days (Pereira and Grimes 2002) (see Figure 8.2).

CHAPTER 8 The Courts and Criminal Trial Procedure

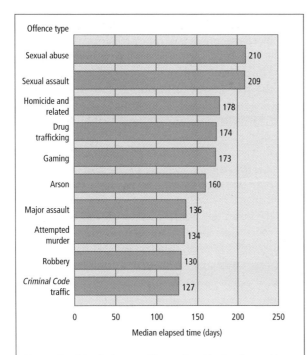

Offence type

	Median elapsed time (days)
Sexual abuse	210
Sexual assault	209
Homicide and related	178
Drug trafficking	174
Gaming	173
Arson	160
Major assault	136
Attempted murder	134
Robbery	130
Criminal Code traffic	127

Notes: Combined, the ten offences listed in the chart with the longest median case elapsed times represent 13% of the cases heard in adult criminal court. Data do not include New Brunswick, Manitoba, British Columbia, and Nunavut.

Source: Statistics Canada, *Juristat*, Catalogue 85-002, vol. 22, no. 1, February 2002, p. 3.

FIGURE 8.2

Median Time Elapsed from First to Last Adult Criminal Court Appearances, Case Types with the Longest Processing Times, Nine Provinces and Territories in Canada, 1999–2000

with the other factors, including "the standard maintained by the next comparable jurisdiction in the country."

2. *The explanation for the delay.* Two key factors were identified: (a) the conduct of the Crown and (b) systematic or institutional delays. In addition, the accused cannot unduly cause a delay in the proceedings, although if the accused were to make a deliberate attempt to delay the trial, the courts would not rule in her favour, and the burden of proof would lie with the accused.

3. *Waiver.* In this situation, the accused indicates that she has understood that she has a s. 11(b) guarantee and has waived the right provided by that guarantee.

4. *Prejudice to the accused.* The Crown will proceed in those cases in which, despite a long delay, no resulting damage was suffered by the accused.

The impact of the *Askov* case was enormous. Approximately 100 000 criminal charges were permanently stayed in Ontario alone, including a number of cases involving charges of sexual assault, assault, and fraud. Within two years, however, the Supreme Court of Canada reconsidered the issue of speedy trial. In *R. v. Morin* (1992) it ruled that a delay of between 14 and 15 months in a case involving charges of impaired driving did not violate s. 11(b) of the *Charter*. In this case, the Supreme Court changed its direction by ruling that the protection of society was served by allowing "serious cases to come to trial, that administrative guidelines are not limitation periods, and the importance of evidence of prejudice" (Stuart 1995: 347). Since the *Morin* ruling, the number of cases stayed due to unreasonable delay has fallen dramatically (see Figure 8.2). This change came about primarily because provincial governments provided more resources to the courts and investigated other strategies, such as diversion programs. Most cases in Canada are now heard within one year of the first court appearance. In fact, many cases are dealt with in a single appearance, usually within the first four months of the initial court appearance.

The Right to a Public Trial

Do members of the media have the right to attend trials? While this issue is not addressed explicitly by the *Charter*, s. 2(b) guarantees freedom of the press and other forms of mass media. However, freedom of the press is limited by s. 1 of the *Charter*, where it has been held that freedom of the press is not an absolute. A discussion of the most fundamental rights accused persons possess in the Canadian legal system follows.

While most criminal trials are open to reporting by the media, a public trial is for the benefit of the accused. Section 11(d) of the *Charter* states that any person charged with an offence has the right "to be presumed innocent until proven guilty according to law in a fair and public hearing." This means that justice cannot be served by secret court trials. But, as noted earlier, the accused can request the judge to order a ban on the publication of certain evidence emerging in a preliminary inquiry. In such a case, the name of the accused can be published, but specific evidence presented in court cannot be published, as "this might jeopardize the ability of the accused to receive a fair trial" (Boyd 1995: 141). The rationale is that the media could give out information that biases potential jurors or judges. As a result, great care is taken to protect the accused.

These cases typically involve issues concerning the effect of pretrial publicity and whether publicity will influence the right of the accused to a fair trial. The Supreme Court ruled in *Dagenais v. Canadian Broadcasting Corp.* (1994) that the right to a fair trial does not take precedence over the right to a free press. The Court ruled that the first test for a publication ban is the determination of whether it is necessary to prevent "a real and substantial risk to the fairness of the trial." Freedman and Burke (1996: 257) studied the effect of pretrial publicity in the Paul Bernardo case, a case they aptly described as "one of the most sensational cases in Canadian history." In their study of 155 adults who acted as mock jurors, they found only a limited negative effect of pretrial publicity on their verdict, leading the researchers to conclude "there was no relation between the amount heard and ratings of guilt or verdicts either before or after the trial account."

Another important issue is whether criminal trials should be televised as a matter of right. In 1981, in the United States the U.S. Supreme Court removed all constitutional obstacles to the use of television over the complaints of the accused. As a result, during the summer of 1995 many Canadians watched live television coverage of the O.J. Simpson trial, though they could view only artists' sketches of the Paul Bernardo trial.

According to s. 486(1) of the *Criminal Code*, a judge has the right to exclude the public for all or part of the trial if she feels it is in the "interest of public morals, the maintenance of order or the proper administration of justice." Exclusion is most commonly ordered when a child or mentally challenged person is about to testify and the judge feels exclusion will assist the witness.

One of the most controversial decisions a judge can make is to exclude the media. Rarely are members of the media banned from the courtroom. It is more common for a Superior Court judge to issue a nonpublication order to protect "the integrity of the court." In addition, s. 486(3) expressly allows a trial judge to ban the publication of anything that would identify the names of the complainant or witnesses in trials involving sexual offences.

THE CRIMINAL TRIAL

A criminal trial is a formal process that strictly follows rules of evidence, procedure, and criminal law. The formality and rigidity implied by this definition stands in sharp contrast to trials shown in many television shows and movies, which present the courtroom as a "no-holds-barred" arena in which defence lawyers and prosecutors ask leading questions, act in a prejudicial manner, and win cases through courtroom trickery. In reality, each criminal trial follows a particular procedure that must be observed by all parties involved. As a result, trials are complicated events, and the judge has to make decisions about technical questions of procedure and about what evidence is allowed.

The key actors are the prosecutor and defence lawyer, who present their case as persuasively as they can and in a manner that they hope is most likely to lead to an adjudication in favour of their client. Prosecutors use police reports, testimony from witnesses and victims, and physical evidence in an attempt to persuade the court the defendant is guilty. The defence lawyer tries to point out the limits and problems in the prosecutor's case, and at the same time presents evidence beneficial to the accused. The defence lawyer tries to ensure that his client's constitutional rights are protected. Since only one side can win, both the prosecutor and the defence lawyer will assess the trial in order to see if an appeal is necessary.

The Opening Statement

Once the jury has been selected and the trial begins, a court employee reads the criminal charges to the jurors. Both the prosecutor and defence lawyer then have the right to make opening statements to the jury. In Canada, the prosecutor presents the first opening statement. This statement usually includes a summation of the criminal charges, the facts of the case, and the Crown's plan on how it will proceed. However, the prosecutor cannot be biased or impartial in her opening comments, since the prosecutor's role is to assist the jury in arriving at the truth. As a result, Crown prosecutors have a duty to be impartial, and this duty precludes any notion of winning or losing. They must guard against stating information likely to excite and inflame the jury against the accused. Nor may they "express a personal opinion as to the guilt of the accused or state that the Crown … [is] …. satisfied as to the accused's guilt" (Salhany 1986: 274).

The defence does not have to make an opening statement if he does not wish to. The defence lawyer too outlines the case but informs the jury of how he intends to show that the defendant is innocent of all charges. This plan entails describing how he will prove the prosecution's case to be inadequate.

Prosecutors cannot promise evidence that they will not bring to court. If they mention the name of a particular witness and the testimony they expect from that witness, and this individual does not appear, the judge may rule the statement was prejudicial toward the accused and subsequently set aside any verdict of guilt. In addition, the prosecutor cannot mention any evidence that she knows will be inadmissible and cannot mention any prior record of the accused.

If the trial does not involve a jury, the opening statements can be brief, as the judge is probably knowledgeable about the case, the appropriate rule of law, and some of the evidence that may already have been discussed in a preliminary inquiry.

All evidence submitted in the court in an attempt to prove the defendant innocent or guilty must meet the highest standard of proof. The standard is "guilty beyond a reasonable doubt," and it is viewed as the basis for reducing the risk of mistaken conviction if there are questions about certain facts presented during the trial. The standard goes hand in hand with the belief that it is better to release 100 guilty persons than to convict one who is innocent.

Trial Evidence

Once the opening statements have concluded, the prosecution starts its case by presenting evidence. Usually the first evidence to be presented is testimony provided by sworn witnesses (for example, police officers, medical examiners, victims, etc.). This type of testimony consists of reports from the witnesses on anything that they saw, heard, or touched. Sometimes it involves the opinions of witnesses; for example, an eyewitness may give an opinion on whether the defendant appeared confused. Expert witnesses are specialists in certain areas that apply to the case. For example, a medical examiner can give expert testimony on the time of death or on how injuries occurred. No more than five expert witnesses may be used by the prosecution or defence without the approval of the judge.

When the prosecution finishes her questioning, the defence has the right to cross-examine the witness. Cross-examination may focus on the oral and written statements of the witness. Testimony is but one form of evidence that may be used during a trial. Other types of evidence are

- *Real evidence.* This type of evidence consists of exhibits such as weapons, clothing, fingerprints, etc. Real evidence must be original. However, photographs and duplicates may be introduced as evidence.
- *Direct evidence.* This type of evidence consists of the observations of eyewitnesses.

A courtroom located in Vancouver allows lawyers to present video evidence on CDs, which jurors can view on individual monitors.

- *Circumstantial evidence.* This type of evidence proves a subsidiary fact from which the guilt or innocence of the accused may be inferred.

All evidence presented in court is governed by the rules of evidence. The judge acts as an impartial arbitrator and rules on whether certain types of evidence are allowed into the trial. Judges may decide to exclude certain evidence. One such type of excluded evidence is known as hearsay evidence. This is information that a witness hears from someone else. The courts have ruled that such information represents a denial of the defendant's right to cross-examination, since witnesses do not have the ability to establish the truth of the information.

The Defence Lawyer's Presentation of Evidence

The defence lawyer has the right to introduce any number of witnesses at a trial or none at all. If he does introduce a witness, the prosecution has the right to cross-examine that individual. One of the most critical decisions a defence lawyer makes is whether to have his client give testimony under oath. During a criminal trial, the defendant has the right to be free from self-incrimination (that is, the right to remain silent), which means the accused has the right not to testify.

The Closing Argument

Section 651 of the *Criminal Code* determines whether the prosecution or defence presents its closing argument first. If the defence presents evidence or the defendant testifies, the defence must address the jury before the prosecution does. If no defence evidence is called, the prosecutor presents her evidence first. During their closing arguments, both prosecution and defence are allowed to offer reasonable inferences about the evidence and show how the facts of the case prove or disprove the defendant's guilt. However, they are not allowed to comment on evidence not used during the trial.

The Charge to the Jury

After the defence lawyer and prosecutor make their final presentations to the court, the judge instructs, or charges, the members of the jury on the relevant principles of law they must consider when deciding the guilt or innocence of the defendant. The judge includes information such as the elements of the alleged offence, the evidence required to prove each charge, and the degree of proof required to obtain a guilty verdict. It is essential for the judge to clearly explain the relevant laws and evidence requirements as well as the meaning of reasonable doubt. In addition, judges must instruct the jury on the procedures they should use when making their decision. These instructions are important, since they may prove to be the grounds for an appeal.

These instructions seem simple and reasonable. However, in reality they may confuse jurors and lead them to make incorrect evaluations of the evidence or to select the wrong verdict. The final instructions given to the jury apply to issues of evidence and testimony and usually include mention of

1. the definition of the crime with which the defendant is charged:
2. the presumption of the defendant's innocence;
3. the burden of proof that lies with the prosecution; and
4. the fact that if, after discussion, there remains reasonable doubt among the jurors as to the guilt or innocence of the defendant, he must be acquitted.

The judge also instructs jurors about the possible verdicts they might consider. While the jury may reach a verdict on the guilt or innocence of the defendant on the original charge, it usually has the option to decide on the degree of the offence in many cases (for example, second-degree murder or manslaughter).

The Verdict

After the judge reviews the case and the charges, the jury moves to a separate room to consider the verdict. The jury verdict in a criminal case must always be unanimous. Juries may take a few hours, a number of days, or many weeks to review all aspects of the case before they reach a decision.

If a jury remains deadlocked after a lengthy deliberation, it may return to the courtroom and inform the judge of the situation. The judge may request the jurors to return to the jury room for a final attempt to arrive at a verdict; in most cases the judge specifies a time limit. If all reasonable attempts to reach a verdict fail, a hung jury results. In such cases, the judge dismisses the jury and declares a mistrial. It is then up to the prosecution to decide whether to retry the case, a decision that must be made within a specified time period. If a new trial is ordered, a new jury will be appointed.

If the jury reaches a verdict of guilty, the judge sets a sentencing date. The judge can request a presentence report from a probation officer before the sentence is imposed. In such cases, the defence lawyer can start the process of appeal. Defendants may be released while awaiting sentencing or held in custody.

The jury has no role in sentencing except in cases of second-degree murder. In such cases, the jury can make a recommendation to the judge that the length of time before parole be increased from 10 years to a longer period, which cannot exceed 25 years. However, this is a recommendation only, and the trial judge is not bound to accept it.

One of the important roles of a jury is jury nullification. Nullification takes place when a jury does not follow the court's interpretation of the law in every situation, thereby nullifying (that is, suspending) the requirements of strict legal procedure. In a typical case of nullification, a jury decides to disregard what the judge told them about specific aspects of the law or evidence because it considers the application of the law to the defendant to be unjust.

Jury nullification can occur in two ways. The first is when a verdict of guilty is reached and the judge decides the verdict is erroneous. In such a case, the judge may refuse to abide by the verdict and may instruct the jury to acquit the defendant. The second occurs when the judge requests a jury to arrest its verdict of guilty and acquit the accused.

APPEALS

Canada's criminal justice system allows all those convicted of a crime a direct criminal appeal. Both the defendant and the prosecution may appeal the decision in a case. The convicted individual has the right to appeal his conviction, or the sentence, or his not being found mentally unfit to stand trial (because of a mental disorder), or his being held criminally responsible (because of a mental disorder).

If the trial involved an indictable offence and was heard by a provincial judge, by a federally appointed judge without a jury, or by a judge and jury, the appeal is taken to the provincial Court of Appeal. The accused may appeal his conviction if it involves a point of law (the trial judge makes an incorrect legal ruling), a question of fact (the trial judge draws the wrong inference from the facts of the case), or the length of the sentence. The prosecution may appeal an acquittal on issues involving a point of law or a sentence but not on the basis of questions of fact. In addition, the terms of an appeal for the prosecution depend on whether the trial involves an indictable or summary conviction offence. In

a summary conviction case, the prosecutor can appeal against a dismissal or the sentence. In an indictable offence case, the prosecution can appeal the sentence, if the accused was acquitted, if it was found that the accused was not criminally responsible on the basis of a mental disorder, or if the accused was found to be unfit to stand trial (Mewett 1992).

There are limits to the length of time that may pass before an appeal is filed, but extensions can be obtained for a variety of reasons. During an appeal it is not uncommon for the convicted individual to apply for bail or another form of pretrial release.

The Appeal court can order a new trial or acquit the convicted individual if it finds that the trial judge made an error in law, that the verdict was unreasonable and not supported by the evidence, or that a miscarriage of justice took place. If it appears that the position of the prosecutor is no longer valid, the Appeal Court usually grants an acquittal. But if it decides there is still enough evidence for the prosecutor to argue the case, it will order a new trial.

If the Appeal Court decides the appeal registered by the prosecution is valid, it normally grants a new trial. However, it can convict and sentence the accused if the trial was by judge alone and enough evidence was presented to the court.

For summary conviction offences, the convicted individual usually appeals a conviction or sentence to a federally appointed judge in a Superior Court. Again, the accused may be released pending the outcome of the appeal. It is rare for a summary conviction offence to be heard by the Supreme Court of Canada, and then only if the case involves an important legal issue.

SUMMARY

Our court systems are organized at the federal and provincial levels. Because the accused is presumed innocent until proved guilty, it is up to the prosecutor to prove guilt beyond a reasonable doubt. The major actors in the courts are the judge, the prosecutor, and the defence lawyer. The prosecutor represents the interests of the state, while the defence lawyer provides essential services to his client. The prosecutor uses evidence collected by the police to convince the court that the defendant is guilty, while the defence lawyer attacks the prosecution's case.

An important part of the trial is the selection of members of the public to serve as jurors. Both lawyers may challenge any prospective juror on the basis of cause or for peremptory reasons.

Trials are conducted in accordance with rules of evidence and criminal procedure. These rules are enforced by judges who, during trials, act as arbitrators in any issues that arise. Evidence must be reliable and relevant, otherwise it is inadmissible.

The issue of discretion is an important factor at this stage of the criminal justice system. Since the number of cases in which individuals are charged with crimes far exceeds the number of courts, plea-bargaining becomes important in the day-to-day functioning of our criminal justice system. Many cases are never heard formally in a courtroom because they are plea-bargained. Note, however, that in some jurisdictions (Ontario, for example) police overcharging is a more significant cause of plea-bargaining than is shortage of court resources. Many jurisdictions have charge-approval mechanisms to prevent overcharging by police.

Discussion Questions

1. Should the prosecutor have absolute discretion over which cases are heard in court? Why or why not?

2. What are some of the undesirable features of plea-bargaining?

3. Do you think the right to a jury trial should be expanded to all defendants?

4. Should criminal court trials in Canada be televised, as they are in the United States?

5. How are jurors selected? Should factors such as the race, gender, and social class of the accused be considered when selecting jurors?

6. What are the arguments for and against the appointment of judges? The election of judges?

7. Why should a speedy trial be a legal right for defendants?

8. Should all defendants accused of a criminal offence be allowed to plea-bargain for a reduced sentence in exchange for a guilty plea?

9. Should judges be formally required to participate in all plea bargains? Give your reasons.

10. What are the disadvantages for a defendant who does not receive interim release? What are the advantages for those who receive it?

11. Should victims be given more power so their concerns are heard at all stages of the trial, not just at sentencing?

12. Do you think that a defence lawyer should be morally obliged to represent a person who may have committed a crime?

Suggested Readings

Arcaro, G. 2000. *Criminal Investigation: Forming Reasonable Grounds.* Scarborough, Ont.: Nelson Thomson Learning.

Balkan, J. 1997. *Just Words: Constitutional and Social Wrongs.* Toronto: University of Toronto Press.

Borovoy, A. 1988. *When Freedoms Collide.* Toronto: Lester, 1988.

Cairns, A. 1992. Charter *versus Federalism: The Dilemmas of Constitutional Reform.* Montreal: McGill-Queen's University Press.

Russell, P.H. 1987. *The Judiciary in Canada: The Third Branch of Government.* Toronto: McGraw-Hill Ryerson.

References

Alschuler, A. 1968. "The Prosecutor's Role in Plea Bargaining." *University of Chicago Law Review:* 50–112.

Besserer, S., and R.C. Grimes. 1996. "The Courts." In L.W. Kennedy and V.F. Sacco, eds., *Crime Counts: A Criminal Event Analysis.* Scarborough, Ont.: Nelson Canada.

Boland, B., P. Mahanna, and R. Scones. 1992. *The Prosecution of Felony Arrests, 1998.* Washington, D.C.: Bureau of Justice Statistics.

Bowal, P. 2002. "Ten Differences." *LawNow* 26, no. 6: 9–11.

Boyd, N. 1995. *Canadian Law: An Introduction.* Toronto: Harcourt Brace Canada.

Campbell Research Associates. 1992. *Review and Monitoring of Child Sexual Abuse Cases in Hamilton-Wentworth, Ontario.* Ottawa: Department of Justice.

Canadian Bar Association. 1987. *Code of Professional Conduct.* Ontario: Canadian Bar Association.

Cullen, F., W.J. Maakestad, and G. Cavender. 1987. *Corporate Crime under Attack: The Ford Pinto Case and Beyond.* Cincinnati: Anderson.

Desroches, F.J. 1995. *Force and Fear: Robbery in Canada.* Scarborough, Ont.: Nelson Canada.

Ericson, R. 1981. *Making Crime: A Study of Detective Work.* Toronto: University of Toronto Press.

Ericson, R., and P.M. Baranek. 1982. *The Ordering of Justice: A Study of Accused Persons as Defendants in the Criminal Process.* Toronto: University of Toronto Press.

Feeley, M. 1981. *Felony Arrests: Their Prosecution and Disposition in New York Court.* New York: Vera Institute.

Freedman, J.L., and T.M. Burke. 1996. "The Effect of Pretrial Publicity." *Canadian Journal of Criminology* 38: 253–70.

Friedland, M.L. 1965. *Detention before Trial.* Toronto: University of Toronto Press.

Gomme, I.M., and M.P. Hall. 1995. "Prosecutors at Work: Role Overload and Strain." *Journal of Criminal Justice* 23: 191–200.

Greene, I. 1995. "Judicial Accountability in Canada." In P.C. Stenning, ed., *Accountability for Criminal Justice: Selected Essays.* Toronto: University of Toronto Press, pp. 355–75.

Greene, I. , C. Baar, P. McCormick, G. Szablowski, and M. Thomas. 1998. *Final Appeal: Decision-Making in Canadian Courts of Appeal.* Toronto: James Lorimer & Co.

Griffiths, C.T., J. Klein, and S.N. Verdun-Jones. 1980. *Criminal Justice in Canada.* Vancouver: Butterworths.

Grosman, B. 1969. *The Prosecutor: An Inquiry into the Exercise of Discretion.* Toronto: University of Toronto Press.

Hann, R.G. 1973. *Decision Making in the Criminal Court System: A Systems Analysis.* Toronto: Centre of Criminology.

Jacoby, J. 1979. "The Charging Policies of Prosecutors." In W. McDonald, ed. *The Prosecutor.* Beverly Hills: Sage, pp. 75–97.

Karp, C., and C. Rosner. 1991. *When Justice Fails: The David Milgaard Story.* Toronto: McClelland and Stewart.

Law Reform Commission of Canada. 1990. *Controlling Criminal Prosecutions: The Attorney General and the Crown Prosecutor.* Ottawa: Law Reform Commission of Canada.

———. 1989. *Plea Discussions and Agreements.* Ottawa: Law Reform Commission of Canada.

———. 1984. *Questioning Suspects.* Working Paper 32. Ottawa: Minister of Supply and Services.

———1975. *Criminal Procedure: Control of the Process.* Ottawa: Minister of Supply and Services Canada.

Martin, J. 1970. "The Role and Responsibility of the Defence Advocate." *Criminal Law Quarterly* 12.

McCormick, P., and I. Greene. 1990. *Judges and Judging: Inside the Canadian Judicial System.* Toronto: J. Lorimer.

Mewett, A.W. 1992. *An Introduction to the Criminal Process in Canada,* 2nd ed. Scarborough, Ont.: Carswell.

Osborne, J.A. 1983. "The Prosecutor's Discretion to Withdraw Criminal Cases in the Lower Courts." *Canadian Journal of Criminology* 25: 55–78.

Peiera, J., and C. Grimes. 2002. *Case Processing in Criminal Courts, 1999/00.* Ottawa: Canadian Centre for Justice Statistics.

Roach, K. 1999. *Due Process or Victims' Rights: The New Law and Politics of Criminal Justice.* Toronto: University of Toronto Press.

Russell, P. 1987. *The Judiciary in Canada: The Third Branch of Government.* Toronto: McGraw-Hill Ryerson.

Salhany, R.E. 1986. *Arrest, Seizure, and Interrogation,* 3rd ed. Toronto: Carswell.

Stuart, D. 1995. "Prosecutorial Accountability." In P.C. Stenning, ed., *Accountability for Criminal Justice: Selected Essays.* Toronto: University of Toronto Press, pp. 330–54.

Stuart, D., and R.J. Delisle. 1995. *Learning Canadian Criminal Law.* Scarborough, Ont.: Carswell.

Swartz, M.A. 1973. Quoted in J. Caplan, *Criminal Justice.* Mineola, N.Y.: Foundation Press.

Vidmar, N. 1999. "The Canadian Criminal Jury: Searching for a Middle Ground." *Law and Contemporary Problems* 62: 141–72.

Vinglis, E., H. Blefgen, D. Colbourne, P. Culver, B. Farmer, D. Hackett, J. Treleaven, and R. Solomon. 1990. "The Adjudication of Alcohol-Related Criminal Driving Cases in Ontario: A Survey of Crown Attorneys." *Canadian Journal of Criminology* 32: 639–50.

Wheatley, J.R. 1974. "Plea Bargaining: A Case for Its Continuance." *Massachusetts Law Quarterly* 59: 31–41.

Wheeler, G. 1987. "The Police, the Crowns, and the Courts: Who's Running the Show?" *Canadian Lawyer* (February).

Willcocks, P. 1999. "Delays Excessive, Sex-Abuse Accused Goes Free." *The Globe and Mail,* 28 January, A4.

Court Cases

Dagenais v. Canadian Broadcasting Corp. (1994), 94 C.C.C. (3d) 289 (S.C.C.)

R. v. Askov (1990), 59 C.C.C. (3d) 449 (S.C.C.)

R. v. Barnes (1991), 63 C.C.C. (3d) 1 (S.C.C.)

R. v. Beare (1988), 45 C.C.C. (3d) 57 (S.C.C.)

R. v. D. (S.) (1992), 72 C.C.C. (3d) 575 (S.C.C.)

R. v. Hansen (1977), 37 C.C.C. (2d) 371 (Man. C.A.)

R. v. L. (T.P.) (1987), 37 C.C.C. (3d) 1 (S.C.C.)

R. v. Mankwe, [2001] 3 S.C.R. 3

R. v. Meddoui (1990), 61 C.C.C. (3d) 345 (Alta. C.A.)

R. v. Morin (1992), 71 C.C.C. (3d) 1 (S.C.C.)

R. v. Parks (1993), 15 O.R. (3d) 324, 24 C.R. (4th) 81 (Ont. C.A.)

R. v. R. (M.E.) (1989), 49 C.C.C. (3d) 475 (N.S. C.A.)

R. v. Thompson (1990), 59 C.C.C. (3d) 225 (S.C.C.)

R. v. Williams (1996), 106 C.C.C. (3d) 215 (B.C. C.A.)

Sentencing and Punishment

CHAPTER OBJECTIVES

✓ Explain and contrast the four major goals of criminal sentencing.

✓ Outline the various sentences available to a judge.

✓ Know the recent changes to sentencing in Canada.

✓ Explain why there is a difference between the sentence handed out by a judge and the actual sentence served by the offender.

✓ Explain why alternatives to sentencing, such as Aboriginal healing circles, appeared in Canada.

✓ List the major forms of punishment available to judges.

Once an accused person is convicted at the end of a criminal trial, the court must adjudicate an appropriate sentence. Our criminal justice system operates on the belief that justice at sentencing must prevail; that is, guilty people must be punished for the crime. This stage is one of the most controversial, since the public is concerned about the type and length of punishment. Some people argue that sentences are too short; others believe they are too long.

Sentencing is the process by which judges impose a punishment on a convicted criminal. The punishments available to the sentencing judge depend on the offence committed by an offender, but judges have a wide variety of punishments from which to select. Sentences can include incarceration, fines, community service orders, or probation. Allegations about disparity and discrimination in sentencing have led to the demand for controlling judicial discretion as well as the introduction of alternative sanctions. When an individual is convicted, a punishment must be handed out. The question then becomes what is the appropriate sentence to indicate the disapproval of society?

One of the most controversial cases in recent Canadian sentencing history is *R. v. Gladue* (1999). This case involved s. 718.2(e) of the *Criminal Code* (see below), which states "all available sanctions other than imprisonment that are reasonable in the circumstance should be considered for all offenders, with particular attention to the circumstances of aboriginal offenders." In this cases, Jamie Tanis Gladue, an Aboriginal woman, was charged with the second-degree murder of her husband. She had reason to believe that he was having an affair, and an argument ensued, during which Ms Gladue stabbed him in the heart with a knife. Following the preliminary inquiry and the selection of the jury, she pleaded guilty to the charge of manslaughter. She was then sentenced to three years in prison with a 10-year firearms prohibition, a sentence typically handed out to those convicted of manslaughter in Canada.

The trial judge noted a number of mitigating factors about Ms Gladue (see below). These included her supportive family, the alcohol therapy she had been undergoing since the incident, educational upgrading, her remorse, and her guilty plea. Aggravating factors included the fact that she stabbed her husband twice, had intended to seriously harm him, and had committed a serious crime (Lash 2000).

When handing down the sentence, the trial judge noted that Ms Gladue was Cree but that she lived off a reserve and was therefore not entitled to the special consideration due to her on account of her Aboriginal status as stipulated in s. 718.2(e). The case was appealed to the British Columbia Court of Appeal on the basis of her attempts to "rehabilitate herself" since the offence, the 17 months she had waited prior to her trial to start, and that the trial judge failed to consider her Aboriginal status. Again Ms Gladue lost. She then appealed the verdict to the Supreme Court of Canada. The Supreme Court considered only one factor in her appeal—whether or not the trial judge gave appropriate attention to Ms Gladue's Aboriginal status. The justices decided that Ms Gladue should receive a conditional sentence (see Chapter 10) of two years less a day, to be served in the community. In reaching their judgment the justices commented about the discrimination experienced by Aboriginals in the criminal justice system, noting also "the excessive imprisonment of Aboriginal people is only the tip of the iceberg insofar as the estrangement of the Aboriginal peoples from the Canadian justice system is concerned."

This decision was quickly followed by two similar cases, also in British Columbia. In the first, a Métis woman who had stabbed her common-law husband to death was given a conditional sentence, enabling her to look after her five-year-old daughter. And, in July 1999, the British Columbia Supreme Court used the same section to reduce a life sentence to 20 years imprisonment for a 37-year-old Métis man. However, the courts do not always accept applications for a reduced sentence based on s. 718.2(e). For example, in 2000, a judge in Nanaimo, British Columbia, rejected a defendant's Aboriginal status as a reason for reducing her 10-year sentence for fatally abusing her stepdaughter (Bailey 2000). This sentencing provision has been criticized since its introduction (*National Post* 1998; Humphreys 2001; Seeman 2001) because some critics feel it violates the principles of proportionality and equality introduced in Canada's sentencing law in 1996 (Brodeur and Roberts 2002).

THE PURPOSE OF SENTENCING

Sentencing is considered by many to be the most important stage in the criminal justice system, since it is at that point that the offender is punished. But punishment covers a wide spectrum of sentences in Canada, including fines, probation, community service, imprisonment, an intermittent sentence, or a recognizance to keep the peace. As well, a judge may combine certain of these punishments—for example, a fine and a probation order—into what is known as a split sentence. Perhaps due to the number of sentencing options open to judges,

sentences have come under much criticism. Critics argue sentences are too lenient or too long. It is rare that everyone agrees on their appropriateness in any given criminal case.

Sentencing involves handing out a punishment to the convicted offender. Punishing criminals serves two ultimate purposes: (1) the "deserved infliction of suffering on evil doers" and (2) the "prevention of crime" (Packer 1968: 36–37). Although this statement appears straightforward, it raises many questions. For example, how do we determine what is a "deserved" punishment? How can we be certain that punishment will "prevent" crimes? How can we know that convicted offenders are "rehabilitated"? Should sentences of incarceration be shorter than longer? And what is the overriding purpose of sentencing: the protection of society or the benefit of offenders? To answer these questions, we need to consider the four, basic philosophical reasons for sentencing. While these goals are presented as separate and distinct from one another, sentences in Canada can reflect a combination of them (Havemann 1986; Doob 1992).

Deterrence

By punishing an offender, the state indicates its intent to control crime and deter potential offenders. Deterrence, the oldest of the four main sentencing goals, refers to the protection of society through the prevention of criminal acts. This is accomplished by punishing offenders in accordance with their offence. Too lenient a sentence might encourage more people to engage in criminal activity because they would not fear the punishment for their offence; too severe a sentence might reduce the ability of the criminal justice system to impose punishment that is regarded as fair and impartial, and might actually encourage more criminal activity. For example, if all convicted robbers were to receive a minimum of 10 years for their crimes, they may kill their victims if those victims are the only witnesses able to identify them. For the deterrence approach to work, it must strike a balance between fear and justice among both offenders and law-abiding citizens.

There are two types of deterrence: specific and general. Specific deterrence attempts to deter, through punishment, an individual offender from committing another crime (or recidivating) in the future. General deterrence refers to a sentence that is severe enough to stop people from committing crimes. To date, there is some evidence to show that specific deterrence works, but only in certain instances, such as domestic violence (Sherman and Berk 1984). However, many more studies have found that specific deterrence does not stop people from committing a second crime once they serve their sentence for a first offence (Wheeler and Hissong 1988; Fagan 1989). General deterrence, by punishing an offender, is intended to make an impact on the members of society. Specific deterrence is intended to discourage individuals from engaging in behaviour that had earlier led to their conviction and sentencing; it is predicated on an individual's wish to avoid the pain of punishment in future.

The objectives of general and specific deterrence may be incompatible with each other. For example, a man who assaults his wife may best be deterred from spousal assault by participating in anger-management therapy. This sentence may not be in the best interests of general deterrence, however, if the punishment is not perceived as adequate to deter members of society from engaging in the same behaviour. Deterrence can be difficult to achieve because it relies on the certainty and speed of punishment. If the punishment for a crime is harsh but the risk of being apprehended is low, it is doubtful that potential offenders will be deterred.

Selective Incapacitation

If an offender is considered to be a significant risk to society, he may be sentenced to a long term in prison. Incapacitation as a punishment justifies long sentences, because those so punished are considered serious threats to the safety of society. Incarcerating those individuals (referred to as "chronic" offenders) who commit the most heinous and/or the greatest number of criminal offences is thought to reduce the crime rate. In essence, the goal of the incapacitation approach is to prevent future crimes by imprisoning individuals on the basis of their past criminal offences.

While the incapacitation and deterrence approaches both focus on punishing criminals for the express purpose of protecting society, incapacitation differs from deterrence because it favours much longer sentences. Supporters of incapacitation argue it is an effective crime prevention approach. Ehrlich (1975) stated that a 1 percent increase in sentence length leads to a 1 percent decrease in the rate of crime. Zedlweski (1987) concluded that for every dollar spent on incarcerating an offender, there is a $17 saving to society in terms of social cost. Critics of this approach believe it is flawed since it does not include proportionality (see Chapter 3) for specific types of criminal offences. That is, how can we be sure that punishing a robber to life imprisonment will reduce the crime rate? Perhaps a much shorter punishment would assure that she would not commit another robbery after she is released from prison. Another argument is that incapacitating criminals protects society only while the offender is in prison. Some argue that after offenders have served their prison

This is a view of the men's maximum security unit of the Saskatchewan Penitentiary in Prince Albert, Saskatchewan.

terms, they may actually be more predisposed to committing more crime (Clear 1980).

Rehabilitation

A sentencing approach that emphasizes rehabilitation is based on the belief that many (but not all) offenders can be treated in such a way that, once released, they will live crime-free lives in their communities. Supporters of rehabilitative sentences argue it is fairer and more productive to treat certain offenders rather than punish them without treatment. The purpose of this sentencing approach is to treat the social and psychological problems of offenders. Since every offender is potentially different in the type and length of treatment he needs, supporters of this approach argue that a variety of programs be available to assist in the treatment. Rehabilitation-based sentencing is predicated on reform in the future rather than for the criminal act committed.

The success of rehabilitation programs has been the subject of much debate. Many argue that a "get tough" approach (i.e., a deterrence or incapacitation approach) to sentencing and punishment will be more successful in controlling crime. However, recent studies point out that the rehabilitation approach is successful, particularly when treatment programs and offender needs are matched effectively (Andrews et al. 1990). Rehabilitative sentences, in contrast to those based on the deterrence and incapacitation approaches, do not always include imprisonment. In fact, offenders may be sentenced to serve their punishment in the community if appropriate services are available there.

Justice

According to the justice model, offenders should be punished no more or less severely than their actions warrant. Specifically, the severity of their sentence should depend on how serious their crime was, i.e., the essence of punishment should be to punish offenders with fairness and justice, that is, in proportion to the gravity to their criminal offence. Offenders should be punished because they deserve to be: their punishment should fit the crime. This approach specifies that all punishments be equally and fairly given to those with the same number of prior criminal convictions and who have committed the same crime. The focus is on the crime committed rather than any attribute of the individual. Extralegal factors such as race, gender, and social class are not considered. Different individuals who commit the same offence may receive a different sentence but only because of mitigating or aggravating factors. The actual sentence imposed is based on the crime committed; it is not concerned with any future projections of the likelihood of treatment success or reduction in the crime rate.

The justice model differs from the deterrence and incapacitation approaches because

1. it focuses on an offender's past behaviour as the rationale for sentencing rather than on her future criminality and the protection of society, and
2. it believes that sentences, while determinate, should be shorter than longer.

This means that for a specific criminal offence, justice model advocates, for example, support a sentence of five years (with no parole) in contrast to supporters of the deterrence and incapacitation approaches who prefer a longer sentence (also with no parole). In theory, then, the justice model favours a sentencing approach with shorter periods of punishment (including community-based punishments).

HOW DO JUDGES DECIDE ON A SENTENCE?

Many people argue that if someone commits a serious crime, he should receive a lengthy sentence. If this doesn't happen, judges are criticized for being too lenient. Judges do not reach their decision on a sentence in an arbitrary way, however. Their options are restricted by law (these restrictions are referred to as the "structure of sentencing"). For example, it is impossible for a judge to sentence an offender to life imprisonment for a summary conviction offence, since that sentence is outside what is allowed by law. Judges, however, have certain parameters within which they can individualize sentences on the basis of the offender (such as taking into consideration his prior record) as well as the circumstances surrounding the crime. Judges are limited in their options, since they do not have the ability to use

discretion in every case. In some instances, such as first- and second-degree murder and manslaughter, fixed minimum sentences apply, and judges cannot change them.

What is the source of judicial discretion? Is it the result of the personal preferences of a particular judge, the legal seriousness of the crime, the defendant's race, the quality of the arguments given by the defence attorney and Crown prosecutor during the trial, or perhaps the impact of the crime on the victims? All of these factors may in some way contribute to the judge's decision.

If you were a judge with the responsibility for deciding which offenders are incarcerated or stay in the community, how would you decide? What criteria would you use in making your decision? Criminal sentences in Canada vary widely, from a discharge to life imprisonment. This variation originates in the *Criminal Code*, which sets out the maximum punishment for each offence. When you make your sentencing decision, it is of concern not only to the offender but also to the community, the police, and the victims. And of course your decision may be a mistake. What happens, for example, if you decide that a convicted offender receives probation but while he is serving that sentence he commits a series of violent crimes? Would you change your sentencing approach in future or would you view the probation order and its consequences as an aberration since it hadn't happened before?

Judges have a number of sentencing options available to them, as we've seen, so a judge who decides on a sentence must first determine what she hopes to accomplish with the sentence. Sentencing has at least one of the following objectives: deterrence, selective incapacitation, justice, or rehabilitation. These are important to the sentencing of offenders because our system of justice is supposed "to accomplish some social utility beyond merely solving crimes and catching criminals" (Anderson and Newman 1993: 288). Two factors are important here: sentencing and dispositions.

Sentencing has been defined as "the judicial determination of a legal sanction to be imposed on a person found guilty of an offence" (Canadian Sentencing Commission 1987: 153). According to Roberts and Cole (1999: 4), this brief definition includes "all the traditional elements, namely that the sanction must be legal, it must be imposed by a judge, and it can follow a criminal conviction." It needs to be distinguished from the actual sentence (the disposition) imposed on the offender. A disposition refers to "the actual sanction imposed in sentencing" (Law Reform Commission of Canada 1974: 4).

Of course, before an offender receives a disposition, he must plead guilty or be found guilty in a court of law. If he has commited an offence and admits to it, one assumes he will be found guilty. The issue then becomes the type and length of the disposition. If the crime involves a serious, violent act, is it not reasonable to expect a lengthy period of imprisonment as the disposition? Though one expects this to be true, the events of the court trial and the factors surrounding the commission of the offence may have significant weight in determining the final disposition.

Punishments can vary widely across Canada, from probation to life imprisonment. Although almost everyone agrees offenders "should be punished in some way, there is far less consensus about the purpose of punishment" (Roberts and Cole 1999: 5). The foundations of these purposes are found in the guiding forces of our criminal justice system (see Chapter 3). Any sentence can reflect one of these purposes or a combination of them. If any specific purpose of sentencing exists, it is closest to specific deterrence—that is, to reduce "the crime rate by stopping the criminal activities of apprehended offenders and deterring others from committing crimes" (Anderson and Newman 1993: 288). How we can best way to achieve this is, of course, open to opinion and debate.

Forms of Punishment

Judges in Canada have a number of dispositions available when they decide to punish a convicted offender. These sentences (or dispositions) include

- *Imprisonment.* Whether for the purpose of deterrence, incapacitation, rehabilitation, or justice, one type of punishment used in Canada both today and historically is the imprisonment of convicted offenders. A sentence of imprisonment can be served in either a federal or provincial correctional facility (see Chapter 11). In recent years, governments have tried to limit sending offenders to prison unless they have committed the most serious offenders.
- *Intermittent sentences.* These sentences allow offenders to serve their sentences on a regular basis (such as weekends) in order to allow them to continue to engage in other activities (e.g., employment). They are limited to a maximum of 90 days by law.
- *Fines.* Fines can be levied by judges in combination with incarceration and probation or independently of other types of punishments. When the judge decides to punish an offender by ordering him to pay a fine only, it indicates the judge considers the offender not to be a threat to the community and one who doesn't have to be supervised in his community.
- *Restitution and community service.* While fines are payable to a government, restitution and community

· when you give service in kind - Restitution

service are paid to injured parties (these punishments are also referred to as "reparations"). Restitution is a payment made directly to the victim(s) while community service attempts to make offenders do something that will benefit the community.
- *Probation.* Probation is a criminal sanction in which offenders are allowed to spend their sentence (or part thereof) in the community under supervision as long as they follow certain conditions set by the court (see Chapter 10).
- *Restorative justice.* When offenders have committed a nonserious crime, some judges feel that by having the offender and victim meet and discuss the offence, the relationship between them will be "healed."
- *Absolute and conditional discharges.* When an offender receives an absolute or conditional discharge, he is not considered to have been convicted of an offence. A conditional discharge means that an offender is discharged with conditions and is supervised as if he were on probation. An absolute discharge means he does not need any supervision.
- *Community-based sanctions.* This approach emphasizes the use of noncriminal alternatives to traditional punishments. These include referrals to substance abuse or behavioural modification programs.

The Sentencing Process

When a judge decides to sentence a convicted offender, she relies on information provided by other persons. A presentence report is valuable for judges when they are considering the sentence. Compiled by a probation officer, these reports discuss relevant information about the crime and its impact upon the victim(s), as well as a large amount of personal data concerning the offender. This personal information is not admissible at trial, but it gives the judge a view of the offender, including whether or not he is employed, the degree of family support, and his level of education. In addition, prosecutors and defence lawyers may propose a sentence to a judge (this is usually worked out during a conference), although the judge does not have to accept their recommendation.

A judge will also look at other factors when deciding on a sentence. The most important of these are the seriousness of the offence and whether or not there were any mitigating or aggravating factors (see Exhibit 9.1). Usually, the more serious the offence, the longer the sentence. Mitigating circumstances refer to those circumstances that permit a shorter sentence to be given, while aggravating circumstances include such things as the prior record of an offender, the degree of violence used, and whether any weapons were used during the offence. If a judge determines there were aggravating

EXHIBIT 9.1   Aggravating and Mitigating Circumstances

AGGRAVATING CIRCUMSTANCES
- Previous convictions of the offender
- Gang activity
- Vulnerability of the victim
- Planning and organization
- Multiple criminal incidents
- Use or threatened use of a weapon
- Brutality

MITIGATING CIRCUMSTANCES
- First-time offender
- The employment record of the individual
- Rehabilitative efforts since the offence was committed
- Disadvantaged background
- Guilty plea and remorse
- The length of time it took to prosecute or sentence the offender
- The character of the offender

factors (see Exhibit 9.1) involved during the crime, she may decide to make the offender serve a longer period of time in a correctional facility before he is allowed to make an application for parole.

SENTENCING LAW IN CANADA

In 1994 Justice Minister Allan Rock introduced Bill C-41, which proposed to reform the sentencing system as well as intermediate punishments (see Chapter 10). On 3 September 1996, Bill C-41 (known as the sentencing reform bill) was proclaimed, bringing about a significant change in the sentencing system in Canada. The bill had three objectives:

1. "to provide a consistent framework of policy and process in sentencing matters;
2. to create a system of sentencing policy and process approved by Parliament, and
3. to increase public accessibility to the law relating to sentencing" (Daubney and Parry 1999: 33).

It also introduced conditional sentences as an option for judges when they sentenced someone who was convicted (see Chapter 10).

Bill C-41 contained a statement of the purpose and principles of sentencing (s. 718). The following are excerpts:

The fundamental purpose of sentencing is to contribute, along with crime prevention initiatives, to respect for the law and the maintenance of a just, peaceful and safe society by imposing just sanctions that have one or more of the following objectives:

(a) to denounce unlawful conduct;
(b) to deter the offender and other persons from committing offences;
(c) to separate offenders from society, where necessary;
(d) to assist in rehabilitating offenders;
(e) to provide reparations for harm done to victims or to the community; and

(f) to promote a sense of responsibility in offenders, and acknowledgment of the harm done to victims and to the community.

These objectives include all of the traditional purposes of sentencing such as deterrence, justice, incapacitation, and rehabilitation. Significantly, s. 718(e) indicates the federal government's interest in the area of restorative justice as it relates to the "reparation for harm done to victims and the community and in promoting a sense of responsibility in offenders and acknowledgment of the harm done to the victims and to the community" (Daubney and Parry 1999: 34).

Section 718 also includes the statement concerning the fundamental principle of sentencing, which states that a sentence must be proportionate to the seriousness of the offence and the degree of responsibility of the offender. This section also introduced a number of other sentencing principles (see Exhibit 9.2).

SENTENCING PATTERNS IN CANADA

What sentences do convicted offenders receive for their criminal actions? A recent analysis of sentencing practices used information from eight jurisdictions across Canada in during 2000–2001, representing over 80 percent of all cases reported to the police for those years. The information used comes mostly from those cases heard in provincial courts (only three provinces reported the cases heard in Superior Court), but these account for the majority of all cases tried in Canada, since only 3 percent of cases in these jurisdictions were transferred to the Superior Courts. The provincial adult courts in these eight jurisdictions heard 375 466 cases involving 816 449 charges in 2000–01, a decrease from the 446 086 cases heard in 1994–95. The average number of charges during this same period has increased slightly, from 1.97 to 2.17. The likelihood of being sentenced to a period of incarceration for committing a criminal offence has

EXHIBIT 9.2 The Principles of Sentencing in Canada

Section 718.2 of the *Criminal Code* specifies a number of sentencing principles:

(a) a sentence should be increased or reduced to account for any relevant aggravating or mitigating circumstances relating to the offence or the offender, and, without limiting the generality of the foregoing,

   (i) evidence that the offence was motivated by bias, prejudice or hate based on race, national or ethnic origin, language, colour, religion, sex, age, mental or physical disability, sexual orientation, or any other similar factor,

   (ii) evidence that the offender, in committing the offence, abused the offender's spouse or common-law partner or child, or

   (iii) evidence that the offender, in committing the offence, abused a position of trust or authority in relation to the victim

   (iv) evidence that the offence was committed for the benefit of, at the direction of or in association with a criminal organization; or

   (v) evidence that the offence was a terrorism offence

(b) a sentence should be similar to sentences imposed on similar offenders for similar offences committed in similar circumstances;

(c) where consecutive sentences are imposed, the combined sentence should not be unduly long or harsh;

(d) an offender should not be deprived of liberty, if less restrictive sanctions may be appropriate in the circumstances; and

(e) all available sanctions other than imprisonment that are reasonable in the circumstances should be considered for all offenders, with particular attention to the circumstances of aboriginal offenders.

remained relatively stable since 1994–95, about 34 percent (Brookbank and Kingsley 1998; Thomas 2002).

This study of adult criminal court statistics during 2000–2001 revealed a number of important findings about sentencing in Canada, including

- The median length for all cases receiving a prison sentence was 30 days, a figure that has been almost stable since 1996–97.
- The two most common offences heard in adult criminal court were common assault (12 percent of all cases) and impaired driving (12 percent).

- A conviction was recorded in 61 percent of all cases heard in adult criminal court.
- The highest conviction rate for a crime against the person was sexual abuse (64 percent), followed by robbery (60 percent) and major assaults (55 percent) (see Figure 9.1).
- The highest conviction rate for a crime against property was break and enter (69 percent), followed by property damage/mischief (64 percent) and theft (63 percent) (see Figure 9.2).
- Probation was the most common sanction, imposed in 44 percent of cases resulting in conviction. Fines were the second most common sentence, accounting for 37 percent of all cases. Incarceration in a federal or provincial correctional facility was imposed in 35 percent of cases.
- Eighty-three percent of all cases heard in adult court involved males.
- Cases heard in adult criminal court involved adults between the ages of 18 and 24 years 31 percent of the time when the age of the accused was known, while 29 percent of the cases involved 25- to 34-year-old people (Thomas 2002).

ISSUES IN SENTENCING

Some members of the public argue that judges are too lenient in the punishing of offenders, which has led researchers to study public opinion about sentencing. Another issue of concern is that of sentencing variation among judges and provinces. Should sentence severity depend on the judge who hears a case, or the jurisdiction in Canada where the case is heard? Finally, what are other jurisdictions doing in an attempt to control judicial variation in sentencing? Is it possible to eliminate sentencing variation by implementing different sentencing laws? When differences in sentences are found (particularly when they involve sentencing disparity and sentencing discrimination), it is common to blame judicial discretion.

Sentencing Disparity

Sentencing disparity occurs when similar crimes do not receive similar punishments. The Canadian Sentencing Commission (1987) identified three types of sentencing variation:

1. from case to case, where the same judge imposes different sentences for similar offenders convicted of the same offence committed in similar circumstances;

2. from judge to judge, where different judges impose different sentences in similar cases; and

3. from court to court, where different courts in a particular jurisdiction use different standards for what is considered an appropriate sentence in specific cases.

The Sentencing Commission interviewed 400 judges, who indicated they felt variation existed among their sentencing practices, largely due to differences in personal attitudes. In addition, over 80 percent of approximately 700 Crown prosecutors and defence lawyers believed unwarranted variation existed in sentences within their jurisdictions, and almost 90 percent stated that they felt there was unwarranted variation across Canada.

Another reason given for sentencing disparities in Canada is geographical location. Whether or not con-victed offenders are incarcerated and for how long often depends on where they committed the crime. During 2000–01, the highest incarceration rate was in Prince Edward Island, where 59 percent of convicted cases resulted in a term of imprisonment, followed by Ontario (41 percent) and Yukon (37 percent); the lowest rate was in Saskatchewan (22 percent) (see Figure 9.3). The reason commonly given to explain the much higher rate in Prince Edward Island is that first-time offenders convicted of impaired driving are frequently incarcerated; in 2000–01, 91 percent of all impaired-driving convictions resulted in incarceration of the convicted offender.

A study conducted by Roberts and Birkenmayer (1997) discovered significant variation in sentencing patterns among provinces. The amount of variation depended on the type of offence under study. They reported that the rate of incarceration for the offence of "theft under" ranged from a low of 4 percent in

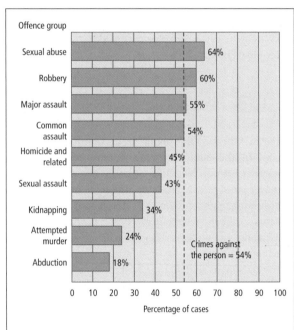

Note: The calculation of conviction rates excludes 1836 (2.3%) Crimes Against the Person cases with final decisions of "Commit for Trial in Superior Court" and "Re-election to Provincial Court." Adult Criminal Court Survey data are not reported by New Brunswick, Manitoba, British Columbia, Northwest Territories, and Nunavut.

Source: Statistics Canada, *Juristat*, Catalogue 85-002, vol. 22, no. 2, March 2002, p. 7.

FIGURE 9.1

Conviction Rates for Cases with Crime against the Person as the Most Serious Offence in the Case, Eight Provinces and Territories in Canada, 2000–01

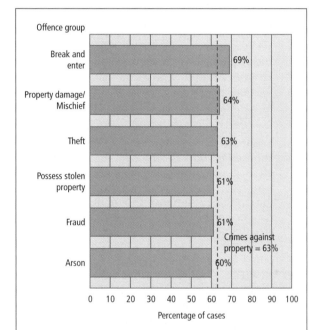

Note: The calculation of conviction rates excludes 1836 (2.3%) Crimes Against the Person cases with final decisions of "Commit for Trial in Superior Court" and "Re-election to Provincial Court." Adult Criminal Court Survey data are not reported by New Brunswick, Manitoba, British Columbia, Northwest Territories, and Nunavut.

Source: Statistics Canada, *Juristat*, Catalogue 85-002, vol. 22, no. 2, March 2002, p. 8.

FIGURE 9.2

Conviction Rates for Cases with a Crime against Property as the Most Serious Offence in the Case, Eight Provinces and Territories in Canada, 2000–01

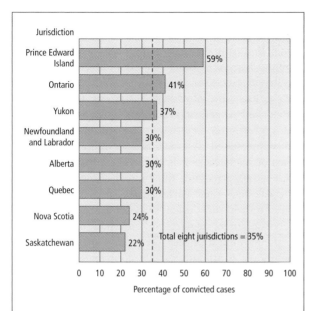

Jurisdiction

Prince Edward Island: 59%
Ontario: 41%
Yukon: 37%
Newfoundland and Labrador: 30%
Alberta: 30%
Quebec: 30%
Nova Scotia: 24%
Saskatchewan: 22%

Total eight jurisdictions = 35%

Percentage of convicted cases

Note: Includes cases completed in Superior Courts in Prince Edward Island, Alberta, and Yukon. Information from Quebec's 140 municipal courts (which account for approximately 20% of federal statute charges in that province) are not yet collected. Adult Criminal Court Survey data are not reported by New Brunswick, Manitoba, British Columbia, Northwest Territories, and Nunavut.

Source: Statistics Canada, *Juristat*, Catalogue 85-002, vol. 22, no. 2, March 2002, p. 10.

FIGURE 9.3

Percent of Convicted Cases Sentenced to Prison for the Most Serious Offence in the Case, Eight Provinces and Territories in Canada, 2000–01

Newfoundland to a high of 26 percent in Yukon. Compared to the variation discovered in offences of other types, the variation in this one was fairly slight, due largely to "legally relevant factors as well as the fact that the monetary limit of this criminal offence places a constraint on the variability in offence seriousness" (Roberts and Birkenmayer 1997: 6). Other offences were found to have a greater sentencing range. For example, incarceration rates for breaking and entering ranged from 26 percent in the Northwest Territories to 78 percent in Prince Edward Island.

Courthouse Norms

Another explanation for sentencing disparity focuses upon individual courtroom work groups and highlights the different sentencing practices of different judges for similar crimes. Hogarth (1971) studied the sentencing patterns of 71 magistrates in Ontario and found a good deal of variation in their sentencing decisions. He found that judges' penal philosophies and attitudes determined what they considered important during a trial, ultimately influencing both the type and length of sentences they imposed. Hogarth estimated that the legal facts of a case accounted for only 9 percent of the sentencing variations found in his study. The most famous study in this area was conducted by Palys and Divorski (1986), who studied judicial variation in sentencing by presenting 206 Canadian provincial court judges with five hypothetical cases and requesting that they indicate what sentence they would impose on the offender. While judges were found to vary in their sentencing decisions in all five cases, the greatest differences were discovered in a case involving assault causing bodily harm. The judges' sentences varied from a $500 fine plus six months' probation to five years in a federal institution.

Sentencing Discrimination

Sentencing discrimination occurs when the length of a sentence is influenced by extralegal factors, such as the defendant's race, gender, social class, or any other factor not directly related to the criminal offence (see Chapter 1). Studies investigating the possibility of discrimination in sentencing in Canada have focused on two minority groups: Aboriginals and blacks. LaPrairie (1990), in her study of the overrepresentation of Aboriginals in correctional facilities in Canada, reported that while they are overrepresented in Canadian correctional facilities, it is not due to discriminatory sentencing practices. Others (e.g., Renner and Warner 1981; Clairmont 1989; Clairmont et al. 1989) all reported that they found some sentencing discrimination against blacks. Williams (1999: 212) found that the variables of unemployment and detention before trial "did have a discernable effect in that both were associated with higher imprisonment rates." That is, judges who use such extralegal factors such as unemployment and being held in detention before trial as reasons for incarcerating convicted offenders "are likely to discriminate against black men without ever intending to do so" (Williams 1999: 212).

Public Opinion and Sentencing

Research conducted in a number of Western countries in recent years indicates that members of the public select harsher sentences than judges do. Studies have long pointed out the wide gap that exists between the sentences imposed by judges and those the public would have handed out in the same cases. However, research comparing the relative punitiveness of public and judicial attitudes toward the punishment of offenders has come to a different conclusion (Roberts 1988; Roberts and Doob 1989). In the study conducted by Roberts and Doob (1989), 62 percent of the public and 63 percent of the judiciary agreed on which offenders should be incarcerated. These same researchers discovered that when they presented the public with sufficient information about different sentencing options available to judges, the members of the public became *less* punitive than judges. The public recommended incarcerating a total of 81 863 offenders in the study, whereas judges had incarcerated a total of 92 415.

But does the public agree with judges about which offences should lead to incarceration? When Roberts and Doob compared the rank-orderings of the public with the actual actions of the judiciary on 10 offences, they found substantial differences between the two groups. Of the ten offences, the public suggested more punitive sentences for five (arson, assaulting a police officer, forgery, theft over $5000, and fraud over $5000) and gave virtually the same response for two offences (possession of a dangerous weapon and kidnapping). Those offences for which the judiciary gave more punitive responses were robbery, perjury, and break and enter.

While it appears that the public may be more punitive than judges when sentencing offenders, they tend to support a variety of sentencing goals. For example, one Canadian study discovered that when a crime was judged relatively minor, the sentencing goal supported by most of the public was deterrence. However, the public responded differently when presented with serious violent crimes. For violent crimes such as robbery and sexual assault, the public showed little approval for deterrence; selective incapacitation received the most support (Canadian Sentencing Commission 1987). Kaukinen and Colavecchia (1999), using data collected by the 1993 General Social Survey, found that the socioeconomic status of individuals is an important predictor of public attitudes toward sentencing. Higher-status respondents were dissatisfied with the ability of the courts to assist victims of crime (see below) while individuals belonging to lower socioeconomic groups most often expressed dissatisfaction with the ability of the courts to protect the legal rights of the accused.

The most recent General Social Survey, conducted in 1999, attempted to document the attitudes of Canadians toward the courts and sentencing. Less than 25 percent of those Canadians sampled felt the courts were doing a good job of determining whether or not the accused is guilty (21 percent), helping the victim (15 percent), and providing justice quickly (13 percent). Forty-one percent considered the courts to be doing a good job at ensuring a fair trial for the accused. In terms of sentencing, most Canadians are in favour of community-based sanctions, but only for certain individuals, such as first-time offenders. For repeat offenders, this preference changed to favouring a term of incarceration in a correctional facility. For example, 68 percent of Canadians stated that an offender found guilty of a repeat break and enter should serve a prison term. This figure almost paralleled the number of repeat offenders for break and enter sentenced to a prison term by the courts (63 percent) during 1998–99. In comparison, for a repeat offender convicted of an assault, 63 percent of the public indicated they preferred a prison sentence, whereas the courts in 1998–99 incarcerated 29 percent of such offenders (Tufts 2000).

Sentencing Guidelines

Sentencing guidelines attempt to control judicial variation in sentencing. Supporters of the guidelines argue that sentencing systems that allowed the discretionary powers of judges to remain unchecked led to disparity in sentencing decisions. A policy favouring sentencing guidelines attempts to eliminate sentencing disparity by controlling judicial discretion at the sentencing stage. Guidelines will state that sentencing should be done without regard to the race, gender, or social or economic status of the defendant. In their original form, guidelines allow judges to make sentencing decisions based solely on two factors: (1) the severity of the crime for which the offender was convicted, and (2) the prior record of the offender. As a result, guidelines regulate both the decision to commit an offender to prison and the length of the prison term. Guidelines are constructed to imprison those convicted of serious violent crimes as well as those who have long criminal records. Most property offenders would not be imprisoned until they had been convicted of a number of offences; instead, they would be given alternative sanctions, to be served in the community.

Another popular aspect of this sentencing rationale is that it ignores all characteristics of the offender, because it focuses only on the act for which the offender is convicted in court. Because the gender, race, age, and social class of the offender is irrelevant to the sentence, advocates of this approach point out that it is fair and equal to all.

Sentencing guidelines were recommended by the Canadian Sentencing Commission (1987) in its attempt to eliminate some of the problems associated

Lucille Poulin, escorted by a supporter, heads to Supreme Court in Charlottetown on 25 October 2002. Poulin was convicted of assaulting five children in her care at a religious commune in rural Prince Edward Island.

with sentencing in Canada at the time. Some of the problems identified by the commission were

- Maximum penalties are unrealistically severe and do not always reflect the relative seriousness of offences.
- Mandatory minimum sentences create injustices by unnecessarily restricting judicial discretion without accomplishing other functions ascribed to them.
- Systematic information about current sentencing practice is lacking. For policy makers and sentencing judges alike, easily accessible information does not exist (Stuart and Delisle 1995: 903).

As a result of these problems, the Canadian Sentencing Commission (1987) recommended a "fundamental overhaul" of the sentencing practices in Canada. The recommended changes were

1. a new rationale for sentencing (which was achieved through the introduction of Bill C-41);
2. elimination of all mandatory minimum penalties (other than for murder and high treason);
3. replacement of the current penalty structure for all offences other than murder and high treason with maximum penalties of 12 years, 9 years, 6 years, 3 years, 1 year, or 6 months. In exceptional cases, for the most serious offences that carry a

maximum sentence of either 12 or 9 years, provision is made to exceed these maximums;

4. elimination of full parole release (other than for sentences of life imprisonment);
5. provision for a reduction of time served for those inmates who display good behaviour while in prison. The portion that can be remitted would be reduced from one-third to one-quarter of the sentence imposed;
6. an increase in the use of community sanctions. The commission recommends greater use of sanctions that do not imply incarceration (for example, community service orders, compensation to the victim or community, and fines, which do not involve any segregation of the offender from the community);
7. elimination of "automatic" imprisonment for the fine default to reduce the likelihood that a person who cannot pay a fine goes to jail;
8. creation of a presumption for each offence respecting whether a person should normally be incarcerated or not. The judge could depart from the presumption by providing reasons for the departure;
9. creation of a "presumption range" for each offence normally requiring incarceration (again the judge could depart by providing reasons); and
10. creation of a permanent sentencing commission to complete the development of guideline ranges for all offences, to collect and distribute information about current sentencing practice, and to review and, in appropriate cases, to modify (with the assent of the House of Commons) the presumptive sentences in light of current practice and appellate decisions.

Do sentencing guidelines actually achieve their goals of fairness and equity? Initial analyses of sentencing guidelines have been implemented in the United States, where the federal government and a number of states have introduced them (in fact, the Canadian Sentencing Commission used the approach taken by the state of Minnesota as a guide for many of its policy recommendations). Miethe and Moore (1985) studied the impact of defendants' social class on sentences during the first year of the Minnesota sentencing guidelines. They found judges were following the guidelines by giving greater weight to offence-based characteristics, such as the use of a weapon and the severity of the criminal action. Differential treatment of offenders on the basis of race, employment status, and gender declined, as did variations among judicial jurisdictions. In addition, the researchers found that tighter controls on judicial discretion did not lead to greater discretion upstream in the criminal justice system—as in, for example, increased prosecutorial discretion. Four years later, in a follow-up study, they found that judges substantially reduced sentence disparity. Miethe and Moore also reported that some variations appeared; for example, they found judges and prosecutors bent the structure of the guidelines. Judges sometimes departed from the guidelines (about 10 percent of the time), while prosecutors changed their charging and plea-bargaining practices to circumvent the guidelines that they felt were unreasonable. Other researchers (e.g., Kramer et al. 1989) reported results confirming these research efforts.

However, studies conducted during the 1990s found considerable variation emerging in the application of the guidelines. D'Alessio and Stolzenberg (1995) found more deviation from sentencing guidelines the longer they were in effect. They discovered that judges were not giving first-time violent offenders prison terms, despite the guidelines' stipulating a period of incarceration. In addition, Frase (1991) reported that prosecutors increasingly circumvented sentencing guidelines by reducing the charges or by recommending leniency because of offender-based criteria, such as family background or race.

These studies tell us that the elimination of disparity and discrimination at the sentencing stage is very difficult to attain, at least to date. Yet s. 718.2 of the *Criminal Code* instructs judges to "take into consideration" a number of principles, including that "a sentence should be similar to sentences imposed on similar offenders for similar offences committed in similar circumstances." As Brodeur and Roberts (2002: 82) suggest, since "this is a codified sentencing principle—one of just a few—in our view judges should take it seriously indeed."

Victim Participation in Sentencing

In the 1980s a significant issue was raised in Western legal systems: the right of victims to participate in the trial, typically by way of victim impact statements (see Exhibit 9.3). Proponents of this approach argued that integrating victims into the court system by guaranteeing their rights would be an important step for our legal system, since it would recognize the victim's wish for status in court proceedings (Hall 1991). Others felt the recognition of victims would increase their dignity, underscore that a real individual had suffered at the hands of a criminal, and promote fairness by giving victims the right to be heard in court (Henderson 1985; Kelly 1984; Sumner 1987).

Opponents of victims' rights argued that establishing victims' rights as legal rights would challenge the very basis of the adversarial legal system, particularly the idea that crime is a violation against the state rather than against individual persons (Ashworth 1993). Others pointed out that recognizing victims in our legal system would result in too much pressure on the judge, vindictiveness on the part of the victim, more court delays, longer trials, substantial increases in legal costs to the state, and disparity in sentencing. Some argue judges themselves are reluctant to take into consideration the feelings and concerns of victims when it comes to sentencing offenders. The courtroom is their domain, and while outsiders can inform the judiciary of their experiences, there is no guarantee that the victims will have any influence on their decision (Rubel 1986; Grabosky 1987; Miers 1992).

Since 1989, when the federal government enacted Bill C-89, victims in Canada have had the right to file a victim impact statement, a document that invites victims to detail the effect of the crime on them. The statement is then forwarded to the judge for consideration in sentencing. When these forms were introduced, it was hoped they would have a significant influence on the sentencing decision. They were an attempt to bring victims back into the criminal justice system by giving them an opportunity to have an influence on the sentencing of those convicted of a crime, either through a written statement or by speaking before a judge in the courtroom, to inform the court about the impact of the crime and, in some cases, to advocate the sentence the offender should receive.

The effect of these statements on sentencing is largely unknown, since it is rare for a judge to mention a victim impact statement. However, some judges have made it a habit to mention them in certain cases, particularly those in which they feel that aggravating circumstances in the offence severely traumatized the victim, leading judges to hand out tougher sentences.

During the 1980s and 1990s provincial governments across Canada also passed victims rights' legislation. The first jurisdiction to introduce a victims' bill of rights in Canada was Manitoba in 1986. Since then, all other provinces and the federal government have passed some type of victim legislation. For example, in June 1996 Ontario proclaimed Bill 23 (known as the *Victim's Bill of Rights*). It outlined the principles and standards for the treatment of victims in the criminal justice system, and included increasing access to information for the victim, the right to have property involved in a criminal offence returned as quickly as possible, and the victim's right to having input into sentencing. The federal government expanded its legislation on victims in September 1996,

EXHIBIT 9.3   Rights of Victims in Canada

In May 1988 Parliament passed Bill C-89, sanctioning victims' rights and entitlement. These rights are defined as follows:

1. A victim has

    • the right to be treated with courtesy, compassion, dignity and respect for the privacy of the victim;
    • the right to access social, legal, medical, and mental health services that are responsive to the needs of the victims' dependents, spouse or guardian; and
    • the right to have property stolen from a victim returned to the victim as soon as possible.

2. Subject to the limits imposed by the availability of resources and to any other limits that are reasonable in the circumstances of each case, a victim has:

    • the right to be informed of:

    (i)   the name of the accused,
    (ii) the specific offence with which the accused is charged,
    (iii) the scope, nature, timing and progress of prosecution of the offence,
    (iv) the role of the victim and other persons involved in the prosecution of other offence and of any opportunity to make representations on restitution and the impact of the offence on the victim,
    (v)   court procedures, and
    (vi) crime prevention measures;

    • the right to be informed by law enforcement, court, health and social services personnel, at the earliest possible opportunity of the services, remedies and mechanisms to obtain remedies available to a victim; and
    • while waiting to give evidence at a proceeding in respect to an offence, the right to be kept apart, where necessary, from the accused and the accused's witnesses to ensure the safety of the victim, and the victim's family and to protect them from intimidation and retaliation.

    On 15 April 1999 amendments were tabled to the *Criminal Code* that would strengthen the rights of victims of crime in the criminal justice system:

    • ensure that victims are informed of their opportunity to prepare a victim impact statement at the time of sentencing;
    • ensure that victims have the choice to read the victim statement aloud;
    • require that victim impact statements be considered by courts and review boards fol-

lowing a verdict of not criminally responsible on account of mental disorder;

    • extend to victims of sexual or violent crime up to age 18 protections that restrict personal cross-examination by self-represented accused persons;
    • require police officers and judges to consider the victim's safety in all bail decisions;
    • allow victims and witnesses with a mental or physical disability to have a support person present when giving testimony; and
    • make it easier for victims and witnesses to participate in trials by permitting the judge to ban publication of their identity where it is necessary for the proper administration of justice.

The effect of victim impact statements on the criminal justice system varied across the six study sites. For example, in Victoria, B.C., few victim impact statements were used in court when their use was controlled by prosecutorial discretion. Prosecutors indicated that they did not use them because they felt they contained no new information, that too many were vague or contained largely irrelevant information, that they were of doubtful accuracy, and that they contributed to higher operating costs of the criminal justice system. In Toronto, prosecutors felt victim impact statements could have a significant role in court, and, as a result, two-thirds of the victim impact statements in Toronto were entered into court trials as exhibits, and one-third were used as Crown submissions.

For all Crown prosecutors, victim impact statements had the greatest impact in sexual assault and sexual abuse cases. In addition, these statements were considered helpful in raising prosecutors' awareness of the long-term emotional impact on victims, which had not been captured in other documents available to prosecutors (Roberts 1992: 67). Victim statements had some impact on judges. Of the 13 judges who responded to the question "Have victim impact statements actually affected sentences that you have passed?", seven judges responded positively and six answered no. However, in British Columbia, Roberts (1992: 77) reported a "minor change" in sentences imposed by judges in cases where a victim impact statement was used, while "occasionally sentences have been dramatically higher."

According to Roach (1999: 291), these low rates of victim participation indicate that victim impact statements "have not emerged as a major criminal justice issue" in this country and that these low rates of participation may be the result of victims' reluctance "to expose their suffering to adversarial challenge."

when Bill C-41 was passed. Amendments to the *Criminal Code of Canada* specifically codified the rights of victims of crime in order that their participation be increased and that they receive greater benefits in the sentencing process in several ways, including the admissibility of victim impact statements, restitution to victims, and victim participation in some parole hearings (Bacchus 1999).

Do victim impact statements make a difference at sentencing? To evaluate this policy, the Department of Justice conducted studies in six Canadian cities during 1986 (Giliberti 1990). Part of the study evaluated the effect of victim impact statements on victims. To their surprise, researchers discovered no difference between the degree of victims' satisfaction with justice when their impact statements were used in court and when they were not. According to the victims, the most important feature of the program was the opportunity it gave them to discuss the offence and its effects and to have this information given to the court, to be given useful feedback about the case, and to be able to contact someone should they experience any difficulty. Researchers also discovered that victim impact statements led to victims' being better informed about what was happening in their case as it progressed through the system. However, it was reported that the impact of this program was the same for participants and nonparticipants in terms of the level of their participation in the criminal justice system, their satisfaction with how the case was handled, and their future reporting of incidents to the police. The majority of victims were found to hold negative attitudes toward sentencing both before and after their cases.

SENTENCING AND HEALING CIRCLES

In recent years, much attention has been given to the overrepresentation of Aboriginals in the federal and provincial correctional systems. Quigley (1994: 270) has summarized the implications of this overrepresentation:

- Aboriginal accused persons are more likely to be denied bail. This likelihood in turn tends to increase the likelihood of incarceration on conviction.
- Aboriginal offenders are more likely to be committed to jail for nonpayment of fines. In Saskatchewan during the 1992–93 fiscal year, almost 75 percent of admissions to jails for fine default were Aboriginals.
- Aboriginal offenders are less likely to receive probation as a sentence than are non-Aboriginal offenders.

From this evidence, Quigley (1994: 271) recommended an attempt "to decrease the preponderance of Aboriginal people within the prison system." One proposal has been to reintroduce sentencing and healing circles, in which a group of elders participates with a judge in the sentencing process in an attempt to heal the accused, the victim, and the community.

The nature of sentencing circles varies across Canada, but some features are common to all. Quigley notes that modern sentencing circles are in fact a hybrid of the traditional form of Aboriginal community justice and the Western legal system. In essence, judges retain the right to give final approval to a sentence imposed by a sentencing circle. What is different, however, is the process by which the sentence is arrived at. According to Quigley (1994: 288), the difference is that "sentencing circles are a variation in procedure, not necessarily a change in the substance of sentencing." The sentencing circle operates on a basis similar to that of the Western legal system in some ways. For example, any dispute on a factual matter is resolved by calling for evidence and by examination and cross-examination of witnesses. What differs is that, through discussions within the sentencing circle, "respected members of the community, the victim, the police, the accused, the family of the accused, Crown and defence counsel, and the judge try to jointly arrive at a decision that is acceptable to all."

There is some variation in the type of offences allowed to be heard by sentencing circles although, in most cases, these offences are minor in nature, such as property crimes. Serious violent crimes are usually not allowed to be heard by a sentencing circle, although there are exceptions, such as the Community Holistic Circle Healing found in Hollow Water (see Chapter 3).

Beyond the type of offence, there are a number of other criteria considered important for determining whether or not a sentencing circle will be held. These were determined in *R. v. Joseyounen* (1995), which set out the following criteria:

- The accused must agree to be referred to the sentencing circle.
- The accused must have deep roots in the community in which the sentencing circle is held and from which the participants are to be drawn.
- There are elders or respected nonpolitical community leaders willing to participate.
- The victim is willing to participate and has not been coerced into participating.
- The court should determine beforehand if the victim is suffering from battered woman syndrome.
- If she is, she should receive counseling and be accompanied by the support team in the circle.
- Disputed facts must be resolved in advance.
- The case is one in which the court is willing to depart from the usual range of sentencing.

Aboriginal Ganootamaage Justice Services of Winnipeg volunteers take part in a healing circle for a 20-year-old shoplifter (not shown in photo) at the Aboriginal Centre in September 1998. The sentence they handed down was the first by a healing circle under a new Manitoba program for Aboriginal offenders.

Once a sentence is agreed on, it is not automatically accepted by the Western legal system. For example, the Saskatchewan Court of Appeal overturned the sentence handed down by a sentencing circle to Ivan Morin. Morin, a 34-year-old Métis, was convicted in 1992 of robbing a gasoline station of $131 and choking a female attendant. He was sentenced to jail for 18 months instead of the six to eight years requested by the Crown. The Crown's sentence was proposed on the basis of Morin's 34 prior criminal convictions, which ranged from drunk driving and small-time break-ins to attempted murder and kidnapping. Still, the trial judge accepted the recommendation of the sentencing circle. The Crown appealed the case. The appeal was based largely on the opinion that Morin was using the sentencing circle to receive the lightest sentence possible and showed neither real remorse nor interest in rehabilitation. The Saskatchewan Court of Appeal, in its review of the case (*R. v. Morin* (1995)), noted that judges should accept the decisions of sentencing circles in cases where

1. the accused agrees to be referred to a sentencing circle;
2. the accused has deep roots in the community in which the circle is held;
3. the elders are willing to support the offender; and
4. the victim voluntarily participates.

Since Morin appeared to be trying to take advantage of the lighter sentences associated with sentencing circles, the court of appeal decided to accept the argument presented by the Crown and increased the sentence. Such appeals, however, are rare.

The benefits of sentencing circles are many. According to a court in Yukon, the benefits of sentencing circles involve numerous modifications to the decision-making process:

1. The monopoly of professionals is reduced.
2. Lay participation is encouraged.
3. Information flow is increased.
4. There is a creative search for new options.
5. The sharing of responsibility for the decision is promoted.
6. The participation of the accused is encouraged.
7. Victims are involved in the process.
8. A more constructive environment is created.
9. There is greater understanding of the limitations of the justice system.
10. The focus of the criminal justice system is extended.
11. There is greater mobilization of community resources.
12. There is an opportunity to merge the values of Aboriginal nations and the larger society (*R. v. Moses* (1992)).

CHAPTER 9 Sentencing and Punishment

Despite the enthusiasm for the potential for healing circles, some have been cautious in their support (Clairmont 1996; Roberts and LaPrairie 1996; LaPrairie 1998). Clairmont studied three such programs in three different communities and concluded that "in all programs the objectives relating to victims and community reconciliation have proven elusive to date." Clairmont notes that it is particularly important for these programs to involve the community at large. LaPrairie (1998) reports that victims often feel healing programs to be less positive experiences than do the offenders. In addition, only about 30 percent of the families of offenders and victims considered the way offenders had been dealt with to be appropriate. As LaPrairie notes, "these findings are not … to suggest a lack of merit in the projects identified above or in pursuing local justice in aboriginal communities … [but] to identify the need for greater clarity in the development and delivery of local justice services."

SUMMARY

The sentencing of a convicted person is one of the most crucial decisions made in our criminal justice system. In Canada judges have considerable discretion in deter-mining the length of a sentence, and their decision reflects how they wish the accused to be punished. However, in most cases the decision of the judge is not final, since the members of the parole board may decide to grant full parole before the completion of the sentence.

The object of a sentence is to reduce crime by incarcerating criminals and deterring others from committing crimes. Deterrence, selective incapacitation, rehabilitation, and the justice model all vary in terms of emphasis on how best to deal with offenders through sentencing.

The Canadian government has attempted in recent years to shift the focus of sentencing to a justice model perspective. The Canadian Sentencing Commission was formed in 1987 to investigate the problems with the current sentencing approach and to suggest an alternative approach that is both coherent and consistent. A number of significant problems have been identified in the sentencing patterns of judges. These include discrimination and disparity, with the result that a structured approach to sentencing is favoured by some. In addition, alternate sanctions for Aboriginals have been introduced to attempt to reduce their overrepresentation in the correctional systems across Canada.

Discussion Questions

1. Why is sentencing considered by many to be the most critical phase in our system of justice?

2. What are some of the arguments for and against using factors other than the crime itself in deciding an appropriate sentence for a convicted offender?

3. Compare the different types of sentence affiliated with each of the different models of criminal justice. What are the benefits and disadvantages of each?

4. Are there any crimes for which the Canadian government should pass mandatory sentencing laws?

5. Should public opinion affect sentencing decisions made by judges?

6. Should Canada have a well-defined sentencing policy? If so, what would be the impact of such a policy?

7. Should victims have a greater role in the sentencing of offenders? How could victims be given a greater role?

8. What are the benefits and drawbacks of Aboriginal sentencing circles?

9. Should Canada reintroduce the death penalty as a sentence for first-degree murder? Using the United States as your example, do you think that the death penalty deters crime? Explain your answer.

Suggested Readings

Roberts, J., and D.P. Cole, eds. 1999. *Making Sense of Sentencing.* Toronto: University of Toronto Press.

Roberts, J., and L. Stalans. 1997. *Public Opinion, Crime and Criminal Justice.* Boulder, Colo.: Westview Press, 1997.

Ruby, C. 1994. *Sentencing*, 4th ed. Toronto: Butterworths.

Tonry, M. 1996. *Sentencing Matters.* New York: Oxford University Press.

Walker, N. 1991. *Why Punish?* Oxford: Oxford University Press.

References

Anderson, P.R., and D.J. Newman. 1993. *Introduction to Criminal Justice*, 5th ed. Toronto: McGraw-Hill Ryerson.

Andrews, D.A., I. Zinger, R. Hoge, J. Bonta, P. Gendreau, and F. Cullen. 1990. "Does Correctional Treatment Work? A Clinically Relevant and Psychologically Informed Meta-Analysis." *Criminology* 28: 393–404.

Ashworth, A. 1993. "Victim Impact Statements and Sentencing." *Criminal Law Review:* 498–509.

Bacchus, S. 1999. "The Role of Victims in the Sentencing Process." In J.V. Roberts and D.P. Cole, eds., *Making Sense of Sentencing*. Toronto: University of Toronto Press, pp. 217–29.

Bailey, I. 2000. "Woman Gets 10 Years for Death of Stepdaughter." *National Post*, 12 August, A4.

Blumstein, A.J., J. Cohen, S.E. Martin, and M. Tonry. 1983. *Research on Sentencing: The Search for Reform*. Washington, D.C.: National Academy Press.

Brodeur, J.P., and J.V. Roberts 2002. "Taking Justice Seriously." *Canadian Criminal Law Review* 7: 77–91.

Brookbank, C., and B. Kingsley. 1998. *Adult Criminal Court Statistics, 1997–98*. Ottawa: Juristat.

Bureau of Justice Statistics. 2000. *Prisoners in 2000*. Washington, D.C.: U.S. Department of Justice.

Campbell, A.K. 1990. "Sentencing Reform in Canada." *Canadian Journal of Criminology* 32: 387–95.

Canadian Sentencing Commission. 1987. *Sentencing Reform: A Canadian Approach*. Ottawa: Minister of Supply and Services.

Clairmont, D. 1996. "Alternative Justice Issues for Aboriginal Justice." *Journal of Legal Pluralism and Unofficial Law* 36: 125–58.

———. 1989. *Discrimination in Sentencing: Patterns of Sentencing for Assault Convictions*. Halifax: Royal Commission on the Donald Marshall, Jr., Prosecution.

Clairmont, D., W. Barnwell, and A. O'Malley. 1989. *Sentencing Disparity and Race in the Nova Scotia Criminal Justice System*. Halifax: Royal Commission on the Donald Marshall, Jr., Prosecution.

Clear, T. 1980. *Harm in Punishment*. Boston, MA: Northeastern University Press.

D'Alessio, S.J., and L. Stolzenberg. 1995. "The Impact of Sentencing Guidelines on Jail Incarceration in Minnesota." *Criminology* 33: 283–302.

Daubney, D., and G. Parry. 1999. "An Overview of Bill C-41 (The *Sentencing Reform Act*)." In J.V. Roberts and D.P. Cole, eds., *Making Sense of Sentencing*. Toronto: University of Toronto Press, pp. 31–47.

Doob, A.N. 1992. "Community Sanctions and Imprisonment: Hoping for a Miracle but Not Bothering Even to Pray for It." *Canadian Journal of Criminology* 32: 415–28.

Ehrlich, I. 1975. "The Deterrent Effect of Capital Punishment: A Question of Life and Death." *American Economic Review* 65: 397–417.

Fagan, J. 1989. "Cessation of Family Violence: Deterrence and Dissuasion." In L. Ohlin and M. Tonry, eds., *Crime and Justice: A Review of Research*, vol. 11. Chicago: University of Chicago Press, pp. 100–51.

Frase, R.S. 1991. "Sentencing Reform in Minnesota, Ten Years After." *Minnesota Law Review* 75: 727–54.

Giliberti, C. 1990. "Study Probes Effectiveness of Victim Impact Statements." *Justice Research Notes* 1: 1–8.

Grabosky, P.N. 1987. "Victims." In G. Zdenkowski, C. Ronalds, and M. Richardson, eds., *The Criminal Injustice System*, vol. 2. Sydney, Australia: Pluto Press, pp. 143–57.

Hall, D.J. 1991. "Victim Voices in Criminal Court: The Need for Restraint." *American Criminal Law Review* 28: 233–66.

Havemann, P. 1986. "From Child Saving to Child Blaming: The Political Economy of the *Young Offenders Act*, 1908–1984." In S. Brickey and E. Comack, eds., *The Social Basis of Law*. Toronto: Garamond Press, pp. 225–42.

Henderson, L.N. 1985. "The Wrongs of Victims' Rights." *Stanford Law Review* 37: 937–1021.

Hogarth, J. 1971. *Sentencing as a Human Process*. Toronto: University of Toronto Press.

Humphreys, A. 2002. "Going Easy on Native Criminals a Mistake." *National Post*, 28 March, A4.

Jacoby, J.E., and C.S. Dunn. 1987. National Survey on Punishment for Criminal Offenses. Paper presented at the National Conference on Punishment for Criminal Offenses, Ann Arbor, Mich.

Justice Report. 1990. Vol. 7, no. 3. Ottawa: Canadian Criminal Justice Association.

Kaukinen, C., and S. Colavecchi. 1999. "Public Perceptions of the Courts: An Examination of Attitudes toward the Treatment of Victims and Accused." *Canadian Journal of Criminology* 41: 365–84.

Kelly, D.P. 1984. "Victims' Perceptions of Criminal Justice." *Pepperdine Law Review* 11: 15–22.

Kramer, J.H., R.L. Lubitz, and C.A. Kempinen. 1989. "Sentencing Guidelines: A Quantitative Comparison of Sentencing Policy in Minnesota, Pennsylvania, and Washington." *Justice Quarterly* 6: 565–88.

LaPrairie, C. 1998. "The 'New' Justice: Some Implications for Aboriginal Communities." *Canadian Journal of Criminology* 40: 61–79.

———. 1990. "The Role of Sentencing in the Over representation of Aboriginal People in Correctional Institutions." *Canadian Journal of Criminology* 32: 429–40.

Lash, J. 2000. "Case Comment: *R. v. Gladue*." *Canadian Woman Studies* 20: 85–91.

Law Reform Commission of Canada. 1974. *Studies on Sentencing: Working Paper 3*. Ottawa: Information Canada.

Manson, A. 2001. *The Law of Sentencing*. Toronto: Irwin Law.

Miers, D. 1992. "The Responsibilities and the Rights of Victims of Crime." *Modern Law Review* 55: 482–505.

Miethe, T.D., and C.A. Moore. 1989. *Sentencing Guidelines: Their Effect in Minnesota*. Washington, D.C.: U.S. Department of Justice.

———. 1985. "Socioeconomic Disparities under Determinate Sentencing Systems: A Comparison of Preguideline and Postguideline Practices in Minnesota." *Criminology* 23: 337–64.

National Post. 1998. "Equal under the Law." 14 December, A15.

Ontario Commission on Systemic Racism in the Criminal Justice System. 1995. *Report of the Ontario Commission on Systemic Racism in the Criminal Justice System.* Toronto: Queen's Printer.

Packer, H.L. 1968. *The Limits of the Criminal Sanction.* Palo Alto, CA: Stanford University Press.

Palys, T.S., and S. Divorski. 1986. "Explaining Sentencing Disparity." *Canadian Journal of Criminology* 28: 347–62.

Quigley, T. 1994. "Some Issues in the Sentencing of Aboriginal Offenders." In R. Gosse, J.Y. Henderson, and R. Carter, eds., *Continuing Poundmaker and Riel's Request.* Saskatoon: Purich, pp. 269–98.

Renner, K., and A. Warner. 1981. "The Standard of Social Justice Applied to an Evaluation of Criminal Cases Appearing before the Halifax Courts." *Windsor Yearbook of Access to Justice* 1: 62–80.

Roach, K. 1999. *Due Process and Victims' Rights: The New Law and Politics of Criminal Justice.* Toronto: University of Toronto Press.

Roberts, J.V. 1988. "Public Opinion about Sentencing: Some Popular Myths." *Justice Report* 5: 7–9.

Roberts, J.V., and A. Birkenmayer. 1997. "Sentencing in Canada: Recent Statistical Trends." *Canadian Journal of Criminology* 39: 459–82.

Roberts, J.V., and D.P. Cole. 1999. "Introduction to Sentencing and Parole." In J.V. Roberts and D.P. Cole, eds., *Making Sense of Sentencing.* Toronto: University of Toronto Press, pp. 3–30.

Roberts, J.V., and A.N. Doob. 1989. "Sentencing and Public Opinion: Taking False Shadows for True Substances." *Osgoode Hall Law Journal* 27: 491–515.

Roberts, J.V., and C. LaPrairie. 1996. "Circle Sentencing: Some Unanswered Questions." *Criminal Law Quarterly* 39: 319–55.

Roberts, J.V., and A. von Hirsch. 1999. "Legislating the Purpose and Principles of Sentencing." In J.V. Roberts and D.P. Cole, eds., *Making Sense of Sentencing.* Toronto: University of Toronto Press, pp. 48–62.

Roberts, T. 1992. *Assessment of the Victim Impact Statement Program in British Columbia.* Ottawa: Department of Justice, Research and Sentencing Directorate.

Rubel, H.C. 1986. "Victim Participation in Sentencing Proceedings." *Criminal Law Quarterly* 28: 226–50.

Seeman, N. 2001. "Two Kinds of Justice is No Justice at All." *The Globe and Mail,* 6 December, A23.

Sherman, L.W., and R. Berk. 1984. "The Specific Deterrent Effects of Arrest for Domestic Assault." *American Sociological Review* 49: 261–72.

Stuart, D., and R.J. Delisle. 1995. *Learning Canadian Criminal Law,* 5th ed. Toronto: Carswell.

Sumner, C.J. 1987. "Victim Participation in the Criminal Justice System." *Australian and New Zealand Journal of Criminology* 20: 195–217.

Thomas, M. 2002. *Adult Criminal Court Statistics 2000/01.* Ottawa: Canadian Centre for Justice Statistics.

Tufts, J. 2000. *Public Attitudes toward the Criminal Justice System*. Ottawa: Canadian Centre for Justice Statistics.

Wheeler, G., and R. Hissong. 1988. "Effects of Sanctions on Drunk Drivers: Beyond Incarceration." *Crime and Delinquency* 34: 29–42.

Williams, T. 1999. "Sentencing Black Offenders in Ontario." In J.V. Roberts and D.P. Cole, eds., *Making Sense of Sentencing*. Toronto: University of Toronto Press, pp. 200–16.

Williams, T., and K. Kalm. 1990. "General and Specific Measures of Public Attitudes toward Sentencing." *Canadian Journal of Behavioural Science* 22: 327–37.

Zamble, E. 1990. "Public Support for Criminal Justice Policies: Some Specific Findings." *Forum on Corrections Research* 2: 14–19.

Zedlewski, E.W. 1987. *Making Confinement Decisions*. Washington, D.C.: Government Printing Office.

Court Cases

R. v. Gladue, [1999] 1. S.C.R. 688

R. v. Joseyounen, [1995] 6. W.W.R. 438 (Sask. Prov. Ct.)

R. v. Morin (1995), 42 C.R. (4th) 339 (Sask. C.A.)

R. v. Moses (1992), 11 C.R. (4th) 357 (Y.T. Terr. Ct.)

CHAPTER 10

Alternatives to Prison: Probation, Conditional Sentences, and Intermediate Sanctions

CHAPTER OBJECTIVES

✓ Outline the major forms of intermediate sanctions: intensive supervision programs, home confinement and electronic monitoring, and day fines.

✓ Evaluate whether the goals of intermediate sanction programs—reducing prison populations and prison costs and increasing safety—are being achieved.

✓ Discuss whether deterrence-based programs work.

✓ Consider whether intermediate punishment sanctions would be beneficial if introduced in Canada.

✓ Discuss the importance of alternatives to prisons and how they affect the number of individuals incarcerated in Canada.

T his chapter reviews the main alternatives to imprisonment used in Canada and/or in other western nations today: probation, conditional sentences, and three types of intermediate punishment—intensive supervision probation, home confinement and electronic monitoring, and day fines. Both probation and conditional sentences are forms of community-based sanctions, but while probation has existed in Canada for over a century, conditional sentences were not implemented until 1996 as part of the package of reforms proclaimed when Bill C-41 was passed (see Chapter 9). Intermediate punishments have been handed down in the United States for three decades and are starting to appear or be considered for use in Canada. For example, most provinces now have some form of intensive supervision probation, and three provinces have published the results of their pilot projects on home confinement and electronic monitoring. With estimates that the federal and provincial prison populations will exceed 45 000 by 2004 (Foran 1995), these programs will no doubt come under increasing scrutiny by various provincial and federal authorities in the next few years. This chapter reviews intermediate punishments programs in the United States and provides some basis on which to judge them and decide whether they are appropriate for use in Canada.

On 25 April 2001, Kimberly Rogers pleaded guilty in a Sudbury, Ontario, court to welfare fraud. She admitted to the judge that between 1996 and 1999 she had received loans from the Ontario Student Assistance Plan in order that she could attend community college. At the same time, however, she was also receiving over $13 000 in general welfare assistance from the provincial government. Both the Crown prosecutor and defense attorney requested the judge to give her a conditional sentence of community service work. Since Ms Rogers was pregnant, the judge decided instead to sentence her to six months of home confinement that required her to remain in her apartment at all times with the exception of medical and religious purposes and for shopping for the necessities of life, all of which he ruled had to be done on Wednesdays, between 9 a.m. and 12 noon. The judge also ordered her to repay the welfare money she received. After her conviction, she was also cut off from social assistance, but in June she won a continuance of her payments, pending a constitutional challenge before the Ontario Court of Appeal (Blatchford 2002: A10).

Less than four months later, on 9 August 2001, her body was discovered in her second-floor walkup apartment in Sudbury. A number of factors—the 30°C heat and the fact that she had been confined to a period of six months of home confinement—contributed to her death. Within two weeks of her death, *The Globe and Mail* commented that her fate was "a 21st-century Dickens story," describing her punishment as "straight out of a 19th-century Charles Dickens novel" (Blatchford 2002: A1). When she died, Ms Rogers was reported to be receiving $520 a month in benefits, from which 10 percent ($52) was being "clawed back" by provincial authorities as a repayment for welfare fraud. Since her rent was $450 a month, she had about $18 a month for all her other expenses. The provincial coroner conducted an autopsy and on 15 August 2001, announced that "the circumstances (of her death) are not ones which indicate death due to heat stroke" (Blatchford 2002: A10). Later, it was reported by the *National Post* that Ms Rogers had "overdosed on the prescription drug she took for depression, though whether deliberately or accidentally isn't known ..." (Blatchford 2002: A10). To what degree the sentence of home confinement contributed to Ms Rogers' death may never be known, but it does raise issues about the fairness of such sentences. For example, if she had been wealthier, could she have afforded an apartment with air conditioning, which would likely have made her sentence much more bearable? This and other questions can be raised about many of the types of sentences discussed below; although they are intended to keep people out of a correctional facility, do they have the same impact on all persons who receive such a sentence or do they have a more deleterious impact on those who are poor?

PROBATION

Probation is based on the idea that certain offenders pose no danger to society. A judge gives probation at the sentencing, after suspending the offender's sentence; however, a judge cannot suspend a sentence for an offence that has a specified minimum punishment. A probation order can be imposed either as a single sentence or as a "split sentence," that is, when an offender is required to complete another punishment—for example, pay a fine or serve a period of time not exceeding two years in a correctional facility—before going on probation. The maximum length of a probation order for adult offenders is three years. Belanger (2001) found that during 1999–2000 probation was used in 40 percent of all single conviction cases and 49 percent of all

multiple conviction cases (that is, cases resulting in two or more sentences). When a judge gives probation as the sole punishment, the average sentence length is more than one year (434 days). When probation is used for cases involving more than one conviction, the average sentence length is longer (556 days).

Probation typically involves an offender being released into the community under the supervision of a provincial probation service. It is, in essence, a contract between an offender and the state in which the former promises to abide by the conditions mandated by the court. If the offender breaks the conditions of probation, a federal statute, or the *Criminal Code*, a breach of probation has occurred.

Compulsory conditions of probation include remaining within a particular jurisdiction, reporting to a probation officer as required, keeping the peace, keeping authorities informed about changes of residence and employment, and refraining from contact with criminal associates (Birkenmayer 1995). The court may impose other conditions deemed reasonable "for protecting society and for facilitating the offender's successful reintegration into the community" (s. 732.1(3)(h)). Judges may impose optional conditions, such as drug counseling, avoiding contact with children (for example, if a child molester is placed on probation), or performing a specified community service order.

Judges have considerable discretion in determining whether to give probation. Section 731 of the *Criminal Code* states that

> Where an accused is convicted of an offence, a court may, having regard to the age and character of the offender, the nature of the offence and the circumstances surrounding the commission
>
> (a) ... suspend the passing of sentence and direct that the offender be released on the conditions prescribed in a probation order...

Probation has been a common punishment and it's consistently being revised. For example, when Bill C-41 (see Chapter 9) was proclaimed it included probation as a punishment for firearm offences. However, s. 100 of the *Criminal Code* creates prohibition orders against the possession of firearms, ammunition, or explosive devices. These orders are imposed on offenders convicted or discharged in connection with offences involving violence, threats of violence, or firearms. Courts are now required (s. 731.1) to consider ss. 109 and 110 of the *Criminal Code* before imposing a probation order (Daubney and Parry 1999).

Bill C-41 also made allowances for the long-term supervision (sometimes referred to as "super probation") of certain offenders in the community. Section 753.1 of the *Criminal Code* is concerned with individuals whom the courts find to be dangerous offenders. If a judge decides there is a possibility that offenders will be a high-risk threat to the safety of a community or that they might reoffend once released, she can order the offender to be placed on probation while in the community for a period of up to 10 years. The supervision may be attached to parole, and would begin after parole has been successfully completed.

The Use of Probation as a Sanction

Probation is the most common form of community sanction in Canada. Of the 228 267 cases in 1999–2000 that resulted in a conviction, there were 72 289 probation orders (a decrease of 8 percent compared to the previous year). Of these cases, 75 percent had a probation sentence length between six and 24 months; the median length was one year. The most common single-conviction cases receiving a probation sentence in nine provinces and the territories during 1999–2000 were common assault (79 percent), assault with a weapon (level II) and arson (both at 78 percent), and sexual assault (level I) (76 percent) (see Figure 10.1).

Eligibility for Probation

Many people believe probation is granted to first-time offenders who commit a minor property offence. However, probation is a common sentence given to individuals convicted of violent offences. There are two reasons the majority of violent criminals are given a sentence of probation: (1) the violent crimes that most commonly receive probation are less serious and therefore warrant a lenient response, and (2) the offender's prior criminal record. According to Roberts (1999) over 67 percent of all violent crimes were considered by judges to be relatively minor incidents. He also points out that "property offenders are more likely to have prior convictions than violent offenders … [and] … are more likely to have been sentenced to probation in the past. This may discourage judges from imposing probation on this second (or third) occasion" (Roberts 1999: 95).

Studies of probation orders show that both the sentencing of offenders to probation is increasing and that the median length of probation orders is growing longer. In 2000–01, for example, nine offences had a median probation sentence of 18 months or longer. The types of offences that led to long probation orders are typically serious in nature, and probation is usually imposed in combination with incarceration. Most vio-

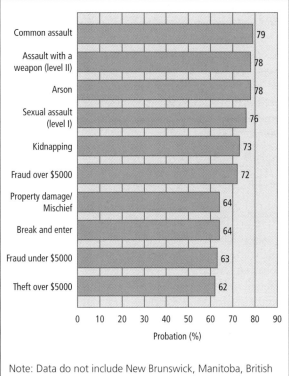

Note: Data do not include New Brunswick, Manitoba, British Columbia, and Nunavut. Calculation of means excludes cases where length of prison is unknown.

Source: Statistics Canada, *Juristat*, Catalogue 85-002, vol. 21, no. 10, December 2001, p. 10.

FIGURE 10.1

Probation Rates for Single-Conviction Cases, Canada, 1999–2000

lent crimes (e.g., attempted murder, robbery, kidnapping, sexual assault, and sexual abuse) receive the longest probation terms, usually around two years in length. Two other violent offences—abduction and common assault—have a median probation length under two years (Thomas 2002).

Sex offenders receive longer probation orders than those given to all violent offenders. In 1997–98, 72 percent of the probation orders granted to sex offenders exceeded one year in length (29 percent of these orders exceeded two years). In comparison, 47 percent of probation orders given to all violent offenders exceeded one year (9 percent of these were in excess of two years). Less than 4 percent of probation terms for sex offenders were for periods of less than six months. Overall, the median probation term in 1997–98 for both sexual assault and other sexual offences was two years, twice as long as the median probation term for violent offence cases (Integration and Analysis Program 1999). Arson is the only crime besides violent offences to have a median period of probation of two years or more.

Seventy-five percent of offences in the category of crimes against persons (that is, violent crimes) received a term of probation order, compared with 55 percent in the crimes against property category, 38 percent of other *Criminal Code* offences, 20 percent of traffic offences, and 37 percent of all drug-related offences. It should be noted that of all the violent criminals who received probation during 2000–01, 32 percent also received a prison sentence (Thomas 2002).

Who Gets Probation?

Thirty-nine percent of all male offenders received probation in 1999–2000 compared to 45 percent of all female offenders. When the probation rates for both violent and property crimes categories are combined, the probation rate was 42 percent for males and 54 percent of females. Differences are also found when the average lengths of probation sentences for males and females are compared: males receive longer probation terms than females. For example, for the offence of common assault and break and enter, males received an average of 428 days and 514 days of probation, respectively, compared to 370 days and 457 days for females. Females received longer probation terms for the offences of arson, fraud under $5000, and impaired driving (Belanger 2001). Twelve percent of probationers across Canada were Aboriginal (a decrease from 16 percent in 1992–93), with the western provinces having the highest rate of Aboriginals on probation.

Breaches of Probation

Breaches of probation are common. In 1997–98 there were 11 329 breach of probation cases heard in adult criminal courts in nine Canadian jurisdictions (Brookbank and Kingsley 1998). Unemployed young males with a low income, a prior criminal record, and a history of instability are most at risk to be rearrested while on probation (Morgan 1994). Female probationers with stable marriages, higher levels of education, and either part- or full-time employment are most likely to succeed while on probation, as compared with those who are single, have completed lower levels of education, and are unemployed. A number of factors are consistently related to those who receive probation: prior record, a previous probation sentence, and a prior period of incarceration (Morgan 1994).

Stephen Chung leaves court in Hamilton after receiving a conditional sentence. He pleaded guilty of one count each of fraud and uttering a false document in what is believed to be Canada's largest case of medicare fraud ($4 million) by an individual.

The high number of breaches of probation became a major issue in the early 1990s during debates about sentencing reform. Many felt changes were necessary to those sections of the *Criminal Code* pertaining to probation since the sanctions available for breach of probation were ineffective and commonly led to plea bargains. Daubney and Parry (1999: 36) point out that the issues associated with probation included concerns that "supervision was too often ineffective, due to a lack of ability to change conditions of probation to suit the case, and the overall authority of the probation officer." Bill C-41 addressed these problems by revising some of the provisions related to the enforcement and administration of probation.

THE CONDITIONAL SENTENCE OF IMPRISONMENT

One of the most controversial sections of Bill C-41 was the creation of the conditional sentence. The conditional sentence is a sentence of imprisonment of less than two years that the offender serves in the community under optional and mandatory conditions. Section 742.1 states that a conditional sentence may be imposed where

(a) the *Criminal Code* does not set a minimum term of imprisonment;
(b) the court imposes a sentence of less than two years; and
(c) the court is satisfied that allowing the offender to serve the sentence in the community would not endanger the safety of the community and would be consistent with the fundamental purpose and principles of sentencing as set out in ss. 718 to 718.2 of the *Criminal Code*.

The goal of the conditional sentence was to create a true alternative to imprisonment in the hope that it would reduce the number of individuals incarcerated (Daubney and Parry 1999; Reed and Roberts 1999). When a court imposes a conditional sentence, it "has essentially imposed the community for jail as the place where the sentence is to be served, as long as conditions set out in its order are respected" (Daubney and Parry 1999: 42). Roach (2000: 26) points out that conditional sentences "were defined as sentences of imprisonment that should be served under strict conditions in the community."

Mandatory conditions include law-abiding behaviour, appearing before the court when ordered, remaining within a specific set of boundaries unless the court grants its permission to leave, and informing the court or supervisor of any change in address or occupa-

tion. Optional conditions include those that are possible in most probation orders, such as attending a treatment program and providing support and care for dependants. The most common options used to date are curfews, mandatory medical or psychiatric treatment, and orders preventing offenders from contacting other persons. The least-used option is home confinement and electronic monitoring (Roberts et al. 2000).

Conditional sentences are situated between incarceration and probation in terms of punishment by sentencing judges *(R. v. Proulx* (1999)). This means conditional sentences "can and should reflect aims of penal policy that are appropriate to both incarceration and probation" (Roberts and Healy 2000: 309). While probation is designed to focus on rehabilitation as its primary objective, conditional sentences are intended to fulfill the principles of denunciation and rehabilitation (Lonmo 2001).

The Use of Conditional Sentences

In the 43-month period between the proclamation of Bill C-41 on 6 September 1996—when the conditional sentence became one of the courts' sentencing options—and 31 March 1999, judges imposed conditional sentences against 58 734 offenders. The average length of conditional sentences alone granted during this period was eight months. When a conditional sentence was combined with probation, 70 percent of offenders received a sentence of 12 months or more. Across Canada, conditional sentences were most commonly ordered for crimes against property (39 percent), followed by 31 percent for violent crimes, 11 percent for drug offences, 8 percent for administration of justice offences, 7 percent for "Other *Criminal Code*," and 4 percent for driving offences. A study by Roberts et al. (2000) of judges' views on conditional sentencing reports that judges would impose conditional sentences more often if more support services were available in the community, although 67 percent of the judges felt that conditional sentences were less effective than jail in deterring crime.

Nationally, females received almost 19 percent of all conditional sentences. Offenders aged between 31 and 40 received the highest number of all conditional sentences (33 percent), and 70 percent of offenders given a conditional sentence had a prior record.

On average, Aboriginal offenders received 17.5 percent of all orders. Aboriginals received just over 67 percent of all conditional sentences imposed in Saskatchewan in that two-year period and 44.7 percent of those in Manitoba. This is in keeping with s. 718.2(e)

Jurisdiction	Year	Number of Conditional Sentences	Percent Females	Percent Aboriginal	Median Age
Newfoundland	1996–97	212	30	1	25
	1997–98	304	25	7	31
Prince Edward Island	1996–97	4	–	—	..
	1997–98	29	10	..	..
Nova Scotia	1996–97	242	16	2	31
	1997–98	476	14	3	30
New Brunswick	1996–97	185	20	..	27
	1997–98	596	19	..	29
Quebec	1996–97	2 555	14	3	32
	1997–98	3 983	14	4	32
Ontario	1996–97	1 940	23	7	33
	1997–98	4 293	25	7	33
Manitoba	1996–97	..	..	..	..
	1997–98	526	..	..	..
Saskatchewan	1996–97	445	16	78	29
	1997–98	928	29	73	29
Alberta	1996–97	1 004	27	22	..
	1997–98	1 343	26	22	..
British Columbia	1996–97	1 064	15	15	31
	1997–98	2 080	16	16	32
Yukon	1996–97	22	23	23	30
	1997–98	50	20	93	29
Northwest Territories	1996–97	..	..	..	..
	1997–98	..	..	..	..
Provincial/Territorial Total[1]	1996–97	7 673	19	12	34

1. Conditional sentences were introduced in September 1996.
.. figures not available
— amount too small to be expressed
– nil or zero

Source: Statistics Canada, *Juristat*, Catalogue 85-002, vol. 19, no. 4, April 1999, p. 11.

of the *Criminal Code*, which states in part that "all available sanctions other than imprisonment that are reasonable in the circumstance should be considered for all offenders, with particular attention to the circumstances of aboriginal offenders" (LaPrairie 1999) (see Chapter 9).

Only limited data is currently available on breaches of conditional sentences. Relying on the information provided by seven jurisdictions, LaPrairie (1999) reports that the overall breach rate was 17.5 percent, with a high of 26 percent in British Columbia to a low of 15 percent in Ontario. Fifty-six percent of these breaches were for violating a mandatory condition, 36 were for reoffences and the remaining 8 percent involved breaches of an optional condition. Forty-four percent of these breaches resulted in either partial imprisonment or imprisonment for the rest of the order; 26 percent resulted in nothing

being done to the offender; 20 percent led to "amending conditions," and the remaining 7 percent of cases involved an "unknown" response.

Roberts (1999) raises the issue of disparity in the use of conditional sentences. He argues that the broad discretionary powers granted judges may lead some of them to view the same case in different terms. One judge might decide that placing the offender on a conditional sentence may pose a threat to the community and would therefore give the offender a prison sentence, whereas another judge might not interpret the case in the same way, reasoning that the offender should be given a conditional sentence. As Roberts (1999) notes, provinces have taken different approaches to the issue of conditional sentences and, as a result, disparities have emerged among the provinces (see Table 10.1). For example, the Saskatchewan Court of Appeal ruled in

TABLE 10.2 Number and Percentage Distribution of Convicted Cases with Conditional Sentences by Offence Group and Jurisdiction, 1999–2000

| | Total | | | Convicted cases with a conditional sentence | | | | | | | | |
| | Convicted Cases | Cases with a conditional sentence | | Newfoundland | | Ontario | | Alberta | | Yukon | |
Offence Group	#	#	%	#	%	#	%	#	%	#	%
Total Offences	157 222	5481	3.5	248	5.2	4264	4.0	899	2.4	70	8.9
Criminal Code Total	140 173	4843	3.5	217	5.5	3716	3.9	843	2.5	67	9.0
Crimes Against the Person	28 821	1432	5.0	69	7.6	1104	5.2	226	4.1	33	22.4
Crimes Against Property	42 024	2293	5.5	95	6.9	1698	6.2	486	4.4	14	9.3
Other *Criminal Code* Violations	42 130	879	2.1	41	4.3	739	2.5	84	0.9	15	6.1
Criminal Code Traffic	27 198	239	0.9	12	1.6	175	1.1	47	0.6	5	2.5
Other Federal Statute Total	17 049	638	3.7	31	4.1	548	4.8	56	1.7	3	6.7

Note: Total convicted cases includes those for the four jurisdictions listed in this table.

Source: Statistics Canada, *Juristat*, Catalogue 85-002, vol. 21, no. 10, December 2001, p.11.

support of conditional sentences while the Court of Appeal in Alberta viewed the role of conditional sentences in a more conservative manner.

The Impact of Conditional Sentences

Have conditional sentences reduced the number of offenders sentenced to a period of imprisonment? When conditional sentences were introduced, supporters of this new type of sentence felt that incarceration rates would decrease. Critics argued that it would do the opposite: namely that judges would sentence offenders who would have previously received to probation to the "more severe" conditional sentences. The first analysis (Reed and Roberts 1999) indicated that they were helping decrease the use of incarceration, although the authors felt that caution was necessary before attributing this decrease to the introduction of conditional sentences. Yet, this decline in custodial

admissions "cannot be attributable to the introduction of conditional sentence, since ... admissions to custody had been declining for several years before conditional sentences were introduced" (Reed and Roberts 1999). Fewer offences are being committed, and as a result fewer charges are being laid; therefore fewer offenders are admitted to correctional facilities. But Reed and Roberts went on to point out that the best way to assess the impact of conditional sentences is to compare sentences of admission to both federal and provincial correctional facilities, since the percentage of these admissions "should have declined by the number of conditional sentences imposed" (Reed and Roberts 1999: 9).

Their analysis indicates that the total number of sentences of imprisonment handed down has changed little since conditional sentences were introduced in late 1996. Reed and Roberts found that, in the year prior to the establishment of conditional sentences, 35 percent of sentences imposed in eight jurisdictions across Canada involved a term of imprisonment; in 1997–98, with over

TABLE 10.3 Cases with a Conditional Sentence by Length of Sentence and Jurisdiction, 1999–2000

| | Total convicted cases | | | Length of conditional sentences | | | | | | | |
| | # of conditional sentences | % of total | 3 months or less | % | >3–6 months | % | >6–12 months | % | >12–24 months | % |
Jurisdiction										
Newfoundland	248	5.2	46	18.5	26	10.5	87	35.1	89	35.9
Ontario	4264	4.0	1435	33.7	1569	36.8	863	20.2	397	9.3
Alberta	899	2.4	99	11.0	296	32.9	281	31.3	223	24.8
Ontario	70	8.9	41	58.6	19	27.1	7	10.0	3	4.3

Source: Statistics Canada, *Juristat*, Catalogue 85-002, vol. 21, no. 10, December 2001, p.11.

22 000 conditional sentences imposed, the proportion of terms of imprisonment remained at 35 percent. Roach (2000: 26), after looking at the first two years of the use of conditional sentences, commented that the data "strongly suggests conditional sentences have resulted in net widening." However, Belanger (2001), after examining data on what type of sentences (e.g., custody, probation and conditional sentences) offenders received reported that the number of sentences to a term of custody dropped from 60 percent to 49 percent while the probation orders increased from 40 percent to 42 percent. This led Belanger (2001: 13) to conclude that "these data would imply that net widening is not occurring at the national level" (see Tables 10.2 and 10.3).

INTERMEDIATE SANCTIONS

Community corrections have traditionally used rehabilitation as a means to deal with offenders. Probation officers have been regarded as caseworkers or counselors whose primary responsibility is to assist offenders to adjust to society. Offender surveillance and control are minimal when compared to the levels of security and control required within the formal criminal justice system. During the past two decades, intermediate sanctions have been introduced in an attempt to introduce more control over those offenders released into the community.

Intermediate sanctions include programs usually administered by probation departments such as intensive supervision probation, home confinement, fines, electronic monitoring, and restitution orders. These sanctions are also referred to as "judicially administered sanctions" because it is judges who in most cases sentence offenders to these programs. Intermediate sanctions are outgrowths of justice model–based policies (see Chapter 3). One of the biggest issues with these programs if a large number of offenders serving these types of sentences recidivate and subsequently are placed into a correctional setting, because the savings would not be as large and the number of inmates would increase. If intermediate sanctions are to be successful, care must be taken to maintain a high quality of programs as well as the type of offenders who participate in them.

Intermediate sanctions were first introduced in the belief they would reduce prison overcrowding and substantially reduce the costs of placing offenders within the correctional system. Early advocates also believed such programs would protect the community by exerting more control over offenders than traditional probation services. It was hoped that the overall effect of these new forms of punishment would also deter potential offenders from committing crimes and assist in the rehabilitation of offenders by using mandatory treatment orders, reinforced by mandatory substance-abusing tests and the firm revocation of violators (Byrne et al. 1992).

Why are intermediate punishments so popular? First, there is the strong belief that the costs associated with these programs are somehow lower. The direct cost of administering and supervising an intermediate punishment program is generally thought to be much less than that of running a prison. Indirect cost savings result when offenders on intermediate sanctions are required to find employment, thereby generating income, paying taxes, and participating in community service projects and other such activities that would not be possible if they were imprisoned (Rackmill 1994).

Second, some jurisdictions require participants to help pay for the costs of the program. Byrne et al. (1989) point out that intensive supervision probationers usually have to pay a probation supervision fee of $10 to $50 per month, as well as any court-ordered fines and restitution payments. Intermediate punishments also save money by diverting large numbers of offenders from prison. Collectively, this would save millions of dollars each year.

Third, intermediate punishments can also result in sentences that are seen as fair, equitable, and proportional (Morris and Tonry 1990). Sending violent criminals to prison makes sense, but shouldn't those convicted of fraudulent offences be given a lighter punishment, albeit one that maintains some degree of control? Such a system, Tonry and Will (1990) argue, establishes fairness and equity in sentences not involving incarceration, as it can increase the punishment for those who are reconvicted of an offence but for whom a prison sentence is inappropriate. Intermediate punishments also provide stronger control than normal community supervision. In theory they lead to greater deterrence too, because the greater amount of surveillance makes it likely that anyone violating the terms of the program is caught and punished. Further, offenders under intermediate punishment should also commit fewer offences, because the conditions of the program limit their opportunities to engage in such activities. According to Petersilia and Turner (1993), closer surveillance will likely uncover more technical rule violations.

Critics argue that the benefits of intermediate punishments have not been achieved. Instead, they argue, these programs have brought about a new era of punitive punishments that simply incarcerate more offenders than before (Morris and Tonry 1990). Clear (1994) believes these new punishments reflect what he calls the "penal harm movement," a series of seven interrelated components based on the assumption that crime rates can be reduced if more offenders are punished and placed under the control of criminal justice agencies. His argument is related to net-widening as it believes more, not fewer, offenders will be placed into these programs.

The components of the "penal harm movement," when combined, create what Clear called the "punishment paradigm." The components in this paradigm are

1. The "root causes" of crime, such as social inequality, racism, and poverty, cannot be changed or have no relevance to the causes of crime.
2. Any programs developed and implemented to combat the root causes of crime are misplaced and will not reduce the crime rate.
3. Criminals will be deterred only if the criminal justice system ensures that they receive enough pain for their wrongs.
4. Prisons are an effective means of reducing crime because they keep criminals off the street.
5. Society will be much safer with large numbers of criminals in prison.
6. Offenders in the community should be controlled, not incarcerated, through a variety of programs known as intermediate punishments, such as house confinement, electronic monitoring, and intensive probation supervision.
7. If crime rates do not decrease, more punishment, community control, and prisons will be needed.

Intensive Supervision Probation

Intensive supervision probation (ISP) is the most common form of intermediate punishment today. It can be used across jurisdictions or for a specific program. For example, when Manitoba instituted its high-risk probationer program it contained an intensive supervision component. The popularity of ISPs stems from their perceived ability to reduce prison populations, eliminate the need for building costly new prisons, and prevent the negative impact of imprisonment on offenders. As well, they are seen as promoting public safety by ensuring that all offenders are subject to intensive surveillance, thereby reducing the opportunities for involvement in criminal activities (Petersilia 1987b).

What makes ISP so different from regular probation? The most commonly cited advantage is the small probation officer–client ratios, usually 15 to 40 clients per probation officer. According to Thompson (1985), other elements that characterize ISP programs are the following:

1. *Supervision is extensive.* Probation officers have multiple weekly face-to-face contacts with offenders, as well as collateral contacts with employers and family members and frequent arrest checks.
2. *Supervision is focused.* Monitoring activities concentrate on specific behavioural regulations governing curfews, drug use, travel, employment, and community service.
3. *Supervision is ubiquitous.* Offenders are frequently subjected to random drug tests and unannounced curfew checks.
4. *Supervision is graduated.* Offenders commonly proceed through ISP programs in a series of progressive phases—each of which represents a gradual tempering of the proscriptions and requirements of ISP—until they are committed to regular supervision as the final leg of their statutory time on probation.
5. *Supervision is strictly enforced.* Penalties for new arrest and noncompliance with program conditions are generally swift and severe.
6. *Supervision is coordinated.* ISP offenders are usually monitored by specially selected and trained officers who are part of a larger specialized, autonomous unit.

ISP programs are not designed for leniency but rather as punishment. As one policy-maker stated in reference to these programs, "we are in the business of increasing the heat on probationers … to satisfy the public's demand for just punishment … Criminals must be punished for their misdeeds" (Erwin 1986: 24).

ISP programs are not easy to participate in, because they usually involve several contacts with a probation officer every week, residence only in approved locations, random drug and alcohol tests, and one year's minimum involvement. In fact, due to the intrusive nature of these programs, many offenders choose not to participate when given the chance, even if the alternative is prison. Petersilia and Turner (1993) report that 25 percent of the Oregon offenders they studied who were eligible for an ISP program preferred prison instead.

Evaluations of ISPs

The results of these two state programs led to the rapid increase of ISPs across the United States and, to a lesser degree, Canada. Expectations were high. As Petersilia (1993) points out, the rapid expansion of ISP programs was based on a number of assumptions about how prison overcrowding, costs, and crime control would be affected if these programs were introduced. The first assumption was that a significant number of people are medium-risk offenders who should neither be placed on routine probation nor sent to prison. As a result, they should be placed in the community, but under more stringent conditions than those of regular probation programs.

The second assumption was that ISPs were cost-effective because fewer people would be sentenced to prison. It was also believed that ISPs could affect judges' overall sentencing practices; once they understood that these medium-risk offenders would be under tighter system control while serving their sentence in the community, judges might be willing to place these offenders into ISP programs.

The third assumption was that ISPs provide stronger crime control than regular probation but less control than prison. It was firmly believed that participants on ISPs would be deterred from committing crimes due to the tighter surveillance.

Three major findings consistently appeared in evaluations of ISPs. First, most ISP participants were not prison-bound offenders. In reality, many of the offenders who ended up on ISPs should have been placed into regular probation programs. This problem, from the perspective of those who created ISPs, was caused not by the original guidelines that outlined who was to be placed in these programs but rather by judges who ignored those guidelines and misused the intent of ISPs. Judges placed lower-risk offenders on ISPs and as a result ISPs "widened the net," since the proportion of people who went into regular probation programs and prison remained the same.

Second, ISP participants increased their rearrest rates after being placed under increased supervision. Instead of reducing criminal activity, ISP programs actually increased incarceration rates and system costs. Petersilia and Turner (1993) found little difference in rearrest rates after one year (38 percent for ISP participants and 36 percent for regular probationers). The study also revealed a much higher percentage of ISP participants were arrested for technical violations (70 percent versus 40 percent of regular probationers) and that, as a result, 27 percent of ISP participants were sent to a correctional facility after one year, compared with 19 percent of regular probationers.

The third finding that appeared in evaluations of ISP programs was that recidivism rates were reduced in those ISPs that included a rehabilitative component. Byrne and Kelly (1989: 37), for example, found that "58 percent of the offenders who demonstrated improvement in the area of substance abuse successfully completed the one year at risk, as compared with only 38 percent of those who did not improve." The researchers found that crime control could be achieved, but through the use of rehabilitation measures on the ISP programs.

Jolin and Stipak (1992) reported that drug treatment led to a significant reduction in offenders' drug use (from 95 percent at the time they started the program to 32 percent at the completion of the program). Latessa (1995) discovered that high-risk clients fared no worse, and sometimes better, than random samples of regular probationers when they participated in ISPs with a treatment component. Finally, treatment-based ISPs have been found to have a lower rate of recidivism than a matched group of regular probationers (21 percent versus 29 percent), a finding attributed to the fact that ISP participants received "significantly more treatment services" (Gendreau et al. 1994: 34). Gendreau and Little (1993), after systematically reviewing 175 evaluations of intermediate sanction programs concluded that "in essence, the supervision of high-risk probationers and parolees must be structured, [be] intensive, maintain firm accountability for program participation, and connect the offender with prosocial networks and activities."

HOME CONFINEMENT AND ELECTRONIC MONITORING

Home confinement (HC) and electronic monitoring (EM) are designed to restrict offenders to their place of residence. In home confinement offenders stay at their place of residence instead of in a correctional facility. In addition, the offender maintains family ties, continues employment, and can take advantage of community programs and resources.

A significant concern about HC is the issue of surveillance. How can correctional officials guarantee that offenders are following their probation orders and remaining at home during the designated times? This issue was solved by electronic monitoring, which informs officials at a central location if the offender is not following her home confinement agreement by violating a curfew order. By increasing the certainty of detection, it is hoped that EM will deter those sentenced to HC from reoffending.

As with ISP, HC and EM became popular within a few years. For example, in 1986 a total of 95 offenders were on EM programs in the United States. One year later this number increased to 2300 and, by 1992, 1200 different agencies were controlling over 45 000 monitorees (Maxfield and Baumer 1990). The interest in EM is largely due to projected cost savings together with effective surveillance of offenders released to serve their sentence in the community.

Canada has been slow to introduce house arrest and EM as standard components of its offender control system despite the ruling in *R. v. Proulx* (2000) that conditional sentences should include house arrest as the "norm, not the exception." In addition, the same ruling "virtually mandated the use of electronic monitoring as part of many conditional sentences" (Makin 2000: A8). Criticisms have been directed toward provincial governments for the slow rate of introduction of EM programs.

Electronic Monitoring Technology

Until recently, the most common form of EM technology did not involve any interaction or communication between those being monitored and those controlling the equipment. This system, referred to as a continuously signalling system, consists of three components. The offender wears a transmitter (usually on the ankle) that constantly emits a signal that is monitored by personnel in a central office. A receiver–dialer is attached to the telephone at the monitored location, usually the offender's place of residence. The receiver–dialer receives the signal from the transmitter and dials the central computer at the monitoring centre, where a computer records the absence or presence of an offender in his home during a designated time period. If the central computer discovers that the offender is not at home at the designated time, it prints out a message. When this occurs, a supervising officer is contacted and the authorities called (Ball, Huff, and Lilly 1988; Schmidt 1998).

In the second major form of EM, periodic calls are made to the offender's residence, and the offender's presence is verified using what is known as programmed contact equipment. A wide variety of equipment can be used for verification. In the system known as an "electronic handshake," the offender wears a device that is to be inserted into a piece of equipment attached to the telephone. Voice verification technology requires the offender to repeat certain words for which a voice-print was made when the offender entered the program. Another device is similar in design to a wristwatch, and beeps when the monitoring agency decides to randomly call the offender. When the offender receives the call, he calls a special telephone number and establishes his "caller ID" by pressing a button attached to the equipment. Other types of systems are used, including a drive-by system and a newly developed program that has the ability to track the offender by using a Global Positioning System.

Evaluations of Electronic Monitoring Programs

Low-risk offenders have been the traditional target group of HC and EM programs (Brown and Roy 1995). When these programs were first instituted in a large-scale manner in the United States, they were almost exclusively used for cases of driving while impaired (DWI) and driving under suspension (DUI). Successful program completion rates were high, with rates of 80 percent to 90 percent quite common. For example, in their analysis of EM programs for DWI and DUS offenders over a seven-year period, Lilly et al. (1993) found that the rate of successful completion exceeded 97 percent. According to the researchers, this rate of success is impressive, given the higher rates of EM violations during the early months and the increased surveillance of program participants. Research has consistently found a positive relationship between the age of traffic offenders and their EM success rates. In the Lilly et al. (1993) study, for example, the success rate for individuals 17–40 ranged between 74 and 84 percent, while the rate for those over 40 was between 85 and 92 percent.

The first Canadian use of EM occurred in British Columbia (British Columbia Department of Corrections 1995). Started as a pilot project in Vancouver in 1987, it was intended to provide a cheaper alternative to incarcerating selected offenders. In the initial study, 92 individuals in the Vancouver region were placed in an EM program. Only nonviolent offenders were allowed to participate, and the majority of the offenders (90 percent), had been convicted for DWI and DUS, and all had at least one prior conviction. While the EM sentences varied between 7 and 90 days, almost 50 percent of the program participants were placed on the program for 10 to 15 days. All offenders completed their EM sentence successfully. These results led to an expansion of the program and, by 1992, EM was available throughout the province except in sparsely populated areas. By 1996, there were approximately 300 offenders participating in EM programs. Reports at that time indicated that the program was indeed cheaper than sending offenders to a correctional facility (Mainprize 1992; 1995).

These success rates have led policy-makers to experiment with placing more serious offenders on HC and EM programs. Newfoundland conducted an EM program operating with higher-risk offenders in which the offenders were required to attend an intensive treatment program. After one year, the recidivism rate (defined as rearrest, reconviction, and imprisonment/reimprisonment) for the group was 26.7 percent, lower than that for probationers and a group of inmates. This extra programming "may explain the lower than expected recidivism rate for this group" (Bonta et al. 2000: 72).

To date, most EM programs in Canada are found in British Columbia, Saskatchewan, and Newfoundland. Four provinces—Alberta, Quebec, New Brunswick, and Nova Scotia—do not use EM; the other provinces use it, but only on a limited basis. For example, in the fall of 1999, Ontario had only 65 to 70 offenders participating in its EM program. The use of EM in Canada is limited due to its unavailability to the judiciary or to political concerns about public safety. In British Columbia, for example, EM is a decision made by correctional authorities only when inmates are being released from custody. Another reason is the concern held by provincial authorities about law and order and public safety issues rather than issues about reintegrating low-risk offenders back into the community. Many judges, given the appropriate type of offender and criminal offence, may decide to use EM if it was available as a sentencing option, especially for conditional sentences. For example, in 1999 the Ontario Court of Appeal commented that EM could be used more often, a decision that is not shared by provincial authorities (Makin 1999).

Has EM been successful in Canada? In a recent evaluation of the EM programs in British Columbia, Saskatchewan, and Newfoundland, Bonta et al. (1999) compared a total of 262 participants in EM programs with a group of offenders who were either incarcerated or placed on probation. The recidivism rate for the individuals placed on EM was 26.7 percent for the EM participants, 33.3 percent for the probationers, and 37.9 percent for those placed into custody. However, the researchers found the EM participants had lower recidivism rates due to the fact that they were lower-risk offenders and were therefore better risks not to recidivate. When the researchers introduced into their analyses the risk levels of all the offenders they studied, the differences in the recidivism rates could not be attributed to the type of sanction. With this discovery the researchers concluded that EM programs do not reduce the recidivism of offenders more effectively than custody or probation. It also raised questions about net-widening, specifically whether EM programs are targeting low-risk offenders who would have received a community sanction. The researchers' findings led them to question whether EM programs are more cost-effective, whether they really contribute to greater public safety, and whether attempts to reduce criminal behaviour are better served by treatment programs.

Other criticisms of EM have been raised in the United States. In their study of drinking drivers on HC and EM, Baumer et al. (1990) uncovered no significant differences in recidivism rates of high-risk probationers supervised by EM and those under "manual" supervision (20.5 percent for EM and 18.3 percent for the manual supervision program). They also found that 42 percent of each group had violated the terms of their programs by being absent when they should have been at home. This led the researchers to conclude that EM programs do not guarantee reduced recidivism rates compared with manual programs. In another study comparing EM program participants with offenders under manual supervision, Brown and Roy (1995) found the experimental group to be more likely to complete their home confinement sentence, although the difference in the rate of failures (18 versus 22 percent) was not substantial. One of the conclusions of this study was that EM was more effective when used with a specific type of offender, namely those who were unemployed and unmarried.

The Impact of Home Confinement and Electronic Monitoring Programs

Clear and Hardyman (1990) stated that early supporters of intermediate punishment programs such as ISP had exaggerated claims that such programs would bring about a revolution in corrections—that is, better crime control, reduced prison populations, fiscal savings, and greater public safety. Of course, more modest claims—for example, that there are little, if any, cost savings, and only a minimal increase in public safety—would lead to diminished support for these programs, and thus the implementation of these programs would be in question.

Because ISP, as well as HC and EM programs, have been viewed as panaceas to the control of crime, little attention was initially placed on the clarity of these programs' goals, making it difficult for researchers to state whether a program has been successful in reaching its goals. As Tonry (1990: 180) has commented, ISP programs have succeeded, not in terms of achieving their stated goals, but rather in serving "latent bureaucratic, organizational, political, professional, and psychological goals of probation departments and officers."

Bonta et al. (2000: 73) believe that the impact of EM varies with the intended outcomes. If such a program is designed purely to achieve program completion, then the surveillance and control nature of EM "may ensure that offenders complete a period of supervision without incident." In fact, they found that completion rates were high on the various provincial programs regardless of the amount of time offenders spent on them (from an average of 37.3 days in British Columbia to 71.6 days in Newfoundland and 139.3 days in Saskatchewan). However, if the desired outcome of an EM program is to reduce recidivism, Bonta et al. state that "EM has questionable merit."

FINES

Since 1996–97, the imposition of sentences involving fines has decreased in Canada. In 2000–01, 37 percent of convicted cases received a fine, compared to 44 percent in 1996–997. In addition, during these same years there has been a trend of higher fines: in 1996–97, 21 percent of all fines were for over $500; in 2000–01, this had increased to 42 percent. The median amount for all fines in 1996–97 was $300; in 2000–01, the median amount had increased to $400 (see Table 10.4) (Thomas 2002). In Canada, fines can be imposed alone or in conjunction with other sanctions, with the exception of two offences: if the offence carries a minimum or a maximum penalty of more than five years, the offender cannot receive a fine alone. Not surprisingly, fines are rarely used as the most severe sanction in the category of crimes against the person.

According to adult court statistics for 1999–00, fines were most commonly imposed when they were used as a single sanction; 45 percent of offenders required to pay a fine received no other punishment. Slightly more than one-third of all fines (36 percent) were imposed in impaired driving cases. A fine was imposed in 41 percent of cases with convictions; however, only 2 percent of offenders who received a prison sentence had to pay a fine as well. Fines were used in 19 percent of single conviction cases involving violence (the average fine amount was $419). Figure 10.2 illustrates the single conviction cases involving *Criminal Code* offences that have fines imposed most frequently. The highest average fine amount ($656) was found in the offence of impaired driving (86 percent of these cases involved a fine at sentencing) (Belanger 2001).

Questions about the fairness of fines have surfaced over the past few decades in Canada. In most jurisdictions, judges receive little guidance about how and on whom to impose fines, but it is agreed that once the facts of a case are considered, judges use fines as a sanction in an appropriate manner. For example, low-risk offenders are more likely to receive a fine instead of incarceration as a sanction. However, judges often make decisions with little information about the offender's ability to pay, which results in a significant number of people defaulting on paying the fines imposed on them and ending up in a provincial or territorial correctional facility. In 1997–98, just over one-fifth (22 percent) of

all admissions to these facilities were for failing to pay a fine. Although this was a 4 percent reduction from the previous year, Reed and Roberts (1999) indicate that admissions to custody for fine default have decreased in Canada only slightly over the past 15 years. In 1981–82, for example, 29 percent of all admissions to provincial and territorial facilities were for fine default. Jurisdictions in Canada vary in their use of incarceration for those who default on a fine; in 1997–98 the number of individuals incarcerated in a provincial facility for failing to pay a fine ranged from 1 percent in Newfoundland and 2 percent in Ontario to 33 percent in Alberta and 57 percent in Quebec.

Some provincial governments created fine option programs in the 1970s in an attempt to create alternatives for people who could not pay the fines imposed on them by the court. (Community service was a common option.) According to the report on fines made by the Law Reform Commission (1975), fines can have a discriminatory impact upon poor offenders. The

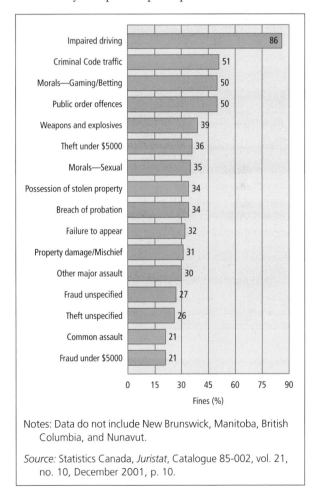

Notes: Data do not include New Brunswick, Manitoba, British Columbia, and Nunavut.

Source: Statistics Canada, *Juristat*, Catalogue 85-002, vol. 21, no. 10, December 2001, p. 10.

FIGURE 10.2

Fines in Selected Single-Conviction Offences, Nine Provinces and Territories in Canada, 1999–2000

TABLE 10.4	Convicted Cases by Median Prison and Probation Sentence and Fine Amount, Selected Provinces and Territories in Canada, 1996/97 to 2000/01

	1996/97			1997/98			1998/99			1999/00			2000/01		
	Prison	Probation	Fine	Prison	Probation	Fine	Prison	Probation	Fine	Prison	Probation	Fine	Prison	Probation	Fine
Offence Group	median (days)	median (days)	median ($)	median (days)	median (days)	median (days)	median (days)	median (days)	median ($)	median (days)	median (days)	median ($)	median (days)	median (days)	median ($)
Total Offences	40	365	300	40	365	300	45	365	300	30	365	300	30	365	400
***Criminal Code* Total**	30	365	300	30	365	350	31	365	350	30	365	400	30	365	500
Crimes Against the Person	90	365	300	90	365	300	90	365	300	90	365	300	90	365	300
Homicide and related	2190	730	250	2555	730	275	2190	913	525	2190	725	500	2780	540	700
Attempted Murder	900	1080	500	1148	730	0	1080	1095	11750	1620	1095	1000	1935	730	9400
Robbery	540	730	300	540	730	350	540	730	300	540	730	300	540	730	400
Kidnapping	180	730	1500	180	730	425	270	730	350	180	730	500	393	730	500
Sexual Assault	270	730	500	270	730	500	360	730	500	300	730	500	360	730	500
Sexual Abuse	180	730	500	222	730	500	210	730	500	240	730	500	360	730	500
Major Assault	90	540	300	90	540	300	90	540	350	90	450	325	90	540	400
Abduction	180	730	125	89	720	450	30	730	600	180	453	50	30	365	0
Common Assault	30	365	250	45	365	300	45	365	300	45	365	300	36	365	300
Crimes Against Property	60	365	200	60	365	200	60	365	200	60	365	200	60	365	250
Break and Enter	180	730	300	180	720	300	180	540	300	180	540	300	180	540	375
Arson	270	730	500	270	730	325	285	730	300	300	730	500	270	730	400
Fraud	60	450	200	60	365	200	70	365	200	60	365	250	60	365	250
Possess Stolen Property	60	365	300	60	365	300	60	365	300	60	365	300	60	365	300
Theft	30	365	200	30	365	200	30	365	200	30	365	200	30	365	200
Property Damage/Mischief	30	365	200	30	365	200	30	365	200	30	365	200	30	365	200
Other *Criminal Code* Violations	30	365	200	30	365	200	30	365	200	30	365	200	24	365	200
Weapons	60	365	200	90	365	200	60	365	250	60	365	250	60	365	250
Administration of Justice	20	365	150	20	365	150	20	365	150	17	365	150	15	365	150
Public Order Offences	15	360	200	15	360	200	30	360	200	30	360	200	20	360	200
Morals—sexual	15	365	200	10	365	200	12	365	200	10	365	200	10	365	250
Morals—gaming	3	360	750	7	360	750	16	360	1000	90	360	1000	75	365	1500
Unspecified *Criminal Code*	30	365	200	30	365	200	30	365	200	30	365	200	30	365	250
***Criminal Code* Traffic**	30	360	500	30	360	500	30	360	200	30	360	600	30	360	700
Other *Criminal Code* traffic	30	365	500	35	360	500	30	360	500	45	360	500	30	360	600
Impaired Driving	30	360	500	30	360	500	30	360	500	30	360	600	30	360	700
Other Federal Statute Total	70	365	150	80	365	150	90	365	200	60	365	200	60	365	200

Notes: Revised figures for 1996/97, 1997/98, and 1998/99. Revisions were made to the calculation of median prison sentence lengths in 1999/00 and the previous three years were recalculated using the same formula. Excludes cases where the length of prison was not known, and cases where the length was specified as indeterminate. Cases sentenced to life imprisonment were recoded to 9125 days (or 25 years) for the calculation of sentence length medians.

Adult Criminal Court Survey data are not reported by New Brunswick, Manitoba, British Columbia, Nunavut for all years, and Northwest Territories for 1996/97 and 2000/01.

Source: Statistics Canada, *Juristat*, Catalogue 85-002, vol. 22, no. 2, March 2002, p. 12.

Commission noted that 57.4 percent of Aboriginal admissions to provincial institutions in Saskatchewan in 1970–71 were for nonpayment of fines, as compared with 24.7 percent of non-Aboriginal admissions. The inability to pay fines is a significant reason why Aboriginal offenders are overrepresented in provincial and territorial correctional facilities; since Aboriginals experience high rates of unemployment (between 60 and 90 percent) in their communities, fines are not reasonable options for them (Frideres and Robertson 1994: 110). As the Alberta Task Force on the Criminal Justice System and Its Impact on the Indian and Metis People of Alberta (Alberta 1991) stated, the use of custody for fine defaulters does not fulfill the principle of proportionality and the purposes of sentencing, such as the protection of the community and deterrence.

One solution for avoiding the incarceration of fine defaulters was to have defence counsel introduce information about the accused's ability to pay a fine into the court record, subject to cross-examination by the Crown prosecutor. It was also possible for a judge to request this information to be included in a presentence report. Bill C-41 simplified the process of including such information when it introduced the provision that the court "may fine an offender under this section [s. 734] only if the court is satisfied that the offender is able to pay the fine." If the offender cannot pay, other alternative sanctions are to be considered, including probation, a conditional sentence, an absolute or conditional discharge, or incarceration.

Another alternative is day fines. The concept of day fines was first introduced in Finland in 1921 and is based on the idea that fines can be a sentence that satisfies the idea of proportionality by assessing an offender's net income as well as the seriousness of the crime. Day fines (in contrast to the current fixed-fine system) are weighted by a daily-income value taken from a chart similar to an income tax table; the offender's number of dependents is also considered. Evaluations of day fine programs in the United States have found that they are generally successful, increasing the amount of money collected from fines while at the same time reducing the number of arrest warrants for failure to pay. Even if the fine could not be paid in full, most offenders paid at least some of the amount they owed to the state (Hillsman (1990).

INTERMEDIATE SANCTIONS: HOW WELL DO THEY WORK?

In 1985, intermediate sanctions were called the future of corrections (Sawyer 1985). But have they lived up to this original potential? Over 15 years later, we have the ability to examine whether they have reached their goals, particularly in the areas of reducing prison populations, saving money, and deterring crime. The results of several Canadian and U.S. evaluations are reviewed below in order to assess the success or failure of these programs.

Do Intermediate Sanctions Reduce Prison Crowding?

This issue is perhaps the most critical for introducing intermediate sanction, as advocates argue that the number of offenders incarcerated will decrease. However, as Morris and Tonry (1990: 223–34) point out, this position is based on the belief that most individuals convicted of a serious crime are sent to prison, an assumption they point out is incorrect because "most felonies never were or are not now punished by imprisonment." They claim that offenders placed on intermediate sanctions would usually be placed on regular probation programs or on suspended sentences rather than being sent to prison. In addition, evaluations of intermediate sanctions have revealed high rearrest rates for offenders, with the result that some states report at best only a 50 percent success rate of offenders completing the program (Erwin and Bennett 1987). Researchers have also discovered that intermediate sanctions have had only a minor impact on the total prison population. For example, Petersilia (1987a) found that Georgia's ISP (intensive supervision probation) "saved" 186 prison beds in a year, a number Tonry (1990) estimates would be unlikely to significantly reduce prison crowding. Petersilia (1987b), in her review of five electronic monitoring programs, discovered that the majority of the individuals who ended up in them were not from prison, but rather were on regular probation programs. With few exceptions, "participants in the program had only been convicted of misdemeanors" (Johnson et al. 1989: 156–57).

Are Intermediate Sanctions a Cost-Saving Alternative?

One of the most common arguments for implementing intermediate sanction programs is that they cost less than incarceration programs. Most of these arguments are based on average per-offender costs, which many have pointed out is a misleading unit of analysis on which to evaluate the financial savings of an intermediate sanction program. One reason for this is the length of time offenders are sentenced to prison or to an intermediate sanction program. Morris and Tonry (1990) point out that directly comparing costs is misleading because if the average offender serves 12 months on an intermediate sanction program at a total cost of $3000 but would otherwise have served three months in prison at a final cost of $4000, the intermediate sanction program costs more, not less.

Comparing per-offender costs is also misleading because there is an assumption that all offenders are diverted into intermediate sanctions from prison. However, many intermediate sanction participants (a figure that varies from 50 percent to 80 percent, depending on the type and location of the program) are diverted from regular probation programs. According to Tonry (1990: 182), intermediate sanction programs "costs per day are six times higher than the cost of ordinary probation." Moreover, the higher the number of individuals placed into an intermediate sanction program directly from the courts, the lesser the savings because fewer people are being taken out of prison.

Furthermore, most cost comparisons look only at the costs of building a new prison but ignore the cost of operating an intermediate sanction program, which is labour-intensive. If 25 offenders on an intermediate sanction program require the hiring and training of four to eight new employees, this "increases direct outlays in the form of salaries and expanded overhead expenses, but also produces longer-term financial commitments in the form of employment benefits and pensions" (U.S. General Accounting Office 1990: 27).

When all costs, both direct and marginal, are factored in, any savings may be limited. For example, Petersilia and Turner (1993: 309) studied 14 programs and reported that in "no site did intermediate sanction programs result in cost-savings during the one year follow-up period." This was due mainly to the large number of technical violations, revocations, and incarcerations and the cost of court appearances, resulting in costs up to twice as high as those for routine probation and parole supervision.

In their study of home confinement in Arizona, Palumbo et al. (1992) discovered that, due to organizational operating problems, the actual cost of the program exceeded the cost of prison. They determined that the key factor in the higher rate of costs was that while the intermediate sanction programs were increasing the number of program participants, the prisons remained overcrowded. As Palumbo et al. (1992: 238) report, if "an alternative is not used as a way of reducing the total number of prison beds in use, or to eliminate some of these institutions, then alternatives to incarceration cannot be cost-effective." This reasoning is supported by Tonry (1990: 180), who, after analyzing the full potential of the cost-saving measures of intermediate sanction programs, came to the conclusion that "only when the numbers of people diverted from prison by a new program permit the closing of all or a major part of an institution or the cancellation of construction plans will there be substantial savings."

Another argument made for the cost-effectiveness of intermediate punishments is that many of them charge a fee to the offenders participating in them. Renzema and Skelton (1990: 14) point out that, in the programs they reviewed, approximately 67 percent of all offenders pay fees. The average cost is $200 a month, with probationers paying "an average of $155 a month while inmates pay an average of $228 a month. A few programs charge clients as much as $15 a day for monitoring."

Tonry (1990) points out a significant error made by those who evaluate the cost savings of intermediate sanction programs: they fail to include the cost of recidivists in their analysis. Since offenders on these programs may be caught for technical violations or new crimes and be sent to prison, the additional time incarcerated also has to be factored into any comparison of costs. With recidivism rates at about 40 to 50 percent, taking incarceration time into account in the cost-benefit analysis would substantially increase the costs of these programs.

Can Intermediate Sanctions Control Crime?

The third major issue raised by advocates of intermediate sanction programs is their effectiveness in controlling crime. They argue that more intensive supervision will, of necessity, reduce crime. Basing their arguments on the recidivism rates reported in early evaluation studies, they stress that these programs have the potential both to "control offenders in the community and to facilitate their growth to crime-free lives" (Morris and Tonry 1990).

However, some studies have discovered that many offenders released from intermediate sanction programs committed serious crimes once they were released into the community. Even low-risk offenders on intermediate sanction programs have been found to reoffend at a high rate on release. For example, almost 27 percent of offenders in three provinces recidivated, although they had lower risk levels than either the inmates or probationers they were being compared to. According to Bonta et al. (2000), the lower recidivism rate of those involved with EM programs is explained by the lower risk of the offender. Numerous studies (Petersilia and Turner 1993; Wallerstedt 1984) have found that individuals released from programs often have high recidivism rates and that many of their offences are serious crimes. In addition, many researchers have reported that these programs fail to result in any reduction in crime rates. Pearson (1986: 443–44), for example, concluded that "we can be confident that intermediate sanction programs at least did not increase recidivism rates."

In one of the most comprehensive analyses of its kind, Petersilia and Turner (1993) reported that in the 14 intermediate sanction programs they studied, no participants were rearrested less often, had a longer time before being rearrested, or were arrested for less serious offences than those individuals on regular probation. When the researchers included technical violations in their recidivism measure, "the record for intermediate sanction programs looks somewhat grimmer" (Petersilia and Turner 1993: 310–11). Approximately 65 percent of the offenders on these programs recorded a technical violation, in comparison with 38 percent of those offenders on regular probation. The researchers also found no support for the argument that offenders arrested for technical violations reduced the incidence of any future criminal acts.

Do Intermediate Sanctions Work?

The concerns raised about alternative sanctions do not mean that they should be abandoned. Perhaps there was too great an expectation that these programs would somehow "save" the current correctional crisis by reducing prison populations and recidivism and making communities safer. As Finckenhauer (1982) has noted, the history of corrections is filled with great expectations but, at the same time, littered with failed panaceas. New programs are attractive because they always promise to do so much, at a minimal cost. When programs are poorly conceived and implemented and, as a result, fail to reach their goals, it is not surprising that they are labelled as another program that "didn't work."

Yet a number of important lessons can be learned by examining the rise and growth of alternative correctional programs, particularly the rapid growth in intermediate sanctions. The number of offenders entering the correctional system is beyond the control of criminal justice officials. Political demands for tougher penalties and a "war on crime" can have a significant impact on the operation of all facets of our criminal justice system. The police are under more pressure to arrest and charge more alleged criminals; the courts are under more pressure to deal with these alleged offenders more speedily. But when offenders enter the correctional system, often with long sentences, correctional officials have a hard time knowing where to put them.

The justice model underlies these intermediate sanction programs. The results to date have revealed not only that specific programs do not reach their objectives, but also that the justice model belief that alternative sanctions are the best way to deal with minor offenders is open to question. However, evidence shows that some intermediate punishment programs, when merged with rehabilitation-based principles, achieve more favourable results (Gendreau et al. 1994).

Researchers who have evaluated programs and have seen the high rates of recidivism in these programs recommend the inclusion of rehabilitation. For example, in their study of the Florida Community Control Program, Smith and Akers (1993: 228) noted that "a more persuasive model might move back in the direction of community reintegration and propose that occupation skill enhancement, education, substance abuse treatment, behavior modification and other practices be added to the principle of closely supervising home confinement." And in their analysis of the 14 sites experimenting with intermediate supervision probation, Petersilia and Turner (1993: 321) report that in the three California locations included in their study, offenders who "received counseling, held jobs, paid restitution, and did community service were arrested 10–20 percent less often than were other offenders."

These comments are consistent with a growing literature on the importance of introducing effective rehabilitative components into intermediate sanction programs. Any such program would have to identify which offenders would receive treatment. This means that the principles of risk, need, and responsivity must be introduced (see Chapter 12) (Andrews et al. 1990). As Petersilia and Turner (1993: 320) point out, placing drug-dependent offenders into an ISP (intensive supervision probation) program that "forbids drug use, provides frequent drug testing, and provides no assured access to drug treatment virtually guarantees high violation rates." The potential for intermediate sanctions with a strong rehabilitative component exists, but only if they "provide the opportunity to channel offenders into treatments that address criminogenic needs—sources of criminality that are not targeted and affected by surveillance and punishment" (Cullen et al. 1995).

SUMMARY

Intermediate sanctions have developed rapidly to service the needs of both the social control system and offenders. These types of sanctions fall between incarceration and probation, filling a need for the state to have a significant amount of control over offenders, but, at the same time, enable offenders to live in the community. This allows governments to save money and give the appearance that sentences are more fair.

The most common form of intermediate sanction is intensive supervision probation, which is characterized by close contact between probation officers and their clients. Home confinement is increasing in popularity, and is usually accompanied by an electronic monitoring device. Day fines are another alternative, usually directed toward offenders who are unable to pay a fixed fine due to their employment status.

To date, advocates say that these programs have successfully met their goals. Researchers are much more cautious in their conclusions, although they have identi-fied many program components as being crucial factors in reducing future criminality. Despite their successes or failures, these programs continue to be used in the hope that they will be low-cost, high-security alternatives to traditional approaches of punishment.

Discussion Questions

1. Is home confinement a "real" punishment? Explain your answer.

2. Compare and contrast "regular" probation with intensive supervision probation.

3. Do intermediate punishments reduce crime? Give reasons for your answer.

4. What are the most successful aspects of intermediate punishment programs?

5. Why do you think Canada has been slower to introduce intermediate punishments than the United States?

6. Compare and contrast EM programs that use the continuously signalling system with EM programs using programmed contact equipment.

7. Do intermediate punishments really assist in reintegrating offenders back into society? Explain.

8. Discuss the goals of intermediate punishments. Why were they introduced?

Suggested Readings

Byrne, J.M., A.J. Lurigio, and J. Petersilia, eds. 1992. *Smart Sentencing: The Emergence of Intermediate Sanctions.* Newbury Park, Calif.: Sage.

Ellsworth, T., ed. 1996. *Contemporary Community Corrections,* 2nd ed. Prospect Heights, Ill.: Waveland Press.

Hartland, A.T., ed. 1995. *The Search for Effective Correctional Interventions.* Newbury Park, Calif.: Sage.

Morris, N., and M. Tonry. 1990. *Beyond Prison and Probation: Intermediate Punishments in a Rational Sentencing System.* New York: Oxford University Press.

Smykla, J., and W.L. Selke. 1995. *Intermediate Sanctions: Sentencing in the 1990s.* Cincinnati, Ohio: Anderson.

Tonry, M., and K. Hamilton, eds. 1995. *Intermediate Sanctions in Overcrowded Times.* Boston, Mass.: Northeastern University Press.

References

Alberta. 1991. *Report of the Task Force on the Criminal Justice System and Its Impact on the Indian and Metis People of Alberta,* vol. 1. Edmonton.

Andrews, D.A., J. Bonta, and R.D. Hoge. 1990. "Classification for Effective Rehabilitation: Rediscovering Psychology." *Criminal Justice and Behavior* 17: 19–52.

Ball, R.A., C.R. Huff, and J.R. Lilly. 1988. *House Arrest and Correctional Policy: Doing Time at Home.* Newbury Park, Calif.: Sage.

Baumer, T.L., R.I. Mendelsohn, and C. Rhine. 1990. *The Electronic Monitoring of Non-Violent Convicted Felons: An Experiment in Home Detention: Executive Summary.* Washington, D.C.: National Institute of Justice.

Belanger, B. 2001. *Sentencing in Adult Criminal Courts 1999/00.* Ottawa: Canadian Centre for Justice Statistics.

Birkenmayer, A. 1995. *The Use of Community Corrections in Canada: 1993–1994.* Ottawa: Juristat.

Blatchford, C. 2002. "Overdose, Not Heat, Killed Welfare Recipient." *National Post,* August 15, A1–A10.

Bonta, J., J. Rooney, and S. Wallace-Capretta. 1999. *Electronic Monitoring in Canada.* Ottawa: Public Works and Government Services Canada.

Bonta, J., S. Wallace-Capretta, and J. Rooney. 2000. "Can Electronic Monitoring Make a Difference? An Evaluation of Three Canadian Programs." *Crime and Delinquency* 46: 61–75.

British Columbia Department of Corrections. 1995. "British Colombia Corrections Branch Electronic Monitoring Program." In K. Schulz, ed., *Electronic Monitoring and Corrections: The Policy, the Operation, the Research.* Burnaby, B.C.: Simon Fraser University, pp. 53–58.

Brookbank, C., and B. Kingsley. 1998. *Adult Criminal Court Statistics, 1997–98.* Ottawa: Canadian Centre for Justice Statistics.

Brown, M.P., and S. Roy. 1995. "Manual and Electronic House Arrest: An Evaluation of Factors Related to Failure." In J. Smykla and W.L. Selke, eds., *Intermediate Sanctions: Sentencing in the 1990s.* Cincinnati: Anderson.

Byrne, J.M., and L. Kelly. 1989. *Restructuring Probation as an Intermediate Punishment: An Evaluation of the Implementation and Impact of the Massachusetts Intensive Probation Supervision Program: Final Report.* Washington, D.C.: National Institute of Justice.

Byrne, J.M., A. Lurigio, and J. Petersilia. 1992. "Introduction: The Emergence of Intermediate Sanctions." In Byrne, Lurigio, and Petersilia, eds. *Smart Sentencing.* Newbury Park, Calif: Sage, pp. ix–xv.

Byrne, J.M., A.J. Lurigio, and C. Baird. 1989. "The Effectiveness of the New Intensive Supervision Programs." *Research in Corrections* 2, no. 2: 1–48.

Clear, T. 1994. *Harm in American Penology: Offenders, Victims, and Their Communities.* Albany, N.Y.: SUNY.

Clear, T., and P. Hardyman. 1990. "The New Intensive Supervision Movement." *Crime and Delinquency* 36: 42–60.

Cullen, F.T., J.P. Wright, and B.K. Applegate. 1995. "Control in the Community: The Limits of Reform?" In A.J. Hartland, ed., *The Search for Effective Correctional Interventions.* Newbury Park, Calif.: Sage.

Daubney, D., and G. Parry. 1999. "An Overview of Bill C-41 (The *Sentencing Reform Act*)." In J.V. Roberts and D.P. Cole, eds., *Making Sense of Sentencing.* Toronto: University of Toronto Press, pp. 31–47.

Erwin, B.S. 1987. *Final Evaluation Report: Intensive Probation Supervision in Georgia.* Atlanta, Ga.: Georgia Department of Corrections.

———. 1986. "Turning up the Heat on Probationers in Georgia." *Federal Probation* 50: 17–24.

Erwin, B.S., and L.A. Bennett. 1987. "New Dimensions in Probation: Georgia's Experience with Intensive Probation Supervision (ISP)." *Research in Brief.* Washington, D.C.: U.S. Government Printing Office.

Finckenhauer, J.Q. 1982. *Scared Straight! and the Panacea Phenomenon.* Engelwood Cliffs, N.J.: Prentice-Hall.

Foran, T. 1995. "A Descriptive Comparison of Demographic and Family Characteristics of the Canadian and Offender Populations." *Forum of Corrections Research* 7: 3–5.

Frideres, J.S., and B. Robertson. 1994. "Aboriginals and the Criminal Justice System: Australia and Canada." *International Journal of Contemporary Sociology* 31: 101–27.

Gendreau, P., F.T. Cullen, and J. Bonta. 1994. "Intensive Rehabilitation Supervision: The Next Generation in Community Corrections?" *Federal Probation* 58: 72–78.

Gendreau, P., and T. Little. 1993. "A Meta-analysis of the Effectiveness of Sanctions on Offender Recidivism." Unpublished manuscript, University of New Brunswick, Saint John, N.B.

Gendreau, P., M. Papparozzi, T. Little, and M. Goddard. 1993. "Does Punishing Smarter Work? An Assessment of the New Generation of Alternative Sanctions in Probation." *Forum on Corrections Research* 5: 31–34.

Hillsman, S.T. 1990. "Fines and Day Fines." In M. Tonry and N. Norris, eds., *Crime and Justice: A Review of Research,* vol. 12. Chicago: University of Chicago Press, pp. 49–98.

Integration and Analysis Unit. 1999. *Sex Offenders.* Ottawa: Canadian Centre for Justice Statistics.

Johnson, B.R., L. Haugen, J.W. Maness, and P.P. Ross. 1989. "Attitudes towards Electronic Monitoring of Offenders: A Study of Probation Officers and Prosecutors." *Journal of Contemporary Criminal Justice* 5: 153-64.

Jolin, A., and B. Stipak. 1992. "Drug Treatment and Electronically Monitored Home Confinement: An Evaluation of the Community-Based Sentencing Option." *Crime and Delinquency* 38: 158–70.

Langan, R. 1994. "Between Prison and Probation: Intermediate Sanctions." *Science* 264: 791–93.

LaPrairie, C. 1999. *Conditional Sentence Orders by Province and Territory.* Ottawa: Department of Justice.

Latessa, E. 1995. "An Evaluation of the Lucas County Adult Probation Departments ISP and High Risk Groups." In A.T. Hartland, ed., *The Search for Effective Correctional Interventions.* Newbury Park, Calif.: Sage.

Law Reform Commission of Canada. 1975. *Criminal Procedure: Control of the Process.* Ottawa: Minister of Supply and Services Canada.

Lilly, J.R., R.A. Ball, G.D. Curry, and J. McMullan. 1993. "Electronic Monitoring of the Drunk Driver: A Seven-Year Study of the Home Confinement Alternative." *Crime and Delinquency* 39: 462–84.

Lonmo, C. 2001. *Adult Correctional Services in Canada 1999/00.* Ottawa: Canadian Centre for Justice Statistics.

Mainprize, S. 1995. "Social, Psychological, and Familial Impacts of Home Confinement and Electronic Monitoring: Exploratory Research Findings from British Columbia's Pilot Project." In K. Schulz, ed., *Electronic Monitoring and Corrections: The Policy, the Operation, the Research.* Burnaby, B.C.: Simon Fraser University, pp. 141–87.

———. 1992. "Electronic Monitoring in Corrections: Assessing the Cost Effectiveness and the Potential for Widening the Net of Social Control." *Canadian Journal of Criminology* 34: 161–80.

Makin, K. 2000. "Judge Blasts Ontario's Monitoring of Convicts." *The Globe and Mail,* 28 January, A8.

———. 1999. "Fear Limits Use of Electronic Monitoring." *The Globe and Mail,* 11 October, A3.

Maxfield, M.G., and T.L. Baumer. 1990. "Home Detention with Electronic Monitoring." *Crime and Delinquency* 36: 521–36.

Morgan, K. 1994. "Factors Associated with Probation Outcome." *Journal of Criminal Justice* 22: 341–53.

Morris, N., and M. Tonry. 1990. *Between Prison and Probation: Intermediate Punishments in a Rational Sentencing System.* New York: Oxford University Press.

Palumbo, D.J., M. Clifford, and Z.D. Snyder-Joy. 1992. "From Net-Widening to Intermediate Sanctions: The Transformation of Alternatives to Incarceration from Benevolence to Malevolence." In J.M. Byrne, A.J. Lurigio, and J. Petersilia, eds., *Smart Sentencing: The Emergence of Intermediate Sanctions.* Newbury Park, Calif.: Sage, pp. 229–44.

Pearson, F. 1987a. "Evaluation of New Jersey's Intensive Supervision Program." *Crime and Delinquency* 34: 437–48.

———. 1987b. *Preliminary Findings of Research on New Jersey's Intensive Supervision Program.* New Brunswick, N.J.: Rutgers University Press.

———. 1986. *Research on New Jersey's Intensive Supervision Program: Final Report.* Washington, D.C.: National Institute of Justice.

Petersilia, J. 1998. "A Decade of Experimenting with Intermediate Sanctions: What Have We Learned?" *Federal Probation* 62: 3–9.

———. 1993. "Measuring the Performance of Community Corrections." *Performance Measures for the Criminal Justice System.* Washington, D.C.: U.S. Department of Justice.

———. 1987a. "Georgia's Intensive Probation: Will the Model Work Elsewhere?" In B. McCarthy, ed., *Intermediate Punishments: Intensive Supervision, Home Confinement and Electronic Monitoring.* Monsey, N.Y.: Criminal Justice Press, pp. 15–30.

———. 1987b. *Expanding Options for Criminal Sentencing.* Santa Monica, Calif.: Rand Corp.

Petersilia, J., and S. Turner. 1993. "Intensive Probation and Parole." In M. Tonry, ed., *Crime and Justice: A Review of Research,* vol. 17. Chicago: University of Chicago, pp. 281–336.

Rackmill, S.J. 1994. "An Analysis of Home Confinement as a Sanction." *Federal Probation* 58: 45–52.

Reed, M., and J.V. Roberts. 1999. *Adult Correctional Services in Canada, 1997–98.* Ottawa: Juristat.

Renzema, M., and D. Skelton. 1990. "Trends in the Use of Electronic Monitoring: 1989." *Journal of Offender Monitoring* 3: 14–19.

Roach, K. 2000. "Conditional Sentences, Restorative Justice, Net-Widening and Aboriginal Offenders." In *The Changing Face of Conditional Sentencing: Symposium Proceedings.* Ottawa: Department of Justice, pp. 25–38.

Roberts, J.V. 1999. "Conditional Sentencing: Issues and Problems." In J.V. Roberts and D.P. Cole, eds., *Making Sense of Sentencing.* Toronto: University of Toronto Press, pp. 77–97.

Roberts, J.V., A.N. Doob, and V. Marinos. 2000. *Judicial Attitudes to Conditional Terms of Imprisonment: Results of a National Survey.* Ottawa: Department of Justice.

Roberts, J.V., and P. Healy. 2000. "The Future of Conditional Sentencing." *Criminal Law Quarterly* 44: 309–41.

Roberts, J.V., and R. Will. 1990. *Intermediate Sanctions.* Washington, D.C.: National Institute of Justice.

Sawyer, K. 1985. "Tougher Probation May Help Georgia Clear Crowded Prisons." *Washington Post,* 16 August, A1.

Schmidt, A.K. 1998. "Electronic Monitoring: What Does the Literature Tell Us?" *Federal Probation* 62: 10–20.

———. 1989. "Electronic Monitoring." *Journal of Contemporary Criminal Justice* 5: 133–40.

Smith, L.G., and R.L. Akers. 1993. "A Comparison of Recidivism of Florida's Community Control and Prison: A Five-Year Survival Analysis." *Journal of Research in Crime and Delinquency* 30: 267–92.

Thomas, M. 2002. *Adult Criminal Court Statistics 2000/01.* Ottawa: Canadian Centre for Justice Statistics.

Thompson, D. 1985. *Intensive Probation Supervision in Illinois.* Chicago: Center for Research in Law and Justice.

Tonry, M. 1990. "Stated and Latent Functions of ISP." *Crime and Delinquency* 36: 174–91.

United States General Accounting Office. 1990. *Intermediate Sanctions: Their Impacts on Prison Overcrowding, Costs.*

Wallerstedt, J. 1984. *Returning to Prison.* Washington, D.C.: National Institute of Justice.

Court Case

R. v. Proulx (2000), 30 C.R. (5th) 1 (S.C.C.).

Corrections in Canada: History, Facilities, and Populations

CHAPTER OBJECTIVES

✓ Examine the adult correctional population in Canada today.

✓ Discuss the facilities for women offenders in the federal correctional system.

✓ Discuss the legal rights of inmates.

✓ Understand the effects of being sentenced to prison, including prison violence and suicide.

✓ Outline the main benefits for introducing new-generation correctional facilities.

When offenders are convicted of a criminal offence, they may be sentenced to a period of confinement in a federal or provincial/territorial correctional institution. Canada's correctional system started during the early 1800s in Ontario with the opening of the Kingston Penitentiary. The correctional system has grown over the last 160 years from this single facility to meet the growing number of individuals sentenced to a term of incarceration. Today, there are approximately 151 provincial/territorial correctional facilities, 48 federal institutions, and 15 federal community correctional centres to house inmates.

The operation of such facilities requires governments to supply a number of services, including food, security, programming, and health. One of the most important health issues to emerge during the last decade has been the infectious diseases of HIV-AIDS and Hepatitis C. During the early 1990s, there were 20 known cases of HIV-AIDS; in 2001 there were 217 reported cases. Hepatitis C is more prevalent, accounting for about 30 percent of the prison population (Pachner 2001). According to a Correctional Service of Canada spokesperson, "the testing of inmates is voluntary, but CSC energetically promotes testing for infectious diseases ... treatment and specialists are available to all inmates at federal prisons" (Sutton, in Pachner 2001: 8). In 2001, all 115 inmates who requested treatment for HIV-AIDS were receiving it. At the same time, only 39 inmates were getting treatment for Hepatitis C due to "limited access to specialists."

However, Ralf Jurgens, executive director of the Canadian HIV-AIDS legal network, stated that "while there have been big improvements over the past 10 years ... they have not been doing everything that they can. We really know that there is a serious situation" (Jurgens, in Prachner 2001: 8). Jurgens believes that all correctional systems, not just the federal correctional system, have a moral and legal responsibility to prevent the spread of HIV-AIDS. Improvements can be made in the areas of education, confidential testing, the provision of safe needles, and needle exchange programs and bleach kits.

The issue of infectious diseases has received more attention recently due to a lawsuit from an inmate. Jason Pothier, a 24 year-old federal inmate, is suing the federal government alleging that he contracted the AIDS virus because health measures in prisons "are so abysmal they constitute negligence" (Picard 2001: A1). Pothier, an acknowledged heroin user, said he was denied access to clean needles and methadone (a drug used to help addicts on heroin). As a result, he alleges he contracted the HIV virus and Hepatitis C. He is arguing that his constitutional rights have been violated because health programs in prisons "are far inferior to those in the community." He also states that prison officials "have routinely withheld prescribed medications and on numerous occasions dispensed the wrong medications" (Picard 2001: A1, A5). According to Darrell Kloeze, a lawyer at the Ontario HIV & AIDS Legal Clinic, the loss of liberty accompanying a sentence of incarceration "does not and should not extend to health care" (Kloeze, in Picard 2001: A5). Pothier's court case indicates the changing realities facing correctional facilities, in terms of not only health care issues but also the legal rights of inmates. Some of these issues will be discussed later in this chapter.

Following a discussion of the history of correctional facilities and a profile of the adult correctional population, this chapter covers some of the most important issues facing Canadian corrections today. They include coping with prison life, prison violence, and prison suicide. In addition, the chapter discusses the legal rights of inmates, including the requirement for the Correctional Service of Canada to operate in a fair manner in its treatment of inmates.

A BRIEF HISTORY OF FEDERAL CORRECTIONAL FACILITIES IN CANADA

It is only in recent decades that Canada, like all other western nations, has increased its use of confinement as the main approach to punishing offenders. Between 1832, when the first federal prison was built in Kingston, Ontario, and 1950, a total of eight federal prisons were constructed. During the 1950s, three federal institutions were built, followed by eight in the 1960s, five in the 1970s, and six during the 1980s.

The first prisons in North America were built in the United States. Two different types were originally constructed. The Pennsylvania System reflected a strong Quaker influence: inmates were isolated not only from the outside but also from each other. They had one hour a day to exercise by themselves in an outside yard; they were expected to spend the rest of their time in their small cells, reading the *Bible* provided to them, reflecting on their illegal actions, and "repenting" their crimes (Jackson 1983).

An aerial photograph taken in 1919 of the federal Kingston Penitentiary for Men in Kingston, Ontario

Another style of prison was built in Auburn, New York. Referred to as the Auburn System, this institution held inmates in what is known as the "congregate system." This system was based on the belief that the most efficient way for inmates to reform their actions was through hard work. During the day, inmates worked together both inside and outside the walls, although they were not supposed to talk to each other. Prisoners ate together, but in complete silence. If the inmates were not working or eating, they were locked in their cells. A specific prison architectural style characterized the Auburn system. While the Pennsylvania prison was built on one floor, the Auburn system had a number of floors of cells built on top of each other, in tiers, as they were called (Rothman 1971). The Auburn system, originally built between 1819 and 1823, quickly became the most copied style of prison and ultimately was considered to be the "international prototype of a maximum-security prison" (Anderson and Newman 1993: 349). The Auburn system would become the basis for Canadian prisons. The first prisons were built by provincial authorities; the first was completed in 1835 and was located in Kingston, Ontario, followed by the New Brunswick Penitentiary (1841) and the Nova Scotia Penitentiary (1844). In 1868, the federal government took over all three of these institutions, and then proceeded to build four new facilities during the next 12 years. The Pennsylvania system continued to survive in one particular form: solitary confinement. Most correctional institutions today contain within them areas set aside for more severe forms of punishment for inmates who violated prison rules and regulations or who are considered to be troublemakers.

During the remainder of the 19th century, the federal government operated the prisons under their control in a very harsh manner. Solitary confinement was regularly used (up to 18 months at a time), conditions were harsh, and discipline was extreme. These techniques, it was argued, clearly demonstrated its "superiority (in terms of) the treatment of incorrigibles and criminal crooks" (Jackson 1983: 38–39). At the start of the 20th century, significant changes were introduced into the federal correctional system. These changes included the introduction of parole, training for correctional officials, and the development of inmate classification systems. This resulted in the housing of inmates on the basis of their needs and crimes, and led to the minimum-, medium- and maximum-security designations of correctional facilities (see below). The treatment of inmates was now based on what was called the "policy of normalization," which specified that inmate programs would be in a controlled (not oppressive) environment in order to better represent the conditions in society. Education programs and vocational training were also introduced at this time. In reality, the living conditions of inmates remained harsh, with the continued use of handcuffs and the ball and chain until the early 1930s (Eckstedt and Griffiths 1988).

In 1935, the federal government decided to change its approach toward the treatment of inmates. Gradually it adopted what was called the medical model of corrections, an approach favouring the use of a variety of programs and therapies in the hope they would cure inmates of their problem behaviour. This approach advocates medical solutions for problem behaviour, and treatments are to be prescribed by experts in human nature, such as psychiatrists and psychologists. The long-term impact of this new approach was immense—in 1937, there were eight federal correctional facilities in existence, while by 1961 this number had increased to 19.

In 1963 the medical model began to decline in its importance, to be replaced by the reintegration model. This approach favoured community-based correctional facilities, in particular the elimination of the coercive aspects of "treatment" and the rise of the use of community resources in the correction of offenders. This approach reflects the justice model of corrections (see Chapter 3), which maintains that inmates have to be protected from any potential harmful actions of correctional officials through the introduction of legal rights for inmates and the increased use of community sanctions. This approach dominated until the 1990s when the federal government merged the reintegration model with the psychologically based risk prediction ideology (see Chapter 12). The dominant approach today involves an increased use of community resources, an assessment of offenders' risks and needs when they enter correctional facilities, and a program that addresses any limitations found (see Figure 11.1). In fact, the approach used since the early 1990s by the federal government has become recognized in other countries as the most effective way to treat inmates (see Chapter 12).

A BRIEF HISTORY OF FEDERAL CORRECTIONAL FACILITIES FOR WOMEN

The earliest prison for women in Canada was located in the Kingston Provincial Penitentiary. While the original design specified separate units for male and female inmates, the first two women who were sentenced there were placed in the infirmary. By 1859, 68 women were serving a sentence in this facility, creating a serious problem for administrators. As Faith (1993) points out,

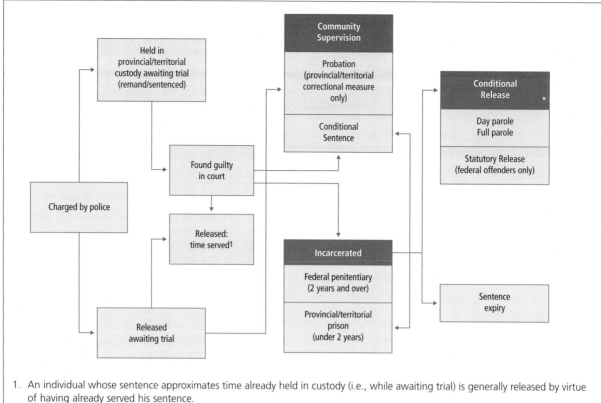

1. An individual whose sentence approximates time already held in custody (i.e., while awaiting trial) is generally released by virtue of having already served his sentence.

Source: Statistics Canada, *Juristat*, Catalogue 85-002, April 1999, p. 3.

FIGURE 11.1

An Overview of Events in the Adult Correctional System

women inmates were viewed as an "inconvenience" to the operation of the prison. Women continued to be moved to various locations within the penitentiary over the years, basically being "confined wherever and in whatever manner best served the administration of the larger male population" (Cooper 1993: 5).

Construction of a separate institution for women inmates was not started until 1914. This facility, known as the Prison for Women, was actually built within the walls of the male prison in Kingston. Construction of a completely separate facility for women was started in 1925 and completed in 1934. This new facility was designated as a maximum-security facility. No outside windows were built into the walls, all letters were censored, and there were no opportunities for education or vocational training that were available to male inmates. Reports of sexual abuse and harsh living conditions led many reformers to demand that conditions be improved.

Beginning in 1938, numerous reports, investigations, and commissions investigated the Prison for Women, and their final reports all shared one point—that the facility be closed. They recommended all

inmates be located in their home provinces or in regional correctional facilities that should be built and operated by the federal government. Many of these reports used substantive ideology to support their demands, that is, that female offenders are different from male offenders, and as a result, should have different programs available to them. Programs are to be woman-centred, that is, all policies must be restructured to reflect the realities experienced by women as distinct from men. The report *Creating Choices: Report of the Task Force on Federally Sentenced Women* (1990) reflected this ideology and advocated "the empowerment of female inmates, meaningful choices, respect and dignity, supportive environments, and shared responsibilities" (Correctional Service of Canada 1990: 126–35). Other recommendations included the need for the federal government to open regional facilities for women, including a healing lodge for Aboriginal women, increase the programming for women, and make the programs more relevant so inmates would be able to reintegrate quickly into society upon their release.

Perhaps the most significant event in the history of federal correctional institutions for both women and

Canada happened in 1994, when "a series of events occurred in the Prison for Women in Kingston ... [which] would go on to define the new 'face' of corrections in Canada" (Erdahl 2001: 43). On the evening of 22 April 1994, an Emergency Response Team comprising male correctional officers from the neighbouring federal facility in Kingston became involved in a "brief but violent physical confrontation with eight female inmates" in order to take them out of their cells in the segregation unit and strip-search them. The next day, these women were sent to a psychiatric centre before being returned to the prison for women.

The news of the treatment of these women became public, and a Royal Commission of Inquiry (known as the Arbour Commission) was created to investigate correctional practices in the prison for women. When it released its final report in March 1996, the Arbour Commission announced a number of significant findings about the federal female correctional facilities, including

1. The Correctional Service of Canada was not responsive to outside criticism and was not prepared to give an honest and fair account of its actions. Instead, it chose to deny any errors in judgment, resist any criticism, and failed to properly investigate allegations of misconduct.
2. The Correctional Service of Canada was part of a prison culture that did not value individual rights; and

3. There was a failure to promote a "culture of rights" by the Correctional Service of Canada (Jackson 2002).

This report led to a significant change in the way the Correctional Service of Canada cares for its inmates. The Prison for Women was ultimately closed as regional facilities were opened.

THE ADULT CORRECTIONAL POPULATION IN CANADA TODAY

In 2000–01, the total correctional caseload (which includes those individuals under some form of supervision in the community) for both federal and provincial institutions was 151 500 offenders. A daily average of 31 547 offenders were held in custody, with 40 percent (12 732 individuals) in federal institutions, 35 percent (10 953 individuals) incarcerated in provincial/territorial facilities, and the remaining 25 percent (7862 individuals) in provincial facilities on remand or temporary detention. The incarceration rate was 133 adult inmates per 100 000 adults during 2000–01, a 2 percent decrease from the previous year.

Since 1990–91, when it was 140 inmates per 100 000 adults, the incarceration rate has decreased by 5 percent in Canada (see Table 11.1) (Hendrick and Farmer 2002).

TABLE 11.1   Trends in Incarceration Rates, 1990/91 to 2000/01

	Provincial/Territorial Incarceration		Federal Incarceration		Total Incarceration	
	Average count per 100 000 adults	% change	Average count per 100 000 adults	% change	Average count per 100,000 adults	% change
1990/91	86	–	54	–	140	–
1991/92	90	4.2	56	3.1	145	3.7
1992/93	91	1.1	58	3.5	148	1.7
1993/94	90	-0.7	62	6.6	151	2.0
1994/95	90	0.4	64	3.3	153	1.5
1995/96	89	-1.7	63	-0.4	152	-0.3
1996/97	87	-2.3	63	-0.4	150	-1.5
1997/98	83	-4.3	60	-4.4	144	-4.3
1998/99	83	0.1	57	-5.5	140	-2.2
1999/00	80	-4.2	56	-2.7	135	-3.6
2000/01	80	0.2	54	-3.1	133	-2.0

Note: Rates may not aggregate to totals due to rounding.
– not applicable

Source: Statistics Canada, *Juristat*, Catalogue 85-002, vol. 22, no. 10, October 2002, p. 4.

TABLE 11.2 Average Daily Count of Offenders in Custody, 2000–2001

	Sentenced Custody	Remand	Other temporary	Total	Incarceration Rate Average count per 100 000 adults
Newfoundland and Labrador	225	54	10	288	69
Prince Edward Island	73	10	3	86	82
Nova Scotia	222	109	10	341	47
New Brunswick[1]	204	71	8	283	48
Quebec	2 011	1 197	16	3 224	56
Ontario	3 737	3 700	188	7 625	83
Manitoba	596	520	– –	1 116	130
Saskatchewan	826	304	0	1 130	150
Alberta	1 323	580	0	1 903	85
British Columbia	1 476	811	199	2 486	79
Yukon	35	18	0	53	235
Northwest Territories	163	28	0	191	684
Nunavut	63	26	0	89	571
Provincial/Territorial Total	10 953	7 428	434	18 815	80
Federal Total	12 732	–	–	12 732	54
Total	23 685	–	–	31 547	133

Note: Rates may not aggregate to totals due to rounding.
– not available for any reference period
– – not available for specific reference period
1. New Brunswick data for 2000/01 are extracted from a new operational system: caution is recommended when making comparisons over time.

Source: Statistics Canada, *Juristat*, Catalogue 85-002, vol. 22, no. 10, October 2002, p. 5.

TABLE 11.3 Trends in Custodial Admissions Rates, 1992/93 to 2000/01

	Provincial/Territorial		Federal		Total	
	Custodial admissions per 10 000 adults charged	% change	Custodial admissions per 10 000 adults charged	% change	Custodial admissions per 10 000 adults charged	% change
1992/93	3766	–	119	–	3884	–
1993/94	3900	3.5	139	17.3	4038	4.0
1994/95	4146	6.3	158	0.5	4285	6.1
1995/96	4163	0.4	142	1.9	4305	0.5
1996/97	4170	0.2	136	-4.5	4306	0.0
1997/98	4222	1.2	139	2.9	4361	1.3
1998/99	4101	-2.8	152	9.2	4254	-2.5
1999/00	4292	4.7	149	-1.9	4442	4.4
2000/01[1]	4406	2.7	150	0.2	4556	2.6

Note: Rates may not aggregate to totals due to rounding.
– not applicable
1. New Brunswick and Manitoba data for 2000/01 (and 1999/00) are extracted from a new operational system: caution is recommended when making comparisons over time.

Source: Statistics Canada, *Juristat*, Catalogue 85-002, vol. 22, no. 10, October 2002, p. 8.

During 2000–01, the lowest provincial incarceration rates were found in Nova Scotia (47 per 100 000 adults), New Brunswick (48) and Quebec (56). In contrast, the highest provincial rates were found in Saskatchewan (150) and Manitoba (130). As Table 11.2 reveals, the territorial incarceration rates are much higher than any of the provinces, but they tend to "fluctuate a great deal due to their relatively small populations" (Hendrick and Farmer 2002).

Table 11.3 indicates the trend in custodial admission rates for provincial/territorial and federal correctional facilities. In 2000–01, most admissions (97 percent) were at the provincial/territorial level. Across Canada, most offenders are admitted to custody for nonviolent offences, but this varies by according to jurisdiction. In 2000–01, violent crime admissions accounted for a larger proportion of the sentenced admissions compared to property offences in Manitoba (46 percent versus 21 percent) and Saskatchewan (31 percent versus 19 percent). In contrast, some provinces had a much smaller proportion of violent crimes to property offences: Prince Edward Island (10 percent versus 32 percent), Alberta (9 percent versus 22 percent) and British Columbia (16 percent versus 27 percent).

Almost 75 percent of admissions to sentenced custody in the provincial/territorial correctional system are for three months or less. During 2000–01, 48 percent of admissions to provincial/territorial custody were for less than one month, and 26 percent for between one and three months. The median time served was the lowest in Quebec (28 days) and the highest in Saskatchewan (119 days). In the federal system, 47 percent of those sentenced to custody were serving a sentence of between two and less than three years, while 21 percent were serving a sentence between three and less

than four years (see Table 11.4). Four percent of federal admissions were for life imprisonment in 2001–02, a figure that has been stable since 1990–91 (Hendrick and Farmer 2002).

In federal correctional institutions, males accounted for the vast majority of admissions (95 percent) in 2000–01 and 91 percent of all admissions to provincial/territorial facilities. In the federal system, the median age of sentenced offenders was 32 years of age, slightly more than for the provincial/territorial system. Regardless of the type of jurisdiction, the most common profile of an inmate in Canada is a male between the ages of 18 and 34. Aboriginals comprised 19 percent of all admissions to provincial/territorial facilities and 17 percent of correctional facilities admissions.

THE ROLE OF CORRECTIONAL INSTITUTIONS IN CANADIAN SOCIETY

Correctional facilities are built to make society a safer and better place. What goes on behind the walls is important in the sense that it is here that the goals of punishment discussed in Chapter 10 take over. Exactly what is used as a guiding philosophy of the correctional system depends on the operating preferences (e.g., deterrence, rehabilitation) of correctional facilities. Three general models of correctional facilities describe the different ways of thinking about prisons since they were first introduced.

- *The custodial model.* This model is based on the idea that prisoners are to be incarcerated for the purposes of incapacitation and deterrence. Any decision is made in the context of maintaining maximum security and discipline. In addition, there is tight control over inmates in all phases of their lives in prison. This model was the first to emerge, and the early prisons built in Canada reflected this style of thinking and operation.
- *The rehabilitation model.* This model emphasizes the ideal of individualized treatment. Concerns about security and control are secondary to the well-being of inmates. Treatment programs are available (and many times forced upon them) for inmates in order to assist them in changing their criminal and antisocial behaviours. This model came into popularity in the 1950s but it began to fade in popularity in the 1970s with the emergence of the critique of rehabilitation brought about by the work of Robert Martinson and his colleagues (see Chapter 12).

TABLE 11.4	Length of Aggregate Sentences, Sentenced Admissions, 2000–2001		
Provincial/Territorial Sentenced Custody		**Federal Custody**	
	%		%
31 days or less	48	2 years <3 years	47
>1 to 3 months	26	3 years <4 years	21
>3 to 6 months	12	4 years <5 years	12
>6 to 12 months	6	5 years <10 years	14
>12 months	8	10 years or more but not Life	2
		Life	4

Note: Percentage distribution may not aggregate to totals due to rounding.

Source: Statistics Canada, *Juristat*, Catalogue 85-002, vol. 22, no. 10, October 2002, p. 10.

- *The reintegration/risk reduction model.* In this model, corrections attempts to prepare inmates to integrate them back into the broader society. Correctional facilities that have taken this approach help inmates work on their specific needs and risks so they will not engage in criminal behaviour once they are living in the community. Responsibility and accountability are stressed during their incarceration and time on conditional release programs. This model is the most influential approach in Canada today.

FEDERAL AND PROVINCIAL/TERRITORIAL CORRECTIONAL INSTITUTIONS

In 2000, there were 52 federal correctional facilities for females and males (excluding halfway houses, also referred to as community correctional centres) operating under the jurisdiction of the federal Correctional Service of Canada. Forty-five of these are penitentiaries, and are classified as single-level security institutions. The remaining seven are classified as multilevel security institutions (Hendrick and Farmer 2002). Five facilities are located in the Atlantic region, Quebec has 12, Ontario has 14, the Prairie region has 13, and the Pacific region has 8. Twelve institutions for male inmates are classified as minimum-security facilities, 20 are medium-security facilities, and 10 are maximum-security facilities. The capacity of these facilities varies from 78 to 501 inmates, with an average of 259 inmates. The average capacity of minimum-security facilities is 121 inmates, while medium- and maximum-security institutions have average capacities of 377 and 235, respectively.

Until recently, the only federal facility for women in Canada was the Prison for Women, located in Kingston, Ontario, with an average population of 115. Beginning in 1978, approximately one-third of all federally sentenced women have been permitted to serve their sentences in provincial facilities in their own province through Exchange of Service Agreements. In the late 1980s, however, the federal government appointed the Task Force on Federally Sentenced Women to study the quality and quantity of programs and facilities for women in the federal correctional system; the task force also looked at the needs of women offenders, as well as their experiences, particularly with regard to physical and sexual abuse. One of the central goals of the inquiry was to evaluate whether the correctional model used for the male prison population is appropriate for women. The final report of the task force, entitled *Creating Choices: Report of the Task Force on Federally Sentenced Women* (Correctional Service of Canada 1990), recommended that the Prison for Women be replaced by five new correctional facilities for women, all of which would feature community-based programs.

The federal government now operates five women's facilities across Canada (Correctional Service of Canada 1997). Regional facilities are located in Truro, Nova Scotia; Joliette, Quebec; Kitchener, Ontario; Edmonton, Alberta; and Burnaby, B.C. Until recently, maximum-security women inmates were not placed in the regional facilities but rather in maximum-security women's units in existing male institutions. These maximum-security women's units were located in Springhill, Nova Scotia; at the Regional Reception Centre in Quebec; and in the Saskatchewan Penitentiary. In the Pacific region, the Burnaby Correctional Centre for Women accommodates women offenders of all security classifications under a joint federal/provincial agreement.

Since the mid-1990s, the federal government has introduced at least nine healing lodges for Aboriginal offenders. Healing lodges are designed to offer services and programs reflecting Aboriginal culture. Aboriginal offenders' needs are addressed through Aboriginal teachings and ceremonies, with an emphasis on spiritual values. Almost all of these healing lodges are found in locations away from urban environments. The first healing lodge opened in 1995 by the federal government was the 30-bed Okimaw Ohci Healing Lodge, located in Maple Creek, Saskatchewan, for Aboriginal women inmates. Since that time, eight more have been opened for Aboriginal males. They are the Pe Sakastew Centre (located near Hobbema, Alberta); the Prince Albert, Saskatchewan Grand Council Spiritual Healing Lodge; the Stan Daniels Healing Centre (in Edmonton); the Elbow Lake Healing Village (near Chehalis, B.C.); the Ochichakkosipi Healing Lodge (in Crane River, Manitoba), the Willow Creek Healing Lodge Natawihokamik (near Duck Lake, Saskatchewan); the Wasekun Healing Centre (near Montreal); and the Some Ke' Healing Lodge (near Yellowknife). In addition, in 1999, the federal government opened the first healing lodge within the walls of a federal correctional facility, in Stony Mountain Institution, a medium-security facility located north of Winnipeg. Inmates do not live in this lodge, but they go to the facility for Aboriginal programming, spiritual teachings, and ceremonies.

In 1996 there were 151 provincial/territorial correctional facilities in Canada. Ontario had the largest number of facilities (47), followed by British Columbia and Quebec (19 each); Prince Edward Island and Yukon operated the fewest number of facilities (two each). Provincial/territorial institutions use different classification systems for their correctional facilities. Just over half (52 percent) of all provincial/territorial facilities are described as correctional centres. Another 27 percent are classified as jail/detention centres, 16 percent as alternative minimum-security facilities, and 5 percent as remand centres (Robinson et al. 1998).

Security Levels

Since the major objective of correctional institutions is confinement, the primary factor in determining the classification level of an inmate is security. On a general level, security has three components:

1. the likelihood that an inmate will escape or attempt to escape;
2. the likelihood that an inmate will place a correctional officer or another inmate in danger; and
3. the likelihood that an inmate will attempt to violate institutional rules (Anderson and Newman 1993).

Until 1981–82, the Correctional Service of Canada employed a classification system of offenders that was based on the likelihood that an offender would escape from an institution and the potential harm to the community if he did. According to the Correctional Service of Canada, the three levels of security were defined as follows:

1. *Maximum security.* The inmate is likely to escape and would cause serious harm in the community.
2. *Medium security.* The inmate is likely to escape but would not cause serious harm in the community.
3. *Minimum security.* The inmate is not likely to escape but, if he did, would not cause harm in the community. (Eckstedt and Griffiths 1988: 191)

When they enter a federal correctional institution inmates receive a security classification by parole officers of the Correctional Service of Canada. This is followed in most cases by an interview with a placement officer who assesses the inmate to determine his security needs. However, this initial assessment does not necessarily determine the type of security-level facility to which the inmate will be sent. An inmate classified as maximum-security may be sent to a medium-security institution, depending on his prior record as well as the type of programs offered by the institution.

Maximum-security facilities are usually surrounded by high fences or walls (depending on when they were built), usually around 20 feet high and surrounded by guard towers at strategic positions. Intrusion detection systems ensure that the perimeter is not "compromised." Parts of the facility are separated by gates, fences, and walls, and inmates are usually required to have special permission forms when they move between sections of the institution outside normal times of movement. A number of inmates live in solitary confinement, either due to behavioural issues or out of concern that they will be attacked by other inmates, usually as a result of their crimes (for example, sex offenders). Maximum-security facilities usually have a number of educational and treatment programs, such as adult basic education, high-school equivalency courses, and various skills-development programs, such as carpentry. In 1996, 20 percent of all male inmates were serving a sentence in a federal maximum-security institution. In the provincial/territorial correctional systems, 39 percent of all male inmates and 46 percent of all female inmates were classified as maximum-security (Finn et al. 1999).

Medium-security institutions are typically enclosed by chain-link fences topped with barbed and razor wire. Compared with maximum-security facilities, medium-security institutions allow more freedom of movement for inmates. Many of these facilities have modern surroundings and training centres; they also have a variety of educational and treatment facilities available. In 1996, the majority (64 percent) of all male inmates and 8 percent of all female inmates in the federal system were classified as medium-security; in the provincial/territorial correctional systems, 13 percent of all male inmates and 7 percent of all female inmates were classified as medium-security (Finn et al. 1999).

Minimum-security prisons usually have no fences or walls around them. In fact, an inmate could walk out of the facility since security around the facility is much more relaxed. There are no armed guards, no towers, no barbed wire, nor any electronic surveillance equipment to ensure prisoners stay within the institution. Staff and inmates often mingle and are indistinguishable from each other since prison clothes are not issued. Inmates are also housed in better living arrangements, in private or semi-private rooms. In addition, inmates may be on work-release programs that allow them to hold jobs during the day. In 1996, 6 percent of all female inmates and 14 percent of all male inmates at the federal level were housed in minimum-security facilities, as were 13 percent of all female inmates and 8 percent of all men in provincial/territorial correctional systems (Finn et al. 1999).

On 31 March 1997, the Correctional Service of Canada reported that 20 percent of all male and female inmates serving a custodial sentence in the federal system were in a maximum-security institution. The majority of offenders were in a medium-security or minimum-security institution (63 and 14 percent, respectively), and the remaining 3 percent were in multilevel facilities (Robinson et al. 1998).

Forty percent of all provincial/territorial inmates and 3 percent of federal inmates were placed in what are referred to as multilevel security facilities (Robinson et al.

1998). A multilevel facility combines the features of two or more of the security levels described earlier in this section. Some facilities use the same buildings to accommodate inmates classified at different security levels, while other facilities operate separate structures for each level of security (Robinson et al. 1998). The majority (86 percent) of female inmates within the federal system are housed in multilevel security institutions, as are 41 percent of all male inmates and 35 percent of female inmates in the provincial/territorial correctional systems.

Starting in 1981–82 the Correctional Service of Canada has operated on the basis of seven security levels. Level 1 facilities are community correctional centres, while level 2 institutions have such minimum-security facilities as forestry and work camps. Levels 3, 4, and 5 represent medium-security facilities, while level 6 represents a maximum-security institution. Level 7 is the highest level of security risk, and is reserved for violent offenders who are placed into what are referred to as special handling units, or "super-max" institutions.

Federal female offenders are classified according to a different scale, the Security Management System, approved for the new women's federal facilities in April 1995. The guidelines govern the daily management of each facility, as well as the inmates' participation in programs and activities and freedom of movement inside each facility. This system focuses on the majority of the female population in federal institutions, rather than on the few who persistently commit crimes in a violent and aggressive manner. It contains six management levels, of which five are related to security classification and one is used exclusively for admission status (Finn et al. 1999).

NEW-GENERATION CORRECTIONAL FACILITIES

Serious offences, including drug use, suicides, assaults, attempted murder, and attacks on correctional officers, appear within correctional facilities. Some prison officials recognized these issues and began to develop a new way to approach the housing, guarding, and treatment of convicted offenders. These officials believed that how the correctional facility is operated is just as important as why it is built. As a result, some correctional facilities in Canada have moved away from a traditional design toward a structure that is referred to as a "new-generation" facility.

In the traditional correctional facility design, cells are located in what is known as a linear design, that is, they are placed on a long hallway. To supervise inmates when they are in their cells, correctional officers have to

The Central North Correctional Centre in Penetanguishene, opened in fall 2001, is the first privately operated provincial correctional facility in Canada.

walk up and down these corridors, and their ability to see beyond the specific cell they are looking at is extremely limited. As a result, many inmates misbehave or engage in illicit activities since they are not under the surveillance of correctional authorities.

"New-generation" facilities are very different; the physical structure is based on a podular design, that is, each "pod" contains 12 to 24 one-person cells extending from a common area. These cells are usually situated in a triangle, enabling correctional officers to be in the centre of the triangle and have visual access to all, or nearly all, the living units and common areas. Daily activities, such as eating and recreational activities, take place in this common area. Other types of facilities are located within the pod, such as treatment and interview rooms, which allow correctional officers greater access to and contact with inmates. Another change in these facilities is the provision of comfortable furniture and rugs, as well as a "communal" room that allows inmates to get together to watch television, listen to a radio, or make a telephone call.

The podular design also differs from the traditional model because it allows the unit to be managed by a direct supervision model (see Exhibit 11.1). This involves continuous physical contact between correctional officers (who are stationed within the actual pod), prison authorities, and inmates. During the day, inmates are allowed only in common areas and can be in their cells only with permission. The benefits of this model are that it allows correctional officials to both identify problematic behaviour quickly and observe the daily actions of each inmate. Prison officials report that the new-generation facilities have led to a dramatic reduction in the number of violent incidents as well as escapes (Zupan 1991).

Female Inmates

Most women remanded or sentenced to a correctional facility in Canada today enter provincial/territorial institutions. The majority of provincial sentences for women are for six months or less, and almost 40 percent are for 14 days or less. Thirty percent are jailed due to their failure to pay fines, and more than 25 percent of all women are serving a sentence in a provincial institution for a property offence, mostly shoplifting or fraud charges. Less than 10 percent had committed a violent offence, the majority of these being minor assault charges. Approximately 25 percent of the women in provincial correctional institutions were repeat offenders, usually having been sentenced previously for such criminal offences as drinking, prostitution, theft, and fraud (Finn et al. 1999).

A small number of women are sentenced to a term in a federal institution: in 1996 only 2 percent of all federal inmates were female; one year later, the Correctional Service of Canada (1997) reported that a total of 357 women were incarcerated in federal correctional institutions. A profile of these women indicates that they share many demographic characteristics with male offenders. Most (51.5 percent) are 20–34 years of age, single (56 percent), possess a Grade 9 level of education or less (46 percent), were unemployed at the time of their offence (80 percent), and were serving their first penitentiary term (74 percent). Nineteen percent were living in a common-law relationship and 11 percent were married at the time of their offence. Fifty-eight percent of federally sentenced women were serving a sentence of six years or less.

Female inmates are convicted and placed into a correctional facility for different and fewer offences than men. In 1996, 38 percent of all female inmates in provincial/territorial correctional institutions were serving a sentence for only one offence, compared with 33 percent of males. At the federal level, more than one-half (55 percent) of female inmates, compared with 26 percent of men, were serving a sentence for one offence. In addition, women in provincial/territorial facilities had a less extensive record than men. Fifty percent of all women in the provincial/territorial system had either no, or only one, prior adult conviction, compared with 36 percent of male inmates. The percentage of men who had five or more prior convictions was almost double that of women (21 percent versus 12 percent, respectively) (Finn et al. 1999). In the federal system in 1997, 87 percent of women serving a term had either no or only one previous term of federal incarceration, in comparison with 71 percent of male inmates, and 4 percent of women had more than three prior terms, compared

EXHIBIT 11.1 Supervision Models

According to prison officials, there are six objectives of the direct supervision model:

1. Staff, rather than inmates, will control the facility and inmates' behaviour.
2. Inmates will be directly and continuously supervised and correctional officers will direct and control the behaviour of all inmates.
3. Rewards and punishments will be structured to ensure compliant behaviour.
4. Open communication will be maintained between the correctional staff and inmates.
5. Inmates will be advised of the expectations and rules of the facility.
6. Inmates will be treated in a manner consistent with proper standards of conduct, and will be treated in a fair and equitable way regardless of their personal traits or crimes they committed.

There are also seven behavioural dimensions necessary for the effective supervision and control of inmates in the pods. Many of these dimensions were developed from the general principles found in effective personnel supervision. These dimensions are

1. Resolving inmate problems and conflicts.
2. Building positive rapport and personal credibility with inmates.
3. Maintaining effective administrative and staff relations.
4. Managing the living unit to assure a safe and humane living environment.
5. Responding to inmate requests.
6. Handling inmate discipline.
7. Supervising in a clear, well-organized, and attention-getting manner.

Sources: Nelson and O'Toole (1983); Gettinger (1984); Zupan (1991).

with 10 percent of the men (Correctional Service of Canada 1997).

Female and male inmates differ in terms of the offences for which they were sent to a correctional facility (see Table 11.5). Women sentenced to a correctional facility are less likely than male inmates to be incarcerated for a violent crime. This was true for both provincial/territorial facilities (where 28 percent of women were incarcerated for a violent crime, compared with 34 percent of men) and federal facilities (where 64 percent of women were incarcerated for a violent offence, compared with 74 percent of men). The most serious offence committed by the majority of women

TABLE 11.5 Distribution of Offence Types by Gender,[1] Federal and Provincial Inmates, October 1996

		Crimes against the Person						
	Number of Inmates[2]	Homicide/ Attempt Murder	Sexual Assault	Serious Assault	Minor Assault	Robbery	Other Violent	TOTAL
		percent						
Provinces/Territories								
Male	20 043	3	7	6	5	9	3	34
Female	1 453	5	2	6	3	9	2	28
CSC								
Male	13 619	24	14	4	–	24	7	74
Female	210	37	1	10	–	13	3	64
Total Male	33 662	12	10	5	3	15	4	50
Total Female	1 663	9	2	7	3	10	2	33

		Property Crimes				
	Number of Inmates[2]	B&E	Theft	Fraud	Other Property	TOTAL
		percent				
Provinces/Territories						
Male	20 043	19	8	4	6	37
Female	1 453	8	13	11	6	37
CSC						
Male	13 619	12	1	–	2	15
Female	210	–	4	1	2	7
Total Male	33 662	16	5	2	4	28
Total Female	1 663	7	12	10	5	34

		Other *Criminal Code* (CC/Federal Statutes)					
	Number of Inmates[2]	Weapons Offences	Admin. of Justice	Impaired Offences	Drug Offences	Other CC/Fed.	TOTAL
		percent					
Provinces/Territories							
Male	20 043	3	4	6	6	11	30
Female	1 453	2	4	5	9	13	34
CSC							
Male	13 619	–	–	1	8	2	11
Female	210	–	–	–	27	1	29
Total Male	33 662	2	2	4	5	8	22
Total Female	1 663	2	4	4	12	12	34

Notes:
– nil or zero
1. Only the most serious offence (MSO) is recorded.
2. Missing data for 2153 provincial/territorial inmates (9%) and 33 CSC inmates (1%).

Source: Statistics Canada, *Juristat*, Catalogue 85-002, vol. 18, no. 8, June 1998, p. 10.

serving a sentence in a provincial/territorial institution was either a property crime or Other *Criminal Code*/Federal Statute offence (36 percent each). Most women who were serving a sentence of less than two years had committed a drug-related offence. In the federal correctional system, the two largest groups of women were those serving a sentence for homicide/attempted murder (37 percent) and those whose most serious offence was drug-related (27 percent) (Finn et al. 1999). According to Shaw (1991), about two-thirds of federally sentenced women have a serious problem with drug or alcohol abuse.

For violent crimes only (data is incomplete for other offences), female inmates had a different victim–offender relationship than their male counterparts. In 1996 the largest proportion of victims were in the category of "other" relationships (26 percent); adult strangers (25 percent) and spouses/ex-spouses (21 percent) comprised the next largest groups. Female inmates were less likely than males to have victimized a spouse, ex-spouse, or known child. The largest proportion of victims for male offenders were spouses or ex-spouses (28 percent).

To facilitate the reintegration of federally sentenced women into the community, an attempt was made to introduce innovative programs into each of the regional centres. For example, at the Truro Federal Women's Facility (which has a maximum capacity of 30 offenders), the program goals were "community oriented, holistic, women-centred, culturally sensitive, supportive of autonomy and self-esteem, and oriented toward release" (LeBlanc 1994: 12). Programs take place both on- and off-site, with an emphasis on off-site programming if the offender does not pose a risk to the community. All programs are aimed at helping women make informed and meaningful decisions about their lives. In addition, the Truro facility contains a multifaceted children's program. Some children are allowed to visit their mothers on a temporary basis, while others live with their mothers in the institution (LeBlanc 1994).

Aboriginal Inmates

Aboriginals represented 2 percent of the national population in 2000–01, but comprised 19 percent of provincial/territorial inmates and 17 percent of federal inmates. According to the 1996 Canada Census, the percentage of Aboriginal inmates with a Grade 9 education or less was almost four times greater than that of the general population. Aboriginal inmates had a 24 percent unemployment rate, compared with 10 percent for all persons in Canada (Statistics Canada 1996).

Aboriginal inmates share some of the demographic traits of other provincial/territorial and federal inmates. Most (56 percent) were single or living in a common-law relationship (35 percent) at the time they committed the offence for which they were sentenced to prison. Fifty-four percent were serving their first term in a federal institution, and 59 percent were serving a sentence of less than six years. However, there were a number of significant differences between Aboriginal and non-Aboriginal inmates. Aboriginals were younger than non-Aboriginals in both the provincial/territorial correctional facilities (29 compared with 32 years of age) and federal facilities (31 compared with 35 years of age). Thirty-three percent of Aboriginals were serving their sentence in a provincial/territorial facility (versus 31 percent of non-Aboriginals), and 56 percent in federal facilities (as compared with 43 percent). Seventy percent of Aboriginals in provincial/territorial facilities were unemployed at the time of their arrest, compared with 47 percent of non-Aboriginal inmates; in federal facilities the ratio was 53 percent Aboriginals to 40 percent non-Aboriginals (Finn et al. 1999).

Table 11.6 reveals that, at the provincial/territorial and federal levels, the majority of both Aboriginal and non-Aboriginal offenders are serving a sentence for a violent offence; however, a higher percentage of Aboriginal offenders (81 percent) than non-Aboriginal offenders (66 percent) are serving a sentence for committing a violent offence.

In terms of victim–offender relationships, a slightly larger percentage of Aboriginals than non-Aboriginals knew their victims (70 percent versus 66 percent). The largest percentage of victims of Aboriginal inmates were spouses/ex-spouses (31 percent), strangers (30 percent), and friends (13 percent). This can be compared with the most common victims of all

Okimaw Ohci Spiritual Lodge

	Number of Inmates[2]	Crimes against the Person						
		Homicide/ Attempt Murder	Sexual Assault	Serious Assault	Minor Assault	Robbery	Other Violent	TOTAL
		percent						
Provinces/Territories								
Aboriginal	3 941	3	8	12	7	8	2	40
Non-Aboriginal	17 406	4	6	5	5	9	3	32
CSC								
Aboriginal	1 964	23	20	10	–	21	4	79
Non-Aboriginal	11 865	24	12	3	–	25	8	72
Total Aboriginal	5 905	10	12	11	5	12	3	53
Total Non-Aboriginal	29 271	12	9	4	3	16	5	48

	Number of Inmates[2]	Property Crimes				
		B&E	Theft	Fraud	Other Property	TOTAL
		percent				
Provinces/Territories						
Aboriginal	3 941	18	8	2	7	35
Non-Aboriginal	17 406	18	8	5	6	37
CSC						
Aboriginal	1 964	13	1	–	2	16
Non-Aboriginal	11 865	12	1	–	2	15
Total Aboriginal	5 905	16	5	2	5	28
Total Non-Aboriginal	29 271	16	5	3	4	28

	Number of Inmates[2]	Other *Criminal Code* (CC/Federal Statutes)					
		Weapons Offences	Admin. of Justice	Impaired Offences	Drug Offences	Other CC/Fed.	TOTAL
		percent					
Provinces/Territories							
Aboriginal	3 941	2	4	6	6	7	26
Non-Aboriginal	17 406	3	4	6	6	12	31
CSC							
Aboriginal	1 964	–	–	1	2	1	5
Non-Aboriginal	11 865	–	–	1	9	3	13
Total Aboriginal	5 905	2	3	5	5	5	19
Total Non-Aboriginal	29 271	2	2	4	7	8	24

Notes:
– nil or zero
1. Only the most serious offence (MSO) is recorded.
2. Data were missing for 2332 province/territorial inmates (10%) and 33 CSC inmates (1%).

Source: Statistics Canada, *Juristat*, Catalogue 85-002, vol. 18, no. 8, June 1998, p. 10.

non-Aboriginals: strangers (34 percent), spouses/ex-spouses (26 percent), and their child or a child in trust (15 percent) (Finn et al. 1999).

Prison Life

Prisoners are separated from the outside world, experience a life under the constant scrutiny of prison guards and other staff, and are required to follow strict daily regimes or endure strict disciplinary sanctions. Prisons are commonly referred to as "total institutions." According to Goffman (1961), total institutions have four distinct elements:

1. The inmate lives under the watchful eye of a centralized institutional authority.
2. The inmate shares his space with other inmates, who are all treated alike and forced to enact the same routines.
3. All of an inmate's time is tightly scheduled by a body of rules and administrative orders imposed by those in charge.
4. The entire system of enforced activities, and time and space control, is organized around the institutional goals of correction and/or treatment.

Total institutions force inmates to live regimented and dehumanizing lives. Extensive control over the lives of inmates forces them to "fight back" against this authority, leading them to commit more criminal acts. Recently, however, this traditionally accepted view of prisons as total institutions has been challenged. Farrington (1992) argues that prisons can better be described as "not-so-total" institutions, pointing out that Goffman's view is no longer consistent with the one that underlies most modern prisons. He states that prisons are never totally isolated from society, as most require a constant supply of goods and services from the broader society. Prison staff work only in the prison, and by leaving every day, take the prison into the community; they also bring back information from outside the prison and can answer inmates' questions. Furthermore, inmates may maintain contacts with many aspects of their former lives. The trend toward relatively shorter sentences and various programs that allow inmates to leave the prison for brief periods of time mean they have consistent contact with their communities. In addition, the correctional system today, through its emphasis on community corrections, emphasizes reintegration of inmates.

Despite Farrington's view, prisons remain in many ways total institutions. Residents must dress according to institutional rules, and many human activities are strictly curtailed, including family relations, friendships, heterosexual activities, and a choice in deciding the daily activities in which one wants to participate.

Inmate Society

For decades, experts on prisons and prison life have stated that inmates form their own world, with a unique set of norms and rules referred to as inmate subculture (Irwin 1974). The basis of inmate subculture, they argue, is a unique social code of unwritten rules and guidelines that tell inmates how to behave, think, and interact with prison staff and other inmates. Clemmer (1958) introduced the idea of inmate social codes when he wrote about life in a maximum-security prison. He identified a unique language used by prisoners, known as argot (Caron 1982), consisting of such words as "jointman" (a prisoner who behaves like a guard) and "yard" ($100). Clemmer also identified what he termed the "prisonization process"—the manner in which an individual assimilates into the inmate subculture by adhering to norms of behaviour, sexual conduct, and language. According to Clemmer, inmates who become the most "prisonized" are the most difficult to reintegrate into mainstream society.

When studying prisonization, criminologists have looked at two areas: how inmates adapt their behaviour to a life behind bars and how life in a correctional facility changes due to inmate behaviour. For example, Sykes (1958) and Sykes and Messinger (1960) used Clemmer's work to identify the most important aspects of inmate subculture. They discovered what they called a "prison code"—that is, a system of social norms and values established by inmates to regulate inmates' behaviour while serving their sentences in a prison. According to Sykes (1958), these principles include the following:

1. Don't interfere with inmates' interests, such as never betraying another inmate to authorities.
2. Don't lose your head, and refrain from emotional displays (e.g., arguing) with other inmates.
3. Don't exploit other inmates.
4. Be tough and don't lose your dignity.
5. Don't be a sucker, make a fool of yourself, or support guards or prison administrators over the interests of the inmates.

Sykes and Messinger identified the major theme of the inmate social code as prison or group solidarity. The greater the number of inmates who follow the inmate code, the greater the stability of the prison population, resulting in less prison violence.

Cooley's (1992) research on prison victimization in Canada attempted to discover if the inmate social code existed in five institutions. After interviewing 117

CHAPTER 11 Corrections in Canada: History, Facilities, and Populations inmates, Cooley concluded that the inmate code, as traditionally defined, did not exist in the five institutions studied. What he did find, instead, was a set of informal rules of social control. The most important informal rules of social control are

1. *Do your own time.* These rules define the public and private realms of prison life. They encourage group cohesion by defining proper prison behaviour, which promotes order and minimizes friction. They also discourage prisoners from asking for help from others.

2. *Avoid the prison economy.* These rules warn inmates of the consequences of conducting business in the informal prison economy. High interest rates exist in this economy, and if debts aren't paid off, physical violence may occur. These rules promote social cohesion by warning inmates of the consequences of not paying debts.

3. *Don't trust anyone.* These rules, which caution inmates to be wary of whom they associate with, are a consequence of the existing informant, or "rat," system. The fewer people to whom a prisoner divulges personal information, the better. But, if you find some other inmates you can trust, support and help them so they will respond in kind to you.

4. *Show respect.* This set of rules prescribes how inmates should interact with each other during their daily activities. These rules contribute to the social cohesion in the prison by defining appropriate and inappropriate conduct between prisoners. They also determine a prisoner's status within the prison hierarchy, and those who follow the rules are respected. Those who violate the rules may be physically assaulted (Cooley 1992: 33–34).

According to Cooley, these rules can bring the inmate population closer or isolate them. The resulting environment can best be described as partially unstable, in the sense that the prison is neither in conflict nor in consensus. The informal social control system described by Cooley creates an inmate's status within the prison. Lifers and serious violent offenders usually maintain a high status, unless an inmate loses by engaging in behaviour not accepted by the other inmates. For example, while Donald Marshall was imprisoned at the medium-security federal institution located at Springhill, Nova Scotia, he was told that another inmate, a "greenhorn," hadn't delivered some MDA (a powerful hallucinogenic drug) to him. When Marshall confronted the other inmate, it became obvious that the new inmate didn't know about "the code that applied when a greenhorn had a 'beef' with a lifer" (Harris 1986:

279). When the other inmate refused to admit he hadn't delivered the drug, Marshall knocked him unconscious.

This inmate social code has changed over the years. In the earliest studies of inmates, researchers concluded that an unwritten set of rules guided inmate conduct. A prisoner's position in a prison was determined by whether he followed the prison code—those who failed to do so were ignored and rejected by the prisoners who followed the code. Nevertheless, most of these rejected inmates were considered to be relatively safe from the violent actions of others unless they "ratted out a con." Starting about two decades ago, however, correctional facilities started to change as the prison code lost some of its status as a force in maintaining social relationships among inmates. This was due to the increase in younger offenders and drug offenders who were originally viewed by those embedded in the traditional prison code as only "looking out for themselves" and unwilling to follow the code and pay homage to other inmates. As a result, violence started to increase among inmates. But with the increase of gangs in prisons in Canada and other western countries, the traditional prison code has been replaced by one in which loyalties to the gang are most important. As a result, there has been an increase of inmate-on-inmate violence. In response to the gang members now found in the federal system, the Correctional Service of Canada has started to send inmates in Quebec who are linked to rival gangs to different areas within prison facilities. Maximum-security inmates, for example, are typically sent to Donnacona Institution, where Aisle 119 is reserved for members and associates of the Bandidos Motorcycle Club and Aisle 240 for the members of the Hells Angels. There is also evidence that gang violence is escalating between other gangs members serving time across Canada, a situation that may lead to "tremendous violence" within prisons (Humphreys 2002: A3).

According to Dobash et al. (1986), women inmates experience prison and the pains of imprisonment differently compared to male inmates. Ishwaran, Neugbauer, and Neugbauer (2001: 135) point out that female inmates "cope with the loss of emotional relationships by developing and maintaining significant relationships of 'pseudo families' with other prisoners." Hannah-Moffat (2001: 233) points out that "one manifestation of the pains of imprisonment experienced by female inmates is self-injurious behaviour." Self-injurious behaviour (or self-harm as it is also called) has been found to be a serious problem among women in the Canadian correctional system. Presse and Hart (1996) reported that, in their study of 26 patients in the Intensive Healing Program at the Prairie Regional Psychiatric Centre, 19 had self-injured. And the 1990

Survey of Federally Sentenced Aboriginal Women in the Community reported that Aboriginal women continued to slash themselves after being released in order to relieve their tension and feelings of anger. Fillmore and Dell (2001: 105) point out that to effectively deal with self-injurious behaviour, it is important to interconnect "the health concerns of self-harm [with] the broader issues of poverty, child care support, housing, education, job training, employment, discrimination, and racism."

Another difference experienced by women who are sentenced to a term in a correctional facility is the disruption of their family life. At the time of their offence at least 50 percent of all incarcerated female offenders were living with at least one of their children. As a result, many had to make special child-care arrangements with family or friends. Some lost custody of their children to the authorities. While many provincial governments have some type of policy regarding mother and child contact, this was not so for federally sentenced women until recently. Shaw (1991), in her survey of federally sentenced women, reported that separation from children and concerns about child custody were a major source of anxiety for incarcerated women. The federal government's Task Force on Federally Sentenced Women reported that approximately 70 percent were mothers, many of whom were sole supporters of their children. In addition, most women had a limited education background and few marketable skills, and were either on social assistance or working at low-paying jobs when they were arrested (LeBlanc 1994). When the regional centres for federally sentenced women were opened, the Mother–Child Program was created, which allows for the option of children living with their mothers in the facility (Watson 1995).

PRISON VIOLENCE

Conflict leading to violence is an ever-present reality of prison life. Violence can involve different sets of actors: inmate versus inmate, staff versus inmate, inmate versus staff. According to official data, major assaults on inmates by other inmates declined yearly from 1983–84 until 1988–89, but started to increase dramatically during 1989–90, a trend that has continued. The Correctional Service of Canada produces the equivalent of official police reports (i.e., the Uniform Crime Reports) but the actual occurrence of such incidents that happen within the walls is not known and so the true picture of violence in prison is not available. Between 1995–96 and 1997–98, for example, 144 major assaults among inmates were recorded. In addition, there were 10 major assaults by inmates on correctional staff members, 9 murders by inmates, 8 hostage takings, and 13 major fights among inmates (Correctional Service of Canada 1998).

Attacks on staff members varied between one and 10 annually between 1984–85 and 1991–92. On average, there are two to four serious assaults on staff each year. Furr (1996) examined the characteristics of sexual assaults on female prison staff in the federal correctional system by studying 11 inmates who had committed (or attempted to commit) at least one sexual assault against a female staff member. He found that these inmates had committed serious crimes that had resulted in severe physical harm to the victims, including murder or attempted murder. Many inmates suffered from psychoses, severe personality disorders, or mental/behavioural instability, and most had been identified as at high risk to sexually assault a female staff member—in some cases, they had warned the staff members about their risk before attacking them. The majority of these assaults on the female staff occurred after the inmate had experienced hopelessness, including being rejected for a conditional release program by the National Parole Board.

Violence can also involve all the inmates in a correctional facility. Culhane (1985) documented nine examples of prison violence in Canada between 1975 and 1985. She describes the degradation of inmates by prison officials, and the resulting prisoner violence. One such incident occurred at Archambault Prison, north of Montreal, in 1972. Although 50 inmates were identified as having actively participated in the riot, between 75 and 150 were sent to solitary confinement. These inmates were accused of "participating passively" and therefore "had to pay the social price." Complaints about this treatment reached the attention of federal politicians; a federal inquiry failed to materialize because the guards who had allegedly been involved denied that they had participated, and there was a lack of corroborating evidence (Culhane 1985; Ruby 1985).

Prison Suicide

Inmate suicide is the leading cause of death in Canadian prisons. Burtch and Ericson (1979) reported that between 1959 and 1975 the suicide rate of inmates in Canada's federal institutions was 95.9 per 100 000 inmates, compared with 14.2 per 100 000 nonprison males in Canada. Between 1983 and 1992, 128 of the 265 offenders who died while in federal custody committed suicide (Fogel 1992). In 1991–92, six Aboriginal women committed suicide at the Prison for Women in Kingston, Ontario; as Grossmann (1992) notes, this is an alarmingly high rate in an institution that houses approximately 110 individuals.

Concern over these suicide rates led to the Correctional Service of Canada's creation of a suicide prevention program. In order to gain as much information as possible about male and female inmates who had committed suicide, Green et al. (1992) studied 133 suicides that occurred between 1977 and 1988. They discovered that most suicides were male (129, or 97 percent) and 115 (or 80 percent) were white. The study also revealed that suicide was distributed among all age groups. In terms of marital status, one-half of suicides were single, 38 percent were married or living in common-law relationships, and 12 percent were divorced. Sixty percent had no children, 14 percent had one child, and the rest had two or more children.

The researchers reported that hanging was the most common method (80 percent) of inmate suicide. Almost all of the suicides occurred within an inmate's own cell. In terms of offence and sentence characteristics, 51 individuals had committed a nonsexual offence of violence as their most recent offence, 34 had a robbery or weapons offence, 25 had a property offence, and only one individual was a first-time offender. Green and his colleagues discovered that a high number of suicides occurred early on in a sentence—25 percent within 90 days of sentencing and 50 percent within a year of sentencing.

In an attempt to rectify this situation, the Correctional Service of Canada developed a comprehensive approach for assessment, prevention, intervention, treatment, support, evaluation, research, and training of staff. Specific actions include

1. providing a safe, secure, and humane environment for those who suffer from mental illness and for those who must cope with the stresses of life in a correctional environment;
2. increasing the awareness and understanding of both management and staff concerning suicide and self-injury;
3. developing staff skills to prevent suicide and self-harm, including identifying suicide risk, monitoring pre-indicators, and providing crisis intervention and support services; and
4. developing and implementing support services for survivors, as well as affected staff and inmates.

While these measures may be appropriate for males, Grossmann (1992) argues that they are not applicable to Aboriginal women. She argues that correctional officials should better understand the needs of these women in the context of their socioeconomic position and victimization experiences. Responses to these needs should include a variety of culturally sensitive methods of assistance that would focus on their "violent pasts and various forms of personal victimization, as well as opportunities to redress their education and employment deficiencies" (Grossmann 1992: 412). The Task Force on Federally Sentenced Women (Correctional Service of Canada 1990) recommended assistance to abused women, improved counseling services, more culturally sensitive spiritual supports, and the maintenance of relationships between offenders and their families and communities.

PRISONERS' RIGHTS, DUE PROCESS, AND DISCIPLINE

Before the introduction of the *Charter of Rights and Freedoms* in 1982, inmates had limited legal rights. It was difficult for them to question prison rules and regulations or the decisions of prison officials. Perhaps the most important reason for inmates lacking legal rights was the hesitancy of provincial and federal courts to intervene in the administration of prisons unless there were obvious, excessive, and indiscriminate abuses of power by prison officials. This policy is referred to as the "hands-off doctrine" and consists of three observations:

1. Correctional administration was a technical matter best left to experts rather than to courts ill-equipped to make appropriate evaluations.
2. Society as a whole was apathetic to what went on in prisons, and most individuals preferred not to associate with or know about the offender.
3. Prisoners' complaints involved privileges rather than rights.

In the 1970s, Penitentiary Service Regulations insisted that prison officials provide inmates with certain basic minimum standards, such as the right to adequate food and clothing, essential dental and medical services, and time to exercise. These rights represented only the basic core of the Standard Minimum Rules for the Treatment of Prisoners (1957) adopted by the United Nations, covering such issues as religion, transfers, and disciplinary procedures (MacKay 1986).

At the end of the 1960s prisoners and prisoner-rights advocates challenged this hands-off doctrine in the courts over the issue of due process rights within correctional facilities. In the first such case, *R. v. Beaver Creek Correctional Camp* (1969), an inmate challenged the prison's authority to make disciplinary decisions without providing inmates with due process protections, such as the right to a fair hearing and the right of having legal counsel. The case also challenged the arbitrary powers found within s. 229 of the Penitentiary Regulations, which outlined a number of activities for which inmates could be disciplined.

EXHIBIT 11.2 Special Handling Units: Canada's Supermaximum Institutions?

In the United States approximately 30 states are experimenting with supermaximum prisons, but recently much attention is being given to the supermaximum prison located in Tamms, Illinois. Formally known as Tamms Correctional Center, it isolates all inmates for 24 hours a day. In essence, all programs and services come to each inmate either through a television located in each cell or by individual attention from priests or staff who go to individual cells to talk to each inmate.

Four inmates serving time in Tamms filed a class-action suit that alleged that the structure of Tamms will lead to sensory deprivation based on the nearly total isolation, which leads to "tormenting pain" (Campbell 1999).

The closest any correctional facility in Canada comes to this type of supermaximum prison are special handling units (SHUs). The Correctional Service of Canada opened two special handling units in 1977 to house male inmates "who could not be managed adequately in a maximum-security institution because of the high level of risk and danger they posed to staff and other inmates" (O'Brien 1992: 11). These units were housed in two sections of existing federal correctional institutions, one in Millhaven, Ontario, and the other in the Correctional Development Centre in Quebec. Two institutions were built specifically as SHUs and opened in 1989 in Prince Albert, Saskatchewan, and Ste-Anne-des-Plaines, Quebec.

A new policy on the control of dangerous inmates in the federal system was introduced in 1990. SHUs began to offer limited programs, such as anger management and treatment for substance abuse, and only those inmates who were assessed as high risk to staff and other inmates were sent to these facilities. The objective of SHUs is to safely reintegrate prisoners into a maximum-security prison. This allows other institutions to became safer, thus enabling them to work with larger numbers of offenders in the hope of successfully reintegrating them into society (O'Brien 1992).

In 1991–92, 50 to 60 inmates with an average age of 31.5 years (ranging from 24 to 52 years) entered the Prince Albert SHU. The most common offence for those admitted was first-degree murder (21.1 percent), and the most common sentence was life imprisonment (42.1 percent). At the SHU in Ste-Anne-des-Plaines, Quebec, the average age of inmates was 33 years, with a range of 22 to 55 years; their common offence was second-degree murder and robbery (20.6 percent each), and 26.5 percent were serving a life sentence. Of those admitted to the Quebec SHU, 32.4 percent were serving their first federal sentence.

In 1998, the SHU in Prince Albert closed. Since the end of 1999 about 70 inmates have been held in the SHU in Ste-Anne-des-Plaines, which has a capacity of 90 inmates. Inmates are divided into groups of five or six on each floors (also known as "ranges"). This facility is the only one in Canada where correctional officers are allowed to carry firearms and live ammunition during their patrols. Inmates in an SHU are not totally isolated from each other, as they are allowed to exercise within a small group and to watch a communal television. Some inmates are locked in their cells for 24 hours a day, but only because they refuse to participate in any programs or to take advantage of the limited work activities available.

Sources: O'Brien (1992); Campbell (1999); Humphreys (2002).

The Ontario Court of Appeal ruled that while natural justice also applied to inmates, there were situations in which prison officials had the right to place an inmate in segregation without proper due process safeguards and the possibility of a review of the administrative decision in question. However, while the court ruled that administrative decisions were reviewable when they involved questions about the civil rights of inmates, this case involved a decision purely administrative in nature and therefore wasn't reviewable by the courts.

The first case to significantly challenge the administrative power of prison officials was *R. v. McCann* (1975). Jack McCann had been placed in solitary confinement in the B.C. Penitentiary for 754 days under the authority of s. 2.30(1)(a) of the Penitentiary Service Regulations, which states

> Where the institutional head is satisfied that for the maintenance of good order and discipline in the institution … it is necessary or desirable that the inmate should be kept from associating with other inmates.

McCann argued that his period in solitary confinement infringed on his right to freedom from cruel and unusual treatment or punishment under s. 2(b) of the *Canadian Bill of Rights* (Jackson 1983). The court held that prison administrators had the right to place inmates in solitary confinement with no prior hearing, unless their civil rights were in jeopardy. But it ruled that the use of solitary confinement in this case did, in fact, constitute "cruel and unusual punishment" (Jackson 1983: 101–33).

However, the Supreme Court of Canada, in *Martineau v. Matsqui Institution (No. 2)* (1979), formally recognized that "The rule of law must run within penitentiary walls." It also stated that although prison officials are making administrative decisions, they are still subject to the duty to act fairly. In this case, two inmates at the Matsqui Institution in British Columbia had been found guilty of being in a cell where they shouldn't have been. They argued that "they were not provided with a summary of evidence against them; that the evidence of each was taken in the absence of the other; that the conviction was for an offence unknown to law; and that Martineau was never given an opportunity to give evidence with respect to the charge" (Jackson 1983: 126–27). As a result of this ruling, all those who make administrative decisions concerning the rights or liberties of inmates have a duty to act fairly (Pelletier 1990).

The Duty to Act Fairly

What does it mean to "act fairly," especially for inmates in a correctional facility? The duty to act fairly involves two basic rights: (1) the right to be heard, and (2) the right to have an impartial hearing. As Pelletier (1990: 26) notes, the right to be heard means that all citizens have the right "to be informed of the allegations made against them and to respond to those allegations." The right to an impartial hearing means that "a decision must not be rendered against a person for discriminatory or arbitrary reasons."

In Canada, two areas of legal concern are related to the duty to act fairly: (1) administrative segregation (or solitary confinement) and (2) discipline of inmates.

What are the powers of prison officials to place inmates into administrative segregation? Obviously, some situations, such as prison riots, may require immediate segregation. But what about other situations? In *R. v. McCann* (1975), which was the first case to argue the fairness of the decision to segregate, Mr. Justice Heald ruled that the decision to place an inmate in solitary confinement was "purely administrative" and therefore not subject to legal review.

This interpretation was reinforced by the decision in *Kosobook v. Canada (Solicitor-General)* (1975). In this case, the complainants had been told that they were placed into solitary confinement after an administrative inquiry into the stabbing of an inmate, but no charges

had been laid against them. They argued that their segregation was a denial of natural justice and their right to an unbiased tribunal, the result of a decision made in an arbitrary manner, and an infringement of the *Canadian Bill of Rights*. They claimed that they had not been provided with due process projections and that, as a result, they had been held in arbitrary detention. The judge ruled that the prison authorities did not have any judicial or quasi-judicial functions, but rather performed the role of an administrative body. As a result, they could not violate the *Canadian Bill of Rights*.

However, in *Martineau v. Matsqui Institution (No. 2)* (1979) the Supreme Court of Canada ruled that correctional officials are under a duty to act fairly when making disciplinary decisions. In essence, the Supreme Court concluded that the rule of law must be upheld within correctional facilities. As a result of the ruling in the *Martineau* case, the Correctional Service of Canada changed its policies to fit more closely with the fairness doctrine. For example, in terms of administrative segregation, inmates now have the right to be heard within the correctional context, and prison authorities are obliged to (1) inform an inmate, in writing, of the reasons for the placement in segregation within 24 hours following this placement; (2) notify an inmate in advance of each review of the placement into segregation, in order to permit the inmate to present his case at a hearing in prison; and (3) advise the inmate, in writing, of decisions concerning his status.

SUMMARY

The ideas underlying our contemporary correctional institutions have their origins in the United States during the 19th century. Two competing systems emerged: the Pennsylvania system and the Auburn system. While both approaches treated their inmates with great discipline and rigidly enforced rules, the Auburn system, which allowed groups of inmates to work together and then isolated them at night, formed the basis of the Canadian correctional system.

Canada's federal and provincial/territorial correctional populations have declined slowly since 1995–96. In addition to those serving a sentence in a correctional facility, more than 119 000 offenders are serving a sentence in the community.

At present, over 40 federal correctional facilities operate in Canada. They are classified according to security level, and significant differences exist between them when it comes to their physical appearance and the amount of freedom given to inmates. Five new regional facilities for federally sentenced women are now operational and provide new and innovative programs designed specifically for women. Many of the programs take place in the community.

Until recently, little information was available about prison society. Certain codes or rules exist for inmates to follow, but the prison environment is very unstable since changes are always occurring. There is much violence in Canadian prisons, and many inmates attempt to isolate themselves from other inmates and situations they feel may lead to violence.

Today, inmates have significant, although limited, legal rights. Inmates can take their grievances to various officials and request a hearing. Various courts, including the Supreme Court of Canada, have recognized that inmates possess these rights, and have ruled in their favour in many cases.

Discussion Questions

1. Do you think that reintegration is a positive approach to dealing with inmates? Why or why not?

2. Discuss the issue of prisoners' rights and the evolution of law concerning such rights in Canada.

3. Should we build more federal prisons in Canada?

4. Describe the classification of inmates and correctional facilities. Do you think that there is a better way to classify offenders?

5. Discuss the special issues concerning the needs of female offenders.

6. Discuss the needs of Aboriginal offenders. Do you think they can be met by the existing correctional systems? Do you think any changes should be made?

7. Discuss the process of "prisonization." What are the negative aspects of this process? Can we change it?

8. Can prison violence ever be eliminated?

9. What is the best way to solve the issue of gangs in Canadian correctional facilities?

Suggested Readings

Eckstedt, J.W., and C.T. Griffiths. 1988. *Corrections in Canada: Policy and Practice,* 2nd ed. Vancouver: Butterworths.

Faith, K. 1995. *Unruly Women: The Politics of Confinement and Resistance.* Vancouver: Press Gang Publishers.

Jackson, M. 1983. *Prisoners of Isolation: Solitary Confinement in Canada.* Toronto: University of Toronto Press.

McMahon, M.W. 1992. *The Persistent Prison? Rethinking Decarceration and Penal Reform.* Toronto: University of Toronto Press.

References

Anderson, P.R., and D.J. Newman. 1993. *Introduction to Criminal Justice,* 5th ed. Toronto: McGraw-Hill Ryerson.

Burtch, B.E., and R.V. Ericson. 1979. *The Silent System: An Inquiry into Prisoners Who Suicide/and Annotated Bibliography.* Toronto: Centre for Criminology, University of Toronto.

Campbell, M. "Buried Alive?" *The Globe and Mail,* 7 December, R1, R2.

Caron, R. 1982. *Go-Boy!* Toronto: Hamlyn.

Clemmer, D. 1958. *The Prison Community.* New York: Holt, Rinehart, and Winston.

Cooley, D. 1992. "Prison Rules and the Informal Rules of Social Control." *Forum on Corrections Research* 4: 31–36.

Cooper, S. 1993. "The Evolution of Federal Women's Prisons." In E. Adelberg and C. Currie, eds., *Women in Conflict with the Law: Women and the Criminal Justice System*. Vancouver: Press Gang Publishers.

Correctional Service of Canada. 1998. *Performance Report for the Period Ending March 31, 1998*. Ottawa: Correctional Service of Canada.

———. 1997. *Corrections in Canada*. Ottawa: Correctional Services Canada.

———. 1990. *Creating Choices: Report of the Task Force on Federally Sentenced Women*. Ottawa: Correctional Service of Canada.

Culhane, C. 1985. *Still Barred from Prison: Social Injustice in Canada*. Montreal: Black Rose.

Dobash, R.P., R.E. Dobash, and S. Gutterridge. 1986. *The Imprisonment of Women*. New York: Basil Blackwell.

Eckstedt, J.W., and C.T. Griffiths. 1988. *Corrections in Canada: Policy and Practice*, 2nd ed. Toronto: Butterworths.

Erdahl, E. 2001. "History of Corrections in Canada." In J.A. Winterdyk, ed., *Corrections in Canada: Social Reactions to Crime*. Toronto: Prentice-Hall, pp. 27–48.

Faith, K. 1993. *Unruly Women: The Politics of Confinement and Resistance*. Vancouver: Press Gang Publishers.

Farrington, K. 1992. "The Modern Prison as Total Institution? Public Perception versus Objective Reality." *Crime and Delinquency* 38: 6–26.

Fillmore, C., and C. Dell. 2001. *Prairie Women, Violence and Self-Harm*. Winnipeg: The Elizabeth Fry Society of Manitoba.

Finn, A., S. Trevethan, G. Carriere, and M. Kowalski. 1999. *Female Inmates, Aboriginal Inmates, and Inmates Serving Life Sentences: A One-Day Snapshot*. Ottawa: Juristat.

Fogel, M. 1992. "Investigating Suicide." *Forum on Corrections Research* 4, no. 3: 8–9.

Forum on Corrections Research. 1992. "Violence and Suicide in Canadian Institutions: Some Recent Statistics." *Forum on Corrections Research* 4: 3–5.

———. 1991. "An Historical Overview of the Construction of Canadian Federal Prisons." *Forum on Corrections Research* 3: 3–4.

Furr, K.D. 1996. "Characteristics of Sexual Assaults on Female Prison Staff." *Forum on Corrections Research* 8: 25–27.

Gettinger, S.H. 1984. *New Generation Jails: An Innovative Approach to an Age-Old Problem*. Washington, D.C.: National Institute of Corrections.

Goffman, E. 1961. *Asylums*. New York: Doubleday.

Green, C., G. Andre, K. Kendall, T. Looman, and N. Potovi. 1992. "A Study of 133 Suicides among Canadian Federal Prisoners." *Forum on Corrections Research* 4: 20–22.

Grossman, M. 1992. "Two Perspectives on Aboriginal Female Suicides in Custody." *Canadian Journal of Criminology* 34: 403–16.

Hannah-Moffat, K. 2001. "Limiting the State's Right to Punish." In J.A. Winterdyk, ed., *Corrections in Canada: Social Reactions to Crime.* Toronto: Prentice-Hall, pp. 151–69.

Harris, M. 1986. *Justice Denied: The Law versus Donald Marshall.* Toronto: Totem.

Hendrick, D., and L. Farmer. 2002. *Adult Correctional Services in Canada, 2000/01.* Ottawa: Canadian Centre for Justice Statistics.

Humphrey, A. 2002. "Prisoner 'Tried to Hurt Mom.'" *National Post,* 16 August, A3.

Ishwaran, S., S. Neugbauer, and R. Neugebauer. 2001. "Prison Life and Daily Experiences." In J.A. Winterdyk, ed., *Corrections in Canada: Social Reactions to Crime.* Toronto: Prentice-Hall, pp. 129–50.

Jackson, M. 2002. *Justice behind Walls: Human Rights in Canadian Prisons.* Vancouver: Douglas & McIntyre.

———. 1983. *Prisoners of Isolation: Solitary Confinement in Canada.* Toronto: University of Toronto.

LeBlanc, T. 1994. "Redesigning Corrections for Federally Sentenced Women in Canada." *Forum on Corrections Research* 6: 11–12.

Lonmo, C. 2001. *Adult Correctional Services in Canada, 1999–00.* Ottawa: Canadian Centre for Justice Statistics.

MacKay, A.W. 1986. "Inmates' Rights: Lost in the Maze of Prison Bureaucracy?" *The Correctional Review* 1: 8–14.

McCorkle, R.C. 1992. "Personal Precautions to Violence in Prison." *Criminal Justice and Behavior* 19, no. 2: 160–73.

Meddis, S.V., and D. Sharp. 1994. "Prison Business in a Blockbuster." *USA Today,* 13 December, 10.

Morris, N., and M. Tonry. 1990. *Between Prison and Probation: Intermediate Punishments in a Rational Sentencing System.* New York: Oxford University Press.

Nelson, W.R., and M. O'Toole. 1983. *New Generation Jails.* Boulder, CO: Library Information Specialists, Inc.

O'Brien, R.L. 1992. "Special Handling Units." *Forum on Corrections Research* 4: 11–13.

Pachner, K. 2001. "Infectious Diseases Outpacing Prison Health Services." *RCMP Gazette,* 64: 8.

Pelletier, B. 1990. "The Duty to Act Fairly in Penitentiaries." *Forum on Corrections Research* 2: 25–28.

Picard, A. 2001. "Inmate Sues Ottawa for Contracting AIDS in Jail." *The Globe and Mail,* 20 August, A1–A5.

Presse, L.D., and R.D. Hart. 1989. "Variables Associated with Parasuicidal Behaviour of Female Offenders During a Cognitive Behavioural Treatment Program." *Canadian Psychologist*: 40.

Reed, M., and J.V. Roberts. 1999. *Adult Correctional Services in Canada, 1997–98.* Ottawa: Juristat.

Robinson, D., F.J. Porporino, and W.A. Millson. 1998. *A One-Day Snapshot of Inmates in Canada's Adult Correctional Facilities.* Ottawa: Juristat.

Rothman, D.J. 1971. *The Discovery of the Asylum.* Boston: Little, Brown.

Ruby, C.C. 1985. "Violence in and out of Prison." *The Globe and Mail,* 29 June, E6.

Shaw, M. 1994. "Women in Prison: A Literature Review." *Forum on Corrections Research* 6, no. 1: 13–18.

———. 1991. *Survey of Federally Sentenced Women: Report of the Task Force on Federally Sentenced Women on the Prison Survey.* Ottawa: Corrections Branch, Ministry of the Solicitor General of Canada.

Statistics Canada. 1996. *The Justice Data Factfinder.* Ottawa: Juristat.

Stolz, B.A. 1997. "Privatizing Corrections: Changing the Corrections Policy-Making Subgovernment." *Prison Journal* 77: 92.

Sykes, G. 1958. *The Society of Captives.* Princeton, N.J.: Princeton University Press.

Sykes, G., and S. Messinger. 1960. "The Inmate Social Code." In R. Cloward et al., eds., *Theoretical Studies in the Social Organization of the Prison.* New York: Social Science Research Council, pp. 6–9.

Taylor, C.J. 1979. "The Kingston, Ontario Penitentiary and Moral Architecture." *Histoire Sociale/Social History* 12: 385–408.

Zupan, L.L. 1991. *Jails: Reform and the New Generation Philosophy.* Cincinnati: CJ Anderson.

Court Cases

Kosobook v. Canada (Solicitor General) (1975), [1976] 1 F.C. 540 (Fed. T.D.)

Martineau v. Matsqui Institution (No. 2) (1979), [1980] 1 S.C.R. 602

R. v. Beaver Creek Correctional Camp (1968), 2 D.L.R. (3d) 545 (Ont. C.A.)

R. v. McCann (1975), 29 C.C.C. (2d) 337 (Fed. T.D.)

Richardson v. McKnight, 117 S. Ct. 2100 (U.S. Tenn. 1997)

CHAPTER 12

Community Reintegration

CHAPTER OBJECTIVES

✓ Understand the different community sanction programs that exist today in Canada.

✓ Understand the operation and purpose of the "faint hope" clause.

✓ Examine the rates of recidivism for the community sanction programs.

✓ Look at the relationship between recidivism rates and the race, gender, marital, and employment status of offenders released on community sanction programs.

Although some people would like to see criminals put away in prison forever, the reality is that over 90 percent of offenders are released back into society. Some offenders are placed on probation as soon as they are sentenced or shortly thereafter, while others—considered good risks not to reoffend—are ultimately released on some type of conditional release program such as parole. The beliefs about the role of conditional release programs in the criminal justice system have changed dramatically over the past few decades. As will be discussed below, these programs were once criticized as "not working," while today they are seen by correctional officials as a necessary component of having offenders become law-abiding citizens after their sentences are completed.

This chapter begins with a brief discussion about the history of conditional release programs in Canada and how the approaches underlying these programs have changed in recent decades, from one that emphasized rehabilitation (based on the medical model) to one that focuses on reintegration/risk prediction. The chapter then outlines this reintegration model and how it is practised in the federal system of corrections today and presents a discussion of some of the issues related to reintegration, such as the importance of risk prediction. The role of the National Parole Board and the *Corrections and Conditional Release Act* (1992) are also reviewed. Finally, the different types of conditional release programs and the recidivism rates of participants are reviewed.

According to Freeze (2001a), over the past few years millions of dollars have been claimed in at least 20 lawsuits made against Canada's parole board and corrections agency for crimes committed on parole. In these lawsuits, damages as high as $10 million have been awarded, although in most case when a settlement is reached, it is usually for less than $1 million. The claims all share a similar argument: that officials should have kept prisoners locked up since it would have made the community safer.

Some of these cases include a $10 million claim filed in 1998 by the family of a 17-year-old woman in Ottawa beaten to death; three claims filed in 2000 totaling $6 million by three women and a man who allege a parolee went on a rampage of rapes and abductions in May 1999; and a $3.5 million claim by an individual whose throat was slashed by a paroled double-murderer (Freeze 2001b).

In defending itself against these lawsuits, the federal government argued that it cannot be held financially accountable for the crimes committed by parolees. However, in 1995, a judge made a public award of $394 000 to a woman who had been sexually assaulted by a sex killer who had escaped from a minimum-security correctional facility. In his ruling, the judge ruled that the federal government holds a "duty of care" toward the victim. According to Freeze (2001a: A7), since this case public decisions by judges "have been rare and the government has preferred to settle with victims for undisclosed amounts."

COMMUNITY RELEASE UNDER ATTACK

Starting in the early 1970s, all forms of community sanctions, particularly parole, came under attack from an outraged public who felt that any program that placed offenders into the community as part of their sentence was soft on criminals. In response, these criticisms were followed by a series of policy changes developed by criminal justice practitioners who argued that all forms of community sanction were too discretionary and failed to protect the due process rights of the offenders. Critics of the changes also asserted that the rehabilitation ideal and its related treatment programs that were designed to reintegrate offenders into the community were misplaced. For those reasons, parole was abolished in a number of American states, starting with Maine in 1975. By 1984 the number of states without parole had increased to 11, although in the following year Colorado reinstated parole after having removed its parole board in 1979. The Canadian Sentencing Commission (1987) also recommended the elimination of parole in its report, but its proposals were never implemented.

Nothing Works

In 1974 Robert Martinson published an article that was to have a tremendous impact on the way in which community sanctions would operate in the following decades. Entitled "What Works? Questions and Answers about Prison Reform," the article questioned the very existence of rehabilitation. This essay was drawn from a larger work (Lipton, Martinson, and Wilks 1975) that assessed 231 evaluation studies of treatment programs that operated between 1945 and 1967. At the end of his article, Martinson (1974: 25) commented that with "few and isolated exceptions the rehabilitative efforts that have been reported so far have had no appreciable effect on recidivism."

Yet in his last section—"Does Nothing Work?"—he pointed out that the studies reviewed were no doubt flawed in many ways, which led to the inability to find any significant treatment successes. Martinson reasoned

that their failure to discover any successful treatments was grounded in large part in the lack of sophistication of both the methods and statistics used in the studies. As a result, it was almost impossible for researchers to detect either the positive effects of or the problems with the internal quality of the programs, such as therapeutic integrity. Nevertheless, Martinson (1974: 49) wrote that it may be impossible for rehabilitation-based programs to overcome or reduce "the powerful tendencies of offenders to continue in criminal behaviour."

Most people who read Martinson's article failed to heed his acknowledgment that there may indeed be positive effects of rehabilitation in the future. Instead, the phrase "nothing works," as Walker (1984: 168) notes, became an instant cliché for critics and exerted enormous influence on both popular and professional thinking. Five years later, Martinson (1979: 244, 252) clarified his position:

> Contrary to my previous position, some treatment programs do have an appreciable effect on recidivism … some programs are indeed beneficial. New evidence from our current study leads me to reject my original conclusion … I have hesitated up to now, but the evidence in our surveys is simply too overwhelming to ignore.

Though his original article is one of the most frequently cited in criminology, his second remains virtually ignored (Cullen and Gendreau 1989). By the time his second article appeared, the critique of rehabilitation was too powerful and entrenched. Martinson himself, after reviewing the few research projects on parole, concluded that when parolees and nonparolees were compared, parole had at best only a delaying effect on recidivism (Waller 1974). This doubt cast on the benefits of parole led to questions concerning the grounding of parole in rehabilitation (Canadian Sentencing Commission 1987).

DISCRETION AND DISPARITY

Another issue raised by critics of community sanctions was the immense discretionary power held by parole boards. These critics were concerned not only with the arbitrariness of many parole board decisions but also the inability of the boards to develop criteria that could help them predict which offenders were ready to be released into the community. Parole authorities were accused of knowing little about the criminal personality and of making contradictory decisions (Frankel 1972).

Because parole boards often shortened the sentences of offenders by releasing them on a conditional

EXHIBIT 12.1 Federal Policy on Offender Reintegration

One purpose of the *Corrections and Conditional Release Act*, in keeping with one of the purposes of the federal correctional system, is to assist in the rehabilitation of offenders and their reintegration into the community as law-abiding citizens through the provision of programs in penitentiaries and in the community. Offender reintegration is defined as all activity and programming conducted to prepare an offender to return safely to the community and live as a law-abiding citizen. To understand offender reintegration, one must understand the variables considered in decisions about releasing offenders to the community. For each offender, the Correctional Service does the following:

- collects all available relevant information about the offender, including items such as the judge's reasons for sentencing and any victim impact statements
- assesses the offender's risk level (the likelihood that he or she will reoffend) and criminogenic needs (life functions that lead to criminal behaviour)
- reduces the offender's risk level by increasing his or her knowledge and skills and changing the attitudes and behaviours that lead to criminal behaviour

- develops and implements programs and individual interventions that effect change in areas that contribute to criminal behaviour
- in cooperation with the offender, develops a plan to increase the likelihood that the offender will function in the community as a law-abiding citizen
- motivates and helps the offender follow the correctional plan and benefit from correctional programs and interventions
- monitors and assesses the offender's progress in learning and changing
- makes recommendations to the National Parole Board as to the offender's readiness for release and the conditions, if any, under which he and she could be released
- after release, helps the offender respect the conditions of the release and resolve day-to-day living problems
- makes required programs and interventions available in the community
- monitors the offender's behaviour to ensure that he or she is respecting the release conditions and not indulging in criminal behaviour
- if required, suspends the offender's release, carries out specific intervention, and reinstates or recommends revocation of the release as appropriate

Source: Thurber (1998).

---

release program (e.g., parole) they became, in essence, the main sentencing agent in the criminal justice system. The Canadian Sentencing Commission (1987: 240), after examining statistics on both the original sentences and subsequent parole board decisions across Canada, came to the conclusion that "there is a substantial difference between the sentence a judge hands down and the length of time an offender actually serves in prison."

This discretion, critics argue, leads to disparity in the time served by offenders. Specifically, the Canadian Sentencing Commission (1987: 240) noted that "offenders serving longer sentences are more likely to get released on parole than are offenders sentenced to shorter terms." Harman and Hann (1986: 27–29), for example, reported in their study of persons sentenced for manslaughter between 1975–76 and 1981–82 that the percentage of the prison sentence served before parole release ranged between 51 and 64 percent. They also found that more individuals convicted of manslaughter were released on parole than those convicted of break and enter.

CONDITIONAL RELEASE PROGRAMS IN CANADA

There are numerous types of conditional release programs currently being used in Canada today. Most are in a state of flux in the sense that demands for tighter control of offenders in the community by citizens have led correctional officials to change definitions of who gets on these programs in order to tighten security and enhance public safety.

A BRIEF HISTORY OF CONDITIONAL RELEASE IN CANADA

The earliest form of conditional release in Canada was known as "remission," and its important role was included in the first *Penitentiary Act* (1868). This program utilized a point system, allowing offenders to receive an early release at the maximum rate of six days per month for good behaviour. Merit (and demerit) points were awarded for good behaviour and attitude as well as for industrious work. A few years later, this policy was changed to allow an inmate to receive a bonus of up to 10 days remission once he had earned 72 days under the existing scheme (i.e., had been a "model" inmate for one year). This formula (which had the potential of releasing inmates after serving three-quarters of their sentence) remained in practice until 1961.

The *Ticket-of-Leave Act* (1899) was the first piece of legislation involving the conditional release program of parole. This act specified that inmates could gain a form of early release (known as "clemency") that was independent of earned remission. Clemency gave the Governor-General of Canada the power to release an inmate early under certain conditions. In essence, this program introduced a system of administrative discretion of release and reduced the time served to a greater extent than that allowed under the policy of remission (Ryan 1990; Carrington 1991). The first parole officer (who worked for the Salvation Army) was appointed in 1905. In 1913, the Remission Service of Canada was created and placed under the control of the federal Department of Justice.

From the early 1900s to 1958, the ticket-of-leave system gradually changed to resemble the modern parole system. In 1958 the *Parole Act* was proclaimed and the authority to grant release and to issue revocation orders was transferred to the newly formed National Parole Board. This board operated on the premise that "interviews between Board members and inmates do not serve a sufficiently useful function … the Board should not be required to grant inmates an opportunity for a personal interview" (Cole and Manson 1990: 171). All information in support of parole applications was collected from a variety of sources and then submitted in written form. However, the *Parole Act* provided little guidance on the criteria that the members of the National Parole Board would consider when reviewing an application for early release. This new piece of legislation introduced a significant change: the realization that there should be a statutory term of parole supervision in the community prior to inmates completing their sentences. At this same time, the policy of "temporary absence" was also introduced, which allowed inmates to be released into the community for relatively short periods of time.

Over the next decades, the federal government commissioned numerous reports concerning parole and other forms of conditional release. Most of these recommended increasing the conditional release system, and, as a result, new policies were gradually introduced (such as mandatory supervision and day parole). One of the most significant reports was produced by the Ouimet Committee (1969), which recommended that the system of parole be expanded in order to assist offenders to reintegrate back into the community. In the late 1980s, however, the Canadian Sentencing Commission (1987) recommended that the system of full parole be abolished (it also recommended that a system of earned remission be retained). This recommendation was not followed by the Canada Sentencing Commission; the following year the Daubney Committee proposed that the conditional release system be expanded but that the system of earned remission be abolished. Of these two reports, the recommendations made by the Daubney Committee had a greater impact on the system of conditional release.

The Reintegration Approach

Today, the Correctional Service of Canada has expanded the conditional release system so that most, although not all, inmates are released into the community prior to the end of their sentence. This reintegration is based on two factors. The first is the belief that only the most serious offenders should be sentenced to a period of incarceration in the federal system and, second, that the use of alternative sanctions (such as conditional sentences) be maximized. According to Latessa and Allen (1997: 28), reintegration is "a broad correctional ideology stressing the acquisition of legitimate skills and opportunities by criminal offenders, and the creation of supervised opportunities for testing, using, and refining those skills, particularly in community settings."

The reintegration approach takes the position that the major predictors of recidivism are known and that each individual offender has to be assessed in terms of these predictors in order to develop programs that will enhance his reintegration to society. These major predictors of recidivism are

1. "antisocial/procriminal attitudes, values, beliefs and cognitive-emotional states (that is, personal cognitive supports for crime";
2. "procriminal associates and isolation from anti-criminal others (that is, interpersonal supports for crime)"; and
3. antisocial personality orientations such as low self-control, impulsiveness, risk-taking and ego-centrism (Andrews 1995: 37).

Recidivism is also predicted by a history of anti-social conduct going back to childhood; by poor childhood training by parents, such as inadequate support and supervision; and by "low levels of personal educational, vocational or financial achievement," including

Lucie McClung, the first woman to be appointed Commissioner of the Correctional Service of Canada, favours reintegrating inmates into the community.

an "unstable employment record" (Andrews 1995: 37). Some of these predictors are static but most are dynamic, that is, the majority of these predictors of recidivism can be changed. These dynamic factors are called "criminogenic needs."

To determine the chances for an offender recidivating, the risks and needs of each offender are assessed when he enters a federal correctional facility. This in turn leads to the selection of the proper response (or responsivity) by correctional personnel.

The Correctional Service of Canada has practised this approach for over a decade. The major legislation guiding the Correctional Service, the *Corrections and Conditional Release Act*, has as one of its main goals the reintegration of offenders into the community (see Exhibit 12.1 on page 287).

During the Offender Intake Assessment (or OIA) an extensive amount of information is collected, including an offender's prior criminal record, her potential for violence, and the nature of her most recent offence. During the OIA, a criminal risk assessment and an identification of the offender's case needs are developed by parole officers. These two assessments form the basis of the Correctional Plan Overview, which evaluates the total case record of an offender (it is typically

updated every six months). These records become the basis of the Custody Rating Scale (CRS) which is used to determine the security classification of an offender (see Figure 12.1).

The Offender Risk Assessment and Management Process is based upon the risk and need of each offender. (The National Parole Board also evaluates offenders who have applied for early release on a conditional release program; see below.) A risk assessment identifies those individuals most likely to reoffend and their needs so correctional officials can develop a personalized plan to assist the offender during incarceration. The Correctional Service of Canada implemented the Offender Risk Assessment and Management strategy in 1986 and all inmates, except some offenders who may receive a very early release date, are assessed (Taylor 1998).

The Theory of Risk Assessment

The theory of risk assessment underlies the OIA. This theory focuses upon the social psychology of criminal behaviour and states that individual and social/situational factors combine to create in offenders values, cognitions, and personality contexts that facilitate criminal behaviour. To a large extent, these ways of thinking and behaving are learned and reinforced, and ultimately lead to individual differences in criminal actions.

The three key principles of risk assessment are risk, need, and responsivity. The first principle, risk, states that higher levels of service should be allocated to the higher-risk cases. However, as Andrews (1989: 14) points out, "the belief persists that treatment services, if effective at all, only work for lower risk cases." Thus, high success rates for low-risk offenders on a conditional release program may be incorrectly interpreted to mean that the offenders benefited from treatment. This may not be so because, being low-risk, they may have had high success rates even without treatment. As Andrews (1989: 19) points out, "such errors involve confusing the predictive accuracy of pretreatment risk assessments with the issue of who profits from it." If high-risk offenders are improperly assessed as low-risk, they will no doubt have high recidivism rates. In his research on probation supervision programs in Ottawa, Kiessling (1989) discovered higher-risk cases in a regular supervision program had a recidivism rate of 58 percent, compared with 31 percent of high-risk cases placed in a high-risk supervision program. Therefore, it is essential to have a correct determination of risk in order to match the offender with the type of program from which she will benefit.

The essential component of the risk assessment is the determination of which risks are considered static factors and which are considered dynamic factors. Static factors include the prior record of an offender and her prior record (if any) when placed on a conditional release program). Dynamic factors (sometimes referred to as "need" factors) involve those characteristics of an offender that can be changed through correctional programming. These include level of education, the level and type of cognitive thinking skills, occupational skills and interpersonal skills. Dynamic factors differ from static factors because they can be changed. Some needs may be viewed as criminogenic, that is, if they are not dealt with, there is a significant chance that an offender will reoffend after release.

The second principle, need, asserts "if correctional treatment services are to reduce criminal recidivism, the criminogenic needs of offenders must be targeted" (Andrews 1989: 15). These needs vary among individuals, but the following are needs that can be dealt with in a rehabilitative program:

- change antisocial attitudes
- change antisocial feelings
- reduce antisocial peer associations
- promote formal affection/communication
- promote formal monitoring and supervision
- promote identification and association with anticriminal role models
- increase self-control, self-management, and problem-solving skills (Andrews 1989: 15).

Responsivity is the third principle, and it deals with the selection of appropriate targets for change and styles of service. Responsivity factors are individual targets that affect the treatment goals (Bonta 1995: 36). According to Andrews (1989), two ideas are central to the success of responsivity: (1) the styles or types of service that work for offenders, and (2) within offender groups, any special responsivity considerations. In essence, this principle addresses effective correctional supervision and

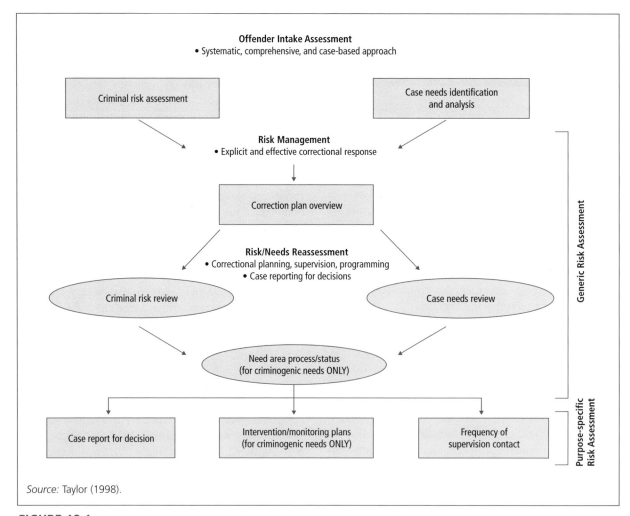

Source: Taylor (1998).

FIGURE 12.1
The Offender Risk Assessment and Management Process

counseling and assumes that all offenders are different. Characteristics such as verbal skills, communication style, inadequate problem-solving skills, and poor social skills become important not only in classifying offenders but also in the way offenders themselves respond to efforts to change their behaviour, thoughts, and attitudes (Bonta 1995).

Research in this area has found that the typical response involves many risk factors, in order that offenders receive training in prosocial attitudes. An important part of this principle is matching offenders to parole officers' characteristics. Research indicates parole officers who scored higher on interpersonal sensitivity and awareness of social rules received higher scores from their clients and were also more likely to display prosocial behaviour and disapprove of antisocial behaviour (Andrews 1980; Andrews and Kiessling 1980).

The Case Management Process

Case management is defined as "a systematic process by which identified needs and strengths of offenders are matched with selected services and resources in corrections" (Enos and Southern 1996: 1). The essential objectives of this system are to

- provide for the systematic monitoring of an offender during his confinement;
- facilitate the graduated release of an offender back into the community; and
- prevent an offender from reoffending after he has been released into the community.

This system establishes a program for each inmate that

1. provides for a level of structure in order that any needs are dealt with;
2. balances the protection of the community with the need for offender rehabilitation;
3. prepares an inmate for successful reintegration back into the community; and
4. assists in the effective supervision while an offender is serving his conditional release program. Exhibit 12.2 shows the case management process.

THE NATIONAL PAROLE BOARD

The National Parole Board (NPB) plays a significant role in the conditional release of inmates into the community. While it once held significant discretionary powers under the *Parole Act* (see above), the board gradually changed its approach due to concerns about the lack of due process guarantees and procedural safeguards

---

EXHIBIT 12.2 The Five Phases of the Case Management Process

I. Initial Assessment and Institutional Placement

- identification of inmate risks/needs
- development of correctional plan

II. Correctional Planning and Institutional Supervision

- correctional plan initiated
- institutional programs (work, treatment, skills upgrading)
- institutional transfers
- institutional releases (temporary absences, work releases)
- ongoing monitoring of inmate progress

III. Preparing Cases for Release Decisions

- institutional progress reports
- community assessments

IV. Parole Board Decision and Release

- temporary absences, day/full parole, statutory release

V. Community Supervision

Source: Griffiths and Cunningham (2000).

---

for inmates during parole hearings. For example, the Report of the Task Force on the Release of Inmates (1973) criticized the criteria for parole release for being vague and unclear, with the effect that "neither inmates nor members of the Board are able to articulate with any certainty what positive and negative factors enter the parole decision" (*Report of the Task Force on the Release of Inmates* 1973: 32). The task force proceeded to recommend that offenders be allowed to appear before the parole board members, giving them "the opportunity to hear from the decision-makers themselves the reasons for their decision" (*Report of the Task Force on the Release of Inmates* 1973: 34). The reasons for any decision were now to be written down and a copy given to the applicant. Additional procedural safeguards were also introduced into the *Parole Act*—namely, the granting of a parole hearing when requested and written reasons for the rejection of an application. In addition, the National Parole Board (1981) published a list of factors that parole board members could consider during a hearing. These include

- the criminal record, kinds of offences and their pattern, and the length of crime-free periods between convictions;

- the nature of the current offence and its seriousness;
- the understanding the inmate appears to have of the situation that brought him to prison, and what he has done about it;
- the effort the inmate has made while in prison to take training and to take advantage of educational and employment upgrading activities;
- the institutional behaviour and offences of the inmate;
- the previous parole violations, if any, of the inmate; and
- the plans the inmate has for employment or training and how definite they are.

"Schedule offences" are an important component of the legislation governing the federal correctional system (the *Corrections and Conditional Release Act*, which replaced the *Parole Act*). These are offences under the *Criminal Code* prosecuted by way of indictment. Offences found in Schedule I are violent crimes, such as murder, attempted murder, sexual offences, and offences of criminal negligence in which the result was severe harm or death. Severe harm may be either physical or psychological. Schedule II offences are offences under the *Controlled Substances and Drugs Act* and the *Food and Drugs Act* and are prosecuted by way of indictment. Offences included in Schedule II include all drug offences and conspiracy to commit a drug offence (charges for simple possession are excluded). The importance of these schedules lies in their influence on the classification of offenders, types of programming, the need for a psychiatric or psychological assessment, and consideration for a conditional release program (Leonard 1999).

Today, before offenders leave a federal correctional facility on a conditional release program, they agree to a correctional plan developed by the National Parole Board with the assistance of correctional officials (such as institutional parole officers). The correctional plan outlines an individualized risk management strategy for each offender and specifies those interventions and monitoring techniques required to address the risks associated with the offender's reoffending. It commonly involves the placing of certain restrictions on his movement and activities, and it specifies certain constructive activities, such as jobs and counseling.

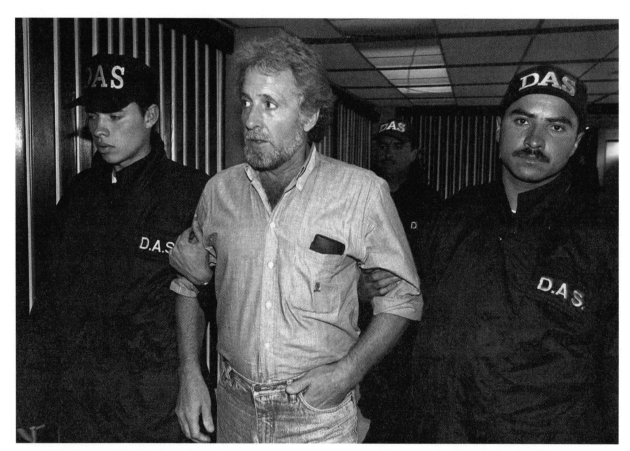

Raymond Boulanger, a pilot for the Cali, Columbia, cocaine cartel, was sentenced to 23 years in prison after being found guilty of landing 4 tonnes of Columbian cocaine at an airfield in Northern Quebec. He received day parole in 1998, under the new federal guidelines that allow first-time federal inmates convicted of nonviolent crimes to receive day parole at the one-sixth point of their sentence.

The assumption behind this approach is that people become involved in crime because of problems in their lives, such as lack of employment opportunities due to a lack of job training and skills, substance abuse, lack of skill in anger management, and so on. The correctional plan is based on information selected from risk assessment evaluations conducted by the Correctional Service of Canada as well as the case management group to which the offender belongs while in custody (Correctional Service of Canada 1997).

The release of an offender into the community entails addressing three related issues: supervision, programming, and community involvement. Supervision is the direct monitoring of and communication with offenders once they are back in the community. This is usually conducted by parole officers or trained volunteers, depending on the offender involved. Not all offenders are adequately supervised, however, according to the 1999 report by the federal Auditor General. He conducted a random sample of 150 offenders under community supervision in five major urban centres and reported that 10 to 20 percent "were not contacted with the required frequency" (Bellavance and Alberts 1999: A6). Supervision alone does not, in the opinion of the Correctional Service of Canada, help offenders change. Therefore, it is combined with "programming," which requires the supervised offender to participate in programs designed to meet his needs. These programs are located in the community, with the idea that they will assist in the reintegration of the offender (Correctional Service of Canada 1997).

CONTEMPORARY COMMUNITY SANCTIONS IN CANADA

Despite the fact that the law specifies offenders must receive penalties for their crimes, it also allows for the mitigation of sentences. Some offenders serve time in either a provincial or federal institution, of course, but the majority remain in the community—at home and at work—under the supervision of probation or parole officers. During 2000–01, over 151 000 adults were under the jurisdiction of the various federal and provincial correctional agencies in Canada. Of these, almost 120 000 (about 80 percent) were under some type of community sanction.

On conditional release programs, offenders complete their sentence in the community after serving time in a correctional institution. A major difference between probation (see Chapter 10) and a conditional release program is that probation is imposed by a judge after an individual is convicted of an offence. A conditional release program, on the other hand, is not a sentence imposed by the court but a release decision made by correctional authorities or a parole board after an offender has completed part of his sentence in a correctional institution.

Conditional release programs were implemented as a result of dissatisfaction with the role of prisons. Prisons are considered to be too expensive to operate, have harmful effects, disrupt family relationships, and have success rates about the same as probation and conditional release programs. The cost of operating a correctional institution, as we have pointed out, is high. Food, medical and dental services, vocational and literacy training, 24-hour security, and escorted leaves are expensive. Community sanctions, however, are much lower in cost. Guards are not needed, and capital costs are lower since no expensive security devices are required. The offender is usually working and paying taxes, family support, and, in some cases, restitution to victims.

In addition, community sanctions are thought to mitigate the harmful effects of incarceration on individuals. Life in a correctional institution does not resemble life in society. Violence, lack of employment skills and training, and a controlled environment have led many to conclude that prisons do more harm than good. Community sanctions allow offenders to maintain connections to society, allowing them to work, be in supportive relationships, and take advantage of community resources. Finally, those who receive community sanctions usually have lower recidivism rates, since they are considered lower risks. So placing these individuals in a correctional facility could be counterproductive, as it would disrupt their lives and families, and make it more difficult for them to reintegrate into society.

RISK OF RECIDIVISM

Despite the introduction of these procedural changes, the National Parole Board came under increasing public criticism for its release decisions, especially after a series of homicides in 1987–88 by individuals on conditional release programs. To some members of the public at the time, offenders released into the community were potential high-risk offenders.

However, studies of inmates placed into a community release program found that rates of recidivism related to the type of conditional release program offenders were placed on. For example, a profile of readmissions to federal correctional institutions over a six-year period showed a substantial difference between recidivism rates for those on full parole and those on mandatory supervision. Of the 8751 offenders released on full parole, 30 percent were readmitted, compared to

58 percent of the 17 769 offenders placed on mandatory supervision.

The majority of offenders returned to a federal institution for violating the terms of their conditional release did so within 12 months of their release. Within 24 months, 81 percent of all offenders who failed on full parole or mandatory supervision were readmitted. After 24 months, however, the risk of returning to a federal institution dramatically declined. According to the Correctional Service of Canada (1990: 12), "after the two-year follow-up point, the number of offenders returning to federal institutions dropped to 2 percent and gradually tapered off each subsequent year. At the six-year follow-up point, fewer than 1 percent of offenders were readmitted." This study revealed that for those offenders on mandatory supervision, the critical point for readmission to a federal institution occurs within six months of release, while for offenders on full parole the second six-month period is the most critical.

Because of concerns about recidivism rates, the Correctional Service of Canada instructed the National Parole Board to shift its focus to risk factors as the prime consideration when considering release of offenders. This change was introduced in November 1986, when the National Parole Board identified its primary purpose as the protection of society. To achieve this goal, the board made risk assessment of future crimes by offenders after release its major focus (National Parole Board 1987). In 1988 the National Parole Board released its policy on prerelease detention, which was intended to identify the criteria for parole board decisions.

These policies were based on three key assumptions: first, that risk to society is the fundamental consideration in any conditional release decision; second, that the restrictions on the freedom of the offender in the community must be limited to those that are necessary and reasonable for the protection of society and the safe reintegration of the offender; and, third, that supervised release increases the likelihood of reintegration and contributes to the long-term protection of society (National Parole Board 1988; Bottomley 1990; Larocque 1998).

In 1992 the *Corrections and Conditional Release Act* replaced the *Parole Act*. This change brought about goals designed to increase the commitment to conditional release into the community. The new act also identified the fundamental principles that would guide corrections in the changing social and legal contexts of Canadian society. The Correctional Service of Canada is now guided by a statement of principles that states, first, that the purpose of the federal correctional system is to maintain "a just, peaceful and safe society" (Haskell 1994: 45). This purpose is to be achieved by the following means:

(a) carrying out sentences imposed by courts through the safe and humane custody and supervision of offenders; and

(b) assisting the rehabilitation of offenders and their reintegration into the community as law-abiding citizens through the provision of programs in penitentiaries and in the community (s. 3, *Corrections and Conditional Release Act*).

In addition, those who drafted the *Corrections and Conditional Release Act* wanted to enhance for all concerned—offenders, correctional staff, and the public—an understanding and appreciation of the principles and purposes behind correctional decision-making. As a result, there is now improved guidance for the National Parole Board as it carries out its mandate. It was hoped that the board would become "more consistent and straightforward in its functioning" (Haskell 1994: 46).

To achieve its goals, the *Corrections and Conditional Release Act* authorizes the disclosure of all relevant information to offenders (subject to certain limited exceptions) when a decision adversely affects their conditional release application. In addition, the act allows for the disclosure of some information to victims, in the hope that this will "lead to greater awareness of the legitimate reasons behind decisions that may appear arbitrary, inappropriate or even unfair" (Haskell 1994: 46). The act also requires the release of all information to the National Parole Board about the offender's background that could affect the board's conditional release decision. This information includes the nature of the offences as well as police and prosecution files and sentencing information.

Risk Assessment

The *Corrections and Conditional Release Act* requires the National Parole Board to distinguish different types of offenders on the basis of risk factors. All board members are required to "specifically assess whether an offender will commit an offence, in particular a violent offence, while on conditional release" (Sutton 1994: 21). To enhance their decision-making ability, board members are now required to have training in risk assessment and knowledge of relevant research.

National Parole Board decisions are therefore made on the basis of risk assessment, risk prediction, and risk reduction. They are based on a general knowledge of the social-psychological perspective on criminal conduct, including the assumption that criminal behaviour is, in most cases, learned behaviour. When making decisions about conditional release, parole board members make assessments in five areas of an offender's situation (Sutton 1994: 22):

1. behavioural history;
2. the immediate situation;
3. mental and emotional outlook favourable to criminal activity;
4. pro-criminal social supports; and
5. other personal factors, including level of development, self-regulation, problem-solving skills, impulsivity, and callousness.

The Task Force on Reintegration of Offenders, formed by the Correctional Service of Canada in 1997, reported that the service is legally mandated to use the least restrictive measures consistent with protecting the public. As such, the task force recommended implementing a risk-related differentiation process that places offenders into one of three categories on the basis of a risk/needs rating. This categorization is accomplished during the Offender Intake Assessment process. The three levels are

1. release-oriented intervention for low-risk offenders;
2. institutional and community intervention for moderate-risk offenders; and
3. high-intensity intervention for offenders in the high-risk category (Correctional Service of Canada 1997).

In an effort to assess the significance of these principles in their application to recidivism rates, Brown and O'Brien (1993) described a study that involved a panel of psychologists and psychiatrists and their assessments of 69 randomly selected federal offenders in a forensic unit of a Canadian hospital. The most common offences were murder (41 percent of the offences), a sexual offence (20 percent), and assault or manslaughter (19 percent). The panel used 15 recidivism risk factors—three demographic factors and 12 clinical factors—to complete their assessments. On the basis of risk scores, 26 offenders were identified as "good risks" for release into the community, and all were successful in completing their terms on parole. Recidivism risk factors therefore assisted in releasing these high-risk offenders on parole. However, the success of these offenders on parole was in large part the result of treatment services delivered in the context of risk principles in a community setting.

Conditional Release Programs

Conditional release programs include full parole, day parole, statutory release, and temporary absences. Full parole allows offenders to serve a portion of their sentence in the community until it has expired. Most inmates in the federal correctional system can apply to the National Parole Board for full parole after they have served one-third of their total sentence or seven years, whichever is shorter. Offenders who are subject to longer eligibility requirements include those serving life sentences or sentences of preventive detention. Offenders serving a sentence of two years less a day in a provincial institution are eligible to apply for parole after serving one-third of their sentence. Ontario and Quebec are the only provinces that operate their own board of parole. The National Parole Board has authority over all provincial inmates in those provinces that do not have their own provincial parole board (Eckstedt and Griffiths 1988; Birkenmayer 1995). Once offenders are released on full parole, they are placed under the supervision of a parole or probation officer and are required to follow general and specific conditions similar in nature to those granted probationers. As with all types of conditional release, offenders can be reincarcerated if they fail to fulfill the conditions of their parole or break the law.

Day parole differs from full parole in that it is granted only for short periods of time, to a maximum of four months and renewable for a period of up to one year. Most offenders in both federal and provincial correctional facilities become eligible for day parole six months before they are eligible for full parole. The National Parole Board has the authority to grant day parole to offenders in both federal and provincial correctional institutions. Provincial parole boards do not have the power to grant day parole.

Temporary absences (TAs) are granted for four main reasons, namely medical, compassionate, administrative, and family and community-contact. They grant absences that can last from a few hours up to 15 days. A TA is granted when an offender requires medical treatment not available in a correctional facility. An example of a compassionate TA is when a family member falls seriously ill or dies. Family and community-contact TAs are granted to allow offenders to participate in community activities that contribute in their adjustment in the community. An administrative TA is given when an offender needs to make contact with community agencies prior to her release (Grant and Belcourt 1992).

TAs may be either escorted or unescorted. An escorted TA may be granted at any time after sentencing; an offender on an escorted TA must be accompanied by a representative of the correctional facility. TAs are the responsibility of the superintendent of the institution, under the authority of the Correctional Service of Canada.

Federal offenders not granted parole may, under statutory release, be released into the community before the expiration of their sentence. Though provincial inmates can gain early release for earned remission (good behaviour) and not be supervised in the community, federal offenders released under statutory release are supervised in the community as if they were on parole. However, all inmates leaving a correctional institution on statutory supervision must, before their release, have their cases reviewed by the National Parole Board. The Corrections and Conditional Release Act allows the board to detain an offender on statutory supervision beyond and up to the normal release date. Further, the board has the power to specify that an offender released on statutory supervision live in a community residential facility if it feels the offender will be a threat to the community or will commit a crime before the termination of his sentence.

The National Parole Board does not grant parole to every applicant; in fact, in most years fewer than 50 percent of applications are successful. Just over 40 percent of federal and provincial applicants for full parole were successful in 2000–01. Of the 4028 male federal inmates who applied for full parole in 2000–01, only 1638 applicants (41 percent) were successful. And of the 228 women serving a federal sentence who applied for full parole, 172 (75 percent) were successful. The number of provincial inmates in British Columbia, Ontario, and Quebec who are released on full parole has declined from 1995–96 to 2000–01. In 1995–96, there were 3616 offenders on provincial parole while, in 2000–01, this number had decreased to 2237 (Correctional Service of Canada 2001).

It is possible that an inmate will never be released on a conditional release program; in such cases the inmate is detained until his warrant expiry date. Detainees fall into one of three categories. The first category contains those convicted of offences included in Schedule I of the *Corrections and Conditional Release Act*. This category is particularly likely to contain offenders who are thought likely to commit another offence causing death or serious injury if released into the community on a conditional release program. The second category too contains those convicted of offences found in Schedule I, specifically sexual offences involving children. The third category contains those convicted of Schedule II offences. This category is most likely to contain those believed likely to commit a serious drug offence while on a conditional release program. According to statistics provided by the National Parole Board, the number of inmates detained has increased from 184 in 1991–92 to a high of 484 in 1995–96, and then it has steadily decreased to 215 in 2000–01. According to Leonard (1999), detainees have committed a variety of offences, from violent sexual offences to crimes that did not involve any sexual activity whatsoever.

THE EFFECTIVENESS OF CONDITIONAL RELEASE PROGRAMS

There is much disagreement over the effectiveness of conditional release programs in Canada today. Much of this debate focuses on the operation and administration of parole. Roberts (1988), in his study of attitudes toward the National Parole Board, found two-thirds of Canadians considered the board to be too lenient. Another study conducted by the Canadian Criminal Justice Association (1987) discovered that most members of the public felt the board released too many offenders. Adams (1990: 11) found most Canadians were negative toward parole. Most of the people he interviewed said that offenders "get off too soon, that parole is virtually automatic after one third of the sentence and that the nature of the offender's crime and concurrent risk to society are not given proper consideration." Adams also reported that while parole is actually part of the offender's sentence, it is "not viewed generally by the public as part of the 'punishment' for a crime."

Since offenders commit different types of crimes and have different criminal backgrounds, is it fair to treat all offenders on conditional release programs the same way? In addition, offenders have their conditional release orders revoked for different reasons: for a technical violation, such as missing a curfew, perhaps, or for a conviction for an indictable offence while under the supervision of the parole board. The National Parole Board measures the effectiveness of conditional release on the basis of three factors:

1. the rate of success;
2. the number of charges for serious offences committed by offenders while on release in the community, by release type, in eight offence categories that emphasize violent crimes (murder, attempted murder, sexual assault, major assault, hostage-taking, unlawful confinement, robbery, and so-called sensational incidents such as arson); and
3. post-warrant expiry recidivism.

Recidivism Rates

A key factor in assessing the success of an offender on a conditional release program is the recidivism rate (see Table 12.1 on page 298). In general, recidivism is the readmission, because of a violation, of an offender to an institution. It is usually expressed as a rate between the number of readmissions and a particular period of time, usually the period during which the offenders are still under the supervision of correctional authorities.

The two most common categories in which recidivism is measured are technical violations and convictions for new offences. A technical violation occurs when an offender breaks a condition of his release program. A technical violation does not count as a new criminal offence. Nouwens et al. (1993) illustrate the concept of technical violation by discussing a "fraud offender who was told to abstain from alcohol and drugs while on release [and who] decides to celebrate his newfound freedom by getting drunk at a party. The police are called … and find out the offender is on parole." Other examples of technical violations include failing to stay within a specified geographical location or failing to maintain a job.

Recidivism rates are considered to be the most important criteria by which the success or failure of a conditional release program is judged. In 1996–97, the success rate of male offenders on full parole was 89.2 percent. Of the 2279 male offenders on parole, parole was revoked in only 247 cases. Of the cases revoked, 205 were for nonviolent offences and 42 were for violent offences. The success rate of women offenders on full parole (92.7 percent) was slightly higher than the success rate for male offenders. Only nine cases of women's parole were revoked, all for nonviolent offences.

During the same period, rates of success were much higher for offenders on day parole. The success rate for women on day parole was 98.6 percent; for males it was 96.4 percent. Only 108 of the 3004 males and 2 of 139 female offenders had their day parole revoked (26 males had their day parole revoked for violent offences; of the 2 cases involving women, both were for nonviolent offences).

Offenders released on statutory release had the highest recidivism rates among offenders in the three conditional release programs, though the rates were not dramatically different than those in full parole. The success rate for men on statutory release was 87.9 percent (608 failures in 5009 cases), and for women it was slightly lower—85.4 percent. One hundred and seven men had their statutory release revoked for a violent crime, while only two women committed a violent offence (Correctional Service of Canada 1997).

Recidivism rates can also be measured over the different lengths of time that offenders are on a conditional release program. Nouwens et al. (1993) compared the short-term and long-term recidivism rates of 1000 federal offenders. Short-term recidivism was measured by looking at those offenders released over a three-year period (1 April 1990 to 31 March 1993). The percentage of supervised offenders readmitted to a correctional facility for technical violations was 2.8 percent, while 2 percent were readmitted for a new offence.

Long-term recidivists were defined as those offenders released during a 10-year period (1 April 1975 to 31 March 1985). During this 10-year period, 15 418 offenders were released on full parole. Of these, 72 percent (11 704 offenders) completed their sentence without being returned to custody for any reason. After these individuals had completed their parole, approximately 10 percent committed a new offence, for which they returned to the federal correctional system. During the same period, 27 124 offenders were released on mandatory supervision. Fifty-seven percent completed their sentence successfully, while 24 percent had their release revoked for technical violations, and 19 percent were readmitted for a new offence. Thirty-four percent of those offenders who successfully completed their statutory supervision were readmitted to a federal institution after their sentence had finished.

Nouwens et al. (1993) also studied the readmission rate by type of conditional program release for 1000 offenders admitted to federal custody for a new offence between 1 April 1988 and 31 March 1989. By 30 June 1993 almost 92 percent of these offenders were released on some form of conditional release. During this period the overall readmission rate was 37.1 percent. However, the highest rate of readmission was for those released on statutory supervision (46.6 percent), almost double the rate for those released on full parole (25.1 percent).

But are different types of offenders more successful on conditional release programs than others? Are those who commit a violent crime, such as murder, bad risks for parole, or are those convicted of a sex offence at higher risk of recidivism? Edwin (1992) investigated the recidivism rates of 2900 homicide offenders released between 1975 and 1990 to determine their success rate on full parole. Of these offenders, 658 were convicted of first- or second-degree murder. The vast majority (77.5 percent) successfully completed their conditional release program, while 13.3 percent were incarcerated for a technical violation of their full parole and 9.2 percent for the commission of an indictable offence. Of the 69 indictable offences committed by the released offenders, 21 (30.4 percent) were narcotics offences, 12 (17.5 percent) were property offences, 6 (8.7 percent) involved robbery, and 17 (24.6 percent) were for other *Criminal Code* offences (Edwin 1992: 7).

Edwin also studied the full parole and supervision success rate of 2242 offenders convicted of manslaughter between 1 January 1975 and 31 March 1990. Almost all of these offenders (93 percent) were released on a conditional release program. Forty-seven percent were released on full parole and 53 percent on statutory supervision. Twenty-two percent of those released on full parole were reincarcerated: 14.6 percent for a technical violation, 6.5 percent for an indictable offence, and 0.5 percent for a summary conviction offence. Of those released on mandatory supervision, 41 percent had their full parole revoked. Thirty-one percent were revoked for a technical violation of the conditions of their parole order, 10 percent for an indictable offence, and 1 percent for a summary offence.

There is much public concern about the release of "special needs" offenders, such as those diagnosed with mental disorders, on conditional release programs. Porporino and Madoc (1993) compared the recidivism rates of 36 male federal offenders identified as having a mental disorder with a matched group of 36 federal offenders without mental disorders. During the four-year study, almost as many offenders with mental disorders were released (67 percent) as those without (75 percent). But offenders with mental disorders were more likely to be released on mandatory supervision (83 percent), while offenders without mental disorders (44 percent) were released more often on parole. In addition, Porporino and Madoc (1993: 17) reported "a tendency for mentally disordered offenders to serve more time before release and a greater proportion of their sentence."

The study looked at recidivism at two points during the release period: six and 24 months after release. No significant differences were found in the recidivism rates between the two groups during the first six months of conditional release, although more offenders without mental disorders were returned to custody for a new offence or a new violent offence. After 24 months, however, those with mental disorders were more likely to have their conditional release suspended due to concern about the probability of further violent offences (Madoc and Brown 1994: 11). In contrast, offenders without mental disorders were more likely to have their conditional release revoked for the commission of a new offence.

The National Parole Board uses post-warrant-expiry recidivism rates as indicators of long-term effectiveness. However, offences committed after warrant expiry are beyond the control of the National Parole Board. According to Larocque (1998: 22), information concerning the recidivism rates of federal offenders after "warrant expiry on SR [statutory release] indicates that offenders reaching warrant expiry on statutory release are 3 to 4 times more likely to be readmitted to a federal institution than offenders who complete their sentence on full parole." In addition, recidivism rates are higher for all groups of offenders who have been in the community for longer periods, regardless of the type of conditional release program they were in.

Conditional Release and Due Process

Other critics have focused on the lack of explicit criteria used in the decisions to grant parole. This led to confusion on the part of inmates who wished to improve themselves and subsequently improve their chances of being granted parole. There were also concerns about the fairness of parole hearings, in particular "the absence from parole of due process requisites such as the right to a hearing, to know the nature of complaints against one, and to be informed of the reasons for adverse decisions" (Bottomley 1990: 339). These issues led to what has been referred to as the "pains of parole," a term used to describe the "anxiety, fear, loss of dignity, excessively limited freedom, [and] uncertainty of one's future" (Mandel 1975: 520–26).

In 1977 the Sub-Committee on the Penitentiary System in Canada (1977: 151) concluded that inmates are under the impression that the Parole Board does not, in all circumstances, treat them fairly. "The records contain many examples of inmates whose parole has been revoked because they arrived a few minutes late and who were charged with being unlawfully at large … It is, therefore, extremely disconcerting to hear of inmates having their paroles suspended and revoked for essentially trivial questions."

These concerns about the role of the National Parole Board were echoed by the late Chief Justice

TABLE 12.1	Charges for Serious Offences by Release Type					
Release Type	1992–93	1993–94	1994–95	1995–96	1996–97	1997–98
Day parole	73	68	64	15	12	26
Full parole	55	79	69	43	50	37
Statutory release	98	93	123	107	133	125
Total	226	240	256	165	195	188

Source: Larocque (1998), p. 21.

Laskin, who commented in the case of *R. v. Mitchell* (1976), a case involving the matter of parole revocation:

> The plain fact is that the Board claims a tyrannical authority that I believe is without precedent among administrative agencies empowered to deal with a person's liberty. It claims an unfettered power to deal with an inmate, almost as if he were a mere puppet on a string.

In 1978 new regulations under the *Parole Act* guaranteed inmates serving a sentence of two years or more a series of due process safeguards—a hearing, disclosure of information, and reasons for the denial of parole. Nevertheless, these safeguards did not eliminate the perception that the decisions made by the National Parole Board were unfair and that disparity continued to exist, albeit in a more subtle manner (Casey 1986).

Confusion about parole board decisions continued among offenders. Eckstedt (1985) found that, five years after the new regulations came into effect, offenders who requested parole hearings continued to question the fairness of board decisions. In an attempt to rectify this situation, reforms were recommended and legal changes made. Perhaps the most significant statement came from the Canadian Sentencing Commission (1987: 244–45), which recommended that parole in Canada be abolished because it violates the principle of proportionality, introduces uncertainty into the sentencing process, and transfers the decision-making power of judges. Others are content to apply the *Charter of Rights and Freedoms* to specific cases as they come forward (Cole and Manson 1990).

Today the *Corrections and Conditional Release Act* (s. 147) allows for appeals within 60 days of the decision when an inmate's application for parole is denied. Grounds for appeal include the National Parole Board's making a decision that fails to observe a principle of fundamental justice; an error of law; a breach or failure to apply a policy adopted to respect ethnic, cultural, and linguistic differences; a failure to respond to the special needs of women and Aboriginals; a decision based on incomplete information; and the failure to act with appropriate jurisdiction (Leonard 1999). A judicial review is also possible, at both the federal level and the provincial.

The Faint Hope Clause

In July 1976 Canada abolished capital punishment with the passage of Bill C-84. This bill established mandatory life sentences, with parole eligibility specified for those convicted of first- and second-degree murder (25 years and 10 to 25 years, respectively). Bill C-84 also stipulated that offenders convicted of first- and second-murder be eligible for a judicial review after serving 15 years of their sentence, and, if successful in their application, be able to participate in a conditional release program. Section 745.6 of the *Criminal Code* was a component of Bill C-84 and was added to the *Criminal Code* when it passed.

This section, now commonly referred to as the "faint hope clause," allowed offenders who served at least 15 years of their sentence to apply for a reduction in the amount of time they had left to serve before the parole eligibility date specified in their sentence. As Roberts and Cole (1999: 284) point out, s. 745.6 was included in the *Criminal Code* "out of recognition of the fact that inmates who have served well over a decade in prison may have changed," adding that "once applications began to be heard by juries, the section became possibly the most controversial provision in the *Criminal Code*."

The faint hope clause states that any offender still serving a sentence after 15 years has the right to apply for a judicial review of parole eligibility. Application is made to the chief justice in the province or territory in which the conviction occurred. The chief justice determines if the offender is eligible to apply, and, if so, informs the provincial Justice minister of the decision. A two-stage process then begins: (1) a preliminary hearing followed by (2) the actual hearing.

The preliminary hearing considers such issues as the evidence to be allowed as well as more mundane matters such as transportation and living facilities. The hearing is adversarial in nature, and the applicant is present. A jury determines if the application has merit and decides on one of three options: (1) no change or reduction in the period before parole eligibility, (2) a reduction in the number of years of imprisonment prior to eligibility of parole, and (3) termination of ineligibility for parole, allowing the applicant immediate eligibility for parole. If the jury selects the third option, it does not mean the offender is released right away, but rather that he can apply to the National Parole Board for release prior to the original eligibility date (Brown 1992).

Under the original legislation, no clear guidelines were available to assist juries in making their decisions. According to s. 745.6(2), juries were able to consider such issues as "the character of the applicant, his conduct while serving his sentence, the nature of the offence for which he was convicted and such other matters as the judge deems relevant in the circumstances." If the jury rejected the application, the Supreme Court of Canada would possibly hear an appeal, although s. 745 made no provision for such an action. If the Supreme

Court decided in the applicant's favour, a second hearing was ordered. In addition, juries did not have to be unanimous in their decision, as only two-thirds of the jurors had to agree to allow an applicant to proceed to a hearing by the National Parole Board.

In December 1996, s. 745.6 was revised by Parliament (through the passing of Bill C-45), largely as a result of the application for early release from serial killer Clifford Olson. Olson gained national and international notoriety in the early 1980s when he received $100 000 from authorities to reveal the locations where he had buried the bodies of 11 of his murder victims in the lower mainland of British Columbia. Public outrage over the application was so great that it became an issue during the 1997 federal election.

As a result, this subsection of the *Criminal Code* was revised (and the revision was called the "Olson Amendment"). No longer are multiple murderers able to apply for early release. Note, however, that very few cases involving multiple victims are ever processed, and those are unlikely to be approved by a jury. Superior Court judges now have to review all applications and be convinced that they have a reasonable prospect of success (Roberts and Cole 1999). Another change makes it mandatory that the jury must be unanimous in its decision. And when a jury unanimously decides that the number of years to be served is to be reduced, they have to decide by a two-thirds majority that a certain number of years must be served before the inmate can apply to the National Parole Board for a possible reduction in time to be served. If a jury decides that no reduction in time is to be granted, they may set another date of application. If they don't set a date, the inmate has to wait for another two years before he can apply again. These changes were made retroactive, to include all individuals who had committed their crimes before Bill C-45 was passed. In addition, Bill C-41 (proclaimed in 1995) made it possible for the families of victims to submit victim impact statements as evidence. (While such information was admitted previously, it was done so at the discretion of the judge.)

Between the first judicial review and 4 June 2000, there were 103 successful applications for a reduction in time served before parole by a jury. Of these, 84 applications (81.6 percent) led to a reduction in the time to be served for offenders by the National Parole Board. One interesting aspect of s. 745(6) is that not every inmate eligible for early release had applied for a hearing. By 3 June 2000, 80 percent of all possible applicants had in fact not applied. It is thought that this low number is the result of the belief held by inmates that the chance of gaining early release is extremely low (Stein 2001).

RISK FACTORS FOR RECIDIVISM

Andrews (1989) reviewed the literature on recidivism and concluded that the findings from prior research were consistent in outlining characteristics that indicate an increased risk of crime. These characteristics include having associates who have criminal tendencies or who are antisocial in nature; procriminal attitudes, values, and beliefs; generalized difficulties or trouble in relationships with others; and being male. The more risk factors present, the greater the likelihood of reoffending. According to Andrews (1989: 13), research has established "beyond question, that systematic risk assessment allows the identification of lower and higher risk groups … [and that] offenders in higher risk groups will be responsible for a majority of the recidivistic offenses."

Of course, predictions are not always accurate. Some individuals identified as high risk may never reoffend, while some identified as low risk will. In an attempt to improve risk classification of offenders, risk assessment criteria have been developed on the basis of behavioural and objective criteria. Behavioural criteria involve cognitive–behavioural and social learning models, including the modelling and reinforcement of anticriminal behaviour, graduated practice of new skills, role-playing, providing resources, and concrete verbal suggestions (Andrews et al. 1990). Objective criteria, the most commonly used to compare offenders on conditional release programs, include such measures as race, drug abuse history, and employment status.

Studies by Antonowicz and Ross (1994) and Robinson (1995) have concluded that low-risk offenders have a similar, if not better, response to treatment than high-risk offenders. Andrews (1996) has identified four significant risk factors: antisocial cognitions, antisocial associates, antisocial personality complex, and a history of antisocial behaviour.

Most research on success in conditional release programs compares recidivists and nonrecidivists on a number of standard objective criteria, including gender, race, age, marital status, and employment.

Gender

Most comparisons of male and female offenders on conditional release report some difference in their recidivism rates. In general, females appear to have lower recidivism rates than males. Bonta et al. (1992), in their analysis of 2985 male and 81 female recidivists released from federal custody during 1983–84, discovered that 36 percent of the women committed a further offence within three years of their release compared with a rate of 49 percent for the males. In the case of temporary absences, Grant and Belcourt (1992) reported women were less likely to fail on this program (0.01 percent) than males (1.0 percent). However, Lefebvre (1994), in her analysis of 929 males and 44 females on day parole during 1990–91, found the overall failure rate for women was 30 percent, compared with 27 percent for male offenders.

The reason for parole revocation varied among females and males: 5 percent of females committed a new offence, compared with 10 percent of males. This result supports the conclusion reported by Belcourt, Nouwens, and Lefebvre (1993), who reported in their analysis of 968 females released from federal custody over a 10-year period that 50 percent were readmitted for a technical violation while 21 percent had their release revoked for a new offence. Blanchette and Dowden (1998) state that federally sentenced women released on either full or day parole have higher success rates on day and full parole than those released on statutory release or on the expiration of their warrant.

Proper programming has a significant influence on lowering the rate of recidivism among federally sentenced women. Two hundred and fifty-one federally sentenced women were studied (143 who were substance abusers were compared with 108 nonabusers), all of whom were released on either day or full parole. The researchers found that the substance abusers were at greater risk of being returned to a correctional facility. However, participation in drug treatment programs while in custody was "associated with reduced returns to custody for substance abusers; the rate approximated that of female non-abusers" (Dowden and Blanchette 1998: 29).

Race

Members of racial minority groups are overrepresented in the Canadian federal prison system. In 1991, 12 percent of all admissions to federal institutions and 19 percent of all admissions to provincial facilities were Aboriginal, despite the fact that less than 3 percent of the Canadian population is Aboriginal (Canadian Centre for Justice Statistics 1991). During this same period, Caucasians in this prison population increased 6.1 percent, from 10 315 to 10 946.

Most research reveals that Aboriginals released on conditional release programs have recidivism rates higher than those of their Caucasian counterparts. Bonta et al. (1992) reported in their analysis of 282 male Aboriginal inmates an overall recidivism rate of 66 percent. They reported that 84 percent of these Aboriginals had been previously incarcerated. Aboriginals placed on mandatory supervision during the three-year study had a much higher recidivism rate (75 percent) than those released on full parole (33 percent).

Belcourt et al. (1993) studied the success of Aboriginal female offenders in all forms of conditional release programs. They report that Aboriginal women were overrepresented in the group returned to a correctional facility after release. Forty-four percent of the Aboriginal women offenders were readmitted, compared with approximately 19 percent of non-Aboriginal female offenders.

Grant and Belcourt (1992), in their study of temporary absences, found Aboriginals to be underrepresented in all TA programs except for compassionate TAs. However, they note that these differences can be explained in large part by legal variables, namely the fact that Aboriginals are more likely to have been convicted of serious violent offences and to have served a greater number of multiple federal prison sentences. Given these facts, Grant and Belcourt conclude that Aboriginal peoples "may therefore represent a greater risk to the community and, as with other offenders in these categories, are less likely to be granted TAs."

The reasons for these differences between Aboriginal and non-Aboriginal offenders have concerned the Correctional Service of Canada, various federal government committees studying conditional release programs, and independent researchers. The Daubney Committee (1988: 214), for example, noted that it appears "Native inmates are often not as familiar with release preparation and the conditional release system as other inmates." Zimmerman (1992: 401) reports that Aboriginals "often waive the right for early release." She attributes this in part "to subtle encouragement by case management officers" (1992: 409). As a result, Aboriginal offenders are the least likely of all groups in the federal correctional system to be released on parole. This is in part due to certain parole criteria being "inherently weighted against aboriginal offenders" (Zimmerman 1992: 408), i.e., jobs and counseling available in community.

Aboriginals who are granted parole are more likely to find themselves returned to prison before the expiration of their conditional release program, a fact thought to be the result of the inappropriate conditional release requirements placed on them, more stringent enforcement of release conditions, and inadequate support on their release.

Ellerby (1994: 23) points out that these higher recidivism rates have made the reintegration of Aboriginals into the community on conditional release programs both "difficult" and "challenging." Culturally specific practices were incorporated into the treatment process in the hope that they "would help aboriginal offenders address their offending and develop the insight and skills necessary to avoid or manage the factors that place them at risk of re-offending" (Ellerby 1994: 24). Starting in 1987, the Forensic Behavioural Management Clinic in Winnipeg began to include traditional healing practices into their treatment of both Aboriginals and non-Aboriginals participating in their programs. These programs involve elders and present an opportunity for offenders to take part in pipe ceremonies and sweat lodge ceremonies. The introduction of this program has made treatment more meaningful for the program participants.

Age, Marital Status, and Employment

Sherman et al. (1992) reported that recidivism may be higher among those who are unemployed and unmarried. Citing research from domestic violence studies, they argue that neither race nor a record of prior offences had an impact on reducing recidivism. Instead, they found that "arrested persons who lacked a stake in conformity were significantly more likely to have a repeat offence than their counterparts who were not arrested" (Sherman et al. 1992: 682). This finding suggests that those with a higher stake in conformity are more likely to complete their conditional release program.

Lefebvre (1994) found that the overall failure rate of her sample of day parolees was inversely related to age. For the youngest group (18 to 25 years) it was 41 percent, followed by 25 percent for those 26 to 40, and 14 percent for those over 40. The rate of failure due to the commission of a new offence was 15 percent for the youngest group, 9 percent for those between 26 and 40, and 5 percent for the oldest group. Similar findings were discovered by Bonta, Lipinski, and Martin (1992), who found that recidivists were, on average, three years younger (26) than nonrecidivists at the time of sentencing. In their study of female offenders, Belcourt et al. (1993) found a similar trend. Twenty-nine percent of those between 18 and 25 were readmitted, compared with 22 percent of those between 26 and 30, 20 percent of those between 31 and 45, 16 percent of those aged 46 to 60, and 11 percent over the age of 60.

In relation to marital status, Lefebvre (1994) found offenders who were married or involved in common-law relationships at the time of their offence had a lower failure rate (22 percent) than those divorced or separated (28 percent) or single (29 percent). Studies by researchers such as Bonta et al. (1992) have consistently found recidivism rates for single, divorced, or separated offenders to be higher than for those who are married.

Lefebvre (1994) studied the impact of employment status and education on recidivism. She found that the overall failure rate for day parolees declined as the offender's level of education increased, from 29 percent for those with a Grade 8 education or less to 19 percent for those with postsecondary education. She also found that those who were employed at the time of their offences were twice as likely to be successful on conditional release programs than those who were unemployed (16.8 percent versus 33.9 percent, respectively).

HOW INMATES VIEW RECIDIVISM

Most criminological research uses recidivism as an indicator of the success or failure of correctional programs to prepare offenders to live a crime-free existence in the community or as a predictor of future criminal behaviour. However, Zamble and Porporino (1988) argue that both these approaches may be "incomplete because they fail to acknowledge that institutional treatment is not a one-way causal process but rather the outcome of interaction between the correctional system and offenders." Besozzi (1993) interviewed 25 offenders serving their first sentence in a federal institution, although most had prior records and had served sentences in either a juvenile or a provincial institution. At the beginning of the study, most inmates indicated that they hated prison life and, once released, did not want to return. Some even mentioned that their time in prison would deter them from reoffending when they returned to the outside. This attitude quickly changed for most, however, as, on reflection, "the correctional institution became less awful and the determination not to reoffend became less resolute. The deterrent effect of prison seemed to vanish" (Besozzi 1993: 37).

Besozzi (1993: 35) also discovered inmates "have developed their own theories to explain why 'they always come back.'" One significant theory formulated by inmates is that the very nature of the correctional facility and the parole supervision system are important "causes" of failure. By this, inmates mean that prison staff are not there to help but rather to ensure that inmates fail when they are released. Programs in the prison are simply viewed "as a way to get out sooner, not as a way to improve the odds of success on the outside" (Besozzi 1993: 37). This view comes from the inmates' conception of prison as a place in which to be punished, not as a place in which to be rehabilitated or to solve the problems that will likely make them reoffend on release.

Some of these feelings derive from the fact that prison is a negative environment. Most inmates interviewed were unsure of how much they had changed, if at all, while in prison. As one inmate stated when contemplating the reality of leaving prison, "I think I will be more aggressive than before, when I get out. Oh yes, that's for sure, because you experience a lot of unfairness here" (Besozzi 1993: 37). Another reason given for the negativity associated with prisons is the fact that, although inmates want to change, prisons lack the resources, both in terms of quality and quantity, to assist them. This was particularly true for offenders at the beginning of their sentence (Zamble and Porporino 1988). "The strongest criticisms of the correctional system came from inmates who knew they needed to change, went to prison hoping for some qualified help and think they didn't receive it" (Besozzi 1993: 37).

Some offenders did indicate that they had changed, but that change was brought about through their own effort, not as a result of any effort from the staff. Most of these offenders isolated themselves from the other inmates and thought about how they would live on the outside so as not to reoffend. According to one inmate, his time in prison was a "positive experience" and gave him the "opportunity to think a lot … to question values and attitudes" (Besozzi 1993: 37).

Overall, most inmates had vague and ambiguous feelings about their chances of survival on the outside. According to Besozzi, this uncertainty was due to the fact that they had not developed a well-defined identity, as they alternately saw themselves as law-abiding citizens and criminals. The second reason was their uncertainty caused by the lack of clarity in the aims of the correctional system.

SUMMARY

Conditional release programs can be traced back to 1868, when a formal system of parole was first implemented. Today conditional release programs consist of various parole programs, including full parole, day parole, and temporary absences. Probation, however, is the largest conditional release program, in terms of the number of offenders taking part, currently practised today in Canada. During the past 20 years, largely as a result of increased legal rights for prisoners, these programs developed so as to allow prisoners better access to both probation and the various conditional release programs.

In recent years prison authorities have started to emphasize risk factors as the most significant consideration when considering which offenders to place in these programs. Once offenders are placed in these programs they must follow a set of rules or conditions. If they violate one, their release may be revoked and they will be returned to a correctional facility. The Canadian courts have extended legal rights to all those applying for or who are in these programs. If an individual is not allowed to participate in a program, he must be told why he was rejected. In addition, if an individual's conditional release is revoked, the individual has the right to a full hearing on the issue and the right to legal counsel.

Discussion Questions

1. Discuss the use of conditional release in Canada. Should more people be placed in these programs?

2. What is the current role of the National Parole Board? How has it changed over time?

3. Discuss the factors that influence the decision to grant parole.

4. What is the purpose of probation?

5. What are some of the problems associated with probation orders?

6. What type of offenders are most likely to reoffend?

7. Discuss the risk factors used in the decision to grant parole.

8. Should we continue our statutory supervision policy? What purposes does this policy serve?

Suggested Readings

Andrews, D., and J. Bonta. 1998. *The Psychology of Criminal Conduct,* 2nd ed. Cincinnati: Anderson.

Cole, D.P., and A. Manson. 1990. *Release from Imprisonment: The Law of Sentencing, Parole, and Judicial Review.* Toronto: Carswell.

Culhane, C. *Still Barred from Prison.* 1985. Montreal: Black Rose Books.

Faith, K. 1993. *Unruly Women: The Politics of Confinement and Resistance.* Vancouver: Press Gang Publishers.

Gottfredson, D.M., and M. Tonry, eds. 1987. *Prediction and Classification: Criminal Justice Decision Making.* Chicago: University of Chicago Press.

References

Adams, M. 1990. "Canadian Attitudes toward Crime and Justice." *Forum on Corrections Research* 2: 10–13.

Andrews, D.A. 1996. "Criminal Recidivism Is Predictable and Can Be Influenced: An Update." *Forum on Corrections Research* 8: 42–45.

———. 1995. "The Psychology of Criminal Conduct and Effective Treatment." In J.M. McGuire, ed., *What Works: Reducing Offending.* West Sussex: John Wiley, pp. 35–62.

———. 1989. "Recidivism Is Predictable and Can Be Influenced: Using Risk Assessments to Reduce Recidivism." *Forum on Corrections Research* 1: 11–17.

———. 1980. "Some Experimental Investigations of the Principles of Differential Association through Deliberate Manipulations of the Structure of Service Systems." *American Sociological Review* 45: 448–62.

Andrews, D.A., and J. Bonta. 1998. *The Psychology of Criminal Conduct,* 2nd ed. Cincinnati: CJ Anderson.

Andrews, D.A., and J.J. Kiessling. 1980. "Program Structure and Effective Correctional Practices: A Summary of the CaVic Research." In R.R. Ross and P. Gendreau, eds., *Effective Correctional Treatment.* Toronto: Effective Correctional Treatment.

Andrews, D.A., I. Zinger, R.D. Hodge, J. Bonta, P. Gendreau, and F.T. Cullen. 1990. "Does Correctional Treatment Work? A Clinically Relevant and Psychologically Informed Meta-Analysis." *Criminology* 28: 369–404.

Antonowicz, D., and R.R. Ross. 1994. "Essential Components of Successful Rehabilitation Programs for Offenders." *International Journal of Offender Therapy and Comparative Criminology* 38: 97–104.

Belcourt, R., T. Nouwens, and L. Lefebvre. 1993. "Examining the Unexamined: Recidivism among Female Offenders." *Forum on Corrections Research* 5: 10–14.

Bellavance, J.D., and S. Alberts. 1999. "20% of Criminals on Parole Lack Supervision." *National Post,* 21 April, A6.

Besozzi, C. 1993. "Recidivism: How Inmates See It." *Forum on Corrections Research* 5: 35–38.

Birkenmayer, A. 1995. *The Use of Community Corrections in Canada: 1993–1994.* Ottawa: Juristat.

Blanchette, K., and C. Dowden. 1998. "A Profile of Federally Sentenced Women in the Community: Addressing Needs for Successful Reintegration." *Forum on Corrections Research* 10: 40–43.

Bonta, J. 1995. "The Responsivity Principle and Offender Rehabilitation." *Forum on Corrections Research* 7: 34–37.

Bonta, J., C. LaPrairie, and S. Wallace-Capretta. 1997. "Risk Prediction and Re-Offending: Aboriginal and Non-Aboriginal Offenders." *Canadian Journal of Criminology* 39: 127–44.

Bonta, J., S. Lipinski, and M. Martin. 1992. "The Characteristics of Aboriginal Recidivists." *Canadian Journal of Criminology* 34: 517–22.

Bottomley, A.K. 1990. "Parole in Transition: A Comparative Study of Origins, Developments, and Prospects for the 1990s." *Crime and Justice: A Review of Research,* vol. 12. Chicago: University of Chicago Press.

Brown, G. 1992. "Judicial Review: How Does It Work and How Does It Affect Federal Corrections?" *Forum on Corrections Research* 4: 14–16.

Brown, R.J., and K.P. O'Brien. 1993. "How Do Experts Make Parole Recommendations and Are They Accurate?" *Forum on Corrections Research* 5: 3–4.

Canadian Centre for Justice Statistics. 1991. *Adult Correctional Services in Canada.* Ottawa: Statistics Canada.

Canadian Criminal Justice Association. 1987. *Attitudes toward Parole.* Ottawa: Canadian Criminal Justice Association.

Canadian Sentencing Commission. 1987. *Sentencing Reform: A Canadian Approach.* Ottawa: Minister of Supply and Services.

Carrington, D.O. 1991. *Crime and Punishment in Canada: A History*. Toronto: McClelland and Stewart.

Casey, M. 1986. "Parole: A Purely Personal View." *The Correctional Review* 1: 19–20.

Cole, D.P., and A. Manson. 1990. *Release from Imprisonment: The Law of Sentencing, Parole, and Judicial Review*. Toronto: Carswell.

Correctional Service of Canada. 1997. *Basic Facts about Corrections in Canada*. Ottawa: Solicitor General of Canada.

———. 1990. "A Profile of Federal Community Corrections." *Forum on Corrections Research* 2: 8–13.

Cullen, F.T., and P. Gendreau. 1989. "The Effectiveness of Correctional Rehabilitation: Reconsidering the 'Nothing Works' Debate." In L. Goodstein and D. MacKenzie, eds., *American Prisons: Issues in Research and Policy*. New York: Plenum, pp. 23–44.

Daubney Committee. 1988. *Taking Responsibility: Report of the Standing Committee on Justice and Solicitor-General on Its Review of Sentencing, Conditional Release and Related Aspects of Corrections*. D. Daubney, chair. Ottawa: Queen's Printer.

Dowden, C., and K. Blanchette. 1998. "Success Rates for Female Offenders on Discretionary versus Statutory Release: Substance Abusers and Non-Abusers." *Forum on Corrections Research* 10: 27–29.

Eckstedt, J.W. 1985. *Justice in Sentencing: Offenders' Perceptions*. Ottawa: Canadian Sentencing Commission.

Eckstedt, J.W., and C.T. Griffiths. 1988. *Corrections in Canada: Policy and Practice*, 2nd ed. Toronto: Butterworths.

Ellerby, L. 1994. "Community-Based Treatment of Aboriginal Offenders: Facing Realities and Exploring Realities." *Forum on Corrections Research* 6: 23–25.

Edwin, G. 1992. "Recidivism among Homicide Offenders." *Forum on Corrections Research* 4: 7–9.

Enos, R., and S. Southern. 1996. *Correctional Case Management*. Cincinnati: CJ Anderson.

Frankel, M.F. 1972. *Criminal Sentences: Law without Order*. New York: Hill and Wang.

Freeze, C. 2001a. "Victims Sue Ottawa for Crimes Committed by Convicts." *The Globe and Mail*, 26 December, A1–A7.

———. 2001b. "National Parole Board Pays the Price." *The Globe and Mail*, 28 December, A7.

Grant, B.A., and R.L. Belcourt. 1992. *An Analysis of Temporary Absences and the People Who Receive Them*. Ottawa: Correctional Service of Canada.

Griffiths, C.T., and A. Cunningham. 2000. *Canadian Corrections*. Scarborough, Ont.: Nelson Thomson.

Harman, W.G., and R.G. Hann. 1986. *Release Risk Assessment: An Historical Descriptive Analysis*. Ottawa: Solicitor General of Canada.

Haskell, C. 1994. "The Impact of the *Corrections and Conditional Release Act* on Community Corrections." *Forum on Corrections Research* 6: 45–46.

Kiessling, J. 1989. Cited in D.A. Andrews, "Recidivism Is Predictable and Can Be Influenced: Using Risk Assessments to Reduce Recidivism." *Forum on Corrections Research* 1: 11–17.

Larocque, B. 1998. "Federal Trends and Outcomes in Conditional Release." *Forum on Corrections Research* 10, no. 2 (May): 18–22.

Latessa, E.J., and H.E. Allen. 1997. *Corrections in the Community*. Cincinnati: CJ Anderson.

Lefebvre, L. 1994. "The Demographic Characteristics of Offenders on Day Parole." *Forum on Corrections Research* 6: 11–13.

Leonard, S.G. 1999. "Conditional Release from Imprisonment." In J.V. Roberts and D.P. Cole, eds., *Making Sense of Sentencing*. Toronto: University of Toronto Press, pp. 259–76.

Lipton, D., R. Martinson, and J. Wilks. 1975. *The Effectiveness of Correctional Treatment*. New York: Praeger.

Madoc, L.L., and S.L. Brown. 1994. "Sex Offenders and Their Survival Time on Conditional Release." *Forum on Corrections Research* 6: 14–17.

Mandel, M. 1975. "Rethinking Parole." *Osgoode Hall Law Journal* 13: 501–46.

Martinson, R. 1979. "Symposium on Sentencing: Part II." *Hofstra Law Review* 7: 243–58.

———. 1974. "What Works? Questions and Answers about Prison Reform." *Public Interest* 35: 22–54.

National Parole Board. 1988. *National Parole Board Pre-Release Decision Policies*. Ottawa: Ministry of Supply and Services.

———. 1987. *Briefing Book for Members of the Standing Committee on Justice and Solicitor General*. Ottawa: National Parole Board.

———. 1981. *A Guide to Conditional Release for Penitentiary Inmates*. Ottawa: National Parole Board.

Nouwens, T., L. Motiuk, and R. Boe. 1993. "So You Want to Know the Recidivism Rate." *Forum on Corrections Research* 5: 22–26.

Porporino, F.J., and L.L. Motiuk. 1993. "Conditional Release and Offenders with Mental Disorders." *Forum on Corrections Research* 5: 17–19.

Roberts, J.V. 1988. "Early Release from Prison: What Do the Canadian Public Really Think?" *Canadian Journal of Criminology* 30: 231–49.

Roberts, J.V., and D.P. Cole. 1999. "Sentencing and Early Release Arrangements for Offenders Convicted of Murder." In J.V. Roberts and D.P. Cole, eds., *Making Sense of Sentencing*. Toronto: University of Toronto Press, pp. 277–94.

Robinson, D. 1995. "Federal Offender Family Violence: Estimates from a National File Review Study." *Forum on Corrections Research* 7: 15–18.

Ryan, H.R.S. 1990. "Foreword." In D.P. Cole and A. Manson, eds., *Release from Imprisonment: The Law of Sentencing, Parole, and Judicial Review*. Toronto: Carswell, pp. v–x.

Sherman, L.W., D.A. Smith, J.D. Schmidt, and D.P. Rogan. 1992. "Crime, Punishment, and Stake in Conformity: Legal and Informal Control of Domestic Violence." *American Sociological Review* 57: 680–90.

Stein, K. 2001. *Section 745.6—The "Faint Hope Clause."* Ottawa: Department of Justice.

Sub-Committee on the Penitentiary System in Canada. 1977. Report. Ottawa: Supply and Services Canada.

Sutton, J. 1994. "Learning to Better Predict the Future: National Parole Board Risk-Assessment Training." *Forum on Corrections Research* 6: 20–22.

Task Force on the Release of Inmates. 1973. Report. Ottawa: Information Canada.

Taylor, G. 1998. "Preparing Reports for Parole Decisions: Making the Best Use of Our Information—and Time." *Forum on Corrections Research* 10, no. 2 (May): 30–34.

Thurber, A. 1998. "Understanding Offender Reintegration." *Forum on Corrections Research* 10: 14–18.

Walker, S. 1984. *Sense and Nonsense about Crime*. Belmont, Calif.: Wadsworth.

Waller, I. 1974. *Men Released from Prison*. Toronto: University of Toronto.

Zamble, E., and F. Porporino. 1988. *Coping, Behavior and Adaptation in Prison Inmates*. New York: Springer-Verlag.

Zimmerman, S. 1992. "'The Revolving Door of Despair': Aboriginal Involvement in the Criminal Justice System." *University of British Columbia Law Review*: 367–426.

Court Case

R. v. Mitchell, [1976] 2 S.C.R. 570

CHAPTER 13

Youth Justice

CHAPTER OBJECTIVES

✓ Understand why the *Juvenile Delinquents Act* was passed and the differences between the way it treated juveniles and the way the criminal justice system treated adults.

✓ Explain how the *Young Offenders Act* changed the nature of the juvenile justice system in Canada.

✓ Discuss the limitations of the *Young Offenders Act* and how the *Youth Criminal Justice Act* tries to correct these issues.

✓ Understand youth crime trends and custodial rates since the *Young Offenders Act* was proclaimed in 1984.

✓ Explain how young offenders can appear in adult court.

✓ Understand why the *Youth Criminal Justice Act* was passed and the changes it has introduced to the youth justice system.

YOUTH JUSTICE VERSUS CRIMINAL JUSTICE

Youths between 12 and 17 in Canada today are treated separately from adults in our criminal justice system. Police services commonly have officers who specialize in youth crime or have special units that deal exclusively with young offenders. Many youths who are arrested are never sent to youth court, but instead choose to participate in alternative measure programs. A separate court—youth court, with specialized judges and prosecutors—hears cases involving youths. And convicted youths serve their terms of custody in institutions separate from those that house adult offenders.

These differences are the result of historical views of youths and their behaviour in our society. At the beginning of the 20th century some concerned groups (referred to as "child savers") argued that young people should be treated differently from adults by the criminal justice system. These groups thought that young persons who broke the law were in fact themselves victims of neglect and improper care in the home. A youth who broke the law was indicating that his parents had lost control of him, and the state had to intervene in order to protect its best interests. This led to the creation of a separate criminal justice system that gave the state power to intervene in the lives of youths. This system is based on the idea of *parens patriae*—literally, the *state as a parent*.

The idea behind *parens patriae* was that young people should be treated differently from adults by the criminal justice system. The focus was not on punishment but rather on assisting young offenders to learn to control themselves and to prevent them from engaging in other criminal activity in order to become law-abiding citizens. The emphasis was therefore on treatment rather than punishment. The label of "delinquent" was not to be used as a term that referred to a youth as a criminal but to an individual who needed special consideration from the state.

Ontario enacted the first laws in Canada that formalized the notion of *parens patriae* in 1893. This legislation was entitled *An Act for the Prevention of Cruelty to, and Better Protection of Children*, also referred to as the Children's Charter (Sutherland 1976). Canada enacted its first piece of federal juvenile legislation (the *Juvenile Delinquents Act*) in 1908.

The *Juvenile Delinquents Act* (JDA) stated that, in order for a youth to be considered a delinquent, he had to break a law and be punished in a special court that heard only cases involving youths (juvenile court). Delinquency was defined on the basis of age. No child or youth could be held legally responsible for his actions unless he had reached the age of seven. Provinces selected the upper age limit, which was between 14 and 17. A "delinquent act" was defined as the violation of any federal, provincial, or municipal law for which the punishment was a fine or imprisonment or a term in an industrial school or reformatory (Bell 1999).

Under the *parens patriae* approach, delinquent acts were not considered criminal nor were delinquents considered criminals. Children who violated the law could not be found guilty of a criminal act and would not be treated as adults. Instead, juvenile proceedings—more informal than adult criminal proceedings—were designed to establish whether the child in question needed treatment. The legal theory of *parens patriae* "recognizes that children who violate the law are in need of the same care and treatment as are law-abiding citizens who cannot care for themselves and require state intervention into their lives" (Siegel and Senna 1997: 19).

Considerable discretion was built into the operation of the juvenile courts in order to achieve a treatment focus. For example, the terms used in adult criminal courts were modified to make juvenile court proceedings seem different from those of a criminal court trial. The term "petition" was substituted for criminal complaint, trials became "hearings," and pleas became "true" or "not true" rather than "guilty" or "not guilty." Hearings were held in private, in order to protect the reputation of the accused, and the rules of due process used to guide adult court procedural issues were dispensed with. Judges were granted considerable discretionary power to determine the appropriateness of testimony and evidence without being challenged on the grounds of illegality of the proceedings. They were also given a wide range of sentencing dispositions, which gave them much power to make decisions in the best interests of the child—the power, essentially, of a "pseudoparent" (Leschied 1995).

Between the first decade of the 20th century and the late 1960s the JDA and the juvenile courts operated with little change. One significant alteration took place in 1924, however, when the JDA was revised to include more offences within its purview. The revision created the status offence—that is, juveniles could be arrested and referred to juvenile court and even institutionalized for activities not considered criminal for adults, such as truancy, incorrigibility, running away from home, violating a curfew law, purchasing or drinking alcoholic beverages, and engaging in various sexual activities.

Further, a delinquent was redefined as "any child who violates any provision of the Criminal Code or of any bylaw or ordinance of any municipality, or who is guilty of sexual immorality or any similar form of vice, or who is liable by reason of any other act to be committed to an industrial school or juvenile reformatory under the provisions of any Dominion or provincial statute" (West 1991: 33).

Criticisms about the JDA culminated in the 1960s and 1970s, forcing the federal government to reevaluate this legislation. Some argued there were not enough crime control policies and due process protections built into the act. In 1967 a draft titled Children's and Young Persons Act was published to facilitate discussion about changing the JDA. This draft was followed in 1970 by Bill C-192 (An Act Respecting Young Offenders and to Repeal the JDA), but it never passed the House of Commons. In 1975 a report titled Young Persons in Conflict with the Law made recommendations about the future of Canada's juvenile justice system. Two years later, in 1977, the federal Solicitor General issued Highlights of Proposed New Legislation for Young Offenders. The *Young Offenders Act* was passed in 1982, and it came into force on 2 April 1984.

Four pressing concerns led to these developments. The first was the rising rate of juvenile delinquency, which was largely considered to be the result of the ineffectiveness of the JDA. Critics pointed out that a juvenile typically had to commit several offences prior to having a hearing in juvenile court. Critics argued that the solution was longer sentences as well as greater accountability on the part of those involved in the juvenile justice system. The second major criticism was aimed at the extensive discretionary power granted by the JDA to the juvenile court.

The third criticism concerned the issue of net-widening, specifically the belief that the programs espoused by the JDA tended to push youths further into the juvenile system rather than solve the root problems of juvenile offending. The JDA was criticized for assisting the offenders only as they progressed through the various stages of the juvenile justice system. As a result, the level of state intervention escalated accordingly. The fourth criticism concerned the high cost of running the juvenile court. In the 1960s the cost of

EXHIBIT 13.1 The Legal Rights of Youths: Search and Seizure

R. v. M. (M.R.) (1998)

An issue connected with search and seizure (see Chapter 2) is the right of school officials and police to search students and their possessions on school property. If authorities believe that a student is violating the law, that student's locker may be searched. But is it possible for school officials to search and seize illegal items from a student's locker without a warrant? Are such cases unreasonable and therefore in violation of rights accorded the student by the *Charter of Rights and Freedoms*?

FACTS OF THE CASE

Students told a junior-high-school vice principal in Nova Scotia that a 13-year-old student was planning to sell drugs that night on school property during a school dance. The vice principal asked the individual in question and his companion to report to the office, where the vice principal asked each if he was in the possession of drugs and advised them that he was going to search them. A plainclothes RCMP officer, who had been called by the vice principal in accordance with school policy, was present but said nothing while the vice principal spoke to the students and searched them. The vice principal took a bag of marijuana from one of the students, and then gave it to the RCMP officer. The officer advised the youth he was under arrest for possession of marijuana. The police officer read the youth his police caution and his right to legal counsel, as well as his right to contact a parent or adult. The accused attempted unsuccessfully to telephone his mother and informed the officer that he did not wish to contact anyone else. The officer and the accused then proceeded to the accused's locker, which the officer searched. The officer discovered no illegal item in it.

The trial judge concluded that the vice principal was acting as an agent of the police and held that the search violated the accused's rights to be free from unreasonable search and seizure under s. 8 of the *Charter of Rights and Freedoms*. He excluded the evidence found in the search, and since the prosecution offered no other evidence the charge against the accused was dismissed. The verdict was appealed. The Nova Scotia Court of Appeal allowed the appeal and ordered a new trial. At his second trial the youth was convicted. He then appealed to the Supreme Court of Canada.

DECISION

In an 8–1 decision, the Supreme Court of Canada held that the appeal should be dismissed. It held that the prohibition against illegal search and seizure applies to school officials as well as to law enforcement officials. Teachers are not merely substitute parents but agents of the state who are required to carry out state policy and law. Nevertheless, students do not give up their constitutional rights when they walk onto school property, and, in the case of a search, students have the right to privacy with respect to one's person and they should expect that privacy.

However, this reasonable expectation of privacy may be diminished in some circumstances. This expectation is lower for a student at school than it would be in some other circumstances, since students know that teachers and school authorities are responsible for providing a safe environment and maintaining order and discipline within the school. According to the Supreme Court, the possession of drugs and dangerous weapons challenges the ability of school officials to fulfill their responsibilities. School officials have to be able to respond quickly and reasonably—and this may involve school officials searching students and seizing prohibited items. Where the criminal law is involved, evidence found by a teacher or other school official should not be excluded because the search would have been unreasonable if conducted by the police.

According to the majority of the Supreme Court justices, the requirement of a warrant or some other form of prior authorization would be impractical and unworkable in the school environment. Teachers must be able to act quickly to deal with problems as they arise in school in order to protect their students and to maintain the orderly atmosphere required for learning. The search of a student should depend on its reasonableness, the scope of the search, the age and sex of the student, and the behaviour that prompted it. In view of this standard, the vice principal's search was justified, because the report he had received created a reasonable suspicion that the student had marijuana in his possession.

The Supreme Court of Canada outlined the approach to be taken by teachers when considering searches:

1. A warrant is not essential in order to conduct a search of a student by a school authority.
2. The school authority must have reasonable grounds to believe that there has been a breach of school regulations or discipline and that a search of a student would reveal evidence of that breach.

Continued on next page

operating the criminal justice system as a whole began to skyrocket, and governments sought ways to save money. The government saw the criticisms of the JDA as ideas that could lead to savings. One such idea was that the system should intervene as little as possible in the lives of youths. The book *Radical Nonintervention* (1973), by Edwin Schur, caught the attention of governments, particularly its argument that youths processed through the juvenile court system are stigmatized. Schur's solution to this problem was to divert as many offenders out of the juvenile system as possible, decrease the reliance on juvenile custodial institutions, and decriminalize status offences.

Although all of these criticisms helped bring about the demise of the JDA, the strongest was that youths lacked due process protections readily available to adults. This meant that youths could not secure defence counsel, that evidentiary standards were often lacking, and that few treatment programs were available. As a result, the operation of the juvenile justice slowly started to change. Gradually it became less discretionary and more concerned with the legal rights of youths.

These changes were hastened by the introduction of the *Charter of Rights and Freedoms* in 1982 (see Exhibit 13.1). Questions were raised about the applicability of the *Charter* to youths in conflict with the law.

So, when the *Young Offenders Act* (YOA) was passed, it emphasized the justice model (see Chapter 3) at the expense of the rehabilitation of young persons. The main focus of the YOA was the due process rights of the accused, including the understanding that the youth court would limit itself to the trying of young persons who were charged with violating the law, as well as the introduction of due process safeguards. To achieve these goals, the YOA contained four guiding principles:

1. young people must assume responsibility for their illegal behaviour;
2. society has a right to protection from illegal behaviour;
3. youths are entitled to traditional legal rights and some additional protections; and
4. young people, because they are by definition not mature, have special needs and should not be held accountable in the same manner or to the same extent as adults.

Between 1984 and 1997 considerable debate surrounded the YOA, with the result that significant changes were introduced, notably to sanctions as well as juvenile transfers to adult court (see Table 13.1). In 1986 the first amendments were made to the YOA, all of which strengthened its deterrence aspects. These changes came about as a result of intensive lobbying efforts by the police, provincial Attorneys General, and some federal politicians who believed the YOA was too soft. These amendments included increasing youth court sentences for murder, introducing victim impact statements into youth court, and imposing conditional supervision following an order of custody whenever a judge feels stricter controls are necessary for the benefit of the youth or the protection of the public. The police were also allowed to access juvenile records for investigative purposes, and the names of young suspects at large could be published with the permission of the court.

Other criticisms concerning the YOA were made over the ensuing years, and Dell (1999) divides them into three categories. First was the insufficient attention given to the prevention of youths from engaging in criminal activity; second was the inadequate measures used to deal with the most violent offenders and offences; and third was the system's too-heavy reliance on custody as a response to youth crime.

Finally, in 1998 the Federal Youth Justice Strategy was announced. It contained three broad aims:

1. to address the limitations of the YOA;
2. to reform the youth justice system and legislation; and
3. to address the root causes of youth crime.

TABLE 13.1	Chronology of Canada's Youth Justice Legislation

1908	*Juvenile Delinquents Act*:
	• child welfare approach
	• significant judicial discretion

1984	*Young Offenders Act* (YOA):
	• emphasis on youth responsibility, protection of society, special rights, and youth needs

1986	amendments to YOA:
	• technical amendments to custody placements
	• changes to enhance police powers

1992	amendments to YOA:
	• increased maximum sentence from three to five years for murder
	• clarified rules for transferring youth to adult court

1995	amendments to YOA:
	• increased maximum sentence to 10 years for murder
	• created presumption of transfer for 16- and 17-year-olds charged with serious violent offences to adult court

1996 (August)	Federal–Provincial–Territorial Task Force on Youth Justice Report:
	• reviewed the YOA and made recommendations, some of which contradicted those made by the standing committee
	• report referred to the House of Commons
	• recommended allowing victim impact statements in court
	• recommended information-sharing among youth justice professionals

1997 (April)	review of the YOA:
	• report referred to the House of Commons Standing Committee on Justice and Legal Affairs for consideration

1997 (August)	review of the youth justice system
	• 14 recommendations

1997 (August)	Meeting of First Ministers:
	• with exception of Quebec, called for meaningful amendments to the YOA
	• committed to improving preventive and rehabilitative programs for young offenders

1997 (December)	proposed amendments to the YOA

1998 (May)	Federal Youth Justice Strategy announced

2002	*Youth Criminal Justice Act* introduced

Source: Adapted from Dell (1999), p. 46.

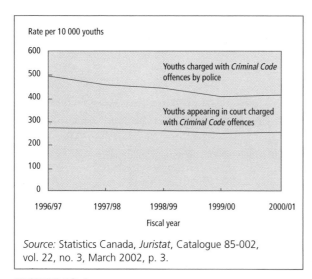

Source: Statistics Canada, *Juristat*, Catalogue 85-002, vol. 22, no. 3, March 2002, p. 3.

FIGURE 13.1

The Trends in Police and Court Data Closely Correspond, Showing Decreasing Involvement of Youths in the Criminal Justice System

This led to the introduction of the *Youth Criminal Justice Act* in 2002 (see below).

TRENDS IN YOUTH CRIME

The rate at which youths were charged with *Criminal Code* offences in Canada increased by 1 percent in 2000–01 compared to the previous year. This was the first year since 1992 there was an increase in the number of youths charged with a criminal offense; from 1992 to 1999, the rate of youths charged with a *Criminal Code* violation declined by 31 percent (see Figure 13.1).

Property crime continues to be the most common category of youth offending. During 2000–01, 40 percent of all *Criminal Code* offences committed by youths fell into this category. The two most common property offences heard in youth court (both of which made up 24 percent of the total youth court caseload) were "theft $5000 and under" and "breaking and entering." Since 1996–97, the total number of property crime offenses processed through youth court decreased by 23 percent, including breaking and entering (–35 percent), possession of stolen property (–31 percent) and theft (–22 percent) (deSouza 2002).

Twenty-two percent of all youth court cases involved violent crimes. Almost one-half of the violent crime category comprised minor assaults (46 percent), while murder, manslaughter, and attempted murder accounted for less than 1 percent of all youth crimes heard in youth courts across Canada in 2000–01. The remaining major categories of offences heard in youth

court were "Other *Criminal Code* offences (18 percent), *Young Offenders Act* offences (12 percent), drug-related offences (7 percent) and other federal statute offences (less than 1 percent)" (deSouza 2002: 4). Figure 13.2 presents the 10 most common principal charges heard in youth courts during 2000–01. It reveals that a very small group of offences accounts for the largest proportion of the youth court caseload—the five most common offences accounted for 57 percent of the total caseload. Among the most commonly held beliefs about youth crime in Canada today are that

- it is increasing dramatically;
- more serious violent crimes are being committed by youths;
- youths are involved in crime at an earlier age;
- youths receive lenient sentences; and
- the number of youths charged by the police is increasing.

These beliefs are not necessarily true. In 2001, for example, there was an almost 31 percent decrease in the charges laid against youths as well as a 6 percent decrease in the total number of charges of sexual assaults. The rate at which youths were charged with robbery, however, increased by 9.5 percent. Youths charged with property crimes decreased by 3.3 percent in 2000–01 compared to the previous year; the property crime rate in Canada has

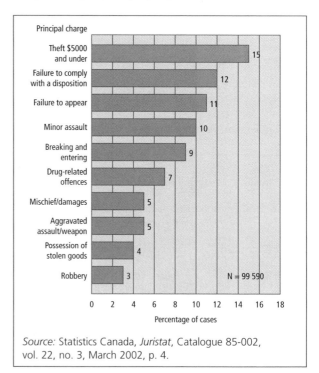

Source: Statistics Canada, *Juristat*, Catalogue 85-002, vol. 22, no. 3, March 2002, p. 4.

FIGURE 13.2

Few Offences Accounted for the Largest Proportion of the Youth Court Caseload 2000–2001

now decreased for 10 consecutive years. The rate of "Other *Criminal Code*" offences increased by a total of 5.6 percent in 2001, largely driven by increases in the rates of "offensive weapons" (+8.8 percent), failure to appear (+7 percent), and "mischief" (+1.9 percent). However, Savoie (2002: 20) points out that between 1991 and 2001 the total number of youths charged with serious violent crimes (such as homicide or sexual assault) or a crime involving potential violence (such as "offensive weapons") was extremely low compared to crimes involving a minimal amount of violence such as minor assault or a property crime.

Sprott (1996) points out that these perceptions may be the result of the media. She studied all reports of youth crime published in three Toronto daily newspapers for a period of two months and reported that 94 percent of the stories featured violent criminal activity. In contrast, the Canadian Centre for Justice Statistics reported that, of the youth cases heard in Ontario during 1995, only 22 percent of the principal charges involved a violent crime.

Sinclair and Dell (1999), using national statistics between 1992 and 1997, pointed out that while the number of youths charged by the police consistently decreased (a trend that continued until 2000, when there was an increase of 1.4 percent), these significant decreases were rarely noted by the mass media, which preferred to focus on the more extreme forms of violent acts committed by youths. And according to the research conducted by Lee and Leonard (1995: 1), the "phenomenon of serious youth violence is actually so infrequent that it tends to elude statistical analysis." Similarly, Moyer (1996: 2) concluded from her analysis that "the type of offenses which result in system involvement shows that the vast majority of juvenile criminal behavior involved is not, by any definition, very serious in nature."

Age is a significant factor in the type of crime committed by youths. Youths charged with a property crime are more likely to be younger than youths charged with a violent crime. In 1997–98, 12- and 13-year-olds were more likely to be involved in the theft of goods valued at $5000 and under, common assault, and mischief; 16- and 17-year-olds were more likely involved in offences related to the failure to comply with a disposition, drugs, and possession of stolen property.

Older youth (i.e., 16- and 17-year-olds) are also more likely to appear in youth court than youths from all other age groups. In 2000–01 they accounted for 51 percent of all cases, while 15-year-olds accounted for 22 percent, 14-year-olds accounted for 15 percent, 13-year-olds accounted for 7 percent, and 12-year-olds accounted for 3 percent. The use of sanctions to deal with convicted young offenders has increased. The use

of secure custody, open custody, and probation increased in 2000–01 (continuing a trend that started in 1992–93) while the use of fines, community service orders, and absolute discharges have generally decreased. Finally, no apparent pattern was noted in the number of youths transferred to adult court between 1991–92 and 1996–97. The number ranged from a low of 55 in 1992–93 to a high of 120 in 1996–97 (there were 86 such cases in 2000–01).

There has been much speculation in recent years about increasing rates of violent crime committed by young female offenders. Dell and Boe (1997) analyzed data on female young offenders between 1992 and 1996 and found no evidence of an increase in the number of female young offenders charged by the police. They report that the national rate of violent crime among female youths remained constant during this period, at 44 charges per 10 000 female youths. This rate was one-third that of charges against young males for violent crimes. More recently, Savoie (1999) reported that in 1998 the violent crime rate of female youths increased to 47 charges per 10 000 female youths but at the same time it remained at one-third the rate at which young males were charged. The most common violent crime charge against female youths in 1998 was common assault (67 percent of all violent crime charges), though common assault accounted for less than half (46 percent) of violent crime charges against male youths that year.

Youth Court Caseloads

An indicator commonly used to measure youth crime in Canada is the caseload of youth courts in each province and territory. Thus, the caseload trends presented in this chapter reflect the court process and response to youth crime rather than the actual prevalence of criminal activity among youths. Since 1992–93 the number of cases heard in youth courts in Canada has decreased. For example, in 2000–01, there was a 2 percent decrease from the previous year and a 10 percent decline since 1996–97 (see Table 13.2).

During 2000–2001, youth courts across Canada heard 99 590 cases. These cases reflect one of three different types of federal statute offences: violations of the *Criminal Code*, the *Young Offenders Act*, or federal drug laws. The cases heard in youth court involving the *Criminal Code* in 1997–98 included property crimes (40 023 cases), violent crimes (21 760 cases), "Other *Criminal Code* offences" such as failure to appear in court and escape from custody (18 264 cases), *Young Offenders Act* offences (12 447 cases), drug-related offences (6967 cases) and other federal statute offences (129 cases).

Youth Court Decisions and Dispositions

Sixty percent of cases heard in youth court in 2000–01 ended in a conviction. Of the remaining cases, proceedings were stayed or withdrawn in 36 percent, and 4 percent of the cases ended in an acquittal. These proportions have remained the same since 1996–97. Some provincial variation exists in the total number of cases heard in youth court that result in a conviction, from a low of 44 percent in Yukon to a high of 87 percent in New Brunswick. These differences can be explained in part by different charging practices. According to Hendrick (1999), the higher proportions of cases stayed and withdrawn in certain provinces reflect charges set aside pending the successful completion of alternative measure programs.

In 2000–01 the most common disposition in all youth court cases was probation (48 percent). The next most frequent dispositions were secure custody and open custody (17 percent each), a community service order (7 percent), fines (6 percent), absolute discharges (2 percent) and all other sentences (3 percent). The percentage of cases that result in a community service order

is low because such orders are most frequently used as a condition of probation or used along with a more serious disposition, such as open or secure custody.

Many differences existed between the dispositions for female and male young offenders. About 50 percent of convictions for male and female young offenders resulted in a term of probation, although probation was slightly more common for females (54 percent) than males (47 percent). Differences appeared in other sentences also, including both types of custody for males (36 percent for males, 28 percent for females). The gender differences for all other sentences were slight (deSouza 2002).

Secure and open custody cases were the most serious sentences in 34 percent of youth court sentences across Canada (see Table 13.3). A sentence of custody was handed down in 94 percent of murder/manslaughter and attempted murder cases, in 62 percent of attempted murder cases, and in 53 percent of robbery cases. The only property crime that was close to 50 percent custody dispositions was theft over $5000 (48 percent). Certain administrative offences resulted in higher proportions of sentences of custody also, notably escape from custody/unlawfully at large (89 percent) and failure to comply with a court disposition (42 percent). Of the

---

TABLE 13.2 Cases Heard in Youth Court by Principal Offence Category, 1996/97 to 2000/01

Offence Category	1996–97	1997–98	1998–99	1999–2000	2000–01	% change from 1996–97 to 2000–01
Total Cases (number)	110 065	110 882	106 665	102 061	99 950	
% change in the number of cases*	–	1%	-4%	-4%	-2%	-10%
Violent Crimes (number)	23 044	23 711	23 564	22 937	21 760	
% change in the number of cases*	–	3%	-1%	-3%	-5%	-6%
Property Crimes (number)	51 767	49 602	45 566	41 122	40 023	
% change in the number of cases*	–	-4%	-8%	-10%	-3%	-23%
Other *Criminal Code* Offences[1] (number)	18 285	19 316	19 421	18 718	18 264	
% change in the number of cases*	–	6%	1%	-4%	-2%	0%
Drug-related Offences (number)	5 353	4 549	4 716	5 394	6 967	
% change in the number of cases*	–	-15%	4%	14%	29%	30%
YOA Offences (number)	11 335	13 442	13 289	13 763	12 447	
% change in the number of cases*	–	19%	-1%	4%	-10%	10%
Other Federal Statute Offences (number)	281	262	109	127	129	
% change in the number of cases*	–	-7%	-58%	17%	2%	-54%

Notes:
* refers to the previous year
– not applicable
1. includes cases involving traffic offences

Source: Statistics Canada, *Juristat*, Catalogue 85-002, vol. 22, no. 3, March 2002, p. 10.

TABLE 13.3   Sentences in Youth Courts, 2000–2001

	Total Cases	Most Significant Sentence						
		Secure Custody	Open Custody	Secure and Open Custody	Probation	Fine	Community Service Order	Other[1]
		%	%	%	%	%	%	%
Canada	60 041	17	17	35	48	6	7	5
Newfoundland and Labrador	1 381	25	17	41	52	2	1	3
Prince Edward Island	170	15	35	50	39	5	0	6
Nova Scotia	2 176	1	35	37	53	4	5	1
New Brunswick	1 780	20	14	35	57	6	0	3
Quebec	7 952	16	12	28	56	3	9	5
Ontario	18 919	19	21	41	47	3	4	4
Manitoba	3 846	21	14	35	47	7	5	7
Saskatchewan	5 707	21	14	34	49	4	10	3
Alberta	10 721	16	10	26	39	16	13	6
British Columbia	6 799	13	22	35	54	3	2	5
Yukon	157	27	25	52	36	4	4	4
Northwest Territories	264	30	27	57	32	5	6	0
Nunavut	169	14	17	30	62	1	1	7

1. "Other" includes compensation, pay purchase, compensation in kind, restitution, prohibition, seizure, forfeiture, conditional discharge, absolute discharge, essays, apologies, and counselling programs.

Source: Statistics Canada, *Juristat*, Catalogue 85-002, vol. 22, no. 3, March 2002, p. 13.

20 809 cases resulting in both an open and secure custody disposition, 34 percent resulted in sentences of custody for less than one month, 44 percent for one to three months, 15 percent for four to six months, and 6 percent for more than six months.

The median length of a custodial sentence was one month. The longest median custodial sentence was for murder and manslaughter convictions (24 months), followed by attempted murder (17 months), aggravated assault (five months), and breaking and entering (three months). The percentage of youth court cases involving custodial sentences less than three months in length has increased from 71 percent in 1992–93 to 79 percent in 2000–01. The most common sentence length for probation was 12 months (56 percent of all probation orders) (Hendrick 1999).

Since 1992–93, repeat offenders have accounted for approximately 45 percent of all youth court cases. Compared with those individuals who appeared in youth court for the first time, repeat offenders were more likely to have been charged with property crimes. In 2000–01, 53 percent of repeat offenders were charged with a property offence and 24 percent for a violent crime. In contrast, 47 percent of first-time offenders were charged with a property offence and 29 percent were charged with a violent crime. According to Hendrick (1999: 9), these differences may be attributed to police use of diversion and alternative measure programs for first-time offenders. First-time offenders during 2000–01 were more likely to receive probation; 62 percent of convictions for first-time offenders led to a probation order compared to 35 percent of repeat offenders).

Repeat offenders were more likely than first-time offenders to receive a sentence of custody (51 percent versus 20 percent). These offenders accounted for 39 percent of all youth court convictions in 2000–01. Males were more likely to be repeat offenders than females (22 percent of all repeat offenders were male versus 17 percent of the female caseload).

ALTERNATIVE MEASURES

The YOA established the use of alternative measures to ensure that young persons "who would otherwise proceed to court are dealt with through non-judicial, community-based alternatives" (Kowalski 1999: 1). These programs—which include personal service to a victim, financial compensation, community service, personal or written apologies, and educational sessions—are used to divert young offenders who have been accused of less serious offences out of youth court, allowing the offenders to keep their criminal record clean. At the same time, alternative measures hold youths accountable for their actions. These programs are also used to reduce the numbers of youths flowing through the youth court system.

Alternative measures divert about 20 percent of all cases from youth court. In 2000–01, 24 002 youth cases resulted in the use of alternative measures. In all Canadian jurisdictions, more youths were processed through the youth court system than through alternative measures programs. The national average was three youths in court for each involved in an alternative measures program.

Although Quebec considers all offenders to be eligible for participation in an alternative measures program, in all other provinces and territories, alternative measures are used only in connection with less serious offences. It is usual for offenders convicted of murder, manslaughter, attempted murder, major assaults, sexual assault, offences involving domestic violence, drug offences, and offences involving impaired driving to be ineligible for alternative measures programs (Kowalski 1999: 8).

Offenders most commonly placed in alternative measures were those convicted of property offences (73 percent), "Other *Criminal Code*" offences (15 percent), and violent crimes (8 percent), while the remaining 4 percent were convicted of federal statute offences and other types of offences. Youths convicted of theft under $5000 accounted for 57 percent of all youths placed into an alternative measure program, followed by youths convicted of mischief (11 percent of all youths sentenced to alternative measures), "other property offences" (9 percent), common assault (7 percent), and break and enter (5 percent).

Alternative measures programs are usually reserved for first-time offenders, as we've seen. Almost all (89 percent) individuals placed in an alternative measures programs in 1998–99 were first-time offenders. Nine percent had committed one previous offence, and the remaining 2 percent had committed two previous offences.

The most common alternative measures program assigned to youths was community service (22 percent), followed by an apology (17 percent), other alternative measures (15 percent), and social skills improvement and essay/presentation/referral (11 percent each). The majority of cases in alternative measures programs were successfully completed during 1998–99. Ninety-three percent of all youths completed their alternative measure, while 1 percent partially completed their programs in 1998–99 (Kowalski 1999).

Alternative measures are not being continued in the *Youth Criminal Justice Act* (YCJA). Instead, the YCJA introduces a greater range of diversionary measures (see Exhibit 13.2).

EXHIBIT 13.2 The *Youth Criminal Justice Act*: Extrajudicial Measures

The alternative measures provisions are not being continued in the YCJA. Instead, the Act recognizes a broader range of diversionary measures. Extrajudicial measures are set out in the Act according to the following principles:

a) extrajudicial measures are an effective way to address youth crime;

b) extrajudicial measures allow for effective and timely interventions focused on correcting offending behaviour; and

c) extrajudicial measures are presumed to be adequate to hold a young person accountable for his or her offending behaviour if the young person has committed a non-violent offence and has not previously been found guilty of an offence.

Specifically, the Act includes warnings, police and crown cautions, referrals and extrajudicial sanctions. These sanctions are comparable to the current alternative methods.

The YCJA also states that extrajudicial measures be designed to provide an effective and timely response to offending behaviour outside the bounds of judicial measures. In addition, the Act encourages the youth and the victim/community to be involved in the design and implementation of the programs followed by participation in decisions related to accountability and reparation.

Source: Statistics Canada, *Juristat*, Catalogue 85-002, vol. 22, no. 8, October 2002, p. 4.

Custody

In Canada there are two levels of custody for young offenders. Secure custody is characterized by locks, bars, fences, and the close monitoring of the movement of youths in the institution. Open custody is characterized by facilities that offer guidance and assistance to youths. Open custody thus places a duty on provinces to create a program that allows the young person to improve her behaviour. The provision of such opportunities became an issue in Nova Scotia, where the judge ruled (in *Re B. (D.)* (1986)), that "ordering the youth to remain in a single room, even though it is fairly large with a television set available, cannot in today's philosophy of providing programmes to assist youths to understand their problems, be considered an appropriate facility and one of open custody." The judge also stated that open custody has to provide young offenders "a real measure of hope for their rehabilitation and reform …"

The power of youth courts to decide whether to place a youth in custody is found in s. 20 of the YOA.

Section 24 defines these powers by specifying that custody is to be used as a last resort. Under the YOA, the maximum sentence for offenders in either open or secure custody is usually two years. This can be increased to three years if the crime would normally carry a maximum sentence in adult court. Further, the crime of first-degree murder carries a maximum sentence of 10 years (the last four years may be served in the community) and that of second-degree murder seven years (the last three may be served in the community) (Hendrick 1999).

When sentencing a youth to a term in custody the judge must decide between open and closed custody by determining whether the young person poses a risk to the public as well as considering the needs of the offender and the offender's previous record. Before making any disposition involving custody, the judge must order a predisposition report, which is required to include certain elements stipulated in s. 14(2) of the YOA. These include an indication of the availability and appropriateness of community services and facilities for young persons, the relationship between the young person and the young person's parents, and the degree of control and influence of the parents over the young person.

The YOA distinguishes between open and closed custody. According to s. 24.1(1), the setting for open custody may be (1) a community residential centre, group home, child-care institution, or forest or wilderness camp, or (2) any other facility designated by the Lieutenant Governor in Council of a province. The setting for secure custody, in contrast, is any place or facility designated by the Lieutenant Governor in Council in a province for the secure containment or restraint of the youth. It is important to add that the definitions of open custody and closed custody are not precise; the courts have given provincial governments discretion, since part of the definition is the power of designation. Some open custody facilities are similar in operation to closed custody facilities, though the power of provincial governments to dictate what should be considered an open custody facility is not absolute.

An increase in the number of custody orders has been apparent since the inception of the YOA, especially in the area of open custody in the past five years. In 1983–84, a total of 14.2 percent of all dispositions involved custody (8.0 percent for open custody, 6.2 percent for closed); five years later, the total had reached 20.9 percent (9.7 percent for open custody, 11.2 percent for closed). In 2000–01, custody was ordered in 34 percent of all cases (17 percent for open custody, 17 percent for closed).

Judges are sentencing more youths to open custody because of its perceived benign nature and because in so doing the state provides services that provide for the best interests of the child. However, according to Corrado and Markwart (1988: 111), open custody—though an attractive sentencing option because it is "less onerous" than closed—may lead to net-widening.

Provinces and the territories differ in the frequency with which they use custody of either type, from a high of more than 57 percent of all convictions in Newfoundland and Labrador to a low of 26 percent in Alberta. In 2000–01 there were 21 014 cases resulting in a custodial disposition. Across Canada, custody was the most common sentence ordered in cases involving murder and manslaughter (94 percent of each of these cases), escape from custody and being unlawfully at large (89 percent), attempted murder (62 percent), robbery (53 percent), and failure to appear/comply with a court disposition (42 percent).

In terms of the length of custody orders, 34 percent of offenders were sentenced to less than one month in custody, 44 percent to between one and three months, 15 percent to between four and six months, and 6 percent to more than six months. In 2000–01, the median sentence length for cases resulting in secure custody was 30 days, while for open custody it was slightly longer at 34 days (deSouza 2002). During 1997–98 the highest median custodial sentence length (24 months) was for cases of murder and manslaughter, followed by attempted murder (17 months), aggravated assault (five months), breaking and entering (three months), and motor vehicle theft and possession of stolen property (two months). Repeat offenders were three times more likely to be given a term in custody than first-time offenders (Hendrick 1999).

Transfer to Adult Court

In recent years there has been much concern about violent crimes committed by youths (see Exhibit 13.3). This concern has led to demand that some youths receive an adult sentence. Some believe that placing the offending youth into a juvenile facility would not be a deterrent and that the best way to deal with the situation is to transfer the youth to adult court.

Under the *Young Offenders Act* (as it was enacted in 1984), s. 16 specified that a youth could be transferred to adult court if various criteria were met. Two of the most important were (1) the youth must be at least 14 years old at the time of the alleged offence and (2) the crime must have been a serious indictable offence such as murder, manslaughter, armed robbery, break and enter, or sexual assault. The youth court was further directed by s. 16(2) to take into account the following factors:

1. the seriousness of the offence and the circumstances in which it was allegedly committed;
2. the age, maturity, character, and background of the young person including previous findings of criminal activity and guilt;
3. the adequacy of the *Young Offenders Act* and the adequacy of the *Criminal Code* to meet the circumstances of the case;
4. the availability of treatment or correctional resources;
5. any representations made to the court by or on behalf of the young person or the prosecution; and
6. any other factors that the court considers relevant—issues such as mental illness, involvement of the accused with others, etc.

The transfer to adult court was not automatic, because when serious charges were brought before youth court the legislation required the youth court judge, before hearing any plea, to ask the Crown prosecutor and the defence counsel if they wished to have the case transferred to adult court. If the prosecutor agreed but the defence lawyer disagreed, a special transfer hearing would then be scheduled. During this special hearing, the prosecution had to present evidence to support the argument that the transfer was necessary for two reasons: the protection of society and the best interests of the accused.

Under the original provisions of the YOA a youth could serve a sentence handed down in adult court in a youth facility until the age of 21, but only with the approval of the provincial director of corrections. Some judges were reluctant to send youths to adult court because of the possibility of longer sentences and the possibility that they might have to serve most if not all their sentence in adult correctional facilities. In the decade following the introduction of the YOA, these issues were constantly highlighted. As a result, considerable variation appeared among provinces in terms of their use of juvenile transfers. Manitoba and Alberta had relatively high transfer rates; the rest of the provinces and territories had low rates. This discrepancy has been explained as a function of whether provinces decided to emphasize "the protection of society," as Manitoba and Alberta did, or "the needs of the young person" (Bala 1994).

Changes were made to laws governing transfer hearings during the 1990s. The first changes occurred in 1992, when amendments were made to s. 16 of the YOA. These amendments specified, among other things, the length of time a youth convicted of murder

---

EXHIBIT 13.3 Legislative Attempts to Control Serious Violence among Youths: Bill C-37

In 1995 concerns about youth violence and the public perception that the YOA was soft on violent crime led the federal government to introduce amendments. These amendments culminated in the passing of Bill C-37, a key component of which was the introduction of longer sentences designed to protect the public and provide greater supervision over young offenders convicted of committing violent crime. Bill C-37 places the onus on the young person, his/her counsel, or the Attorney General to show why a case of serious violence should proceed in youth court. If a convincing case cannot be made, cases of murder or attempted murder, manslaughter, or aggravated sexual assault are automatically heard in adult court if the offender was 16 or 17 years of age at the time of the offence.

If the case is not transferred to adult court and a conviction is secured:

- for first-degree murder the maximum sentence is ten years, of which a maximum of six years is to be served in custody and the remainder on conditional supervision;
- for second-degree murder the maximum sentence is seven years, comprising four years in custody and the remainder on conditional supervision; and
- for first- or second-degree murder, the young person has the option of electing trial before a youth court judge or trial by Superior Criminal Court judge and jury. If an election is not made, the election will have been deemed to be Superior Court.

If the case is heard in adult court and the accused is:

- convicted of first- or second-degree murder and under 16, the penalty is life imprisonment without parole for between five and seven years, or five years if the judge does not set parole ineligibility;
- 16 or 17 and the offence is first-degree murder, the penalty is life without parole for 10 years, and
- 16 or 17 and the offence is second-degree murder, the penalty is life with no parole for seven years.

Source: Statistics Canada, *Juristat*, Catalogue 85-002, vol. 15, no. 7, March 1995, p. 4.

---

could serve before being eligible for parole. If a youth was transferred to adult court and found guilty of first-degree murder, he would serve a maximum of 10 years before becoming eligible for parole. If convicted of second-degree murder, the youth would become eligible for parole in five years. In addition, youths convicted of crimes in adult court would be allowed to serve their sentence in a youth facility unless it was felt that doing so would create public safety issues.

In 1995 the law governing transfers to adult court was once again changed. First, the amendments specified that 16- and 17-year-olds charged with murder, manslaughter, attempted murder, or aggravated sexual assault were to be tried in adult court unless an application was granted to enable the case to be heard in youth court. If an application was made to have the case heard in youth court, it was up to the young person to show that the objectives of protection of the public and best interests of the youth could be met in a youth facility. If both objectives could not be determined satisfactorily, in the opinion of a youth court judge, the protection of the public remained paramount and the youth must be tried in adult court.

In 1999, the proposed *Youth Criminal Justice Act* (see below) made two recommendations in the area of transfers to adult court. First, the act proposed the group of offenders be expanded to include repeat young offenders who have a pattern of convictions for serious violent offences. The second recommendation was to decrease the age limit to include 14- and 15-year-olds. Further, the new act proposed to alter the transfer process to adult court for offenders whose cases are not automatically heard in adult court. Unlike the current system, in which a transfer hearing takes place prior to the trial, it is now proposed that adult sentences will be given after the trial has occurred and the young offender has been found guilty. Prosecutors will have to indicate their intention to seek adult sentences before the trial begins. The young offender then elects to be tried in provincial youth court or by a Superior Court judge alone or by a Superior Court judge with a jury. No matter which court is chosen, all have access to the full range of adult sentences following conviction when the required criteria are met. When the *Youth Criminal Justice Act* was passed, it left to each province to determine the age at which a youth can be transferred to adult court for a charge involving serious crimes such as murder and sexual assault. Provinces can decide to lower the age limit to a minimum of 14 or leave the age at 16 if they so desire. What is the impact of transferring juveniles to adult court? Most of the empirical studies have reported on the American experience. One consistent finding has been that each year in the United States over 10 000 youths are transferred to adult court. Most of the youths were charged not with violent crimes but with property and public (that is, drug and alcohol) offences, most pleaded guilty in adult court, and most were more likely to receive a probation sentence than a period of confinement. It takes over two and a half times as long to process a transfer case through the adult legal process than to hear the case of a youth who is tried in youth court.

Finally, it was reported that the belief that youths transferred to adult court would receive better treatment was not always well founded; most of the youths finished their sentence without receiving any treatment at all (Feld 1987; Fagan 1995).

ALTERNATIVE CUSTODIAL FACILITIES FOR YOUTHS

Boot Camps (Shock Incarceration)

The increased interest in boot camps reflects the pattern of development for other intermediate punishments described by Morris and Tonry (1990). As with other intermediate punishments, a few supporters were able to establish experimental boot camps, and the initial evaluations, which reported lower recidivism rates, received much interest. As a result, in the 10 years following the first opening of a boot camp in Georgia in 1983, 36 states had begun operating boot camps (Mackenzie 1994: 1).

A number of criteria separate boot camps from other correctional institutions, such as wilderness camps. First, boot camps are highly structured and include military drills, physical training, and hard labour. Second, the program targets young persons (usually males) between the ages of 16 and 24 who are convicted of nonviolent offences and who do not possess an extensive prior criminal record. Third, the length of time served by offenders ranges from three to six months, with the average stay being approximately 4.5 months (Camp and Camp 1993).

Boot camp participants are typically awakened as early as 4 a.m. They dress in uniform and exercise for one hour before breakfast. They attend school classes until 11 a.m., when lunch is served. More physical training follows, then dormitory clean-up and counseling sessions. After a 4:30 p.m. dinner, more counseling is provided. At 7 p.m. a variety of organized sports are played. An hour is reserved for personal activities such as washing and writing letters. Television is available at this time, but only programs considered to be educational in content are permitted. Lights are out at 9:30 p.m. The same routine is followed all week, with the exception of Sundays when inmates are allowed visitors for three hours in the afternoon.

Although boot camps share a military approach to discipline, they vary widely in their other program components. These variations are based on different ideas about how the program can achieve the desired goals. Mackenzie and Ballow (1995) studied 11 different boot camp programs and reported variations in number of participants, number of days served, placement authority, type of program entry and exit (voluntary or forced), as well as the type and amount of counseling offered to program participants. Other variations included location (that is, whether participants were housed in part of a larger prison or in a separate facility), intensity of release supervision, and type of aftercare during community programs. The researchers concluded that no unified "model" boot camp exists.

Boot camps became popular very quickly due largely to claims of significant reductions in recidivism rates. Studies have found that these initial claims were largely inflated, and most evaluations report that the recidivism rates of those who successfully complete their term in a boot camp were similar to those who were placed into regular probation or diversion programs. A study by Mackenzie et al. (1995) found no differences in recidivism rates between those who completed a boot camp program and their comparison group counterparts in eight U.S. states. Mackenzie and Souryal (1995), in a study of boot camps in six states, found regular probationers less likely than boot camp graduates to be rearrested for a crime. In addition, successful boot camp participants were more likely to be reincarcerated for new offences at a higher rate than regular probationers.

There is some evidence, however, that boot camps can influence some offenders' behaviour more positively than regular probation. First, after release from custody, but still under supervision in the community, graduates of boot camps were involved in more positive activities in the community. The key element appears to be maintaining an aftercare program in the community for at least five months, a program component that leads to significant reductions in recidivism rates. Second, unlike those individuals incarcerated in traditional custodial facilities or placed on regular probation, boot camp participants indicated that their experience led to significant positive changes in attitude and behaviour. The benefits of boot camps included improved physical health and educational opportunities, as well as appropriate therapeutic programming (Mackenzie and Shaw 1990; Mackenzie, Shaw, and Souryal 1992; Bourque et al. 1996).

Another goal of boot camps is the reduction of prison populations. Boot camp supporters claim that this can occur in two ways:

1. lower recidivism rates for boot camp graduates, who might have committed many more crimes if they hadn't been "shock incarcerated"; and
2. through the reduction of time that offenders spend in prison, since boot camp participants are usually returned to the community much earlier than those incarcerated.

Mackenzie and Souryal (1995) reported that certain factors affected the ability of boot camps to reduce prison crowding, including restrictive eligibility and suitability criteria (stricter criteria divert fewer prison-bound offenders), and length of the program (programs that keep participants in boot camps longer are less likely to reduce prison crowding), as well as the size of the program and graduation rates (smaller programs and those that graduate fewer offenders keep fewer offenders out of prison). If boot camps are to reduce prison overcrowding, programs must be carefully designed and controlled (Mackenzie and Piquero 1994).

Claims that boot camps can positively influence some offenders' behaviour and reduce prison crowding can, in fact, be realized, but only if the program design is properly developed and implemented. Researchers who analyzed successful boot camps point out that staff commitment, program integrity, and the timing of program integrity are the key factors involved in making participants into prosocial individuals (McCorkle 1995; Lutze 1998).

THE *YOUTH CRIMINAL JUSTICE ACT* (YCJA)

On 29 May 2001, Bill C-7, the *Youth Criminal Justice Act*, was passed by Parliament; it will replace the YOA in April 2003. This legislation was the result of criticism directed toward the YOA, in part from those who argued that there was too much emphasis in the act on the use of custody as a response to youth crime, and that the act largely ignored other intervention approaches (rehabilitation, for example) that are possibly more effective, meaningful, and facilitative in terms of their showing young offenders the impact of their crimes on the victim as well as the community. In addition, there was concern that the approach taken by the YOA was not succeeding in instilling basic values such as respect for others, responsibility, and accountability. Concerns were also directed at the steady increase in the number of repeat offenders who committed violent offences.

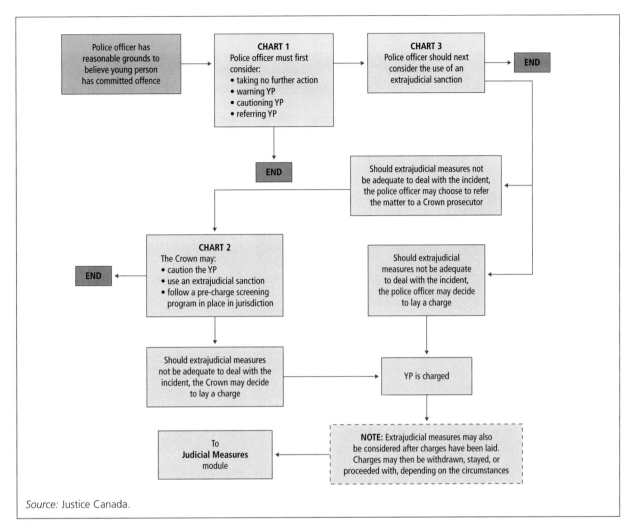

FIGURE 13.3
YCJA, Sections 4–14, Extrajudicial Measures—Summary Diagram

These issues led the federal minister of Justice to request, in 1996, the Standing Committee on Justice and Legal Affairs to conduct a review of the YOA and the operation of the youth justice system. As a result of this review, a new youth justice strategy was proposed. The preamble to the proposed act mentions the hope that the new legislation reduces "the over-reliance on incarceration for nonviolent offenders."

In addition, it recognizes the importance of rehabilitation and reintegration. Public protection, however, continues to be the primary goal of the youth justice system. The proposed legislation also recognizes the importance of addressing specific offenders, such as repeat offenders who commit violent offences, and of taking a broader, integrated approach that involves prevention, alternatives to the courts, and new approaches to punishment.

In order to accomplish this new strategy, the committee focused on three complementary areas:

- *Prevention.* The need to address the root causes of crime, support youth, encourage community efforts to reduce crime, promote crime prevention, and introduce effective alternatives to the formal youth justice system.
- *Meaningful consequences for youth crime.* The need for specific measures for violent and repeat offenders, to help young offenders understand the impact of their actions and allow them to make good on the harm done to victim and community.
- *Intensified rehabilitation.* The need for measures for violent and repeat young offenders that are more firm, more controlling, and more effective in providing treatment and support for rehabilitation and reintegration. While this approach is to be applied to all young offenders, it is particularly important to violent young offenders.

The YCJA extensively reworks the youth justice system. As illustrated in Figures 13.3 through 13.6, the youth justice system now involves a greater use of alternatives throughout each stage of the youth justice system in the hope that more youths will stay in the community and not repeat their criminal acts.

The key elements of the YCJA involve changes to major components of the YOA. For example, the Statement of Principles and Objectives of the YOA was found to be both unclear and sometimes in conflict with itself. The new legislation includes a statement of principles and objectives that clearly points out that the protection of society is the main goal of all criminal law, including youth justice law.

The statement also makes it clear that prevention, meaningful consequences of crime, and rehabilitation are all essential and complementary components of a youth justice system that is effective in protecting the public. This statement includes sections that specify youths are to be held accountable for their actions, that youths are to be treated differently from adults, and that violent youths are to be treated differently from non-violent youths.

The YCJA contains several measures that address the problem of violent and repeat young offenders, including the age and range of offences that can lead to a youth having his case heard in adult court (see the discussion of transfers to adult court above). In addition, a special sentencing option is to be made available to judges when they consider the disposition of the most violent and high-risk youths. This small group of offenders may require a combination of longer periods of supervised control and intensive rehabilitation programs that deal with the risk they pose to society.

Other new measures found in the YCJA include the provision of a broader range of community-based sentences that emphasize responsibility to the victim and community. A similar proposal is found in the area of alternative measures, where the federal government hopes that alternatives such as police cautioning, diversion programs, and restorative justice programs (see Chapter 14) can become more effective and efficient as responses to some youth crime.

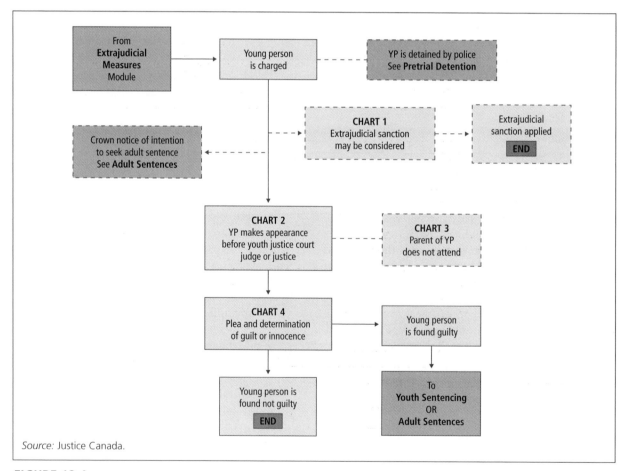

Source: Justice Canada.

FIGURE 13.4
YCJA, Sections 23–27, 32–37, Judicial Measures—Summary Diagram

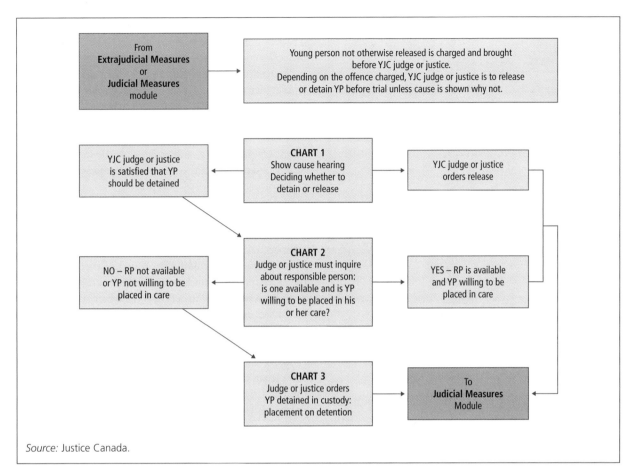

FIGURE 13.5
YCJA, Sections 28–31, *Criminal Code*, Part XVI—Summary Diagram

Parental Responsibility for Juvenile Crimes

Is it possible for the law to make someone responsible for another person's criminal actions? It is, and most laws in this respect are found in the area of youthful offences. Indeed, the law has long recognized the family to be a central factor in delinquency. Since parental discipline and control are assumed to be closely associated with youth crime, some American jurisdictions are now making parents responsible for their child's criminal behaviour.

These laws are not without precedent, since variants of them have existed in one form or another in both Canada and the United States throughout the 20th century. The first parental-responsibility law was enacted by Colorado in 1903, and it penalized parents for "contributing to the delinquency of a minor." Laws such as this allow the courts to punish parents in juvenile courts for behaviours associated with or suspected of encouraging their child's delinquency.

Supporters of this type of legislation believe that the conditions in the family unit are the best predictor of a child's behaviour and that parents are responsible for teaching their children the importance of subscribing to social values. One of the 42 states in the U.S. that has enacted this type of law was California, where the state government made it a misdemeanour offence when parents failed "to exercise reasonable care, supervision, protection and control over their children." California expanded this law in 1988 as a part of an attempt to control gangs with its *Street Terrorism and Prevention Act*. Persons convicted of violating of this law face a maximum penalty of a $2500 fine and one year in prison. This law was upheld by the California Supreme Court in July 1993, at which time it was ruled that the law sets a standard of behaviour for parents attempting to guide and control their children. In 1995 three other states—Wyoming, Arizona, and Louisiana—enacted comparable laws, creating the crime "improper" or "negligent" parental supervision, with penalties similar to those in the California legislation.

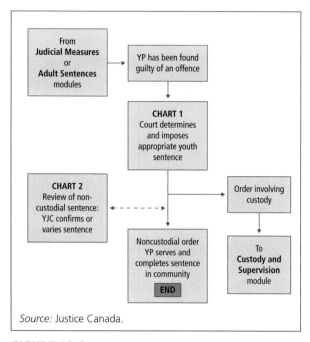

Source: Justice Canada.

FIGURE 13.6

YCJA, Sections 38–60—Summary Diagram

Some states have enacted legislation allowing for the criminal punishment of parents who violate parental-responsibility statutes. Perhaps the most widely reported case took place in Elgin, Illinois, when in May 1992 a judge sentenced a mother to 30 days in jail for failing to keep her Grade 2 daughter in school. Other parents have been ordered to serve time in classrooms with their chronically truant children. After analyzing these and other cases, Geis and Binder (1991) concluded that laws making parents responsible for the criminal actions of their children are "nasty and vicious." They also argue that there is no empirical study to date that has attempted to evaluate the claim that parental-responsibility laws reduce the crime rate of youths.

Another approach to this issue makes parents civilly responsible for the actions of their children. Parents whose children break the law may be required to pay for the damages caused by those children. In the United States, all states with the exception of New Hampshire and New York have parental-liability laws in their statutes, albeit with limits on how much money can be paid out. The average maximum recovery amount for all jurisdictions is $4100. Vermont has the lowest maximum fine—$250—while Texas has the highest at $15 000.

Manitoba was the first Canadian province to permit victims of property crimes to sue the parents of youths who committed an offence. This legislation—*The Parental Responsibility Act*—was enacted in the fall of 1997 and allows parents of young offenders to be sued to a maximum of $7500 for compensation for their child's illegal actions. This law places the onus on the parents of the offender to prove they weren't negligent in looking after and supervising their child. However, it is up to the victims to gather the evidence, complete the necessary paperwork, and make sure the defendants are properly served with the appropriate papers. If the complainant wins the case and the defendants don't pay them the amount awarded, it is up to the complainant to obtain a garnishment order.

In the first two years after this legislation was proclaimed, only 10 cases have involved legal proceedings. Parents have been held liable in two of the 10 cases. Of the other eight, none has reached a court hearing: two were adjourned indefinitely and the other six were either dismissed or discontinued (Kuxhaus 1999).

Ontario introduced its *Parental Responsibility Act* in 2000, and it deals only with claims of up to $6000 for property damages. It places the burden on parents to show that they exercised "reasonable supervision" over the child when the incident occurred. This law created great controversy when it was introduced since it assumes that any damage or loss was intentionally caused unless a parent can persuade a judge otherwise (*The Globe and Mail* 2000).

SUMMARY

At the beginning of the 20th century in Canada, there was no federal legislation governing juveniles. By the end of the century the *Young Offenders Act*, in place for just 16 years, was being superseded by the *Youth Criminal Justice Act*. Despite the impending introduction of the new act, the YOA had introduced a virtual revolution in the area of juvenile justice in Canada. Youths now have the same rights as adults, special facilities, and diversion programs (that is, alternative measures). Despite these changes, many people became critical of the YOA and demanded that it be made tougher.

As a result, amendments were made to the YOA concerning the length of sentences and the laws governing transfers to adult court. The success or failure of the *Youth Criminal Justice Act* remains to be seen, but it has introduced more legislation concerning prevention measures and support for rehabilitation programs than were available in the YOA.

Discussion Questions

1. What does *parens patriae* mean?

2. How do statistics concerning young offenders differ from those collected for adults?

3. How has the juvenile justice system evolved over the course of the 20th century?

4. Should youths be protected by the same due process rights afforded adults?

5. Should transfer hearings for youths be extended to 14- and 15-year-olds who commit serious crimes?

6. Should the length of sentences for all youths be lengthened? If so, by how much?

7. Is it a good idea to expand alternative measures to include all young offenders except those who commit serious violent crimes?

8. Do you think parental-responsibility laws help reduce youth crime? Do you think these laws are a good idea?

Suggested Readings

Bell, Sandra J. 1999. *Young Offenders and Juvenile Justice: A Century after the Fact.* Scarborough, Ont.: ITP Nelson.

Chesney-Lind, M., and R. Shelden. 1992. *Girls, Delinquency, and Juvenile Justice.* Pacific Grove, Calif.: Brooks/Cole.

Corrado, R., N. Bala, R. Linden, and M. LeBlanc, eds. 1992. *Juvenile Justice in Canada: A Theoretical and Analytical Assessment.* Toronto: Butterworths.

Dell, C.A., and R. Boe. 1998. *Female Young Offenders in Canada*, rev. ed. Ottawa: Correctional Service of Canada, Research Branch.

Lescheid, A., P. Jaffe, and W. Willis, eds. 1991. *The Young Offenders Act: A Revolution in Canadian Juvenile Justice.* Toronto: University of Toronto Press.

Platt, A. 1969. *The Child Savers.* Chicago: University of Chicago Press.

Schur, E. 1973. *Radical Nonintervention: Rethinking the Delinquency Problem.* Englewood Cliffs, N.J.: Prentice-Hall.

References

Bala, N. 1994. "What's Wrong with the YOA Bashing? What's Wrong with the YOA? Recognizing the Limits of the Law." *Canadian Journal of Criminology* 36: 247–70.

Bell, S. 1999. *Young Offenders and Juvenile Justice: A Century after the Fact.* Scarborough, Ont.: ITP Nelson.

Carrington, P. 1995. "Has Violent Youth Crime Increased? Comment on Corrado and Markwart." *Canadian Journal of Criminology* 37: 61–74.

Corrado, R.R., and A. Markwart. 1988. "The Prices of Rights and Responsibilities: An Examination of the Impacts of the *Young Offenders Act* in British Columbia." *Canadian Review of Family Law* 7: 93–115.

Dell, C.A. 1999. "Young Offender Legislation in Canada: A Commentary." *Forum on Corrections Research* 11: 47–50.

Dell, C.A., and R. Boe. 1997. *Female Young Offenders in Canada: Recent Trends.* Ottawa: Research Branch, Correctional Service of Canada.

deSouza, P., 2002. *Youth Court Statistics, 2000/01.* Ottawa: Canadian Centre for Justice Statistics.

Engler, C., and S. Crowe. 2000. *Alternative Measures in Canada, 1998–99.* Ottawa: Canadian Centre for Justice Statistics.

Fagan, J. 1995. "Separating the Men from the Boys: The Comparative Advantage of Juvenile versus Criminal Court Sanctions on Recidivism among Adolescent Felony Offenders." In J.C. Howell, B. Krisberg, J.D. Hawkins, and J.J. Wilson, eds., *A Sourcebook of Serious, Violent, and Chronic Offenders.* Thousand Oaks, Calif.: Sage.

Feld, B.C. 1987. "Juvenile Court Meets the Principle of Offense: Legislative Changes in Juvenile Waiver Statutes." *Journal of Criminal Law and Criminology* 78: 471–533.

Geis, G., and A. Binder. 1991. "Sins of Their Children: Parental Responsibility for Juvenile Delinquency." *Notre Dame Journal of Law, Ethics and Public Policy* 5: 303–22.

Hendrick, D. 2001. *Youth Custody and Community Services in Canada, 1999/00.* Ottawa: Canadian Centre for Justice Statistics.

———. 1999. *Youth Court Statistics 1997–98.* Ottawa: Juristat.

Kong, R. 1998. *Canadian Crime Statistics, 1997.* Ottawa: Canadian Centre for Justice Statistics.

Kowalski, M. 1999. *Alternative Measures for Youth in Canada.* Ottawa: Juristat.

Kuxhaus, D. 1999. "Do Laws against Parents Work?" *Winnipeg Free Press,* 16 November, A1, A3.

Lee, N., and T. Leonard. 1995. "Serious Violent Offences and Offenders in Youth Court." In C.A. Dell and R. Boe, eds., *Female Young Offenders in Canada: Recent Trends.* Ottawa: Research Branch, Correctional Service of Canada.

Leschied, A. 1995. "The *Young Offenders Act* in Review: A More than Modest Proposal for Change." *Forum on Corrections Research* 7: 37–40.

Marinelli, J. 2002. *Youth Custody and Community Services in Canada, 2000/01.* Ottawa: Canadian Centre for Justice Statistics.

Moyer, S. 1996. *Report of the Federal–Provincial–Territorial Task Force on Youth Justice: A Profile of the Youth Justice System in Canada.* Ottawa: Ministry of Justice.

Savoie, J. 2001. *Crime Statistics in Canada, 2001.* Ottawa: Canadian Centre for Justice Statistics.

———. 1999. *Youth Violent Crime.* Ottawa: Juristat.

Schur, E. 1973. *Radical Nonintervention: Rethinking the Delinquency Problem.* Englewood Cliffs, N.J.: Prentice-Hall.

Siegel, L.J., and J.J. Senna. 1997. *Juvenile Delinquency,* 3rd ed. Minneapolis–St. Paul: West.

Sinclair, R.L., and C.A. Dell. 1999. "Recent Trends in Youth Crime." *Forum on Corrections Research* 11: 39–42.

Sprott, J.B. 1996. "Understanding Public Views of Youth Crime and the Youth Justice System." *Canadian Journal of Criminology* 38: 271–90.

St-Amand, C., and P. Greenberg. 1996. *Youth Custody and Probation in Canada, 1994–95.* Ottawa: Canadian Centre for Justice Statistics.

Sutherland, N. 1976. *Children in English-Canadian Society: Framing the Twentieth-Century Consensus.* Toronto: University of Toronto Press.

The Globe and Mail. 2000. "Who's A Bad Parent, Then?" 17 August, A12.

Tremblay, S. 1999. *Crime Statistics in Canada, 1998.* Ottawa: Juristat.

West, G. 1991. "Towards a More Socially Informed Understanding of Canadian Legislation." In A. Leschied, P. Jaffe, and W. Wills, eds., *The* Young Offenders Act. Toronto: University of Toronto Press.

Court Cases

R. v. M. (M.R.), [1998] 3 S.C.R. 393

Re B. (D.) (1986), 27 C.C.C. (3d) 468 (N.S. T.D.)

CHAPTER 14

Contemporary and Future Challenges in the Canadian Criminal Justice System

CHAPTER OBJECTIVES

✓ Discuss the limits of legal rights in Canada, particularly as they apply to inmates.
✓ Understand the importance of community-based approaches throughout the criminal justice system.
✓ Explain the merits of sentencing enhancements for particular types of crimes.
✓ Discuss whether inmates should serve most of their sentence prior to their release on a conditional release program.
✓ Discuss the use of restorative justice in our criminal justice system and whether there are limits to the use of such programs.

The Canadian criminal justice system undergoes continuous change. Many of the topics discussed in this text are the result of problems perceived in a specific area, such as sentencing, and beliefs that a new policy or law will improve our criminal justice system. Of course, there is rarely unanimity on the changes that should be made and how they should be made. This chapter discusses a variety of issues, some of which are currently under debate in the legal system or in justice committees. Some are being put to practical use in other countries while in Canada they're being considered by officials or interest groups in terms of their applicability to our country. One such case involves enhanced sentencing for hate crimes, a policy already introduced into the sentencing policies of many other western countries.

One of the greatest threats for individuals comes through the uses of technology. For example, in November 2002, federal authorities in the United States broke up what they called the biggest identity-theft case in history when they charged three men with the theft of information from more than 30 000 people. Many victims had their bank accounts drained and their credit rating ruined. Losses were initially estimated at US$2.7 million, but experts believed that many more millions would be reported lost before the case came to trial. The scheme started in 1999 when a help-desk worker at a software company sold passwords and codes for downloading consumer credit reports to an unidentified individual. He received $30 for each report, each of which was passed to at least 20 more people, all of whom set out to make money from the information they had received. With more than 15 000 credit reports stolen, there was ample opportunity to do just that (Associated Press 2002: B2).

ENHANCED HATE CRIME SENTENCING

(Contributed by Helmut-Harry Loewen)

In the early-morning hours of 4 January 1998, Nirmal Singh Gill, 65, was kicked and beaten to death on the grounds of the Sikh Temple in Surrey, British Columbia, where he worked as caretaker. After an extensive three-month police investigation involving wiretaps, surveillance, and police officers posing as outlaw bikers, five male skinheads belonging to a racist group called White Power were arrested. The police investigation showed that aside from bragging about the killing of the elderly immigrant, the five neo-Nazis were planning to inaugurate a "racial holy war" by going on a shooting rampage against Indo-Canadian children in Surrey, a city in which Punjabi is the first language of 40 000 of its 300 000 residents. Among the evidence produced during the trial was a letter written in prison by one of the defendants, Nathan Leblanc, to convicted murderer John King, who is on death row in Texas for the dragging death of an African-American man. Leblanc wrote of King's hate crime: "You should be given a medal!"

After the defendants pleaded guilty to manslaughter, the Crown presented evidence at the sentencing hearings in November 1999, demonstrating that the killing was motivated by racial hatred. The Crown called for life sentences for all five defendants, basing its position on sentencing provisions introduced by Parliament to the *Criminal Code* in 1995 (see Chapter 9). Section 718.2 of the *Criminal Code* specifies that certain principles be taken into account in the sentencing phase. Among the aggravating circumstances leading to enhanced sentences is "evidence that the offence was motivated by bias, prejudice or hate based on race, national or ethnic origin, language, colour, religion, sex, age, mental or physical disability, sexual orientation, or any other similar factor" (s. 718.2(a)(i)). While the judge did not accede to the Crown's call for life imprisonment, he did impose increased penalties of 18 years incarceration for two of the defendants and 15 for the others, minus three years counted as time already served. In imposing the sentences, the judge noted that a balance needed to be struck between protecting society from the dangers posed by racially motivated violence and securing the fundamental right to freedom of expression.

In multicultural societies such as Canada's, with its racially and ethnically diverse population, the issue of hate or bias crimes has garnered increasing interest from the criminal justice system, social scientists, human rights advocates, and the media. Though hate-motivated violence against racial or ethnic minorities reaches back to the late-19th and early-20th centuries in Canada, when race riots instigated by organized anti-Asian mobs destroyed Vancouver's Chinatown, the concern with defining hate crimes and drafting anti-hate legislation did not emerge until after World War II, in the wake of disclosures about the extent of Nazi atrocities against Jews and other targeted populations of Europe. In 1948 the United Nations passed the landmark Convention on the Prevention and Punishment of the Crime of Genocide, which formulated principles for conceptualizing crimes motivated by ideologies of racial supremacy. Subsequent hate laws in many countries were based on the parameters established in the U.N. convention and in its International Convention on the Elimination of all Forms of Racial Discrimination (1966).

In the 1960s, in response to concerns expressed by Jewish and African-Canadian citizens, the government of Canada directed a special parliamentary committee to study the problem of hate propaganda and to make recommendations on the drafting of provisions in the Criminal Code for identifying and punishing certain hate-motivated crimes. In drafting its recommendations, the committee noted that even though the number of those involved in such activity may be small, "the effects are likely greater than present numerical estimates would suggest" and that ongoing racial harassment may provide "the seedbed from which a more dangerous and more widespread prejudice can flower tomorrow" (Canada 1996: 18).

Scholars and law enforcement officials have recognized that criminal activity motivated by racial prejudice and other expressions of bias merits special attention for the "disproportionate harm" inflicted not only on the victim but in the community to which the victim belongs (Roberts 1995). Studies of assaults motivated by hate note the greater degrees of physical injury that result in comparison with injuries suffered in assaults that are not bias-motivated (Levin and McDevitt 1993). Hate-motivated attacks also often involve multiple offenders, which reinforces the vulnerability felt by victims. The effect of such crimes is thus not restricted to the victim. "A hate crime resembles no other crime. The effects of hate crime reach beyond the immediate victim or institution and can damage society and fragment communities" (Sanderson 1991: 43).

Hate or bias crime has been defined on three levels. First, in terms of a general definition, it is a crime in which the offender is motivated by a characteristic of the victim that identifies the victim as a member of some group toward which the offender feels animosity (Garofalo and Martin 1991: 17). Second, municipal police agencies in Canada have adopted various definitions of hate crime. While most police agencies agree that a hate crime is a criminal offence motivated by the offender's hate or bias against a victim's racial or ethnic origin, nationality, religion, or sexual orientation, some include reference to disability and gender in their list of identifiable groups. The various law enforcement definitions differ too in the degree to which hate or bias is the motivation—whether hate or bias is the sole motivation or merely a part in defining the class of criminal offence. A final set of definitions, introduced in 1970 with amendments to the stipulated four hate-related offences: advocating genocide, public incitement of hatred; willful promotion of hatred; and a prohibition on possession of hate propaganda for the purpose of its dissemination. These offences are found in Part VIII, ss. 318–320, of the *Criminal Code*, which deals with propaganda.

Section 318 makes it an indictable offence to advocate or promote genocide. In keeping with the United Nations definition of genocide, the *Criminal Code* specifies "acts committed with intent to destroy in whole or in part any identifiable group" by "(a) killing members of the group; or (b) deliberately inflicting on the group conditions of life calculated to bring about its physical destruction." An "identifiable group" is defined as "any section of the public distinguished by colour, race, religion or ethnic origin." This provision recognizes that genocide involves actions (such as killing) and intentions (mental state), and that it is a criminal act to argue in favour of or to encourage a course of action that has genocidal intent. To date, the only case in Canada to have been instituted under this provision was *B'nai Brith v. Harcus* (1992), which involved alleged members of the Manitoba Knights of the Ku Klux Klan who were also charged with related offences after undercover Winnipeg police officers infiltrated the group. Charges were stayed in this case after the disclosure that one of the investigating officers had perjured herself. For a criminal proceeding to be instituted under this and the next section, the Attorney General must give consent.

Section 319 creates two hate-related offences. Section 319(1) prohibits making statements in a public place that incite hatred against any identifiable group and that may lead to a breach of the peace. Section 319(2) stipulates the offence of willfully promoting hatred against any identifiable group by communicating statements other than in private conversation. Section 319(7) defines the central terms relating to both offences under s. 319:

> 'communicating' includes communicating by telephone, broadcasting or other audible or visible means; 'identifiable group' has the same meaning as in Section 318; 'public place' includes any place to which the public have access as of right or by invitation, express or implied; 'statements' includes words spoken or written or recorded electronically or electromagnetically or otherwise, and gestures, signs or other visible representations.

In a high-profile case involving James Keegstra, an Alberta teacher, a conviction was secured under s. 319(2). Keegstra was accused of promoting hatred against Jews by alleging that the Holocaust was a fabrication concocted by a sinister conspiracy to destroy Christian civilization. The Supreme Court ruled that although s. 319(2) infringes on the guarantees of freedom of expression in the *Charter of Rights and Freedoms* s. 2(b), it is nonetheless a justifiable and reasonable limit on that freedom, given the harm to intergroup relations caused by such hate speech (*R. v. Keegstra* (1990)).

Section 320 is a provision related to the previous two in that it provides for a warrant to seize copies of hate propaganda that are possessed for the purpose of sale or distribution. Under the prior authorization of judicial warrant, and with no requirement that a formal prosecution be brought forward, any writing, visible sign, or other representation whose communication would constitute an offence under s. 319 may be seized. If a judge determines the material to be hate propaganda, it is ordered forfeited to the Crown for disposal as directed by the Attorney General.

Critics of hate crime legislation have noted a number of problems. Given the lack of consensus on how various law enforcement and human rights agencies in Canada define hate crime—both in terms of degree of intent and groups included—some researchers and organizations have called for police agencies to adopt a uniform definition.

A related problem is the absence of any national mechanism with which to collect statistics on the extent of the problem. Because of discrepancies among the various definitions of hate crime, it is difficult to gather reliable data on reported incidents. Aside from statistical data gathered by some municipal police forces and human rights groups such as the League for Human Rights of B'nai Brith (which collects annual data on anti-Semitic incidents), no obligatory collection of hate crime statistics currently exists to determine the scope of such activity. Even if new reporting mechanisms are introduced, it is widely recognized that because of various factors, including minorities' mistrust of the police, fears of further humiliation, and the threat of additional victimization, "of all forms of criminality, hate crimes are likely to be among the most underreported offences" (Roberts 1995: 14).

Ideological conflicts over differing interpretations of rights are a further area of disagreement. Canada has ratified international mechanisms that secure human rights in general and that protect minority populations such as women, racial and ethnic minorities, Aboriginal peoples, and people with mental and physical disabilities. To cite one example: Canada is signatory to the *United Nations Declaration on the Elimination of all Forms of Racial Discrimination*, which states in Article 4 that hate propaganda is illegal, that states should criminalize the dissemination of ideas based on racial supremacy or racial hatred, and that all organizations promoting such ideas should be declared illegal. While Canadian law has no provision to criminalize the formation of or membership in a hate group, Canada has endorsed these general moral principles, which are embedded in its *Criminal Code* provisions.

At the same time, however, the *Charter* affirms the rights of free expression of ideas and freedom of association. The debate over hate propaganda legislation thus involves two contrasting interpretations of rights. One view claims that freedom of speech has a position of priority over all other rights and freedoms, since the right to express dissenting and unpopular ideas is fundamental to a democracy. This libertarian view contrasts with the egalitarian one, which argues that curbs on hate speech are necessary to protect minority groups from the harmful effects of hate speech. As Kallen (1998: 4) notes,

> From the egalitarian view, all persons and groups must be equally protected against the willful promotion of hatred and against defamatory attacks which deny their right to human dignity. Freedom of speech, from this view, does not mean the right to vilify. Insofar as hate propaganda has no redeeming social value and is inherently harmful both to target groups and the social order, restrictions on freedom of expression explicitly designed to curb hate-mongering represent "reasonable limits."

Since their inception in parliamentary deliberations in the 1960s and 1970s, hate crimes legislation—and related enforcement matters—have emerged as issues worthy of close scrutiny by the criminal justice system, minority communities, and antiracism activists. Despite state and community efforts to monitor and track hate crime in Canada, it remains a complex problem that will continue to present challenges in the 21st century. New forms of technology, such as the Internet, which facilitate the globalization of hate, are already presenting law enforcement agencies with jurisdiction problems; national borders are barriers of little or no consequence to the dissemination of hate propaganda. In France, courts have already heard cases involving 13 neo-Nazi skinheads charged in England and France with hate crimes committed with a Web site serviced by an Internet provider based in British Columbia. A Canadian federal human rights tribunal commenced hearings over the Zundelsite, a Web site that promotes Toronto-based neo-Nazi publisher Ernst Zundel's denial of the Holocaust from an Internet provider based in California. Such cases demonstrate that combating hate crimes in the 21st century will require strategies and solutions that grow out of and yet go beyond the frameworks established in the wake of the genocidal horrors of the 20th century.

SPECIALIZED COURTS: THE TORONTO DRUG TREATMENT COURT

Specialized courts have jurisdiction over specific types of offenders and offences in the criminal justice system. The benefits of this approach include removing many cases from the existing court system as well as allowing court personnel to become experts in a particular area. Specialized courts involve youth court, which addresses crimes committed by persons aged 12 to 17 (see Chapter 13) and domestic violence courts (which involve such criminal offences as child, elder, and spousal abuse and assault).

Although it has been in operation in the United States and western European nations for some time, the drug treatment court has recently been introduced to Canada. It stands in contrast to the most common approach to preventing the selling and consumption of illicit drugs in both Canada and the United States, which is known as "supply-side enforcement." This means that law enforcement agencies are the primary criminal justice agency to wage the "war on drugs"; that is, they have the authority to detect those individuals growing and/or selling drugs with the intention of reducing the supply of illegal drugs. This in turn has led to other criminal justice agencies becoming involved in the "war on drugs"; for example, the courts are charged with ensuring that convicted drug offenders receive certain types of sentences and that special legislative provisions are used, in particular the federal *Proceeds of Crime (Money Laundering and Terrorist Financing) Act*, which allows the police to forfeit monies and/or material objects (such as vehicles) obtained through the use of monies made through the selling of illicit drugs.

This approach has been questioned over the years by those who argue that preventive programs are a better approach. As a result of their efforts, a variety of preventive programs are used across the country, most commonly aimed at preventing school-age youths from using drugs. One such example is DARE (Drug Abuse Resistance Program). This elementary school program gives students the skills to resist peer pressure to experiment with drugs and alcohol. Some say this program is a failure, while others argue that, given the right type of person providing the program, it can be successful.

As stated above, specialized drug courts have been introduced, first in Toronto and later in Vancouver, to combat the drug problem. These courts follow a similar approach to that in the United States in the late 1980s and are based on the premise that treatment will do more to lower recidivism rates of drug offenders than will incarceration (Finn and Newlyn 1994). The Canadian model follows the general model developed for drug courts in the United States where there are over 600 currently in operation. Nonviolent offenders being processed through the court system as a result of their drug-related activities can be diverted from the criminal courts into a drug court and therapeutic programs. This involves the defendant's waiving his right to a speedy trial, as he is immediately placed into a drug treatment program. These programs most commonly involve frequent meetings with the presiding judge, treatment at a designated substance abuse centre, and a constant monitoring of the individual through urinalysis, reports from treatment providers, etc. If the defendant completes the program, the original charges are dismissed. If he does not complete the program, the charges are reinstated and the offender is returned to the criminal justice system for normal processing.

The key components of drug treatment courts include

1. the integration of alcohol and treatment services with the justice system;
2. a nonadversarial approach;
3. accessibility to a continuum of alcohol, drug, and other related treatment and rehabilitation services;
4. abstinence (which is monitored by frequent testing);
5. ongoing judicial interaction with each participant; and
6. creating partnerships between drug courts, public agencies, and community-based organizations (Olson et al., 2001).

The Toronto Drug Treatment Court started on 1 December 1998 and by the end of its first year of operation had supervised 110 drug addicts (Makin 1999). By the summer of 2000, 22 persons had successfully completed the program. The court's target group is nonviolent offenders who are addicted to crack cocaine, heroin, or cocaine. Addicts can apply for the program after they have been charged with possession or trafficking in small quantities of crack cocaine, heroin, cocaine, and/or have been charged with a prostitution-related offence. Addicts who have been charged with selling drugs for financial gain or who have been charged with selling drugs in a location frequented by youths, such as a school, are not allowed in the program (Bindman 2002).

Before an individual is allowed on the program, he is evaluated to ensure he has no background of violent crime and that he is willing to seek treatment. Only 20 percent of those considered for the program succeed in being seriously considered for the program. If an offender is admitted to the program, he is placed on bail to begin treatment. As part of this program, he must

The staff of Canada's first drug court, located in Toronto

consent to urine tests and must appear in front of a drug court judge as often as twice a week to discuss his progress. There are two avenues that a participant may take. The first is for those offenders with little or no criminal record who are charged with simple possession of cocaine or heroin. If they are selected for this particular approach, they will enter the Drug Treatment Court prior to their plea. Once they successfully complete the program, any charges will be withdrawn or stayed. The second approach (which is used in 90 percent of cases) involves those offenders who have more serious records or charges. As a condition of entering the program they must plead guilty and sign a consent form waiving various constitutional rights such as the right to be tried within a specific amount of time. If the participant successfully completes the program, he will be given a noncustodial sentence (usually probation with a list of conditions). If he fails to complete the program, he must appear in criminal court again for sentencing (Chiodo 2001). Drug treatment courts are unique in two respects. First, the court is nonadversarial (for example, a Crown prosecutor can praise a participant doing well on the program) and, second, all participants must stay in court after they report on their progress, listening to other participants talk about their addictions and treatment.

Participants remain in the program between 12 and 16 months. Phase I of the program can be completed in as little as three months (once the participant has been drug free for three months, completed employment and life skills courses, and possesses a stable job and home life). Of the first 75 participants admitted to the program, 42 (56 percent) were participating in the program one year later. Of the clients who were no longer involved in the program, 20 (27 percent) were expelled, 4 (5 percent) withdrew, and 8 (11 percent) were terminated from the program due to their failure on some component of the program (e.g., failure to appear for treatment court as scheduled).

Besides providing benefits to those drug offenders who complete the program, drug courts also represent a significant savings for taxpayers. The cost of treatment in drug courts in the United States has been estimated to be $3500 per year, while the cost of incarcerating an offender is estimated at between $18 000 and $25 000 per year.

In addition, those who have successfully completed the program have been found to have much lower rates of recidivism—lower than 10 percent compared to about 30 percent for those who have been incarcerated (Bindman 2002).

CYBER CRIME: THE ISSUE OF IDENTITY THEFT AND ONLINE PORNOGRAPHY

Cyber crime refers to those crimes that occur on the virtual community of the Internet. The so-called "location" of these crimes—cyber space—raises many new issues for the criminal justice system, such as the enactment of laws and the prosecution of offenders because cyberspace allows individuals to communicate, provide and receive information, and sometimes commit crimes while anonymous. Although there are many different types of cyber crime, including cyber stalking, cyber consumer fraud, and hacking, this section focuses on identity theft, which has been referred to as the "crime of the new millennium" and "a major scourge of the information age" (Marron 2002).

Identity Theft

Identity theft occurs when an individual steals a form of identification, such as a name, date of birth, or Social Insurance number, and uses that information to access the victim's financial resources. This type of activity existed before the use of the Internet became common. In its earliest forms, thieves watched people at public telephones in order to "steal" their calling card numbers or to find a bank credit card receipt. In both cases, the object was to quickly use the information before the victim was aware that he had been victimized.

How easy is it to steal someone's identity? Many birth or death announcements placed in a newspaper include the maiden name of a mother, the most common password used in the banking system across Canada. From this piece of information alone a thief can start to construct a person's identity by finding other bits of information about the unsuspecting victim, such as a telephone number, address, and place of employment. Then, he can easily obtain a photo identification (perhaps from a library) and get government offices to issue a Social Insurance number, birth certificate, and driver's licence (Clark 2002).

The increased use of the Internet has turned identity theft into the fastest-growing financial crime in Canada and the United States. The Internet allows criminals to steal information off-line and then use stolen credit cards online while protected by anonymity. Identity theft is widespread in Canada—between October 2001 and June 2002 there were 5352 victims found across Canada with reported losses of approximately $6 million. It is estimated that this figure will increase to $20 million once each victim totals his final losses. The potential for identity theft is large—in 2001, it was estimated that there are about 1.4 million more Social Insurance numbers in circulation than there are persons in Canada, indicating the potential of large-scale abuse (Clark 2002). In comparison, there are a reported 700 000 to 750 000 victims a year (Marron 2002). It is also estimated that each individual victim in the United States spends an average of 175 hours of personal time and over $800 to clear her name and restore her credit rating.

Current laws used to protect individuals from theft are difficult to apply in cyberspace. As a result, new laws must be passed to address these issues. The Ontario government introduced one such law in 2001. This law increased the fine for impersonating to $50 000 (from $1000) and tightened government control over such official identity documents such as birth certificates. One police official in Canada believes that there has to be a different way to establish our identity rather than obtaining various pieces of identification that collectively create our self, perhaps by introducing a single national identity card (Clark 2002).

Online Pornography

The Internet is also the location of a massive amount of pornography. The pornography industry has made huge profits from the Internet; it is estimated that the online sex industry generates over $100 million each year in Canada and over $1 billion in the United States (*Business Week* 2000). The problem of online pornography usually takes one of two forms. The first is the illegal exposure to online surfers of sexual images or invitations and the second is the trafficking of pornographic photographs and videos. The Internet has facilitated this increase in the pornography industry for a number of reasons, including

- *Speed:* The Internet is the quickest means of sending visual materials over long distances. Pornographers can deliver the information faster and more securely than by using the mail system.

- *Security:* Any illegal materials placed in the hands of a mail carrier can be potentially discovered. This risk is significantly lower when the Internet is used. For example, passwords can be used to protect an Internet site, thereby keeping the site secure.
- *Anonymity:* Anonymity is the most important protection offered by the Internet to those in the online pornography industry and their customers (Graham 2000).

Due to the above, lawmakers and the courts face a challenge in controlling the online pornography industry. According to a survey conducted by the Crimes against Children Research Center at the University of New Hampshire, one in five children between the ages of 10 and 17 it surveyed had been the object of a sexual solicitation over the Internet during the year prior to the survey. The study concluded that girls were targeted at almost twice the rate of boys, and that fewer than 10 percent of the total number of incidents were reported to the authorities (Foss 2002).

In an attempt to control such activities, the Canadian government passed Bill C-15A in June 2002, which contained provisions designed to protect children from individuals who use cyberspace to victimize children. This bill addressed three areas—sexual exploitation, Internet luring, and child pornography—to protect children. The *Criminal Code* was changed in the following ways:

- *Internet Luring and Child Pornography:* It is now illegal for an individual to communicate with a child over the Internet for the purpose of committing a sexual offence against that child as well as to transmit, make available, export, and access child pornography.
- *Child Sex Tourism:* This bill amended the child sex tourism law (passed in 1997) in order to simplify the process of prosecuting Canadians who sexually exploit children in other countries.
- *Enhanced Judicial Powers:* This bill now permits judges to order both the deletion of child pornography posted in computer systems in Canada and the forfeiture of any materials used during the commission of a child pornography offence. Judges can now keep known sex offenders away from children by using prohibition orders, long-term offender designations, and one-year peace bonds for offences related to child pornography and the Internet.

It wasn't long before the first individuals were charged with the new offence of Internet luring. One such case involved the Winnipeg Police Service charging a 22-year-old male who allegedly made contact with a 13-year-old female in an Internet chatroom and then persuaded her to meet him. He then allegedly took the victim to his home, where they engaged in sexual activity. In order to charge the alleged perpetrator with Internet luring, the police had to gain the approval of the Massachusetts Attorney-General to gain access to the text of the conversations made by the victim and perpetrator since the texts were recorded by a Boston-area Internet service that hosted the chatroom (Foss 2002). A number of other charges were also laid in this case, including sexual assault and sexual interference.

COMMUNITY JUSTICE

Community justice focuses on the belief that crime not only involves an offender, an incident, or a case that needs to be processed through the criminal justice system, but also is a social problem that affects the life within a community. At first glance, community justice appears to share a similar focus to that offered by restorative justice (see the discussion on this topic later in this chapter) but besides a focus on community empowerment, it is quite different. Community justice is viewed by Clear and Karp (1999) as all those activities that include community in their processes, particularly neighbourhood-level operations, problem-solving, decentralization of authority and accountability, and citizen involvement within the justice process. Three major areas of community justice have emerged: community policing (see Chapter 6), community-oriented lawyering, and community courts.

Community-Oriented Lawyering

Another innovation in the court system involves community-based lawyering. Some lawyers have started to move away from reactively processing cases presented to them and instead work in partnership with other criminal justice agencies and communities in order to address the problems faced by residents of neighbourhoods. This work is called community-oriented lawyering.

The goals of community-oriented lawyering include preventing and reducing disorder and crime, restoring victims and communities to more effective and healthier functioning, and empowering local citizens. And though prosecution is still an activity employed by prosecutors, for community-oriented lawyers it is only one tactic that can be used to solve problems in neighbourhoods and communities. Prosecutors are taking a leadership role in building connections and initiatives that bring together citizens, businesses, government agencies, and other criminal justice agencies in the community for the purposes of reducing crime and increasing safety (Coles and Kelling 1998). This means they are developing

TABLE 14.1   Traditional Practice and Community Lawyering Compared

	Traditional Case Orientation	New Community Orientation
Unit of work	• Crimes • Cases • Complaints	• People • Problems • Relationships
Definition of success	• Win cases • Uphold rule of law • Be fair and impartial	• Reduce severity of the problem • Improve quality of life for individuals and micro-communities • Restore relationships
Community role	• Source of clients • Complainants • Political support	• Influences priorities and witnesses • Helps define what constitutes success • Necessary partner
Extent of inter-agency collaboration	• Limited to high visibility cases, "issue du jour"	• Frequent, intensive
Tools	• Investigation • Negotiation • Litigation	• Community mobilization • Training (e.g., police, citizens) • Civil remedies • Negotiated voluntary compliance • Motivating agency cooperation
Favourite question	• What happened?	• What's happening?

Source: Connor (2000), p. 29.

accountability at the neighbourhood level by implementing tactics that include

1. refining their core capabilities in order to enhance the prosecution of violent and repeat offenders;
2. helping set standards for the selective prosecution of offenders and offences in the context of neighbourhood priorities;
3. relying on civil law and the use of civil initiatives as well as criminal law and criminal sanctions; and

4. using diversion and alternatives to prosecution, sentencing, and incarceration such as mediation, treatment, community service, and restitution to victims.

In the same way that community policing introduced a distinctive approach to law enforcement, community-oriented lawyers have started to redefine the role of lawyers. According to Connor (2000), the most important factor in this redefinition is that some lawyers noticed the changes in policing and the positive results occurring as a result of the introduction of community policing initiatives. From the police they learned it was possible, in some cases, to change their strategy and pursue an approach that favours prevention in order that the cycle of crimes brought about by drug addiction, child abuse, and untreated mental illness be eliminated.

To achieve the goals of community-oriented lawyering, a new approach was needed (see Table 14.1). Most significant here is that the traditional approach has been to ask, "What happened?" while the new approach attempts "to reshape what will happen" (Connor 2000: 28). Community-oriented lawyers approach their jobs by focusing on the problems of particular people and places rather than just crimes and legal cases. As Connor (2000: 28) points out, these lawyers "think beyond the individual drug sale to the drug market itself; beyond the civil action for termination of parental rights to the woman who seems trapped in a cycle of abusive relationships."

In addition, the definition of success has changed. No longer is winning the case the only desired outcome, as increasing neighbourhood safety, preventing crime, and improving the quality of life have all become important considerations. In order to achieve these goals, community-oriented lawyers listen to the victims themselves as well as to service providers, local residents, and criminal justice agents who work in the community, such as police officers who work in community storefronts (see Exhibit 14.1). Other changes include the sharing of information and the making of decisions based on the feelings and concerns of other members of the community. Another significant change is that court processing is a tool, not an end in itself. Instead, other types of activity are used, such as employing nonadversarial solutions and negotiating outcomes between the parties involved.

How can the effectiveness of community-oriented lawyers be measured? Like success in community

---

EXHIBIT 14.1 Community Prosecution

In 1990 the district attorney of Multnomah County, in Portland, Oregon, assigned a senior deputy district attorney to work for one year on a neighbourhood-based prosecution project in Portland's inner-city Lloyd District. This district was characterized by citizens as unsafe, and this perception was compounded by gang and drug problems in adjoining communities.

The attorney and the Lloyd District business leaders created a business association and created a public safety committee. The committee produced a report that called for better lighting, the coordination of private security, and intensified public law enforcement. In connection with this last point it underscored the need for more police officers and a more visible police presence. One of the recommendations made by the committee was unique: a request for the assignment of a special assistant deputy prosecutor (ADA) to the district.

The committee wanted the ADA to address its concern about the lack of consequences in the downtown courts for criminal activity that adversely affected the district and its business. The committee was so supportive of this idea that it raised private monies in order to hire an ADA. As a result, the district attorney approved a one-year pilot project on the condition that public funds would be used if the program proved successful. This was known first as the Neighborhood Prosecutor Project, but its name was soon changed to the Neighborhood District Attorney (NDA) Project.

This change was more than just a renaming. It was the result of the realization on the part of the ADA who was hired that the job entailed more than just prosecuting offenders. Indeed, as the job evolved, the ADA became more involved in ways in which the street behaviour and low-level disorder that threatened neighbourhood safety could be put into place. Soon the role of the ADA involved providing answers, giving feedback, and explaining various aspects of the official criminal justice system, especially the legal constraints prohibiting the police from doing what local citizens wanted them to do in certain situations to make the neighbourhood safer. The core activity of the ADA soon became devising alternative responses to the legal system.

The alternatives included the use of the law in innovative ways, such as resorting to civil remedies, developing new resources, getting people to work together in new ways, and negotiating to bring diverse community interests together to discuss issues. In order to accomplish this, the ADA became a facilitator, legal counsellor, problem solver, and community advocate. As Boland (1996: 40) states, "only a network of police, citizens, the local government, and 'downtown justice' can get this job done. In this new approach to reducing crime, the flexibility needed to get the job done requires a new organizational arrangement." Perhaps the best indication of the success of the NDA is the fact that it quickly expanded to other parts of Portland, and in all parts it was successful.

Source: Boland (1996).

CHAPTER 14 Contemporary and Future Challenges in the Canadian Criminal Justice System policing, success in community-oriented lawyering will include traditional outcome measures—in this case the conviction of criminals in a court of law. But it will also include several other measures, such as the degree to which certain neighbourhood problems are solved and the effectiveness of civil sanctions and negotiated agreements used in lieu of prosecution. Other possibilities include evaluating the perceptions of safety by the residents in a designated area, increasing the involvement of citizens in crime prevention and crime reduction, improving case management procedures used by the police, and improving the ability of individual citizens and neighbourhood groups to solve problems (Coles and Kelling 1998).

Community Courts

Community courts are decentralized courts that respond directly to community concerns rather than wait for serious crimes to be committed. They share certain features that create a strong connection between unruly conduct and the adjudication process. Among those features are citizens' advisory committees, citizen volunteers, and programs that involve the community more closely in the adjudication process.

According to Rottman (1996), three different models exist for today's community-focused courts. The first is Navajo Peacemaking, an approach that uses Navajo traditions and principles in the judicial process. The integration of Navajo customs is most evident in the Peacemaker division of the Navajo Nation judicial branch, which emphasizes nonadversarial processes in dispute resolution. The formal aspects of this process include a peacekeeper, who is a person recognized for ability and wisdom, the parties in disagreement, their extended families, and Navajo religious ceremonies. Peacemaking gains its authority from the community.

All Peacemaker sessions take a similar approach and have addressed problems that range from marital discord to land dispute. Peacemaking is a ceremony. First, basic rules are established, prayers are made, all those in attendance become involved in the questions and answers, a problem-solving statement is developed by the peacemaker, agreements are made, and prayers are offered once again. It is important to emphasize that there are no winners or losers, but only agreed-upon decisions. Generally these sessions last two or three hours, but some have gone on for much longer (Rottman 1996; Zion 1998).

The second approach noted by Rottman involves the return of certain types of criminal cases to communities through the use of local or "branch" courts. The Midtown Community Court (MCC), located in Manhattan, New York City, is perhaps the most famous

example of this approach. In the MCC, only minor offences are heard.

But this is not just another court trial using the same actors and the same rules in a criminal courtroom that just happens to be located in a community. Instead, the community plays a significant role and is viewed as having a major role to play in the process and decision. In the MCC, community groups provide opportunities and the supervision of sentences that are served in the community. In addition, they provide other resources and services, such as treatment, support, and education. Eventually a community advisory board was created and a mediation board developed for disputes within the community to be resolved outside the traditional legal process.

The third type of community court recognized by Rottman is the community justice centre. The community justice centre "significantly expands traditional notions about the role of courts and tests the extent to which they are capable of serving as catalysts for change" (Rottman 1996: 50). The centre comprises local agencies that supervise community service sentences and local residents' groups that become involved in the legal process, and it coordinates and makes recommendations for programs and services to those who need them. The Red Hook Community Justice Center, in Brooklyn, New York, generally hears misdemeanour criminal cases but also hears such felony cases such as domestic violence and juvenile delinquency. In addition, it also hears civil cases such as landlord–tenant disputes and small claims.

According to Rottman, the three types of community-based justice programs discussed above share certain elements. First, they all practise some type of restorative-based justice (see below). Second, community courts treat those involved as real individuals rather than as abstract legal persons. Third, community resources are used in the adjudication of disputes.

THE POLICE AND PRISON PRIVATIZATION MOVEMENTS

The Police

One of the most interesting aspects of policing that has developed over the past few decades is the growth of the private-security sector (Shearing and Stenning 1981; Cunningham and Taylor 1985; Shearing 1992). The private-security sector was larger than the public-police sector throughout the 1990s. For example, in 1996 there were 59 090 police officers across Canada and 82 010 private-security personnel. This difference represents a 1 percent decrease in the total number of police officers between 1991 and 1996 but a 4 percent increase in the private-security sector during those same years (Swol 1998). Private security comprises private investigators and security guards. In 1996 there were 69 780 private-security guards and 12 230 private investigators. Part of the dramatic increase in the private-security sector is due to private-security personnel now doing some of the work traditionally thought to be the exclusive domain of the public police.

There are significant differences between the personnel who work for private security and the public police. First, more women are employed in the private sector. In 1996 women comprised 21 percent (2550) of all private investigators and 20 percent (14 065) of all private-security guards, compared to 13 percent (7490) of all police officers. Second, a considerable age difference exists between individuals employed in the various sectors. A much higher percentage of private-security personnel are under the age of 25 and over the age of 55 than in the public police. Almost 70 percent of all police officers were between the ages of 25 and 55 in 1996, compared to 50 percent of private investigators and 38 percent of security guards. Third, police officers have attained a higher level of education than their counterparts in the private sector. In 1996, 81 percent of police officers had some education greater than a high school diploma, compared to 66 percent of private investigators and 53 percent of security guards. Further, 14 percent of police officers had received a university degree, compared to 10 percent of private investigators and 7 percent of security guards. Fourth, visible minorities make up a larger part of private-sector security guards. In 1996, 6 percent of private investigators and 11 percent of security guards were members of visible-minority groups, compared to 3 percent of all police officers. Finally, police have significantly higher incomes than private security. In 1996, the average of police officers across Canada was $53 795, nearly twice that of security guards (Swol 1998).

Private police forces provide security to many private organizations, including shopping centres, industrial facilities, banks, and business organizations. The bulk of this work is visible: personnel wear distinct uniforms and are either located in a conspicuous location in a building or walk a specific perimeter. Other security personnel conduct their work in an undercover capacity. Some organizations hire security personnel to work alongside regular employees in an attempt to uncover criminal activity. In addition, they monitor hidden surveillance cameras of employee work and rest areas in an attempt to detect employee wrongdoing.

How did private policing and security forces become such a major force? As early as 1972 governments in North America were interested in the growth of private security. The U.S. Department of Justice had commissioned the Rand Corporation to conduct the first study of private policing (Kakalik and Wildhorn 1972). The report identified private security as an "industry" that provides a "service to the public." Accordingly, private policing was seen as an "asset," "making a significant contribution to the American economy" and relieving taxpayers of substantial costs if the public police were to expand their services to include those provided by private police.

Over 10 years later, another significant research project investigated the growth of private-security forces. This study was conducted by the Hallcrest Corporation and funded by the U.S. government to study the growth and issues posed by private police forces that had emerged since the Rand study. The authors of the report stated that by 1985 "Americans will easily spend $20 billion per year for products and services to protect themselves—more than they'll spend to support all enforcement agencies (federal, state, local) in the United States" (Cunningham and Taylor 1985: 163).

The authors of the report identified three responses to resistance about private police forces. First was a real structural change occurring in contemporary society involving the expansion of enclosed private industries and developments. These places required security, and security was to be provided by private police forces (while public places were patrolled by the public police forces). Second, much of the resistance to private policing stemmed from concern voiced by the public police, largely to do with the loss of personnel. Finally, the authors pointed out, private security agencies "police" areas and conduct themselves in ways that are outside the realm of public police forces (Shearing 1992).

In Canada, a report for the Solicitor General of Canada by Normandeau and Leighton (1990) recommended that Canadian policing policy include "new strategic partnerships" that integrate the potential of all types of policing in order to better preserve the peace in communities.

Some argue that the continued growth in the number of private-security personnel and the decline of public policing has come about largely because citizens have doubt about the ability of public police forces to protect them and their property. This doubt can lead to a several issues; for example, Reiss (1988) and Moore (1992) argue that the increase of private policing can lead to (1) a distribution of security based on who can afford it, (2) less respect for the rights of those detained, and (3) a lower level of professional competence.

Another concern is that many criminal offences discovered by the private police are not referred to the public system. Many are dealt with privately, outside the protections guaranteed to citizens by the *Charter of Rights and Freedoms*. This public–private split leads to concern about the possibility of two criminal justice systems operating at once: one public and the other private.

Will the private system be as concerned about the rights and protections of the public as the public system (Cunningham, Strauchs, and Van Meter 1990)?

Private Prisons

Although prisons have always been controversial in our society, proposed private prisons have become a current issue in Canada. Such prisons would be built and operated by private corporations specializing in corrections, and would serve the purpose of saving large amounts of money for both federal and provincial governments.

In the spring of 1995 New Brunswick signed a contract with a private corporation specializing in the building and management of correctional facilities—Wackenhut Corrections Corporation of Palm Beach Gardens, Florida—to build and operate a young-offender facility. At the same time, it announced that it was exploring the possibility of calling for proposals to build and possibly operate an 80-bed adult facility. The Nova Scotia government then released a press statement stating that it was looking at the feasibility of involving the private sector in operating its nine provincial correctional centres. Both provincial governments cited cost savings as their rationale in exploring the private prison alternative. New Brunswick noted it could save as much as 15 percent of the costs of building and operating a facility, while Nova Scotia stated it was looking for ways to reduce the provincial debt. In the United States, cost savings are estimated at approximately US$10 for each inmate per day (Cox 1995). While the government of New Brunswick later decided to staff the new facility with provincial employees, it raised issues concerning private prisons in Canada.

While Canada and other countries, including Great Britain, Australia, and France, have experimented with privatizing prisons, the only country to have implemented such prisons is the United States, where it is estimated that 3 percent of prisons and jails are now privately run. In 1991 the Corrections Corporation of America (the largest contractor of private prisons), operated 14 secure adult facilities and three juvenile facilities, totaling about 48 000 beds; Wackenhut operated eight adult facilities and 3200 beds. Now more than 50 private correctional facilities housing adult inmates are operating in the United States. Most are minimum- or medium-security institutions and most have been built in the three states—California, Florida, and Texas—that have the largest inmate populations. In addition to running correctional facilities, private corporations are involved in designing and constructing correctional facilities, and maintain that they can build a facility twice as quickly and 20 percent cheaper than a state government can. The private sector is also involved in the financing of new construction; traditionally, prisons and jails are owned by government and funded by taxpayers, but due to fiscal strategies during the 1980s, private corporations became involved with the financial construction of facilities.

In all other countries that are experimenting with private prisons, such as Great Britain and Canada, citizen approval of debt for capital projects is not required. As a result, private financial support of prisons is "less attractive ... because the cost of raising capital is higher when the debt instruments are not backed by the full faith and credit of the government" (McDonald 1992: 391). Experiments with private prisons were conducted largely as a result of claims that private contractors could relieve governments of the costs of running these facilities while maintaining the same level of custody and quality of services. State governments, facing large increases in the number of inmates, the high costs of constructing prisons (up to $75 000 per bed) and demands by the public to reduce taxes, turned to private prison contractors in the hope that they would be able to construct and then operate prisons at a cheaper cost than the state.

At first, these claims by private prison contractors seemed to be borne out (Meddis and Sharp 1994). However, a 1996 study by the U.S. General Accounting Office (GAO), the investigative unit of Congress, compared studies of public and private prisons on the basis of two factors: (1) cost of operation and (2) quality of service. The final report concluded that the results were mixed. The GAO found that some private operations were cheaper and yet able to provide quality services, while other private facilities were more costly to operate and/or offered poorer quality of services. It concluded that these studies provided little guidance for jurisdictions intent on reducing the costs of their prisons.

Nevertheless, advocates of privatization believe that private prisons have distinct advantages in terms of cost-effectiveness. First, they are more productive because they are private and not caught in public sector bureaucracy and red tape. Second, there is a strong belief that private prisons are efficient, which encourages greater productivity among employees. There is greater risk-taking in terms of productivity and implementation of cost-cutting measures. In addition, these institutions are able "to buy in larger quantities of discounts and from a wider range of possible suppliers," thereby reducing the costs of supplies (McDonald 1992: 399).

Critics of privately operated prisons argue that prisons are not institutions that can be operated on a balance sheet. They believe that the labour-intensive nature of prisons does not allow for significant amounts of technological innovations that will reduce costs.

Instead, they argue, cost savings will come at the expense of reliable and well-trained employees, and any advantage private corporations may hold over their public-sector counterparts may be reduced if their employees unionize.

Furthermore, critics argue that privately run prisons will not be committed to providing quality programs for inmates. Charging that the private sector is more interested in "doing well" than in "doing good," an American Bar Association committee wrote that "conditions of confinement will be kept to the minimum that the law requires" (American Bar Association 1986: 6).

Supporters of private prisons argue that private correctional corporations have demonstrated that they perform the same services as government-run facilities at a cost 10 to 15 percent lower. However, Shichor (1995) argues that there is no consensus on the cost savings achieved by private prisons. Supporters argue that labour costs are saved by flexible staffing, by electronic surveillance used in lieu of human surveillance, and by substituting fringe benefits with profit-sharing arrangements (Logan 1990). Critics, on the other hand, argue that these practices may lead to reduced safety within these institutions and in less security for surrounding communities (DiIulio 1991).

All researchers who have studied both public and private correctional institutions have commented on the difficulty of making direct comparisons. Even advocates of privatization believe that private prisons will not always be cheaper than public-sector facilities, but that their strength resides in their ability to be more innovative and implement changes more quickly and more efficiently. Though in Canada the move toward intermediate sanctions, as well as greater use of conditional release programs and community alternatives, seemed to signal an end, for now, to any thought of adult private prisons, the provinces have taken a much closer look at this issue. In New Brunswick, a private prison contractor designed a new Youth Training Facility. The first operational adult provincial correctional facility to be built and operated by a private prison contractor is located in Ontario. The privately owned Management & Training Corporation (MTC) of Utah operates Ontario's newest provincial correctional facility, located in Penetanguishene, Ontario. This facility has capacity for 1184 maximum security adult inmates (1152 males and 32 females). The facility features six interconnected octagonal pods, with each pod containing six living units (two offenders are housed in each cell), an enclosed exercise area, and program and visiting areas. MTC was awarded a five-year contract worth $170 million for its bid of just under $80 per inmate per day—a bid that was $60 lower than the average provincial cost (Pachmar 2001).

CORRECTIONS: THE OLDER INMATE

Individuals between 20 and 39 years of age are overrepresented in the adult federal and provincial/territorial custodial populations. Robinson et al. (1998) report that on 5 October 1996, 22 percent of all provincial/territorial male inmates were between the ages of 20 and 24. In contrast, only 9 percent of the federal correctional population were in the same age category. In the federal system, the age groups of 25 to 29 and 30 to 34 were the most overrepresented. Eighteen percent of male federal inmates were between the ages of 25 and 29 (though only 10 percent of Canada's total male population were in this age group) and 21 percent were between 30 and 34 (though only 12 percent of the total Canadian male population were in this age group). Overall, 68 percent of all federal male inmate were under the age of 40, while 84 percent of provincial/territorial inmates were in the same category (Robinson et al. 1998).

The findings for the age of females incarcerated were similar to males. For example, 72 percent of all federal female inmates were under the age of 40, while 73 percent of all females incarcerated in provincial/territorial facilities were under the age of 40.

Richard Sauve won his legal fight to have the right to vote extended to all federal inmates.

That most of Canada's inmates are under the age of 40 should not obscure the fact that our correctional population is getting older. The average age of an offender serving a sentence in a provincial/territorial institution in 1997–98 was 32, while in the federal system the average age was 33. These average ages represent a significant increase since 1991–92, when the average age was 28. The number and proportion of inmates in Canada's federal correctional facilities who are over the age of 50 is increasing also, reflecting the gradual aging of Canadians. This phenomenon is reflected in various statistics. For example, in 1992–93 the average age of persons admitted to custody in the federal system was 32, and in 1996–97 it was 36.

When we refer to older offenders, we refer to offenders who are 50 years of age or over. In 1996 older offenders in Canada ranged from 50 to 90 years of age. The largest group of older offenders (45 percent) is between the ages of 50 and 54, followed by those who are 55 to 59 (28 percent) and 60 to 64 (15 percent). Twelve percent were 65 years of age or over. The most common offences to lead directly to the incarceration of older offenders were sexual (38 percent of all offences), homicide (24 percent), and robbery (13 percent).

The issue of older offenders is most acute in Canada's federal system, as the number of inmates there is gradually increasing. The number of lifers serving sentences in federal correctional facilities has increased over the past few years. In 1996, 1527 older offenders were serving a period of incarceration in Canada's federal correctional facilities, an increase of 10 percent from 1993.

Three types of older offenders are identified. The first group includes those who were incarcerated while young and have stayed in prison since then. In 1996, 155 (10 percent) of all older offenders fell into this category. The second category contains those individuals who are chronic offenders and who were incarcerated numerous times prior to their latest sentence of imprisonment. Two hundred and sixty-one (17 percent) of all older offenders fell into this group. Most are serving time for property crimes. The third category of older offenders contains those individuals who are serving their first term of imprisonment late in life. For most of their life they were law-abiding but became involved in crime later (Aday 1994). This category comprises the majority (1111, or 73 percent) of older inmates in Canada's prisons (Robinson et al. 1998).

Older offenders pose special problems for the correctional system; while growing old in prison and serving a long sentence, older offenders have special needs and problems that set them apart from the rest of the adult offender population (Walsh 1989; Cowles 1990). Among these issues are medical attention,

An ever-increasing number of elderly inmates in Canada are serving time in a correctional facility. John McKee, 73, is serving a seven-year sentence for sexual offences.

adjustment to imprisonment, programming, prison environment, peer relationships while in prison, family relationships, and parole issues (Uzoaba 1998). A study of older inmates in California discovered that 80 percent had a chronic health condition, 38 percent had hypertension, 28 percent had heart disease, and 16 percent had cataracts (Zimbardo 1994). Donzinger (1996) estimated that the cost of looking after the typical inmate in a state facility in the U.S. averages about $22 000 per year but that for older inmates it rises to about $60 000. Some observers estimate that health care costs for the United States federal system will increase by 10 to 20 percent during the first decade of this century (Bradley 1990). Some argue that older inmates provide a stabilizing influence on younger inmates in correctional facilities (Cavan 1987).

Despite the high costs of incarceration, some (for example, Goetting 1983; Walsh 1992) argue that it is inconsistent to argue that older inmates be excused from serving time in a federal institution simply because costs are high. They argue that the needs of older inmates will not create a heavy financial burden on the correctional system. But they also point out that there has to be recognition that older inmates need to receive programs designed to meet their needs.

In addition to health issues is the issue of specialized care in prison. To date, prisons have operated with young offenders in mind. But some observers (for example, Vito and Wilson 1985; Wilson and Vito 1988) speculate prisons will become geriatric centres and special staff will have to be trained to look after these inmates. Morton (1993: 44) recommends that specialized staff be trained to identify physical disabilities in older inmates, to develop policies on managing the special needs of older inmates, to be sensitive to the physical and emotional difficulties experienced by older inmates, and to begin developing solutions that apply to specific institutions.

The issue of adjustment to prison life on the part of older prisoners is a contentious one. Some argue that older inmates experience more psychological and emotional problems, a concern that Vito and Wilson (1985) believe is not addressed by correctional systems. However, others (for example, Teller and Howell 1981) argue that older offenders are better adjusted, less impulsive, and less hostile than those who are younger. Sabath and Cowles (1988) found that older offenders who maintain family contacts are better adjusted than those who don't, and there is general agreement that first-time older offenders are better adjusted in prison than those who have served at least one previous term of incarceration (Aday and Webster 1979; Teller and Howell 1981).

Other issues facing older inmates arise when they leave a correctional facility. They are by then used to prison life and have established social networks. How do they survive in the outside world? Many of their friends may have died or forgotten about them, so questions involving care and a place to stay become paramount. As Hassine (1996: 97) points out, the elderly inmate represents "a growing underclass of dependents in a world of change."

A special category of older offenders includes those who spend many years in prison and are generally referred to as "lifers." In 1997–98, 2433 inmates were serving a life sentence—18 percent of the total federal inmate population. The median age of lifers was 39 in 1997–98, compared to 33 for nonlifers. Lifers were more likely than nonlifers to be non-Aboriginals, single, less educated, and unemployed when they committed the offence that led to their incarceration in a federal institution (Finn et al. 1999). These individuals will in all probability spend some of their older years in a federal institution, and pose particular challenges for federal correctional authorities.

RESTORATIVE JUSTICE

Restorative justice refers to activities within the criminal justice system that are directed at repairing the injury to the victim and the community as opposed to focusing solely on the adversarial relationship between state and offender. In contrast, our criminal justice system is based on the idea that the sanction for a particular crime must be closely related to the crime and that the offender should be punished in a way that deprives him of any gain. Supporters of restorative justice prefer a system that focuses on making the victim whole rather than the struggle between prosecution and defence to win the case. The restorative justice model attempts, in other words, to shift the focus from the prosecutor to a system that helps those who were victimized by the offender.

The coining of the term "restorative justice" is usually credited to Albert Eglash (1975), who identified three types of justice:

1. retributive justice, which is based on punishing the offender;
2. distributive justice, which focuses on the therapeutic treatment of offenders; and
3. restorative justice, which is based on restitution.

The first two types of justice differ from restorative justice in that they focus on the actions of offenders, deny victim participation, ignore the ramifications of the offence within a community context, and expect any participation on behalf of the offender to be passive. Restorative justice, in contrast, focuses on the involvement of victims and offenders as well as concerns about the community in the process of reparation and rehabilitation.

Others have expanded on this concept. Zehr (1990) sees restorative justice as a process that attempts to restore the victim and community and to rebuild ruptured relationships. Others, such as Morris (1994), talk about "transformative" justice, described as a system that emphasizes that crime is not just a violation of people and relationships but an opportunity to have those people and relationships explore the causes of the event in question, repair the relationship between the offender and victim, and increase the level of safety within the community. Whatever the emphasis, restorative justice is viewed as a new model of criminal justice, or, as Zehr (1990) describes it, a new "lens."

As we saw earlier, key aspects of the adversarial system are the quality of the evidence, proving guilt beyond a reasonable doubt, and protecting the legal rights of the accused. In addition, prosecutors assess cases on the basis of the likelihood of a successful outcome. Restorative justice advocates believe that it is more important to focus on the impact of the crime on the victim. In order to allow for such a shift in our criminal justice system, Parliament made revisions to the *Criminal Code* to allow for alternative sanctions. Bill C-41 (see Chapter 9), when it was proclaimed in 1995, authorized alternative measures (s. 717 of the *Criminal Code*) that can be used "to deal with a person alleged to have committed an offence only if it is not inconsistent with the protection of society...." These programs include restitution, community service, personal services to the victim, and mediation, among others. If these programs are to be used, three conditions must be satisfied:

1. The measures are part of an authorized program.
2. The person considering their use is "satisfied that they would be appropriate, having regard to the needs of the person alleged to have committed the offence and the interests of society and of the victim."
3. The alleged offender consents to participate and accepts responsibility for the act or omission that forms the basis of the alleged offence.

Restitution Programs

Restitution is the most common form of restorative justice. In this approach, the offender pays restitution in an attempt to repair some of the harm experienced by the victim. Paying money is the most common type of restitution; other types are returning property or performing a service for the victim. In each type of restitution the victim is compensated for his loss either directly or indirectly. The goal of restitution services is to serve as a mechanism that restores the victim to his previous condition and at the same time punishes the offender.

Restitution programs that require the offender to pay some amount of money to the victim, though they have widespread support, are not often used in our justice system. This is because many offenders are poor, possess few job skills, and have less than a high school education. Under the restorative justice model, however, it is possible for the offender to repair the harm experienced by the victim in another way, such as fulfilling a community service order. A community service order is an attempt to hold an offender accountable for his actions when he is not able to pay money to the victim. As a condition of release, then, the offender is required to work for a designated organization (for example, a nonprofit organization) for a certain number of hours.

Section 738 of the *Criminal Code* allows the court to order the accused to make restitution to the victim if the amount is "readily ascertainable." If the offence involved physical harm to the victim, the maximum amount to be paid is actual monetary loss, which includes loss of income. Section 739 permits the court to order the offender to make restitution to any "secondary victim." This means that if the offender steals something of value and then sells it to another, unsuspecting person, the judge can order the offender to reimburse that second victim.

Mediation Programs

In our adversarial system of justice it is rare after a crime has been committed for the victim and offender ever to speak to each other. They may see each other, but it is usually in court, where the victim can observe the offender but not engage in face-to-face discussion.

Instead, the prosecutor speaks on behalf of the victim and the defence lawyer represents the accused. This system further distances the victim from the offender. One of the major strengths of the mediation process is that both the victim and offender have to agree voluntarily to participate; if one party is reluctant or refuses, no meeting takes place.

A mediation program (also referred to as a Victim–Offender Reconciliation Program, or VORP) is a forum in which the victim and offender meet in an "atmosphere of structured informality" within a neutral setting (Wright and Galaway 1989: 2). During the meeting, the offender and victim discuss their version of events and how the offence has affected them. In addition, they are able to ask each other questions and talk about their feelings. They can discuss ways in which justice can be restored in a fair and equitable manner. The outcome of this meeting may involve a written or verbal apology, restitution, community service, personal service, or a combination of these. Once an agreement is reached, it is put in writing and the victim and offender discuss a timetable for restitution and how it will be enforced if the agreement is not followed.

Umbreit (1994) and Umbreit and Niemeyer (1994) enumerated four benefits of such programs. First, mediation gives victims direct input into the criminal justice system, allowing them to be heard in an environment where their participation had traditionally been as observer only. Second, it permits victims and offenders to discuss a variety of issues on a personal basis, rather than through lawyers or not at all. Third, it allows victims to attain closure on the physical harm or psychological trauma they experienced during the criminal act by exercising some degree of control over the final outcome. Fourth, it forces offenders to see victims as people with emotions and fears that are similar to their own feelings.

After the completion of VORPs, victims have reported feeling empowered and that justice is achieved. Another important finding is the reportedly high rate of successful restitution agreements and the low rate of recidivism.

Repairing Harm to the Victim

Some of these programs emerged as specific community responses to problems in the existing criminal justice system. The range of these initiatives varies with the needs and resources of each community. Some include sentencing circles (see Chapter 9) and restorative justice–style programs that are based on a holistic view of justice. They are based on the notion of popular justice that is dealt with by the community rather than by specialized actors such as judges and prosecutors.

LaPrairie (1994) identifies three central components of this approach:

1. the use of informal community processes rather than the representatives or members of the western legal system;
2. the involvement of victims in the process; and
3. the treatment of crime as a social injury rather than an injury solely to the offender.

A holistic view of justice involves a shift from the involvement in most cases of outsiders to the involvement of community members, an approach that focuses on reestablishing harmony following any rift in the social order. A core concept is shame. The public identification of offenders, as well as the appearance of the offenders in the community to acknowledge their actions, are essential components.

A number of different programs have been established using this approach. These programs are now part of the larger justice system and are typically called Community Justice Forums or Family Group Conferences. While differences exist in the way they are conducted, all share certain activities. One is that both the victim and offender agree to participate, and they may invite family and friends to accompany them to the conference or forum.

The conference itself is considered a meeting between these two communities or groups. The group discusses what happened, the consequences for everyone attending the meeting, and what should be done to repair the harm. Agreement on a plan to rectify the situation is reached. Supporters of this approach feel that this meeting has a positive impact on the offender, since the offender has to take responsibility and offer help to the victim.

SUMMARY

This chapter raised a number of contemporary and future issues facing the Canadian criminal justice system. These issues range from specific concerns, such as the drug courts, to broader questions, such as restorative justice and community-based prosecutions. It is clear that our justice system will continue to evolve during the next few years.

All the changes discussed raise fundamental questions about the role of our justice system. Changes will occur in all areas. And this means that controversy will occur as various groups vie for their ideologies. How the issues are resolved will depend, of course, on how governing bodies react.

Discussion Questions

1. Should lawyers practise community justice lawyering in Canada? What problems would they encounter from the existing criminal justice system?

2. Should the various levels of governments spend more money on the police, particularly for the hiring of new police officers in the RCMP and municipal police forces?

3. What are some of the problems that could emerge from the introduction of community courts?

4. Should restorative justice be used only for minor crimes, leaving most violent and serious property crimes to be heard in the established criminal courts?

5. Should restorative justice be oriented primarily toward the adjudication of young offenders?

6. Should restorative justice programs be used for young persons under 12 years of age?

7. Should we increase the maximum length of our sentences for violating our hate crime laws?

8. What are some of the difficulties involving the enforcement of the new Canadian laws designed to protect children from offences committed on the Internet?

Suggested Readings

Barrett, S.R. 1987. *Is God Racist? The Right Wing in Canada.* Toronto: University of Toronto Press.

Karp, D., ed. 1998. *Community Justice.* Lanham, Md.: Rowman and Littlefield.

Kinsella, W.P. 1993. *Web of Hate: Inside Canada's Far Right Network.* Toronto: HarperCollins Publishers.

McCarthy, B., and R. Langworthy, eds. 1988. *Older Offenders: Perspectives in Criminology and Criminal Justice.* New York: Praeger.

Nolan, James L., ed. 2002. *Drug Courts in Theory and Practice.* New York: Adline de Gruyter.

Rigakos, G.S. 2002. *The New Parapolice.* Toronto: University of Toronto Press.

Van Ness, D., and K.H. Strong. 1997. *Restoring Justice.* Cincinnati: CJ Anderson.

References

Aday, R.H. 1994. "Aging in Prison: A Case Study of New Elderly Offenders." *International Journal of Offender Therapy and Comparative Criminology* 38: 79–91.

Aday, R.H., and E.L. Webster. 1979. "Aging in Prison: The Development of a Preliminary Model." *Offender Rehabilitation* 3: 271–82.

Associated Press. 2002. "US Breaks Huge Identity-Theft Case." *Winnipeg Free Press,* 26 November, B2.

Bindman, S. 2002. "Canada's First Drug Court Breaks the Cycle of Drugs and Crime." *LawNow* 26: 13–15.

Boland, B. 1996. "What Is Community Prosecution?" *National Institute of Justice Journal* (August): 35–40.

Bradley, S. 1990. "Graying of Inmate Population Spurs Corrections Challenges." *On the Line* 13: 5.

Bureau of Justice Statistics. 1996. *Corrections Statistics.* Washington, D.C.: Government Printing Office.

Business Week. 2000. "Everything Has a Price ..." 10 July, 10.

Canada. 1996. *Report of the Special Committee on Hate Propaganda.* Ottawa: Queen's Printer.

Cavan, R.S. 1987. "Is Special Treatment Needed for Elderly Offenders?" *Criminal Justice Policy Review* 2: 213–24.

Chiodo, A.L. 2001. "Sentencing Drug-Addicted Offenders and the Toronto Drug Court." *Criminal Law Quarterly* 45: 53–99.

Clark, T. 2002. "Ontario Laws Toughened to Combat Identity Theft." *The Globe and Mail,* 9 February, A8.

Coles, C., and G. Kelling. 1998. "Prosecution in the Community: A Study of Emergent Strategies. A Cross-Site Analysis." Paper presented at J.F. Kennedy School, Harvard University, Program in Criminal Justice, September.

Connor, R. 2000. "Problem-Solving Lawyers." *National Institute of Justice Journal* (January): 26–33.

Cowles, E.L. 1990. "Programming for Long-Term Inmates." Executive Summary. *Long-Term Confinement and the Aging Inmate Population: A Record and Proceeding.* Washington, D.C.: Federal Bureau of Prisons.

Cragg, W. 1992. *The Practice of Punishment: Towards a Theory of Restorative Justice.* New York: Routledge.

Cunningham, W.C., J.J. Strauchs, and C.W. Van Meter. 1990. *Private Security Trends 1970 to the Year 2000: The Hallcrest Report II.* Boston: Butterworth Heinemann.

Cunningham, W.C., and T.H. Taylor. 1985. *The Hallcrest Report: Private Security and Police in America.* Portland, Ore.: Chancellor.

DiIulio, J.J. 1991. "The Duty to Govern: A Critical Perspective on the Private Management of Prisons and Jails." In D.C. McDonald, ed., *Private Prisons and the Public Interest.* New Brunswick, N.J.: Rutgers University Press.

Eglash, A. 1975. "Beyond Restitution: Creative Restitution." In J. Hudson and B. Galaway, eds., *Restitution in Criminal Justice: A Critical Assessment of Sanctions.* Minneapolis: International Symposium on Restoration.

Finn, P., A. Newlyn, and C. Gray. 1994. "Miami Drug Court Gives Drug Defendants a Second Chance." *Judicature* 77, no. 5.

Finn, A., S. Trevethan, G. Carriere, and M. Kowalski. 1999. *Female Inmates, Aboriginal Inmates, and Inmates Serving Life Sentences: A One-Day Snapshot.* Ottawa: Juristat.

Foss, K. 2002. "Winnipeg Man among First Charged with Internet Luring." *The Globe and Mail,* 14 September, A9.

Garofalo, J., and S.E. Martin. 1991. "The Law Enforcement Response to Bias-Motivated Crimes." In N. Taylor, ed., *Bias Crime: The Law Enforcement Response.* Chicago: Office of International Criminal Justice.

Goetting, A. 1983. "The Elderly in Prison: Issues and Perspectives." *Journal of Research in Crime and Delinquency* 20: 291–309.

Graham, W.R. 2000. "Uncovering and Eliminating Child Pornography on the Internet." *Law Review of Michigan State University Detroit College of Law,* Summer.

Hassine, V. 1996. *Life without Parole.* Los Angeles: Roxbury.

Kakalik, J.S., and S. Wildhorn. 1972. *Private Security in the United States.* Washington, D.C.: U.S. Department of Justice, National Institute of Law Enforcement and Criminal Justice, Law Enforcement Assistance Administration.

Kallen, E. 1998. "Hate on the Net: A Question of Rights/A Question of Power." *Electronic Journal of Sociology* 3 (http://www.sociology.org/content/vol003.002/kallen.html); accessed 1998.

LaPrairie, C. 1994. *Seen but Not Heard: Native People in the Inner City,* vol. 3. Ottawa: Department of Justice.

Levin, J., and J. McDevitt. 1993. *Hate Crimes.* New York: Plenum Press.

Lilly, R.J., and P. Knepper. 1993. "The Corrections–Commercial Complex." *Crime and Delinquency* 39: 150–59.

Logan, C.H. 1990. *Private Prisons: Cons and Pros.* New York: Oxford University Press.

Makin, K. 1999. "Drug Treatment Court Helps Addicts Turn Their Lives Around." *The Globe and Mail,* 1 December, A7.

Marron, K. 2002. "Identity Thieves Plunder the Net." *The Globe and Mail,* 28 June, E1–E2.

Moore, M.H. 1992. "Problem-Solving and Community Policing." In M. Tonry and N. Morris, eds., *Modern Policing.* Chicago: University of Chicago Press, pp. 90–158.

Morris, R. 1994. *A Practical Path to Transformative Justice.* Toronto: Rittenhouse.

Morton, J.B. 1993. "In South Carolina: Training Staff to Work with Elderly and Disabled Inmates." *Corrections Today* 55, no. 1: 42–47.

Normandeau, A., and B. Leighton. 1990. *A Vision of the Future of Policing in Canada: Police Challenge 2000.* Ottawa: Solicitor General of Canada.

Olson, D.E., A.J. Lurigio, and S. Alberts. 2001. "Implementing the Key Components of Specialized Drug Treatment Courts: Practice and Policy Considerations." *Law & Policy* 23: 171–96.

Patchmar, K. 2001. "Ontario Introduces Private Prison to Canada." *RCMP Gazette* 63: 30–31.

Reed, M., and J. Roberts. 1999. *Adult Correctional Services in Canada, 1997–98.* Ottawa: Juristat.

Reiss, A.J. 1988. *Private Employment of Public Police.* Washington, D.C.: U.S. Department of Justice, National Institute of Justice.

Roberts, J.V. 1995. *Disproportionate Harms.* Canada: Department of Justice.

Robinson, D., F.J. Porporino, W.A. Millson, S. Trevethan, and B. MacKillop. 1998. *A One-Day Snapshot of Inmates in Canada's Adult Correctional Facilities.* Ottawa: Juristat.

Rottman, D.B. 1996. "Community Courts: Prospects and Limits." *National Institute of Justice Journal* (August): 46–51.

Sabath, J., and E.L. Cowles. 1988. "Factors Affecting the Adjustment of Elderly Offenders in Prison." In B. McCarthy and R. Langworthy, eds., *Older Offenders: Perspectives in Criminology and Criminal Justice.* New York: Praeger.

Sanderson, P.M. 1991. "Investigation of Religious Bias-Motivated Crimes." In N. Taylor, ed., *Bias Crime: The Law Enforcement Response.* Chicago: Office of International Criminal Justice.

Shearing, C.D. 1992. "The Relation between Public and Private Policing." In M. Tonry and N. Morris, eds., *Modern Policing.* Chicago: University of Chicago Press, pp. 399–434.

Shearing, C.D., and P. Stenning. 1981. "Modern Private Security: Its Growth and Implications." In M. Tonry and N. Morris, eds., *Crime and Justice: An Annual Review of Research,* vol. 3. Chicago: University of Chicago Press.

Shichor, D. 1995. *Punishment for Profit: Private Prisons/Public Concerns.* Thousand Oaks, Calif.: Sage.

Swol, K. 1998. *Private Security and Public Policing in Canada.* Ottawa: Juristat.

Teller, F.E., and R.J. Howell. 1981. "The Older Prisoner: Criminal and Psychological Characteristics." *Criminology* 18: 549–55.

Thomas, C.W., and D. Bolinger. 1999. *Private Adult Correctional Facility Census,* 12th ed. Gainesville, Fla.: University of Florida Center for Studies in Criminology and Law.

Umbreit, M. 1994. *Victim Meets Offender: The Impact of Restorative Justice and Mediation.* Monsey, N.Y.: Criminal Justice Press.

Umbreit, M., and M. Niemeyer. 1994. "Victim–Offender Mediation: From the Margins toward the Mainstream." *American Probation and Parole Association Perspectives,* Summer.

Uzoaba, J.H.E. 1998. *Managing Older Offenders: Where Do We Stand?* Ottawa: Correctional Service of Canada, Research Division.

Vito, G., and D. Wilson. 1985. "Forgotten People: Elderly Inmates." *Federal Probation* 49: 18–24.

Walsh, C.E. 1992. "Ageing Inmate Offenders: Another Perspective." In C.A. Hartjen and E.E. Rhine, eds., *Correctional Theory and Practice.* Chicago: Nelson-Hall.

———. 1989. "The Older and Long-Term Inmate Growing Old in the New Jersey Prison System." *Journal of Offender Counselling Services and Rehabilitation* 13: 215–48.

Wilson, D., and G. Vito. 1988. "Long-Term Inmates: Special Need and Management Considerations." *Federal Probation* 52: 21–26.

Wright, M., and B. Galaway, eds. 1989. *Mediation and Criminal Justice: Victims, Offenders, and Community.* Newbury Park, Calif.: Sage.

Zehr, H. 1990. *Changing Lenses: A New Focus for Criminal Justice.* Scottsdale, Pa.: Herald Press.

Zimbardo, P.G. 1994. *Transforming California's Prisons into Expensive Old Age Homes for Felons.* San Francisco: Center on Juvenile and Criminal Justice.

Zion, J.W. 1998. "The Dynamics of Navajo Peacemaking." *Journal of Contemporary Criminal Justice* 14: 58–74.

Court Cases

B'nai Brith v. Harcus (1992) [unreported]

R. v. Keegstra, [1990] 3 S.C.R. 697

GLOSSARY

Absolute jurisdiction indictable offence. Offences for which the accused has to be tried by a provincial court judge unless the judge determines the case must be tried another way. These offences are found in s. 553 of the *Criminal Code.*

Actus reus. The illegal act. It involves either the commission of an act, such as an assault, or the failure to act, such as failing to take proper safety measures.

Adjudication. The determination of guilt or innocence of the accused by a judge.

Administrative law. The laws created by administrative agencies (in the form of rules, regulations, orders, and decisions) in order that they can carry out their responsibilities and duties.

Adversarial system. The procedure used to determine truth in a criminal court system. According to this system, the burden is on the state to prove the charges against the accused beyond a reasonable doubt.

Aggravating circumstances. Any circumstances accompanying the commission of a crime that may justify a harsher sentence.

Appeal. A review of lower court decisions or proceedings by a higher court.

Appearance notice. Issued to the accused requiring him to appear in court on a specific date and time. An appearance notice is issued to the accused instead of arresting him.

Arraignment. The process in which the accused hears the formal charges laid against him and pleads either guilty or innocent.

Arrest. The taking into custody of a person thought to have committed a crime. The legal requirement for an arrest is "reasonable and probable grounds."

Assembly-line justice. The idea that the criminal justice process is similar to a production line that handles most cases in as routine a manner as possible.

Auburn prison system. The prison system developed in New York in the 19th century that favoured a tier-based prison facility and congregate working conditions for inmates.

Beyond a reasonable doubt. The standard used to determine the guilt or innocence of an accused.

Boot camp. A short-term militaristic-style correctional facility in which youths and young adults are exposed to intensive physical conditioning and discipline.

Broken window theory. The approach used to refer to the idea that community disorder leads to criminal behaviour.

Case law. The judicial application and interpretation of laws as they apply in any particular case.

Charge a jury. When the judge informs a jury of the relevant evidence of a case and the types of decisions the jury can reach about the accused.

Charge-bargaining. A prosecutor's decision to reduce the number of charges against the accused in return for a plea of guilty and for information.

Classical approach. An approach to the study of criminology that emphasizes reforming laws and improving the criminal justice system as the best way to resolve the crime problem.

Common law. Early English law, developed by judges, based on local customs and feudal rules and practices. Common law formed the basis of the standardized criminal law system in England.

Community policing. A police strategy that emphasizes the reduction of fear, community involvement, decentralization of the police force, neighbourhood police stations, and order maintenance as an alternative approach to fighting crime.

Concurrence. Forms the legal relationship between the guilty mind and the illegal act.

Corpus delecti. The body of circumstances that must exist for a criminal act to have occurred.

Courtroom work group. The informal social organization of the courtroom, comprising the prosecutor, defence attorney, judge, and other court workers. The informal relationships among the members of this group have far-reaching implications for the treatment of the accused in our criminal justice system.

Custodial interrogation. The questioning of a suspect after that person has been taken into custody. Before any interrogation begins, the individual must be read his rights.

Custody. The forceful detention of an individual.

Cyber crime. A crime that occurs online, in the virtual community of the Internet, as opposed to the physical world.

Cyber stalking. The crime of stalking, committed in cyberspace.

Deadly force. Force applied by a police officer that is likely or intended to cause death.

Deprivation model. The theory that states that inmate aggression is the result of the frustration inmates experience at being deprived of freedom, consumer goods, etc. that are common outside prison.

Determinate sentencing. A period of incarceration fixed by legislature that cannot be reduced by a judge or correctional officials.

Deterrence. The prevention of crime before it occurs by threatening individuals with criminal sanctions.

Deterrence, general. A crime control policy that aims to stop potential law violators from engaging in illegal behaviour. It favours certain policies—such as long prison sentences—that underscore the fact that the pain associated with crime outweighs the gain.

Deterrence, specific. A crime-control policy that advocates punishment severe enough to convince convicted offenders never again to engage in criminal behaviour.

Deterrence model. One of the four main models of criminal justice. It envisions a criminal justice system with no discretion, more police, and longer prison terms. It is related to the crime control model and classical school of criminology.

Directed patrol. A police patrol strategy. Police officers are told to spend much of their patrol time in certain areas, to use certain tactics, and to watch for certain types of offences.

Discretion. The use of individual decision-making and choice to influence the operation of the criminal justice system. All the major institutions of the criminal justice system—police, courts, corrections—make decisions that influence the outcome of cases.

Disparity. The lack of uniformity in sentencing, which leads to concern about discrimination against particular groups in society. Disparity involves arbitrary differences between sentences against offenders convicted of the same crime.

Drug courts. Courts whose jurisdiction is limited to drug offences. Offenders selected receive treatment as an alternative to incarceration.

Election indictable offence. An offence for which the accused (or his lawyer) may decide on what type of criminal court he wishes to be tried in.

Electronic monitoring (EM). A system designed to ensure an offender completes the terms of a court order. EM is the regulatory aspect of home confinement.

Employment equity. The federal government policy that stresses that minorities should be represented in the work force.

Fact-bargaining. A type of plea-bargaining in which the prosecutor decides not to introduce certain facts about the offence or offender into the court record.

Fine. One of the most common sentences in Canada. Failure to pay a fine is one of the most common reasons for the incarceration of offenders.

First-degree murder. Planned and deliberate murder—though it does not have to be planned or deliberate when the victim is a police officer, a prison guard, an individual working in a prison, or a similar individual acting in the course of duty.

Foot patrol. A type of police patrol linked to community policing. It takes police officers out of cars and places them on a beat, which allows them to strengthen ties with community residents.

Full parole. The early release of an inmate from prison subject to conditions established by a parole board. Full parole can be granted to inmates after they serve one-third of their sentence, unless their sentence specifies otherwise.

Habeas corpus. A judicial order requesting that a state representative (e.g., a police officer) detaining another give reasons for the capture and detention. It is a legal device used to request a judicial review of the reasons for an individual's detention and the conditions of detention.

"Hands-off" doctrine. The unwritten policy favouring noninterference by the courts in the administration of correctional facilities.

Home confinement. A type of intermediate punishment that allows offenders to live at home while serving their sentence.

"Hot spots." Concentrated areas of high criminal activity that draw the interest of the police.

Hybrid offence. An offence that may proceed either as an indictable or summary conviction offence. The decision on how to proceed is usually made by the Crown prosecutor.

Identity theft. The theft of identity information, such as a name, driver's licence, Social Insurance Number, etc. This information is typically used to access the victim's financial resources.

Incarceration. Occurs when an offender receives a sentence that stipulates that he spend time in either a provincial or federal correctional institution.

Indictable offence. An offence for which the accused must, or has the right to, choose between a trial by judge and a trial by jury, with the exception of a few minor offences.

Infanticide. One of the four types of murder. It was introduced in 1948, and only a woman can be charged. The *Criminal Code* defines an infant as a child under one year of age.

Information, to lay an. One lays an information when one presents to a judge a sworn written allegation alleging the individual named in the document has committed an offence. Informations are also used to obtain search warrants.

Intermediate sanctions. Sanctions that are more restrictive than probation and less restrictive than imprisonment.

Judicare. A type of legal aid practised in Canada that combines elements of the public defender and judicare models.

Judicial Interim Hearing. The condition(s) of pretrial release, typically set by a justice of the peace, in order that an accused lives in the community prior to her trial. Also referred to as "bail."

Jury. A group of individuals whose function is to determine guilt or innocence of the accused. A jury comprises 12 citizens.

Justice model. A model of criminal justice that emphasizes legal rights, justice, and fairness. A main feature of this model is that any punishment should be proportional to the seriousness of the crime.

Legal aid. A government-supported system that allows individuals who are earning below a certain amount to receive free legal services.

Legalistic. An approach that stresses the type of crime committed as opposed to any extraneous factors such as the race or social class of the offender.

Lower court. A general term used to describe those courts that have jurisdiction over summary conviction offences. Most pleas are made in these courts.

***Mala en se* offences.** Actions, such as murder, sexual assault, robbery, and theft, that are made illegal by statutes as the actions violate basic moral values.

***Mala prohibita* offences.** Actions, such as pollution and traffic laws, that are made illegal because they conflict with current norms and public opinion.

Management of demand. A police organizational strategy that categorizes requests for service and analyzes them as to their priority, resulting in differential police responses.

Manslaughter. Unintentional homicide requiring either criminal negligence or an unlawful act.

Mens rea. A prerequisite of criminal conduct is the "guilty mind." *Mens rea* is based on the belief that people can control their behaviour and choose between right and wrong. It commonly is used to refer to the intent to commit a crime.

Mitigating circumstances. Any circumstances accompanying the commission of a crime that may justify a lighter sentence.

New-generation jail. A type of correctional facility distinguished architecturally from its predecessors by a design that encourages interaction between inmates and correctional officers.

Parens patriae. A doctrine that holds that the state has a responsibility to look after the well-being of children and to assume the role of a parent, if needed.

Parole. The conditional release of an inmate from his unfinished sentence of incarceration into the community. The decision to parole an individual is made by a parole board, which determines the conditions of the release.

Pennsylvania system. A prison system developed in the 19th century that emphasized solitary confinement for all inmates so they could reflect on individual penitence.

Podular design. The architectural style of the new-generation jail. "Pods" usually contain between 12 and 24 one-person cells, and a communal room that allows for social interaction.

Preliminary inquiry. An inquiry made by a provincial court judge in a case involving an indictable offence in order to determine if there is enough evidence to order the accused to stand trial.

Pre-sentence report. An investigation usually conducted by a probation officer before the sentencing of a convicted offender. The report typically contains information about the offender's personal background, education, previous employment, and family as well as interviews with family members, neighbours, and employer.

Prisonization. The socialization process through which a new inmate learns the accepted norms and values of the prison population.

Private prisons. Correctional facilities operated by private corporations.

Probation. A sentence that allows a convicted offender to serve his sentence in the community, subject to certain conditions for a designated time period.

Problem-oriented policing. A style of policing that emphasizes a focus on a specific crime problem. It features a proactive rather than reactive approach to fighting crime.

Procedural law. The rules that define the operation of criminal proceedings. It specifies the methods that are to be followed in obtaining warrants, conducting trials, sentencing convicted offenders, and reviewing cases by Appeal Courts. Its main purpose is to describe how substantive offences are to be enforced.

Public defender. A type of legal aid. Legal aid lawyers are employed by a provincial government to help with the legal defence of an accused.

Recidivism rate. The repetition of criminal behaviour. It is measured by criminal acts committed by persons under correctional supervision or technical violations of individuals on probation or parole.

Rehabilitation. A correctional philosophy that emphasizes the treatment of conditional offenders and their reintegration into the community.

Rehabilitation model. One of the four criminal justice models. It differs from the other models in its support of discretion in the system and the treatment of the offender.

Reintegration. The goal of corrections that focuses on preparing the offender for a return to the community.

Revised Uniform Crime Reports. Reports that record incident-based criminal events. Each crime incident is analyzed for a number of individual characteristics (e.g., the relationship between offender and victim). (*See also* Uniform Crime Reporting System.)

Revocation. The withdrawal of probation or parole orders due to the commission of a new offence or the violation of any condition set out in a parole or probation order.

Search warrant. An authorization granted to police officers by a judge that authorizes officers to search a specific place.

Second-degree murder. Any murder that is not first degree is second degree. The maximum punishment for second-degree murder is life imprisonment.

Selective incapacitation. The incarceration for long periods of time of a select group of "chronic" offenders who commit numerous violent offences.

Selective incapacitation model. One of the four criminal justice models. It emphasizes long prison sentences for the small number of individuals who chronically commit violent crimes. It rejects any type of favourable discretionary actions for those offenders.

Sentence-bargaining. A form of plea-bargaining that involves the reduction of a sentence in return for a plea of guilty or information.

Sexual assault. Classified as a violent crime. Legislation introduced in 1983 created three levels of sexual assault, which emphasize that these offences involve physical violence directed against an individual.

Social service. A view held by some police officers that their prime function is to assist the public in as many ways as possible. A purely legalistic approach is rejected except in extreme cases.

Specialty courts. Those courts having jurisdiction over one specific area of criminal activity, such as domestic violence or illegal drugs.

Stare decisis. A common law doctrine under which judges are to follow those precedents established by prior decisions.

Statute law. Laws created by legislatures in a response to changing social conditions and public opinion.

Statutory release. A program designed to release most incarcerated offenders who have not been able to obtain full parole and have served two-thirds of their sentence.

Summary conviction. Minor offences tried on the basis of the information without other pre-trial formalities.

Summons. An order by the court requiring the appearance of the accused or a witness before it.

Superior Court. The court where most indictable offences are tried, either by judge or by judge and jury.

Supreme Court exclusive indictable offence. Involves those individuals who are charged with first- or second-degree murder. The case is tried by a federally appointed judge and jury.

Suspended sentence. A prison term that is delayed by a judge's order while the convicted offender is involved in community treatment. If this treatment is successful, the individual is allowed to remain in the community.

Temporary absence (TA). Permits the release of offenders from federal institutions so they can access programs and various services within the community.

Temporary absence, escorted. An offender's permitted temporary absence, for a brief period, from a correctional facility, on the basis of having an escort.

Temporary absence, unescorted. An offender's permitted temporary absence, for a relatively long period of time, from a correctional facility, in order to integrate that individual into the outside community.

Total institution. Institutions that eliminate all daily and normal inmate contact with the outside world.

Uniform Crime Reporting System. National crime statistics maintained by the RCMP in Ottawa. Offences are grouped into three categories: crimes against the person, crimes against property, and "other" crimes. (*See also* Revised Uniform Crime Reports.)

Venir. The group of citizens called for jury duty, from which all juries are selected. This is also referred to as jury array. The purpose of the venir is to eliminate persons who are unqualified to be jurors.

Victim Impact Statement. The option given to the victim of a crime to complete a form and detail what has happened to that victim as a result of the crime. If the victim decides to fill out the form, it is placed in the case file and may have an impact on the case, particularly at the sentencing stage.

Victimless crime. Crimes for which there are no complainants or victims. It refers to consensual social exchanges punished by criminal law (e.g., drug use and selling sex).

Warrant. An authorization that grants an individual, usually a police officer, to do what is specified in the warrant (e.g., to arrest someone).

Warrantless search. Those conditions that allow an individual, usually a police officer, to search a place without a warrant (e.g., doctrine of plain view).

Watchman. A style of policing that emphasizes a reactive style of policing rather than a proactive or preventative style.

PHOTO CREDITS

p. 8   CP/Calgary Herald(Colleen Kidd)

p. 13   CP(Jonathan Hayward)

p. 14   CP(Jonathan Hayward)

p. 40   CP(Richard Lam)

p. 46   CP/Montreal La Presse(Remi Lemee)

p. 49   CP/Le Journal de Montreal

p. 66   CP/Colorado Springs Gazette

p. 71   Deborah Baic

p. 94   Global TV

p. 98   CP(Louis Lanzano)

p. 99   Jeff Sallot

p. 108   CP(Richard Lam)

p. 113   CP/Toronto Star(Sean White)

p. 119   Glenn Baglo/Vancouver Sun

p. 147   John Maloney/The Gazette

p. 148   CP(Jeff McIntosh)

p. 164   Global TV

p. 168   Fred Lum/The Globe and Mail

p. 188   CP PHOTO

p. 192   CP(Tom Hanson)

p. 204   CP(Jacques Boissinot)

p. 215   CP(Thomas Porter)

p. 223   CP(Andrew Vaughan)

p. 227   CP(Joe Bryksa)

p. 238   Patti Gower/The Globe and Mail

p. 260   National Archives of Canada/PA-30472

p. 268   Courtesy of Ontario Ministry of Correctional Services

p. 271   Courtesy of Correctional Service of Canada

p. 289   Courtesy of Correctional Service of Canada

p. 292   © AFP/CORBIS/MAGMA

p. 335   Department of Justice Canada

p. 343   Bernard Clark

p. 344   Jon Murray/Vancouver Province